ACCOUNTING
IN A BUSINESS CONTEXT

Aidan Berry & Robin Jarvis Fifth edition

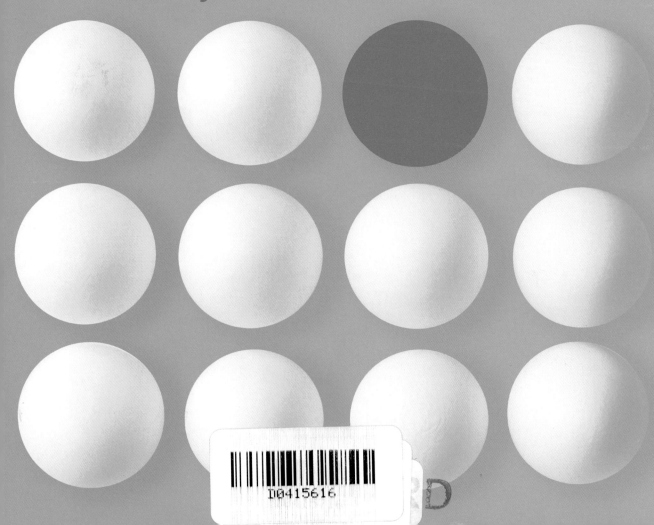

ACCOUNTING
IN A BUSINESS CONTEXT
Aidan Berry & Robin Jarvis Fifth edition

AIDAN BERRY
Professor and Dean of Brighton Business School
University of Brighton

ROBIN JARVIS
Professor of Accounting,
Brunel University and
Head of SME Affairs at the
Association of Chartered Accountants (ACCA)

SOUTH-WESTERN
CENGAGE Learning™

Australia • Brazil • Japan • Korea • Mexico • Singapore • Spain • United Kingdom • United States

SOUTH-WESTERN
CENGAGE Learning

Accounting in a Business Context
Fifth edition
Aidan Berry and Robin Jarvis

Publishing Director: Linden Harris

Publisher: Brendan George

Development Editor: Annabel Ainscow

Content Project Editor: Lucy Arthy

Production Controller: Eyvett Davis

Marketing Manager: Amanda Cheung

Typesetter: KnowledgeWorks Global Limited, India

Cover design: Adam Renvoize

For product information and technology assistance, contact **emea.info@cengage.com**.

For permission to use material from this text or product, and for permission queries, email **emea.permissions@cengage.com**.

The Author has asserted the right under the Copyright, Designs and Patents Act 1988 to be identified as Author of this Work.

British Library Cataloguing-in-Publication Data
A catalogue record for this book is available from the British Library.

ISBN: 978-1-4080-3047-9

Cengage Learning EMEA
Cheriton House, North Way, Andover, Hampshire, SP10 5BE United Kingdom

Cengage Learning products are represented in Canada by Nelson Education Ltd.

For your lifelong learning solutions, visit
www.cengage.co.uk

Purchase your next print book, e-book or e-chapter at
www.cengagebrain.com

Printed in China by RR Donnelley
2 3 4 5 6 7 8 9 10 – 14 13 12

BRIEF CONTENTS

PART I FINANCIAL ACCOUNTING   1

PART II MANAGEMENT ACCOUNTING   317

v

CONTENTS

CASE STUDIES

ACKNOWLEDGEMENTS

We are grateful to all our colleagues who have provided useful feedback on previous editions and made helpful suggestions for improvement. Particular thanks are due to those reviewers who gave us thoughtful comments on the strengths and weaknesses of the previous editions and our proposals for this fifth edition:

- Brian Holdstock (University of Brighton)
- Jill Lyttle (Queen's University Management School, Queen's University Belfast)
- Anne Ullathorne (Birmingham Business School, University of Birmingham)
- Petteri Vilen (Tampere University of Applied Sciences, Finland)

Finally, we should acknowledge those people, colleagues, friends and family who supported us, put up with our moods under pressure and probably gave thanks that once again we were locked in our studies and out of their hair.

PREFACE TO THE FIFTH EDITION

As was the case with previous editions, the fifth edition has been written primarily to meet the needs of business and non-accounting students, but will also be suitable to use with some accounting 'specialist' groups. It balances the need to know how to use accounting information with enough knowledge of how the accounting statements or reports were created to understand their strengths and limitations.

The approach adopted is to begin with the simple; to build knowledge, reinforce the learning and add new levels of complexity to create a deep understanding of the concepts, principles and techniques involved. In developing this edition we have listened carefully to the feedback from lecturers and students and considered thoroughly the suggestions of a number of reviewers, some of which have been incorporated in this new edition. We have retained what we consider to be the strengths of previous editions, namely a clear step-by-step approach to knowledge acquisition, the use of the worksheet for illustrating the double-entry process in a holistic way and for illustrating the link between the various standard financial reports. In all chapters clear learning outcomes have been identified and set out at the start of the chapter. Each chapter now has activities added in addition to the key concepts, real world case studies, review questions and problems for discussion and analysis. To help the learner we have provided answers to some activities, a selection of review questions and problems at the back of the book. We have updated the case studies bringing in examples from USA and Europe and have revised the text to reflect the introduction of International Financial Reporting Standards concentrating as far as possible on the requirements of the International Financial Reporting Standard for Small and Medium Sized Entities and incorporating the terminology from that standard throughout the text. We thought long and hard about the new format suggested in the standard and felt that with the increasing internationalization of our student body and the commercial world on balance it would be appropriate to adopt the suggested format as we anticipate that this will be increasingly adopted by preparers of financial reports. We have added further review questions and problems for discussion and analysis. In recognition of feedback from previous readers, we have included solutions to some of the review questions and problems at the back of this edition, so enabling students to check their own work and understanding. In addition, we have made additional questions available to students and lecturers on the accompanying website at **www.cengage.co.uk/berryjarvis5**.

In terms of content, the major new features are the greater emphasis on the fact that we are looking at small business reporting in an international context, the introduction of a section on flexible budgeting and further earlier introduction of the cash flow statement, clarification of the link between the cash flow statement the worksheet, statement of financial position and income statement, using the same step-by-step approach to learning that has proved successful in previous editions. We believe that in this edition we have retained and built on the strengths of the previous editions, have clarified our learning philosophy and produced a book that is accessible, readable and up to date.

WALK THROUGH TOUR

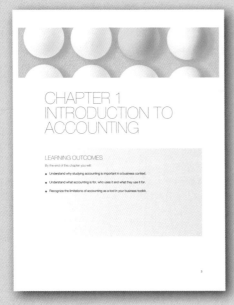

Learning outcomes Listed at the start of each chapter, these highlight the key outcomes covered by each chapter.

Key Concepts Highlighted throughout the text.

Activities Quick activities are dispersed throughout the text, to test the reader's knowledge and encourage active learning.

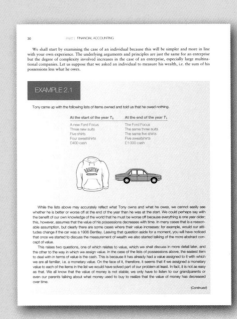

Examples Examples are dispersed throughout the text to illustrate practical application.

Case Studies Engaging use of case studies throughout the text.

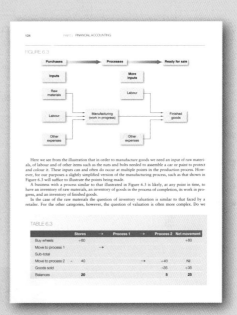

Figures and tables Clearly set out on the page, to aid the reader with quick conceptualization.

Summary The end of each chapter has a summary of the main points and key concepts covered.
References and **Further reading** Provide helpful directions to further sources of information.

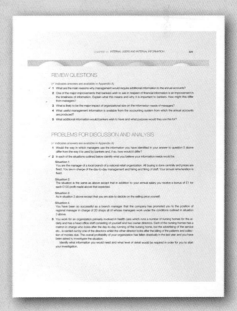

Review questions Short questions which encourage students to review their understanding of the main topics and issues.
Problems for discussion and analysis More in-depth problems to test students' knowledge and understanding, and prompt useful discussion.

About the website

All of our Higher Education textbooks are accompanied by a range of digital support resources. Each title's resources are carefully tailored to the specific needs of the particular book's readers. Examples of the kind of resources provided include:

- A password protected area for instructors with, for example, a testbank, PowerPoint slides and an instructor's manual.
- An area for students including, for example, useful weblinks.

To discover the dedicated digital support resources accompanying this textbook please go to: **www.cengage.co.uk/berry5**

For students

- Company summaries
- Weblinks for case studies

For lecturers

- PowerPoint slides
- Instructor's manual
- Testbank of multiple choice questions

PART I
FINANCIAL
ACCOUNTING

CHAPTER 1
INTRODUCTION TO ACCOUNTING

LEARNING OUTCOMES

By the end of this chapter you will:

● Understand why studying accounting is important in a business context.

● Understand what accounting is for, who uses it and what they use it for.

● Recognize the limitations of accounting as a tool in your business toolkit.

In this chapter we will ask and answer some questions about accounting. The first and perhaps most important to you at this stage is: Why study accounting? So we will start with that and then move on to discuss our approach to helping you understand accounting and how you can use it. We will then answer some more questions such as: What is accounting? Who uses it? What do they use it for? Where is it going? What are its limitations?

WHY STUDY ACCOUNTING?

Whether you intend to go into business, work in the public or voluntary sector or simply live off your accumulated wealth you are going to need to manage some resources to survive. At a simple level as a student you will need to know how much money you are going to receive from loans, bursaries, grants, family and other sources so that you can see if that matches what you are going to spend over the next few years on fees, books, living expenses, rent, food electricity and transport. To do this you can list all the money coming in and all the money going out and see if it balances and, if it does not, take appropriate action by either increasing your income by getting a part time job or decreasing your expenditure by replacing that car with a bike! If you are anything like a typical student you will find that you also need more sophisticated information on when the money comes in and when you have to pay it out so you might draw up some sort of forecast that tracks when money is expected and when bills have to be paid – a personal budget which you can use to keep track of whether you are living within your means or not. So, at a personal level we all use a basic form of accounting in our everyday life to make decisions on whether to buy clothes, books, go out for an evening or move in to a luxury penthouse flat.

ACTIVITY 1.1

Spend a few minutes thinking about where your money is going to come from and what your expenses are likely to be in the next few years.

You might have thought of money coming in from student loans, bursaries, your family, part-time or vacation jobs. You should have thought about expenditure on rent, books, food, transport, phone bills, holidays, clothes, entertainment, etc.

We can therefore see that for a business which has many thousands more transactions than we do as an individual the need to have some sort of system that tracks what is earned and what is spent is vital. The owners of the business they need to be able to decide whether to keep their money invested in that business or withdraw it and invest it elsewhere. If they also run the business they will need information for all sorts of decisions. Their marketing manager may come in with an idea for a new advertising campaign, the production manager with a proposal to buy some new machinery, the IT manager with a proposal to upgrade the communications system, while the personnel manager has a new all singing all dancing staff development scheme. As the owner and chief executive the first thing you might want to do is to get these ideas expressed in some common terms like how much will they cost and how much more profit will we make by implementing each of these ideas. You can then look and see whether they are all good ideas, whether they need you to raise additional finance, how you might do that, which scheme you should support and which you should give priority to.

As you can see from this quick discussion a business leader will always be in a position where she or he has to make decisions about alternative investments as, in general, money is not in unlimited supply and all actions ultimately cost money to implement. Without working out the costs and the likely benefits decisions will be ill informed and your business will not survive. Hopefully, you will also have recognized that accounting is not an add on to the real business it is vital to informed decision making about marketing, staffing, investment in new production techniques and delivery systems, in other words, all the processes that keep businesses and organizations working and producing wealth to pay wages and other forms of return to those who invest their time and resources in that endeavour.

OUR APPROACH TO THE STUDY OF ACCOUNTING

Although when we think of business big names spring to mind, for example in food retailing we might think of Sainsbury, Asda, Tesco, Morrisons, Waitrose, Carrefour, Auchan, Aldi. In reality, however, although these supermarket giants probably have the lion's share of total sales there are hundreds of thousands of small businesses out there, the corner shops that stay open all hours and provide an alternative to the out of town or edge of town supermarket. This pattern is mirrored across many business sectors.

ACTIVITY 1.2

Can you think of small businesses you might have had or are likely to have dealings with over the next few years?

Those you are likely to have on your list may be bicycle repair shops, independent garages, taxis, hairdressers, computer repair specialists, internet cafés, clubs, pubs, restaurants, florists, specialist shops for presents, jewellers, florists, quirky clothes shops, etc.

Whichever country you choose in the world, even the developing world, you will find that the majority of businesses are classified as small businesses. In general, in most developed countries, a figure in excess of 90% of businesses being classified as small would not be a bad estimate. These businesses may be very sophisticated or very simple, but in general they are more likely to be simple than a large conglomerate like BP, Total, Saab, Toyota or Virgin Atlantic. In general terms they are subject to less regulation and what is there is readily accessible. They provide a simple mechanism for building from a simple model of a street trader to a more sophisticated business and exploring how accounting can be adapted from very simple principles to deal with complexity.

So we will start with a small simple business. Using a simple equation, a worksheet that mirrors a spreadsheet package like Excel, and with the help of a clear understanding of the definitions of the technical terminology of accounting, income, expenditure, assets and liabilities, and some simple addition and subtraction, we will enable you to produce accounting information that you can understand and use to make personal and business decisions.

WHAT IS ACCOUNTING?

In order to understand the role and importance of accounting in the context of business organizations it is first necessary to decide what the word 'accounting' means. If you were to look up the word 'account' in *Roget's Thesaurus,* you would be directed to words such as report and narration. Further investigation would reveal that it is also referred to as commercial arithmetic, double-entry book-keeping, etc. These alternatives imply totally different things: a report is something that conveys information for a particular purpose, whereas commercial arithmetic implies a mechanical exercise following agreed rules or principles.

In practice, although accounting is normally seen as a series of figures, which may give the impression that it is only a form of commercial arithmetic, these are, in fact, merely a convenient way of summarizing and reporting information that would be indigestible in narrative form. For example, if you were asked to provide a report giving details of the value of everything you own, it would be simpler to use figures to represent the value rather than words. However, there are certain things that do not lend themselves to summaries in numerical terms. An example may be the value of good health, the value of lead-free petrol or even the value of a qualification such as a degree.

Apart from problems concerned with what can be reported and what should be reported, other problems need to be considered, for example whether it can be reported in a numerical format and whether that is the best and most understandable format. We also need to consider whom the report is for and what it is to be used for. For instance, you may give a totally different account of your car's capabilities to a prospective buyer than to a mechanic to whom you had taken it for repairs. So we can see that the question of defining accounting has many facets. We shall look at these issues in more detail later in this chapter. Prior to that, in order to get a better idea of what accounting is generally thought to be about, let us examine some of the more useful of the many definitions contained in the accounting literature.

A definition that is commonly quoted is that produced by the American Institute of Certified and Public Accountants (AICPA) in 1941:

Accounting:
is the art of recording, classifying and summarizing, in a significant manner and in terms of money, transactions and events which are in part at least, of a financial character, and interpreting the results thereof.

This definition implies that accounting has a number of components – some technical (such as recording of data), some more analytical (such as interpreting the results) and some that beg further questions (such as 'in a significant manner': significant to whom and for what?).

Let us consider another definition offered by AICPA:

Accounting:
is the collection, measurement, recording, classification and communication of economic data relating to an enterprise, for purposes of reporting, decision making and control.

This gives us a clue to the fact that accounting is closely related to other disciplines (we are recording economic data) and it also gives us some clue as to the uses of accounting information, i.e. for reporting on what has happened and as an aid to decision making and control of the enterprise.

Another part of the same document sees accounting as:

Accounting:
a discipline which provides financial and other information essential to the efficient conduct and evaluation of the activities of any organization.

This suggests that the role of accounting information within an organization is at the very core of running a successful organization. Thus, as we have already noted, accounting can be seen as a multifaceted activity which not only records and classifies information but also provides an input to the decision-making processes of enterprises.

The latter point is brought out more clearly in the later definition provided by the American Accounting Principles Board in 1970 (APE No. 4):

Accounting:
is a service activity. Its function is to provide quantitative information, primarily financial in nature, about economic entities that is intended to be useful in making economic decisions, in making reasoned choices among alternative courses of action.

Accounting has, of course, moved on since the 1970s; there is increased pressure for more environmental reporting and corporate social reporting as well as issues around corporate governance (how an organization is run and controlled on behalf of its stakeholders) in the wake of scandals such as Enron, Lehman Brothers and Northern Rock. Thus, although the key points of these definitions, summarized in Key Concept 1.1, remain true, there are subtle changes in interpretation. For example, accounting is no longer solely about quantitative information as this often needs to be explained in narrative form and some reporting does not easily lend itself to quantification. Similarly, although most of the information still relates to financial performance, annual reports of organizations now contain information that is not financial and relates to other areas such as governance, social responsibility and environmental impact. In the case studies in this chapter and throughout the book we will provide you with examples of what is contained in annual reports. As an example of the wealth of information now contained in the Annual Report, the 2008 BP annual report contained over 100 pages of information before starting the section on financial information.

Returning to our discussion of our definitions of accounting we can distill some key points for that discussion about what a useful definition contains as shown in Key Concept 1.1.

KEY CONCEPT 1.1

Accounting

The important points made in these definitions are that

- accounting is generally about quantitative information;
- the information is likely to be financial;
- it should be useful for making decisions.

The fact that accounting was described in the AICPA definition above as a service activity reinforces the point made earlier that, in order to understand the usefulness of accounting, we need to know who uses accounting information and what they use it for.

FOR WHAT PURPOSE IS IT USED?

This question can be answered on two levels at least: that of the individual and that of the enterprise. If we take the level of the individual first, as you will have worked out from the discussion so far and through Activity 1.1, accounting information could be used to assist in planning future levels of expenditure, to help control the level of expenditure, to help raise additional finance (e.g. student loans, mortgages, hire purchase) and to decide the best way to spend their money. Thus, at the level of the individual, accounting can have three functions: planning, controlling and decision support.

At the level of the enterprise it is used to control the activities of the organization, to plan future activities, to assist in raising finance, and to report upon the activities and success of the enterprise to interested parties.

You will note that the major difference between the two is that in the case of an enterprise, apart from its uses in planning, controlling and decision making, which are all internal activities or functions, accounting also has what we could describe as an external function – that of providing information to people outside the enterprise. This became more important when the idea of joint stock companies started to take off in the 19th century; incidentally, the first of these appears to have been founded in around 1250 when some of the people of Toulouse formed a company called the *Société des Moulins du Bazacle* which had 96 parts or shares which were traded at a price that varied according to economic conditions and the output of the mills along the Garonne river. The increase in number and importance of joint stock companies and the increasing gap between ownership and management meant that the need for external reports by the managers (agents) to the owners also became more apparent. This reporting function is now met through the medium of annual accounts or financial reports and is often referred to as financial accounting. The external users may use the information contained in the financial report as part of their decision process, which necessarily requires that the information contained in these reports is useful for decisions or to evaluate what management has done with the money invested in the business, normally referred to as stewardship. Apart from meeting the needs of external users, the system that produces the financial accounting reports also meets some of the needs of internal users, for example to see the results of plans implemented in the last year. This requires information on the actual outcomes. This can then be evaluated against the projected outcomes, reasons for differences identified and appropriate actions taken. Other needs of management are met through reports based upon information provided by the internal accounting system. The internal accounting system, which may be in addition to the system which underpins the financial reporting system, is often referred to as the management accounting function. The major difference is that management accounting, as the name implies, is primarily directed towards providing information of specific use to managers, whereas financial accounting information, which is often produced in summary form, has many users apart from managers.

WHO USES ACCOUNTING INFORMATION?

Whether accounting information relates to the activities of an individual or to a business enterprise, its users can be placed in two broad categories:

1   those inside the enterprise – the managers or, in the case of a small business, the owner;

2   those outside the enterprise, including shareholders, banks, the government and tax authorities.

Internal users

The major internal user is the management of an enterprise. For a small enterprise this is likely to be the owner or a small number of individuals in the case of a partnership. However, many businesses are much larger and these may be owned by numerous individuals or groups of individuals, as is the case with large enterprises such as Mazda, Nokia, Marks & Spencer, Sainsbury or BP. In many cases the major investors are themselves owned by others, as is the case with the major financial institutions. In this situation it is extremely unlikely that the actual owners would or could take an active part in the day-to-day running of the enterprise. Consider the chaos if all the people who own shares in Samsung tried to take an active part in the day-to-day running of that business. Instead, these owners or shareholders delegate the authority for the day-to-day running to a group of directors and managers.

These directors and managers are involved in the routine decision-making and are the equivalent of the owner in a small business in terms of their information needs. These needs are normally met through unpublished reports of various kinds. These reports are generally based on information provided through both the financial and the management accounting systems. The exact nature of the reports will vary from enterprise to enterprise. For example, a department store may require information about the profitability of each of its departments, whereas for a factory producing a small number of different products the information required is more likely to be about the profitability of each product.

The form of the report will also vary depending on its purpose. For example, if management wishes to control what is going on, it will need a report on the past transactions and performance, probably measured against some predetermined standard. For planning purposes, however, a forecast of what is likely to happen in the future will be more important. These different forms of reports and ways of grouping information are normally referred to under the generic heading of management accounting, and this form of accounting will be the focus of the second half of this book. At this stage it is worth briefly summarizing the different categories of management accounting reports. To do this we need to make some broad generalizations about the needs of managers and to categorize those needs in some meaningful way. In practice, of course, there is a certain amount of overlap between the categories but we need not concern ourselves with this at present. The categories will be discussed in greater detail in Chapters 13–19. The broad categories that we have referred to in terms of the needs of managers are as follows:

Planning   The need to plan activities so that the finance can be raised, marketing and promotional campaigns set up and production plans agreed. This is the planning function.

Control   The need to control the activities of the enterprise, which may include setting sales targets **and** ensuring that they hold an adequate supply of goods to meet demand. It will also include identifying where targets have and have not been met so that the reasons for the failure to achieve the targets can be identified. This is referred to as the control function.

Decision making   The need to make specific decisions (Should we produce the item ourselves or buy it in? How much will it cost to produce a particular item? How much money will we need in order to run the enterprise?). This is the decision support function.

In addition to these three major components of their role top managers as agents of the owners are also concerned with ensuring that all the assets of the business are in existence, are utilized appropriately and effectively to further the aims of the business.

A moment's reflection will lead us to the conclusion that the area of management accounting is a vast area in its own right and so, rather than getting deeply involved at this stage, let us first look at the other broad area we identified – the needs of users outside the enterprise, the external users. We shall, of course, be returning to the needs of internal users in more detail, in Chapter 13.

External users

We need to establish who the external users are. Fortunately, over the years there have been many reports which have addressed this question. However, although the lists of users have been repeated in many reports they are generally derived from those contained in *The Corporate Report*, published by the Institute of Chartered Accountants in England and Wales (1975). The list below, taken from *The Corporate Report*, includes most of the accepted users of external financial reports (see Key Concept 1.2):

- the owner(s) (shareholders in a company);
- those who lend the enterprise money (e.g. the bankers);
- those who supply the enterprise with goods (suppliers);
- those who buy goods from the enterprise (customers);

- the employees of the enterprise;
- the government;
- the general public.

KEY CONCEPT 1.2

Financial accounting

Financial accounting can broadly be thought of as that part of the accounting system that tries to meet the needs of the various external user groups for decision useful information. This it does by means of the annual financial report which usually takes the form of a statement of financial position also commonly referred to as the balance sheet, the income statement, also known as the profit and loss account and the cash flow statement.

These groups are normally provided with information by means of published annual reports. In order to decide to what extent the annual reports meet the needs of the external users and to understand more fully the importance of accounting, we shall briefly discuss the needs of the external users listed above.

Owners/shareholders

As we have said, in the case of a small enterprise the owners are likely to be actively engaged in the day-to-day operations of the enterprise. In these small enterprises, therefore, the owners' needs will often be met by the management accounting information and reports. As the enterprise grows, however, it is likely that the owners will become divorced from the immediate routine operation and therefore will not have access to the management accounting information, which in any case may be too detailed for their requirements. This is the case in companies quoted on the Stock Exchange. It is also going to be the case in a number of other businesses where the functions of management are carried out by people other than the owners.

In all these cases the owner needs to know:

- whether the enterprise has done as well as it should have done;
- whether the managers have looked after, and made good use of, the resources of the enterprise.

In order to evaluate whether the enterprise has done well and whether resources have been adequately used, there is a need to be able to compare the results of one enterprise with the results of others. Information of this type is normally based on past results and under certain conditions it can be provided by financial accounts.

Owners also need to know:

- how the enterprise is going to fare in the future.

Financial accounting is unlikely to provide this information for a variety of reasons, in particular because it is largely if not exclusively based on the past and takes no account of future uncertainties. Past results may be taken into account as one piece of information amongst many when trying to predict the future, but in a changing world it is unlikely that past results will be repeated because conditions will have changed.

ACTIVITY 1.3

Clearly accounting information as a predictor of the future depends on the ability to use the information in the accounts and combine it with other 'external' information about the way the world is changing. In the telecoms industry a decade ago phones were wired, telephone boxes were commonplace, calls were routed via landlines and telephone operators, mobile phones were hardly even an emerging technology. Spend a moment thinking how these changes may have affected your interpretation of the accounting information had you known they were on the horizon?

Taking each of these changes in turn we could see that the use of mobile phones increased the market out of recognition so sales forecasts based on landline technology would have been wildly out. They made telephone boxes almost obsolete so reducing the demand for engineers to repair these, operators were no longer needed as technology had replaced them. So the staffing costs would have been completely different to today where the costs might be associated with high street shops and salespeople. This in effect means that because of the extent of technological change in this industry the financial accounts on their own would not be useful for predicting future sales, costs or profits.

Although there are limitations on the usefulness of the information contained in annual reports, these are often the only form of financial report available to an owner who is not involved in the day-to-day activities of the business. Owners therefore have to base their decisions on this information which despite its inadequacies has as its fundamental objective being useful for decision makers. Thus, for example, a shareholder, who is after all a part owner, may use the accounting information contained in the annual report, by comparing the results of the business with those of another business, to decide on whether to sell his or her shares. In doing so the shareholder will be assessing the return he or she gets from investing in one business as compared to another having due regard to the financial information contained in the accounts and to external factors such as the riskiness of the investment compared to available alternatives. In practice, the involvement of the shareholder in this process of making comparisons, in the case of a quoted company, is likely to be fairly indirect. This is because most of the information contained in the annual reports will already have been looked at by the owner's professional advisers, who may be accountants, stockbrokers or financial analysts. The investor and owner are therefore likely to make the decision based on the professional advice they receive rather than relying upon their own interpretation of the information contained in annual reports. This is not to say that they will rely exclusively on expert information or that they will not use the information provided in the annual reports for their decision. The reality is likely to be a mixture, the balance of which will depend on the degree of financial sophistication of the shareholder or owner, i.e. the less sophisticated they are the more reliance they will have to place on their external advisers. If as an investor your target portfolio includes the smaller business, however, then the more you know and understand what is and what is not in the annual accounts and how they are prepared the better.

Lenders

People and organizations only lend money in order to earn a return on that money. They are therefore interested in seeing that an enterprise is making sufficient profit to provide them with their return (usually in the form of interest). This information is normally provided by means of an income statement. They are also interested in ensuring that the enterprise will be able to repay the money it has borrowed; hence, they need to ascertain what the enterprise owns and what it owes and how money flows in to and out of the enterprise. This information is normally provided in the statement of financial position or balance sheet and cash flow statement.

In practice, research (Berry *et al.*, 1987, 1993, 2004) has shown that bankers operating in the UK use a mixture of different approaches to arrive at the lending decision. The choice of approach has been shown to be related to the size of the enterprise. In the case of smaller enterprises the 'gone concern' or security-based approach, which emphasizes the availability of assets for repayment in the event of the business going bust, predominates and the emphasis is clearly on the balance sheet now also called the statement of financial position. However, with very large businesses the approach adopted is more likely to be the 'going concern' approach, where the emphasis is more clearly focused on the profitability of the enterprise. The importance of published accounting information in the form of annual reports for this group cannot be overemphasized: nearly 100% of respondents to surveys (Berry *et al.*, 1987; Berry and Robertson, 2006) said that the reports were very important and always used in making a lending decision. The more recent survey by Berry and Robertson (2006) found that for bankers the cash flow statement was the most important statement of the three primary financial statements.

Suppliers of goods and services

Goods and services can be supplied on the basis either that they are paid for when they are supplied or that they are paid for at some agreed date in the future. In both cases the supplier will be interested to know whether the enterprise is likely to stay in business and whether it is likely to expand or contract. Both of these needs relate to the future and as such can never be adequately met by information in the annual report as this relates to the past.

Suppliers of goods who have not been paid immediately will also be interested in assessing the likelihood of getting paid. This need is partially met by the annual report, as the statement of financial position or balance sheet shows what is owned and what is owed and also gives an indication of the liquidity of the assets. The reason why we are tentative about its use in this way is that often the information is many months out of date by the time that it is made public, as it is only published annually.

ACTIVITY 1.4

Have a quick look at the needs identified so far and see what, if any, are common.

You will probably have identified profitability and liquidity as factors that users have in common. The differences between users are to do with emphasis and power to obtain information.

Customers

Like suppliers, customers are interested in an enterprise's ability to survive and therefore to carry on supplying them with goods. For example, if you are assembling cars you need to be sure that the suppliers of your brakes are not going to go bankrupt. The importance of this has increased with the introduction of techniques such as just-in-time management. The customers in this situation will need to see that the enterprise is profitable, that it owns enough to pay what it owes, and that it is likely to remain in business and supply components efficiently and on time. Some of these needs are met at least partially by the income statement, the statement of financial position and the cash flow statement.

The employees

Employees depend on the survival of the enterprise for their wages and therefore are interested in whether the enterprise is likely to survive. In the long term, an enterprise needs to make a profit in order to survive. The income statement may assist the employee in making an assessment of the future viability of the company.

The employee may also be interested in comparing how well the enterprise is doing, compared with other similar enterprises, for the purposes of wage negotiations, although the accounts are only useful for this purpose if certain conditions are met. The accounts can also be used internally for wage negotiations as information about the company's level of profitability and ability to pay can be obtained from them.

The government and regulatory bodies

The government uses accounting information for a number of purposes, the most obvious of which is the levying of taxes. For this purpose, it needs to know how much profit has been made. This information is provided in the income statement. The government also uses accounting information to produce industry statistics for the purposes of regulation and in the light of the banking crisis, the demise of MG Rover and the actions of the Phoenix Four the government is becoming more directly involved in regulation through the Financial Services Authority, The Pension Regulator and similar bodies. It is also worth bearing in mind the other sources of regulation for example the Stock Exchange which requires compliance with a code of corporate governance – see Case Study 1.1 for an example of disclosure of information in respect of Next and their compliance with the requirements.

CASE STUDY 1.1

Next plc Annual Report 2009

Combined Code compliance
The Group complied throughout the year under review with the provisions set out in Section 1 of the June 2006 FRC Combined Code on Corporate Governance.

The Board of Directors
Commentary
Under this heading the Board provides an overview of its responsibilities and how it carries out those responsibilities, communication frequency of meetings and who attends.

(Continued)

Audit Committee

Commentary

Under the code of practice all quoted companies must have an independent audit committee; its remit is described in the extract below.

Example text from report

The Committee considers financial reporting and reviews the Group's accounting policies and annual statements. In particular, any major accounting issues of a subjective nature are discussed by the Committee. The Committee also reviews internal and external audit activity and the effectiveness of the risk management process; significant risk issues are referred to the Board for consideration.

Remuneration Committee

Commentary

Under the code of practice all quoted companies must have an independent remuneration committee to determine the pay of senior management and report to shareholders.

Example text from report

This committee determines the remuneration of the executive directors and reviews that of senior management. A Remuneration Report is included in this Annual Report.

Nomination Committee

Commentary

Under the code of practice all quoted companies must have a separate nomination committee and the extract below provides an overview of the remit of this committee.

Example text from report

The Committee consists of the Chairman and four independent non-executive directors, including the senior non-executive director. The Committee meets as required to fulfill its duties of reviewing the Board structure and composition and identifying and nominating candidates to fill Board vacancies as they arise.

Other headings on which reports are included in the governance section of the annual report of NEXT include:

Directors' conflicts of interest
Chairman
Chief Executive
Management delegation
Performance evaluation
Risk management
External auditors
Personal use of company assets
Relations with shareholders
Going concern

It should also be borne in mind that in certain cases these roles are combined with other functions, for example that of owner (the National Health Service), customer (defence procurement) or public watchdog (environmental protection boards). Equally, it can have any one of these and other roles such as regulatory roles. For all these purposes the government uses accounting information.

ACTIVITY 1.5

Have a quick search on the internet and see what you can find out about the Phoenix Four.

You should have found a wealth of information that should have convinced you that there is a need for accounting information and regulation and that there is also a need for continuous improvements to be made in both these areas.

At this point we can sum up what we have identified so far in terms of information needs of the various users in the form of Table 1.1

TABLE 1.1

User group	Future profitability	Current profitability	Efficiency	Risk business and financial	Value of assets	Liquidity
Owners	X	X	X	X	X	
Preference shareholders	X	X				
Lenders	X	X	X		X	X
Suppliers & customers	X	X				
Employees	X	X	X			X
Government		X				

The general public

Although the general public may use some of the information contained in Table 1.1 it may also require many different types of information about enterprises in both the public and private sectors. Much of this information is not supplied directly by financial accounts. For example, the public might be interested in the level of pollution resulting from a particular activity. This information is not at present always provided within enterprises' annual reports; however, accounting reports may be useful in informing the public of the ability of an enterprise to absorb the additional costs of providing pollution controls. On the other hand, certain information provided in financial accounts may be of more direct relevance, e.g. the profitability or otherwise of the few remaining nationalized industries or state-controlled bodies, e.g. Health Trusts. It is now the norm and indeed the International Standard on Financial Reporting for Small and Medium Size Entities (IFRS-SMES) (2009) which recommends good practice means you will see within the annual report of an organization three types of basic financial statement specified in Key Concept 1.3:

KEY CONCEPT 1.3

Key financial statements

- the statement of financial position or balance sheet;
- the income statement or profit and loss account;
- the cash flow statement.

In addition if businesses follow the requirement of the IFRS-SMES there will be lots of other information including details about total gains and accounting policies, which you will be introduced to over the course of the next 12 chapters.

Starting with the statement of financial position or balance sheet, this can be seen as a measure of the accumulated wealth at a point in time. Although this is a simple definition, as we will see in Chapter 2 how we measure that wealth is not as straightforward as it might appear at first sight. If we view the statement of financial position or balance sheet as a measure of the accumulated wealth at a point in time, then in a dynamic world we would expect this to change over time and the income statement and cash flow statement can both be seen as ways of depicting that change in wealth over time. The income statement measures any profit or loss generated in the period, whereas the cash flow statement shows the movements in cash over the period. We will discuss each of these statements in more detail later. It is worth noting that when companies comply with the IFRS-SMES they will also be required to produce a statement of comprehensive income which includes gains not included in an income statement, a statement of changes in equity, a statement of significant accounting policies and notes to the accounts all of which will be explained in due course

Although all annual reports will have the three core statements identified in Key Concept 1.3 above, it is usually the case that enterprises, especially large enterprises, will use the annual report to provide additional information to shareholders and other users. Some examples of the ways in which financial reports are used for presenting both financial information and other information of interest to users is illustrated in Case Studies 1.1 through to 1.4 all of which are taken from the annual reports of major companies. The report in Case Study 1.2 relates to environmental issues in the supply chain, the actual stores and the logistics of getting supplies to the stores. As can be seen from these limited extracts the Carrefour group takes environmental and sustainability issues seriously and puts them at the core of business decisions.

CASE STUDY 1.2

Environmental issues

Commentary

Below are some headlines and extracts from the annual report and accounts of the French supermarket chain Carrefour talking about aspects of their policies and business practices and impacts on the environment.

(Continued)

Extracts from the 2008 Annual Report

The Carrefour Group strives to limit the environmental impact of its activities.

Creating a virtuous dynamic for the globe is Carrefour's daily challenge.

Making positions clear The Carrefour Group is revising its business practices to protect natural resources. Its consumer ranges particularly reflect this effort: GMO-free own-brand food products in Europe; garden furniture made from non-threatened, exotic wood species; a complete ban on selling Mediterranean bluefin tuna in Europe as of 2008, and support for the creation of sustainable sourcing for palm and soy oil.

Fewer kilometres driven Upstream, the Group's warehouse deliveries are increasingly reliant on alternative forms of transport. In 2008, Carrefour France shipped over 40% of its imported merchandise by river borne and rail transport. Now that Carrefour has five consolidation platforms throughout Europe, suppliers can deliver to a single location. Carrefour then takes it from there, using fully loaded multi-supplier trucks for warehouse deliveries. Downstream, transport rounds are being increasingly streamlined. In Italy, a software program adjusts the daily delivery schedule to fluctuations in the volume of orders. As a result, the number of kilometres travelled has dropped by 5% and the amount of fuel burned by 7%. In 2008, logistics services, in cooperation with stores, decided to change the way stores are supplied on a daily basis by keeping pace with the real needs of each store department. This policy will be expanded Group-wide in 2009.

Carrefour's warehouses are also coming up to speed on sustainable development. In France, 55 audits were conducted in 2008. In 2009, two sites will undergo a carbon assessment, allowing them to identify key environmental impacts and act accordingly.

Another area on which companies increasingly report either as part of the annual report or as a separate report is that of corporate social responsibility and how the company is fulfilling its role in that regard. It is now an area that is itself spawning a new industry of consultants and advisers. In short corporate social responsibility takes a wider view than simply reporting to the owners of the business; it addresses a wider audience of stakeholders which we have referred to as users. This part of the annual report is used to include a commentary on how the company has addressed those wider needs and responsibilities. The activities that fall under this broad umbrella may include looking after employees' rights and welfare, involvement in the local and regional community and giving back to society.

CASE STUDY 1.3

John Lewis Partnership

Commentary

The John Lewis Partnership is widely known and is a genuine partnership with employees being co-owners of the business. This is why it refers to its partners rather than shareholders in the following extract from the Annual Report which is concerned with its record on corporate social responsibility.

(Continued)

John Lewis Partnership – extract from 2008 Annual Report

Corporate Social Responsibility (CSR) Treating our Partners as individuals, with respect, honesty and fairness, sharing the rewards and responsibilities of ownership and conducting our business with integrity and courtesy are key aspects of the way we work. This drives our environmental policies, our involvement with local communities and our approach to responsible sourcing and trading.

The Partnership has made a commitment to annually benchmark our CSR performance with other leading UK businesses. The Partnership achieved platinum level status in the most recent Business in the Community (BITC) Corporate Responsibility Index. Platinum ranking is awarded to those companies reaching a score equal to or above 95%. In 2008, our CSR performance was independently recognized at the BITC Awards for Excellence, where we received six 'Big Tick' awards for the following programmes: Waitrose Education; Waitrose Local and Regional Sourcing; Waitrose Responsible Sourcing and the Waitrose Foundation; the Golden Jubilee Trust (all reaccreditations); the John Lewis Newcastle vocational placement scheme; and John Lewis Glasgow school mentoring programme. These awards are made to companies demonstrating excellence in the way that they organize and integrate their responsible business practices and can show a positive impact both on society and business.

As we have said, the area of corporate social responsibility (CSR) has become a major area of focus for businesses and many companies produce separate reports. In Case Study 1.4 we have taken two extracts from the 36 page report on CSR produced by Santander.

CASE STUDY 1.4

Santander Annual Report 2008

Extracts from the Corporate Social Report
Commentary

The first of these extracts is the introduction to the document from Lord Burns the Chairman of the group and it provides an overview of how Santander view the remit of CSR and this provides not only an overview of SCR activities but puts it into the context of how the business and global economy are impacting. The second extract concerns what they are doing with Universities and higher education.

Introduction to Santander CSR 2008 Despite a very difficult economic environment in 2008, Abbey's business performed well and we continued to make good progress on our CSR activities.

This was the second of our three year CSR plan, and our focus was on seven priority areas – financial inclusion, employee diversity, volunteering, corporate donations, environmental impacts, climate change and supplier engagement. We made considerable progress on the majority of these and continued to invest in our new flagship programme Santander Universities which saw partnerships established with a further 21 UK institutions.

(Continued)

To support our customers, we invested further in our range of value for money products and services including launching a 'First Home Saver' account paying a market leading 8% for savings of between £100 and £300 a month in a commitment to first time buyers. We also launched a dedicated 'Passport to Balancing Your Life' pack for employees bringing together a new range of policies to support employees in achieving a positive work-life balance.

Our focus on encouraging staff in community activities increased the take up of our 'Community Days' team challenges and this year 47 projects were supported around the UK. With the launch of our first 'Charity of the Year' in 2008 we were able to raise over £140 000 for Great Ormond Street Hospital and in total our community contributions reached £4.9 million. Our efforts to reduce the environmental impacts of our day-to-day business continued and an investment of almost £7 million in new technology and equipment helped to contribute to a reduction in energy of 18% resulting in CO_2 emissions of 4.02 tonnes per employee.

2009 is expected to be another difficult year for the UK economy with further market deterioration that will present ongoing challenges. However, Abbey continues to benefit from the strength of Santander and we remain confident that our business will grow. We are committed to maintaining our CSR programme activities. With an enhanced presence in the marketplace, we recognize that our position as one of the largest financial companies in the UK carries with it an increased responsibility to society.

During 2009, we will review our programme to ensure our CSR activities are aligned to the expectations of our stakeholders and we will look to integrate the Alliance & Leicester and Bradford & Bingley CSR initiatives taking the best of each to support our goal of becoming the best commercial bank in the UK.

Lord Burns

Universities Santander believes that investing in higher education and research is the most powerful means of promoting the development and prosperity of society. As a result, the 'Santander Universities' scheme was launched in 1996 as the cornerstone of the group's CSR policy.

By establishing partnerships with universities across Latin-America and Europe, the Group has developed a unique collaborative network with global reach. The programme was launched in the UK in 2007 bringing the benefits of Santander Universities to ten institutions.

2008 saw the further expansion of Santander Universities in the UK and by the end of the year agreements were established with a total of 31 institutions, equating to £1.8 m pledged in support for the higher education sector.

The agreements, for an initial three year period, are bespoke in order to meet each university's needs and priorities. The most common areas of investment are for staff and student international mobility, research, and knowledge transfer.

The partnership agreements cover a broad range of collaboration themes and between Santander Universities and the individual institutions CEO lectures, sports programmes, 'dragons dens', choir tours, visiting fellows and fresher awards have all been facilitated.

UK programme highlights
- 190 international scholarships and research awards.
- 150 post-graduate scholarships to the UK.
- 48 non-academic community awards.
- 18 enterprise and entrepreneur awards.
- eight business incubators.

(Continued)

Fostering entrepreneurship Support for practical enterprise and entrepreneurship is a key strand of the Santander Universities programme. In 2008, with the growing demand for innovative business solutions to climate change and environmental challenges, Santander Universities has been keen to foster research and development projects in this area.

At the University of Bath, Santander Universities sponsored the launch of an MBA project 'Entrepreneurship in Action'. The first prize of £3000 went to the plan believed to have the best commercial potential: 'Cambio' – a business idea **centred** on generating renewable energy from organic waste products.

Oxford Brookes University's environmental motorsport team has developed a hybrid vehicle that took part in Silverstone's Formula Student Competition in July 2008. The 'green' car combines the use of petrol and electricity to provide a more environmentally friendly alternative to traditional rally and racing vehicle fuels. The use of biofuels is one of the main areas of study for research and development within the motor industry and Santander Universities has provided sponsorship for the Oxford Brookes students to support their cutting edge work towards the development of more sustainable energies.

Extending value The Santander Universities model not only provides scholarships and event sponsorship but also responds to the banking needs of the university community through the development of targeted products and services.

This year saw the launch of a Santander international student account, a solution to the often lengthy process international students face when opening a bank account on arrival in the UK.

With the Santander account, students only need to provide the letter of acceptance from the university and one further form of identification to open an account.

And in order to make banking more accessible for the university community seven Santander Universities branches were opened in 2008: Bath, Essex, Leeds, Loughborough, Southampton, London and Oxford Brookes.

Global Santander Universities in 2008 700 collaboration agreements with Universities in 20 countries including Spain, Portugal, Morocco, China, USA, Russia, UK and across Latin-America.

– 2 820 academic, financial and technological collaboration projects funded.

– 4m university smart cards in circulation.

– 14 665 scholarships, internships and awards.

– 6 840 international mobility scholarships.

– 35 business incubator projects.

– 300 new university businesses.

Two major global projects are also part of the Santander Universities programme:

– Universia, the largest online university network, with 1100 universities in 11 countries.

– The Miguel de Cervantes Virtual Library, the most important Hispanic literature internet portal with the largest volume of Spanish content and number of users in the world.

The breadth and richness of content have made both projects a consolidated source of knowledge and advice for university communities around the world.

LIMITATIONS OF ACCOUNTING INFORMATION

First, and perhaps most importantly, it has to be stressed that accounting is only one of a number of sources of information available to decision makers. It may be the case that other sources of information are just as important if not more important than the information contained in the accounts as the recent banking crisis served to underline. You will have an opportunity to examine this in more detail in the Problems for discussion and analysis section at the end of this chapter. However, to give you a flavour of what we are talking about, research with bankers (referred to earlier) shows that a banker's personal interview with the client is as important as financial information. This is probably because accounting generally only reports on financial items, i.e. those that can be expressed in financial (monetary) terms, whereas the information that bankers are trying to derive from the interview is more qualitative, e.g. an impression of the ability of the applicant to run a successful business. The concern with non-quantitative information is also reflected within the annual reports of quoted companies, as is evidenced by the increasing size of the report (70–200+ pages is not unusual) and the range of information provided. Information of the type shown in Case Studies 1.1 to 1.4 are examples of such information; there would also be information on products, activities, future plans, etc., all provided in narrative form. It is also possible that the information which accounting provides is only of secondary importance, as would be the case where new technology has made the precise costing of a product irrelevant because the product is obsolete. The relative importance of various sorts of information is illustrated in Case Study 1.5.

Even given the role of accounting information in relation to other information, we also have to bear in mind that, in general, financial accounting information relates to the past and the decisions that need to be taken relate to the future. Thus, unless the past is a reasonable predictor of the future, the information may have limited value for this purpose. In the real world, because of the impact of such things as changes in technology, innovations, changing fashions and inflation, the past is unlikely to be a good predictor of the future; a recent example of these difficulties was estimating the costs of and income from the Millennium Dome in London.

CASE STUDY 1.5

GlaxoSmithKline

Commentary

The relative importance of financial and other information varies from organization to organization. For example, GlaxoSmithKline (GSK) is a leading research-based pharmaceutical company, and some of GSK's most valuable assets are the people it employs to research and develop pharmaceuticals and the patents to produce them. It is often difficult to quantify in precise financial terms the value of such assets, but this does not make them any less vital to the survival of the company. A future medical breakthrough or discoveries of detrimental side-effects of a product are just as important information as the financial results of the organization.

GSK values intellectual property and research and development (R&D) as vital assets to the continuing success of the company. Intellectual property refers to the resource of an individual's creativity and innovation. It is interesting to see that whilst in 2003 intellectual property was associated with 'human capital' by 2009 GSK had moved to a more legalistic view of what intellectual property is.

(Continued)

Extract from GlaxoSmithKline (GSK) Annual Report 2009

Intellectual property Intellectual property is a key business asset for our company, and the effective legal protection of our intellectual property (via patents, trademarks, registered designs, copyrights and domain name registrations) is critical in ensuring a reasonable return on investment in R&D.

Extract from GlaxoSmithKline plc Annual Report 2003 GlaxoSmithKline people are fundamental to the success of the business. Their skills and intellect are key components in the successful implementation of sound business strategy. This is the human capital that maximizes the potential of the Group's scientific, commercial and financial assets.

GlaxoSmithKline regards its intellectual property as a key business asset. The effective legal protection of intellectual property is critical in ensuring a reasonable return on investment in R&D.

The continued development of commercially viable new products is critical to the Group's success.

Apart from these problems, there is also the question of what is and what is not included in the financial accounts. For instance, some items which it is generally agreed should be included in financial reports are often difficult to measure with any accuracy and the figures therefore become more subjective. A good example of this problem is an unfinished building. How do we decide on a figure to represent some that is only half complete? A visit to Ireland in 2009/10 would have revealed the extent of the problem as developers built new housing developments around the big cities to cater for the burgeoning demand arising from the boom economy only to be left with estates of non saleable houses when the global recession hit. Another example is the problem of deciding how long something is going to last, e.g. a motor car clearly loses value the older it gets. We might decide that a car ceases to be useful to the business after four or five years, but this is to some extent an arbitrary decision as there are many older cars that still serve a useful purpose. In addition to the problem of deciding how long things will last or what stage of completion they have reached, certain items are difficult to quantify in terms of value and are not easily included in financial reports. For example, the value of a football club is dependent on its ability to attract supporters; this in turn is dependent on its ability to succeed, which is dependent on the abilities of the players, etc. However, although it is doubtful that an exact value could be placed on a player, as this value will vary with the player's fitness etc., it's undoubtedly true that each player has a value on the transfer market. As such, a cost can be established if we buy a player, which gives an indication of the value of the player, but what if we grow our own star players through the cadet team?

In addition to the questions raised above, there are many environmental factors which need to be taken into account but which cannot be adequately included in accounts, although they may be quantifiable in money terms. Examples are the potential market for the product, the impact of European Union (EU) quotas, tax restrictions and environmental issues. If these were to be included in the annual reports of a business it could lead to a loss of competitive advantage.

Finally, we have to deal with the fact that accounting information is expressed in monetary terms and assume that the monetary unit is stable over time. This is patently not the case and, although there has been much discussion on the problem of accounting in times of inflation, no agreed solution has yet been found.

We can conclude from the discussion above that, although it is clear that accounting provides some information that is useful to decision makers, we must bear in mind:

1   that the information is only a part of that necessary to make 'effective' decisions;

2   that accountancy is as yet an inexact science and depends on a number of judgments, estimates, etc;

3   that the end result of the accounting process can only be as good as the inputs and in times of rising prices some of these inputs are of dubious value;

4   that accounting systems can be counterproductive, e.g. the maximization of a division's profit may not always ensure the maximization of the profit of the enterprise.

Nevertheless, it is clear that accounting is vital to the running of a healthy and prosperous enterprise, and arguably it is also an essential prerequisite for a prosperous economy. Before leaving this chapter, it would therefore be useful to look at accounting both in terms of its uses within the business and in the wider context of the business and its environment.

Accounting uses within the business

The accounting department, like, for instance, the personnel department and the marketing department, operates in theory in an advisory capacity only, providing information for managers to make the decision. In practice, however, the financial elements controlled by the accounting function and the information it generates are so central to the operation of the enterprise that the influence of accounting is often all pervasive. Although it is essential to the smooth running of the business, it does not have as direct an impact as, for example, the buying department or the production line. Its effects are generally more subtle, although they may in certain instances be very obvious. For example, if the accounting information indicates that expenses are running at too high a level, this may have dramatic repercussions in other functional areas. Training and recruitment budgets may be instantly frozen, producing a significant impact on the work of the personnel department and other operating departments, and affecting both staffing and skills levels. Alternatively, a decision may be taken to stop expenditure on a current advertising campaign, thus having a direct effect on the work of the marketing department.

Accounting is also unusual in that it can have unintended effects; for example, if sales representatives are judged solely on their sales, this may lead them to sell goods to customers who are unlikely to pay in order to achieve the sales targets set. It can also be a very dangerous tool if used in the wrong way; for example, targets could be set to achieve cost savings on a production line with no account taken of the effect on quality or employee safety. Similarly, if it is used by people who do not understand its limitations, it can lead to wrong decisions. If, for example, a person was unaware that accounting as generally used takes no account of rising prices, goods could be sold at less than they cost to produce.

The importance of accounting within a business should not be underestimated. It provides the basic information by which managers and owners can judge whether the business is meeting its objectives. Its importance is shown by the high salaries that accountants can command and by the prevalence of accountants on the boards of directors of our major public companies.

Accounting information is used within a business to evaluate and shape alternative strategies such as making a component or buying it in from a supplier, thus shaping business plans and activities. At the same time, it is itself a function of the type of activity that an organization engages, its size and the strategies that the organization adopts. For example, the accounting system that would be appropriate for a business consultant who does one job at a time and who can clearly identify the amount of time and the expenses relating to that job would not be appropriate for a manufacturing plant which may use one building and many machines to produce multiple products all at the same time. In the latter case, to be able to identify the materials used and the labour inputs for a specific product would require a much more sophisticated system of accounting. Accounting systems are to a large extent variable and depend on the type of activity or activities in which a business is engaged and on the levels of activity.

Clearly, the organization's goals will have a major impact on the accounting system used; for example, to develop an accounting system with the primary purpose of measuring profit would be wholly inappropriate for a charitable organization. Similarly, the requirements in terms of accounting reports will be very different in the case of a workers' cooperative, the health service and a profit-oriented company. The cooperative members are more likely to be interested in their pay and their share of the surplus generated than in the enterprise profitability. Shareholders in a company, on the other hand, are likely to be more interested in judging overall profitability and comparing that with alternative investments. In the case of the health service, it is clearly the case that the owners, i.e. the general public, are interested in the service received. The costs are important but they are not the primary concern. You can think of similar examples in the transport sector where there is a concern for safety as well as profitability as evidenced by the cessation of air travel in most of Europe in April 2010.

Apart from the nature of the organization, the way in which an organization is structured will have an impact on the type of accounting system that is needed. For example, if a brewery operates all of its pubs by putting managers into them, it will need an accounting system that allows for the payment of regular salaries and bonuses based upon achieving preset targets. These targets are normally set in terms of barrelage and so it will need to know what the normal barrelage for each pub is; it will also need to know the mark-up on spirits, soft drinks, etc., and the approximate mix of sales in order to ensure that its managers are not pocketing the profits. If, however, it sets its organization up so that each pub has a landlord who is a tenant of the brewery, the system required will be different as in this case the landlord is not paid a salary or bonus – his wages instead come from the profits he makes from selling the beers, wines and spirits.

We have already alluded to the effect of the size of the organization on the accounting system. However, it is worth reiterating that the larger and more disparate the organization is, the greater is the need for organizational controls through a system of accountability which makes managers responsible for the performance of their divisions and which provides reports that can be used by senior managers to evaluate the performance of their subordinates and of the organization as a whole. As we have already mentioned, it is vital that the accounting system is tailored to the needs of the organization; otherwise, it will not allow management to control the organization and indeed may have dysfunctional effects. In the case of small businesses it is sometimes the case that little formal accounting information is available on a day-to-day basis. This may be because the operations are sufficiently simple not to warrant a formal system, e.g. a window cleaner knows how many houses or businesses are dealt with each day and therefore does not need much more information. In more complex small businesses, the lack of formal systems is more likely to be because the owner does not have the skills to produce the information and the costs of hiring in the necessary expertise are perceived as outweighing the potential benefits. It is often the case in small businesses that the only time that accounting reports are produced is at the end of the year to meet the needs of the tax collector and when the bank demands them as a prerequisite to granting a loan or extending an overdraft facility.

Finally, before summarizing the main points covered in this chapter, it is worth briefly discussing accounting in the context of the environment, which we referred to earlier in the chapter. As we said, accounting is also affected by its environment. This could be at the level of legislation, regulatory standards (e.g. International Accounting Standards, corporate governance codes), the impacts of new technology and new business processes, such as just-in-time, and, at a macro level, the economy. An example of the latter is a country suffering from hyperinflation has of necessity to use costs other than original costs in its accounting reports because the value of the monetary unit in which accounting information is expressed is changing so quickly.

SUMMARY

In this chapter, we have tried to give a flavour of what accounting is and how it pervades both the internal workings of organizations and the external environment. It can be seen to be at one level a functional area of business and at an external level an important determinant of business survival through its effect on shareholders, lenders, employees, etc. We have indicated that there is no perfect accounting report that will meet the needs of all users and that the needs of users vary depending on the purpose to which the report is put. For example, in the case of a small business the owner may wish to show a low profit to reduce the potential tax bill but may need to show a high profit in order to convince the banker to lend the business money. We have tried to indicate that accounting will only be useful if it is used correctly and if its limitations are understood. A failing business will still fail even though it has an excellent accounting system; on the other hand, potentially successful businesses have been allowed to go bankrupt either because the accounting system did not give the warning signs that it should have done or gave them too late or because management did not have sufficient understanding of the accounting signals to recognize the warning signs.

Before moving on, you should work through the review questions and problems to ensure that you have understood the main points of this chapter.

REFERENCES

Berry, A., Citron, D. and Jarvis, R. (1987) *The Information Needs of Bankers Dealing with Large and Small Companies, Certified Accountants Research Report 7*, London: Certified Accountants Publications.

Berry, A., Faulkner, S., Hughes, M. and Jarvis, R. (1993) *Bank Lending: Beyond the Theory*, London: Chapman & Hall.

Berry, A., Grant, P. and Jarvis, R. (2004) 'European bank lending to the UK SME sector: an investigation of the approaches adopted', *International Small Business Journal*, 22(2):115–122.

Berry, A. and Robertson, J. (2006) 'Overseas bankers in the UK and their use of information for making lending decisions: changes from 1985', *British Accounting Review*, 38(2):175–191.

The Corporate Report ASC (1975), London: Institute of Chartered Accountants in England and Wales.

International Accounting Standards Board (IASB) (2003) *International Accounting Standard 1. Presentation of Financial Statements*, London: International Accounting Standards Board.

REVIEW QUESTIONS

(✓ indicates answers are available in Appendix A)

✓ **1** For what purposes is accounting information used?

    (a) by the individual,

    (b) by the enterprise.

✓ **2** Who are the users of accounting information and which accounting reports do they normally use?

3 What are the needs of internal users? Can you identify any other needs of internal users; if so, can you suggest how these would be met?

✓ **4** What are the limitations of accounting information?

5 Examples were given for some of the limitations. Can you give examples of your own?

6   What are the major determinants of a useful accounting system?

7   What are the likely effects of organizational size on published financial information?

PROBLEMS FOR DISCUSSION AND ANALYSIS

(✓ indicates answers are available in Appendix A)

✓ **1**   It was pointed out that accounting information is only a part of the input to the decision-making process. In order to expand your understanding of the role of accounting information, for the situation outlined below

(a) identify the accounting information that would be relevant, and

(b) identify any other information that would be relevant.

Head & Co. is in business making navigation equipment and wishes to diversify into the production of hang-gliders. The existing business is based in London but the owners may be willing to move. The owners have little knowledge about the market for hang-gliders but feel that there is money to be made in that field.

2   Tack was left some money in his mother's will and decided that he should give up his job and go into business for himself. Whilst the lawyers were still sorting out his mother's estate he started looking round for a suitable business. After a short time he identified a small bacon-curing business that he felt was worth investing in. He was still uncertain how much his mother had left him but thought that it was probably between £40 000 and £50 000. The bacon-curing business was for sale for £100 000 and so assuming that he could finance the remainder he engaged an accountant to check over the books of the existing business and report back to him. As proof of his good faith, he deposited with the business agents £1000 which he had in savings.

The report from the accountant confirmed his initial impression that the business was worth investing in and so he paid the accountant's modest fee of £500 in full. At this stage he discussed his plans more fully with his bank manager, who was impressed with the professional approach taken by Tack.

The bank manager pointed out that Tack had no business experience and therefore was a high risk from the bank's point of view. However, in view of their long-standing relationship, the bank was prepared to take a chance and said that it would lend Tack 40% of the purchase price.

On the basis of this, Tack signed a conditional agreement to buy the bacon-curing business. A short time after this he received from the lawyers a letter stating that his inheritance from his mother amounted to only £30 000.

He could not raise the additional finance to purchase the bacon-curing business and so withdrew from the agreement, recovered his £1000 deposit and purchased a yacht with the intention of doing charter work to the Caribbean.

Required

Discuss the point at which, in your opinion, the accounting process should begin, giving reasons for your point of view. You should pay particular attention to the dual needs of Tack as an individual and as a potential owner of the business.

3   In Case Study 1.2 we identified a firm that produced environmental information and in Case Studies 1.3 and 1.4 we identified examples of corporate social responsibility reporting. Identify, with reasons, industries where you might expect to find this information, visit their websites and provide examples of environmental and social responsibility reporting.

4   In Case Study 1.5 GlaxoSmithKline made the following statements:

Intellectual property is a key business asset for our company, and the effective legal protection of our intellectual property (via patents, trademarks, registered designs, copyrights and domain name registrations) is critical in ensuring a reasonable return on investment in R&D. (2009 report)

GlaxoSmithKline people are fundamental to the success of the business. Their skills and intellect are key components in the successful implementation of sound business strategy. This is the human capital that maximizes the potential of the Group's scientific, commercial and financial assets.

GlaxoSmithKline regards its intellectual property as a key business asset. The effective legal protection of intellectual property is critical in ensuring a reasonable return on investment in R&D. (2003 report)

Explore how these major assets of GlaxoSmithKline could be represented in the form of financial information.

CHAPTER 2
WEALTH AND THE MEASUREMENT OF PROFIT

LEARNING OUTCOMES

By the end of this chapter you will:

- Understand the relationship between income and wealth.

- Be aware of the problems associated with measuring wealth and their impact on the measurement of income.

- Be able to measure income and wealth using different measurement bases and compare the outcomes.

This chapter explains the relationship between wealth and profit measurement. It then introduces some of the alternative measures of wealth available and illustrates the impact the choice of measurement system can have on the resultant profit measure.

In Chapter 1, we established that there are a number of different users of accounting information, each of whom needs different information for different purposes. However, there are some items of information that are required by most users. These relate to what an enterprise owns and what it owes, and to how it has performed or is performing – in other words, a measure of performance. The former information, i.e. about what an enterprise owns and what it owes, could be termed the worth of the enterprise or its wealth. This measure of wealth or worth relates to a point in time. The other information required is about the way in which the enterprise performed over a period of time. This performance during a period can be measured as a change in wealth over time. Thus, if you increase your wealth you have performed better, in financial terms, than someone whose wealth has decreased over the same period of time. This measurement of changes in wealth over time is referred to in accounting terminology as profit measurement. In this chapter we shall be looking at the ways in which accountants can measure wealth and profit, and discussing some of the merits of the alternatives available. We shall also examine in some detail the way in which the choice of a measurement system affects the resultant profit and wealth measures. To do this, we need to start by defining profit or wealth, as these two ideas are directly linked. A definition of profit that is widely accepted by accountants is based around the definition of an individual income put forward by the economist Sir John Hicks (1930), who stated:

Income is that amount which an individual can consume and still be as well off at the end of the period as he or she was at the start of the period.

KEY CONCEPT 2.1

Income and wealth

A relationship exists between income, or profit, and wealth. The definition above suggests that income can be derived by measuring wealth at two different points in time and the difference between the two figures is the income or profit. An alternative view proposed by other economists suggests that wealth is derived from income. These alternative views are probably both right as the relationship is to some extent circular, as depicted below. The different views taken by various economists really relate to how you break into the circle.

This definition can be illustrated diagrammatically as shown in Figure 2.1.

We can see from Figure 2.1 that we can arrive at the profit for the first period by measuring wealth at the start of the period, i.e. at time T_0, and subtracting that figure from our measurement at the end of the period, i.e. T_1. Similarly, the profit for the second period can be measured by subtracting the wealth at time T_1 from the wealth at the end of period 2, i.e. at time T_2.

FIGURE 2.1

It should also be clear from Figure 2.1 that wealth is static and represents a stock at a particular point in time. Thus, wealth 0 is the stock of wealth at time T_0, wealth 1 is the stock of wealth at time T_1 and wealth 2 is the stock of wealth at time T_2.

KEY CONCEPT 2.2

Wealth

Wealth is a static measure and represents a stock at a particular point in time. This stock can change over time. Hence, the wealth measured at the start of a period will not necessarily be equal to the wealth measured at the end of the period. The difference between the two is the profit or loss for that period of time.

If we look at the way in which profit is depicted in Figure 2.1, it is apparent that profit is a flow over time, i.e. to measure the profit earned over a period of time it is necessary to measure the stock of wealth at the start and end of that period.

KEY CONCEPT 2.3

Profit

Profit represents the difference between the wealth at the start and at the end of the period. Unlike wealth, which is essentially a static measure, profit is a measure of flow that summarizes activity over a period.

To summarize, we have shown that we can express the profit for the first period, i.e. from time T_0 to time T_1, as:

$$\text{profit period } 1 = \text{wealth } 1 - \text{wealth } 0$$

Similarly, we can express the profit for the second period, i.e. the period between time T_1 and time T_2, as:

$$\text{profit period } 2 = \text{wealth } 2 - \text{wealth } 1$$

We have also established that the profit is derived by measuring the wealth of an individual, or an enterprise, at two points in time. On the face of it, this is reasonably straightforward, but let us now look in more detail at what we are trying to measure and how we are to measure it.

We shall start by examining the case of an individual because this will be simpler and more in line with your own experience. The underlying arguments and principles are just the same for an enterprise but the degree of complexity involved increases in the case of an enterprise, especially large multinational companies. Let us suppose that we asked an individual to measure his wealth, i.e. the sum of his possessions less what he owes.

EXAMPLE 2.1

Tony came up with the following lists of items owned and told us that he owed nothing.

At the start of the year T_0	At the end of the year T_1
A new Ford Focus	The Ford Focus
Three new suits	The same three suits
Five shirts	The same five shirts
Four sweatshirts	Five sweatshirts
£400 cash	£1 000 cash

While the lists above may accurately reflect what Tony owns and what he owes, we cannot easily see whether he is better or worse off at the end of the year than he was at the start. We could perhaps say with the benefit of our own knowledge of the world that he must be worse off because everything is one year older; this, however, assumes that the value of his possessions decreases with time. In many cases that is a reasonable assumption, but clearly there are some cases where their value increases: for example, would our attitudes change if the car was a 1906 Bentley. Leaving that question aside for a moment, you will have noticed that once we started to discuss the measurement of wealth we also started talking of the more abstract concept of value.

This raises two questions, one of which relates to value, which we shall discuss in more detail later, and the other to the way in which we assign value. In the case of the lists of possessions above, the easiest item to deal with in terms of value is the cash. This is because it has already had a value assigned to it with which we are all familiar, i.e. a monetary value. On the face of it, therefore, it seems that if we assigned a monetary value to each of the items in the list we would have solved part of our problem at least. In fact, it is not as easy as that. We all know that the value of money is not stable; we only have to listen to our grandparents or even our parents talking about what money used to buy to realize that the value of money has decreased over time.

(Continued)

ACTIVITY 2.1

Can you think of any situations where you found the value of your money had changed over time?

If you go on holiday outside the UK you will have seen that the value of the pound relative to Euro or the US dollar changes from one year to the next.

If we leave the problem of the changing value of money aside and we use money as a measure of value, then we have no problem with the value of the cash in the bank, but what of the other items? What is the value of the car, for example? Is it worth less because it is one year older, and if so how much less? The same line of argument can be applied to the suits and shirts, but in the case of the sweatshirts we do not even know whether they are the same sweatshirts; clearly, there must be at least one that has been acquired during the year as he has five at the end compared with four at the beginning. We also have yet to establish whether the age is important for the purposes of arriving at a value. In order to be able to decide on that question we need first to look at the possibilities available to us.

Although numerous alternatives are put forward, many are combinations of those dealt with here. We shall limit our discussion to the most commonly quoted possibilities. For convenience, and in order to help understanding, we shall first deal with those that relate to cost and then discuss those that are based on some concept of value. We start with original cost, then look at historic cost and finally discuss replacement cost.

The definitions of the terms will be explained later in this chapter. The important point to note at this stage is the relationship between wealth and profit, and the way in which a change in the measurement of one affects the other. This will be explored in more detail, using the example of Tony, later.

KEY CONCEPT 2.4

Original cost

The cost of the item at the time of the transaction between the buyer and seller.

ORIGINAL COST

The original cost of an item is the cost at the time of the transaction between the buyer and the seller. It should be noted that we have made a number of assumptions about there being a willing buyer and willing seller which do not need to concern us at this point. Leaving those problems aside, on the face of it this seems to be a fairly easy figure to arrive at. It is in fact not so easy. Consider the case of this book. Is the original cost the price you paid in the bookshop? Or is it the price the bookshop paid the publisher? Or do we go back even further to the cost to the publisher? Or further still to the cost to the authors? Each of these is a possible measure of the original cost, but the question is: which is the right cost? The answer is that the cost is the cost to the individual or enterprise on which you are reporting. This cost is normally referred to as the historic cost.

> **KEY CONCEPT 2.5**
>
> **Historic cost**
>
> The cost incurred by the individual or enterprise in acquiring an item measured at the time of the originating transaction.

HISTORIC COST

Historic cost is the cost incurred by the individual or enterprise in acquiring an item measured at the time of the originating transaction. It is extremely important as it underpins most but not all current accounting practice. We can see that the historic cost of the book to you will be different from the historic cost to the bookshop. The book shop will buy it at a cheaper price usually about one third cheaper in the case of textbooks. This extra one third of the price is, of course, what keeps the bookshop in business. But let us take our example a stage further. Let us assume that, for whatever reason, at the end of the year you decide you no longer need this book; you therefore decide to sell it. In this situation you will probably find that the book is no longer worth what you paid for it and therefore the historic cost is no longer a fair representation of the book's worth or of your wealth. In order to tackle this problem, when measuring your wealth at the end of the year you could write the historic cost down to some lower figure to represent the amount of use you have had from the book. Accounting follows a similar process and the resulting figure is known as the written-down cost or carrying value. It can be described as the historic cost after an adjustment for usage. The adjustment for usage is commonly referred to as depreciation, and there are a number of ways of arriving at a figure for it, which we shall deal with in Chapter 8.

The problem with historic cost and written-down historic cost is that with the value of money and goods changing over time it is only likely to be a fair representation of value at a particular point in time, i.e. at the point of the original transaction. At any other point it will only be a fair representation of value by chance unless the world is static, i.e. with no innovation etc. Clearly this is not the case and so we should look for alternative measures. One such alternative to the original or historic cost of an item is its replacement cost. This is certainly more up to date and allows for the changes that will take place in a non-static world.

> **KEY CONCEPT 2.6**
>
> **Replacement cost**
>
> The amount that would have to be paid at today's prices to purchase an item similar to the existing item.

REPLACEMENT COST

The replacement cost of an item is the amount that would have to be paid at today's prices to purchase an item similar to the existing item. It is often very relevant as those of us who have had cars written off will know. In those cases the amount that the insurance company pays out often bears no relationship to what it would cost to replace your car, because yours was better than average or had just had a new engine put in. The problem that arises in using replacement cost is first that you have to want to replace the item. You may not want to replace a textbook that you used at school as it would no longer be of use to you. Even if we assume that you do want to replace the item, you may find that it is difficult to identify the replacement cost. Think of a specialist item such as Windsor Castle!

It may be that even if you could replace an item with an exact replica you may not wish to do so. For example, you may wish to obtain a newer version or one with extra functions. The most obvious example of this kind is the replacement of computer equipment, which is constantly expanding in power whilst its size and its price are generally decreasing. This leads us to the same problem that we had with historic cost in that the replacement cost of a computer does not take into account the age of the machine that we actually own. The solution is the same as for historic cost: estimate the effect of usage and arrive at a written-down replacement cost.

As we can see, there are distinct problems in using either historic cost or replacement cost. In a number of situations these are unlikely to be useful measures of value or wealth.

ACTIVITY 2.2

Can you think of situations when historic cost and replacement cost are unlikely to be useful?

In the case of historic cost you might have thought of Zimbabwe where the unit of currency changes value on a daily basis or you may have thought more generally about things that would cause the price to change, new innovations, changes in taste, etc. Some of these are equally applicable to replacement cost especially where the change means that the item is unlikely to be replaced.

Before reading the next section on alternative measures based on value rather than cost, it is worth spending a few minutes thinking of the situations in which historic cost and replacement cost are appropriate and those situations when they are unlikely to be suitable. This is important, because any measure is only useful if it is the appropriate measure to do the job in hand.

For example, although the acceleration of a car may be important in certain circumstances, it is irrelevant for an emergency stop. Similarly, the historic cost or replacement cost of a motor car is unlikely to be useful if we wish to sell the car as the selling price will be governed by other factors. The alternatives to these cost-based measures are measures which are related to value. However, as we shall see, value-based measures also have their own set of problems.

ACTIVITY 2.3

In each of the following examples can you think why historic cost and replacement cost **might** be irrelevant?

A mobile phone

A trident submarine

A coal fired power station

A CD player.

In some of these examples the first question is whether you would want to replace the item, whether technological change has had an effect or whether a change in society's attitude may have an effect as might be the case with the use of coal-fired power stations and the drive to more environmentally friendly sources of power. Similarly, post-cold war the whole question of the need for nuclear weapons is up for debate.

KEY CONCEPT 2.7

Economic value

Economic value is, or would be, an ideal measure of value and wealth.

The value of the expected earnings from using the item in question discounted at an appropriate rate to give a present-day value.

ECONOMIC VALUE

The economic value of an item is the value of the expected earnings from using the item discounted at an appropriate rate to give a present-day value. The problem is not in defining the measure but in actually estimating future earnings, as this implies knowledge of what is going to happen; problems of foreseeing technological change, fashion changes and suchlike make the estimation of future earnings problematic. Even if we assume that this can be done, we are then left with the question of finding an appropriate rate at which to discount the estimated future earnings. The problem here is that each individual may wish to use a different rate depending on his or her circumstances. For example, a millionaire may not worry very much if money is available in a year rather than immediately, but if you have no money to buy your next meal the situation is entirely different. We should not totally discount the possibility of using this measure because of these problems, since with the use of mathematical techniques relating to probability it is still a useful tool in decision making. In fact, it is the basis underlying techniques such as net present value which are often used in investment appraisal decisions which we shall discuss in more detail in Chapter 20.

KEY CONCEPT 2.8

Net realizable value

The net realizable value is an alternative measure of value to economic value.

NET REALIZABLE VALUE

The net realizable value is the amount that is likely to be obtained by selling an item, less any costs incurred in selling. On the face of it, such a measure should be easily obtainable but in practice the amount for which an item can be sold will vary with the circumstances of the sale. The problems of arriving at the net realizable value are apparent in the second-hand car market, where there is a trade price and a range of retail prices. Another good example is the house market, where independent valuations can differ by as much as £50 000 on a property worth between £350 000 and £400 000. Apart from the problem of arriving at a value, other factors will affect the net realizable value. For example, if you are hard up you may be prepared to accept less than the market value in order to get a quick sale. The value in the latter situation is known as the forced sale value, and is the most likely value where circumstances are unfavourable to the seller. If, on the other hand, the market conditions are neutral between buyer and seller, then the net realizable value is likely to be the open market value.

It should be clear from the above that plenty of alternative measures are available, each of which has its own problems. If you remember, the starting point for this discussion was that we wished to establish whether Tony was better off at the end of the period than he was at the start. Had he made a profit? The problem is not one of finding a concept of profit, as there are plenty within the economics literature apart from the one that we have already referred to which was provided by Hicks [see, for example, Fisher's (1930) income concept and that of Friedman (1957)]. The problem is in fact one of measurement, as most of these concepts rely either on a measurement of future income streams or on the measurement of wealth.

We have already pointed out that to measure future income streams is extremely difficult in the real world because of the effects of uncertainty. This then leaves us with the alternative of measuring wealth and leads us to the question of finding the most appropriate measure. As we have seen, all the measures put forward so far have inherent problems, and it may be that the solution lies in combining one or more of these measures to obtain the best measure. For the purposes of this introductory text it is probably unnecessary to probe this area in greater depth but some references are given at the end of the chapter which will provide further background for those interested in pursuing the topic. Before leaving this area completely, let us reconsider the example based on the wealth of Tony and assign some values to see what effect the choice of measure will have.

Time T_0

Description	Historic cost (£)	Replacement cost (£)	Net realizable value (£)
Ford Focus	10 800	10 800	9 000
Suits	450	560	60
Shirts	75	75	10
Sweatshirts	100	100	20
Cash	400	400	400

If you study the figures carefully, you will notice that the only figure common to all three columns is the cash figure. Apart from the cost of the suits, the replacement cost and the historic cost are also identical. In reality this will always be the case at the time when the goods are bought, but it is unlikely to be so at any other time. In this example, the fact that the replacement cost of the suits is different from the historic cost indicates that some, or all, of these suits were bought when the price of suits was lower than it was at the start of the year in question. In other words, the point in time at which we are measuring is different from the date of acquisition and, as we said, in these circumstances the replacement cost is likely to differ from the historic cost.

You should also have noticed that the net realizable value is lower than the historic cost and replacement cost, even though some of the items were clearly new at the start of the year. Once again, this is obviously going to be the case in most situations, because personal goods that are being resold are effectively second-hand goods, even though they may not have been used. The situation for a business enterprise is not necessarily the same because sometimes the goods are bought not for use but for resale, e.g. by a retailer or wholesaler. In these cases the net realizable value of the goods bought for resale should be higher than the cost – otherwise the retailer would not stay in business very long!

Let us now look at Tony's situation at the end of the year and assign some values to the items owned at that time. We shall then be in a position to measure the profit or increase in wealth and to use this as a basis for discussion of some of the problems of measurement which we referred to earlier.

Year T_1

Description	Historic cost (£)	Replacement cost (£)	Net realizable value (£)
Ford Focus	10 800	11 200	8 000
Suits	450	600	40
Shirts	75	90	5
Sweatshirts	100	100	15
Cash	1 000	1 000	1 000

You will notice that the figures have changed in all cases except under historic cost, where, with the exception of the cash, they are the same as at the start of the year. This highlights one of the problems with this measure, in that it only tells us what an item costs and gives no clue as to what it is worth.

It is also worth looking more closely at the car. As you can see, the replacement cost is higher than at the start of the year. You will also see that the replacement cost is higher than the net realizable value. This is because of two things. First, costs would be incurred in selling the car and the amount that you would get would be reduced by these costs. Second, the replacement cost is the cost of replacing a brand new car, whereas Tony actually has a one-year-old car available for sale.

Let us now look at what we get in terms of our measures of wealth and profit, starting with historic cost.

Historic cost

Description	Year T_0	Year T_1
Ford Focus	10 800	10 800
Suits	450	450
Shirts	75	75
Sweatshirts	100	100
Cash	400	1 000
Total	11 825	12 425

We can now measure the profit under historic cost as we have a figure for wealth at the start and end of the year. Thus, using the formula:

$$\text{wealth 1} - \text{wealth 0} = \text{profit}$$

we get:

$$£12\,425 - £11\,825 = £600$$

Let us look at what would happen if we used replacement cost rather than historic cost.

Replacement cost

Description	Year T_0	Year T_1
Ford Focus	10 800	11 200
Suits	560	600
Shirts	75	90
Sweatshirts	100	100
Cash	400	1 000
Total	11 935	12 990

We can now measure the profit under replacement cost as we have a figure for wealth at the start and end of the year. Thus, using the formula:

$$\text{wealth 1} - \text{wealth 0} = \text{profit}$$

we get:

$$£12\,990 - £11\,935 = £1\,055 \text{ profit}$$

In other words, according to the replacement cost figures, we are £1055 better off at the end of the year than we were at the start. Of course, the problem here is that the replacement cost of the car and the suits, shirts, etc., relate to new goods whereas Tony owns a one-year-old car, one-year-old suits, etc. In effect, this means that the gain shown by replacement cost is illusory. If we took into account the fact that, for example, the replacement cost of a one-year-old car was, say, £10 000 and assumed the other figures were correct, we would find that the replacement cost profit was now as follows.

Description	Year T_0	Year T_1
Ford Focus	10 800	10 000
Suits	560	600
Shirts	75	90
Sweatshirts	100	100
Cash	400	1 000
Total	11 935	11 790

Thus, using the formula:

$$\text{wealth } 1 - \text{wealth } 0 = \text{profit}$$

we get:

$$£11\,790 - £11\,935 = -£145 \text{ loss}$$

Here we find that the resultant figure is negative, which means that Tony has made a loss rather than a profit.

Finally, let us see what the situation would be if we were using the net realizable value to arrive at our measures of wealth.

Net realizable value

Description	Year T_0	Year T_1
Ford Focus	9 000	8 000
Suits	60	40
Shirts	10	5
Sweatshirts	20	15
Cash	400	1 000
Total	9 490	9 060

We can now measure the profit under net realizable value as we have a figure for wealth at the start and end of the year. Thus, using the formula:

$$\text{wealth } 1 - \text{wealth } 0 = \text{profit}$$

we get:

$$£9\,060 - £9\,490 = -£430 \text{ loss}$$

Using net realizable value as the basis of measuring wealth, we find that Tony is worse off at the end of the year than he was at the start.

You may well be wondering at this point which is the correct answer, and this takes us back to the question of who is to use the information and for what purpose it is to be used. Clearly, this varies from case to case; however, it is more important at the present time that you understand that differences arise depending on the valuation method adopted. You may feel that as Tony is clearly worse off at the end of the first year than he was at the start (he no longer has a brand new car), adjusted replacement cost or net realizable value are the better alternatives. However, you must bear in mind that we are trying to measure the amount that can be spent whilst maintaining wealth and that there is therefore a hidden assumption that Tony wants to maintain the wealth he had at the start.

This may not in fact be the case because of changes in circumstances. He may, for example, have been banned from driving, which would mean that he does not want to replace his car. The net realizable value model would be more useful now as he would probably want to sell the car. However, although he has lost his driving licence he will still need to go out even if only to buy food. He is going to need to wear some clothes, and so to value these on the assumption that they are going to be sold is not a defensible position.

CONCLUSION

We have seen that there are a number of alternative ways of measuring a person's wealth and that each has its own problems. One of the most commonly cited problems with both replacement cost and net realizable value is that they are subjective, which is true in many cases. This is one reason why accounts are still prepared using historic costs even though, as we have seen with the simple example of Tony, this can lead to irrelevant information being produced and wrong decisions being taken. Another reason that is often cited for retaining historic cost in the accounts is that it is a system which is based on what was actually spent and owners of enterprises need to know what money has been spent on. But to what extent can the advantage of historic cost make up for its deficiencies as a measure of wealth and therefore as the basis of the profit measure? This question is and has been the subject of much debate and that debate will continue for many years to come. In 2010 there were over 40 international accounting standards in force of which at least eight recommended the use of fair value as an alternative to historic cost. However, for our purposes, we only need to be aware of the problems associated with using each of the alternatives because they may well lead to different decisions being made. The fact that these alternatives are not just theoretical views with no practical significance is illustrated in Case Study 2.1, which draws attention to an alternative presentation used by BP in 2008 to show the profit for the year measured on a replacement cost and historic cost basis.

CASE STUDY 2.1

BP plc

Commentary

In the annual report for the year ended 31 December 2008, BP plc included within its annual report a reconciliation of the profit for the year, as measured in historic cost terms, with the replacement cost profit for the year. As you can see the historic cost profit attributable to the BP shareholders is $21 157 million while the replacement cost profit for the same period is $25 593 million, a difference of $4436 million or over 20%. You can also see that the volume of the difference varies greatly from year to year with 2006 only having a tiny difference relatively and 2007 showing a lower profit under replacement cost than under historic cost.

(Continued)

Extract from the annual report of BP plc for the year ended 31 December 2008
Information about this report

This document constitutes the Annual Report and Accounts of BP plc for the year ended 31 December 2008 in accordance with UK requirements and is dated 24 February 2009. This document also contains information that will be included in the company's *Annual Report on Form 20-F 2008* in accordance with the requirements of the US Securities and Exchange Commission (ISEQ). Such information will be supplemented and may be updated at the time of filing that document with the SEC or later amended, if necessary.

The Annual Report and Accounts for the year ended 31 December 2008 contains the Directors' Report, including the Business Review and Management Report, on pages 2–76 and 89–100, 102 and 191. The Directors' Remuneration Report is on pages 77–87. The consolidated financial statements are on pages 101–190. The report of the auditor is on page 103 for the group and page 192 for the company.

BP Annual Report and Accounts 2008 and *BP Annual Review 2008* may be downloaded from www.bp.com/annualreport. No material on the BP website, other than the items identified as *BP Annual Report and Accounts 2008* and *BP Annual Review 2008*, forms any part of these documents.

For the year ended December 31

	$million		
	2008	**2007**	**2006**
Profit before interest and taxation from continuing operations	**35 239**	32 352	35 158
Finance costs and net finance income relating to pensions and other post-retirement benefits	**(956)**	(741)	(516)
Taxation	**(12 617)**	(10 442)	(12 331)
Minority interest	**(509)**	(324)	(286)
Profit for the year from continuing operation attributable to BP shareholders	**21 157**	20 845	22 025
Profit (loss) for the year from Innovene operations	**–**	–	(25)
Inventory holding (gains) losses, net of tax	**4 436**	(2 475)	222
Replacement cost profit	**25 593**	18 370	22 222
Replacement cost profit from continuing operations attributable to BP shareholders	**25 593**	18 370	22 247
Replacement cost profit (loss) from Innovene operations	**–**	–	(25)
Replacement cost profit	**25 593**	18 370	22 222
Explorations and production	**38 308**	27 602	31 026
Refining and marketing	**4 176**	2 621	5 161
Other business and corporate	**(1 223)**	(1 209)	(841)
Consolidation adjustments—unrealized profit in inventory	**466**	(220)	65
Replacement cost profit before interest and taxation	**41 727**	28 794	35 411
Finance costs and net finance income relating to pensions and other post-retirement benefits	**(956)**	(741)	(516)
Taxation on a replacement cost basis	**(14 669)**	(9 359)	(12 362)
Minority interest	**(509)**	(324)	(286)

(Continued)

For the year ended December 31

	$million		
	2008	2007	2006
Replacement cost profit from continuing operations attributable to BP shareholders	**25 539**	18 370	22 247
Per ordinary share—cents			
– profit for the year attributable to BP shareholders	**112.60**	108.76	109.84
– Replacement cost profit	**136.21**	98.85	110.95
Dividends paid per ordinary share—cents	**55.06**	42.30	38.40
– pence	**29.988**	20.995	21.104
Dividends paid per American depositary share (ADS)—dollars	**3.304**	2.538	2.304

[a]Replacement cost profit reflects the replacement cost of supplies. The replacement cost profit for the year is arrived at by excluding from profit inventory holding gains and losses and their associated tax effect. Inventory holding gains and losses, for this purpose, are calculated for all inventories except for those that are held as part of a trading position and certain other temporary inventory positions. BP uses this measure to assist investors in assessing BP's performance from period to period. Replacement cost profit is not a recognized GAAP measure.

[b]Effective 1 January 2008, replacement cost profit for the year is determined by excluding from profit inventory holding gains and losses as well as their associated tax effect. Previously, replacement cost profit excluded inventory holding gains and losses while the tax change remained unadjusted and included the tax effect or inventory holding gains and losses. Comparative amounts have been amended to the new basis and the impact of the change is shown in the table below. There is no impact on profit for the year.

for the year ended 31 December

	$ million	
	2007	2006
Replacement cost profit		
– as previously reported	17.287	22.253
– tax effect on inventory gains and losses	1.083	(31)
as amended	18.370	22.222

Case Study 2.1 illustrated that although the international accounting profession has moved strongly towards using historic cost as the basis for financial reporting the debate about what is the best basis has not been fully resolved to the satisfaction of all preparers or users of accounting information. We can trace the argument through decades going back to the 1970s and before when the accounting profession was concerned with accounting for the purchasing power of the monetary unit, through the 1980s when the thinking shifted to current cost accounting which is a hybrid system combining historic cost, replacement cost and net realizable value to arrive at a valuation of assets based on the 'value to the business'. Because we measure profit as the change in wealth over a period each shift in the measurement of assets produced a different profit. In the majority of cases these current cost accounts had disappeared by the turn of the century. However, Case Study 2.2 provides an example of the type of disclosure provided in addition to the historic cost information by the National Grid in 2000 when they were required to produce this supplementary information as a condition of their licence.

CASE STUDY 2.2

The National Grid

Commentary

The National Grid Company plc supplies electricity transmission under a licence. The licensor required as a condition the preparation of current cost versions of the income statement, balance sheet (now referred to as the statement of financial position), cash flow statement and statement of total recognized gains and losses. To illustrate this point, the current cost statement of total recognized gains and losses and the balance sheet of the National Grid in 2000 are reproduced below. As we said above although we no longer see these statements in the UK as a matter of course the debate still goes on and if you look at the inflation rate in a country such as Zimbabwe, where in December 2008 the latest figures put Zimbabwe's annual inflation rate at 516 quintillion per cent. That's 516 followed by 18 zeros, there is clearly a need to look at something other way of measuring value.

Extract from the National Grid Regulatory accounts for the year ended 31 March 2000
Current cost statements of total recognized gains and losses

	Note	Transmission 2000 £m	Transmission 1999 £m	Settlements 2000 £m	Settlements 1999 £m	Inter-connectors 2000 £m	Inter-connectors 1999 £m	Ancillary services 2000 £m	Ancillary services 1999 £m
Current cost operating profit	–	364.2	335	7.2	5.7	46.5	38.4	0.3	0.2
Taxation	–	–		−2.4	−1.4	–	–	–	–
Revaluation of tangible fixed assets	6	−51.5	42.3	–	–	–	–	–	–
Total recognized gains and losses for the year		312.7	378	4.8	4.3	46.5	38.4	0.3	0.2

Balance sheet

	Note	Transmission 2000 £m	Transmission 1999 £m	Settlements 2000 £m	Settlements 1999 £m	Inter-connectors 2000 £m	Inter-connectors 1999 £m	Ancillary services 2000 £m	Ancillary services 1999 £m
Tangible fixed assets	2	4 760.80	4 837.60	1.1	2.5	160.7	174.9	0.2	0.2
Current assets									
Stock		8.4	7.8	–	–	–	–	–	–

(Continued)

	Note	Transmission		Settlements		Inter-connectors		Ancillary services	
		2000 £m	1999 £m	2000 £m	1999 £m	2000 £m	1999 £m	2000 £m	1999 £m
Debtors	3	4 259.10	3 890.20	18.3	19.8	403	344	11	17.7
Cash at bank and in hand		54.2	23.9	3.4	1.2	–	–	–	–
		4 321.70	3 921.90	21.7	21	403	344	11	17.7
Creditors (amounts falling due within one year)	4	−305.4	−292.5	−12.2	−12.7	–	−1.7	−9	−16
Net current assets		4 016.30	3 629.40	9.5	8.3	403	342.3	2	1.7
Total assets less current liabilities		8 777.10	8 467.00	10.6	10.8	563.7	517.2	2.2	1.9
Provisions for liabilities and charges	5	−1.9	−4.5	–	–	–	–	–	–
Net assets employed		8 775.20	8 462.50	10.6	10.8	563.7	517.2	2.2	1.9
Capital employed	6	8 775.20	8 462.50	10.6	10.8	563.7	517.2	2.2	1.9

SUMMARY

We have looked at a definition of wealth and of profit which is commonly used and indeed underpins current accounting practice, and we have found that there are problems in actually measuring wealth. We have looked at four alternative measures: historic cost, replacement cost, net realizable value and economic value. We have shown by way of a simple example that each of the first three produces a different answer and in the course of our discussion we have pointed to some of the problems and assumptions underlying each alternative. At the present time there is no generally accepted right answer, and in fact the most commonly used system is that based on historic cost (although it should be noted that Philips, the electronics giant, has used replacement costs for a number of years). Finally, it should also be pointed out that change is likely to be slow in coming as the present system, based on historic cost, is familiar to all and has, it is said, worked well in the past, although it is unclear what criteria are being used to back up this claim.

REFERENCES

Fisher, I. (1930) *The Theory of Interest*, London: Macmillan.
Friedman, M. (1957) *A Theory of the Consumption Function*, Princeton, NJ: Princeton University Press.
Hicks, J. (1946) *Value and Capital*, Oxford: Clarendon Press.

REVIEW QUESTIONS

(✓ indicates answers are available in Appendix A)

✓ **1** Profit is normally seen as a flow over time, whereas wealth can be described as a stock at a point in time. Explain in your own words the difference between a stock and a flow.

✓ **2** There are a number of different ways in which we can measure wealth. List the alternatives discussed in the chapter together with any drawbacks or problems that were identified with their use.

3 In certain situations we said that written-down cost could be used as an alternative. Explain in your own words the difference between cost and written-down cost, and suggest when the latter would be more appropriate.

4 What effects, if any, do rapid changes in technology have on the appropriateness of each of the alternative ways of assigning a cost or a value to an item?

PROBLEMS FOR DISCUSSION AND ANALYSIS

(✓ indicates answers are available in Appendix A)

✓ **1** Under certain circumstances, only one of the alternative methods of valuation is the most appropriate. Giving brief reasons for your choice suggest the most appropriate value, e.g. historic cost, net realizable value, etc., to be placed on each item in the following.

Jean owns a shop which used to sell clothes, but she has now decided that given the location she would make more money running a restaurant at the same premises. She has obtained planning permission for the change of use and has bought some of the equipment needed but has not yet started trading. She has made a list of the items that the business owns which is reproduced below:

(a) freehold shop;
(b) hanging display for clothes;
(c) a two-year-old car which is essential for the business;
(d) new restaurant tables and chairs;
(e) cash till;
(f) quantity of fashion garments that were not sold in the closing-down sale.

You may find that you need more information or have to make some assumptions. This is normal but you should state any assumptions that you are making.

2 In the example of Tony in the text, no allowance was made for the fact that an item had been in use for some time. Although it is intuitively obvious that the utility of most things declines over time, it is more difficult to identify the extent of that decline over a given period. In addition, even if we could identify the decline in utility and the utility remaining, we still have to assign some monetary amount to both parts. We said that this was done by arriving at a written-down cost or value. For each of the following examples suggest, with reasons, the best method for arriving at the written-down cost or value.

(a) A machine which will produce 10 000 items and will then need to be replaced. Production each year is to be matched to sales and estimates of sales are 1000 units in year 1 and 2500 units in year 2. Sales in the years after that cannot be forecast with any accuracy.
(b) A leasehold property on a five-year non-renewable lease.
(c) A company car.
(d) A laptop
(e) Specialist computer software.

3 Sandra and Ashwin, having recently graduated with degrees in computing, decided to go into business buying and selling computers. They decided to target the student market as they felt this was ripe for exploiting. They were able to get a special deal from a manufacturer in Malaysia to supply 500 computers at £200 each. They then spent an hour per machine setting them up for their customers and provided an after-sales service if required. The costs of shipping the machines to the UK were £15 per machine. At the end of the period they had sold 400 machines at an average price of £300 per machine. However, in the interim the main PC suppliers had launched an upgraded machine which meant that their machines were now 'last generation' and were more difficult to sell, and they believed they would have to reduce their selling price to £150 to sell the remaining machines.

(a) Calculate the wealth at the start and end of the period and the profit for the period on the basis of historic cost and replacement cost.

(b) Comment on which of the two profit figures is the best reflection of the activity during the period and which gives the best indication of the future profits.

4 Two brothers decided to go into business buying and selling beds. Details of their transactions are set out in the case study below.

They initially bought 400 beds at £100 each and a delivery van for £6000. At the end of six months they had sold 300 of the 400 beds for £150 each. Unfortunately, during that time the bed manufacturer had increased the price to £120 each and was their only source of supply. To make matters worse, a discount store had opened in the area and it was selling the same beds at £140 each. The brothers found that on average over the six months they had incurred costs for advertising, petrol, etc., which amounted to £10 for each bed sold.

(a) On the basis of the information above, calculate what the brothers' wealth was at the start and end of the six months, and what profit had been made using historic cost as the basis for your calculations.

(b) On the basis of the information above, calculate what the brothers' wealth was at the start and end of the six months, and what profit had been made using replacement cost as the basis for your calculations.

(c) On the basis of the information above, calculate what the brothers' wealth was at the start and end of the six months, and what profit had been made using net realizable value as the basis for your calculations.

(d) Having calculated the profit for the first six months, discuss whether the profit figure is a useful benchmark for measuring the performance of the business, and also whether it is useful as a guide to future profitability.

CHAPTER 3
THE MEASUREMENT OF WEALTH

LEARNING OUTCOMES

By the end of this chapter you will:

- Understand the importance of the separation of the business from the owner and the application of the business entity principle.

- Understand what a statement of financial position is and understand its component parts.

- Understand the importance and limitations of the statement of financial position.

- Have an understanding of the accounting equation and be able to draw up a simple statement of financial position.

- Be aware of the advantages and thinking behind different formats for the statement of financial position and the current format proposed in the International Financial Reporting Standard for Small and Medium Size Entities.

This chapter explores the concepts of wealth in more detail and relates them to the statement of finan-cial position, previously commonly referred to as the balance sheet. This statement can be viewed as a surrogate wealth measure. The elements of the statement of financial position are defined and the inter-relationships and interdependency of assets, liabilities and owners' equity are explained.

In Chapter 1, we discussed the objectives of accounting reports and the influences of users on financial reporting. We also discussed the limitations of accounting information and the role of accounting in business, its effect on business and some of the factors which influence accounting. In Chapter 2, we examined some possible approaches to income measurement from the point of view both of the econo-mist and of the accountant. We shall now look more specifically at the ways in which accountants measure wealth and income.

We suggested that the problem facing accountants is that of finding an appropriate basis for the mea-surement of wealth. There is also the additional problem that in the real world a system which only measures wealth and derives income from it will not be able to cope with the complexity of present-day enterprises. Consider a large retailing group such as IKEA, Carrefour or Sainsbury: should they have to carry out a valuation of all their premises, vehicles, inventory, etc., on one day of the year? The costs of such an operation would make it prohibitively expensive, even if it was logistically possible. For compa-nies such as Unilever plc, where operations are carried out on a world-wide basis, these logistical prob-lems would be even greater. Such a system would also lead to problems because management or the owners would not be able to make decisions on a day-to-day basis as they would only have information at hand once a year. Because of these problems with annual valuation systems, we need to find separate ways of measuring wealth and income.

The measurement of income will be dealt with in detail in Chapter 4. In this chapter, we concentrate on the problem of the measurement of wealth and the way in which accounting approaches that prob-lem. We shall look in some detail at the use of the statement of financial position as the measure of wealth, at its component parts such as assets and liabilities, and finally at the format in which the state-ment of financial position is presented and the way in which that is influenced by the type of organiza-tion, the regulatory environment and the needs of the users.

THE MEASUREMENT OF WEALTH

In the case of an individual, we have said that wealth can be found by simply listing the items you own, assuming of course that you do not owe anybody money as this will clearly reduce your wealth. To some extent the same can be said for an enterprise, although the level of complexity will, of course, be greater. The way in which this is done for an enterprise is similar to that for an individual but the result-ing statement is called a statement of financial position or balance sheet. You should note that this state-ment relates to a position at a point in time, the reporting date. It is because of this that the analogy with a snapshot is often found in accounting textbooks.

KEY CONCEPT 3.1

The statement of financial position or balance sheet

The statement of financial position is a statement which shows at a point in time, known as the reporting date, all the items (assets) owned by the enterprise and all the amounts owed by the enterprise (liabilities).

The definition is not intended to be comprehensive – it merely provides us with a basic idea of what we are referring to. Before looking at the statement in more detail, it is important to appreciate that, although an enterprise does not exist in the same way as a person, for accounting and for some legal purposes an enterprise is presumed to exist in its own right. It is therefore treated as a separate entity from the person or persons who own or operate it. In broad terms, it is possible to account for any unit which has a separate and distinct existence. It may be that this is a hotel, for example, or a group of hotels or a more complex organization such as Marriott International Inc., which is an organization operating hotels, holiday resorts and associated businesses worldwide. This idea of a separate entity is often referred to in accounting literature as the business entity principle. It applies equally to organizations that are not commonly referred to as businesses such as charitable organizations, clubs and societies. The question of whether the entity should be accounted for separately is related not only to the legal situation but also to the question of whether it can be seen to have a separate existence.

KEY CONCEPT 3.2

The business entity principle

The business entity principle states that transactions, assets and liabilities that relate to the enterprise are accounted for separately from the assets of the owner or owners. It applies to all types of enterprise irrespective of the fact that the enterprise may not be recognized as a separate legal or taxable entity.

Whilst the application of this principle and the reasons for it are fairly self-evident when we are looking at large public companies such as Hewlett Packard or Shell, they are less clear with smaller enterprises such as the corner newsagents or a secondhand car business. If, for example, you decided to set yourself up as a car dealer, for accounting purposes the cars purchased as a car dealer and the money earned as a result of that activity would be treated separately from your own personal car and money. This allows the tax authority to tax you separately on the profits from your business and it also helps you to arrive at the value of your business should you wish at some stage to sell it or take in a partner. The important point to remember is that for each business entity it is possible to account separately and therefore to draw up a statement of financial position at a point in time.

We shall now examine the statement of financial position in more detail.

IMPORTANCE OF STATEMENT OF FINANCIAL POSITION OR BALANCE SHEET

The purpose of a statement of financial position is to communicate information about the financial position of an enterprise at a particular point in time. It summarizes information contained in the accounting records in a clear and intelligible form. If the items contained in it are summarized and classified in an appropriate manner it can give information about the financial strength of the enterprise and indicate the relative liquidity of the assets. It should also give information about the liabilities of the enterprise, i.e. what the enterprise owes and when these amounts will fall.

KEY CONCEPT 3.3

Liquidity

Liquidity refers to the ease with which assets can be converted to cash in the normal course of business.

The combination of this information can assist the user in evaluating the financial position of the enterprise. It should be remembered, however, that financial statements are only one part of the information needed by users and thus the importance of this accounting statement should not be overemphasized.

ACTIVITY 3.1

Can you think of a situation where liquidity becomes really important?

You may have thought of the situation where a business is in trouble and its future is uncertain as was the case of Portsmouth football club in the 2009/10 season when there were doubts about its ability to pay the wages bill which in common with all premiership sides is not inconsiderable but is vital to the entities' survival.

In most cases, enterprises draw up a statement of financial position at least once a year. It could be done more frequently, of course, or indeed less frequently, although convention dictates that a normal accounting period is a year and tax laws and other legislation are set up on that basis. It should also be remembered that because the statement of financial position represents the position at one point in time, its usefulness is limited as the situation may have changed since the last statement was drawn up. For example, you may draw up a statement of financial position every December and so if you looked at the statement in the following October it would be ten months out of date. It may be helpful to think of the business as analogous with a movie and the statement of financial position as a still from that movie. Clearly, in the case of a movie the still does not give a complete picture and the same can be said for the statement of financial position.

We need to know what the statement contains. We have already said that it is similar to an individual's own measurement of wealth. Therefore, if you think how you would measure your own wealth you will realize that you need to make a list of what you own (assets) and take away from that what you owe (liabilities). For an enterprise, this listing of assets and liabilities at a particular point in time is the enterprise's statement of financial position.

Given this information about the contents of a statement of financial position, let us look in more detail at what is meant by assets and liabilities. We shall consider assets by looking at what constitutes an asset and how assets are classified into subcategories.

ASSETS

Although we can find many definitions of assets, some of these are less useful than others. Most contain some of the vital elements of a useful description, but a clear working definition is needed. Given the move towards adoption of International Standards both in the UK and globally we will start with the definition included in the International Accounting Standards Committee's (1989) Framework for the Preparation and Presentation of Financial Statements (Para. 49a) and repeated in the International Financial Reporting Standard for Small and Medium Size Entities (Para. 2.15). The definition is given in Key Concept 3.4.

KEY CONCEPT 3.4

International Accounting Standards – definition of an asset

An asset is a resource controlled by an enterprise as a result of past events from which future economic benefits are expected to flow to the entity. [Para. 2.15 IFRS-SME]

Resource controlled by an enterprise

The use of the word 'controlled' is important as many earlier definitions of assets implied that in order to be an asset something must be owned. In reality most assets are owned, but ownership is not a precondition for the recognition of an asset. For example, a rental agreement for a house that entitles you to occupy the house at a rent of £20 a week obviously confers a benefit if the market rental is, say, £90 a week and thus may be seen as an asset. On the other hand, the fact that an individual or enterprise owns an item does not necessarily mean that there is any future benefit to be obtained. For example, an old motor car that is no longer roadworthy may cease to be an asset, and in fact unless it can be driven to the breaker's yard it may become a liability as you will have to incur costs to get it towed away.

ACTIVITY 3.2

Can you think of items that you still own that you would no longer classify as assets?

You may still have old books, notes, clothes, games, mobiles, etc. which are simply cluttering up space, have little or no value but you have not been bothered to get rid of them. You own these items but they are probably not assets.

As a result of past events

This is in effect shorthand for saying some 'economic' transaction must have occurred which gave rise to the situation where the enterprise was able to control the resource to obtain the future benefits.

Future economic benefits

This is a key term which you need to remember. The clear implication in the term 'future economic benefits' is that, in order to be an asset, there must be some clear expectation that some benefit will be derived by the enterprise either now or in the future. This implies that the item must have some specific usefulness to the enterprise. An item that has no specific usefulness for the enterprise is therefore not an asset. This is particularly important in times of rapidly changing technology as it suggests that the question of what is and what is not an asset can only be decided on the basis of its usefulness to the enterprise. For example, it is fairly obvious that a mine full of gold is an asset for a mining business. However, there will come a point when all the gold has been removed and all that is left is a hole in the ground. The hole in the ground is no longer useful to the mining enterprise and it ceases to be an asset.

However, for a different type of enterprise, e.g. a rubbish disposal business, a hole in the ground is useful. We can therefore conclude that in order to be classified as an asset, an item must be useful to the enterprise itself.

ACTIVITY 3.3

If the price of gold or tin goes up and you own a mine which was uneconomical to extract gold or tin from but now it could be mined profitably does that change your view on whether you have an asset and if so why?

    If you have decided that you now have an asset you will have identified that the deciding factor was not about ownership as that did not change but about future benefits the prospects for which are now positive.

Expected to flow to the entity

This relates to Key Concept 3.2, the business entity principle, i.e. that the future economic benefits must be received by the enterprise at some point in time. It is vital in many cases to be able to separate out the assets of the enterprise from those of the owner. For example, the factory building is likely to be an enterprise asset as the benefits from its use are likely to accrue to the enterprise. However, if the enterprise is a corner shop with residential accommodation, it is somewhat less clear which part of the building is an asset of the business and which is not. In practice, it may well be that some of the goods held for resale are actually physically stored in part the residential accommodation. There is unfortunately no general rule which can be applied and each case must be considered on its merits. The process of distinguishing between the assets of the owner and those of the business is merely an application of the business entity principle referred to earlier. In simple terms, this principle states that the business should be viewed as separate from the owner and therefore accounted for separately.

    Like all definitions, this definition is really shorthand for a fuller definition and there are some assumptions implicit in the application of the definition. These are:

- that the asset must be capable of measurement;
- that the measurement should be in monetary amounts.

    The reason for the second of these assumptions is simply that accounts are drawn up in monetary terms. In reality, there are future resource flows that arise as a result of other factors. For example, the right of a producer of jams to state that its goods are 'By Royal Appointment' may enhance sales and therefore future economic benefits but these additional benefits are neither easily estimated nor capable of being measured in monetary terms. Other examples of items which are clearly of benefit but which are not included for accounting purposes are a good location, a highly motivated work or a reputation for excellent service. You will remember from Chapter 1 that we discussed this problem in the context of the limitations of accounting information.

CURRENT AND NON-CURRENT ASSETS

For accounting purposes, assets are normally separated as far as possible into subcategories. The reasoning behind this is that accounting statements should provide information that is useful in making

ACTIVITY 3.4

Can you think of other areas where a business may have an asset that will give it a future benefit but that benefit cannot easily be measured in monetary terms?

There are lots of examples you may have thought of: reputation, brand name, etc. The problem is can you reasonably be said to control them? We have seen many brands go out of fashion at the whim of the consumer not the business entity and even if they were stable how would you measure the future benefit?

economic decisions. These decisions, it is suggested, can be made more precisely if some indication is given regarding the nature of the assets of the enterprise. The categories that are increasingly being used are current and non-current assets, although you will also see the term fixed assets used in place of or as a subcategory of non-current assets.

Current assets

Although the term current asset is in common usage, a review of accounting textbooks would reveal that the definition of a current asset is not as clear as might be expected. Because of the increasing adoption of International Standards, we will examine the definition adopted there. We will do this in some detail as International Accounting Standards (IAS) and International Financial Reporting Standards (IFRS) identify two types of assets (IAS 1 Para. 57, IFRS-SME Para. 4.5), i.e. current and non-current assets, but only define the latter in terms of what it is not rather than what it is. Thus, if you can demonstrate that an asset is not a current asset then it must be a non-current asset.

The Standards define a current asset as meeting any of four criteria namely:

1   It is expected to be realized in, or is intended for sale or consumption in, the entities' normal operating cycle.

2   It is held primarily for the purpose of being traded.

3   It is expected to be realized within twelve months after the reporting date.

4   It is cash or cash equivalent.

We shall examine each of these criteria in turn.

It is expected to be realized in, or is intended for sale or consumption in, the entities' normal operating cycle

This introduces a number of ideas, the first being that to be an asset it has to be realized, sold or used in the normal operating cycle. So we first need to know what is meant by realized. This is part of the realization principle which will be dealt with in more detail in the next chapter. For the moment we can use as a shorthand definition that a future benefit is expected to flow to the entity. This criterion also identifies that it can be goods held for resale or for consumption. An example of the former would be anything that is intended to be sold; this may be goods in a shop or it may be some shares that the business has bought to use some spare cash. An example of goods held for consumption might be the headed notepaper and stationery that the shop uses in the course of its business. Finally, it is worth noting that this criterion is linked with the term 'operating cycle'. The term operating cycle is easier to understand by looking at one or two examples. In the case of a shop selling clothes, the operating cycle may consist of buying garments and selling them for cash. In the case of an assembly business, the operating cycle may involve more processes such as buying two or more components, assembling them, then selling them and collecting the cash. Hence, the operating cycle has no fixed period but depends on the nature of the business and may in fact extend over a number of years. This would be the case with property development, ship and other heavy construction industries. The fact the operating cycles are of different lengths is not vital as in general terms those assets that are part of the operating cycle are similar and are likely to be items such as inventory, money owed to the business, cash in the bank, etc.

It is held primarily for the purpose of being traded

At first sight this may seem to be very similar to the first criterion, which talks about goods intended for sale. The difference is that the first criterion is concerned with intention and time, i.e. the normal operating cycle, rather than the nature of the asset. This criterion is concerned solely with the nature of the asset. So items under this criterion would include clothes for fashion retailer, fruit and vegetables for a greengrocer, cars for a car showroom, and land and buildings for a property developer.

It is expected to be realized within twelve months of the reporting date

By convention, accounting periods are normally one year, hence the reference to twelve months. This criterion allows us to classify as current assets items such as money owed to us that we expect to receive in the next twelve months.

It is cash or cash equivalent

The final criterion is, in part, self-explanatory in that cash is cash and money in the bank is exactly that cash equivalents is slightly more complex and can be ignored for the present. We shall return to a discussion of cash equivalents in the chapter on cash flow statements.

Having looked at these criteria, for our purposes, therefore, a useful working definition is that given in Key Concept 3.5, which combines these criteria.

KEY CONCEPT 3.5

Current asset

A current asset is one which is either part of the operating cycle of the enterprise or is likely to be realized in the form of cash within one year.

Non-current assets

This is to a large extent a catch-all term to include anything that does not fall within the category of current asset. It encompasses two distinct types of asset known as tangible and intangible assets, in addition to other assets of a long-term nature.

Tangible, financial and intangible assets

Essentially a tangible asset is one that can be touched, i.e. has some physical attributes such as a building or a car. A financial asset is self explanatory: it is a financial investment which may be in the form of a holding of shares in another business entity, an investment in debentures or such like. By contrast, an intangible asset is one that has no physical form but still meets the essential definition of an asset in that it provides future benefits, examples being the copyright on this book, patents and trademarks.

In reality, most tangible non-current assets are likely to fall in the category often referred to in the accounting literature as fixed assets, which broadly comprises property, plant, equipment, furniture and vehicles, whereas intangible assets would include items that are less likely to fall within that category. A fixed asset broadly can be defined as follows.

KEY CONCEPT 3.6

Fixed asset

An asset that is acquired for the purposes of use within the business and is likely to be used by the business for a considerable period of time.

The essential elements of this definition relate to both time, i.e. a considerable period, and intention. If the intention was to sell it or use it or consume it within the operating cycle, then it would meet the criteria for a current asset. A good example of the importance of intention is if we take a physical item with a long life, e.g. a washing machine. If the washing machine was owned by an electrical retailer, such as Comet or Currys, then the intention would be to sell it and as such it would be a current asset. If, on the other hand, it was owned by a launderette, the intention would be to use it in the business to generate income, i.e. future benefits. Hence, in the case of the launderette it would be a fixed asset, whereas in the case of the retailer it would be a current asset. In general, the view taken is that fixed assets are the 'long-term' earnings generators for a business.

Intangible and financial non-current assets

By looking at the definitions of current and fixed assets, it should be clear that it is possible to think of some non-current assets that a business might own that do not easily fit within either category. An example of such an asset is a trademark or a patent on a product or process that has been developed by the enterprise itself. An example of a non-current monetary asset could be an investment in the shares of another enterprise. Although we could give numerous examples, it is sufficient for our purposes at present to recognize that within the category of non-current assets there will be assets which are by their nature and usage different from each other.

Having looked at what constitutes an asset and at the way in which assets are divided into subcategories on the statement of financial position, we can now turn to the other part of the statement – what is owed or, to use accounting terminology, the liabilities.

LIABILITIES

As with the general term assets, a useful working definition of liabilities must contain a number of components. A suitable definition is that contained in the International Accounting Standards. This is reproduced in Key Concept 3.7.

KEY CONCEPT 3.7

A liability

A present obligation of the enterprise arising from past events, the settlement of which is expected to result in an outflow from the enterprise of resources embodying economic benefits. [IAS 1 Para. 49, IFRS-SME Para. 2.15b]

The definition states that the obligation must exist at the present time and when it is discharged the enterprise will have to pay something, which could be in the form of cash or other resources. An example of using other resources would be where you discharge the debt by supplying goods in exchange or providing labour or some other service. Clearly, the definition is worded in such a way that it covers all possible situations. However, a simpler definition which is adequate for our purposes and which is easier to understand and remember is:

Liabilities are what the business owes

An alternative way of looking at them is to view them as claims on the assets of the business.

Current liabilities

Given that we have used a simple definition for liabilities, we can also use a simple definition of current liabilities (Key Concept 3.8). This definition is in fact in line with the heading under which current liabilities are shown in the published accounts of companies. The most common example of a current liability is a bank overdraft, which, in theory at least, may have to be repaid to the bank on demand. Another example is where goods are bought on credit terms and the supplier has not been paid at the reporting date. As was the case with current assets, the International Accounting Standards (IAS 1 and IFRS-SME) identify a set of criteria for defining a current liability. In the opinion of the authors this adds little to the working definition produced below, but those who are interested in investigating this further will find a reference to the relevant standards at the end of this chapter.

KEY CONCEPT 3.8

Current liabilities

Those liabilities falling due for payment with one year.

Non-current liabilities

As was the case with current assets and non-current assets all liabilities that cannot be classified as current are by definition non-current. There are a number of different types of longer term liability which we shall describe in more detail in Chapter 9. The common factor amongst these is that they do not have to be repaid in full in one year; an everyday example of this type of liability is a mortgage on a house. In the case of a business, however, this type of liability may take a number of forms such as a bank loan repayable in three or five years. Liabilities of this sort are longer term liabilities and are normally put under the heading of non-current liabilities.

OWNERS' EQUITY

The owners' equity or share of the capital of the business can be viewed in a number of ways. In a sense it is a liability of the business in so far as it is a claim on the assets. However, it differs from other liabilities in that other liabilities have definite dates by which they are to be paid and are fixed in amount. The owners' equity, on the other hand, is normally left in the business as long as it is required. Another way of viewing the owners' equity is as a residual claim on the assets of the business after all the other liabilities have been settled. In general, however, the owners' equity is normally shown under two headings, i.e. that which is put into the business and that which is earned by the business and left in the business. The latter category we shall refer to as retained profits. In the case of an individual the owners' equity is analogous to wealth, whereas when the owner is a business it is often referred to as capital. As we showed in Chapter 2, the amount of this wealth or capital is dependent on the measure used, i.e. replacement cost, net realizable value, etc. It is therefore better to view owners' equity as a residual claim rather than as capital or wealth as those expressions imply that an absolute measure of owners' equity is possible. In the IFRS-SME this is exactly the approach adopted and equity is simply described as 'the residual interest in the assets of the entity after deducting all its liabilities' (Para. 25c).

KEY CONCEPT 3.9

Owners' equity

Owners' equity is in one sense a claim on the assets of the enterprise. It is different from other liabilities in that the amount cannot necessarily be determined accurately. It can be viewed as a residual claim on the assets of the enterprise after all the other monies owed, the amounts of which are generally known, have been paid off.

THE STATEMENT OF FINANCIAL POSITION

As we have already indicated, the statement of financial position of an enterprise can be viewed as a statement of assets and liabilities at a particular point in time, the reporting date. Because the business is an artificial entity, by definition all its assets belong to someone else. This idea is summed up fairly simply in what is normally referred to as the accounting equation:

$$\text{assets} = \text{liabilities}$$

The equation describes the balance sheet or statement of financial position in its simplest form and must always hold true. However, it uses a very loose definition of liabilities and can be further refined to highlight the differences between pure liabilities and owners' equity as follows:

$$\text{assets} = \text{liabilities} + \text{owners' equity}$$

This equation can be rewritten to highlight the fact that owners' equity is a residual claim on the assets:

$$\text{assets} - \text{liabilities} = \text{owners' equity}$$

Simple statements of financial position

To illustrate the equation above, a simple statement of financial position can be constructed using the information contained in Example 3.1.

Keelsafe, Part 1

Harry Keel had just been made redundant and he decided to start up a small business making safety harnesses which he called Keelsafe Safety Harnesses. For this purpose he purchased:

	£
One industrial sewing machine	550
A quantity of heavy duty webbing material	300
A quantity of sewing materials	100
A second-hand computer	150
A supply of office stationery and letterheads	50
One cutting machine	400

The remaining £50 of his redundancy money was put into a business bank account.

Part 1

At this stage we could draw up a list of assets of the business as follows.

Assets	£
Sewing machine	550
Webbing	300
Sewing materials	100
Computer	150
Stationery	50
Cutting machine	400
Cash in bank	50
	1 600

We could also identify the owner's equity in the business as being £1600, i.e. the amount he put in. Thus, the other side of the equation and indeed the balance sheet or statement of financial position would be:

Owner's equity	1 600
	1 600

Before moving on, it is worth thinking about how we obtained the figure for owner's equity: all we did was to list what Harry's business owned and then, as it did not owe anything to anybody but Harry, the owner, we made the statement of financial position balance by recording the amount the business owed to Harry, the owner's equity.

Let us take this example a bit further.

EXAMPLE 3.1

Keelsafe, Part 2

As the business was just starting, Harry decided that until the business got off the ground he would operate from home and use the garage to manufacture the safety harnesses and the front room of his house as an office. His house had originally cost him £50 000 in 1999.

Part 2

This additional information, on the face of it, presents us with a problem as we do not know how much of the £50 000 relates to the garage and to the front room. We know that the business uses some of the house and that the house is an asset; the question is whether it is an asset of Harry himself or of the business and if it is the latter how should we record it and at what amount. To answer this question we need to go back to our definition of an asset as:

a resource controlled by an enterprise as a result of past events from which future economic benefits are expected to flow.

Bearing in mind the business entity principle, we can see from the definition that the garage is not an asset of the business as the business is viewed as a separate entity from the owner. It is Harry Keel himself who owns both the house and the garage, and he also retains the legal right to enjoy the benefits from their use. Hence, the garage is not an asset of the business as the business has no legal right to use the garage; it therefore does not need to be included in the statement of financial position of the business. A similar argument can be applied to the front room which is being used as an office.

EXAMPLE 3.1

Keelsafe, Part 3

When Harry starts to make up the harnesses he realizes that he needs to buy some fasteners. He therefore approaches a supplier and finds that enough fasteners to fit all the harnesses he can make up with his existing materials will cost him £300. As he has used up all his redundancy money he approaches his bank which agrees to make a loan of £500 repayable in two years to his business, which he has called Keelsafe Safety Harnesses. He borrows the £500, puts it in the business bank account and then buys the fasteners with a cheque drawn on that account.

Part 3

We shall look first at this transaction and then draw up a new statement of financial position. The reason we have to draw up a new statement of financial position is that we are now at a different point in time and you will remember that a statement of financial position shows the position at one point in time only, the reporting date.

The actual transaction on its own can be looked at in two stages.

(Continued)

Stage 1

The first stage is that we borrow the money from the bank. This has two effects: we increase the business assets as the business will get a future benefit from the use of that money, and we also increase the business liabilities as the business now owes the bank £500. This viewed on its own can be depicted as:

$$\text{assets} = \text{liabilities}$$
$$\text{Cash in bank } 500 = \text{Loan } 500$$

Stage 2

If we now look at the second stage where some of the money in the bank is used to buy the fasteners, we can extend Stage 1 and depict this as:

$$\text{Assets} = \text{liabilities}$$
$$\text{Cash in bank } 500 = \text{Loan } 500$$

$$\text{Cash in bank} - 300$$
$$\text{Fasteners} + 300$$

We can see that all that has happened is that we have exchanged one asset for another and the totals on either side of the equation have remained the same.

Before going on to draw up a new statement of financial position, you should note the important principle that we have just illustrated as this will be applied again and again throughout this book. The principle is that there are two sides to every transaction. At the first stage the two sides of the transaction were an increase in assets with a corresponding increase in liabilities, whereas at the second stage there was a decrease in one asset with a corresponding increase in another asset. This principle is often referred to as the principle of duality, which is essentially a grand-sounding title for the principle that all transactions have two sides.

KEY CONCEPT 3.10

The principle of duality

The principle of duality is the basis of the double-entry bookkeeping system on which accounting is based. It states: every transaction has two opposite and equal sides.

Having established this principle, we can now draw up the new statement of financial position of Keelsafe Safety Harnesses. Unlike in the previous statement of financial position, this time we will classify the assets into current and non-current assets, and group these together to make the statement more meaningful. Another way in which we can make the statement more meaningful is to order the assets in descending order of liquidity, i.e. the more difficult the item is to turn into cash the less liquid it is. Hence, the inventory, which consists of fasteners etc., can be seen as less liquid than cash. Similarly the sewing machine as a non-current asset is seen to be less liquid than the inventory.

You will also note that each of the groups of assets is subtotalled and the subtotal is shown separately. The total of all the assets is then shown. It is double underlined to indicate that it is a final total. It is conventional to use single underlining for subtotals and double underlining to denote final totals.

Having classified and listed the assets of Keelsafe, we then show the amounts owed by the business sub-classified into the amount the business owes to others and the amounts it owes to Harry i.e. the residual claim or the owner's equity.

Statement of financial position of Keelsafe Safety Harnesses as at 31 May 2010

	£
Current assets	
Cash at bank	250
Office stationery	50
Webbing material	300
Sewing materials	100
Fasteners	300
	1 000
Non current assets	
One sewing machine	550
One cutting machine	400
Computer	150
	1 100
Total assets	2 100
Non-current liabilities	
Bank loan	500
Total liabilities	500
Equity	
Owner's equity	1 600
Total equity	1 600
Total equity and liabilities	2 100

The statement of financial position has been arranged to emphasize the differences between the various types of assets and Harry Keel's residual claim on the assets after the other liabilities have been paid. It conforms to the accounting equation that assets are on one side and liabilities and owner's equity are on the other side. It should also be noted that as the statement of financial position relates to the business it is headed with the name of the business and as it is drawn up at one point in time, the reporting date.

ACTIVITY 3.5

Before you go any further, re-examine the definitions of current and non-current assets and ensure that you understand why the items in Keelsafe have been classified as they have.

Most of these were straightforward the ones you may have had to think about were the office stationery and the loan. In the former case although not held for trading it is reasonable to assume that a business will only hold a few months supply of stationery. In the latter case we identified in the question that the loan was for two years so it is non-current.

ACTIVITY 3.6

Have a quick look at each of the following items and see if you can classify them.

1   Money in the business bank account

2   Money owed to the business by a customer

3   Wages owed to employees

4   The owner's partners car

5   The factory

6   A mortgage on the factory

7   A mortgage on the owners house

You should have come up with the following:

1 and 2, Yes – current assets, 3 a current liability, 4 and 7 not part of the business, 5 a non-current asset, 6 a non-current liability. If you did not go back and look at what constitutes an asset and liability, what is current and finally what does the business entity principle tell us.

Having done that we can now proceed to examine the determinants of the format of statement of financial positions and the ways in which they can be used, together with their limitations. First, however, it is worth looking at Case Study 3.1, the statement of financial position of Volvo and reading the commentary that accompanies it.

CASE STUDY 3.1

Volvo

Commentary

Volvo is probably most widely known for its cars. However it is also involved in marine and industrial engines, the aero industry, trucks and construction equipment. Its balance sheet or statement of financial position shown below is typical of those produced by most businesses. As you can see, it starts with non-current assets totalling over 105 862 million kroner. These non-current assets are broken down into intangible assets, tangible assets and financial assets. The next heading is Current assets which total 89 750 million kroner and which are classified in descending order of liquidity. These two categories of assets current and non-current produces a figure for total assets of nearly 200 000 million kroner. The next part of the statement essentially looks at the other side of the accounting equation or how these assets are financed. This part is again split into categories of equity

(Continued)

and liabilities with the latter being sub divided between non-current and current liabilities – once again the emphasis in the ordering is on liquidity in this case how soon would these have to be paid. This is one format of the balance sheet or statement of financial position and we will discuss this and other formats in more detail in the section on formats.

Volvo Annual Report 1999
Consolidated financial statements

Consolidated balance sheets, SEK M

		December 31, 1997		December 31, 1998		December 31, 1999	
Assets							
Non-current assets							
Intangible assets	Note 12		3 284		5 778		6 618
Tangible assets	Note 12						
Property plant and equipment		30 793		36 207		19 788	
Assets under operating leases		13 501	44 294	22 285	58 492	12 337	32 125
Financial fixed assets							
Shares and participations	Note 13	4 583					
Long-term sales-financing receivables	Note 14	13 967					
Other long-term receivables	Note 15	9 012	27 562	10 989	38 928	20 089	97 119
Total non-current assets			75 140		103 198		105 862
Current assets							
Inventories	Note 16		27 993		32 128		21 438
Short-term receivables							
Sales-financing receivables	Note 17	18 337		22 252		16 496	
Other receivables	Note 18	22 742	41 079	27 943	50 195	22 547	39 043
Marketable securities	Note 19		10 962		7 168		20 956
Cash and bank accounts	Note 20		9 641		13 056		8 313
Total current assets			89 765		102 547		89 750
Total assets			164 815		205 745		195 612
Shareholders equity and liabilities							
Shareholders equity	Note 21						
Restricted equity							
Share capital		2 649		2 649		2 649	
Restricted reserves		16 473	19 122	17 100	19 749	12 553	15 202
Unrestricted equity							
Unrestricted reserves		32 348		41 189		50 268	
Net income		10 481	42 829	8 437	49 626	32 222	82 490
Total shareholders equity			61 951		69 375		97 692
Minority interests	Note 11		899		860		544
Provisions							
Provisions for post-employment benefits	Note 22	3 296		2 936		2 130	

(Continued)

Provisions for deferred taxes		3 912		4 317		**2 218**	
Other provisions	Note 23	15 745	22 953	20 870	28 123	**12 614**	16 962
Non-current liabilities	Note 24						
Bond loans		11 272		15 624		**24 238**	
Other loans		11 663		9 730		**7 984**	
Other long-term liabilities		200	23 135	658	26 012	**292**	32 514
Current liabilties	Note 25						
Loans		18 282		38 876		**21 123**	
Trade payables		15 257		16 317		**11 456**	
Other current liabilities		22 338	55 877	26 182	81 375	**15 321**	47 900
Total shareholders equity and liablities			164 815		205 745		195 612
Assets pledged	Note 26		6 743		5 388		3 930
Contingent liabilties	Note 27		5 406		6 737		6 666

DETERMINANTS OF THE FORMAT OF THE STATEMENT OF FINANCIAL POSITION OR BALANCE SHEET

We shall examine the purpose of the statement of financial position and its limitations. We shall also consider some of the influences affecting the way in which it is presented and the extent to which this is determined by the type of organization and the users of the statements.

Purpose and limitations

The statement of financial position is in essence a list of the assets and liabilities of the enterprise or organization at a point in time. The fact that it represents the position at one point in time, the reporting date, is itself a limitation as it is only relevant at that point in time. At any other time, as we have seen in the case of Keelsafe, a new statement of financial position has to be drawn up. This means that in order for the statement to be useful it should be as up to date as possible, and that its utility diminishes the more out of date it becomes. Similarly, in order that it is an accurate measure of the assets and liabilities the values of those assets and liabilities should be as up to date as possible, and herein lies another limitation.

As we saw in Chapter 2, there are a number of ways in which assets can be valued, some of which are more subjective than others. The right value to choose depends on the purpose for which the statement of financial position is to be used. For example, if we want to know how much each item cost, then the original, or historic, cost would be appropriate. If, on the other hand, we wanted to know how much each item could be sold for, then the net realizable value may be appropriate. Alternatively, if we wanted to know how much the business as a whole was worth, it is likely that neither of the aforementioned would be appropriate. Partly because of the difficulties involved in choosing an appropriate valuation and partly by convention, accountants have traditionally used the historic cost as the basis of valuation of assets although, as we stated in Chapter 2 the use of fair value for some assets is becoming more prevalent and accepted if its prevalence, the International Accounting Standards is taken as a measure of acceptability. Clearly, in certain cases the use of historic cost has led to assets being stated at a figure which bears little if any relation to their current value. The most obvious example of this in recent years has been the changes in prices and values of land and buildings. Because of this, one often sees land and buildings shown in published accounts at fair value or with a note about their value rather than simply showing these at cost. Similarly with financial assets fair value is almost certainly a better measure than their cost as the price fluctuates in some cases on a daily basis.

An allied problem to the changes in the prices of specific assets is the fact that the currency unit of measurement, the euro, pound or dollar, does not itself represent a constant value over time. For example, you cannot buy as many goods with one pound today as you could ten years ago. This once again limits the usefulness of the information contained in the statement of financial position.

Influences on the format of the statement of financial position or balance sheets

The regulatory framework

For very small enterprises, usually owner-managed businesses, there is very little regulatory influence on how what is likely to still be called the balance sheet is produced or the format it follows. Indeed, there is no legal requirement for them to produce annual financial statements, although these may be required, in certain circumstances, by the tax authorities, or by potential lenders of money, e.g. banks. For UK companies, who are required by law to file a copy of their annual accounts with Companies House, there are a number of different sources of regulation that influence the format of the statement of financial position. In the UK and the European Union there are regulations relating to the format of accounts contained in Companies Acts. Traditionally there have been professional bodies which have issued Statements of Standard Accounting Practice (SSAPs) or Financial Reporting Standards (FRS). These professional pronouncements from across the globe are increasingly converging through the work of the International Accounting Standards Committee and we are likely to find a common set of statements and standards in use throughout the world in the future. The only question is when the different systems will converge rather than whether they will converge.

At the present time in some countries the standards are backed by regulation directly or indirectly. In the UK there is something of a compromise whereby the law requires companies to produce accounts that comply with the Companies Acts and generally accepted accounting principles (GAAP) which in effect mean that they must comply with the accepted standards which are increasingly International standards. Whereas in the past this generally applied to large companies with the introduction of the IFRS for small and medium size entities, which constitute over 90% of all businesses, we can expect to see more and more compliance and standardization of reporting around the model suggested in that standard.

For companies quoted on the Stock Exchange, they must also comply with the rules of the particular stock exchange if they want their shares to be traded in that country. In the past that meant complying with country specific requirements which in an increasingly global world was clearly nonsense and thus the move to requiring compliance with internationally accepted standards makes sense. Although this will inevitably mean a change in the terminology used and as not all companies are quoted companies, in reality for a number of years it is likely that some companies will use the terminology from the UK standards and traditions and others will use that from the International Standards. Table 3.1 provides a quick comparison of these two sets of terminology; where the terminology differs, this is shown in italics.

In the remainder of this book we will attempt to use the terminology from the International Standards but we will where appropriate use the more traditional terminology that was prevalent in UK accounting literature. There may be occasions when we have not changed all the references and this is because we are also trying to manage the transition to the new from the old.

TABLE 3.1

International Standards terminology	UK Standards terminology
Statement of financial position	Balance Sheet
Income statement	Profit and loss account
Non-current assets	Fixed assets
• Tangible assets	• Tangible assets
• Intangible assets	• Intangible assets
• Monetary assets	• No heading
Current assets	Current assets
• Inventory	• Stock
• Receivables	• Debtors
Current liabilities	Creditors – amounts falling due within one year
• Payables	• Creditors
Non-current liabilities	Creditors – amounts falling due after one year

Size and type of organization

As we have already indicated, the size and legal status of an organization affect the amount of regulation it is subject to and this in turn has an effect on the format in which that organization has to report. Another factor that impacts on the format of the statement of financial position and other statements contained in the annual report is the type of organization. This may be because it is governed by special regulations, as is the case for banks and other financial service organizations, or because its purpose is different, as would be the case with a charity where the main purpose is not profit maximization and which has no owners and therefore no owners' equity. Other examples of organizations where there is no owners' equity and with which we all interface are local authorities, healthcare trusts and universities.

Impact of users

As we have already mentioned, for smaller businesses the tax authorities and banks may require information in a certain format, normally the same as for companies, that is different from that which the owner, i.e. the internal user, finds useful. We have also seen that when the users include shareholders and the shares are traded on a stock exchange, there are further compliance issues to incorporate into annual reports. It is also worth mentioning at this stage that the users' requirements may be in conflict; for example, an owner may not wish to show large profits and therefore pay more tax but the bank would want to see good profits before lending. The owners may also be of the view that some disclosure is commercially sensitive and therefore would resist efforts to make them disclose that information. In addition, there will always be a constraint caused by uncertainty in respect of whether future economic benefits will arise, whether they can be measured and whether they therefore constitute an asset in the view of the various users of accounts.

CONCLUSION

In this chapter, we have defined the nature, purpose and content of statement of financial position or balance sheet, and have highlighted some of the problems in drawing up such a statement. We have also introduced you to the wider context in which accounting reports can be viewed. It is important before proceeding further that you make sure that you understand the definitions involved and can apply them to real problems. As you have seen, a statement of financial position can take many forms and clearly in a book of this nature there is no necessity to cover all of these. For simplicity, therefore, we shall use one format throughout the book, which is given below. This, as you can see, merely rearranges the accounting equation from:

$$\text{assets} = \text{owners' equity} + \text{liabilities}$$

to:

$$\text{assets} = \text{liabilities} + \text{owners equity}$$

This emphasizes that on the one hand we have the income generating assets of the business and on the other hand we have the mechanisms through which these assets are financed. The basis of this lies in the concept of the entity as a whole being reported on rather than who the report is aimed at. Having said that it still provides some indication of the idea that the equity whilst at one level being a source of finance is also at another level the residual interest in the assets once the liabilities have been paid off. This replaces the previous format of statement that was in common usage and which gave primacy to the owners of the enterprise by deducting the liabilities from the assets to arrive at an amount of net assets equal to the owners' residual interest.

SUGGESTED STATEMENT OF FINANCIAL POSITION FORMAT

Statement of financial position of Simple as at 31 December 2010

	2010 £	2009 £
Current assets		
Cash in hand	20	60
Inventory of raw materials	200	140
Inventory of finished goods	120	80
	340	280
Non-current assets		
Motor vehicles	50	40
Machinery	100	120
Land and buildings	200	200
	350	360
Total assets	690	640
Current liabilities		
Bank overdraft	170	150
	170	150
Non-current liabilities		
Bank loan	150	160
	150	160
Total liabilities	320	310
Owners' equity	100	100
Retained profits	270	230
Total equity	370	330
Total equity and liabilities	690	640

As numerous formats are available and these, to some extent at least, are dependent on the type of organization, we have used the format suggested in the IFRS-SME, which we consider to be appropriate to an introductory-level text.

Reasons for choosing the format above

The statement of financial position is headed with the name of the organization and the date to which the statement of financial position relates. As has already been explained, a statement of financial position relates to one point in time, the reporting date, and that date needs to be clearly stated in the heading. You will also notice that comparative figures are given for the previous year. In some cases, as with Volvo in Case Study 3.1, companies give more than two years comparative figures.

Within the statement of financial position itself we commence with the 'Current assets' which are shown in descending order of liquidity with cash being at the top as it is the most liquid. For example, in order to turn the raw materials into cash, we first have to go through a manufacturing process to get them ready for resale and then sell them, whereas in the case of the inventory which consists of finished goods the manufacturing process has already taken place. Note also that all the current assets are added together and a total is given.

'Non-current assets': these are all tangible fixed assets. These are again shown in descending order of permanence and liquidity. For example, the land and buildings will probably outlast the motor vehicles. They will also take longer to sell if we wished to sell them as we would first have to empty them, whereas the motor vehicles could be sold almost immediately. Once again a total of non-current assets is given and when this is added to the total of current assets a figure for total assets is arrived at.

A similar rationale applies to the other half of the statement with the finance being shown in order of liquidity with the first item being the bank overdraft which in theory at least is repayable on demand. The total for the current liabilities is shown, then the details of the non-current liabilities summing to a total of all liabilities. There is then the owners' equity, again subdivided, in so far as the amounts due to the owners are separately classified between those that the owner contributed to the business and those that the business generated as a result of trading, i.e. the retained profits. Finally the total equity and total liabilities are added together to arrive at a final total matching the total assets in the business.

SUMMARY

In this chapter, we have seen that a statement of financial position is an attempt to show the financial position at one point in time, the reporting date. We have also introduced the idea that a business is viewed for accounting purposes as a separate entity from its owner (the business entity principle). From this starting point, we have gone on to define assets, liabilities and owners' equity, and to look at the accounting equation. Before moving on to the next chapter you should ensure that you have understood what is contained in this chapter by working through the review questions and the problems and case studies given below. As with previous chapters, the answers to the review questions are all within the text.

REFERENCES

IASC (1989) *Framework for the Preparation and Presentation of Financial Statements*. London: Institute of Chartered Accountants.
IASB (2009) *International Financial Reporting Standard for Small and Medium Sized Entities*. London: International Accounting Standards Board.

FURTHER READING

Students who wish to examine the regulatory framework applying to different countries are referred to the latest edition of Nobes, C. and Parker, R., *Comparative International Accounting*, FT Prentice Hall.

REVIEW QUESTIONS

(✓ indicates answers are available in Appendix A)

✓ **1** What are the essential elements of a useful definition of an asset?

✓ **2** What are the implied assumptions underlying the IASC definition of an asset?

3 What are the deficiencies, if any, in the following definition of an asset?
Assets are the things a business owns.

4 What are the essential elements of a useful definition of a fixed asset?

5 Explain in your own words the difference between current and non-current assets, and why it is important to classify assets into subgroups.

6 (a) What are the criteria used by the IASC for classifying a current asset?
(b) How do the first and second criteria differ?

7 What are the differences between tangible and intangible assets?

8 Explain in your own words what a liability is, and the differences between liabilities and owners' equity.

9 What is the purpose of a statement of financial position and what information does it contain?

PROBLEMS FOR DISCUSSION AND ANALYSIS

(✓ indicates answers are available in Appendix A)

✓ **1** (a) Prepare a statement of financial position from the following information.
(b) Comment on the position of the business as shown by that statement of financial position.

	£
Inventory – goods held for resale	6 500
Freehold land and building	34 000
Mortgage on land and building	29 000
Cash in tills	500
Fixtures and fittings	7 600
Office furniture	2 300
Bank overdraft	20 700

	£
Delivery van	3 200
Owners' equity	?

2 (a) Prepare a statement of financial position from the information below.

(b) Comment of the position of the business as shown by the statement of financial position.

	£
Market stall	600
Goods held for resale	2 300
Van	1 800
Cash float	300
Bank loan – three year	3 000
Owners' equity	?

3 Arty has just started an antique business and he has bought the following:

	£
Transit van	10 000
Tools for restoration work	400
Business cards and paper	100
PC and printer	1 200
Furniture for resale	4 000

He has a business bank account with £1300 left in it.

Arty rents a double garage as a storeroom and workshop for £200 a week, paid weekly in advance. He operates the rest of the business from a room at home which he refers to as 'the office'. His house has seven rooms and cost him £85 000 to buy, but is now worth only £70 000.

Arty wants to buy more furniture, so he arranges a three-year bank loan of £1000.

(a) Discuss which of the items above are assets and liabilities of the business.

(b) Clearly identifying any assumptions you make, draw up a statement of financial position for Arty's Antiques after he has taken out the loan.

4 Joan has started her own restaurant using some money left to her by her aunt and by borrowing money from the bank. At the end of the first year she brings you a list of items that she owns and what she owes, and asks you to draw up a statement of financial position. The list is reproduced below.

(i)   She has the deeds to the premises which consist of the restaurant that she purchased for £70 000 and the flat above the restaurant which she bought for £80 000. Joan lives in the flat.

(ii)   Bills for furniture, tables, chairs, etc., which she bought for the restaurant. These amount to £2400.

(iii) Bills for furniture in the flat, which amount to £4500.

(iv)   Bills relating to kitchen equipment in the restaurant, amounting to £4600.

(v)   She has a large amount of wine and drinks in stock for customers which cost her £2300.

(vi)   Tablecloths, napkins, cutlery, tableware, etc., which cost £1200.

(vii) Her bank statement at the end of the year which shows she owes the bank £2800.

(viii) The £5000 receipt for her car, which is a hatchback that she uses to collect supplies for the restaurant and which is also used for deliveries as she does in-house catering for a large local firm of solicitors on a daily basis.

(ix)   The mortgage company's statement showing she owes £50 000 for the restaurant and £35 000 for the flat at the end of the year.

(a) Discuss each item and identify whether it is an asset or a liability and whether it is a business asset or liability.

(b) Draw up the statement of financial position for Joan's business at the end of the first year.

5 In each of the following situations, identify whether the item should be included in the statement of financial position of Transom Trading at 31 December 2010, and if so at what amount and under which heading. Transom Trading is a retailer of motor spares and accessories. In all cases reasons for your decision must be given.

(a) A freehold shop bought in August 2010 for £88 000.

(b) A mortgage of £30 000 taken out to buy the shop in August 2010.

(c) Goods on the shelves at the end of the day on 31 December 2010. These goods had a resale value of £12 000 and had been purchased by Transom Trading for £8000.

(d) Delivery van, costing £15 000, which Transom Trading ordered on 20 December 2010 but which was finally delivered and paid for on 2 January 2011.

(e) Shop fittings which were worth £3000 and had been bought at an auction by Transom Trading for only £1500 prior to opening the shop in August 2010.

(f) A Ford Focus costing £8900 which the owner of Transom Trading had bought in November 2010 for his wife to use. He had found that the Volvo estate which he had bought second-hand in September for £7000 was being used exclusively for collecting and delivering goods for Transom Trading and not as a family car as originally intended.

(g) One cash register which was rented from Equipment Supplies at an annual rental of £200 which was paid on 1 January 2010.

(h) One cash register which Transom Trading had bought in November 2010 for £600.

(i) A bank overdraft which amounted to £6500 on 31 December 2010.

(j) A supply of children's seat belts which the owner of Transom Trading had bought for £600 in September from a market trader in good faith and which were subsequently found to be defective.

6 Using the information in Problem 5 above calculate the owner's equity and draw up the statement of financial position of Transom Trading as at 31 December 2010.

7 Fred owns a garage and has tried to get everything together ready for the business accounts to be drawn up. He has drawn up the list of items below. You are required to identify with reasons the heading under which each item should be classified in the statement of financial position, and the amount at which it should be included.

(a) A motor car bought for resale at a cost of £6500; the retail price was £8000.

(b) Various loose tools for car repairs which cost £700.

(c) Two hydraulic jacks which had each cost £120.

(d) Freehold premises which had cost £40 000.

(e) The cost (£600) of digging and finishing a pit for repairs.

(f) Spare parts held as a general inventory, originally costing £790.

(g) Spare parts bought from the previous owner when the garage was bought. At that time the value was agreed at £600 but it was subsequently discovered that only £200 of these spares were of any use.

(h) Breakdown truck which cost £7000 for the basic truck and £600 to have the crane fitted.

(i) A customer's car worth £1500 which was being held because the customer had not paid an outstanding bill of £300.

(j) Fred's own car which cost £8000. This is used mainly for business but Fred also uses it in the evenings and at weekends for the family.

(k) Customer goodwill which Fred reckons he has built up. He thinks that this would be worth at least £7000 if he sold the garage tomorrow.

(l) A bank loan for £1500 repayable within three months.

(m) A 20-year mortgage on the property amounting to £24 000 which has not been fully repaid. The amount still outstanding is £18 000.

8 Using the information from Problem 7 above, draw up a statement of financial position for Fred's business.

CHAPTER 4
THE INCOME STATEMENT AND THE CASH FLOW STATEMENT

LEARNING OUTCOMES

By the end of this chapter you will be able to:

- Identify revenue and expenses for a period and draw up a simple income statement.

- Understand the principles of accrual accounting where revenue and expenses are allocated to the periods to which the economic activities relate rather than simply when the transaction occurred.

- Understand the definitions of revenue and expenses, the difficulties associated with the recognition of revenue and the importance of the matching principle.

- Understand how a cash flow statement is produced and the advantages that can be gained by identifying different types of cash flows.

In this chapter, we turn our attention to the measurement of profit and cash flows. Profit measurement is formally shown in a financial statement which is referred to as the income statement or profit and loss account. The components of the income statement, revenue and expenses, are defined and contrasted with assets and liabilities in order to illustrate the important differences between the components of the statement of financial position and those of the income statement. We shall also introduce another statement, the cash flow statement, and contrast that with the income statement and statement of financial position.

We have already seen that we can measure profit by measuring wealth at two points in time. We have also shown that the way in which wealth is measured in accounting terms can be roughly equated with what is shown in the statement of financial position, and we have looked at some of the issues arising from the alternative choices in respect of assigning monetary values to wealth measurement.

In this chapter, we shall be concerned with an alternative way of measuring profit, using an income statement – also often called a profit and loss account. From 2005, International Accounting Standards have become widely accepted and the introduction of the International Financial Reporting Standard for Small and Medium Sized Entities (IFRS-SME) in 2009 means that increasingly businesses will report using the terminology from those standards. However, it is likely that for small businesses and in particular sole traders the use of the term profit and loss account will still be seen as the norm for some time to come. In reality, despite the different names, the content is the same so our starting point and approach are very similar to those taken in the previous chapter. We look at what an income statement is, why it is important, why it is produced and what it contains. We then consider some determinants of the content of an income statement and some of the issues that have to be dealt with when drawing up an income statement.

Before leaving this chapter, we shall consider another statement that relates to the flows of resources over the period. This is known as the cash flow statement and throughout this and the following chapters we will be showing you how to produce a cash flow statement and an income statement, and at the same time highlighting the differences between the two when appropriate.

IMPORTANCE OF INCOME STATEMENTS

Unlike a balance sheet or statement of financial position, which communicates information about a point in time, the income statement relates to a period of time. It summarizes certain transactions taking place over that period. In terms of published reports, the period is normally one year, although most businesses of any size produce income statements more regularly, usually quarterly and often monthly accounts. These monthly or quarterly accounts are normally for internal consumption only, although often banks request copies or make the production of such accounts a condition of lending money. The reason why the banks require these accounts on a regular basis is that they need to monitor the health of the business to which they are lending. They want to be confident that the managers of the business are aware of what is happening and taking action to rectify the situation if the business is making losses.

As far as owners and managers are concerned, if they want the business to flourish, there is little point in finding out at the end of the year that the price at which goods or services were sold did not cover what it cost to buy those goods. By that stage it is too late to do anything about it. If a problem is identified at the end of the first month, however, it can be dealt with immediately by putting up prices, buying at a lower price or whatever is appropriate to the particular business.

Clearly, the income statement is a very important statement as it tells you whether a business is profitable or not. We have all heard the expression, 'what is the bottom line?' The bottom line referred to is the amount of profit made by a project or business. By comparing that profit with how much wealth is needed to produce it, you can decide whether to invest in a business. Other factors which need to be taken into account are the risks involved and your own judgement of future prospects in order to decide whether the return as measured by the income statement is adequate. Therefore, it can be argued that the income statement provides some of the basic financial information for a rational decision to be made. We should remember, however, that although most of us think of business as being primarily motivated by profits, this is not always the case. Many small businesses make profits which are unsatisfactory from the point of view of a rational economic assessment, but the owners' motivation may not be profit. They may simply hate working for any boss, or they may value leisure more than additional profits. These are often referred to as lifestyle businesses.

ACTIVITY 4.1

Can you think of other types of organization that are actively trading and making a profit but do not have profit as their primary motive?

You may have identified charities such as Oxfam, Mind or the RSPCA, social enterprises or one-off fundraising events such as Red Nose Day.

Having talked about why an income statement is important, let us now look at what it is and what it contains. We have said that it is a statement covering a period of time, normally one year, and that its purpose is to measure profit, i.e. the increase in wealth. It does this by summarizing the revenue for that period and deducting from that the expenses incurred in earning that revenue. The process is therefore simple, but to be able to do it we need to look at the definition of revenue and expenses.

REVENUE

We will use the definition of revenue included in the International Accounting Standards, in this case IAS 18, and look at it in some detail so that we understand what it means (Key Concept 4.1).

KEY CONCEPT 4.1

Revenue

Revenue is the gross inflow of economic benefits during the period arising in the course of the ordinary activities of the entity when those inflows result in increases in equity, other than increases relating to contributions from equity participants. [IAS 18, Para. 7]

As is usual with definitions, this one seems on the face of it fairly complex. This is because it is trying to cover all eventualities. In most cases, revenue is so obvious that it hits you between the eyes. For example, we would all agree that in a greengrocer's the revenue is going to be the amount that the fruit and vegetables were sold for, and in most cases that amount will all be in cash in the till. However, if we complicate it a bit more and suppose that our greengrocer supplies fruit and vegetables to a couple of local restaurants who settle their bill every month, we find that in order to define revenue we have to include not only cash sales but also the other sales for which we have not been paid. The latter amounts are referred to as 'receivables' or, in some of the older texts in the UK, as 'debtors'. These receivables are shown in our statement of financial position as assets because we shall get a future benefit from them. We shall discuss their treatment in more detail in Chapter 7.

You will note that the definition refers to the inflow of economic benefits and is silent on how these benefits actually flow in to the entity. As we have already seen, it can be in the form of cash or of amounts due to be paid in the future, but what other ways could we get an inflow of economic benefits? In order to explore the answer to that question we will develop further our example of the greengrocer. Let us assume that, in addition to supplying the local restaurants that pay monthly, he also supplies his accountant, but instead of the accountant paying cash the arrangement is that the accountant does the accounts for nothing instead of charging the normal fee of £520 per year. These goods are effectively being sold to the accountant; all that has happened is that instead of the accountant paying the green-grocer £10 per week and then the greengrocer paying the accountant £520 at the end of the year they have simply agreed to exchange one set of economic benefits, the accountant's services, for another set, the greengroceries supplied to the accountant. Hence, the greengroceries 'sold' to the accountant would be included in revenue and the cost of the services provided by the accountant would be included in the expenses.

At this stage, we should have a fair idea of what revenue is: it relates to goods and services sold. However, we need to be careful to ensure that we only include in revenue sales that are part of our ordinary activity. The IFRS-SME usefully separates the definition of income into two components: that concerned with trading, which it refers to as revenue, and that concerned with other gains.

KEY CONCEPT 4.2

Revenue and gains (IFRS-SME)

Revenue is income that arises in the course of the ordinary activities of an entity and is referred to by a variety of names including sales, fees, interest, dividends, royalties and rent. (IFRS-SME, Para. 2.25a)

Gains are other items that meet the definition of income but are not revenue. When gains are recognized in the statement of comprehensive income, they are usually displayed separately because knowledge of them is useful for making economic decisions. (IFRS-SME, Para. 2.25b)

NB: you may note that the second definition introduces the statement of comprehensive income – this is a statement that combines both trading profit and other gains. At this stage you can ignore this. We will deal with it in more detail in Chapter 11.

To illustrate the ideas contained in the definitions in Key Concept 4.2, let us assume that our green-grocer sells one of his two shops: should this be seen as revenue or is it different from selling fruit and vegetables? Clearly, the answer is that it is different, because without a shop the business will cease to exist, whereas one cauliflower more or less does not threaten the existence of the business. Hence, we need to differentiate normal sales of goods and services from 'ordinary activities' from the gains or amounts arising from the sale of what is essentially the fabric of the business. The latter amounts will be dealt with separately and we explore their treatment in more detail in Chapters 8 and 11.

Finally, before leaving our greengrocer illustration, let us assume that, having sold one of the shops, the greengrocer decides to invest the money in some shares or in a building society until such time as a new shop can be found. In this situation the money invested, which is effectively surplus to immediate requirements, will generate an inflow of economic benefits in the form of interest or dividends. This is clearly revenue within the definition provided in Key Concept 4.2 but is different from the main source of revenue in the case of our greengrocer. It would, in this case, be shown separately but included in the total revenue for the period. In certain cases, however, the interest may be the major source of revenue – if, for example, the main activity of a business is lending money. Similarly, dividends may be the main source of revenue for an investment trust.

Returning briefly to Key Concept 4.1 it is worth noting that the definition of revenue requires that these 'inflows result in increases in equity'. So, for example, if we borrow money, there is an inflow of money to the organization but there is also an increase in the liabilities and these effects cancel each other out so there is no increase in equity. In a similar vein, the definition also excludes additional contributions from equity participants as these are simply an increase in assets and an increase in the amount the organization owes to the equity holders.

Hence, we can see that, although broadly speaking revenue is synonymous in many cases with sales, the actual revenue of a business is dependent on the type of business and the particular activity giving rise to the revenue. In the example we have used we have seen that in its simplest form revenue was equal to cash sales. However, for some business activities the distinctions are not so clear and this leads to problems in deciding what revenue relates to a particular period. This, of course, would not be a problem if accounting periods were the same as the period of a business cycle. For example, if a house builder takes 18 months to build and sell a house there is no problem in finding the revenue for the 18 months. Unfortunately, the normal accounting period is 12 months and, as we have pointed out earlier, management and others need information on a more regular basis than that. What, then, is the revenue of our house builder for the first six months, or for the first year? This leads us to the question of when revenue arises and when it should be recognized. To help in answering this we adopt a principle known as the realization principle.

KEY CONCEPT 4.3

The realization principle

The realization principle states that revenue should only be recognized

(a) when the earning process is substantially complete and
(b) when the receipt of payment for the goods and services is reasonably certain.

THE REALIZATION PRINCIPLE

The realization principle is defined in Key Concept 4.3. You may have noticed that, unlike our other definitions, which tend to be fairly precise and all-inclusive, this principle is carefully worded to avoid too much precision. It is meant to provide some basic criteria which can be applied to the particular circumstances. The final decision on whether revenue is recognized is in practice often a matter of judgement rather than fact. Before looking at an example, let us first look at the wording used in the realization principle. First you will see that it talks of process, which implies a period rather than a point in time. It also talks of 'substantially complete', which leaves the question of what is 'substantial': is it two-thirds or 90% or what? The principle also talks of payment being 'reasonably certain'. Once again, this leaves room for the exercise of judgement and raises the question of what is 'reasonable certainty' in an uncertain world.

Obviously, if we sell goods to a reputable customer of long-standing, we are going to be reasonably certain that we shall be paid. If, on the other hand, we sell goods to a shady character, then we may be a lot less confident that we shall be paid. Some further guidance is provided in the International Accounting Standard on the subject of Revenue (IAS 18). This states that revenue should be recognized when:

1   significant risks and rewards of ownership have been transferred to the buyer;

2   managerial involvement and control have passed;

3   the amount of revenue can be measured reliably;

4   it is probable that economic benefits will flow to the enterprise;

5   the costs of the transaction, including future costs, can be measured reliably.

This further clarification is useful as it is more comprehensive. Taking each of these in turn, item 1 is reasonably straightforward but also covers situations where goods are sold on hire purchase or on a type of lease. Although you need to be aware of these types of transaction, for our purposes that level of awareness is sufficient. Item 2 is there to cover situations such as partial sales of companies where, although on the face of it something has been sold, in reality it is still controlled by the enterprise and as such the benefits come to the enterprise. The third and fourth points are self-explanatory and were dealt with when discussing assets in Chapter 3. It is, however, worth noting in the fourth point that we are dealing with probability not certainty. The final point is interesting as although we can measure costs, as we shall see in later chapters there are many ways of measuring cost. It is also worth bearing in mind that measuring future costs is fraught with difficulty, as can be illustrated from the punitive damages being awarded against companies for asbestos-related health problems.

Rather then looking at numerous examples of transactions, which may or may not lead to revenue being realized, let us start by looking in general terms at a production and selling process and examining the possible points at which we could recognize revenue in accordance with the realization principle.

Clearly, it is unlikely that revenue would ever be recognized at point 1 but as we shall see all the other points could be appropriate in different circumstances. If we start at the end of the process,

---

FIGURE 4.1

Point 1	Inputs
	↓
Point 2	Production
	↓
Point 3	Finished goods
	↓
Point 4	Sale of goods
Point 5	Receipt of cash

i.e. point 5, on the face of it this seems to be a safe place to recognize revenue as the earnings process is likely to be complete and payment is certain because the cash has been received. In many cases point 5 is the appropriate point – as for example in the case of our greengrocer. However, he also had some other sales which were paid for monthly in arrears, so those may have to be recognized at point 4 as at that point the earning process is complete and payment is reasonably certain. It is worth noting here that, in the case of our greengrocer, all the criteria in IAS 18 have been met. If we now consider the house builder and use either points 4 or 5, we would get a situation where there was no revenue for the first 17 months but a lot in the 18th month. Of course, in practice even in the case of our builder, money would have been paid on account and it is likely that prior to the end of the contract the criteria laid down in IAS 18 will have been met. The significant factor here is that points 4 and 5 are not necessarily appropriate in all cases.

One could argue that for a shipbuilder points 4 and 5 are inappropriate as money is received throughout a contract and the point of sale is in fact before the production process starts. In this case, as a ship takes a number of years to build, it is also inappropriate to choose point 3 as this would lead to all the revenue arising in one year. Therefore, it may in fact be that point 2 is appropriate if the earning process is 'substantially' complete and, as is likely, payments on account have been received. A similar argument applies to the cases of a property developer or a building subcontractor. In all these cases it is a question of judgement as to whether the earnings process is substantially complete and a judgement about the probability of getting paid. The IAS criteria simply expand these issues, talking of probability of benefits flowing to the enterprise, significant risks and rewards having passed, etc. The one criterion that has not been mentioned so far is whether the costs can be measured reliably; this, together with measuring revenue in some cases, is no mean task. Recent examples such as the Millennium Dome for which revenue estimates were completely wrong and the Scottish Parliament building for which actual costs to date are ten times the original estimate perhaps illustrate that accounting is not an exact science and one can only use one's best judgement.

From the discussion above, it should be obvious that each case needs to be judged on its merits.

ACTIVITY 4.2

You may, like to think about when the appropriate time for revenue recognition would be for the following businesses.

1   a local newsagent;

2   a supplier of components to Ford Motors;

3   a gold-mine where all output is bought by the government at a fixed price;

4   an aircraft manufacturer.

If you have applied the realization principle you should have had little problem with the first example, but the others are more problematic and are discussed more fully at the end of the chapter. If you feel unsure of your own solutions, you may wish to refer to that discussion before proceeding any further.

The problem of when to recognize revenue is very important because profit measurement is based on the revenue for a period and the expenses for that period. Before going on to discuss expenses, we should first discuss how we establish which expenses to include. This is done by means of the matching principle (Key Concept 4.4).

KEY CONCEPT 4.4

The matching principle

We must match the revenue earned during a period with the expenses incurred in earning that revenue.

We can see that the realization principle is of prime importance as it defines the revenue with which the expenses have to be matched. If we include additional revenue then we must also include expenses incurred in earning that additional revenue. On the face of it, this matching is fairly straightforward. However, there are a number of areas where problems arise. These may be to do with timing (as we discuss later) or a combination of timing and uncertainty, as we illustrate in Case Study 4.1.

CASE STUDY 4.1

BP plc

Extract from the principal accounting policies of BP plc for the year ended 31 December 2008

BP Plc 2008

Oil and natural gas exploration and development expenditure Oil and natural gas exploration and development expenditure is accounted for using the successful efforts method of accounting.

Licence and property acquisition costs Exploration licence and leasehold property acquisition costs are capitalized within intangible assets and are reviewed at each reporting date to confirm that there is no indication that the carrying amount exceeds the recoverable amount. This review includes confirming that exploration drilling is still under way or firmly planned or that it has been determined, or work is under way to determine, **that the discovery is economically viable based on a range of technical and commercial considerations and sufficient progress is being made on establishing development plans and timing**. If no future activity is planned, the remaining balance of the licence and property acquisition costs is written off. Lower value licences are pooled and amortized on a straight-line basis over the estimated period of exploration. Upon recognition of proved reserves and internal approval for development, the relevant expenditure is transferred to property, plant and equipment.

Exploration expenditure Geological and geophysical exploration costs are charged against income as incurred. Costs directly associated with an exploration well are initially capitalized as an intangible asset until the drilling of the well is complete and the results have been evaluated. These costs include employee remuneration, materials and fuel used, rig costs, delay rentals and payments made to contractors. **If hydrocarbons are not found, the exploration expenditure is written off as a**

(Continued)

dry hole. If hydrocarbons are found and, subject to further appraisal activity, which may include the drilling of further wells (exploration or exploratory-type stratigraphic test wells), are likely to be capable of commercial development, the costs continue to be carried as an asset. All such carried costs are subject to technical, commercial and management review at least once a year to confirm the continued intent to develop or otherwise extract value from the discovery. When this is no longer the case, the costs are written off.

When proved reserves of oil and natural gas are determined and development is sanctioned, the relevant expenditure is transferred to property, plant and equipment.

Development expenditure Expenditure on the construction, installation or completion of infrastructure facilities such as platforms, pipelines and the drilling of development wells, **including unsuccessful development or delineation wells, is capitalized within property**, plant and equipment and is depreciated from the commencement of production as described below in the accounting policy for Property, plant and equipment.

Commentary

The extract from the accounting principles of BP plc illustrates a number of areas where there are problems of matching expenses and revenue because of conditions of uncertainty. The first of these is licences, which, as you can see from the sections in bold, they need to review annually to establish if they are still worth anything. Under exploration expenditure, again the costs are collected and again are evaluated and written off if the exploration turns out to be a 'dry hole'. Here BP plc like many other companies dealing in the exploration of natural resources and the supply of energy (British Gas, Shell, etc.) has to find the oilfields first and then assess them to decide whether they are worth exploiting or not. The problem is, does an asset exist or not? The acid test for this is whether there is likely to be a future benefit. As can be seen from the note on exploration expenditure, BP plc deals with the question in different ways depending upon the certainty of the outcome. In some cases the expenditure is dealt with as tangible fixed assets. At the other extreme, where it is clear that no future benefit is likely, it treats the expenditure as an expense. This is normal practice within these types of industry, but clearly illustrates the fact that, although accounting rules may assume certainty, reality is not like that. It is all about probability and risk and accounting can therefore only provide an estimation of performance based on assumptions about probability and risk.

EXPENSES

An expense is defined in Key Concept 4.5.

KEY CONCEPT 4.5

An expense

An expense is an expired cost, i.e. a cost from which all benefit has been extracted during an accounting period.

Although the definition of an expense is fairly straightforward, like revenue it is important to recognize that there are two types of expense: the first relating to the 'ordinary activities' and the other relating to 'one-off' transactions. These two types of expense need to be separately identified and treated differently with only those relating to 'ordinary activities' being matched against the income derived from 'ordinary activities' and the other expenses being disclosed separately. The definition itself leads us on to having to define what a cost is. As you will see later, there are numerous ways of arriving at a cost. However, for present purposes we can say that a cost means a money sacrifice or the incurring of a liability in pursuit of the business objectives.

ACTIVITY 4.3

Can you think why it is important to separate out the two types of income and expense and match them carefully?

The answer lies in that idea that what decision makers are interested in is what is going to happen in the future and 'one-off' activities by definition are unlikely to happen in the future but 'ordinary activities' will continue and, assuming all other things are equal (a fairly massive assumption) could provide a useful guide to future revenue and expenses.

Some examples of costs are:

● wages, which normally involve a money sacrifice;

● use of electricity, which normally involves incurring a liability to pay at the end of a quarter;

● purchase of a machine, which will normally incur a money sacrifice or a liability;

● purchase of goods for resale, which will normally incur a money sacrifice or a liability.

Although all the examples can clearly be seen to fit our definition of costs, they are not necessarily expenses of the period. For example, the machinery is likely to last more than one period and so it cannot be seen as an expired cost. Similarly, the goods bought for resale may not be sold during the period and they therefore cannot be seen as an expense of the period, for two reasons. First, the benefit has not expired as we shall be able to sell those goods at some time in the future. Second, they cannot be matched against the revenue earned during the period. There are other situations where the point at which a cost is incurred and the point at which the benefit arises does not coincide. We shall discuss these in more detail shortly.

Before we do that, it is worth emphasizing once again that we are dealing with a separate business entity – remember the business entity principle – Key Concept 3.2 – and only costs relating to the business objectives can ever become expenses. This is very important as in many cases, especially with small businesses, the owner and the business are to all intents and purposes the same, but we are drawing up accounts for the business only. Hence, if we find that a bill has been paid to buy a new double-bed for a newsagent's business, this cost is not an expense of the business because it relates to the owner personally, not the business. Such items often go through a business bank account but need to be separated out and shown as withdrawals of the owner's capital rather than business expenses.

These withdrawals are often referred to in the accounting literature as drawings. We could provide numerous examples of these, some of which are less obvious than others. For example, is the tax and insurance of the car a business expense if the car is also used for family transportation? The guiding principle in making a judgement is whether or not the cost has been incurred in pursuit of the objectives of the business.

We shall return to the discussion of drawings later, but let us now consider some possible situations in which we have to decide whether a cost which is clearly a business cost is an expense of the period. There are three possible situations that we need to discuss. These are where:

- costs of this year are expenses of this year;
- costs of earlier years are expenses of this year;
- costs of this year are expenses of subsequent years.

Costs of this year are expenses of this year

This is the most normal situation and is also the simplest to deal with. It occurs when an item or service is acquired during a year and consumed during that same year.

Note that no reference is made to whether the item acquired has been paid for. It may be that it has still not been paid for even though it has been acquired and used. A common example is telephone calls, which are only paid for at the end of the quarter. The question of the timing of payment is not relevant to the process of matching expenses and revenues.

Costs of earlier years are expenses of this year

These can be divided into those that are wholly used up in the current period and those that are partly used up in the current period.

Wholly expenses of this year

The most obvious example of this is the stock of goods that were in a shop at the start of the year. The cost of buying those goods has been incurred in the preceding year but at the year end the benefit has not expired; they were therefore assets at the year end. However, in the current year they will be sold and thus will become expenses of the current year. The process that has occurred can be illustrated as follows.

If we buy goods in November of year 1 but do not sell them until January of year 2 and we have a year end on 31 December of year 1 then the goods are an asset at that date, i.e. 31 December year 1, as the benefit is not used up. The cost, however, has been incurred in that year. In year 2 the goods are sold and therefore the benefit is used up and there is an expense for the year ended 31 December year 2, although the cost was incurred in the previous year. This can be seen diagrammatically in Figure 4.2.

FIGURE 4.2

A similar situation arises when services are paid for in advance and are not fully used up at the end of the accounting period. For example, if the rent is payable quarterly in advance on 31 March, 30 June, 30 September and 31 December, and the enterprise has a year end on 31 December, then the cost will be incurred in year 1 for the quarter to 31 March, year 2. However, the benefit will be used up in the first quarter of year 2 and therefore the expense belongs to year 2.

These expenses are normally referred to as 'prepaid expenses' and frequently arise in respect of rent and water rates.

ACTIVITY 4.4

Can you think of any examples of things you pay for in advance as different times of the year?

You may have thought of rent, annual subscriptions to clubs and societies, contents insurance, car insurance, road fund licence, etc.

All the examples discussed so far refer to situations where the costs were incurred in the past but the expenses are wholly or partly attributable to the current year. Another category that needs to be considered is where costs have been incurred in the past and only part of the benefit is used up in the current year.

Partly expenses of current year

Other situations that arise for a business are where a cost relates to more than one accounting period. For example, if we assume a 31 December year end and the car insurance of the business is payable on 1 July each year, then half of that cost would be used up and become an expense for year 1 and half would be used up and be an expense of year 2. The crucial test is whether the benefit has been used up at the year end or if there is a future benefit due to the business. The business has an asset worth the unused portion of the services purchased, in our example half a year's car insurance. A similar situation arises if a business buys a car, a machine or some office equipment. It is clearly not appropriate to charge the whole of the costs to the period in which the cost was incurred as the benefits will be there for many accounting periods. These items are referred to as fixed assets and we will return to the treatment of these in detail in Chapter 8. For the moment you need only be aware that they exist and that the principle of matching dictates that they are not treated wholly as an expense of the current period.

ACTIVITY 4.5

Can you think of some everyday examples of long-term assets in use in your home?

You may have come up with a car, a dishwasher, washing machine, computer, printer, scanner, etc. All of these are good examples of consumer durables, the use of which you can benefit from over a number of years.

Costs incurred this year are expenses of subsequent years

Using the example of car insurance, if we are in the first year and the insurance is taken out half way through that year, then some of the cost of the insurance relates to the current year – year one – and some is an asset at the end of year one but will be an expense of year 2.

Other examples are car tax, general insurance and rates. The due date for payment of these will only coincide with the end of the accounting period by chance, and we would not want them to as this would lead to an uneven cash flow. Further examples are goods held in stock or inventory at the year end and fixed assets bought during the year.

Returning to our example of our annual car tax we can see that, if we pay for that in the current year, year 1, on 1 July, then part of that cost will relate to next year, year 2. This is illustrated diagrammatically in Figure 4.3.

Having looked at revenues and expenses, we now need to recap on how these fit together in the income statement before looking at a simple numerical example.

FIGURE 4.3

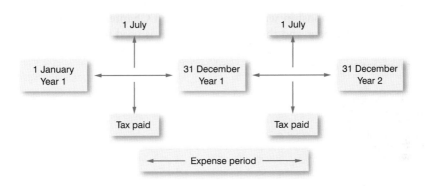

THE INCOME STATEMENT

The purpose of this statement is to measure the profit or loss for the period. It does this by summarizing the revenues for the period, matching the expenses incurred in earning those revenues and subtracting the expenses from the revenues to arrive at the profit or loss. This could be depicted as:

$$R - E = P$$

or:

$$\text{revenue} - \text{expenses} = \text{profit}$$

Before going on to examine what the profit figure could be used for, let us see how this fits with the measurement of wealth described in Chapter 2.

In Chapter 2, we said that profit is the difference between wealth at the start and end of the year, i.e.:

$$\text{wealth } 1 - \text{wealth } 0 = \text{profit } P_1$$

or:

$$W_1 - W_0 = P_1$$

The alternative way of measuring profit was to take expenses from revenue. We said in Chapter 3 that wealth in accounting terms was measured by assets minus liabilities. The resultant figure, i.e. the residual, was referred to as the owners' equity. Thus, we said that at time T_0 the owners' equity is:

$$\text{assets at } T_0 - \text{liabilities at } T_0 = \text{owners' equity at } T_0$$

If we add to the owners' equity at T_0 the profit for the period T_0 to T_1, then the resultant figure will be our wealth at T_1, which will equal our assets minus liabilities at T_1, i.e.:

$$\text{assets at } T_1 - \text{liabilities at } T_1 = \text{owners' equity at } T_0 + \text{profit } P_1$$

or:

$$A_1 - L_1 = O_0 + (R - E)_1$$

This shows us that there is a relationship between the income statement and the statement of financial position; the nature of that relationship will become clearer in Chapter 5. However, let us now look at an example of an income statement and then consider what it is used for, its format and its limitations. In Example 4.1, we use the transactions of Blake's Enterprises, a paint shop, and see what should go into the income statement for the year to 31 December 2010.

EXAMPLE 4.1

Blake's Enterprises

Blake's Enterprises is a new retail paint outlet set up at the start of the year. Its transactions for 2010, its first year, are summarized below.

Dates	Description	Amount (£)
1 January	Purchase of freehold shop	60 000
1 January	Rates for the year	2 000
1 April	Van purchased	8 000
1 April	Van – tax and insurance for one year	600
1 July	Purchase of washing machine	300
Various	Wages to shop assistant for year	6 000
Various	Goods bought and resold	18 000
Various	Goods bought but unsold	4 000
Various	Cash from sales	45 000
Various	Motor expenses and petrol	1 200
Various	Money withdrawn by Blake	6 000

Purchase of freehold
In this case there is an outflow of one resource, money, for an inflow of another resource, the building. The question we need to ask ourselves is whether the benefit arising from this cost has expired during the period.

(Continued)

In this case, although some part of the benefit may have been used up, there is clearly a future benefit from using the building so we have an asset not an expense. At this stage we shall not try to measure the part used up but we should bear in mind that at a later stage we shall need to make such allocations.

Rates for the year

This is clearly a cost and as there is no future benefit to be obtained it is not an asset, therefore as all the benefits have expired it meets the definition of an expense of the year in question and should be included in the income statement.

Purchase of van

As with the freehold shop, the benefit is likely to be available over many periods, i.e. there is a future benefit and we therefore have an asset. We should theoretically allocate to the income statement for the year the amount of the benefit used up in the year. This allocation is done by means of a depreciation charge, which we deal with in Chapter 8. At this stage, therefore, we shall merely note the idea that an allocation should be made.

Van – tax and insurance

This was paid for in advance on 1 April for a full year. At the end of our accounting period, i.e. 31 December, we shall have used nine months' insurance and tax, i.e. nine-twelfths of the total. The expense for the period therefore is $9/12 \times £600$, i.e. £450. The remaining £150 relates to the next year and will provide a future benefit in the form of insurance etc. This £150 is therefore an asset at the end of the year. This and similar items are discussed in more detail in Chapter 7.

Purchase of washing machine

We know that Blake's Enterprises is a retail shop selling paint. It is therefore highly unlikely that the washing machine was bought for use by the business, although it has been paid for out of the business bank account. This is not, therefore, an expense of the business, nor is it an asset of the business as the business will not get any future benefit. It is, in effect, a withdrawal of capital by the owner and should be treated as drawings.

Wages for year

This is clearly a business expense as the wages are paid to the shop assistant and the benefit has been used up. From the information we have, the whole £6 000 relates to the accounting period, and therefore the expense charged for the period should be £6000.

Goods bought and resold

These goods have been sold to customers. They meet with our definition of an expense as the business will get no future benefit from these goods as it no longer owns them. Hence, the whole of the £18 000 is an expired benefit and as such should be charged as an expense in the current year's income statement.

Goods bought but unsold

These goods are still held by the business at the end of the year. The benefit from the goods is still to come in the form of cash when they are sold. These goods held at the year end will provide a future benefit when they are sold and are therefore an asset rather than expense of the period with which we are dealing. Note that the test being applied is whether there is a future benefit or whether the benefit is past. If the former is the case there is an asset; if it is the latter situation then there is an expense.

(Continued)

Cash from sales

This is the revenue of the business for the year and as far as we can tell it is the only revenue. The full amount of £45 000 should be shown as sales revenue in the income statement.

Motor expenses and petrol

Once again the benefit from these has expired. The whole of the £1200 should therefore be charged as an expense to the current year's income statement.

Money withdrawn by Blake

Given the present information, we cannot categorically say whether this is a business expense or not. If it is in effect wages for Blake's work it could be argued that it is a genuine business expense. If, on the other hand, it has simply been withdrawn because Blake has decided to buy a new boat for personal use then it is clearly drawings. For the present we classify it as drawings.

We can now draw up the income statement of Blake's Enterprises for the year ended 31 December 2010.

Income statement of Blake's Enterprises for the year ended 31 December 2010

	£	£
Sales revenue		45 000
Cost of the goods sold		18 000
Gross profit		27 000
Rates	2 000	
Van tax and insurance	450	
Wages	6 000	
Motor expenses	1 200	9 650
Net profit		17 350

You will notice that we have shown a gross profit and a net profit. Gross profit can be defined as sales less cost of goods sold; net profit can broadly be defined as gross profit less operating costs, administrative costs and other charges.

The reason for showing a gross profit is to enable Blake to see that the business is doing as well as it should. Most retail businesses know what percentage of the selling price is profit and what is cost; Blake, for example, has costs of 40% (£18 000) of the selling price (£45 000) and would expect a gross profit margin of 60% (£27 000) of the selling price.

ACTIVITY 4.6

If next year the gross profit margin was only 50%; can you think what might have caused it to reduce?

The answer must lie either with the sales figure or with the cost of goods that have been sold. Problems with the sales figure could arise because not all sales have been included, or because the sales price had to be reduced due to competition or to enter a new market. Similarly the price of the goods bought for resale may have risen or the amount sold could have been incorrectly calculated.

(Continued)

The net profit figure, as can be seen from the definition above, can be affected by numerous expenses. It is the figure often referred to as the bottom line. You may see sets of accounts in which the owners' drawings are deducted from this figure to arrive at a figure of profit retained in the business. The reason for not taking drawings off the net profit figure is similar to the argument for a gross profit in so far as a business will normally incur similar expenses year to year, i.e. Blake will probably need a shop assistant next year, will have to pay rates etc. These amounts will be reasonably constant and the net profit as a percentage of sales should therefore be reasonably constant. The owners' drawings, on the other hand, may fluctuate widely from year to year and therefore to include these in the calculation of net profit would mean that the net profit would also fluctuate widely. This would make any analysis of the performance of the business more difficult than if the drawings are taken after the net profit has been determined.

INFLUENCES ON THE FORMAT OF THE INCOME STATEMENT

Unlike the statement of financial position, which represents the position at the reporting date, the income statement tries to represent a series of transactions over a period of time. Let us look first at what determines the format of the income statement as this also, to some extent, determines its usefulness and its limitations. For this we shall follow a similar format to Chapter 3 in that we shall consider the regulatory framework, the size and type of organization, and the users of the statement. However, as there is considerable overlap between the regulatory framework relating to the statement of financial position and the income statement, we will keep this review brief.

As we have said, in essence the same regulatory framework applies to the income statement as to the statement of financial position, so for very small enterprises, usually owner-managed businesses, there is very little regulation in terms of content or presentation of the income statement. However, the tax authorities, although not necessarily requiring a statement of financial position to be produced, will almost certainly require a statement showing the profit for the period and how it has been arrived at. For incorporated businesses, i.e. companies, as is the case with the statement of financial position, the larger and more complex the organization and its activities the more regulatory authorities it will have to deal with including state laws, national and international financial reporting standards, and stock exchange regulations. There is a clear recognition of size in the regulatory framework. For large companies there are numerous accounting standards, all of which have to be complied with if relevant to the company's business. On the other hand, smaller companies have their own International Financial Reporting Standard for Small and Medium Size Entities (IFRS-SME, 2009), which is less detailed and contains all the regulatory requirements in one document. We will be following the format of that standard throughout this book. For very small companies they may, if they wish, produce an abridged version of the income statement or profit and loss account for lodging with Companies House. It should be noted that the detail of how operating gains and other gains are shown is dealt with in more detail in Chapter 11.

To a limited extent, the type of business activity will determine the presentation and context of the statement. For example, in the case of a retail business such as Blake's Enterprises a gross profit figure may be useful, but in a service business such as a hotel, which is highly labour intensive, the revenue earned may bear little if any relationship to inputs of physical goods. Hence, the type of activity has an effect on what is being reported and how it should be reported. Similarly, the objective of the preparers of information often has an effect on the income statement. If, for example, the accounts are being prepared for tax purposes, the owner may wish to reduce profit, or defer it to the next year if at all possible. On the other hand, if the accounts are to be used to borrow money, then a healthy profit may be what is required to be portrayed. Although we should not give the impression that the profit can be manipulated at will, it is clear from our discussion that there are a number of areas of judgement which allow slightly different results to be obtained from the same basic data. The extent to which manipulation is practised is often limited by the fact that there are a number of conflicting requirements which mean that manipulation of the profit one way for one purpose is detrimental for another purpose. It should also be borne in mind that the income statement can only be as good as the information on which it is based. Thus, for a fish and chip shop whose owner only records every second sale through the till, the accounts will only record those transactions that go through the till.

Finally, it is important to remind ourselves that the type of organization and the organizational goals may make an income statement less relevant and in some cases irrelevant. Examples of industries where there are specific accounting rules include those concerned with exploration and development and those concerned with the provision of financial services. In other cases such as charities and social enterprises where the primary objective is not the generation of wealth *per se*, should the emphasis be on profit or is the prime interest how any surplus monies have been used to further the aims of the charity? Clearly, different statements are appropriate to the needs and aims of different organizations.

Users of accounts

The users of accounts often have different requirements from each other. There is increasing evidence that for smaller entities, whether they are companies or other forms of entity, the income statement is used by the owners for judging the performance of the business. This means that they may want greater detail than would normally be disclosed and so they may produce two income statements, one of which is essentially an abridged and summarized version of the other. Similarly, the regulatory authorities often require specific detailed information. We can safely anticipate that the Financial Services Authority in the UK and its equivalent elsewhere in the world will be looking very carefully at the ways in which banks account for and report profits to say nothing of the disclosure of bonus payments. Similarly the tax authorities will often require detailed information to decide whether a particular expense is allowable against the business profits for tax purposes – the most common example of this in small businesses is entertainment expenses where the tax authorities are particularly concerned that these relate to the business and not just the owner and his or her cronies out for a jolly. Apart from these influences, which lead to greater disclosure of detail, there is the issue of confidentiality influencing disclosure. Clearly a business does not necessarily want its competitors, or indeed its customers, to know how much profit it is making so it will try to limit the amount of detail being disclosed.

The cash flow statement

Before leaving this chapter, we will briefly look at the cash flow statement, which like the income statement is a 'period' statement, i.e. it relates to changes over time rather than a point in time. The cash flow statement, unlike the income statement, which concentrates on increases and decreases in wealth over time, is concerned with the flow of money in to and out of the business entity over time. In simple terms, it shows what money has come in and what has gone out, or as one small business owner described it, 'dosh in and dosh out'. We will return to the cash flow statement in detail both in terms of content and format in Chapter 10. However, in each of the chapters preceding Chapter 10 we will be discussing the effects of the issues under discussion on all three financial statements, i.e. the statement of financial position, the income statement and the cash flow statement. At this stage we simply want to introduce the idea of a cash flow statement in a very simple and crude form.

If we look once again at the transactions of Blake's Enterprises from the point of view of cash inflows, i.e. money coming into the business, and cash outflows, i.e. money going out of the business, we can then draw up a simple cash flow statement.

EXAMPLE 4.2

The information on Blake's Enterprises contained in Example 4.1 is set out below for ease of reference

Blake's Enterprises is a new retail paint outlet set up at the start of the year. Its transactions for 2010, its first year, are summarized below.

Dates	Description	Amount (£)
1 January	Purchase of freehold shop	60 000
1 January	Rates for the year	2 000
1 April	Van purchased	8 000
1 April	Van – tax and insurance for a year	600
1 July	Purchase of washing machine	300
Various	Wages to shop assistant for year	6 000
Various	Goods bought and resold	18 000
Various	Goods bought but unsold	4 000
Various	Cash from sales	45 000
Various	Motor expenses and petrol	1 200
Various	Money withdrawn by Blake	6 000

Purchase of freehold

As we identified previously here there is an outflow of money. We are not concerned at this point on what the money was spent, merely that it genuinely relates to the business entity.

Rates for the year

Once again we have an outflow of money that relates to the business. The fact that in this case it was classified as an expense is irrelevant for the simple cash flow statement we are going to produce.

Purchase of van

This is a similar transaction to the purchase of the freehold shop and there is a clear outflow of money.

Van – tax and insurance

The fact that some of this relates to money paid in advance for next year is of no consequence for the cash flow statement; the fact is that money was paid out during the year and there is therefore a cash outflow.

Purchase of washing machine

Although there is clearly a cash outflow, we have already established that this is likely to be personal rather than related to Blake's Enterprises. However, the cash has gone and this must be reflected as a cash outflow in the form of drawings.

(Continued)

Wages for year
This is clearly a cash outflow.

Goods bought and resold and goods bought but unsold
We are not concerned in cash flow terms with whether the goods were sold or not as the cash outflow relates to buying the goods and we had to buy all the goods so the cash flow relates to the total purchases of £22 000, i.e. £18 000 plus £4000.

Cash from sales
This is a straightforward inflow of cash. In this case all the money was received so all is included in the cash flow statement. If, however, there had been sales included in revenue that were made on credit terms only on those where cash was actually received would there be a cash inflow.

Motor expenses and petrol
Once again there is a clear cash outflow here.

Money withdrawn by Blake
As was the case with the washing machine, there has been a clear outflow of cash which we shall classify as being in respect of drawings.

We can now draw up a cash flow statement of Blake's Enterprises for the year ended 31 December 2010.

Cash flow statement of Blake's Enterprises for the year ended 31 December 2010

	£
Cash inflows	
Sales	45 000
Total cash inflows	45 000
Cash outflows	
Freehold	60 000
Rates	2 000
Van	8 000
Van tax and insurance	600
Drawings (washing machine and cash)	6 300
Wages	6 000
Goods bought (18 000 + 4 000)	22 000
Motor expenses	1 200
Total cash outflows	106 100
Net cash flow	−61 100

As you can see, the cash flow statement, although a period statement like the income statement, does not resemble the income statement in any way. It measures changes in the cash over time, e.g. exchanging cash for the van, and also potential increases in cash. Hence, in its present form as a simple listing of cash inflows and outflows it has little predictive ability. As we shall illustrate later, thinking about the type of cash flow, whether it is a one off, or recurrent and what it is being used for can provide useful information. What the simplified statement that we have drawn up for Blake does tell us in the case of this business is that although it made a profit, as we saw from the income statement, it also spent more in the year than it got in. This may or may not be a cause for concern depending upon how much money the owner has available or can borrow but it does highlight that there may be a cause for concern that is worth investigating.

(Continued)

ACTIVITY 4.7

Looking at the cash flows in the statement above can you create any classifications which would be useful in predicting next year's cash flow?

You may have decided that you would separate out one-off cash flows, e.g. buying the freehold, and ones that vary at the owners whim, e.g. drawings from those that arise as a result of the ordinary trading activities. This would be helpful as you now have an idea of what is recurrent and what is non-recurrent.

SUMMARY

In this chapter, we have identified what revenue is and explained two important principles, i.e. the realization principle and the matching principle. We have also looked at the question of what constitutes a business expense and seen that:

1   expenses are not necessarily the same as costs;

2   all costs must relate to the business before they can even be considered as expenses.

We have also pointed out that the definitions both of assets and of expenses relate to benefits to the business. The important difference is that assets give future benefits, whereas expenses relate to benefits used up in the accounting period. This leads us to a series of questions relating to assets and expenses which may assist in the correct classification of items. These questions may be summarized in the form of a decision tree (Figure 4.4)

Apart from the discussion of the income statement and its components, i.e. revenue and expenses, we have also introduced the concept of a cash flow statement and, utilizing the same example as for the income statement, showed how these two 'period' statements differ in content and uses. We will develop our discussion of cash flow statements and how to make the information they contain more useful later in the book.

Discussion of recognition of revenue

Readers should refer back to Figure 4.1 for the points referred to in the answer below.

1   *A local newsagent*: The business is likely to be mainly cash based so point 5 is probably most appropriate, although this will depend on how many customers buy their newspapers etc., on account.

2   *Supplier of components*: Clearly point 5 is too late as even at point 4 the earnings process is complete and payment is reasonably certain. However, it could be argued that if the component supplier has a fixed contract with Ford, an earlier point, such as the point at which the goods are ready to be delivered, may be appropriate. This may well become closer to the 'norm' if more large firms adopt just-in-time principles as these lead to dedicated inventories being held by their suppliers rather than by them.   *(Continued)*

FIGURE 4.4

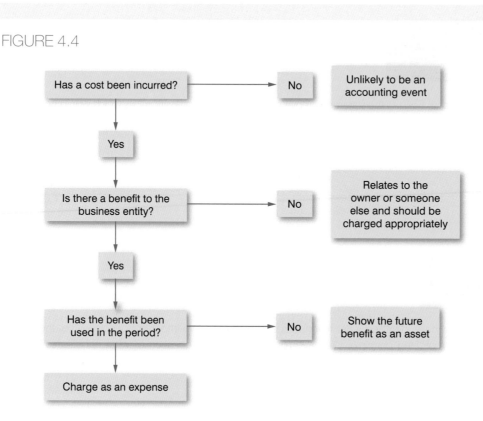

3   *A gold mine*: A similar argument as for the component supplier could be applied here as the earnings process is substantially complete at the point of production and payment is certain as the government buys all output.

4   *An aircraft manufacturer*: Your answer here will depend on the assumptions you have made. If, for example, you assumed that the aircraft manufacturer is making to order then your judgement of certainty of payment would be different than if you assumed that it produced aircraft and then tried to sell them. Similarly, if you thought of an aircraft producer as producing Boeing 757s you may have thought of the production process as spreading over a number of years, in which case point 2 may have been your judgement. If, on the other hand, you thought of the manufacture of light aircraft such as Piper Cubs, you may have assumed a shorter production cycle, in which case point 2 would not be appropriate.

REFERENCES

IASB. (1989) *Framework for the Preparation and Presentation of Financial Statements*. London: International Accounting Standards Board.

IASB. (2008) IAS 1, *Presentation of Financial Statements*. London: International Accounting Standards Board.

IASB. (2009) IAS 18, *Revenue*. London: International Accounting Standards Board.

IASB. (2009) *International Financial Reporting Standard for Small and Medium Sized Entities*. London: International Accounting Standards Board.

FURTHER READING

Readers interested in pursuing the question of when revenue should be recognized may refer to an interesting discussion in J.H. Myers, 'The critical event and the recognition of net profit', *The Accounting Review,* October 1959, pp. 528–532.

Collis, J. and Jarvis, R. (2000) *How Owner-Managers Use Accounts, Research Report,* London: ICAEW.

Collis, J., Jarvis, R. and Skerratt, L. (2001) 'Size and the value of the audit', *Accounting and Business,* 4 (10), November/December, pp. 41–42.

REVIEW QUESTIONS

(✓ indicates answers are available in Appendix A)

✓ **1** In your own words, define revenue.

✓ **2** At what point should revenue be recognized?

3 In your own words, define an expense.

4 How does an expense differ from a cost?

5 'Expenses are always the same as costs for a period.' Discuss the truth of this statement using examples to illustrate your argument.

6 What is the purpose of an income statement and who would use it?

✓ **7** Describe the difference between an expense and an asset.

8 In what circumstances would it be inappropriate to recognize a cost as either an expense or an asset?

PROBLEMS FOR DISCUSSION AND ANALYSIS

(✓ indicates answers are available in Appendix A)

✓ **1** Early in the chapter we produced a generalized five-stage model of the production process. Although that model clearly fits with a manufacturing business, it may be less appropriate to service industries. In each of the following situations provide a possible model of the process and the points at which revenue could be recognized:

(a) the provision of hotel rooms;

(b) a tourist attraction charging a flat, all-inclusive entrance fee, such as a theme park;

(c) a restaurant;

(d) a professional accountancy firm doing a two-stage annual audit;

(e) a package tour operator selling directly to the public.

2 There are two partners in AB & Co., an electrical retailer. They each have withdrawn £5000 from the business in cash during the year. B has also taken a washing machine, which cost £200 and which had a selling price of £280, from the business for personal use. A has been paid wages of £12 000 and B £6000.

Discuss how each of these facts should be dealt with in the accounts, giving reasons for your decisions.

3 Flights of Fancy is a travel agency which deals with flights, package holidays and holiday insurance. When a customer requires a flight booking a £50 deposit is required, with the balance due one month before the flight. For package holidays a deposit of £100 per person is required, with the balance due when the holiday is confirmed. In both cases the tickets are issued 14 days before the start of the holiday or flight, and at that point Flight of Fancy becomes liable to pay the tour operator or airline. In the case of the travel insurance no deposit is required, but the whole premium has to accompany the final payment for the flight or holiday package.

Discuss the point at which Flights of Fancy should recognize the revenue for each of its three services.

4 Bronze Age was the trading name of an antiques business based in Brighton. It operated a business buying, selling and exporting antiques in the UK and abroad. The transactions for the last year were as follows.

(a) Was offered the opportunity to purchase the freehold on the building that the business used for storage and refurbishing the antiques and purchased it for £280 000, incurring legal costs of £2400 to complete the purchase.

(b) Bought antiques that cost £130 000, all of which were sold in the year.

(c) Sales of antiques in the UK amounted to £98 000 and in the export market they amounted to £146 000.

(d) The cost of repairs and refurbishment of the antiques sold was £14 000.

(e) The business owned a van which cost £15 000 last year. The costs of running the van during the year were £2400 including major repairs after the engine had seized up.

(f) Annual tax and insurance on the van was £460.

(g) Business rates for the year amounted to £2800.

(h) Electricity bills for the year were £820, of which £600 had been paid at the year end.

(i) The owner paid wages to his assistant of £16 000.

(j) Delivery costs relating to the overseas sales amounted to £7600, of which all but £1000 had been paid at the year end.

For each of the items above, discuss whether it should be included in the income statement and/or cash flow statement, and on the basis of your decisions draw up an income statement and cash flow statement for Bronze Age for the year.

5 In each of the following situations, discuss whether the item would be included in the income statement for the year to 31 December 2010 and at what amount. The business is that of a builder and builders' merchant.

(a) Sales of general building materials by the builders' merchant to third parties amounted to £26 000, of which £24 000 was received in cash by 31 December 2010 and the remainder was received in January 2011.

(b) Three house conversions were started and completed during the year at a price of £24 000 each. These amounts were received in full by 31 December 2010.

(c) One office conversion which had been 60% complete at the end of 2009 was completed in 2010 at a price of £40 000. Invoices on account amounting to £24 000 had been sent out in 2009.

(d) The building materials sold to third parties during the year had cost £14 000, of which all but £1000 had been paid for by December 2010.

(e) The building materials used on the three houses referred to in (b) had cost £18 000 and had all been paid for by December 2010.

(f) Wages paid in respect of the houses mentioned in (b) amounted to £20 000 for the year.

(g) The costs relating to the office mentioned in (c) were as follows:

Wages paid in 2009	£8 000
Wages paid in 2010	£6 000
Materials used in 2009	£8 000
Materials used in 2010	£7 000

(h) The storemen's wages in the yard amounted to £8000 for the year.

(i) The owner who worked full time in the business paid himself a salary of £9000 and also withdrew £1000 in cash from the business to pay a pressing personal debt.

(j) The motor expenses paid in the year were broken down as follows:

Annual road tax on three vans paid 1 April	£300
Annual insurance on vans paid 1 April	£480*
Repairs and petrol for vans	£600
Annual road tax on owner's car paid 1 June	£100*
Annual road tax on owner's wife's car paid 1 June	£100
Annual insurance on owner's car paid 1 June	£120*
Annual insurance on owner's wife's car paid 1 June	£120*
Repairs and petrol for the two cars	£800

*The charge for road tax had gone up by £20 per vehicle in the previous year and insurance premiums had risen by 20%. All these charges are paid annually in advance.

(k) The following bills were also paid during the year:

Electricity (payable at end of each quarter)	February	£54
	1 May	£451
	August	£451
	November	£60
Rent for one year to 1 April 2011	April 2010	£400*
TV licence to 1 April 2011	1 April 2010	£60*

*The rent had remained the same as in 2009 but the TV licence had gone up from £50 to £60.

6 Based on your decisions, draw up an income statement for 2010 using the information above.

7 Draw up a cash flow statement for 2010 using the information above.

8 Explain why there are differences between the net profit and the net cash flows.

CHAPTER 5
INTRODUCTION TO
THE WORKSHEET

LEARNING OUTCOMES

By the end of this chapter you will:

- Understand the concept of duality and how it applies to the recording of transactions.

- Understand the concept[1] of prudence and its importance in financial statement preparation.

- Be able to record transactions following the principles of double entry using a worksheet as the format for recording those transactions.

- Be able to extract a statement of financial position at the end of a period of time.

- Be able to produce a simple income statement for a period of time.

- Be able to produce a simple cash flow statement for a period of time.

[1]Concept is used here in terms of its meaning as a notion or proposition rather than an accounting concept recognized by the standard setting bodies.

This chapter uses the worksheet as the vehicle to explain and explore the interrelationships between items in the statement of financial position, income statement items and cash flow statement items. The concept of duality, which is central to all double-entry recording systems, is introduced, explained and its use illustrated through the worksheet.

So far we have looked at the measurement of wealth at a point in time through the statement of financial position and at the ways in which profit can be measured using the income statement. We demonstrated that the profit could be measured either from the increase in wealth over a period of time or by using the income statement, or profit and loss account and provided a brief introduction to the third main financial statement, the cash flow statement. Due to the complexity of most business organizations and the number of transactions involved we need a system that records transactions as they happen and from which we can draw the details for inclusion in the statement of financial position, income statement and cash flow statement. As with any good system it needs to have built-in checks and balances to ensure as far as possible that all transactions are recorded and to allow us to trace back any errors to the original source. To do this a form of recording known as double-entry book-keeping was developed. This system is based on a rule known as the principle of duality (see Key Concept 3.10). This principle was discussed in some detail in Chapter 3, and it was further exemplified in our discussion of the accounting equation which we defined as:

$$\text{assets} = \text{liabilities} + \text{owners' equity}$$

We also showed that the owners' equity was increased by the profits made by the business, and we defined profit as:

$$\text{profit} = \text{revenue} - \text{expenses}$$

We can therefore see that if the financial position at the start of the period is stated as:

$$\text{assets at } T_0 = \text{liabilities at } T_0 + \text{owners' equity at } T_0$$

where T_0 indicates the start of the period, then the financial position at the end of the period can be depicted as:

$$\text{assets at } T_1 = \text{liabilities at } T_1 + \text{owners' equity at } T_0 + (\text{revenue} - \text{expenses})$$

Where T_0 indicates the start of the period, T_1 indicates the end of the period and the revenue and expenses are for the period from T_0 to T_1.

These equations show that there is a relationship between assets, liabilities, owners' equity, revenue and expenses. As with all equations we need to ensure that where we make changes within the equation they are balanced by equal and opposite changes. So if we start with an equation that says $5 = 5$ and add 2 to one side we must add 2 to the other so the new equation is $7 = 7$. In accounting terms this means that every transaction recorded must have two entries so that the two sides of the equation stay in balance. This is really an application of the duality principle, which is reproduced below as a reminder of what we have already discussed.

KEY CONCEPT 5.1

The principle of duality

The principle of duality is the basis of the double-entry book-keeping system on which accounting is based. It states that:

Every transaction has two opposite and equal sides.

Let us now summarize how that principle might work in relation to the accounting equation set out below with some simple numbers.

$$\text{assets at } T_1 \ £100 = \text{liabilities at } T_1 \ £20 + \text{owners' equity } £60 \text{ at } T_0 + (\text{revenue} - \text{expenses}) \ £20$$

As you can see each side of the equation totals £100. Let us assume that we have increased one of our assets by £10 then we must either reduce another asset by the same amount so that each side of the equation still totals £100 *or* having increased the left hand side by £10 we must increase the right hand side of the equation by £10 so that the total of each side is £110. This could be done by changing any of the components of the right hand side. The ways in which this might happen are summarised in Key Concept 5.2.

KEY CONCEPT 5.2

Application of the principle of duality

Applying the duality principle to our equation we find that:

If we increase our assets, we must have:

reduced another asset, or
increased our liabilities, or
made a profit, or
increased our owners' equity.

In other words, the principle of duality when applied to the accounting equation holds that both sides of the equation must always be equal.

ACTIVITY 5.1

For each of the transactions that follow, work out the effect on the equation below:

Cash/Bank £5 000 + Cars £4 000 = Equity £6 000 + Profit £1 000 + Liabilities £2 000

1   If the business uses £3000 of its cash to buy another car.

2   If the owner then borrows £3000 from a friend and puts the money in the business bank account.

3   If the business then sells a car which cost £2000 for £2500.

4   If the owner then puts in another £1000 in cash into the business.

You should have come to the following answers – the changes are underlined.

1   Cash/Bank £2 000 + Cars £7 000 = Equity £6 000 + Profit £1 000 + Liabilities £2 000

2   Cash/Bank £5 000 + Cars £7 000 = Equity £6 000 + Profit £1 000 + Liabilities £5 000

3   Cash/Bank £7 500 + Cars £5 000 = Equity £6 000 + Profit £1 500 + Liabilities £5 000

4   Cash/Bank £8 500 + Cars £5 000 = Equity £7 000 + Profit £1 500 + Liabilities £5 000

DOUBLE ENTRY AND THE WORKSHEET

We shall deal with fairly simple examples to illustrate the principles involved. However, it is important to remember that no matter how complex the business these principles still apply. With larger businesses complexity is generally due to the large number of transactions not any inherent complexity in the transactions themselves. Even if we take the example of a high street shop, such as a bakery, we know that there are likely to be a larger number of individual transactions as lots of different customers come in to buy bread and cakes. Therefore businesses have to have sophisticated recording systems to deal with the thousands of transactions that take place during a year. This is why most businesses use various off-the-shelf or bespoke accounting packages to record all these transactions and increasingly even the most basic software will allow some form of analysis and summary reports to be produced. Many will allow reports such as statement of financial position, income statements and cash flow statements to be created with simple commands. The more sophisticated packages will enable tailor-made reports to be produced to meet the particular needs of the users, often the managers of the business. Examples of these types of reports and what they may contain are discussed in the later chapters of this book.

For our purposes, however, we do not need to introduce a high level of sophistication to understand the principles involved and we can set up a perfectly adequate double-entry book-keeping system using spreadsheet software (e.g. Excel). Using a manually produced spreadsheet, which we refer to as a worksheet, we will work through some simple examples that illustrate the basics of double-entry book-keeping.

The worksheet is set out in the form of the accounting equation with columns headed as appropriate. An example of a worksheet is shown below.

Example worksheet

| Description | Assets | | | | = | Equity + Liabilities | |
	Bank/cash	Van	Raw materials	Machine		Equity	Loans
Opening position							
Transaction 1							
Transaction 2							
Transaction 3							
Transaction 4							
Closing position							

At the top of the worksheet we have the accounting equation:

$$\text{Assets} = \text{Equity} + \text{Liabilities}$$

Below that we have descriptions of the assets, the equity and the liabilities each with their own separate column. Next we have the opening position, this is the position when we started the business or at the start of the accounting period, the financial position at T_0. We then record the transaction that take place over the period to end up with the closing position, the financial position at T_1.

Before looking at an example let us briefly discuss the way in which the worksheet has been set up. You will notice that there is a column in which the transaction is identified and described. This identification and description in our case has been done via transaction number. You could include a fuller description; however, the date, the invoice number, the name of the suppliers involved are appropriate.

We shall use the following simple data to illustrate how the transactions are recorded on the worksheet.

EXAMPLE 5.1

Jimbo started up a small manufacturing business and the first transactions were as follows:

Opened a business bank account and deposited £5000 of Jimbo's own money. This can be taken to be the opening position at T_0.

1 Bought a van for £2000;

2 Bought some raw materials for £3000 cash;

3 Got a bank loan of £6000;

4 Bought some machinery for manufacturing for £4000 cash.

Each of these transactions has been entered on the worksheet (version 1) and you should look at that whilst reading the description of what has been done.

Jimbo worksheet version 1

Description	Assets				=	Equity + Liabilities	
	Bank/cash	Van	Raw materials	Machine		Equity	Loans
Opening position	5 000					5 000	
Transaction 1	−2 000	2 000					
Transaction 2	−3 000		3 000				
Transaction 3	6 000						6 000
Transaction 4	−4 000			4 000			
Closing position	2 000	2 000	3 000	4 000		5 000	6 000

Opening position

Jimbo starts the business by putting in £5000. This is the opening position. We record this as £5000 in the bank/cash column as Jimbo expects to get a future benefit from the use of the money and therefore it is an asset. On the other side of our worksheet we have opened a column entitled Equity and we have entered in that column the amount that the owner has put into the business, in effect the amount that the business owes the owner. This is an example of a transaction where we have increased an asset by increasing the equity as previously there was no asset and no equity. Before moving on to the next item you should note that the equation is in balance £5000 on each side. You should also note that what we have here is the detail necessary to draw up the statement of financial position at the start of the period. In fact if we stop at any point in time and total the worksheet we will have the statement of financial position at that point in time, the reporting date, assuming, of course, that all transactions have been recorded.

Transaction 1

The first thing we must do is to establish the nature of the transaction. Here we find that Jimbo has exchanged cash for a van and we need to establish whether this constitutes an exchange of one asset for another or an expense of the business. Applying the simple test:

Does it provide a future benefit or is the benefit past?

We can see that the van is likely to provide a future benefit and therefore what Jimbo has done is to exchange one type of asset for another type of asset. So we have opened another column in which we have recorded the van as an asset and deducted the amount we paid for the van £2000 from the cash column. Thus we

(Continued)

have increased and decreased one side of our equation by the same amount and so if we were to total our worksheet now we would still balance and it would correctly record that the business now owns a van which cost £2000 and has £3000 in the bank rather than the £5000 it started with.

Transaction 2

Next Jimbo used some more cash to purchase some raw materials. Again applying the simple test:

Does it provide a future benefit or is the benefit past?

We can see that again Jimbo has exchanged one type of asset cash for another, raw materials, which will provide a future benefit as we can sell them or use them in the business. We therefore need to record that our asset cash is reduced by £3000 and open a new column in which to record the new asset 'Raw materials' which cost us £3000.

Transaction 3

In this transaction Jimbo borrowed some money and put it in our bank. So we have increased our asset bank/cash by £6000. This money has come from the bank and as such Jimbo owes the bank that money so we open a new column on the other side of the worksheet and record the amount Jimbo owes to the bank. So here we have a transaction which illustrates that the increase in an asset is matched by an increase in the liabilities of the business. Once again if we were to total up our worksheet at this point we would find that it balanced.

Transaction 4

Here Jimbo has exchanged one asset, money in the bank for a machine to help with the manufacturing of the product. Applying the test:

Does it provide a future benefit or is the benefit past?

It is clear that this transaction involves using one asset, our cash, to purchase another asset, machinery. So we have increased one asset by decreasing another. So all that is needed is to open a column for our new asset and show that it cost £4000 and reduce the amount we have in our bank by the same amount.

From the worksheet above it should be obvious that every transaction involves two entries. For example when the owner pays in the money one entry is made in the bank/cash column and another is made in the equity column. It should also be apparent that if all the columns are totalled the worksheet will always balance.

ACTIVITY 5.2

Check here that you understand these points before moving on. If you do not understand then look again at what has been done.

If you still do not understand re-read the section.

It is important that you realize that the balances at the bottom of the worksheet are in this case, and in all cases, the figures that go into the statement of financial position. So, if we were to draw up a statement of financial position at this stage it would look like the one below.

(Continued)

Statement of financial position of Jimbo

Machine	4 000
Van	2 000
Inventory – Raw materials	3 000
Bank/cash	2 000
	11 000
Owner's equity	5 000
Loan	6 000
	11 000

As you can see the balances are those on the bottom line of the worksheet. Before moving on, you may have noticed that in the worksheet all the transactions are ones that only affect the statement of financial position so we cannot at this stage draw up an income statement. However, we can draw up a cash flow statement which in effect summarizes what has been recorded in the bank/cash column of the worksheet. The cash flow statement of Jimbo is provided below.

Cash flow statement of Jimbo

	£
Cash inflows	£
Loan	6 000
	6 000
Cash outflows	
Machine	4 000
Van	2 000
Raw materials	3 000
	9 000
Decrease in bank/cash balances	−3 000

Looking at the cash flow statement you will notice that we have labelled the net cash flow, 'decrease in bank/cash balances' to emphasize the point that in this case the business started with £5000 cash and at the end of these transactions had £2000 in cash.

ACTIVITY 5.3

Check here that you understand these points before moving on. If you do not understand then look again at what has been done.

You should also note that the cash flow statement summarizes the items recorded in the cash column of the worksheet. This is important as it does not change no matter how complex we make the business.

(Continued)

In order to provide a clearer understanding of the way in which the worksheet is used and how revenue and expense items are recorded we shall extend our example by a few more transactions.

Example 5.1 further information

5 Jimbo hired a machine operator who worked on the raw materials (see Transaction 3) and who was paid £500 and turned them into finished goods ready to be sold.

6 Jimbo sold the finished goods for £5000 and received that amount in cash.

Transaction 5

Here, we can see that when Jimbo paid the wages there was an expectation that there would be a future benefit because the operator was going to work on the raw materials and add value by changing them from their original form to a new form. So we could either record these wages as an asset in their own right or add them to the cost of the raw materials and call that finished goods inventory. We shall take the latter course in this example. Thus the entry we need to make is to open a column for 'Finished goods', reduce the cash by £500, and record the £500 spent in the 'Finished goods' column. This is denoted by Transaction 5 (1) on the worksheet extract below.

However, we have said that the cost of the finished goods is the cost of the raw materials plus the wages and at present we have only dealt with the wages. To deal with the raw materials we need to reduce the raw materials column by £3000 and add that amount to the 'Finished goods' column. This is denoted as Transaction 5 (2) on the worksheet extract below.

Jimbo – Transaction 5

Description	Bank/cash	Van	Assets — Inventory: Raw materials	Finished goods	Machine	=	Equity	Loans
Transaction 5 (1)	−500			500				
Transaction 5 (2)			−3 000	3 000				

Transaction 6

Here we have sold all the goods we had and therefore have sales revenue. As these were sold for cash we need to increase our cash/bank column by the £5000. We also need to open a new column on the other side of the worksheet which we will title 'Revenue and expenses' and in this we enter the revenue i.e. sales of £5000. This is shown on the worksheet extract below.

Jimbo – Transaction 6

Description	Bank/cash	Van	Assets — Inventory: Raw materials	Finished goods	Machine	=	Equity	Loans	Revenue & expenses
Transaction 6	5 000								5 000

If at this stage we were to look at the worksheet, Jimbo worksheet version 2 below, and draw up a statement of financial position which is the bottom line of the worksheet it would balance and show us that a profit of £5000 had been made.

(Continued)

Jimbo worksheet version 2

Description	Bank/cash	Van	Inventory Raw materials	Finished goods	Machine	Equity	Loans	Revenue & expenses
Opening position	5 000					5 000		
Transaction 1	−2 000	2 000						
Transaction 2	−3 000		3 000					
Transaction 3	6 000						6 000	
Transaction 4	−4 000				4 000			
Balances	**2 000**	**2 000**	**3 000**		**4 000**	**5 000**	**6 000**	
Transaction 5 (1)	−500			500				
Transaction 5 (2)			−3 000	3 000				
Transaction 6	5 000							5 000
Balance	**6 500**	**2 000**	**0**	**3 500**	**4 000**	**5 000**	**6 000**	**5 000**

However to show a profit of £5000 would be incorrect because we have not applied the matching principle, i.e. we have not shown any expenses incurred in producing the sales of £5000. We can try to identify these expenses directly, as we know they consist of the cost of the raw materials and the wages, i.e. the amount in the 'Finished goods' column.

An alternative approach at this stage would be to look at the balance line for each of our assets and ask ourselves the question:

Is there a future benefit to be obtained or has the benefit expired?

If there is a future benefit then we have an asset; if the benefit has already passed then we have an expense. If we did this in this case, we would have to come to the conclusion that, as we had sold the goods represented by the figure of £3500 in the finished goods column, then these are clearly not an asset any longer and should be charged as an expense of the period. We thus have to make a further adjustment to our worksheet which we show under the heading 'adjustment'. Our new worksheet will now be as follows.

Jimbo worksheet version 3

Description	Bank/cash	Van	Inventory Raw materials	Finished goods	Machine	Equity	Loans	Revenue & expenses
Opening position	5 000					5 000		
Transaction 1	−2 000	2 000						
Transaction 2	−3 000		3 000					
Transaction 3	6 000						6 000	
Transaction 4	−4 000				4 000			
Balances	**2 000**	**2 000**	**3 000**		**4 000**	**5 000**	**6 000**	
Transaction 5 (1)	−500			500				
Transaction 5 (2)			−3 000	3 000				
Transaction 6	5 000							5 000
Adjustment				−3 500				−3 500
Balance	**6 500**	**2 000**	**0**	**0**	**4 000**	**5 000**	**6 000**	**1 500**

(Continued)

If you compare the first, second and third worksheet you will see that we have opened a new column for finished goods next to the raw materials column and both of these are sub-sets of a group of assets called inventory which we shall deal with in more detail in Chapter 6. You should also note that we have also opened a column headed revenue and expenses which, as you will see, collects the items to be included in our income statement. Before leaving this simple example let us extract from the worksheet a statement of financial position at the end of the period, the income statement for the period and the cash flow statement.

Statement of financial position of Jimbo at the period end

Current assets		
Bank/cash		6 500
Inventory	Raw materials	0
	Finished goods	0
		6 500
Non-current assets		
Machinery		4 000
Van		2 000
		6 000
Total assets		12 500
Non current liabilities		
Loan		6 000
Total liabilities		6 000
Equity		5 000
Profit		1 500
Total equity		6 500
Total equity and liabilities		12 500

A careful study of the figures in the statement of financial position and a comparison with the last line of the worksheet will make it clear that the statement of financial position is in fact the bottom line of the worksheet. We have shown the inventory amounts as nil for the sake of clarity. In reality if there are nil balances the headings do not need to be shown.

Income statement of Jimbo for the period

Sales	5 000
Cost of goods sold	3 500
Profit	1 500

You will notice that the income statement is simply a summary of the revenue and expenses column in the worksheet.

Cash flow statement of Jimbo

Cash inflows	£
Loan	6 000
Sales	5 000
	11 000

(Continued)

Cash outflows	£
Machine	4 000
Van	2 000
Raw materials	3 000
Wages	500
	9 500
Increase in bank/cash balances	1 500

As was the case with the earlier cash flow statement this cash flow statement summarizes the cash column and shows that over the whole period from inception there has been a net cash inflow of £1500 since the start of the business.

If we consider what we have done in the example we can see that the system of double entry is merely a convenient way of recording transactions in a logical manner. The system is not complex – all it requires is an understanding of addition and subtraction together with the knowledge that the equation must always be in balance. It also requires the application of our definitions to classify a particular transaction correctly.

ACTIVITY 5.4

If you have had problems in understanding why a transaction is dealt with in a particular way you should return to Chapters 3 pages 49, 54 and 55 and re-read Key concepts 3.4, 3.7, and 3.9 and to Chapter 4 pages 73, 75 and 78 and re-read Key concepts 4.1, 4.3 and 4.4.

Before going on to try an example yourselves it is worth spending some time reflecting on what we have just said by reference to the last example. If we look at any of the columns we can see that there is simply addition and subtraction taking place; a good example is the cash column where we make additions as money comes into the business and make deductions as money is spent.

Another feature of the system that is not so obvious is that if we make mistakes there is an automatic check because in the end the worksheet will not balance. If this turns out to be the case we have two ways of finding the error: we can either do a line by line check to ensure that each of our lines has balanced or we can total the columns at various stages to see where the error is likely to be. For example, if we had an error in the worksheet we have just done we could look at the totals after entering each transaction and see if it balances. Quite often the error is reasonably obvious as the amount involved gives us a clue. The easy way to illustrate this is to put some deliberate errors into the context of the worksheet we have just completed.

SINGLE ENTRY ERROR

Let us assume that we forgot the basic rule that each transaction has two sides and when we paid the wages we simply deducted the £500 from the cash column. Our worksheet would appear as follows:

Jimbo worksheet with single entry error

Description	Assets					=	Equity + Liabilities			
	Bank/cash	Van	Inventory		Machine		Equity	Loans	Revenue & expenses	Check column
			Raw materials	Finished goods						
Opening position	5 000						5 000			0
Transaction 1	−2 000	2 000								0
Transaction 2	−3 000		3 000							0
Transaction 3	6 000							6 000		0
Transaction 4	−4 000				4 000					0
Balances	**2 000**	**2 000**	**3 000**		**4 000**		**5 000**	**6 000**		**0**
Transaction 5 (1)	−500									−500
Transaction 5 (2)			−3 000	3 000						0
Transaction 6	5 000								5 000	0
Adjustment				−3 000					−3 000	0
Balance	**6 500**	**2 000**	**0**	**0**	**4 000**		**5 000**	**6 000**	**2 000**	**−500**

Note that we have added a 'check column' which checks on a line by line basis whether our equation is still in balance. This is easy to do on a spreadsheet as we can simply set up a formula to sum one side of the equation, the assets, and deduct the sum of the other side, the equity, liabilities and revenue and expenses columns. Looking at that column it is clear that the problem is with the wages entry where we have only recorded one side of the transaction. An alternative approach is to add up the two sides of our worksheet and identify the difference and then see if we can spot the error. In this case we find that the assets side totals £12 500, i.e. £6500 + £2000 + £4000, whereas the other side totals £13 000 i.e. £5000 + £6000 + £2000. The difference between the two is £500. We can then look for a transaction involving £500 which, of course, will direct us to the wages as the likely cause of the problem. A third approach is to check that the worksheet balances at various points. In this case we know that prior to entering transaction 4 it balanced Bank/cash £2000 + Van £2000 + Raw materials £3000 + Machine £4000 = £11 000 and on the other side Equity £5000 + Loans £6000 = £11 000.

Thus as illustrated it is easy to make a single entry error but it is usually just as easy to spot what you have done wrong and put it right.

ACTIVITY 5.5

Make sure you understand what has been done so far. If you do not understand this then go back and re-read the example and check the entries on the worksheet line by line to make sure that in each case there is a double entry.

INCORRECT DOUBLE ENTRY

Another common cause of errors is incorrect double entry. In this case two sides are recorded but they do not leave the equation in balance. Let us assume for example that we had got the entry for the wages correct but that we had incorrectly classified the £5000 Jimbo obtained from selling the goods as an increase in cash and an increase in finished goods rather than as sales revenue. The resultant worksheet would then not balance and we would be able to spot the error by identifying the total difference and halving it. In this case, as you will see from the worksheet below, we have assets totalling £21 000 (£6500 + £2000 + £8500 + £4000) and equity and liabilities totalling £11 000. Thus the difference is £10 000 and half of that is £5000. We can then look at each of the transactions involving £5000 and check our entries. Alternatively we can use a check column or a line-by-line check to identify where the error is.

Jimbo worksheet-Incorrect double entry

| Description | Assets | | | | | = | Equity + Liabilities | | | |
| | Bank/cash | Van | Inventory | | Machine | | Equity | Loans | Revenue & expenses | Check column |
			Raw materials	Finished goods						
Transaction 1	5 000						5 000			0
Transaction 2	−2 000	2 000								0
Transaction 3	−3 000		3 000							0
Transaction 4	6 000							6 000		0
Transaction 5	−4 000				4 000					0
Balance	**2 000**	**2 000**	**3 000**		**4 000**		**5 000**	**6 000**		**0**
Transaction 6	−500			500						0
Transaction 6			−3 000	3 000						0
Transaction 7	5 000			5 000						10 000
Balance	**6 500**	**2 000**	**0**	**8 500**	**4 000**		**5 000**	**6 000**	**0**	**10 000**

You will notice that we no longer have a cost of goods sold which is of course logically consistent because, as a result of our error, we no longer have any goods sold. As we have said what we have instead is a worksheet that has assets that total £21 000 while the other side totals £11 000. The difference in this case is £10 000 which is twice the amount involved in the error.

ADDITION, SUBTRACTION AND TRANSPOSITION ERRORS

Another common cause of errors is that we have simply failed to add or subtract correctly. The only way round this problem is to recheck all our totals and all our addition and subtraction. We can reduce the size of that task by balancing our worksheet on a regular basis so that we know where the error is likely to be. A similar problem is a transposition error where, for example, we recorded the total of our cash column as £5600 instead of £6500, i.e. we transposed the order of the 6 and the 5. This is a common error and happens to all of us. In this case we can identify that it may be a transposition error because the difference of £900 is divisible by 9. This will always be the case if we simply transpose two figures, e.g. 45 as 54, 97 as 79, etc. Notice that the difference is divisible by 9 but it does not necessarily have the number 9 in the difference. The difference between 97 and 79 is 18 which is divisible by 9.

Of course if you set all of this up on an electronic spreadsheet and add in a check column which checks what you are doing on a row by row basis you will be able to spot most errors very easily and take appropriate action. However, this approach will not sort all the errors you can make; for example, if you correctly decide that you need to increase one asset and reduce another but do this to the wrong assets you will get a statement of financial position that balances but is wrong. So always look at what you have done and ask yourself is that what I expected?

ACTIVITY 5.6

Before moving on we suggest that you draw up your own worksheet for the following simple set of transactions for Bill and compare them with the answer given. If your answer varies from the one given try to identify what you have done, e.g. classified an item as the purchase of an asset when it was the payment of an expense. Once you are confident with this simple example then move on to the example Jill which contains more entries and see if you can get that right. If not then read the explanations that follow the completed worksheet.

Bill had decided to set up as a market trader, had opened a business bank account and paid in £3 000 of his own money. His transactions for the first month of business were as follows:

1 Bought goods for resale costing £2000 and paid for them.

2 Paid £300 to hire a van to transport them to the market.

3 Paid £100 rental for the market stall.

4 Sold all the goods for cash and received a total of £6500.

Fill in the worksheet below and when you have done that compare your answer with the one on Page 516.

Bill's worksheet for month 1

	Assets		=	Equity + Liabilities	
Description	Bank/ cash	Goods		Equity	Revenue & expenses
Opening balance					
Closing balance					

When you have done this, try Example 5.2 below initially thinking about each transaction and how you would deal with it. You can then compare your approach with our explanations of how we treat that item. Your entries do not necessarily have to be identical with ours as there are many different ways of setting up the worksheet and of arriving at the correct answer to show the position at the end of the month.

EXAMPLE 5.2

Jill decided to start a business selling second-hand cars. She had saved up some money of her own but this was not enough to start and so she had obtained an interest-free loan from her parents. The transactions of the business for the first month were as follows. All transactions were cash transactions.

Day 1   Opened a business bank account and paid in £5000 of her own money.
Day 2   Paid into the bank £6000 that she had borrowed from her parents for use by the business.
Day 3   Found a suitable showroom and paid a fortnight's rent of £300.
Day 4   Went to the car auction and bought the following cars for cash.
           Ford for £3000
           Toyota for £3100
           Mazda for £3800
Day 5   Bought some office furniture for £220.
Day 6   Employed a teenager who was on the dole to clean cars for her at the rate of £10 per car and paid out £30.
Day 8   Placed adverts for all three cars in the local paper. The cost of advertising was £20 per day for each car. She decided that all three should be advertised for two days, and so the total cost was £120.
Day 9   Sold the Ford for £3800 cash.
Day 10   Sold the Toyota for £3900 cash.
Day 11   Returned to the car auction and bought a Renault for £4000.
Day 12   Employed her teenage friend to clean the Renault for £10.
Day 15   Re-advertised the Mazda for three days at £20 per day, total cost £60.
Day 17   Advertised the Renault using a special block advert which cost £75 in total.
Day 18   Paid rent of showroom for the next fortnight amounting to £300.
Day 19   Was offered £4300 for the Mazda.
Day 20   Accepted the offer for the Mazda. Was paid £4300.
Day 22   Sold the Renault for £5200.
Day 23   Went to the car auction and bought a Fiat for £4300.
Day 24   Had the Fiat professionally valeted at a cost of £40.
Day 25   Advertised the Fiat using the special block advert at a cost of £75.
Day 26   Decided that as things were going so well she would repay her parents £500.
Day 27   Took the Fiat on a test drive with a customer and seized the engine.
Day 29   Had the Fiat repaired at a cost of £500.
Day 30   Sold the Fiat for £4700.
Day 31   Paid electricity bill of £40 for the month.

To illustrate the different treatments possible let us consider the transaction on day 3 where Jill paid a fortnight's rent in advance. The question arises whether this is an expense or an asset. Let us consider the alternatives.

On day 3 it is reasonably clear that we have an asset in that we will get a future benefit in the form of the use of the showroom for two weeks. On the other hand, if we are recording the transaction for the first time at the end of the month we can then argue that the transaction is an expense because at that point in time the benefit has expired. Thus, we could record on day 3 the payment and an asset and then re-evaluate all our assets at the end of the month as we have done on our worksheet. Conversely we could wait until the end of the month and just record an expense. We would recommend at this stage that you adopt the former treatment for two reasons: firstly it ensures that you re-evaluate all your assets at the end of the month, and

(Continued)

secondly short-cuts often cause more problems than they are worth if you are unfamiliar with the area. Remember to ask yourself the question:

Is there a future benefit?

Another transaction that should be mentioned is the adverts on day 8 and other days. In these cases a similar dilemma to that already identified with the rent exists. However, there is another problem in that, whereas with the rent we knew that there was going to be a future benefit, in these cases it is far from certain that there will be a future benefit. In other words we do not know when we place the advert whether anyone will reply to it and, even if they do, whether they will buy the car. In these cases we apply a principle known as 'prudence' which says that unless you are **reasonably certain** of the future benefit then you should not recognize an asset. This is similar to the rule for the recognition of revenue Key Concept 4.2 which we discussed in Chapter 4 on page 74. Prudence, however, goes somewhat further as it encourages us to state assets at lower values rather than recognizing an uncertain increase in value, and it suggests that if we think that there is a reasonable chance of a loss we should recognize that loss immediately rather than waiting until it arises.

KEY CONCEPT 5.3

Prudence

Profits should not be anticipated and revenue is not recognized until reasonable certainty exists. However, losses and loss of value of assets should be recognized when they are likely to occur.

ACTIVITY 5.7

Think about the effect of applying prudence – is it likely to lead to profits being understated or overstated?

If we apply prudence we will recognise all losses as soon as they become forseeable and only recognise profit when it is certain so profit is likely to be understated.

As you are probably beginning to recognize, accounting is not just about recording; it is also about exercising judgment within a framework of broad and often very general principles. The important factor to remember as you work through the example above is that you are making judgements and applying the definitions set out in the previous two chapters, and you need to be aware of what you are doing and why you are doing it. You should now attempt to produce your own worksheet and extract an income statement, cash flow statement and statement of financial position.

If your worksheet is correct the balances on the bottom line of your worksheet should be those in the statement of financial position set out below. The income statement follows the statement of financial position and is merely a summary of the revenue and expenses column on the worksheet. The cash flow statement, which follows the income statement, can be viewed as a summary of the cash column.

(Continued)

Statement of financial position of Jill's business at period end

Current assets	
Cash	12 430
Non current assets	
Furniture	220
Total assets	12 650
Non current liabilities	
Loan	5 500
Total liabilities	5 500
Equity	5 000
Profit for period	2 150
Total equity	7 150
Total equity and liabilities	12 650

Income statement of Jill's business for the period

Sales		21 900
Cost of cars sold		18 200
Gross profit		3 700
Expenses		
Rent	600	
Wages	40	
Advertising	330	
Repairs	500	
Valeting	40	
Electricity	40	1 550
Net profit		2 150

Cash flow statement for Jill's business for the period

Cash inflows	
Sales	21 900
Equity paid in	5 000
Loans	6 000
	32 900
Cash outflows	
Expenses	19 750
Loan repayment	500
Furniture purchased	220
	20 250
Net cash inflow	12 650

(Continued)

Even if you find that your answer is correct, before proceeding to the next chapter you should read the explanations for the treatment of the transactions on days 3, 6, 18, 19, 26, 27 and 29 as these are of particular interest and will assist you in the future. If your answer disagrees with ours the full worksheet and explanations are given on Page 517.

SUMMARY

This chapter has introduced you to the worksheet and recalled the concept of duality, which states that for accounting purposes there are two sides to every transaction. We have also shown the importance of asking ourselves some basic questions: what exactly is an asset, an expense, and so forth? Hopefully we have also illustrated that simply by referring back to the definitions contained in Chapters 3 and 4 most if not all the problems you are likely to encounter can be solved.

We have also provided, by means of the worksheet, a simple vehicle for recording, checking and extracting a statement of financial position, income statement and cash flow statement. We have shown that the basis of accounting is very simple as long as you follow the basic principles, and for those times when you do lapse the system used on the worksheet should provide you with a simple and effective check. Finally we have introduced you to the idea that accounting is not a science, that it involves elements of judgments, and we have provided you with the 'prudence' concept as a useful tool to assist in arriving at your judgment.

REVIEW QUESTIONS

1 Describe in your own words what is meant by the concept of duality.

✓ 2 In each of the following cases describe the two entries required on the worksheet.

(a) The owner pays £500 into the business bank account.
(b) A desk is bought for £100 for the business, paid for from the bank account.
(c) The business buys goods for £200.
(d) The rent of the premises of £300 for the first week is paid.
(e) A potential customer makes an offer for the goods of £250.
(f) The wages of the employee amounting to £200 are paid.
(g) The firm receives another offer of £350 for the goods, accepts this offer and is paid immediately.

3 In situations where doubt exists as to whether a transaction has resulted in an asset or expense what questions should be posed?

4 If some doubt still remains how should a choice be made? Explain any principles involved.

5 In your own words describe the concept of prudence.

PROBLEMS FOR DISCUSSION AND ANALYSIS

1 In each of the following situations discuss the potential effect on the business and suggest possible ways in which those effects could be reflected on the worksheet.

(a) The owner starts up a new business and pays £1000 into the business bank account. In addition it is decided that the owner's car will be used exclusively for the business. The car was purchased last year at a cost of £8000 but a similar one-year-old car could be bought for £7500.

(b) Goods previously bought by the business for £500 were sold to a customer for £800. However, prior to taking delivery of the goods the customer changed his mind and decided that he did not want the goods after all.

(c) Another batch of goods which had been bought for £400 and sold for £600 was subsequently found to be faulty. The options available are as follows:

  (i) Give the customer a rebate on the purchase price of £100.
  (ii) Refund the full selling price to the customer and reclaim the goods.

If this course of action is followed a further £140 will need to be spent to rectify the faults.

2 Leech has recently gone into business selling office chairs. Details of her transactions for the first month are given below.

Day 1	Opened a bank account and paid in £5000 of her own money. Transferred the ownership of her car to the business at an agreed price of £2000.
	Rented an office/showroom at a rental of £120 per month and paid one month's rent.
	Bought a desk, chair and other office equipment at a cost of £800.
Day 2	Bought 100 chairs at a price of £35 per chair and paid for them immediately.
Day 3	Received delivery of the chairs.
Day 5	Placed advert in trade paper offering the chairs for sale on the following terms.
	Single chairs £50 per chair including delivery
	Ten or more chairs £45 per chair including delivery
	The advert cost £200 and was paid for immediately.
Day 8	Received separate orders for 12 chairs at £50 each together with accompanying cheques.
Day 9	Paid the cheques into the bank and despatched the chairs. The delivery costs were £72 in total and were paid straight away.
Day 11	Received six orders for ten chairs each at a cost of £45 per chair together with six cheques for £450.
	Banked the cheques and despatched the orders. The delivery charges were £50 for each order, making a total of £300 which was paid immediately.
Day 14	Leech paid herself two weeks' wages from the business, amounting to £150 in total.
Day 16	Bought another 20 chairs for £35 each and paid for them immediately.
Day 21	Paid £150 for car repairs.
Day 23	Received an order for 20 chairs at £45 each; banked the cheque and arranged delivery for £40 which was paid for immediately.
Day 24	Placed a further advert in the trade paper at a cost of £200 which was paid for immediately.
Day 27	Received one order for 15 chairs at a price of £45 each (this order totalled £675) and another order for seven chairs at a price of £50 each (a total of £350). The cheques were banked and the chairs were despatched at a total cost of £100 which was paid immediately.
Day 28	Drew another £150 from the bank for her own wages.
	Sold the remaining six chairs at a price of £250 for all six to a customer who walked into the showroom. The customer paid the £250 in cash and this money was banked. No delivery costs were incurred as the customer took the chairs away.
	Paid the telephone bill of £30 and the electricity bill, £40.

(a) In each situation where there are two possible treatments discuss the arguments in favour of and against each alternative.

(b) Based on the outcome of your discussions draw up a worksheet and enter the above transactions.

(c) Extract a statement of financial position at the end of the month and an income statement and cash flow statement for the month.

(d) Discuss the performance of the business for the period as revealed by the accounts you have prepared, paying particular attention to its cash position and its profitability.

3 Seal has recently gone into business running a small guest-house providing bed and breakfast. Details of the first month's transactions are given below.

Day 1	Opened a bank account and paid in £50 000 of his own money. Transferred the ownership of his car to the business at an agreed price of £2000. Obtained a mortgage from the bank for £140 000 and paid £180 000 to the vendor of the guest-house, the balance of £40 000 coming from the business bank account.
Day 2	Contracted with a firm of decorators to paint and paper all the guest rooms at a price of £1000, payable in cash immediately.
Day 3	Bought furniture for all the guest bedrooms for £2400.
Day 5	Placed advert in local paper saying that the guest-house would be re-opening in one week's time under new management. The advert cost £200 and was paid for immediately.
Day 8	Bought furniture for the dining room and guest lounge for £2800 and paid in cash.
Day 9	Bought tableware, linen, cutlery, etc. for £800.
Day 12	Bought in food to put in inventory at a cost of £80 ready for opening the following week.
Day 14	Opened the guest-house for business and was able to let all eight rooms for the week at £30 per night per room. All the guests paid in advance.
Day 15	Banked the £1680 received from the guests.
Day 20	Replenished the food inventories at a cost of £80.
Day 21	Paid laundry bill of £40.
Day 22	Let all the rooms for the next seven days on the same terms as previously and banked the £1680.
Day 25	Replenished the food inventories at a cost of £80.
Day 26	Received reservations for two rooms for the following week.
Day 27	Paid laundry bill of £40.
Day 28	Drew £300 from the bank for his own wages.
Day 29	Let five rooms for three nights at £30 per night and banked the money.
	Only one of the guests who had made a reservation on Day 26 arrived; this guest paid for three days as he had decided that he was only going to stay until the end of the month. As he arrived in the evening the money was not banked until the following day. Bought enough food to last until the end of the month for £60.
Day 31	Paid the telephone bill, £30 and the electricity bill, £60.

(a) In each situation where there is more than one possible treatment discuss the arguments in favour of and against each alternative.

(b) Based upon the outcome of your discussions draw up a worksheet and enter the above transactions.

(c) Extract a statement of financial position at the end of the month and an income statement and cash flow statement for the month.

(d) Discuss the performance of the business for the period as revealed by the accounts you have prepared, paying particular attention to its cash position and its profitability.

4 Tamsin decided to start a business doing the catering for company functions. She had saved up some money of her own but this was not enough to start so she had obtained a loan from the bank. The transactions of the business, which were all cash, for the first month, were as follows.

Day 1	Opened a business bank account and paid in £1200 of her own money.
Day 2	Received the loan of £1000 from the bank.
Day 3	Found suitable premises and paid £800 for four weeks rent.
Day 4	Went to an auction and bought the following equipment – 50 complete place settings £400, Table linen £300.
Day 5	Had publicity material printed costing £400 which included the cost of sending it out as a mail shot.
Day 6	Bought an old VW Kombi for £900.
Day 8	Placed adverts in the local paper for three days at a total cost of £240.
Day 9	Received her first order worth £800 for a function taking place in two days time.
Day 10	Bought food for the function for £200 and spent the day preparing the food.
Day 11	Hired a couple of friends to help with serving and paid them each £20 for the session. The function was a success and she got paid her £800.
Day 12	Had the table linen laundered at a cost of £30.
Day 15	Received another booking for the next week, this time the price she quoted was £1100 as it was a larger function.
Day 19	Purchased food and drinks for the function at a cost of £450.
Day 20	Employed a friend to help with the preparation for the whole day at a cost of £40.
Day 21	Employed four friends to help with the session for £20 each.
Day 22	Collected her payment of £1100 for the function.
Day 23	Had the table linen laundered at a cost of £60.
Day 24	Bought £50 of replacement place settings as some had been broken when loading the van after the function.
Day 25	Paid £100 for repairs to the Kombi.
Day 26	Placed a block advert in the local paper costing £180.
Day 27	Received bookings for five more functions next month at a price of £900 each.
Day 31	Paid the electricity up to date of £100, the gas bill of £90 and £20 in loan interest.

Required

(a) In each situation where there is more than one possible treatment discuss the arguments in favour of and against each alternative.

(b) Based upon the outcome of your discussions draw up a worksheet and enter the above transactions.

(c) Extract a statement of financial position at the end of the month and an income statement and cash flow statement for the month.

(d) Discuss the performance of the business for the period as revealed by the accounts you have prepared.

CHAPTER 6
INVENTORY

LEARNING OUTCOMES

By the end of this chapter you will:

- Understand what the term inventory means and be able to identify the different forms inventory can take.

- Understand why the determination of inventory levels is important and the effects of inventory levels and values on the income statement and the statement of financial position.

- Be able to apply the concept of prudence to the valuation of inventory.

- Understand the process of matching and the difference between accrual accounting and cash based accounting.

- Understand the acceptable methods for arriving at cost and the application of the rule relating to cost and net realizable value.

- Be able to record inventory and cost of goods sold on a worksheet and produce an income statement, statement of financial position and cash flow statement from basic data.

- Appreciate the need for consistency in the presentation of financial statements.

This chapter takes the reader away from the assumptions adopted in the earlier chapters whereby all transactions took place during the year and all goods bought were sold. This is an unrealistic assumption as most enterprises will hold some goods so that they can meet demand from customers. These goods held to meet customer demand are increasingly referred to as inventory although prior to the adoption of a common set of terminology brought about by countries signing up to the International Accounting Standards the term stock was more commonly used in the UK. Inventory is a broad term which can include raw materials, partially completed goods, known as work in progress, and finished goods. In this chapter the effects of holding inventory at the start and end of the accounting year on the income statement, statement of financial position and cash flow statement are explored and explained. We also explore some of the problems and solutions associated with the determination of a figure for this inventory.

Let us start by examining the simplifying assumptions we have made to date. The first assumption was that no inventory was held at the end of the period. This assumption meant that we had no problem in identifying what had been sold or what it cost. It also meant that the question of whether the goods held in inventory at the end of the period were still worth what we had paid for them did not arise. We also only dealt with single-product businesses which had fairly straightforward processes for converting the goods purchased into saleable commodities. Finally our examples only dealt with start-ups, i.e. businesses in their first year. This meant that the question of how to deal with the inventory held at the beginning of the year did not need to be considered.

Clearly businesses and the real world are more complex than this. Businesses may have multiple processes for converting raw material into final products ready for sale: think of all the components and processes involved in car manufacture. Alternatively they may have multiple product lines: look at the variety of goods on sale at a supermarket. In fact many businesses have a combination of both complex processes and multiple products: look at the range of goods offered by Apple, for example.

In this chapter we shall be relaxing all the assumptions used in the previous chapters and discussing the effects on the statement of financial position, income statement and cash flow statement. We shall also consider:

- the nature of inventory in different types of business;

- the problems arising with more complex businesses, in particular those of work in progress and finished goods;

- the determination of the cost of goods sold during a period;

- the accounting entries needed to record inventory on the worksheet;

- the issues of valuation and how a change in the basis of valuation will affect the statement of financial position and income statement.

Inventory is very important in reality because there is often a high level of resource invested in the inventory. Think about how much needs to be invested to buy all the goods you see on the shelves of a local corner shop let alone a hypermarket. In many businesses this has led to a reappraisal of the way in which they operate and the adoption of techniques such as just-in-time management, which can lead to savings in the costs of holding high levels of inventory (see page 501 for a discussion of this technique). Often the reason that businesses held high levels of inventory was that these were felt to be necessary in order to meet customer demand and to ensure that the production process was not held up. You will see this referred to as buffer stock and there are various techniques available for determining the amount that should be held as well as deciding what size batches to order goods in. This is dealt with in some detail in Chapter 21 pages 496–500 so we will not concern ourselves with those issues here.

It is, however, worth exploring why such techniques are felt to be necessary. If we look at the costs involved in holding high levels of inventory, these are threefold.

- Firstly there is the obvious fact that you have to buy the goods so the more you buy the more money you have tied up not doing anything.

- Secondly there is a cost associated with the space that you use to hold inventory as space costs money.

- Thirdly there is the less obvious cost associated with having to borrow money or find some other form of finance to buy and maintain the inventory level.

The adoption of Just-in-time techniques led to a reappraisal of the production process and demand cycle in order that the level of inventory was reduced to a minimum. A side-effect of this is that many of the large manufacturing firms who have adopted the technique have had to take a closer look at their suppliers to ensure that they have the capability to provide supplies regularly and on time. It has, in some cases, led to a situation where inventory in the form of raw materials or components which were previously held by the manufacturer are now being held by the components supplier, so shifting the cost of holding inventory down the supply chain.

So far we have discussed inventory without really defining the term. Rather than attempting to find one generic definition, which will inevitably become complex and unwieldy, it is easier to look at what comprises inventory as this will lead to a better understanding of the term. Inventory can be said to comprise the following:

1   Goods purchased for resale. For example, packets of cereal are purchased by a supermarket to be sold to their customers; cars are purchased by motor dealers to resell to their customers.

2   Raw materials purchased for incorporation into the product or products being manufactured or assembled for sale, e.g. wood purchased by a furniture manufacturer or steel purchased by a car manufacturer.

3   Consumable goods, which are bought not for resale but for use within the business operation. These could consist of supplies of oil for machine maintenance, supplies of stationery or cleaning materials.

4   Goods in the process of production for sale – these are generally referred to as work in progress examples and could include cars on the production line, partially completed services, construction contracts, etc.

5   Goods that have been through the production process and are awaiting sale, e.g. completed cars at Ford, fully assembled PCs at Hewlett Packard, TVs and CD systems for Sony.

You may have noticed from the examples used that inventory is related to the type of business. For example, cars owned by a furniture manufacturer or retailer such as IKEA will not be classified as inventory because they are held for use in the business and not for resale. You may also have noticed that the third category mentioned is different from the others as it is not held for resale. It is in fact another form of current asset which is only called inventory because it is a stock of items which are held by the business and we have no more suitable term. These first three categories of inventory are often referred to as stocks or raw materials whilst the latter two are frequently referred to as work in progress and finished goods. We will use those terms rather than the general term inventory in this chapter as it is important to differentiate them so that we can identify the issues associated with the measurement of each of these types of inventory.

KEY CONCEPT 6.1

Inventory

Inventories are assets:

1   held for sale in the ordinary course of business;
2   in the process of production; or
3   in the form of materials or supplies to be consumed in the production process or the rendering of services.

International Accounting Standard 2 (Para. 6) 2003

ACTIVITY 6.1

Think of a major high street retailer, a car manufacturer and a property developer and try to identify which of the three types of inventory each would have.

You should have come to the following answers:

Retailer – goods for resale

Car manufacturer – raw materials (steel, tyres, etc.), work in progress (engines, gearboxes cars on the assembly line), finished goods for resale (completed cars)

Property developer – raw materials (bricks, mortar, etc.), work in progress (part completed houses), finished goods for resale (completed houses).

The distinguishing feature of inventory is the intention to resell the item in some form or to use it in a relatively short period of time.

Having looked at some of the ideas that give an indication of what comprises inventory let us now look at work in progress and finished goods. These are both merely different types of inventory – the difference lies in the fact that they have normally gone through some production or assembly process.

KEY CONCEPT 6.2

Work in progress

Work in progress is the term applied to products and services that are at an intermediate stage of completion; for example, if you envisage an assembly line for microcomputers, at any point in time there will be some partially assembled computers somewhere on that production line. An even more obvious example, which we can observe merely by walking round any town centre, is partially completed buildings which are work in progress for some building contractor. A less obvious but equally valid example of work in progress is the time spent to date by an architect on a half-finished drawing.

Finished goods

Finished goods are goods that have been through the complete production or assembly cycle and are ready for resale to the customer. Examples are cars for Toyota, computers for Apple and DVD players for Sony.

In general all these forms of inventory and work in progress fall within the definition of current assets which we adopted in Chapter 3; the reason for distinguishing the three types is that arriving at the cost of the first type of inventory, i.e. raw materials or goods held for resale, is relatively easy compared to something that is part way through or at the end of a process where additional costs such as more components are added together with labour costs for the production or assembly process. Think of car production where there are thousands of components added to the basic chassis at various stages of the production process and imagine stopping the assembly line at a point in time and trying to establish what each partly finished car on that line has cost. If we did this there would be cars at all stages of the production process and therefore all of these part finished cars would have different costs associated with them to say nothing of their values which may be less than their costs at that stage of production.

FIGURE 6.1

Raw materials	Work in process	Finished goods
Car components	Half-assembled car	Completed car

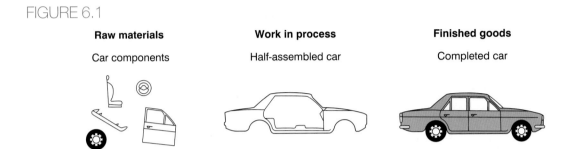

Returning to our definition of current assets, you will notice if you consider the examples given that in some cases the goods will be realized within the year, as is the case for vegetables in a supermarket, and in some cases the reason something is classified as inventory is because it is part of the operating cycle of the business, as in the case of the construction contractor. You will also probably have noticed that the nature of the business is a major determinant of what is and what is not classified as inventory. We shall now explore this aspect of inventory and the question of inventory valuation in more detail.

THE NATURE OF THE BUSINESS AND INVENTORY VALUATION

It is fairly obvious that the nature of the business has an impact on the type of inventory held. We would expect the type of inventory held by a greengrocer to be different from that of a company like IKEA. What may be less obvious is the way in which the nature of the business affects the question of inventory valuation. To illustrate this let us first look at a retailer and a manufacturer and then compare the latter with a provider of services, such as a firm of solicitors.

In the case of a retailing business the inventory held is the goods purchased for resale; because of the nature of the business there is generally little if any change between the goods bought by the business and the goods it sells. Its operating cycle could be seen as shown in Figure 6.2.

If we can establish what the goods cost us when they were bought we can arrive fairly easily at a valuation of inventory by multiplying the cost of each item held by the number of items held. This is because the operating cycle is very simple.

If we now examine the situation of a manufacturing company this is illustrated in figure 6.3 shown on page 124.

FIGURE 6.2

FIGURE 6.3

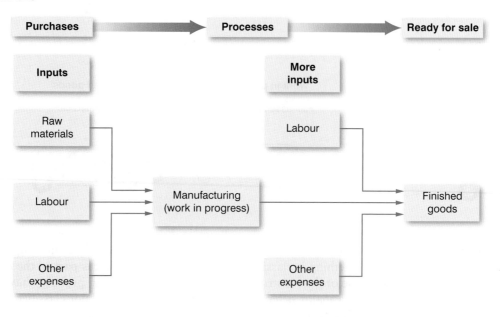

Here we see from the illustration that in order to manufacture goods we need an input of raw materials, of labour and of other items such as the nuts and bolts needed to assemble a car or paint to protect and colour it. These inputs can and often do occur at multiple points in the production process. However, for our purposes a slightly simplified version of the manufacturing process, such as that shown in Figure 6.3 will suffice to illustrate the points being made.

A business with a process similar to that illustrated in Figure 6.3 is likely, at any point in time, to have an inventory of raw materials, an inventory of goods in the process of completion, its work in progress, and an inventory of finished goods.

In the case of the raw materials the question of inventory valuation is similar to that faced by a retailer. For the other categories, however, the question of valuation is often more complex. Do we include the cost of labour in the value of partially completed goods and, if so, which labour? One possible answer would be to include labour involved in the production process and exclude other labour. This is easy in theory but in practice it is not so clear cut. For example, are the foreman and production manager involved in the production process and, if so, what part of their labour cost is attributable to a particular product? The answer to the question of what should and should not be included is vital as it has a direct effect on profit. Alternative approaches to arriving at cost are considered in more detail in Chapters 15 onward. The importance of that discussion cannot be over-emphasized as in some industries where pricing is on a 'cost plus' basis it could be the difference between survival and bankruptcy. If, for example, we quoted a selling price that did not cover all our costs we could end up entering into a contract which could lead to the downfall of the business. Indeed some commentators suggested that the collapse in 1972 of Rolls Royce, perhaps the leading aircraft engine manufacturers in the world at that time, was caused by being tied into a contract where the costs exceeded the selling price of the engines.

The discussion so far has largely related to the manufacturing and assembly sector which is becoming an increasingly smaller proportion of wealth creation in developed economies. But what of the service sector: are the same issues apparent? In this sector the question of inventory valuation can be very straightforward as in the case of a newspaper vendor or much more complex as in the case of lawyers, architects and accountants, for whom the contract to provide services may take many months or even years from inception to completion. If we take the case of lawyers, the inputs will be in the form of labour and expenses such as travelling expenses to see the client and attend court. Thus, in some ways the problem is simplified but here also the question of what costs to include is apparent, what proportion of the secretaries time should be charged to a particular job, what of the costs associated with running the office? It is quite likely that some proportion of the work handled by solicitors will take a considerable amount of time between inception and completion, especially if a case goes to appeal. Thus for some parts of what is referred to as service industry there will be a problem of valuing work in progress when the annual accounts are prepared.

ACTIVITY 6.2

Think of the services provided by an architect or by a firm of accountants where some jobs last over a considerable period of time often involving visits to clients' premises, building sites, or planning departments and identify what costs might be included in work in progress.

Apart from the obvious ones such as direct labour charged to the client, there are likely to be supervisory costs, administrative staff costs, travel costs, printing costs, fees for lodging plans.

THE DETERMINATION OF THE COST OF GOODS SOLD

In previous chapters we assumed that all goods bought in the period were sold in the period and that we could clearly identify the actual goods we sold during the period. In practice despite the introduction of IT based systems many small businesses still do not have adequate records to be able to identify the goods actually sold although this is less true now in retailing with the introduction of affordable electronic point of sales systems (EPOS) which have the capability to update the records of inventory held as goods are scanned at the till. In other small businesses, e.g. a builders' merchant, the costs of accurate records for all items held must be weighed up against the advantages gained from such accuracy. Because of the difficulties involved in recording every item sold and the question of the cost effectiveness of such an exercise some smaller businesses have little if any formal inventory records. Instead they rely on keeping accurate records of purchases and the annual inventory count to establish the cost of goods sold during a period.

This annual inventory count is carried out at the reporting date, and so the inventory figure in the statement of financial position represents a snapshot of the inventory level at that particular point in time. You will notice that in essence what is happening here is what we described in Chapter 2, i.e. the wealth in the form of inventory is measured at two points in time in order to allow us to establish the change over the period. Whilst at first sight this may seem to be an odd way to run a business, it is in fact quite sensible when you consider the impossible job a confectionary manufacturer would have in trying to keep track of every Mars bar, KitKat, or Breaker made. On the other hand if you talk to owners of small businesses you will be surprised at how accurately they can value their inventory simply by looking at what they have in the shop and on the shelves of their storerooms.

What we have just said should not be taken to imply that all retailers have poor inventory records. Clearly, for a business that has accurate and detailed inventory records, arriving at the value of inventory and the cost of goods sold is reasonably simple. Therefore let us look at the situation where detailed inventory movement records are not kept and see how we can arrive at the cost of the goods sold and the cost of those still in inventory at the end of the year. In these cases we need to count the inventory at the start of the year and at the end of the year. From these two figures and the figure for goods purchased during the year we can derive the cost of the goods sold during the year. In other words if we add the purchases to the inventory of goods we had at the start of the year that will tell us the total of the goods we have held during the year. If we then subtract what we have left at the end of the year the resultant figure must be the cost of the goods we have sold during the year, assuming of course that we have allowed for any taken by the owner for personal use etc. This relationship, which is perhaps difficult to describe, can be more easily understood if it is shown in the form of an equation:

$$[\text{Opening inventory} + \text{Purchases}] - \text{Closing inventory} = \text{Cost of goods sold}$$

The information to solve the equation can be derived as follows:

Opening inventory figure – obtained from the statement of financial position at the start of the year

Purchases – from the supplier's invoices

Closing inventory – from a physical inventory count at the end of the year.

As can be seen the inventory figures form a vital component in the calculation of the cost of goods sold. The importance of determining inventory level is examined in Key Concept 6.3.

KEY CONCEPT 6.3

The importance of determining inventory levels

Because the cost of goods sold is, in some cases, calculated by combining the purchases with the inventory figures, the opening and closing inventory levels are vital in determining the cost of goods sold. They therefore have a dual role in the statement of financial position in determining wealth and, through the cost of goods sold, in determining profit.

ACTIVITY 6.3

If the opening inventory is £7000, purchases during the year £23 000 and closing inventory £4000 what is the cost of goods sold?

What would be the cost of goods sold if we found that we had missed another £1000 of closing inventory when we did the count?

If the sales were £40 000 and there were no other expenses what would be the effect of finding the extra £1000 of closing inventory on the final profit figure?

Using the equation: £7000 + £23 000 – £4000 = £26 000
Again using the equation: £7000 + £23 000 – £5000 = £25 000
Original profit = £40 000 – £26 000 = £14 000, revised profit £40 000 – £25 000 = £15 000.

We will now use a worked example to illustrate the use of the equation to deal with inventory and calculate the cost of goods sold and to illustrate the effects on the statement of financial position, income statement and cash flow statement.

EXAMPLE 6.1

The summarized transactions of Tento during the year were as follows.

Sales	£20 000
Purchases	£12 000
Other expenses	£ 6000

The inventory at the end of the period had been counted and was valued at £7000. The financial position of Tento at the start of the period was as follows.

Statement of financial position of Tento at start of period

	£
Current assets	
Cash	11 000
Inventory	5 000
	5 000
Non current assets	
Premises	20 000
	36 000
Owners' equity	36 000
	36 000

Solution 6.1

We start by entering the opening balances on our worksheet, which will now appear as follows.

Worksheet of Tento version 1

	Assets			=	Equity + Liabilities	
Description	**Cash**	**Inventory**	**Premises**		**Equity**	**Revenue & expenses**
Balances	11 000	5 000	20 000		36 000	

If we now enter the transactions for the year and draw up a preliminary total our worksheet will look like this:

(Continued)

Worksheet of Tento version 2

	Assets			=	Equity + Liabilities	
Description	**Cash**	**Inventory**	**Premises**		**Equity**	**Revenue & expenses**
Balances	11 000	5 000	20 000		36 000	
Sales	20 000					20 000
Purchases	−12 000	12 000				
Expenses	−6 000					−6 000
Sub-total	13 000	17 000	20 000		36 000	14 000

The worksheet at this stage shows that we have an inventory of goods of £17 000 whereas we know from our inventory count that what we actually have is £7000. In other words the assets at the end of the year, i.e. the part that will provide a future benefit, are only £7000. Using our equation we can establish that the cost of goods sold during the year was £10 000. This is of course an expense because the benefit is in the past.

The figure of £10 000 was arrived at as follows.

[Opening inventory   +   Purchases]   −   Closing inventory   =   Cost of goods sold
£5 000   +   £12 000   −   £7 000   =   £10 000

Having found that the cost of goods sold is £10 000, we can now enter the cost of goods sold, or cost of sales as it is often called, on our worksheet and draw up our balance at the end of the year. This is done as follows.

Worksheet of Tento version 3

	Assets			=	Equity + Liabilities	
Description	**Cash**	**Inventory**	**Premises**		**Equity**	**Revenue & expenses**
Balances	11 000	5 000	20 000		36 000	
Sales	20 000					. 20 000
Purchases	−12 000	12 000				
Expenses	−6 000					−6 000
Sub-total	13 000	17 000	20 000		36 000	14 000
Cost of sales		−10 000				−10 000
Balances	13 000	7 000	20 000		36 000	4 000

As you will see all that we have done in moving from version 2 to version 3 is to reduce the inventory column by the cost of sales we have calculated using the equation and charged this as an expense to the revenue and expenses column. We would show the calculation included in the worksheet above on an income statement as follows.

Income statement of Tento for the year

	£	£
Sales		20 000
Opening inventory	5 000	
Purchases	12 000	
	17 000	
Less: Closing inventory	7 000	
Cost of sales		10 000
Gross profit		10 000
Expenses		6 000
Net profit		4 000

(Continued)

An alternative simplified presentation would be as follows.

Income statement of Tento for the year

	£	£
Sales		20 000
Cost of sales		10 000
Gross profit		10 000
Expenses		6 000
Net profit		4 000

The latter format, which does not show how the cost of goods sold, is calculated is closer to what you are likely to see in the published accounts of quoted companies.

ACTIVITY 6.4

Take a moment to check back to the worksheet and identify where the figures in the income statement come from.

You will have seen that the figures in the income statement are taken directly from the revenue and expenses column of the worksheet. The income statement is always a summary of the revenue and expenses column of your worksheet.

For completeness we show the statement of financial position and cash flow statement below. You should note that despite the fact that all the cash inflows and outflows related to items included as revenue or expenses the cash flow and the profit are not the same.

Statement of financial position of Tento at end of period

Current assets

Cash	13 000
Inventory	7 000
	20 000

Non current assets

Premises	20 000
	40 000

Owners' equity	36 000
Profits	4 000
	40 000

(Continued)

ACTIVITY 6.5

Look at the figures in the statement of financial position and identify where in the worksheet they come from.

You should have seen that headings are those from the top of the columns and the figures are taken from the bottom line of the worksheet. This is always the case.

Cash flow statement of Tento for the year

Cash inflows	
Cash from sales	20 000
	20 000
Cash outflows	
Purchases	12 000
Expenses	6 000
	18 000
Increase in cash	2 000

ACTIVITY 6.6

Finally take a moment to check back to the worksheet and identify where the figures in the cash flow statement come from.

You will have seen that the figures in the cash flow statement are taken directly from the bank/cash column of the worksheet. The cash flow statement can always be created by summarizing the bank/cash column of your worksheet.

If you compare the net cash flow and the net profit you will see that the increase in cash, the net cash inflow is £2000 and the net profit is £4000. Given that the items in the cash flow statement are also items that are used in the calculation of profit you should understand why these figures differ. The answer lies in the fact that of the £12 000 of goods purchased, for which there was a cash outflow, only £10 000 were sold, the remaining £2000 simply increased the amount of inventory that Tento held. As a general rule we can start to reconcile the cash flow figure and the profit figure by doing a simple reconciliation that looks at the change in the inventory levels. If inventory goes up then clearly some cash is used to buy that inventory if it goes down then it means that some of the goods sold during the period were bought in a previous period and the cash flow would have taken place in the previous period. Based on the simple scenario we have here, the general rule therefore can be stated as in Figure 6.4.

(Continued)

FIGURE 6.4

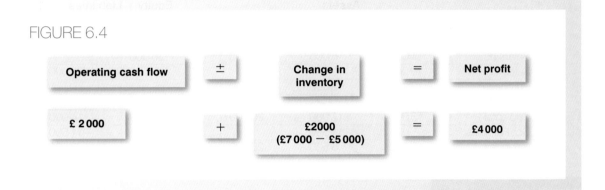

Operating cash flow	±	Change in inventory	=	Net profit
£ 2 000	+	£2000 (£7 000 − £5 000)	=	£4 000

The operating cash flow can be broadly defined as the cash inflows and outflows resulting from the trading activity of the enterprise so would exclude items such as the purchase of non current assets such as premises.

KEY CONCEPT 6.4

Operating cash flow

Operating cash flow is the cash inflows and outflows arising from the trading activities of the enterprise.

Before we move on to the area of valuation it should be noted that, because of the relationship between the statement of financial position and the income statement, an error in the opening inventory figure, the purchases figure or the closing inventory figure will not only change the profit but it will also change the statement of financial position.

For example, if the closing inventory figure had been overstated by £1500 the worksheet would look like the one below and as you can see the balance on the inventory column which goes to the statement of financial position is £5500 compared to £7000 in the previous statement of financial position, i.e. it is £1500 lower. You should also note that because the closing inventory figure is reduced by £1500 the cost of sales has increased by £1500 from £10 000 to £11 500 and this has the effect of lowering the profit by £1500.

Worksheet of Tento version 4

| Description | Assets | | | = | Equity + Liabilities | |
	Cash	Inventory	Premises		Equity	Revenue & expenses
Balances	11 000	5 000	20 000		36 000	
Sales	20 000					20 000
Purchases	−12 000	12 000				
Expenses	−6 000					−6 000
Sub-total	13 000	17 000	20 000		36 000	14 000
Cost of sales		−11 500				−11 500
Balances	13 000	5 500	20 000		36 000	2 500

ACTIVITY 6.7

In Activity 6.3 you worked out what effect a change in the closing inventory figure would have had on the cost of sales and profit. Before moving on think what effect a mistake which overstated the opening inventory would have on the cost of sales and the profit.

An overstatement of the opening inventory would cause the cost of sales to be overstated and the profit to fall. If that is not immediately obvious try putting some numbers in the equation:

[Opening inventory + Purchases] − Closing inventory = Cost of goods sold

VALUATION OF INVENTORY

In general, if prices of goods stay constant over time, tastes do not change and there are no changes in technology, then we would have no problem with inventory valuation. However, fortunately the real world is not like that; this has the advantage that civilization can progress but it creates some problems for accountants (a small price to pay you might think). The question of how changes in prices can affect inventory valuation is wide ranging and is allied to the question of how the cost of inventory is arrived at. We shall therefore first consider the effects of changes in taste and technology; then we shall look at how cost is arrived at before finally considering the effects of price changes.

Changes in technology and taste

We have grouped technology and taste together because although the causes are different the effects on inventory valuation are the same. Let us consider the effect of changes in technology, of which there are hundreds of everyday examples such as the use of microcomputers instead of mainframe machines and the advances in microcomputer technology. Examples of this effect can be found with the price of mobile phones, DVD players, MP3 players, etc., where in a relatively short space of time a new product comes on the market and the prices of the existing products on the market drop dramatically. For the purposes of our illustration let us assume that we are a retailer who had bought ten DVD players at a cost of £200 per machine and were caught by a superior new product coming on the market at a price of £150, meaning that our machines could only be sold at £99. If we valued our closing inventory on the basis of the cost our asset would be shown as £2 000.

However, we said in Chapter 3 that an asset is the right to a future benefit. In our example retailer's situation the future benefit that can be obtained is only £99 per machine, the new retail price. Thus in this case the cost does not reflect the future benefit that we are likely to get. A fairer reflection would be the amount the DVD player could be sold for. However, even the £99 is probably overstating the benefit as there will undoubtedly be some costs incurred in selling the DVD players. If for example these costs were estimated to be £10 per machine, then the amount of the future benefit would in fact be £89. So instead of the asset being recorded at its costs of £2 000 the future benefit is in fact ten times £89, i.e. £890. This is referred to as the net realizable value of the goods.

KEY CONCEPT 6.5

Net realizable value

Net realizable value is defined as the estimated proceeds from the sale of items less the costs of selling these items.

A similar effect would have arisen if the goods could only be sold either at a reduced price or for scrap because of changes in people's tastes (last season's fashions). In each of these cases the cost is not relevant to the future benefit and a better valuation would be the net realizable value. This leads us to the idea that we should compare the cost of an item with what we can get for it and, if the latter figure is lower, use that figure to value our inventory. Expressed in more formal terms this is the valuation rule included as Key Concept 6.6 below.

KEY CONCEPT 6.6

The valuation rule

Inventory should be valued at the lower of cost and net realizable value.

You may well wonder why, if the net realizable value is higher than the cost, that higher value is not used. The reason for this is that the attainment of the higher value is uncertain as tastes may change; thus we apply the prudence principle in these cases. This concept is used in conjunction with the realization principle which we discussed in some detail near the start of Chapter 4. See Key Concept 6.7 below.

KEY CONCEPT 6.7

The prudence concept

Profits are not anticipated and revenue is not recognized until their realization is reasonably certain. Provision is made for all potential losses.

ACTIVITY 6.8

If the net realizable value is lower than the cost what effect would the application of the lower of cost and net realizable value rule have on the closing inventory, the cost of sales and the profit?

The figure for closing inventory would be lower resulting in a higher cost of sales and lower profit.

Having established the general rule for inventory valuation and seen the reasons for the rule, the next question that we need to address is how to establish the cost that is referred to in the rule.

Establishing the cost of inventory

As we have already indicated, the more complex the process involved the more difficult it is to establish the cost of inventory. The problem is what we should and what we should not include. The debate on this subject has been going on for some considerable time in the literature relating to management accounting and will be explored in more detail in later chapters when we discuss the alternative methods that could be used to arrive at cost. Fortunately, for our purposes at present we need only be aware in fairly general terms what the alternative methods are, as the choice between the methods has to some extent been made for us through custom and practice and the rules laid down for companies in International Accounting Standard 2 (IAS 2).

IAS 2 deals with the question of inventory and work in progress (with the exception of construction contracts). Before looking at what that standard lays down let us briefly consider the alternatives. These are best considered by means of a simple example.

EXAMPLE 6.2

Let us assume that a business produces spanners. Each spanner requires £0.30 of steel, and takes 15 minutes labour to produce. The business employs ten people to make spanners and they each produce 140 spanners per week and are paid £140 each per week. We also assume that we have a foreman overseeing our workers who is paid £200 per week and that at the end of the year we have one week's production, i.e. 1400 spanners, in inventory. The question that we have to answer is: what is the cost of the 1400 spanners we have in inventory at the end of the year?

Solution 6.2

One solution might be to establish how much it would cost to produce one extra spanner.

Materials	30 p
Labour £1 per spanner £140 per week divided	£1.00
by 140 spanners produced	
	£1.30

(Continued)

Thus the marginal cost of producing one spanner is £1.30. If we then applied this cost to our inventory we would value our inventory at 1400 × £1.30 = £1 820. This would be the cost using a marginal cost basis.

On the other hand it could legitimately be argued that the cost of producing 1400 spanners, i.e. a week's production, is made up as follows:

Steel 1400 × £0.30	£ 420
Direct labour, ten staff at £140	1400
Foreman's wages	200
Total cost	£2020

The latter method of arriving at the cost is known as absorption costing. A fuller discussion of absorption costing can be found in Chapter 16 page 373 onward.

You will note that the difference between the two is £200, i.e. the foreman's wages are not included on a marginal cost basis.

As we have said, to some extent the choice between the two has been made for us by the requirements of IAS 2 which states that cost shall comprise:

all costs of purchase, costs of conversion and other costs incurred in bringing inventories to their present location or condition. (Para. 10)

The costs of conversion referred to include direct costs (similar to our labour and materials in the example above), production overheads (such as our foreman's wages) and any other overheads that are attributable to bringing the inventory to its present location and condition. An example of these would be the cost to Ford of transporting engines from its production plant to the assembly line factory.

In all the examples we shall deal with we shall adopt a method of arriving at cost which will include all the costs which are obviously attributable to the raw material inventory, work in progress or finished goods. This can be done on the worksheet as illustrated in the following example.

EXAMPLE 6.3

Bertie had his own business which assembled bicycles from a number of components. This involved the following processes:

Process 1   Assembling of frames, saddles and handlebars

Process 2   Adding wheels to the partially completed frames

The first process takes one hour and costs £5 in wages, whilst the second process takes less time and costs £3 in wages, thus to assemble a complete bicycle costs £8 for labour. The frames, saddles and handlebars are bought from one supplier for £40 per set, and the wheels come from a different supplier and cost £20 per set.

We shall assume for simplicity that it is the first year of the business and that Bertie has started with £1000 of his own money. During the year Bertie bought 50 frame sets at a total cost of £2000 and 60 pairs of wheels at a total cost of £1200. He paid wages of £320. He sold 35 bicycles for £140 each, making a total of £4900 in revenue. His only other expenses were the rent of a showroom which cost him £500 for the year.

(Continued)

Let us now look at the manufacturing process in some detail and trace the flow of one of the component parts: the frame sets. We can look at the process in terms of goods flowing through three departments which we shall call stores, where the raw materials are stored, Process 1 where the frames are assembled and Process 2, where the wheels are added and the bikes are ready for sale. These three areas can be equated to inventories of raw material, work in progress and finished goods. If we now trace the flow through the process we can see from Figure 6.5 how the finished product costs are arrived at.

FIGURE 6.5

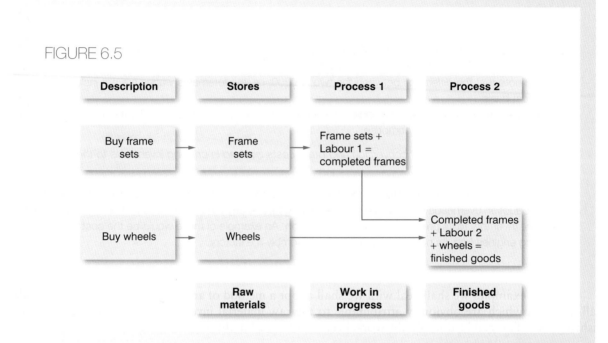

Figure 6.5 shows the assembly process, and we can see that we start with buying frame sets, which we put into the stores. When we are ready to assemble these into completed frames we move them through Process 1, where an additional cost is incurred, i.e. the cost of the labour for this process which we have called Labour 1. At this stage we have work in the process of being completed which we call work in progress, the cost of which is the frame sets plus the labour for assembly so far. We now move the completed frames to Process 2. Here we also get some wheels from the stores and use some more labour, which we identify as Labour 2, to add the wheels to the frames and complete the bikes. These completed bikes we call finished goods, and as you can see the cost of these is the costs incurred in Process 1 plus the cost of the wheels and the labour in Labour 2.

Having explained how the process works, let us now look at some of the detail in the example and see what happens to the 50 frame sets Bertie bought. This is shown in Table 6.1 shown on following page.

The table shows that Bertie starts off with 50 frame sets and puts them in the stores. This represents a net movement of +50, as before he bought the frames he had none. He then moves 40 of the frames to the Process 1 area, leaving ten still in the stores. The net movement is nil, as no more frames have come into the business nor have any gone outside the business; they are simply moving around within the business. The next

(Continued)

TABLE 6.1

	Stores	→	Process 1	→	Process 2	Net movement
Buy frame sets	+50					+50
Move to Process 1	−40	→	+40			Nil
Sub-total	10		40			
Move to Process 2			−40	→	+40	Nil
Goods sold					−35	−35
Balances	**10**		**0**		**5**	**15**

stage is to move the 40 completed frames into Process 2 where the wheels are added. Once again the net movement is nil, as the frames are moving around within the business. The final transaction is that 35 are sold, which reduces the number of frames left in Process 2 to five. The net movement here is -35, as the frames have now moved outside the business. Thus at the end we are left with ten frame sets in stores, none in Process 1 and five in Process 2. This tallies with the fact that Bertie bought 50 and sold 35, leaving 15 at various stages of completion.

The same process could now be applied to the wheels and to labour hours.

If you are not clear on what is happening either go over the table again or alternatively try completing Table 6.2 below for the wheels.

TABLE 6.2

	Stores	→	Process 1	→	Process 2	Net movement
Buy wheels						
Move to process 1		→				
Sub-total						
Move to process 2				→		
Goods sold						
Balances						

Your completed table should look like Table 6.3 shown on page 138. As you will have worked out the wheels only become part of the assembly process at stage 2 of the process and at the end we can see that we have 20 sets of wheels still in their original state, five sets in work in progress and the remaining 35 have been moved to finished goods and been sold.

We are now going to move on to look at the process as a whole and how we account for it in money terms rather than physical units.

At the end of the year he had in inventory five completed cycles, ten untouched frame sets and 20 pairs of wheels.

If we now summarize the information we have been given in total and enter it on our worksheet we can then deal with the closing inventory and the cost of goods sold.

(Continued)

TABLE 6.3

	Stores	→	Process 1	→	Process 2	Net movement
Buy wheels	+60					+60
Move to process 1		→				
Sub-total						
Move to process 2	− 40			→	+40	Nil
Goods sold					−35	+35
Balances	20				5	25

Summary of the information:

	£
Cash at start	1 000
Owner's equity	1 000
Frame sets bought	2 000
Wheels bought	1 200
Wages paid	320
Other expenses – rent	500
Sales revenue	4 900

Our worksheet would now appear as follows.

Bertie's worksheet version 1

	Assets				=	Equity + Liabilities	
	Cash	Frames	Wheels	Wages		Equity	Revenue & expenses
Balance	1 000					1 000	
Frames	−2 000	2 000					
Wheels	−1 200		1 200				
Wages	−320			320			
Rent	−500						−500
Sales	4 900						4 900
Sub-total	1 880	2 000	1 200	320		1 000	4 400

You will notice that the rent of the showroom has been included as an expense. This is a selling expense and therefore could not be classified as an overhead attributable to bringing the goods to their present state and condition if we were valuing inventory.

(Continued)

Turning now to the wages, we were told that each bicycle cost £8 for labour and that he has sold 35 bicycles. The labour in respect of the bikes sold is therefore 35 × £8 = £280. The completed bicycles in inventory cost 5 × £8 = £40 for labour.

If you had done similar calculations for the frames and the wheels and calculated the costs of the bicycles that have been sold, you should have arrived at figures for frames of £1400 and for wheels of £700. If not look at the detailed calculation of the total cost of sales below

The cost of goods sold should be as follows:

Frames 35 × £40	= £1 400
Wheels 35 × £20	= £ 700
Wages 35 × £ 8	= £ 280
Total	= £2 380

Now calculate the amounts to be included in our inventory of finished goods
Your answer should be the same as that given below.

Frames 5 × £40	= £ 200
Wheels 5 × £20	= £ 100
Wages 5 × £ 8	= £ 40
Total	= £ 340

If we now wish to put this on the worksheet we shall first need to open a column for our finished goods and then enter the above information.

Our worksheet will be as follows.

Bertie's worksheet version 2

		Assets				=	Equity + liabilities	
	Cash	Frames	Wheels	Wages	Finished goods		Equity	Revenue & expenses
Balance	1 000						1 000	
Frames	−2 000	2 000						
Wheels	−1 200		1 200					
Wages	−320			320				
Rent	−500							−500
Sales	4 900							4 900
Frames		−1 400						−1 400
Wheels			−700					−700
Wages				−280				−280
Frames		−200			200			
Wheels			−100		100			
Wages				−40	40			
Sub-total	**1 880**	**400**	**400**	**0**	**340**		**1 000**	**2 020**

We shall briefly examine what we have just entered on our worksheet. We have dealt initially with the cost of the goods sold and have transferred the costs of the raw materials, frames and wheels, together with the labour costs associated with the assembly process, to the revenue and expenses column as an expense of the period. You will note that here we have employed the matching principle and matched the costs of assembling 35 bicycles with the revenue earned from selling 35 bicycles. We have then dealt with the bicycles which we have assembled but not sold, our finished goods, and transferred the costs associated with those bicycles

(Continued)

KEY CONCEPT 6.8

Matching principle and accrual accounting

The matching principle is at the heart of accrual accounting and is based on the notion that the revenue for the period should be matched with the expenses incurred in earning that revenue. This leads to a change from cash based accounting, whereby all transactions are charged to the income statement as they are incurred, to accrual accounting whereby items are only charged to the income statement as expenses when the future benefit has been used up.

to a finished goods column. Now if we look at our final balances we find that what is left in inventory is ten frames at £40, 20 pairs of wheels at £20 and finished goods which have cost £340 to get to their present state and condition.

Another way of looking at what is happening in Bertie's business is to see it as a flow through a factory, which is represented by the accounting system. Thus the inputs are the frames, wheels and labour. These together form the work in progress, which then becomes finished goods ready for resale. The parts of the worksheet that relate to this process would therefore look something like the following.

	Raw materials		→	WIP	→	Finished goods	→	Sales
	Frames	Wheels	Wages	Work in progress		Finished goods		Revenue & expenses
Balance								
Frames	2 000							
Wheels		1 200						
Wages			320					
To Work in progress	−1 600			→ 1 600				
To Work in progress		−800		→ 800				
To Work in progress			−320	→ 320				
To Finished goods				−2 720	→	2 720		
To Cost of goods sold						−2 380	→	−2 380
	400	400	0	0		340		

Having dealt with the question of what is included in cost, the last area which we have to consider is the effect of price changes on the cost of goods sold and the closing inventory.

ACTIVITY 6.9

Before moving on try to identify what would have happened had all the 50 bicycles been partially completed, in other words only Process 1 had been completed on the bikes that remained unsold. Assume that there were no other changes in costs.

A worksheet showing that situation is included at the end of the chapter as the answer to Activity 6.9 for you to compare your answer with (see paege 150).

EFFECTS OF PRICE CHANGES

Although we have considered the effect of downward movements in price under the heading of changes in technology we also need to consider the effect of increases in the input price of our inventory, i.e. increases in the prices we pay to our suppliers. As we have already indicated there would be no real problem if all sales could be identified with the actual goods sold. In practice, however, a builders' merchant, for instance, has a pile of bricks and sells them in any order depending on the ease of access. We cannot therefore work out whether a particular brick sold was bought by the builders' merchant when the price of bricks was 30p or whether it was bought after the price had gone up to 33p. It is not feasible or cost effective to trace each brick through the process. We therefore have to find some system that will give a reasonable approximation of the cost of the goods we have sold and of the cost of the inventory remaining. There are of course numerous possibilities at various levels of complexity. For our purposes we shall concentrate on the two methods that are allowed under the International Accounting Standard on Inventory (IAS 2), namely, first in first out and weighted average cost. We will use a simple example to illustrate that depending on the method chosen the profit and the statement of financial position figures can vary considerably.

EXAMPLE 6.4

Barbara started the year with some goods in inventory and bought additional goods as required during the year. The price of the goods she bought rose steadily during the year. The summarized data for her transactions is as follows.

	Units	Cost per unit
Goods in inventory at the start of the year	400	£1.00
Purchases, quarter 1	500	£1.10
Purchases, quarter 2	400	£1.20
Purchases, quarter 3	400	£1.25
Purchases, quarter 4	300	£1.40
Goods sold during the year, 1800 units for a total of £2400		

Using the data above we shall illustrate how the adoption of different valuation rules affects not only the inventory value at the end of the year but also how they affect the cost of sales and therefore the profit. We shall start by considering a method of valuation called first in, first out (FIFO).

First in, first out

The FIFO method is based on the artificial assumption that the first goods bought are the first sold. This means that in effect the inventory held at the end of the period is assumed to be that purchased most recently. It is probably the most common basis of inventory valuation in the UK and there are many situations when it is clearly the obvious choice. This would be the case for any industry or business dealing in consumables.

It should be pointed out that, surprisingly, the choice of method for arriving at the cost of inventory generally has little if anything to do with actual inventory movements.

(Continued)

In our example this method would mean that all of the opening inventory together with that purchased in the first three quarters would be assumed to have been sold together with 100 units bought in the fourth quarter. This would leave a closing inventory of 200 units which were bought in the fourth quarter. The calculation is shown in Table 6.4 below.

TABLE 6.4

FIFO	Purchases			Goods sold		Inventory	
	Units	Unit cost	Total cost	Units	Total cost	Units	Total cost
Goods in inventory at the start of the year	400	£1.00	£ 400	400	£ 400	0	
Purchases, quarter 1	500	£1.10	£ 550	500	£ 550	0	
Purchases, quarter 2	400	£1.20	£ 480	400	£ 480	0	
Purchases, quarter 3	400	£1.25	£ 500	400	£ 500	0	
Purchases, quarter 4	300	£1.40	£ 420	100	£ 140	200	£280
Balances	**2 000**		**£2 350**	**1 800**	**£2 070**	**200**	**£280**

The income statement and statement of financial position would be as follows:

Income statement
Sales revenue (1 800 units)   £2 400
Cost of goods sold   £2 070
Profit   £ 330

Statement of financial position
Inventory (200 units)   £ 280

As you can see the units included in the cost of goods sold include the ones we started with and all those bought in the first three quarters plus 100 units bought in the fourth quarter. The inventory in the statement of financial position consists of 200 of the units bought in the fourth quarter.

Weighted average cost
The weighted average cost method takes the cost of units bought over a period and weights the cost by the number of units. It makes no assumptions about the way in which goods flow through the business. For the purposes of arriving at the charge to the income statement all that is needed is to work out the average cost per unit of inventory and multiply that by the number of units sold. Similarly the closing inventory is arrived at by taking the number of units left in inventory multiplied by the average cost per unit. This leads to a profit and inventory figure which is calculated as shown on the next page.

(Continued)

Weighted average cost		Purchases			Goods sold		Inventory	
	Units	Unit cost	Total cost	Units	Total cost	Units	Total cost
Goods in inventory at the start of the year	400	£1.00	£ 400				
Purchases, quarter 1	500	£1.10	£ 550				
Purchases, quarter 2	400	£1.20	£ 480				
Purchases, quarter 3	400	£1.25	£ 500				
Purchases, quarter 4	300	£1.40	£ 420				
Totals	**2 000**		**£2 350**	**1 800**	**£2 115**	**200**	**£235**
Cost per unit	$\frac{£2\,350}{2\,000}$	=	£ 1.18				

Income statement

Sales revenue (1 800 units)					£2 400		
Cost of goods sold					£2 115		
Profit					£ 285		

Statement of financial position

Inventory (200 units)   £ 235

As you can see the profit figure is £330 using FIFO and £285 using the weighted average cost. The figures for closing inventory included in the statement of financial position are £280 and £235 respectively. You may think that this allows unscrupulous people to manipulate the profit simply by changing the method used. However, this is covered by the requirement to use the same method year on year known as the consistency principle. However, although you can be reasonably certain that a business will be consistent from year to year it does not mean that any two businesses will necessarily have chosen the same method and as such their results will not be directly comparable even though they both comply with the requirements of the International Accounting Standard (IAS2).

KEY CONCEPT 6.9

Consistency

The International Financial Reporting Standard for Small and Medium Sized Entities is quite clear that: 'An entity shall retain the presentation and classification of items in the financial statements from one period to the next.' It then identifies the specific situations under which a change is allowed.

IFRS-SME 2009 Paras.: 3.11 to 3.13

Some of the issues drawn out in the discussion in this chapter are illustrated in extracts from published accounts given in Case Studies 6.1 and 6.2.

CASE STUDY 6.1

Thorntons plc

Extract from the accounts of Thorntons plc for the year ended 27 June 2009

	Group	
	2009	2008
14 Inventories	£000	£000
Raw materials	3 101	2 557
Work in progress	2 715	2 963
Finished goods and goods for resale	19 554	18 787
	25 370	24 307

During the year £415 000 (2008: £80 000) relating to the write down of inventory to net realizable value in prior year was released and reflected in cost of sales

Extract from the accounting policies statement of Thorntons plc
Inventories

Inventories are stated at the lower of cost and net realizable value. Cost includes materials, direct labour and an attributable proportion of manufacturing overheads, based on normal operating capacity, according to the stage of production reached and valued on a FIFO basis.

Net realizable value is the estimated value which would be realized after deducting all costs of completion, marketing and selling. Provision is made to reduce the cost to net realizable value having regard to the age and condition of inventory, as well as its anticipated saleability.

Commentary

Thorntons plc is both a manufacturer and retailer of confectionary, which is reflected in the extract from the accounts; nearly 80% of stocks are finished goods or those bought in ready for resale, however there are also significant levels of raw materials and work in progress. It is also worth noting from the accounting policies statement the inclusion of materials, direct labour and overheads.

In contrast to the situation in Case Study 6.1 the extract from J Sainsbury, Case Study 6.2, does not have work in progress or finished goods.

CASE STUDY 6.2

J Sainsbury plc

Extract from the accounts of J Sainsbury plc for the year ended 21 March 2009

	Group	
	2009	**2008**
16 Inventories	**£m**	**£m**
Goods for resale	689	681

The amount of inventories recognized as an expense and charged to cost of sales for the 52 weeks to 21 March 2009 was £14 490 million (2008: £13 557 million).

Extract from the accounting policies statement of J Sainsbury plc
Inventories

Inventories are valued at the lower of cost and net realizable value. Inventories at warehouses are valued on a first-in, first-out basis. Inventories at retail outlets are valued at calculated average cost prices. Cost includes all direct expenditure and other appropriate attributable costs incurred in bringing inventories to their present location and condition.

Commentary

J Sainsbury plc is a retailer; a significant part of its business relates to consumables. The accounting policies above reflect our discussion of first in first out which is used for inventory held at the warehouses and average cost which is used for inventory at the retail outlets. The fact that inventories held at retail outlets is valued at average cost reflects the perishable nature of food and fluctuating prices of foods.Once again the cost includes direct expenditure plus other atrributable costs.

The extract from the accounts of J Sainsbury plc shows that the main operations of the company are finished goods for resale; note there is no breakdown of raw materials or work in progress as this would be inappropriate for a retailer.

SUMMARY

In this chapter the businesses we have considered have been trading for some time. We have shown how we establish the cost of goods sold during a period and the closing inventory and the effects of these figures on the profit, the statement of financial position and cash flow statement. We have looked at how holding inventory will mean that even if all the transactions are either revenue or expenses the profit will differ from the net cash flow for the period as some of the goods sold may either be bought in the previous period or conversely some of the goods purchased may be sold in the next period. We have also looked at what constitutes cost

(Continued)

when dealing with inventory and have introduced the ideas of marginal and absorption costing. In the latter part of the chapter we have seen that changes in technology can lead to inventory being sold at less than cost and that changes in prices affect both the statement of financial position and the income statement. Finally we have considered two possible methods for arriving at the cost of goods sold during a period and at the closing inventory figure. It can be seen that some of the issues faced in accounting for inventory are often a direct result of the management strategies adopted. For example, just-in-time will affect the amount of inventory held. Other factors at the organizational level that will have an impact are the size of the organization (Tesco or Carrefour are likely to hold a wider range of goods than the corner shop) and the organizational structure: a particular factory may manufacture just one component or a number of components.

REFERENCES

IASB. (2009) *International Accounting Standard 2: Inventories*, London: IASB.
IASB. (2009) *International Financial Reporting Standard for Small and Medium Sized Entities*, London: IASB.

REVIEW QUESTIONS

(✓ indicates answers are available in Appendix A)

✓ **1** What main categories of inventory are likely to be held by a manufacturing business?

2 In arriving at a figure for inventory in a business that manufactures and assembles furniture, what questions would need to be considered?

✓ **3** What would be the effect on the profit if goods costing £6000 were excluded from the opening inventory figure?

4 What are the effects of omitting goods costing £500 from the year end inventory figure?

✓ **5** Why is it necessary to value inventory at the lower of cost and net realizable value?

6 Explain in your own words the difference between absorption costing and marginal costing.

7 Which of the following costs would be appropriate to include in a marginal costing system?

> Director's salary
> Foreman's wages
> Machine operators' wages
> Cost of raw materials

8 Of the costs above which would be appropriate to include in arriving at cost under an absorption costing system?

✓ **9** Name the two methods of inventory valuation allowed under International Accounting Standards and describe the differences between them and the effects of those differences.

10 Think of examples of types of business where one method of inventory valuation would be more appropriate than the others.

PROBLEMS FOR DISCUSSION AND ANALYSIS

(✓ indicates answers are available in Appendix A)

1 Julie had been in business as a market trader for a while and at the start of the month she had £7500 invested in her business of which £5500 was invested in inventory and the remainder was kept in cash or in the business bank account. During the month she had the following transactions.

(a) Bought and paid for further goods for resale amounting to £9000
(b) Paid rent for various market stall pitches totalling £3000
(c) Paid rent for van for month £900
(d) Paid petrol and other expenses amounting to £700
(e) Sold goods for £18 000
(f) At the end of the month she had goods in inventory which had cost £3500
(g) Looking at the goods in her inventory at the end of the month she identifies that some goods that cost her £1200 to buy were water damaged and she estimates that she will only be able to sell these for £400.

Discuss the treatment of each item and then draw up a worksheet, statement of financial position, income statement and cash flow statement for Julie's business for the month.

2 In the situation described in the following example discuss which costs, if any, should be included in the inventory valuation, and at what point in time they should be included.

Hank is in business manufacturing sails. The sail material is purchased in 100 metre lengths and these are delivered to the storeman, who sorts the materials according to quality and width. The material is then issued to the cutting room where five people are employed, one of whom is the cutting room supervisor. After cutting, the material is passed through to the machining room where the sails are sewn up and the hanks etc. are put on. The machining room has seven staff employed full time including a supervisor. From the machining room the sails go through to the packaging department where they are folded, inserted in sail bags and either sent to the despatch department or put into inventory. The packaging department and the despatch department each employ one member of staff working on a part-time basis. The whole operation is under the control of a production manager who also has responsibility for quality control.

3 Discuss the ways in which your answer to problem 2 would be affected by the use of marginal cost basis of inventory valuation.

✓ 4 Gilco had been in business for a year buying and selling home water purifiers. During the year 400 units had been sold and installed. Of these 220 were Model 2 and the remainder were the upgraded model, Model 3. Model 2 is still selling but at a reduced price, which is of course, less than the price of Model 3 as it has fewer features. Since Model 3 was introduced in August the sales of Model 2 have fallen but have now stabilized at ten a month. The stock count at the year end shows that Gilco has 60 Model 3 purifiers and 20 Model 2 purifiers in stock. The price of Model 2 is now £70 and Model 3 is selling at £110. The pattern of purchases for the year is provided below. Gilco estimates that the costs incurred in selling either of the purifiers are £20 per unit.

	Model 2		Model 3	
	Units	Price	Units	Price
Quarter 1	80	£50		
Quarter 2	100	£55		
Quarter 3	60	£55	80	£60
Quarter 4			160	£65

(a) Calculate the cost of the goods sold on a FIFO basis.
(b) Calculate the cost of the goods sold using weighted average cost.
(c) Calculate the figure to be included in the statement of financial position for inventory using a FIFO basis, having regard to the lower of cost or net realizable value rule.

5 Henry has recently gone into business making meat pies. Details of his transactions for the first month are given below.

Day 1   Opened a bank account and paid in £20 000 of his own money.
           Purchased an oven to make pies at a cost of £10 000.
           Paid rent for production space for the first month of £200.

Day 2   Bought the following supplies for cash:
             520 Kg of flour at £1.20 per Kg.
             520 Kg of meat at £2 per Kg.
Day 3   Withdrew £1000 to pay a pressing personal debt.
Day 3 to 31 Made 4000 pies and sold 3900 pies.

Each pie takes 125g of flour and 125g of meat and was sold for £1.
    At the end of the month he still had in inventory the expected 20 Kg of flour, 20 Kg of meat and 100 finished meat pies.

Day 31   Paid himself £1600 wages for the month. He estimates that half his time is spent on
             production and the rest on selling and administration.
             Paid production overheads of £120 for the month.
             Paid administration expenses of £50 for the month.

(a) Draw up a worksheet, statement of financial position, income statement and cash flow statement for Henry's
        business.
(b) Comment on the performance of the business.

6 Using the information in the example below discuss the accounting treatment of each transaction and the possible value of the inventory at the end of the month.
    Stern has recently gone into business assembling hang-gliders. Details of the transactions for the first month are given below.

Day 1   Opened a bank account for the business and paid in £50 000 of his own money.
         Purchases assembly machinery for £40 000 cash.
         Rented factory space at a rental of £200 per month and paid one month's rent in advance.
Day 2   Bought 1000 metres of tubing for the hang-glider frames at a price of £250 per 100 metres and paid
         the £2500 in cash.
Day 3   Purchased 150 sets of material for sails for £20 per set and paid the £3000 immediately. Each hang-
         glider takes one set of sails.
Day 8   Received an order for 20 hang-gliders at £400 each together with a cheque for £8000.
Day 9   Banked the cheque and commenced manufacture of the hang-gliders.
Day 14   Completed manufacture of the 20 hang-gliders and despatched the completed order to the customer,
         paying the delivery charges of £200 immediately.

    At this stage it was possible to do some preliminary calculations relating to the manufacture of each hang-glider. These calculations showed that each hang-glider required the following:

Labour	Sail machining	30 minutes per unit
	Frame assembly	2 hours per unit
	Final assembly	30 minutes per unit
Materials	Metal tubing	4 metres per unit
	Sails	one set per unit

Day 15   Received an order for another 200 hang-gliders at a price of £250 each. Payment is to be made on a
         cash-on-delivery basis.
Day 16   Commenced work on the new order.
Day 26   Purchased another 100 sets of sails and paid for them in cash. The price had gone up to £22 per set,
         making a total of £2200.
Day 30   Paid wages of £800 for the month based on four 40-hour weeks at £5 per hour.
Day 31   Established the position at the end of the month as follows:

Completed hang-gliders ready for delivery	20
Manufactured frames	10

Inventories of materials were as follows:

Steel tubing in inventory	800 metres
Sets of sails in inventory	210 sets

(a) Draw up a worksheet and enter the transactions outlined in the example above.

(b) Draw up a statement of financial position, income statement and cash flow statement for Stern.

(c) Comment on the situation as revealed by the statement of financial position, income statement and cash flow statement of Stern.

7 Spain has recently gone into business manufacturing office chairs. Details of the transactions for the first month are given below.

Day 1   Opened a bank account and paid in £10 000 of own money. Purchased machinery to make the chairs at a cost of £4000 paid for immediately.
Rented factory space at a rental of £200 per month and paid one month's rent in advance.
Bought office equipment at a cost of £400 and paid immediately.

Day 2   Bought 1000 metres of steel tubing at a price of £50 per 100 metres and paid for this immediately.

Day 3   Purchased 250 packs of end fittings for £125, together with a quantity of screws costing £40. Both of these purchases were paid for immediately.

Day 4   Purchased 150 sets of ready-cut seat bases and backrests at a price of £5 per set, and paid for them.

Day 5   Bought upholstery materials and cloth for seat covers for £400 and paid immediately.

Day 8   Received an order for 20 chairs at £50 each together with accompanying cheque.

Day 9   Paid the cheque into the bank and commenced manufacture of the chairs.

Day 14 Completed manufacture of the chairs for order and despatched these to the customer, paying £40 total delivery charges.

At this stage it was possible to do some preliminary calculations relating to the manufacture of the chairs. These showed that each chair required the following:

Labour manufacturing,	2 hours per frame
Upholstering seats and backrests	30 minutes per set
Assembling chairs	30 minutes per chair
Materials per chair	4 metres of metal tubing
	one pack of end fittings
	one set of seat/backrest
	quantity of upholstery materials etc.

Day 15 Received an order for another 200 chairs at a price of £50 each. Payment was to be on a cash-on-delivery basis.

Day 15 Commenced work on the new order.

Day 26 Purchased and paid for another 100 sets of seats and backrests. However, the price per set had gone up to £6.

Day 30 Paid himself wages for the month of £800 calculated on the basis of £200 per week for a 40-hour week.

The position at the end of the month was established as follows.

Completed chairs ready for delivery	20
Manufactured frames	10

In addition there was in inventory

800 metres of steel tubing
210 packs of end fitting
210 seat and backrest sets
half the screws and upholstery materials.

(a) Draw up a worksheet for Spain and enter the above transactions.
(b) Draw up a statement of financial position at the end of the month and an income statement and cash flow
     statement for the month for Spain.
(c) Discuss the performance of Spain's business for the period.

ANSWER TO ACTIVITY 6.10

Description	Cash	Frames	Wheels	Wages	Work in progress		Equity	Revenue & expenses
			Assets			=	Equity + liabilities	
Balance	1 000						1 000	
Frames	−2 000	2 000						
Wheels	−1 200		1 200					
Wages	−320			320				
Rent	−500							−500
Sales	4 900							4 900
Frames		−1 400						−1 400
Wheels			−700					−700
Wages				−280				−280
Frames		−200			200			
Wheels			−100		100			
Wages				−25	25			
Balance	**1 880**	**400**	**400**	**15**	**325**		**1 000**	**2 020**
Wages				−15				−15
Balance	**1 880**	**400**	**400**	**0**	**325**		**1 000**	**2 005**

As you will have seen when undertaking this activity the spreadsheet entries follow the flow of the component parts through the assembly to work in progress or completed goods which are sold. When recording
every transaction you should have asked yourself questions about the nature of the transaction: is it revenue, is there a future benefit, has the benefit been used during the period? You will notice that in our worksheet having allocated the wages to bicycles sold and to those in the process of assembly the wages
column ends with a balance of £15 still in it. Given our assumptions this cannot be attributed either to the
cost of the bicycles or to the work in progress; nor is it an asset at the end of the year as there is no identifiable future benefit. It is therefore treated in the same way as the showroom rent, i.e. as a period expense,
and charged to the income statement. From a management accounting viewpoint this would be seen as a
variation from our budget or plan. We will discuss budgets in more detail in Chapter 19.

CHAPTER 7
AMOUNTS RECEIVABLE
AND AMOUNTS
PAYABLE

LEARNING OUTCOMES

By the end of this chapter you will:

- Be able to deal with trade payables and receivables on the worksheet.

- Understand their impact on the statement of financial position, income statement and cash flow statement.

- Understand why prepayments exist and how to deal with them.

- Understand what accruals are and the need to create them in order to fairly represent the activities of an enterprise during an accounting period.

- Appreciate the differences and similarities between trade receivables, payables, accruals and prepayments.

The progression from a simple cash-based business is taken one stage further in this chapter, where sales on credit and purchases on credit are discussed. The matching principle is explained and the treatment of amounts receivable, sometimes referred to as debtors, and amounts payable, sometimes referred to as creditors are explored in some detail.

In all the examples we have dealt with so far, and indeed in all our discussions, we have always assumed that all transactions are on a cash basis. As we pointed out in Chapter 3, this is unlikely to be the case. Therefore we need to consider how we deal with the situation where a business buys goods from its suppliers on credit terms and supplies goods to customers on credit terms. We need to consider how to deal with the situation where a business has to pay for goods or services in advance, for example insurances, or when it pays after receiving the goods or services, as would be the case with most raw materials and with services such as electricity and telephones.

As these transactions directly affect both the statement of financial position and the income statement, we need a system that deals with them in an appropriate way to ensure that expenses are matched with revenue and that the statement of financial position reflects the position at the reporting date. In other words the system must ensure that the statement of financial position shows the assets held at the reporting date and the amounts owed at that date. The income statement must also record the actual sales for the period and the expenses related to those sales. Not to do so would contravene the matching and realization principles and the accounts would merely reflect the timing of cash receipts and payments rather than the economic substance of the transactions that the business has engaged in during the period. Such a system of accounting is known as accrual accounting. In this chapter we shall examine situations in which the economic substance of the transaction does not occur at the same time as the cash flow and the way in which accrual accounting deals with these situations. In particular we shall look at how it deals with amounts receivable which includes amounts receivable from customers, bad debts and dealing with services for which we have paid in advance which are commonly referred to as prepayments. We shall also discuss amounts owing to suppliers for supplies of goods and services.

TRADE RECEIVABLES AND PREPAYMENTS

In the UK trade receivables were generally referred to as debtors whilst in the American accounting literature, they are often frequently referred to as 'amounts receivable'. The International Accounting Standards use the term 'trade receivables' and you should be aware that all these terms describe the same thing, i.e. money owed to the business for the supply of goods or services. We will use the term trade receivables as it is more descriptive than debtors and its meaning is more transparent. As we say in Key Concept 7.1, trade receivables arise when a business has sold goods for which payment is not received at the point of sale. In this situation we need to recognize the revenue from the sales even though the cash has not yet been received. If, however, we simply entered the sales on the worksheet the accounts would not balance as there would only be one side to the entry. This is in conflict with the principle of duality. We cannot use the cash account for the other side of the transaction as no cash has been received. However, we do have an asset, as we have a right to a future benefit in the form of cash. The way in which accrual accounting solves the problem is to open a column, or account, for this asset which we call 'trade receivables'. Normally this money is received well within a year and therefore you will generally find this asset classified under current assets.

KEY CONCEPT 7.1

Trade receivables

Trade receivables arise when a business sells goods or services to a third party on credit terms, i.e. when goods or services are sold on the understanding that payment will be received at a later date.

PREPAYMENTS

Prepayments or prepaids, as the names imply, are payments in advance. They often arise in respect of such services as insurance, road tax, etc. The payments must relate to the use of such services by the business and not by the owner in a personal capacity, a distinction sometimes difficult to establish in the case of small businesses. The proportion of the payment that relates to benefits still unexpired at the year end will be shown as a current asset in the statement of financial position of the business. Prepayments therefore differ from other receivables in that they relate to payments made by the business rather than to revenue earned from sales. Also, the future benefit will be in a form other than cash receipts.

CASE STUDY 7.1

Rolls Royce plc

Extract from note to accounts for the year to 31 December 2008

11 Trade and other receivables

	2008 £m	2007 £m
Trade receivables	**1 421**	889
Amounts recoverable on contracts	**1 448**	904
Amounts owed by joint ventures	**451**	300
Other receivables	**404**	315
Prepayments and accrued income	**205**	177
	3 929	2 585

Commentary

As you will see from the extract above Rolls Royce plc has a number of different types of receivables and prepayments including trade receivables, amounts owed to them on long-term contracts, which may take longer to collect, amounts owed by members of joint ventures which may be subject to different contractual arrangements, other receivables and prepayments.

We can now look at an example of trade receivables and prepayments.

EXAMPLE 7.1

We assume a business, Pitco, has the following transactions for the period from 1 January to 31 March.

Sales for cash	£6 000
Sales on credit	£4 000
Cash received from credit sales	£3 000
Rent for the quarter, paid 1 January	£ 500
Insurance, year to 31 December, paid 1 January	£1 200

We can see that the revenue consists of the sales for cash and the sales on credit. Of the latter we can calculate that there is still £1000 which has not been received, i.e. £4000 less the £3000 received. This £1000 should be shown as a trade receivable at 31 March, as the benefit has yet to be received. As far as the payments are concerned, the rent is clearly an expense of the quarter as all the benefit from using the premises for the quarter has expired. The insurance premiums paid are for the whole year and so we have to decide what benefit has been used up and what is a future benefit. In this case we have used up three out of the 12 months' benefit and so we have an expense of £300 and a prepayment of £900.

If we put the above information onto a worksheet this will appear as follows.

Pitco worksheet version 1

	Assets			=	Equity + Liabilities	
	Cash	**Trade receivables**	**Prepaids**		**Owner's equity**	**Revenue & expenses**
Cash sales	6 000					6 000
Credit sales		4 000				4 000
Cash from sales	3 000	−3 000				
Rent	−500					−500
Insurance	−1 200		900			−300
Balance	**7 300**	**1 000**	**900**		**0**	**9 200**

You will note that in our worksheet we have shown the credit sales as revenue and recorded at the same time an asset of £4000. This asset was subsequently reduced by the cash received of £3000. You may also have noticed that we charged the rent straight away as an expense and split the insurance premium paid between the prepaid column and the expenses.

An alternative approach would have been to enter both the rent and the insurance as prepayments when they were paid on 1 January and then to consider at 31 March whether they were still assets. This we would do by answering the question: *is there a future benefit?* If we had adopted that approach our worksheet would appear as follows.

Pitco worksheet version 2

	Assets			=	Equity + Liabilities	
	Cash	**Trade receivables**	**Prepaids**		**Owner's equity**	**Revenue & expenses**
Cash sales	6 000					6 000
Credit sales		4 000				4 000
Cash from sales	3 000	−3 000				

(Continued)

		Assets		=	Equity + Liabilities	
	Cash	Trade receivables	Prepaids		Owner's equity	Revenue & expenses
Rent	−500		500			
Insurance	−1 200		1 200			
Balance	**7 300**	**1 000**	**1 700**		**0**	**10 000**
Rent expense			−500			−500
Insurance expense			−300			−300
Final balance	**7 300**	**1 000**	**900**		**0**	**9 200**

As you can see, the end result is the same. The advantage that this presentation has is that it shows clearly what we have done, which always helps in case an error is made. The choice of which presentation to use is personal but we recommend that you use the latter and that you get into the habit of reviewing all the balances, i.e. whether they are still assets or liabilities, before finally extracting a statement of financial position, income and cash flow statement. The advantages of this approach will become more obvious as we proceed through this chapter and the next.

ACTIVITY 7.1

Look at the bank/cash column and the revenue and expenses column. You will note that the balances are different. Can you explain why this is the case?

The business paid out £1200 for insurance of which only £300 related to the accounting period so the £900 prepayment is part of the difference. The other part of the difference is the sales of £1000 which have been recognized for which payment had not been received at the end of the accounting period. These two items together make up the £1900 difference between the profit of £9200 and the cash/bank increase of £7300.

KEY CONCEPT 7.2

Prepayments

Prepayments arise when the business has paid for a service in advance of using it. The key question that must be considered when a payment is made is whether the benefit has been used up or whether there is still some future benefit to be obtained. If there is a future benefit to the business we have an asset; if there is no future benefit we have an expense. The expense must then be matched with the revenue earned in the period in question.

BAD DEBTS

Before leaving the question of trade receivables and prepayments let us consider how we would deal with a situation where, when we come to the end of the quarter and review the balances, we find that some of the amounts owed by customers are not likely to be collectable.

EXAMPLE 7.1 (Continued)

Of the £1000 Pitco is showing as trade receivables, it is likely to receive only £800 because a customer who owed £200 has left the country and is very unlikely to pay up. In this situation the £200 is not an asset as any future benefit expired when our customer skipped the country.

The first question that arises is whether it was a genuine sale. In other words, at the time of making the sale were we reasonably certain that we would receive payment. If the answer is yes, then we have correctly recognized the revenue and the asset. What needs to be done is to deal with the situation that has arisen as a result of later events. This is done by reducing the amount shown as receivables by £200 and charging the £200 as an expense of the period – the entry is described as a bad debt. The worksheet would now appear as follows.

Pitco worksheet version 3

| | Assets | | | = | Equity + Liabilities | |
	Cash	Trade receivables	Prepaids		Owner's equity	Revenue & expenses
Cash sales	6 000					6 000
Credit sales		4 000				4 000
Cash from sales	3 000	−3 000				
Rent	−500		500			
Insurance	−1 200		1 200			
Balance	**7 300**	**1 000**	**1 700**		**0**	**10 000**
Rent expense			−500			−500
Insurance expense			−300			−300
Bad debt		−200				−200
Final balance	**7 300**	**800**	**900**		**0**	**9 000**

It should be noted that the bottom line now represents assets which have a future benefit at least equal to the amount shown.

An example of the problems caused by uncertainty over whether a debt is collectable or not is shown in Case Study 7.2.

CASE STUDY 7.2

Allied Irish Bank plc and Royal Bank of Scotland Group plc

Commentary

The accounts of most companies do not explicitly disclose amounts written off for bad debts. Instead they show the figure of debtors after any bad debts have been taken off. However, in the case of banks this is not the case although finding the figures is no longer as easy as it was as what was clearly labelled provision for bad and doubtful debts, as shown in the extract from Royal Bank of Scotland in 2003 below, is now labelled provisions for impairments in loans and receivables as shown in the Allied Irish Bank extract.

Royal Bank of Scotland Group plc

13 Provision for bad and doubtful debts

	2003 Specific £m	2003 General £m	2002 Specific £m	2002 General £m
At 1 January	3 330	597	3 039	614
Currency translation and other adjustments	−23	−39	−45	−17
Acquisition of subsidiary	44	6	23	–
Amounts written off	−1 519	–	−1 036	–
Recoveries of amounts written off in previous periods	72	–	63	–
Charge to profit and loss account	1 459	2	1 286	–
At 31 December	3 363	566	3 330	597

Allied Irish Bank plc – Annual report 2008

Extracts from the information presented on impairments to loans and receivables in the 2008 Annual Report.

Movements in provision for impairment of loans and receivables

	2008 € m	2007 € m	2006 € m
Total provisions at start of period	744	707	676
Currency translation	−117	−8	−1
Recoveries of previous charge offs	11	13	10
Amounts charged off	−166	−74	−96
Net provision movement	1 833	119	128

(Continued)

	2008 € m	2007 € m	2006 € m
Ireland	1 348	111	73
United Kingdom	363	−1	42
United States of America	12		−1
Poland	101	9	16
Rest of world	9		−2
Recoveries of previous provisions	−11	−13	−10
Total provisions at end of period	**2 294**	**744**	**707**
Provisions at end of period			
Specific	1 148	526	518
General	1 146	218	189
	2 294	**744**	**707**
Amounts include			
Loans and advances to banks	2	2	2
Loans and advances to customers	2 292	742	705
	2 294	**744**	**707**

If you look carefully at the two extracts you will see that they relate to the same thing and that the provision is split between a general provision and a specific provision. The difference between these two is that the specific provision relates to amounts of loans and advances the bank has clearly identified as unlikely to be repaid. The general provision on the other hand is simply an estimate of the proportion of the remainder of the loans and advances that may not be repaid. It is worth noting the trebling of these provisions in 2008 for Allied Irish Bank plc – a clear sign of the crisis that was hitting the banking industry throughout the world.

ACTIVITY 7.2

Looking at Case Study 7.2 you can see that the banks identified specific bad debts and 'general' provisions which are estimates of monies they do not think they will collect in the future. If you were in business what criteria might you use to decide whether a customer is likely to pay or not?

You might look at past track record, how financially sound they are, e.g. public sector bodies are unlikely not to pay although they are often slow payers, or you might get a rating from a credit agency.

Having looked at how receivables and prepayments are dealt with, we can now consider how to deal with the situation in which we receive goods or services before paying for them.

TRADE PAYABLES AND ACCRUALS

When an established business buys goods it rarely pays cash. In fact it is normally only when a business is just starting, or in exceptional cases, that trade credit is not given. The question we have to address is how a business would deal with goods supplied on credit when it may have used them or sold them before it has to pay the supplier. However, before we deal with that question we need to explain the difference between trade payables, other payables and accruals.

Trade payables and indeed other payables, as the names imply, arise when goods or services are supplied to an enterprise for which an invoice is subsequently received and for which no payment has been made at the date of receipt of the goods or services. As we have already said, most established businesses will receive most of their raw materials and components on the basis that payment is due within a certain time period after delivery. At the date at which we draw up a statement of financial position, therefore, we need to acknowledge that there are amounts owing (liabilities) in respect of these supplies.

ACCRUALS

Accruals are in some ways similar to payables in that they relate to amounts due for goods or services already supplied to the enterprise. They differ not because of the nature of the transaction but because, at the time of drawing up the statement of financial position, the amounts involved are not known with certainty. This is usually due to the fact that the invoice for the goods has not been received. A common example of a situation where this arises is telephone bills which are always issued in arrears; other examples are electricity and gas bills. The bills for these are generally received after the end of the quarter to which they relate. In these situations, therefore, all we can do is to estimate what we think is owed for the service the business has used during the period. This estimate may be based on the last quarter or the previous year or on some other basis which the business considers more accurate. An example may help to clarify the treatment of payables and accruals and the differences between the two.

KEY CONCEPT 7.3

Payables and accruals

Payables are amounts owing at a point in time, the amounts of which are known.

Accruals are amounts owing at a point in time, although the precise amount owed is not known with certainty.

EXAMPLE 7.2

For the year to 31 December 201X Archie & Co. had the following transactions:

1 Paid £6000 of Archie's own money into a business bank account together with £5000 borrowed from a friend.
2 Bought 1000 items from a supplier for £12 000.
3 Paid the electricity bills for lighting and heating for three quarters, amounting to £1500.
4 Paid supplier £9000 for some of the items purchased.

If we enter the above transactions on a worksheet and explain how they are dealt with, we can then deal with the other transactions of Archie's business. Our worksheet for the first transactions will look like this.

(Continued)

Archie's worksheet version 1

	Assets		=	Equity + Liabilities			
	Bank	Inventory		Equity	Revenue & expenses	Loan	Trade payables
Item 1	6 000			6 000			
	5 000					5 000	
Item 2		12 000					12 000
Item 3	−1 500				−1 500		
Item 4	−9 000						−9 000
Balance	**500**	**12 000**		**6 000**	**−1 500**	**5 000**	**3 000**

Let us examine each of the transactions in turn.

Item 1

By now we are all familiar with transactions of this type which create an asset and a corresponding liability in the form of money owing either to the owner or to some third party.

Item 2

This is slightly different from the previous examples which have dealt with the purchase of inventory. Up to now we have assumed that the inventory was paid for when we received it. In this case, however, we are only told that during the year we bought items for £12 000. We have no idea, at present, how much we have actually paid out in respect of these items or how much Archie still owes. Therefore we show that he owes money for all the items and open up a column for our trade payables and show £12 000 in that column.

Item 3

Once again this is a familiar item as we receive a bill which is paid for in cash. However, it should be borne in mind that we have in fact only paid for three quarters whereas we have consumed a year's supply of electricity. We therefore need to make some provision for the other quarter. A safe estimate could be that the fourth quarter's bill would be the same as the other quarters, i.e. approximately £500. It may of course turn out to be more or less. We are not attempting 100% accuracy; we just need to give a reasonable picture of the situation.

Item 4

We now know that, of the £12 000 we owe to suppliers, £9000 was paid in the year. We therefore need to reduce our cash by that amount and reduce the trade payables by the same amount.

Let us now return to the question of the electricity bill. We said that we need to make an accrual which we estimated to be £500. Let us see how this affects our worksheet using the balances from the worksheet above.

Archie's worksheet version 2

	Assets		=	Equity + Liabilities				
	Bank	Inventory		Equity	Revenue & expenses	Loan	Trade payables	Accruals
Item 1	6 000			6 000				
	5 000					5 000		
Item 2		12 000					12 000	
Item 3	−1 500				−1 500			

(Continued)

	Assets		=	Equity + Liabilities				
	Bank	**Inventory**		**Equity**	**Revenue & expenses**	**Loan**	**Trade payables**	**Accruals**
Item 4	−9 000						−9 000	
Balance	**500**	**12 000**		**6 000**	**−1 500**	**5 000**	**3 000**	**0**
Accruals					−500			500
Balance	**500**	**12 000**		**6 000**	**−2 000**	**5 000**	**3 000**	**500**

As we can see, an additional column is opened for the accrual, with a corresponding entry in the expenses. The statement of financial position still balances and it now gives a truer picture of the goods we own and the amounts we owe.

Before leaving the subject of receivables and payables here are some more transactions for Archie & Co. which you should try to work through yourself and then compare your answer with the answer shown below.

EXAMPLE 7.2 *(Continued)*

ACTIVITY 7.3

Archie & Co's other transactions in the year to 31 December 201X were as follows.

Item 5   Paid loan interest of £300 in respect of the half year to 30 June 201X.
Item 6   Sold 800 items for £40 000, all on credit.
Item 7   Received £34 000 from customers in respect of sales.
Item 8   Paid £1500 rent for five quarters as rent of the premises is due quarterly in advance.

Note: our answer starts with the balances from Archie's worksheet version 1 and that, for the purposes of presentation, it combines the trade receivables and prepayments in one column and the trade payables and accruals in one column.

(Continued)

ACTIVITY 7.4

Before moving on remember to check that all the assets represent the future benefits.

When we review the position at the year end as shown on our worksheet we find that the asset 'prepaids', included in the receivables and prepaids column is no longer going to give us a future benefit of £1500 as four quarters' rent relate to the year just gone and therefore the benefit has been used. We should also realize that our inventory figure represents 1000 items at £12 each and that, of those, 800 items were sold; therefore our cost of sales should be £9600. Our worksheet will now be as follows.

Archie's worksheet version 3

	Assets			=	Equity + Liabilities			
	Bank	**Inventory**	**Trade receivables & prepaids**		**Equity**	**Revenue & expenses**	**Loan**	**Trade payables & accruals**
Item 1	6 000				6 000			
	5 000						5 000	
Item 2		12 000						12 000
Item 3	−1 500					−1 500		
Item 4	−9 000							−9 000
Balance	500	12 000	0		6 000	−1 500	5 000	3 000
Accruals						−500		500
Balance	**500**	**12 000**	**0**		**6 000**	**−2 000**	**5 000**	**3 500**
Item 5	−300					−300		
Item 6			40 000			40 000		
Item 7	34 000		−34 000					
Item 8	−1 500		1 500					
Balance	**32 700**	**12 000**	**7 500**		**6 000**	**37 700**	**5 000**	**3 500**

ACTIVITY 7.5

Now do the same for the liabilities.

If we do this we find that the interest paid is only for the first half of the year and yet we have had the benefit of the loan for the full year; we therefore need to make a provision or accrual for a further £300. The opening balance figures are taken from the previous closing balance figures on Archie's worksheet, version 3 above.

(Continued)

Archie's worksheet version 4

	Assets			=	Equity + Liabilities			
	Bank	**Inventory**	**Trade receivables & prepaids**		**Equity**	**Revenue & expenses**	**Loan**	**Trade payables & accruals**
Balance	32 700	12 000	7 500		6 000	37 700	5 000	3 500
Rent			−1 200			−1 200		
Cost of sales		−9 600				−9 600		
Interest						−300		300
Balance	32 700	2 400	6 300		6 000	26 600	5 000	3 800

We can now extract the statement of financial position, income statement and cash flow statement for the first year of Archie's business.

Statement of financial position of Archie & Co at 31 December 201X

Current assets	
Cash at bank	32 700
Trade and other receivables	6 300
Inventory	2 400
Total assets	41 400
Current liabilities	
Trade and other payables	3 800
	3 800
Non current liabilities	
Loan	5 000
	5 000
Total liabilities	8 800
Owners equity	6 000
Profit	26 600
Total equity	32 600
Total liabilities and equity	41 400

Income statement of Archie & Co for the year to 31 December 201X

	£	£
Sales		40 000
Cost of goods sold		9 600
Gross profit		39 700
Electricity	2 000	
Loan Interest	600	
Rent	1 200	3 800
Net profit		26 600

(Continued)

Cash flow statement of Archie & Co for the year to 31 December 201X

Cash inflows	
Cash from operations	21 700
Equity	6 000
Loan	5 000
	32 700
Cash outflows	0
Net cash inflow	32 700
Balance at start	0
Balance at end	32 700
Profit	26 600
Less:	
Increase in inventory	2 400
Increase in receivables	6 300
	17 900
Add:	
Increase in payables	3 800
Cash inflow from operations	21 700

Before we move on to examine what happens in the second year of Archie's business it is worth briefly looking at the difference between net cash flow and net profit. You will see from a comparison of the items in the income statement and those in the cash flow statement that the latter contains items that bear no relationship to revenue and expenses, for example the injection of the owner's equity and the loan. You may also notice that even if we strip these items out the net cash inflow is £21 700 compared to the net profit of £26 600. Let us start by looking at cash inflows. Apart from the loan and equity these come from revenue, however the revenue included in the calculation of net profit was £40 000 and of that only £34 000 was received so we would expect, in the absence of any similar items that the cash flow would be £6000 less than the net profit which is £20 600. In fact it is greater than that because of the effect of other items.

Some of this difference is attributable to changes in the inventory level which we discussed in Chapter 6 and the rest can be attributed to changes in the level of payables, prepayments and accruals. Before getting in to a full discussion of what is causing the differences, it is worth just reminding yourselves how the cost of sales is calculated as it will help you when thinking about how the cash flow figure and profit figure is reconciled.

Calculation of cost of sales

[Opening inventory + Purchases] − Closing inventory = Cost of goods sold
£0 +£12 000 −£2 400 = £9 600

We can see here that the cost of sales is made up of three components: the opening inventory, the purchases and the closing inventory. In Chapter 6 we showed that part of the reconciliation of the net profit to the net cash

(Continued)

flow related to the change in inventory levels. So looking first at the change in the inventory level we can see that at the start of the year we had no inventory and at the end of the year we had £2400 in inventory so, assuming we had paid for everything we would expect our cash flow to be £2400 less than the net profit as, using the matching principle, we only charge as expenses the costs of the goods actually sold. This, however, does not explain the whole of the difference. If we look at what happens with our purchases we find that although we had bought £12 000 worth of goods we in fact only paid for £9000 of them so we would expect our cash flow to be higher by £3000. So, if we summarize the effects we have identified to date we have:

	Cash flow statement	Income statement
Starting balance	21 700	26 600
Sales revenue not received (receivables)	+6 000	−6 000
Cash paid for purchases not sold (Inventory)	+2 400	−2 400
Suppliers not paid (Payables)	−3 000	3 000
Balance	27 100	21 200

As you can see from the reconciliation above depending on whether you start with the cash flow or income statement the effects are opposite. You will also have noticed that we have not yet reconciled the two statements. This is because we have not dealt with the impact of prepayments where we pay out the full amount for five quarters so the cash outflow was £1500 but only £1200 of that related to this year and as such the expense charge was £300 less than the impact on cash. The converse is true in the case of accruals as here we charge the full expense even though we have not paid out any cash. In this case the accruals were £800. Thus the full reconciliation is as set out below.

	Cash flow statement	Income statement
Starting balance	21 700	26 600
Sales revenue not received (receivables)	+6 000	−6 000
Cash paid for purchases not sold (Inventory)	+2 400	−2 400
Suppliers not paid (Payables)	−3 000	3 000
Rent paid in advance	+300	−300
Accruals not yet paid	−800	800
Ending balance	26 600	21 700

Now we can see that if we start with the net profit figure and reduce it by increases in inventory and amounts receivable either in cash or other benefits (prepayments) then add any increases in amounts payable, whether invoiced or accrued, we arrive at the increase in the cash flow attributable to revenue and expense related items.

ACTIVITY 7.6

Although this reconciliation may seem complex at this point it is worth spending some time thinking about what has happened and looking back to see the impacts on the cash/bank column and the revenue expenses column on the worksheet.

We will be returning to the subject of cash flows in more detail in Chapter 10.

Before we leave the subject of payables and receivable we will return to the example of Archie and demonstrate what happens in a dynamic business by tracing through what happens in the second year of the business.

EXAMPLE 7.2 *(Continued)*

For the year to 31 December 201Y Archie & Co's transactions were as follows.

1 Bought 1000 items on credit for £12 000.

2 Paid suppliers £14 000.

3 Paid electricity bill of £2300 for last year and three quarters of 201X.

4 Paid loan interest of £600.

5 Sold 1000 items on credit terms for £50 000.

6 Received £46 000 from customers.

7 Paid rent of £1200.

We should briefly discuss some of these items before we enter them on a worksheet.

Let us consider the payments to suppliers and the payment for electricity. In neither of these cases do we know exactly which parts of the payments relate to this year and which to last year. In the former case it does not really matter and in the latter case it is reasonable to assume that £500 relates to last year and £1800 to the first three quarters of this year. As with last year we have to make an estimate of the amount due in respect of the last quarter. Based on the same quarter of the previous year we would estimate £500 but this is clearly too low as, based on the three quarters this year, electricity is now costing £600 a quarter. Therefore a reasonable estimate would be £600.

The loan interest is similar to the situation just dealt with except that in this case there is more certainty that £300 relates to the previous year and £300 to this year. Therefore we need to make an adjustment in respect of the £300 we still owe for the current year.

As far as the cost of sales is concerned there is no real problem as prices have remained constant and we have bought and sold 1000 items in the year.

The situation with trade receivables is the same as for trade payables. We cannot identify the individual payments, but in this particular example it does not make any difference.

Finally, the annual rent is £1200, payable in advance. As the first quarter was paid for last year, this payment relates to three quarters of the current year and one quarter of next year.

After entering these transactions the worksheet should look something like the one below. It is possible to take some short-cuts and get the same answer but you should bear in mind that such short-cuts can lead to errors.

(Continued)

Archie's worksheet 201Y

	Assets			=	Equity + Liabilities			
	Bank	**Inventory**	**Trade receivables & prepaids**		**Equity**	**Revenue & expenses**	**Loan**	**Trade payables & accruals**
Balance	**32 700**	**2 400**	**6 300**		**6 000**	**26 600**	**5 000**	**3 800**
Item 1		12 000						12 000
Item 2	−14 000							−14 000
Item 3	−2 300					−1 800		−500
Item 4	−600					−300		−300
Item 5			50 000			50 000		
Item 6	46 000		−46 000					
Item 7	−1 200		300			−900		
Balance	**60 600**	**14 400**	**10 600**		**6 000**	**73 600**	**5 000**	**1 000**
Cost of sales		−12 000				−12 000		
Rent			−300			−300		
Electricity						−600		600
Interest						−300		300
Balance	**60 600**	**2 400**	**10 300**		**6 000**	**60 400**	**5 000**	**1 900**

It is important to recognize that in the case of accruals and prepayments what appears as a prepayment at the end of one period will cease to be an asset and will become an expense in the next period. Similarly amounts shown as accruals at the end of one period will be paid in the next period and cease to be liabilities. It is also important to recognize that at the end of each accounting period you need to think carefully about whether there are any prepayments made or accruals to be set up for services or goods received for which no invoice has been received by the end of the accounting period.

CASE STUDY 7.3

Unilever plc

Extract from the notes to the accounts of Unilever plc for the year ended
31 December 2008

18 Trade payables and other liabilities

	€ million	€ million
Trade and other payables	2008	2007
Due within one year		
Trade payables	3 873	3 690
Accruals	2 720	2 970
Social security and sundry taxes	341	374
Others	890	983
	7 824	8 017
Due after more than one year		
Accruals	102	138
Others	73	66
	175	204
Total trade payables and other liabilities	7 999	8 221

The amounts shown above do not include any creditors due after more than five years. Trade payables and other liabilities are valued at historic cost, which where appropriate approximates their amortised cost.

Commentary

The extract from the notes of Unilever plc illustrates the kind of items we have been concerned with in this chapter. Note that the accruals are identified separately and they are significant amounts making up over one third of the total liabilities included in the statement of financial position under this heading. It is also worth noting the split between current and non-current, i.e. due after more than one year.

SUMMARY

In this chapter we have dealt with the question of how accruals accounting deals with the problem that, if accounts were prepared on the basis of cash flows, the matching principle would be contravened. We have shown how sales on credit are included as revenue and how the amounts not received at the end of the year are dealt with. These are called receivables and are shown as current assets as they will provide the business with a future benefit. We have also examined the way in which payments in advance can be dealt with in order that expenses are matched against revenue. In addition we have shown how accrual accounting allows bad debts, where the future benefit has expired, to be dealt with. From the point of view of goods supplied to the business we have seen how payables that are outstanding are dealt with and how accruals arise. The principle that is common to all these items is that the accounts should comply with the matching principle. The statement of financial position should record the rights to future benefits and what the business owes at a particular point in time and the income statement should record the revenue earned in the period matched with the expenses associated with earning that revenue.

REVIEW QUESTIONS

(✓ indicates answers are available in Appendix A)

✓ **1** In your own words describe what trade payables are and when they arise.

✓ **2** Explain the difference between trade payables and accruals.

✓ **3** Why are receivables and prepayments classified as current assets?

4 When do prepayments arise and how do they differ from accruals?

5 Explain the matching principle.

6 Why is it necessary to identify receivables and payables?

7 How do receivables affect the income statement?

8 What items would you include when reconciling the profit and the operating cash flow?

PROBLEMS FOR DISCUSSION AND ANALYSIS

(✓ indicates answers are available in Appendix A)

✓ **1** In each of the following situations describe the way that the transaction would be dealt with in the accounts of the business and identify, where appropriate, the effect on the statement of financial position, income statement and on cash flows.

    (a) Purchase of raw materials on credit terms.

    (b) Purchase of production machines for cash.

    (c) Receipts from customers in respect of credit sales.

    (d) Repayment of a loan.

    (e) Payment in respect of research expenditure.

    (f) Sale of goods on credit.

    (g) Payment to a supplier in respect of goods already delivered.

    (h) Payment of wages to clerical workers.

    (i) Payment of wages to production workers.

    (j) Payment of loan interest.

    (k) Payment of an electricity bill from last year.

    (l) Payment of rent quarterly in advance.

    (m) Withdrawal of cash from the business by the owner.

    (n) Receipt of cash from the owner.

    (o) Withdrawal of goods from inventory for personal use by the owner.

    (p) A customer going into liquidation owing money.

2 On 1 June 201X, Jane an ex-university lecturer went into business running short courses for accountancy firms. To start the business she opened a business bank account under the name Abacus & Co and paid £12 000 into the account as capital for the new business. The transactions during the first month were as follows.

    June

    (a) Bought second-hand car for £3000 and paid cash.

    (b) Bought two hundred study manuals from BCP for £2000 and negotiated one month credit terms. These are due to be paid for on 14 July.

    (c) Rented an office in a serviced office building at a monthly rental of £200 and paid three months rent up front.

(d) The office came with pooled secretarial, receptionist and telephone answering service which was billed on the last day of the month based on usage. At the end of the month she received a bill from Bolton Business Centre for £500 which was payable within 30 days.

(e) Arranged with a local design and PR company for the printing and distribution of leaflets advertising her courses to the local accountancy firms. The price agreed was £2000 payable 30 days from receipt of the invoice which arrived on the 29 June.

(f) Delivered two short courses to a mix of students some of whom were paying themselves and some from local firms. Her terms were, as far as possible to get the money up front from the individuals and to let the firms have a month to pay. The detail in respect of these courses is given below.

Customer	Amount	Status
Anna, Barry, Jenny, Sue and Brian	£1 000	Paid
Colin	£ 200	£100 received. £100 still due – being chased.
Patrick	£ 200	All still due – moved address no new address known.
Hopper & Co.	£3 000	One months credit given
Garlic, Ginger & Chives	£2 000	One months credit given

(g) Received an invoice from the University in respect of the lecture rooms used of £1100.

(h) Paid the road tax and insurance for the car for the next 12 months amounting to £660.

(i) At the end of the month she still had 168 study manuals left for future courses. Unfortunately because of a leak in the area where these were being stored two boxes, each containing 20 manuals, had become waterlogged and were only fit for throwing away.

Required

(a) Discuss how each transaction should be treated.

(b) Discuss what if any accruals and prepayments are or should be involved.

(c) Draw up a worksheet, statement of financial position, income statement and cash flow statement.

3 Looking back to Example 7.2 produce an income statement and cash flow statement for 201Y and a statement of financial position at 31 December 201Y.

4 On 1 May 201X Barbara paid £3000 into a business bank account as capital for her new business, which she called Barbie's Bikes. The transactions during May were as follows.

May 3	Bought van for £800 cash.
6	Bought goods on credit from Drake for £700.
8	Paid rent of £120 for the quarter.
14	Bought goods on credit from Gander for £300.
16	Made cash sales of £200.
18	Made credit sales of £400 to Bill's Bikes.
21	Paid the garage account of £20 for petrol and oil.
23	Sold more goods on credit to Swans for £600.
24	Paid Drake £682 after taking advantage of a 2.5% discount for prompt payment.
30	Received £360 from the liquidator of Bill's Bikes and was advised that no more would be forthcoming.
31	Paid monthly salary to shop assistant of £400. Received back from Swans goods with an invoice price of £80 which they had not ordered.

Other information: No inventory count was done at the end of the month but all goods were sold at a price based on the cost price plus one-third.

(a) Discuss how each transaction should be treated.

(b) Discuss what if any accruals and prepayments are or should be involved.

(c) Draw up a worksheet, statement of financial position, income statement and cash flow statement.

CHAPTER 8
NON-CURRENT ASSETS, FIXED ASSETS AND DEPRECIATION

LEARNING OUTCOMES

By the end of this chapter you will have:

- Understood the differences between current and non-current assets.

- Understood the reasons for depreciating fixed assets.

- Understood the most commonly used methods for depreciating assets.

- Understood the effects of depreciation on the statement of financial position.

- Understood the impact of depreciation on the income statement and the cash flow statement and why these effects are different.

- Understood how gains and losses on the sale of fixed assets arise and their impact on the income statement and cash flow statement and why the impacts differ.

- Reinforced your understanding of the differences between cash flows and profits or losses.

Just as the previous chapters extended the simple cash-based system to take into account current assets and current liabilities, this chapter takes the model one stage further and explores assets with longer lives: non-current assets. The problems in arriving at the true cost of these assets are discussed together with the issues of matching the benefits used up in an accounting period with the revenue earned. Various alternative methods of matching benefits used up via depreciation are explored and their limitations illustrated.

In Chapter 3, we discussed the definitions of assets and of current and non-current assets using the definitions included in the International Standards. The underlying distinction that we made between assets and expenses is that an asset relates to present or future benefits whereas an expense relates to past or expired benefits. Thus, we have goods held at the year end shown as an asset and the cost of the goods sold during the year charged as an expense. This applies to all assets in the long run but in the case of non-current assets it takes longer to use up the future benefits than it does with current assets. It is worth, at this point, just reminding ourselves of the definitions we discussed in Chapter 3.

KEY CONCEPT 3.4

International Accounting Standards – definition of an asset

An asset is a resource controlled by an enterprise as a result of past events from which future economic benefits are expected to flow to the entity. [IAS 1, Para. 49(a)]

As you might remember from Chapter 3, the way in which the International Standards dealt with the difference between current and non-current assets was to define current assets and then effectively say that anything that met the definition of an asset but did not meet the definition of a current asset was a non-current asset.

KEY CONCEPT 3.5

Current asset

A current asset is one which is either part of the operating cycle of the enterprise or is likely to be realized in the form of cash within one year.

In Chapter 3, we distinguished two types of non-current assets, namely tangible and intangible assets. We also identified a separate type of tangible asset, namely a fixed asset normally property, plant and equipment. It is with the treatment of fixed assets that we shall be mainly concerned with in this chapter. These were defined in Chapter 3 as shown below.

KEY CONCEPT 3.6

Fixed asset

An asset that is acquired for the purposes of use within the business and is likely to be used by the business for a considerable period of time.

The difficulty that accountants face when dealing with non-current assets is that, unlike current assets, they neither change their form nor become completely used up in the short term. These problems are in some ways similar to those we identified when discussing inventory valuation. In that case we found that there was a problem in allocating costs such as the wages of the foreman and in deciding which part of that cost should be allocated to the costs of the goods sold during the period, i.e. the expired benefit. There was also the question of how much should be allocated to the goods held at the end of the period; this was shown as an asset as there was a future benefit to be derived. The problem can be looked at from a more general angle. From the point of view of the statement of financial position, which tells us what we own at a particular point in time, we have to try to identify the amount of the future benefit left at the end of each year. On the other hand, from the perspective of the income statement, we need to measure the amount of the future benefit used up during the year so that we can match this expense with the revenue earned in that period. Whichever way we choose to look at the problem, we are still left with the issue of how to measure the future benefit to be derived from the use of the asset. This is because the statement of financial position and income statement are linked. You may remember that in Chapter 2 we said that accounting largely adopted a definition of profit based on Sir John Hick's definition of income.

KEY CONCEPT 8.1

Income

Income is that amount which an individual can consume and still be as well off at the end of the period as he or she was at the start of the period.

This we said could be illustrated diagrammatically as in Figure 8.1.

We can see from the diagram that wealth at T_0 plus the profit for the period will give us wealth at T_1. Hence, we can either measure the wealth in the form of future benefits at the end of each period, which brings with it the problems of valuation (as discussed in Chapter 2), or we can try to measure the profit by matching the revenue with the benefits used up during the period, which brings its own attendant problems (as we found with inventory and cost allocation in Chapter 6).

We shall look first at the idea of measuring future benefits with specific regard to all non-current assets and then in more detail at fixed assets. Theoretically, measuring future benefits may be possible. For example, we could measure the benefits to be derived from selling the products or services which our fixed assets help us to produce. In a world in which there is uncertainty, however, this process is far from straightforward, as the Millennium Dome project illustrated dramatically. Apart from the problem of poor estimates and over-optimistic forecasts, which was at the heart of the dramatic differences between the expected and actual revenue from ticket sales for the Millennium Dome, we have to deal with changes in technology and taste. Think, for example, of the difficulty in estimating the future sales of a line of mobile phones where technology and taste are both shortening product life. If we think about the machinery used for creating mobile phones, we are faced with the question of how the

FIGURE 8.1

changes in taste and technology affect the future benefits to be derived from the use of our machinery. We then need to think about the effect of competition on our market share. Similarly, we have to try to take account of the effects of changes in production technology: will it allow competitors with newer equipment to produce the same product at a cheaper price?

In fact, it is extremely difficult to measure the future benefit in the long term as we do not know what changes the future will bring, and therefore we cannot estimate their effects. Traditionally, accounting has solved this conundrum by the simple expedient of valuing assets at cost unless there is reasonable certainty that this value is incorrect, either because it is lower, as would be the case if changes in technology made the fixed assets obsolete, or because it is clearly considerably higher. An obvious example of the type of asset where the value is generally higher than the cost is land and buildings where prices seem to rise inexorably over the long term despite occasional blips such as that caused by the recent recession. There are, of course, many non-current assets where the difficulties of measuring future benefit are even more complex. For example, the value of a patent is largely dependent on two factors: the first is easy to deal with, i.e. that the patent has a defined life, but the second, i.e. that it could be made obsolete by an improved patent, is more difficult to address.

As a result of the problems of estimation and uncertainty around measuring future benefits, accounting avoids approaching profit measurement through asset valuation based on future benefits. This leaves us with the alternative approach, i.e. measuring costs and then measuring expired benefits and matching these with revenues. The problem with this system is that if you were able to tell how much benefit had expired you would then be able to work out what the unexpired or future benefit was. This, we have just argued, is extremely difficult to do in reality because of the problems of uncertainty.

To sum up, we can see that unlike current assets, where the cost and future benefits can be estimated with some certainty, in the case of all non-current assets, whether tangible or intangible, fixed or indeterminate, the future benefits are much more difficult to arrive at. In reality, accounting tries to avoid the difficulty by a fairly rigid application of the prudence concept and by avoiding, as far as possible, including assets that have no direct cost, e.g. the value of a willing workforce, and discouraging the use of value-based measures in the statement of financial position. There are, of course, exceptions to this general rule but it is a useful rule of thumb to work with at this stage.

The other question that arises with non-current assets is how much benefit has been used up during an accounting period. The answer is to use estimates and this is done by charging a part of the asset as an expense each year via a charge known as depreciation. Before moving on to a discussion of depreciation, we will first discuss some other issues relating to non-current assets. These are summarized by the four questions below.

1   How does a non-current asset differ from a current asset?

2   What is the cost of such an asset?

3   Should we be including the asset at cost or value?

4   How should we spread the cost over the useful life?

We need to examine each of these issues if we are to understand what the figures in the statement of financial position and income statement mean.

DIFFERENCE BETWEEN CURRENT AND NON-CURRENT ASSETS

If you look at the definition of a current asset and compare it with the definition of a fixed asset, you will see that the difference is mainly related to 'intention' and the 'nature' of the business. In simple terms, a car used by a sales representative is a non-current asset in a manufacturing business. In the case of a motor dealer, a car is a current asset because it is the 'intention' of the car dealer to sell it and realize cash in the short term. The problem with a definition that relies on the 'intentions' of the business is that these change from time to time as the nature of the business changes or the product changes. This may mean that an asset that was classified as a non-current asset may be reclassified as a current asset or vice versa. An example of a non-current asset that becomes current could be an investment in shares in another company which were being held for strategic purposes, for example building a portfolio for a takeover bid, and which would be classified as a non-current asset. If the company decides not to pursue that strategy and sell the shares, they become a current asset. Case Study 8.1 illustrates a case where items that were previously written off as expenses got reclassified as fixed assets. As these problems rarely arise, we can safely ignore them in this book.

THE COST OF A NON-CURRENT ASSET

On the face of it, the question of what an asset costs should present few if any difficulties. This is true in some cases, but in a great many cases the answer is less clear. For our purposes, it is worth thinking of different types of non-current assets as they present different issues. The first broad type is an asset created by the business. This could be a process or new product which is subject to a trademark or patent, i.e. an intangible asset, or it could be a tangible asset, e.g. a building firm builds it own offices. A second type of non-current asset is one that is bought by the business where we know more precisely what the total cost is, but even here deciding on the cost is not as simple as it might appear.

To illustrate the point, let us look at the situation in which an individual builds or buys a house. If we take the first case first, we know some of the costs, e.g. the price of the land, materials and architects fees, but what cost do we attach to the labour of the individual who builds the house? In the case of someone who buys a house, we could go to the legal contract between the seller and the buyer and we would find within that contract an agreed price. We could therefore argue that the cost is that agreed price, but were you to talk to someone who has recently purchased a house you would find that there were other costs associated with buying that house such as solicitors' fees and surveyors' fees. The question is whether these should be treated as part of the cost of the asset or whether they are expenses. In this particular situation, the way in which an accountant might answer the question is to argue that the amounts involved are not material compared with the cost of the house. This is not really a very satisfactory solution as it merely avoids the question instead of answering it. Accounting does not, in fact, provide a definitive answer to the problem. There are some broad guidelines which accountants use, however. We shall examine some possible examples and identify the basis of the decision.

CASE STUDY 8.1

British Gas plc

Extract from the notes to the accounts of British Gas plc for the year ended 31 December 1994
Commentary
Although this example is dated in time it is still one of the best real life illustrations of the difficulties of defining fixed assets. What we are provided with is an extract from the notes to the accounts of British

(Continued)

Gas plc. This shows that the Board of British Gas decided that, with effect from 1 August 1992, meters which had previously been written off to the profit and loss account (now called the income statement) should be treated as fixed assets. Presumably this was because the Board felt that they fell within the definition of fixed assets. As can be seen from the notes provided, this was one of three changes of accounting policy. The impact of this change on the historic cost profit was to increase that profit by £105 million in 1993 and by £78 million in 1994.

1 Changes in accounting policy

The Board has approved three changes in accounting policy. It has been decided to capitalize all installations of new technology meters. Previously replacement meters were expensed to the profit and loss account. With effect from 1 August 1992, the date of the introduction of the new meter technology, the accounting policy has been amended. The impact of this accounting policy change has been to increase historical cost earnings, but there is no material pre-tax earnings impact in the current cost accounts. In conjunction with this change, the historical cost net book value of meters as at 1 August 1992 is being depreciated over six years, being the estimated remaining service life of the capitalized meters in operation at that time.

Interest charges to finance major capital projects, principally exploration and production and property activities, are now capitalized in accordance with the usual accounting practice in those industry sectors.

Following the restructuring of the UK Gas Business, service contract income is accounted for on an accruals basis rather than on a cash basis.

The financial impact of the above accounting policy changes is given in the tables.

Impact on profit/loss for the financial year

	Current		Historical	
	1994 £m	1993 £m	1994 £m	1993 £m
Capitalization of meters previously charged to replacement expenditure	—	—	81	106
Capitalization of interest previously charged to the profit and loss account	44	54	44	54
Accounting for service contract income	−12	−10	−12	−10

	Current		Historical	
	1994 £m	1993 £m	1994 £m	1993 £m
Less: taxation thereon	32	44	113	150
	−35	−45	−35	−45
Net (decrease)/increase in earnings	−3	31	78	105
Net (decrease)/increase in basic earnings per ordinary share	(0.1p)	0.0p	1.8p	2.4p
1993 – Basic earnings per ordinary share as previously reported		(12.3p)		(6.6p)
– Basic earnings per ordinary share as restated		(12.3p)		(4.2p)

(Continued)

Impact on shareholders' funds

	Current		Historical	
	1994 £m	**1993 £m**	**1994 £m**	**1993 £m**
Tangible fixed assets:				
Capitalization of meters previously charged to replacement expenditure	–	–	231	150
Capitalization of interest previously charged to the profit and loss account	194	150	194	150
Net current assets:				
Accounting for service contract income	−3 103	−391	−3 103	−391
Less: taxation thereon	91	59	322	209
	−3 120	−385	−3 120	−385
Net (decrease)/increase in shareholders' funds	−329	−326	202	124
1993 – Shareholders' funds as previously reported		19 124		7 211
– Shareholders' funds as restated		19 098		7 335

British Gas has also carried out a review of asset lives. Revised asset lives and minor current cost valuation method changes were determined and these changes have led to a reduced current cost depreciation charge of £30 m and an increased historical cost depreciation charge of £14 m. The statement of financial position impact at 31 December 1994 was to increase current cost fixed assets by £130 m and to reduce historical cost fixed assets by £14 m. Prior year comparatives have not been restated as these changes do not constitute a change in accounting policy.

Before doing that, however, we need to explain the idea of materiality. This is a concept often used in the accounting literature and, like a number of other concepts such as prudence, it provides a rule of thumb approach to assist in making judgements. For example, the cost of a car is likely to be material in the case of a small retailer, but in the case of IBM the effect on the fixed assets would be negligible as they are measured in millions of pounds. Hence, materiality is a relative measure and all aspects of the situation need to be looked at before a decision is made.

KEY CONCEPT 8.2

Materiality

Broadly, an item can be said to be material if its non-disclosure would lead to the accounts being misleading in some way.

ACTIVITY 8.1

To understand the idea of materiality being relative rather than absolute try thinking through the following example. A student is doing a business degree and taking five subjects, all of equal weight, one of which is accounting. In accounting there are four tests each carrying 10% of the total mark and an exam which carries the other 60%. In test 1 you find that the marker has missed ten marks out the possible 100 that you could have got.

Think about whether the error is material in respect of:

(a) that test
(b) the mark for the accounting tests
(c) the final mark for accounting
(d) the final mark for the year.

In (a) it is worth 10% so material, in (b) it is only worth 2.5% (one of four tests), probably not material, in (c) it is worth 1%, almost certainly not material, and in (d) it is worth 0.02% certainly not material.

Having introduced the idea of materiality, we can now move on to try to establish the guidelines we referred to above through a series of examples.

EXAMPLE 8.1

A delivery van is purchased by a retailer of office stationery for £7600. The price includes number plates and one year's road fund licence.

Discussion

It is clear that in this example we have a fixed asset. The question is only how much the fixed asset cost. Included in the £7600 is the cost of number plates and one year's road fund licence. The road fund licence is clearly a current asset as it only lasts for one year, whereas the number plates are clearly part of the cost of the fixed asset in that they will remain with the van over its useful life.

EXAMPLE 8.2

Let us now assume that, as the retailer did not have the cash to buy the van outright, it was purchased on hire purchase. The hire-purchase contract allowed the retailer to put down a deposit of £3400 and then make 24 monthly payments of £200. Hence, the total cost of buying the same van would be £8200 compared with the cash price of £7600.

Discussion

The fact that the retailer has decided to finance the purchase in a different way has, on the face of it, added to the cost of purchasing the van. However, this is somewhat misleading as the cost of the van is, in fact, the

(Continued)

same. What has happened in this case is that the retailer has incurred an additional cost which does not relate to the van itself. This additional cost relates to the cost of borrowing money, which is effectively what hire purchase is. If the retailer had borrowed money by a bank loan and then paid cash for the van the cost of the van would have been the cash price and the interest on the loan would be dealt with separately. Hence, in the case of the hire purchase all that needs to be done is to identify the part of the payments that are interest charges and deal with those in the same way as we would deal with interest on loans. In this particular example the interest is £600. The £600 interest would, of course, be charged to the income statement as an expense over the 24 months it takes to pay the hire-purchase company.

EXAMPLE 8.3

A manufacturer bought a second-hand machine for £8000, which had cost £15 000 new. The cost of transporting the machine to the factory was £500 and the costs of installation were £400. When it was installed it was found that it was not working properly and it had to be repaired, which cost £300. At the same time a modification was carried out at a cost of £500 to improve the output of the machine. After two months' production the machine broke down again and was repaired at a cost of £200.

Discussion

The starting point is the basic cost of the machine, which was £8000. The fact that it had originally cost £15 000 when it was new is not relevant. What we need to bring into the accounts of our manufacturer is the cost to that business, not the original cost to the seller. With the other costs, though, the decisions are less clear cut. For example, should the cost of transport be included? One answer would be to argue that in order to obtain the future benefits from the asset we needed to incur this cost and so this is, in fact, a payment for those future benefits. If we followed this line of argument we could then include the costs of installation, the initial repairs and the modifications.

You will have noticed that we referred specifically to the initial repairs rather than all the repairs. The reason for this is that in the first case it could be argued that the reason the business was able to buy the machine cheaply was because it was not working properly. In the second instance, however, the argument is less clear cut, as the repairs might simply be due to normal wear and tear, and should therefore be judged as part of the cost of running the machine in much the same way as we would view the cost of car repairs as a part of the costs of running a car.

We can see from these examples that there is no easy solution to the problem of what should and should not be included in the cost of fixed assets. Each case is judged upon its merits and a decision is made about whether the cost should be included in the expenses for the year or added to the cost of the asset. The broad rule of thumb that can be used to assist in these decisions is in part related to the question of whether to use cost or value. It simply poses the question: has there been an enhancement of the potential future benefits? If there has, then the cost should be added to the asset. If, however, the effect is simply to restore the *status quo*, as is the case with car repairs, then it is more reasonable to treat those costs as expenses of the period in which they arise. This approach conforms to the prudence concept which we have referred to earlier.

COST OR VALUE

As we have just said, the rule of thumb relating to future benefits helps us here. Clearly, if the cost exceeds our estimate of the future benefits, then applying the prudence principle would mean that we show the asset at its value rather than its cost. What then happens if the value exceeds the cost: should we include the asset at its value rather than its cost? Once again there is no simple answer, although over time a set of conventions have emerged which have at their heart the issue of relative certainty. For example, it is generally accepted that property should be valued on a regular basis and shown in the statement of financial position at it value. On the other hand, in the case of investments, which are another type of non-current asset, it is normal practice to include these in the statement of financial position at their cost, although an indication of the value is usually to be found in the notes to the accounts. The difference in the treatments of these two items can be attributed to the relative volatility of the stock market compared with the property market.

THE USEFUL LIFE OF FIXED ASSETS

In our introduction, we mentioned the useful life of the asset and how we spread the cost over the useful life. This raises a number of issues. How do we judge the useful life? What cost do we spread over the useful life? How do we spread it? The last point will be dealt with in our discussion of depreciation, but it is worth examining the other two first. The first point is how we judge the useful life. The answer is that all we can hope for is an approximation of the useful life. The reason we can only approximate comes back to the question of uncertainty in respect of the future. Similarly, if we try to arrive at the cost that we wish to spread over the useful life we could argue that we should take into account anything that we shall be able to sell our asset for when it is no longer viable to use in our business. This amount, the residual value, is only a guess because of the uncertainty involved. In reality it is likely that such issues are sidestepped and that assets are classified into broad groups, which are then assumed to have a useful life based upon either past practice or the norm for the industry. All too often one can visit factories where a vital machine in the production process is no longer included in the accounts because the estimate of the useful life was incorrect.

Having made it clear that there is no magic formula for arriving at either the cost or the useful life, let us now examine the way in which we spread the cost over the useful life. This is done by means of depreciation.

CASE STUDY 8.2

Rolls Royce plc

Extract from the accounting policies note of Rolls Royce plc for the year ended 31 December 2008

Software

The cost of acquiring software that is not specific to an item of property, plant and equipment is classified as an intangible asset and amortized over its useful economic life, up to a maximum of five years.

(Continued)

Property, plant and equipment

Property, plant and equipment assets are stated at cost less accumulated depreciation and any provision for impairments in value. Depreciation is provided on a straight-line basis to write off the cost, less the estimated residual value, of property, plant and equipment over their estimated useful lives. No depreciation is provided on assets in the course of construction.

Estimated useful lives are as follows:

(i)   Land and buildings, as advised by the Group's professional advisors:
    (a) Freehold buildings – five to 45 years (average 24 years).
    (b) Leasehold buildings – lower of advisors'estimates or period of lease.
    (c) No depreciation is provided on freehold land.

(ii) Plant and equipment – five to 25 years (average 14 years).
(iii) Aircraft and engines – five to 20 years (average 17 years).

Commentary

The notes from the accounting policies of Rolls Royce plc illustrate two things. The first is the difficulty in defining cost as by implication in the case of software, which is written down over five years, in some cases it is added to the cost of the plant and equipment. We then see that there are difficulties of defining the useful life of fixed assets. The note shows that even within specific classes of assets Rolls Royce plc uses a range of estimates of the useful life ranging from five years upwards to 45 years in the case of freehold buildings.

You should also note that the method used to calculate depreciation is 'straight line', further discussion on methods of depreciation will follow later in the chapter.

DEPRECIATION OR AMORTIZATION

These two terms mean the same thing; they relate to allocating some of the cost of a non-current asset over the useful life of that asset. We have suggested some reasons for charging depreciation which we shall discuss more fully below. What we have not done is to define depreciation precisely (instead we have tried to give a flavour of what depreciation is). However, no discussion of depreciation would be complete without at least looking at the definition provided in the International Accounting Standard on the subject, IAS 16, Property, Plant and Equipment, and reproduced as Key Concept 8.3.

This definition leads us to the need now to define depreciable amount before we can allocate it. Once again, if we go to the International Standard we find that this contains a definition which is shown here as Key Concept 8.4.

KEY CONCEPT 8.3

Depreciation (amortization)

The systematic allocation of the depreciable amount of an asset over its useful life. [IAS 16, Para. 6]

KEY CONCEPT 8.4

Depreciable amount

The cost of an asset, or other amount substituted for cost, less its residual value.

ACTIVITY 8.2

Thinking back to what you have read can you identify some items that might have been added to or included in the cost of an asset. Here you might have identified delivery costs, legal costs or even software as was shown in the Rolls Royce plc Case Study 8.2

WHY DEPRECIATE?

One reason already mentioned for why we depreciate is to match the revenue earned in a period with the expense connected with earning that revenue. In essence, the argument for matching the cost of goods sold with the sales or of matching expenses with sales is the one being applied here. The major difference is that those other items are ascertainable with a reasonable degree of accuracy, whereas depreciation is only an estimate and subject to all sorts of inaccuracies.

A second and more contentious reason for providing for depreciation is in order to maintain the capacity of a business to continue its production. Clearly, if a machine comes to the end of its useful life the business will need another machine if it is to carry on producing the goods. This, of course, assumes that it would wish to replace the machine, which in itself has underlying assumptions about the product still being produced, the technology in terms of production processes being the same, etc. This question is directly related to our original problem in Chapter 2 of measuring wealth or the state of being well off. Such a measure depends on how you define wealth and whether that changes. For example, a car may be seen as an asset until such time as we run out of petrol reserves; at that stage we may not want to include a car in our measurement of wealth. Therefore, to have retained profits in order to ensure we always had a car would not have been appropriate.

This second reason for providing for depreciation is also contentious because in fact all that accounting depreciation does is to spread the original cost and maintain the original capital. In fact, operating capacity is not maintained through depreciation, as no account is taken of changes in prices, in technology or in consumer demand. Nor is any account taken of changes in the size of the business. This may have implications in terms of economies of scale. We cannot guarantee that we shall have enough money left in the business as a result of our depreciation charges to replace an existing machine with one of equal capacity should we so wish. Having made the point that there is no guarantee that the charges will equal the requirements for replacement because of changes in those requirements and the environment, let us look at how depreciation would maintain capital if the requirements and the environment did not change.

We will start by looking at an example to see what happens if we ignore depreciation and then how it is dealt with in terms of the accounts.

EXAMPLE 8.4

Toni buys a van for £4000 and sets up as an ice cream seller. In addition to the van, £1000 cash is put into the business which is subsequently used to buy stocks of ice cream.

At the end of the first year, the sales have been £6000 and the total expenses including the cost of ice creams, van repairs and running costs were £3000; all the inventory has been sold and so all the money is in cash. Hence, the business has £4000 in cash: the original £1000 plus the money from sales of £6000 less the expenses paid of £3000.

Toni therefore withdraws £3000 on the assumption that the business is still as well off as it was at the start. That is, the business had at the start of the year a van plus £1000 in cash, it still has the van and so there only needs to be £1000 left in for the *status quo* to be maintained. Let us assume for convenience that the situation is repeated for the next three years.

Under these assumptions, the income statements and statements of financial position of the business would be as follows.

Income statements for Toni's business

	Year 1	Year 2	Year 3	Year 4
Sales revenue	6 000	6 000	6 000	6 000
Cost of sales	3 000	3 000	3 000	3 000
Profit	3 000	3 000	3 000	3 000
Withdrawal	3 000	3 000	3 000	3 000
Retained profit	0	0	0	0

Statement of financial position of Toni's business

Balance sheets of Toni's business

	Year 1	Year 2	Year 3	Year 4
Current assets				
Cash	1 000	1 000	1 000	1 000
Non current assets				
Van	4 000	4 000	4 000	4 000
Total assets	5 000	5 000	5 000	5 000
Owner's equity	5 000	5 000	5 000	5 000
Total equity	5 000	5 000	5 000	5 000

If we assume that the van would last four years, we can see that, in fact, the statement of financial position at the end of year 4, assuming it reflects future benefits, should be as follows.

Statement of financial position of Toni's business at end of year 4

Current assets	
Cash	1 000
Non current assets	
Van	Nil
Total assets	1 000
Owner's equity	1 000
Total equity	1 000

(Continued)

As we can see, there is not enough money left in the business to replace the van and in this situation the business cannot continue. If we compare our results with our definition of profit in Chapter 2, it is clear that our profit measure must have been wrong as Toni is not as well off at the end of year 4 as at the beginning of year 1.

The problem has been that the profit has been overstated because no allowance has been made for the fact that the van has a finite useful life which is being eroded each year. If we assume that the cost should be spread evenly over the four years and call this expense depreciation, then our income statements would appear as follows.

Revised income statements of Toni's business

	Year 1	Year 2	Year 3	Year 4
Sales revenue	6 000	6 000	6 000	6 000
Cost of sales	3 000	3 000	3 000	3 000
Gross profit	3 000	3 000	3 000	3 000
Depreciation	1 000	1 000	1 000	1 000
Net profit	2 000	2 000	2 000	2 000
Withdrawal	2 000	2 000	2 000	2 000
Retained profit	0	0	0	0

As can be seen, the net profit has been reduced by £1000 for the depreciation each year and Toni has withdrawn only £2000 each year. The statements of financial position would now be as follows.

Revised statement of financial position of Toni's business

	Year 1	Year 2	Year 3	Year 4
Current assets				
Cash	2 000	3 000	4 000	5 000
Non current assets				
Van	4 000	4 000	4 000	4 000
Depreciation	1 000	2 000	3 000	4 000
Net book value	3 000	2 000	1 000	0
Total assets	5 000	5 000	5 000	5 000
Owner's equity	5 000	5 000	5 000	5 000
Total equity	5 000	5 000	5 000	5 000

The effect of charging depreciation in the income statement was to reduce the net profit, which in turn led to a reduction in the amount available to be withdrawn each year. The reduced withdrawal has led to the cash balance increasing each year by £1000 until at the end of year 4 there is £5000 in the bank and Toni is in a position to replace the van, assuming of course that the price of vans has not changed. If you compare the two sets of statements of financial position there is another change – the fixed asset reduces each year by the amount of the depreciation charge. It is important that you recognize that these two effects should not be mixed up. The increase in cash is as a result of withdrawing less, not as a result of providing for depreciation. The latter does not in itself affect the cash balance, as is obvious if we work through year 1 of this example on a worksheet.

(Continued)

Worksheet showing year 1 of Toni's business

	Assets		=	Equity + Liabilities		
	Cash	Van		Owner's equity	Revenue & expenses	Accumulated depreciation
Start	1 000	4 000		5 000		
Sales	6 000				6 000	
Expenses	−3 000				−3 000	
Depreciation					−1 000	1 000
Withdrawal	−2 000				−2 000	
Balance	**2 000**	**4 000**		**5 000**	**0**	**1 000**

As you can see, the depreciation charge reduces the revenue and expenses column and increases the accumulated depreciation column. It does not affect the cash column in any way.

An alternative way of dealing with depreciation on a worksheet is to reduce the asset column by the depreciation. If we did this, our worksheet would appear as shown below. However, we recommend that wherever possible the worksheet should include a separate column for depreciation as this adds to the clarity and allows one to identify roughly how far through its useful life the asset is at the end of the year. In our example we can see that it cost £4000 and £1000 depreciation has been charged, so we know that we are one-quarter of the way through its estimated useful life.

Alternative worksheet of Toni's business for year 1

	Assets		=	Equity + Liabilities	
	Cash	Van		Owner's equity	Revenue & expenses
Start	1 000	4 000		5 000	
Sales	6 000				6 000
Expenses	−3 000				−3 000
Depreciation		−1 000			−1 000
Withdrawal	−2 000				−2 000
Balance	**2 000**	**3 000**		**5 000**	**0**

In this example, we have assumed that the cost should be spread evenly over the life of the asset. This is known as straight-line depreciation and is one of a number of alternative methods that can be used as the basis for providing depreciation. Each of these alternatives will give a different figure for the depreciation each year and as a result the 'carrying amount', sometimes referred to as the net book value or written-down value, will change. This is illustrated in more detail after our discussion of the most common methods of depreciation. Before going on to that discussion, you need to understand what 'carrying amount' means.

KEY CONCEPT 8.5

Carrying amount

This is the amount at which an asset is recognized after deducting any accumulated depreciation and accumulated impairment losses. [IAS 16, Para. 6]

As you can see, the definition adopted by the International Standard makes no reference at all to value. This is a useful step forward as it avoids any confusion about whether the figure represents what an asset is worth. You may also note that the definition includes both depreciation and 'impairment losses'. At this stage you do not need to worry about these beyond recognizing that in some cases because of changes in technology the carrying amount may exceed the value and this excess would be an impairment loss.

METHODS OF DEPRECIATION

As we have said, there are a number of alternative methods of depreciation, the choice of the appropriate method depending, at least theoretically, on the nature of the asset being depreciated. In practice, however, the only methods in common usage are the straight-line method and the reducing, or diminishing, balance method, and the former is used by most businesses. The reason for this is probably purely to do with simplicity of calculation. In this regard, it would be useful for you to look at the accounting policies statements in published accounts to try to ascertain the reasons underlying the choice of depreciation method. As we shall see in the discussion below, a case can be made for using different methods for different assets or classes of assets. In reality, it may be the fact that assets are put into broad categories, which leads to the predominance of straight-line depreciation which we shall now discuss more fully.

The straight-line method

We have already seen that this is a very simple method, which probably explains why so many companies use it. The assumption, with regard to asset life, that underlies the choice of this method is that the asset usage is equal for all periods of its useful life. The way in which the depreciation charge is calculated is to take the cost of the asset less the estimate of any residual value at the end of the asset life and divide it by the useful life of the asset. Thus, an asset which cost £130 and which has an estimated life of four years and an estimated scrap value of £10 would be depreciated by £30 per year. This was arrived at by using the formula:

$$\frac{\text{cost} - \text{residual value}}{\text{useful life}}$$

In our case this works out as follows:

$$\frac{£130 - £10}{4} = £30 \text{ per annum}$$

Reducing balance method

The reducing balance method, sometimes also referred to as the diminishing balance method, assumes that the asset declines more in the earlier years of the asset life than in the later years. In fact, it is likely that in most cases the cost of repairs will rise as the asset becomes older and so this method when combined with the cost of repairs is more likely to produce a more even cost of using an asset over its full life. It is less frequently used than the straight-line method, probably because it is slightly more difficult to calculate, although with the increasing use of computers this should not really cause any problems. The method applies a precalculated percentage to the written-down value, or net book value, to ascertain the charge for the year. In order to arrive at the percentage we use the following equation:

$$\text{rate of depreciation} = 1 - \sqrt[\text{useful life}]{\frac{\text{scrap value}}{\text{cost of asset}}}$$

Comparison of the two methods

We consider a business that has an asset which has an estimated useful life of three years, its cost was £15 000 and it has an estimated scrap or residual value of £3000.

For the straight-line method, we need to depreciate at £4000 per year, i.e.:

$$\frac{15\,000 - 3\,000}{3} = £4\,000 \text{ per annum}$$

For the reducing balance method, we first need to find the rate of depreciation to apply. In this case it will be 41.5%, which we arrive at by using the equation

$$\text{rate of depreciation} = 1 - \sqrt[3]{\frac{£3\,000}{£15\,000}}$$

This rate is now applied to the carrying amount, i.e. the cost less depreciation to date.

	Straight-line method			Income statement		
Year	Statement of financial position		Income statement	Statement of financial position		Reducing balance method
1	Cost	15 000		Cost	15 000	
	Depreciation	4 000	4 000	Depreciation	6 225	6 225
	Carrying amount	11 000		Carrying amount	8 775	
2	Cost	15 000		Cost	15 000	
	Depreciation	8 000	4 000	Depreciation	9 865	3 640
	Carrying amount	7 000		Carrying amount	5 135	
3	Cost	15 000		Cost	15 000	
	Depreciation	12 000	4 000	Depreciation	12 000	2 135
	Carrying amount	3 000		Carrying amount	3 000	

As can be seen from the example, the charge to the income statement in each year and the accumulated depreciation in the statement of financial position are different with the two methods, although the methods charge, in total, the same amount and come to the same residual value.

Under the straight-line method, the charge to the income statement is £4000 each year and so the accumulated depreciation rises at £4000 a year.

Under the reducing balance method, the charge to the income statement is based on 41.5% of the balance at the end of the previous year. Thus, in year 1 it is 41.5% of £15 000, in year 2 it is 41.5% of £8775 and in year 3 it is 41.5% of £5135.

This can be illustrated by the following chart (Figure 8.2), which shows the impact of each method on the charge to the income statement and clearly shows that the reducing balance method has greater charges in earlier rather than later years.

FIGURE 8.2 Incidence of depreciation charges using the different methods

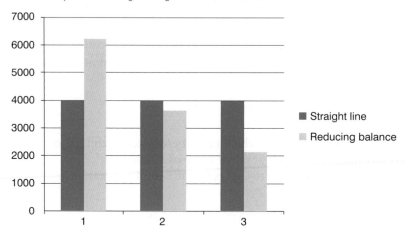

As we have said, both methods achieve the same result in the end as with both methods the asset is written down to its residual value at the end of year 3. It is the incidence of the charge to the income statement which varies, not the total charged. Although in theory the choice of depreciation method should be governed by the nature of the asset and the way in which the benefit is used up, in practice little, if any, attention seems to be paid to this. However, it is worth spending some time understanding when each method would be appropriate. We have said that the straight-line method implies that the benefit from the use of the fixed asset is used up in an even pattern over its useful life. This suggests that it is time which is the determining factor governing the life of the asset rather than the amount of use to which it is put. Thus, if we take the case of a building it is unlikely that the amount of use it gets will materially affect its lifespan and so straight-line depreciation would be appropriate. On the other hand, if we think about the way in which a car engine, for example, wears out this is more likely to relate to usage, i.e. the more miles the car does the more wear and tear there is on the engine. In such a case the straight-line method is unlikely to be the most appropriate method, but we do not have a commonly accepted method that relates directly to usage.

The reducing balance method, however, has characteristics that make it a possible alternative to a direct measure related to usage in that it charges the most benefit used to the early years, as would be the case if the asset were used up by the mileage alone or by the number of hours a machine was run, etc. It is, of course, only an approximation. It is probably not worthwhile from a cost–benefit point of view, however, to measure the number of hours a machine is run for and calculate a precise figure as the total life of the machine and so on are all subject to estimation errors.

We can therefore argue that where the life of the asset relates to time then the straight-line method is likely to be more appropriate, but in the situation where the asset is used up through hours run, mileage or any other measure relating to usage, then the reducing balance method may well give a better approximation of the benefit used up in a period (see Case Study 8.3).

Depreciation and the cash flow statement

You will note that we have not shown a cash flow statement. This is deliberate as depreciation has no effect on the cash flow statement. This can be checked by looking at the entries on the worksheet of Toni's business in Example 8.4 reproduced again below. However, as you can see, it does have an effect on the income statement and as such we have to reconcile these differences in the same way as we did with inventory.

Worksheet showing year 1 of Toni's business

	Assets		=	Equity + Liabilities		
	Cash	Van		Owner's equity	Revenue & expenses	Accumulated depreciation
Start	1 000	4 000		5 000		
Sales	6 000				6 000	
Expenses	−3 000				−3 000	
Depreciation					−1 000	1 000
Withdrawal	−2 000				−2 000	
Balance	2 000	4 000		5 000	0	1 000

From the worksheet, we can see that the balance on the income statement, shown in the revenue and expenses column, is £0 and the change in the cash balance is £1000 (£1000 at the start and £2000 at the end); the difference is the depreciation charge for the year, which needs to be added back to profit to reconcile it with the figure for the net cash flow for the year as shown below.

Reconciliation of profit and cash flow

Net profit	2 000
Add: depreciation	1 000
Less: Withdrawal	−2 000
Net cash flow	1 000

ACTIVITY 8.3

Before moving on just have a look at the worksheet and see the two entries for depreciation – do these affect the bank/cash column.

Clearly the answer is no they do not but they do affect the revenue and expenses column.

SALES OF FIXED ASSETS

Before leaving the discussion of fixed assets and depreciation, we should examine the situation that arises when we sell a fixed asset. It should be obvious from our discussion above that the carrying amount of the asset, i.e. the cost less depreciation to date, is unlikely to bear any resemblance to the market price of that asset. This means that when an asset is sold the selling price will either be less than or exceed the carrying amount and a paper loss or profit will arise. If, for example, we sold the asset used in our previous example at the end of year 2 for £6000, then under the straight-line method there would be a paper loss of £1000 (the carrying amount of £7000 less the £6000 we sold it for). However, if we had been using the reducing balance method we would show a paper profit of £865, i.e. the carrying amount of £5135 compared with the sale proceeds of £6000. We have referred to these as paper profits and losses because what they really are is the difference between our estimates of the future benefit being used up and the actual benefit used up. In other words, they are a measure of the error in our estimates. We shall now look at the way in which these are treated using the worksheet to illustrate the effect on the income statement.

CASE STUDY 8.3

BP plc and British Airways plc

Commentary

For a company such as BP, some of their most valuable assets are the oil and gas fields that they have a right to use. Despite highly developed technology, the company still has to make estimates of the gas and oil contained in these fields. Furthermore, such fields must be depreciated over their useful life to the point where no further reserves remain and decommissioning must commence.

In such situations, straight-line depreciation would be an inappropriate method as the rate at which reserves are depleted depends on the production rate. The following extract illustrates this point.

Extract from the critical accounting policies of BP plc for the year ended 31 December 2008
Depreciation

Development expenditure Expenditure on the construction, installation or completion of infrastructure facilities such as platforms, pipelines and the drilling of development wells, including unsuccessful development or delineation wells, is capitalized within property, plant and equipment and is depreciated from the commencement of production as described below in the accounting policy for Property, plant and equipment.

Oil and natural gas properties, including related pipelines, are **depreciated using a unit-of-production method.** The cost of producing wells is amortized over proved developed reserves. Licence acquisition, field development and future decommissioning costs are amortized over total proved reserves. The unit-of-production rate for the amortization of field development costs takes into account expenditures incurred to date, together with approved future development expenditure required to develop reserves.

Other property, plant and equipment is depreciated on a **straightline** basis over its expected useful life.

Commentary

Production units are preferred as a measure for depreciation as opposed to the estimated useful life measured by time. This example highlights the difficulty in arriving at an appropriate measure for depreciation. It is also worth noting that for all other assets the simple straight line method is used.

British Airways plc Extracts from accounting policies statement for the year to 31 March 2009
Property, plant and equipment

Property, plant and equipment is held at cost. The Group has a policy of not revaluing property, plant and equipment. Depreciation is calculated to write off the cost less estimated residual value on a straight-line basis, over the useful life of the asset. Residual values, where applicable, are reviewed annually against prevailing market values for equivalently aged assets and depreciation rates adjusted accordingly on a prospective basis.

(Continued)

The carrying value is reviewed for impairment when events or changes in circumstances indicate the carrying value may not be recoverable and the cumulative impairment losses are shown as a reduction in the carrying value of property, plant and equipment.

Fleet

Cabin interior modifications, including those required for brand changes and relaunches, are depreciated over the lower of five years and the remaining life of the aircraft.

Aircraft and engine spares acquired on the introduction or expansion of a fleet, as well as rotable spares purchased separately, are carried as property, plant and equipment and generally depreciated in line with the fleet to which they relate.

Major overhaul expenditure, including replacement spares and labour costs, is capitalized and amortized over the average expected life between major overhauls. All other replacement spares and other costs relating to maintenance of fleet assets (including maintenance provided under 'pay-as-you-go' contracts) are charged to the income statement on consumption or as incurred respectively.

Commentary

As you can see British Airways are very clear about the fact that they use the straight line method and that they review their assets at the end of each year to see if there is still the same future benefit and if that has been impaired the asset carrying value is adjusted. It is also worth having a look at what is included in the costs of the fleet and how they deal with brand changes and refitting of interiors, as well as spares held for repairs.

EXAMPLE 8.5

A business bought an asset for £15 000. It estimated the useful life as three years and the scrap or residual value as £3000. The business uses straight-line depreciation. For the purposes of illustration, we shall assume that its sales are £14 000 per year, and the total expenses are £9000 each year for both years 1 and 2. We shall also assume that at the end of year 2 it sold the fixed asset for £6000.

Solution

We can calculate the depreciation charge as £4000 a year for each of the two years.

Worksheet

Year 1	Cash	Asset	Disposal	=	Equity	Revenue & expenses	Depreciation
	Assets			**=**	**Equity + liabilities**		
Asset	−15 000	15 000					
Sales	14 000					14 000	
Expenses	−9 000					−9 000	
Depreciation						−4 000	4 000
Balance	**−10 000**	**15 000**				**1 000**	**4 000**

(Continued)

	Assets			=	Equity + liabilities		
Year 1	**Cash**	**Asset**	**Disposal**		**Equity**	**Revenue & expenses**	**Depreciation**
Year 2							
Sales	14 000					14 000	
Expenses	−9 000					−9 000	
Depreciation						−4 000	4 000
Balance	**−5 000**	**15 000**				**2 000**	**8 000**
Asset		−15 000	15 000				
Depreciation			−8 000				−8 000
Sale proceeds	6 000		−6 000				
Balance	**1 000**	**0**	**1 000**			**2 000**	**0**
Loss on sale			−1 000			−1 000	
Final balance	**1 000**	**0**	**0**			**1 000**	**0**

You will notice when you look at the worksheet that the full depreciation is charged in both year 1 and year 2. The reason for this is that the asset was used for the full year in both years. If it had been used for less than a full year then we should have had to apportion the charge. At the end of year 2, having used the asset for the full year, we decide to sell the asset. As you can see, this involves a number of entries on our worksheet which we shall examine in turn.

For clarity, we have opened a separate column in our worksheet which we have called a 'disposal' column. An alternative way would have been to deal with all the entries in the fixed asset column, but that is more difficult to follow. First, as we have sold the asset we need to transfer the cost, £15 000, and any associated depreciation, in this case £8000, to a disposal column. We receive cash, in this case £6000, in exchange for the asset and so we show the cash in our cash column and in our disposal column. This leaves us with a balance on our disposal column of £1000 which is the amount of the paper loss that we have made. This paper loss is transferred to the revenue and expenses column.

Our worksheet once again shows the correct position as we have no asset or depreciation associated with our asset and our profit to date is reduced to £1000 because of the underestimate or paper loss in respect of the use of the asset for the two years.

The alternative way of dealing with the disposal on a worksheet is as follows.

Note: The worksheet given below starts from the balances at the end of year 2 after the depreciation for the year has been charged but before the disposal of the asset has been dealt with. The major difference is that instead of opening a new account to deal with the disposal all the entries are put through the existing columns or accounts.

Worksheet–alternative presentation

	Assets		=	Equity + liabilities		
	Cash	**Asset**		**Equity**	**Revenue & expenses**	**Depreciation**
Balance (Year 2)	−5 000	15 000			2 000	8 000
Depreciation		−8 000				−8 000
Sale proceeds	6 000	−6 000				
Balance	**1 000**	**1 000**			**2 000**	**0**
Loss on sale		−1 000			−1 000	
Final balance	**1 000**	**0**			**1 000**	**0**

(Continued)

Some find this format easier to follow and work with. The choice of which way the entries are put on the worksheet is in fact irrelevant. It is the principle involved that is important and you may choose the method with which you feel most comfortable.

In published accounts of companies there is a requirement to show the fixed assets, additions and disposals and movements in respect of depreciation in full. An example of such disclosure is given in Case Study 8.4.

EFFECTS ON THE CASH FLOW STATEMENT

Before we look at that, we should once again look at the effects of the sale of the fixed asset on the cash flow statement and how we reconcile the income statement and the cash flow statement. If we produced the cash flow statement and income statement for the second year of Example 8.5, they would look like those shown below.

Income statement for year 2

Revenue	14 000
Expenses	9 000
Gross profit	5 000
Depreciation	4 000
Loss on sale	1 000
Net profit	0

Cash flow statement year 2

Cash inflows

From sales revenue	14 000
Proceeds of sale of fixed asset	6 000
	20 000

Cash outflows

Expenses	9 000
	9 000
Net cash inflow	11 000

We can reconcile these two statements by looking at the operating cash flows i.e. those related to the income statement and the other cash flows caused by the sale of the asset. Hence, we can rewrite the cash flow statement as follows and then reconcile this with the income statement.

Alternative cash flow statement year 2

Operating cash flow	5 000
Proceeds of sale of fixed asset	6 000
Net cash inflow	11 000

The reconciliation would look as follows.

Reconciliation of profit to operating cash flow

Net profit	0
Add back	
Depreciation	4 000
Loss on sale	1 000
Operating cash flow	5 000

ACTIVITY 8.4

Using the worskheet below fill in the entries that would have been made if the asset was sold for £9000.

Worksheet–Activity 8.4

	Assets		=	Equity + liabilities		
	Cash	**Asset**		**Equity**	**Revenue & expenses**	**Depreciation**
Balance (Year 2)	−5 000	15 000			2 000	8 000
Depreciation		−8 000				−8 000
Sale proceeds						
Balance					2 000	0
Final balance						

If you have made the correct entries you should have ended up with a profit of £2000 on the sale of the asset. Your cash column would show a balance £4000 and your revenue and expenses column would also show £4000.

CASE STUDY 8.4

Additions and disposals of fixed assets: Marks and Spencer plc

Extract from the notes to the accounts of Marks and Spencer plc for the year ended 28 March 2009

14 Property, plant and equipment

	Land and buildings £m	Fixtures fittings and equipment £m	Assets in the course of construction £m	Total £m
At 31 March 2007				
Cost	2 468.2	3 653.3	107.5	6 229.0
Accumulated depreciation	(95.3)	(2 089.2)	–	(2 184.5)

(Continued)

	Land and buildings £m	Fixtures fittings and equipment £m	Assets in the course of construction £m	Total £m
Net book value	2 372.9	1 564.1	107.5	4 044.5
Year ended 29 March 2008				
Opening net book value	2 372.9	1 564.1	107.5	4 044.5
Exchange difference	18.4	10.1	5.9	34.4
Additions	82.6	692.8	195.4	970.8
Acquisition of subsidiaries	18.0	11.5	0.2	29.7
Transfers	11.8	110.8	(122.6)	–
Disposals	(73.8)	(5.2)	(0.1)	(79.1)
Depreciation charge	(8.5)	(287.8)	–	(296.3)
Closing net book value	2 421.4	2 096.3	186.3	4 704.0
At 29 March 2008				
Cost	2 525.2	4 473.3	186.3	7 184.8
Accumulated depreciation	(103.8)	(2 377.0)	–	(2 480.8)
Net book value	2 421.4	2 096.3	186.3	4 704.0
Year ended 28 March 2009				
Opening net book value	2 421.4	2 096.3	186.3	4 704.0
Exchange difference	26.3	21.4	8.4	56.1
Additions	45.7	395.2	90.4	531.3
Transfers	32.2	142.4	(174.6)	–
Disposals	(58.4)	(17.3)	–	(75.7)
Depreciation charge	(9.2)	(372.5)	–	(381.7)
Closing net book value	2 458.0	2 265.5	110.5	4 834.0
At 28 March 2009				
Cost	2 566.6	4 811.9	110.5	7 489.0
Accumulated depreciation	(108.6)	(2 546.4)	–	(2 655.0)
Net book value	2 458.0	2 265.5	110.5	4 834.0

The net book value above includes land and buildings of £2458.0 m (last year £2421.4 m), fixtures and fitting of £2265.5 m (last year £2096.3 m) and assets in the course of construction of £110.5 m (last year £186.3 m).

Additions to property, fixtures and fittings and assets in the course of construction amounted to £531.3 m.

Commentary

The note to the accounts gives all the information on the changes in the fixed assets during the year. It breaks the assets down into various classes and for each of these classes of assets shows the additions and disposals during the year together with the associated movements on depreciation provisions. You will see that Marks and Spencer plc comply with the requirement to give comparative information for the previous year by starting with the balances in March 2007 showing the movements for the year and then doing the same for 2008/9. You might also have noted that apart from additions and disposals they give details of assets transferred from assets in construction to land and buildings and fixtures and fittings. Finally you will see that there is an amount for exchange rate differences. You are very likely to see this in the accounts of global companies that own assets in countries where the unit of currency is different from the unit in which they are reporting.

SUMMARY

In this chapter we have reintroduced the definitions of assets and of fixed assets, and we have examined some of the problems associated with arriving at the cost of a fixed asset and estimating the useful life and the residual value. We have also considered the nature of depreciation, why it is charged to the income statement and the way in which it is treated in a statement of financial position. We have seen that there are two methods of depreciation in common usage and we have examined the differences between these and the effects on the income statement and the statement of financial position. Finally, we have discussed and illustrated the way in which a sale of a fixed asset is dealt with via the worksheet, its effect on the cash flow statements and how the profit and operating cash flow are reconciled.

REFERENCES

IASB. (2003) *Presentation of Financial Statements.* London: IASB.
IASB. (2003) IAS 16, *Property, Plant and Equipment.* London: IASB.

FURTHER READING

A full discussion on depreciation is contained in *Depreciation: Depreciating Assets* by W.T. Baxter (Gee, 1981).

REVIEW QUESTIONS

(✓ indicates answers are available in Appendix A)

✓ **1** What is the purpose of depreciation?

2 Why is it unlikely that depreciation will provide for replacement of the fixed asset?

✓ **3** What factors need to be taken into account in determining the useful life of an asset?

4 On what basis do we decide what should and should not be included in the cost of a fixed asset?

✓ **5** Describe what is meant by the carrying amount of an asset.

6 What are the assumptions underlying the two main methods of depreciation?

7 An expense has been defined as a past or expired benefit. In what way does depreciation differ from other expenses?

8 In the chapter we described the profit or loss arising on the disposal of a fixed asset as a paper profit or loss. Explain how this profit differs from that arising on the sale of inventory.

9 What is the effect of depreciation on the cash flows of a business?

10 What is the effect of a sale of a fixed asset for more than its carrying value on

(a) the income for the year and

(b) the cash flows of the business?

PROBLEMS FOR DISCUSSION AND ANALYSIS

(✓ indicates answers are available in Appendix A)

✓ **1** In each of the following situations discuss the most appropriate method of depreciation, giving reasons for your choice.

(a) Land and buildings: The land was purchased for £300 000 and £400 000 was spent on the erection of the factory and office accommodation.

(b) Motor vehicles: The business owns a fleet of cars and delivery vans, all of which were bought new. The owners have decided to trade in the vehicles for new models after four years or 60 000 miles, whichever is sooner. The anticipated mileage figures are 12 000 miles per annum for the cars and 20 000 miles per annum for the vans. Plant and machinery: The plant and machinery owned by the business can be broadly classified into three types as follows:

(c) Type 1: Highly specialist machinery used for supplying roller bearings to Manicmotors Ltd. The contract for supply is for five years, after which it may be renewed at the option of Manicmotors. The renewal would be on an annual basis. The machinery is so specialist that it cannot be used for any other purpose. It has an expected useful life of ten years and the residual value is likely to be negligible.

(d) Type 2: Semi-specialist machinery which is expected to be productive for ten years and have a residual value of 10% of its original cost. However, other firms operating similar machines have found that after the first three years it becomes increasingly more costly in terms of repairs and maintenance to keep machinery of this type productive.

(e) Type 3: General purpose machinery which has an estimated useful life of 80 000 running hours. Based on present levels of production the usage is 8000 hours a year, but as from next year this is expected to rise to 12 000 hours a year if the sales forecasts are correct.

2 Using a worksheet, draw up the statement of financial position, income statement and cash flow statement for the business whose transactions are set out below:

Month 1   Bert put in £9000 of his own money and transferred his own car into the name of the business. At the time of the transfer it would have cost £6000 to buy a new model of the same car but as the car was one year old its second-hand value was only £4000.
The business then bought a machine for £4000, paying for this in cash, and at the same time bought a second machine on credit terms. The credit terms were a deposit of £1000 which was paid in cash and two equal instalments of £900 payable at the start of months 4 and 7, respectively. The cash price of the machine was £2500.

Month 2   Bought raw materials for £3000 and paid cash and made cash sales of £3000.

Month 3   Paid rent in arrears for the three months, amounting to £600 in cash.
Paid wages of £1500 for the three months to date.
Made cash sales of £4000 and purchased more raw materials, again for cash, amounting to £8000.

Month 4   Paid instalment on machine of £900 in cash and made cash sales of £4000.

Months 5–7   Bought raw materials for cash for £2000 and made cash sales of £5000, paid wages for three months of £1500, the rent for three months of £600 and the second and final instalment on the machine of £900.

Months 6–12   Made cash sales of £14000, bought raw materials for cash for £6000, paid wages for six months of £3000 and paid rent for three months of £600.

At the end of the year, Bert has raw materials in inventory which cost £2000. He calculates that the car will last two more years after which he thinks he will be able to sell it for £400. The machines have useful lives estimated at three years and will then be sold for £100 each. Since Bert is not very good with figures, he opts for straight-line depreciation on all the fixed assets.

3 Supercramp's worksheet at 31 March 2010 is given below. During the year to 31 March 2010 the business made a profit of £20 000 before depreciation had been charged and before dealing with items 1–3 below.

Item 1   On 30 September 2009 a new car had been acquired at a cost of £14 000. The amount has been included under the fixed asset total but no depreciation has been charged.

Item 2   The freehold property was purchased on 1 April 2009 and no depreciation has yet been charged.

Item 3   On 31 March 2010 some of the machinery was sold for £9000. The cheque from the purchaser was banked on that day but is not reflected in the bank balance as no accounting entries have been made in respect of this sale. At 31 March 2004 the machinery sold was recorded at cost of £20 000 and had accumulated depreciation of £12 000.

Supercramp follows the following accounting policies in respect of depreciation:

Land	not depreciated
Buildings	4% per annum straight line
Machinery	20% per annum straight line
Cars	25% per annum straight line

In the year of acquisition or disposal assets are depreciated on a time apportionment basis.

Supercramp worksheet

	Assets					=	Equity + liabilities		
	Bank	**Land**	**Buildings**	**Machinery**	**Cars**		**Owner's equity**	**Profit retained**	**Profit for the year**
Balances	18 000	40 000	90 000	55 000	34 000		100 000	117 000	20 000

Required

(a) Discuss how each of the items 1–3 should be treated and the effects on the statement of financial position, income statement and cash flow statement.

(b) Draw up the statement of financial position, income statement and cash flow statement based on the information you have and the adjustments you have made.

CHAPTER 9
FINANCING AND
BUSINESS STRUCTURES

LEARNING OUTCOMES

By the end of this chapter you will be able to:

- Identify the main sources of finance available to a business and explain the characteristics and uses of each of these.

- Understand the alternative sources of finance for small businesses.

- Appreciate the importance of choosing appropriate finance and the impact of financing decisions on risk.

To date, the chapters have largely been concerned with what an organization does with an asset once it has been acquired. In this chapter, we turn our attention to how the business raises the money to acquire its assets. The various types of finance available to different types of organizations are discussed, as are the effects of the finance mix on the returns to the owners.

In this chapter, we shall consider the different forms of finance that a business uses and the effects of the organizational structure upon the sources of finance available. We shall also consider the financing structure of an organization and the effect on financial risk. For these purposes, it is necessary to differentiate between business risk and financial risk.

Broadly speaking, business risk applies equally to all firms in an industry, with some variations relating to size and diversity, i.e. it is industry specific rather than firm specific. Financial risk is more firm specific; it relates to the financial structure of a business, i.e. the way in which it finances its assets.

Before commencing our discussion of the different types of finance, it is important to appreciate that the choice of appropriate finance can be vital to the long-term success of a business. Ideally, the type of finance should match the purpose for which it is to be used. For example, using what is essentially short-term finance for the purchase of a building merely creates problems when the financier has to be repaid. The building is still needed and therefore replacement finance has to be found. Similarly, taking out a loan repayable over 20 years to buy an asset that is only going to be needed for a few years would leave the business in the position of having to pay interest on money it no longer needs. These are, of course, extreme examples, but they do serve to illustrate the point that the finance must be matched with the purpose for which it is to be used.

KEY CONCEPT 9.1

Type of finance

The finance used and the period of that finance should be matched to the period for which it is required and the purpose for which it is to be used.

CASE STUDY 9.1

Northern Rock lessons: How did a few dodgy loans in the US housing market lead to a mini-crisis in Britain's banking system?

A century of advancing regulation, bank consolidation and financial sophistication was thought to have put Dickensian bank 'runs' behind us. Those queues outside Northern Rock branches said otherwise. And they spoke to a deeper fear: that what began as a complex financial crisis in the USA could degenerate into a slowdown or even recession here.

So what is the connection? How did some dodgy loans in the US mortgage market undermine the eighth largest British bank and apparently threaten several others? The link here is a financial mechanism which most of us never have to think about — the inter-bank market. At any one time, different

(Continued)

banks have different requirements for short-term financing. The inter-bank market is the market between banks in which they can borrow from, or lend to, each other to meet their short-term needs. These transactions are secured against collateral such as government bonds. But the market has seized up because of uncertainty about the value of some of the collateral which institutions hold, such as instruments derived from US mortgages, whose value is now hard to determine. If Bank A is suspected of holding a lot of such debt, how can Bank B be sure that a loan to Bank A will be honoured?

Northern Rock fell victim because it depended more than most banks on the inter-bank market, rather than depositors, to fund its operations while also lending on highly attractive terms. In effect, the bank was borrowing short and lending long — the classic recipe for financial disaster. It raised funds by issuing short-term securities secured against its mortgages. This fuelled spectacular growth. But when the credit markets ground to a halt and interest rates rose, it could not raise the cash to fund its operations. Northern Rock's problem was liquidity, not solvency. Unfortunately, depositors did not understand, or did not believe, that this was the case. The financial seizure exposed the shortcomings of Northern Rock's business plan and sparked a textbook crisis of confidence.

(Michael Prest, *Prospect Magazine* 27th October 2007, Issue 139.)

Commentary

The collapse of Northern Rock in 2007 could be seen as heralding the banking crisis that led to a world recession within a matter of years. However, if you read the article above, which is not untypical of many commentaries at the time, you will see in the third paragraph that at the heart of the crisis at Northern Rock was the business model with relied on short-term funds to finance long-term lending. This model worked well but relied on the idea that you might make a loan repayable over 20 years and finance it by borrowing money for say a year and then paying that back and replacing it with another short term loan. For this model to be successful two conditions need to be present. The first of these is that the rate of interest at which you borrow short-term is less than the rate at which you have lent long-term. The second is that there will be short term funds available for you to borrow. Although this was the case initially it did not last. Perhaps if Northern Rock management had followed Key Concept 9.1 they would not have ended up where they did!

Although any attempt to classify different types of finance is problematic, it is useful to look at some broad categories and a division based upon the period of finance is the one we have chosen to use. In considering the various forms of finance, we shall endeavour to follow a pattern of providing a general description of the source of finance, discussing its uses, limitations, costs and availability. Prior to that however, it is worth looking at Figure 9.1 which provides a framework for our discussion.

This figure provides a pictorial representation of the different types of finance available to firms. We will be dealing first with short-term finance or current liabilities as they are called in the accounts, then with medium term finance, which would be included under the heading of non-current liabilities. We will then deal with the other types of non-current liabilities, loans, debentures and leases, which are more long term and can include loans in the form of commercial mortgages periods in excess of 20 years. Finally we will look at equity capital, which is in effect long-term finance provided by investors either through capital injected into the business or retained profits left in the business. This type of finance is normally the most permanent form and any reductions in the injected capital are subject to legal restrictions.

FIGURE 9.1   Sources of finance

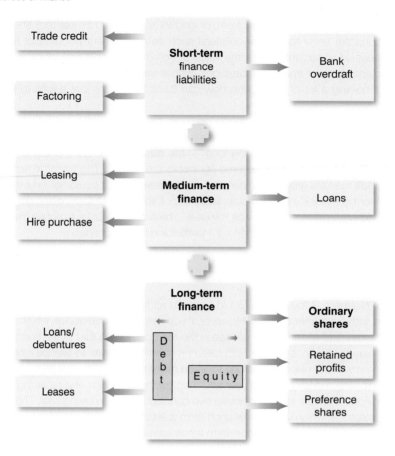

SIZE OF BUSINESS

Although this chapter will cover all types of finance available to businesses you need to remember that the size of the business is an important constraint on the availability of different types of finance. Generally speaking, larger businesses have greater choice, they can sell shares on the stock exchange, issue debentures and obtain loans and financing from lots of different banks. On the other hand, small and medium size businesses tend to have more limited choices and often are not as conversant with what might be available as larger businesses might be. They do, however, use a wide range of finance and interestingly the popularity or use of different sources of finance varies by country, as shown in Table 9.1. The table is based on research carried out in 2006 in five different countries which showed that when raising finance, over 50% of SMEs used their bank as the source of finance. This led to the question of what bank services did the SMEs use, the answer to which is shown in Table 9.1.

TABLE 9.1 Banking services used – country analysis

Country	Current %	Deposit %	Loan %	Mortgage %	Overdraft %	Foreign currency %	International trade services %	Treasury services %	Lease %	Factoring
UK	98	68	31	11	48	34	19	20	29	11
Germany	97	35	56	15	58	9	3	0	32	5
Spain	98	37	33	20	18	11	27	27	50	38
Hong Kong	98	84	49	27	52	74	39	25	27	29
US	97	61	47	20	25	7	10	8	16	16

Source: Banks SMES and accountants: an international study of SME's banking relationships. ACCA research report no. 95

ACTIVITY 9.1

In Table 9.1 there are some considerable differences in the use of, for example, foreign currency services and factoring. Have you any idea why this might be the case?

You may have thought that in the case of foreign currency, Germany, Spain and the United States operate in a large market using one currency, namely the euro and the dollar while the UK and Hong Kong are relatively small markets and therefore even SMEs from those countries trade across the world.

The reasons why factoring is used more in some countries is more of a mystery and an immediate explanation does not spring to mind. A case for some more research here!

SHORT-TERM FINANCE

Conventionally, short-term finance is seen as finance for a period less than a year. It should be used to finance short-term capital requirements such as working capital requirements, i.e. financing inventory and receivables. A number of sources of finance are available, the most common being trade credit, bank overdraft and factoring. It is worth noting that Chapter 21 revisits some of the material covered in this chapter from the viewpoint of working capital management.

Trade credit

We have already come across trade credit in Chapter 7, which dealt with trade receivables and payables. Normally a supplier will allow business customers a period of time after goods have been delivered before payment is required. The period of time and the amount of credit a business gets from its suppliers are dependent upon a number of factors. These include the 'normal' terms of trade of that industry, the creditworthiness of the business and its importance to the supplier. Thus, for example, a small clothing retailer is likely to get less favourable terms than a major group such as Marks & Spencer.

In general, trade credit, which is widely used as a source of finance, provides short-term finance. This is normally used to finance, or partially finance, receivables and inventory. As such, its importance varies from industry to industry. For example, manufacturing industries, where there is greater investment in inventory in the form of raw materials, work in progress and finished goods are more likely to rely on trade credit than service industries. Within an industry there may also be variations. For example, a restaurant is less likely to rely on trade credit than a public house, where a lot of money is tied up in inventory. In fact, within the licensed trade many publicans rely heavily on trade credit and this reliance makes them vulnerable if that credit is not managed effectively. Effective management in a small business setting requires a balance to be struck between taking advantage of trade credit and not being perceived as a slow payer. If too long a period is taken to pay, the supplier may impose less favourable terms next time. The temptation to extend the repayment date can lead to the withdrawal of any period of credit, which means that all supplies have either to be paid for in advance or on a cash-on-delivery basis. Ultimately, too heavy a reliance on trade credit can leave a business vulnerable to the supplier petitioning for bankruptcy or liquidation. Although suppliers are generally reluctant to take such steps, if they believe that they are more likely to recover their money by such a course of action that is what they will do.

Trade credit is often thought of as cost-free credit, which is not strictly true, as often suppliers allow a small discount for early payment. Therefore, taking the full period to pay has an opportunity cost in the form of the discount foregone. This opportunity cost has to be weighed against the availability of funds within the business or the cost of raising additional funds. For trade credit there is generally no requirement for security, which is not the case with other forms of short-term finance, as we shall see.

ACTIVITY 9.2

Recently the author was offered a 3% discount for paying an annual charge of approximately £2000 two months in advance of the due date. Would you have advised him to pay the annual charge two months early?

With current rates of interest on short-term money kept in the bank running at less than 2% per annum a 3% discount for paying two months in advance is a no-brainer assuming that you have the money available. Investing the £2000 for a year would earn £40 or one sixth of that, £8.33 for two months, whereas the discount was £60!

KEY CONCEPT 9.2

Trade credit

Trade credit is a form of short-term finance. It has few costs and security is not required.

Factoring

If a business makes sales on credit, it will have to collect payment from its customers at some stage. Up until that point, it will have to finance those debts, either through trade credit, an overdraft or its own capital. The costs of this finance can be very high and many small businesses will be hard up against their limits in terms of their overdraft and the amount and period of trade credit taken. In order to release the money tied up in receivables, the business can approach a factoring company. These are finance companies which specialize in providing a service for the collection of payments from customers.

Essentially, the way in which the system works is that the factoring organization assesses the firm's customers, in terms of the risk of them going bust and the collectability of the money. It then agrees to collect the money due on behalf of the client business. Once an agreement is reached, the factoring company pays the business in respect of the invoices for the month virtually straight away up to a maximum of 80% of the total trade debt of the business with the remaining 20% being paid when the money is collected. It is then the factoring organization's responsibility to collect the debts as soon as possible. In this form of finance the security provided by the business is in the form of the debts being collected. The factoring company charges for the service in two ways; the first of these is in the form of interest based on the finance provided and the second is by a fee of 2–3% based on turnover for managing the collection of the debts. This form of finance is therefore more expensive than trade credit but can be useful as it allows the business to concentrate on production and sales and improves the cash flow. Factoring, however, is not available to all industries. In some cases this is because it is inappropriate, e.g. most retailing operations, and in others the factoring companies are reluctant to be involved because of a lack of clear legal definitions.

KEY CONCEPT 9.3

Factoring

Factoring provides short-term finance. Costs include an interest charge and a debt management charge. The finance is secured on the receivables.

Invoice discounting

Invoice discounting is in some ways similar to factoring as it is concerned with trade receivables. In this case however, what essentially happens is the business receives around 75–80% of the face value of the invoice and agrees to repay it within a period – up to 90 days. The responsibility for collection remains with the business and the advance has to be repaid at the end of the agreed period even if the debt has not been collected. The advantages, vis-à-vis factoring, are that the costs are less approximately one tenth of the factoring costs, the customer does not know that the business has discounted its invoice and the details of the customers records are kept under the business' control.

ACTIVITY 9.3

Identify the main differences between invoice discounting and factoring.

Invoice discounting has lower costs, is not known by the customer and enables a business to maintain control of their customer's information. On the other hand it does require the business to keep all the accounting records, manage the credit periods and collect the monies due on the appropriate date. All of which could be effectively outsourced to the factoring company.

Bank overdrafts

Banks provide short-term finance for working capital, either in the form of short-term loans or an overdraft. The difference is that a loan is for a fixed period of time and interest is charged on the full amount of the loan, less any agreed repayments, for that period. An overdraft, by contrast, is a facility that can be used as and when required and interest is only charged when it is used. Thus, if a business knows that it needs money for a fixed period then a bank loan may be appropriate. On the other hand, if the finance is only required to meet occasional short-term cash flow needs then an overdraft would be more suitable. We shall discuss loans in more detail under the heading of medium-term finance.

Although many businesses use overdrafts as a semi-permanent source of finance, this is not how the banks would like to see this form of finance used. Bank managers like to see a business bank account, on which an overdraft facility has been provided, 'swinging' between having money in the bank account and using the overdraft. They do not see an overdraft as a form of permanent working capital.

A bank overdraft carries with it a charge in the form of interest and often a fee for setting up the facility. The latter, which is a one-off charge, has become more common in recent years. As far as the interest is concerned, the rate of interest charged is related to the risk involved and the market rates of interest for that size of business. In general, the more risk is involved, the higher the rate of interest. As they operate in a volatile market, small firms tend to be charged higher rates of interest than large firms.

In addition, banks will normally require security, which can take various forms. In the case of a small business the security could be a charge on the assets of the business. In many cases, however, the property is already subject to a charge as it is mortgaged. In these situations the bank may take a second charge on the property or on the owner's home or homes if more than one person is involved. Alternatively, or in addition, the bank may require personal guarantees from the owner or, in the case of a limited company, the directors.

For larger companies, the security may be a fixed charge on certain assets, or a floating charge on all the assets. In the case of very large companies the risk involved is lower and the competition between the providers of finance is greater. Because of this competition, for large companies overdrafts tend to be cheaper and more accessible; security is also less of a factor.

KEY CONCEPT 9.4

Bank overdrafts

Bank overdrafts provide finance only when it is needed. Costs include interest and often a set-up charge. In general, some form of security will be required.

MEDIUM-TERM FINANCE

There are a number of sources of medium-term finance that can be used by a business. We shall limit our discussion to the more common of these, namely medium-term loans, leases and hire purchase.

Loans

As we pointed out, an alternative to overdraft finance for short-term requirements is a bank loan. In general, loans should only be used when finance is required for a known period. Ideally that period should relate to the life of the asset or the purpose for which the finance is to be used. Loans can be obtained for short-term, medium-term or long-term finance. Compared with an overdraft facility, which can be used as and when needed, a loan is more permanent. Repayment of the loan is negotiated at the time the loan is taken out and is generally at fixed intervals. It is often secured in the same way as an overdraft and if the repayment conditions are not met then the lender will take action to recover the outstanding amount.

Bank loans are often granted for a specified purpose and limitations may be imposed regarding the use of the loan and the raising of other finance while the loan is outstanding. Unlike an overdraft, the cost of this form of finance is known in advance as interest accrues from the time the business borrows the money irrespective of the fact that it may not use it straight away. In common with other forms of finance discussed so far, the rate of interest charged and the availability of this source of finance are dependent on the size of the business and the lender's assessment of the risk involved. Thus, in general, the larger and more diversified a business, the easier will be its access to this form of finance.

KEY CONCEPT 9.5

Loans

Loans are generally for a fixed purpose and a fixed period. They have set repayment dates, and costs include interest and set-up fees. They are normally secured on assets.

Hire purchase

An alternative way of financing the acquisition of an asset is through the use of hire purchase. Under a hire-purchase agreement, a finance company buys the asset and hires it to the business. Thus, a business can acquire the asset and use it, even though it has not yet paid for it in full. During the period of the hire-purchase agreement the finance company owns the asset. The hirer has the right to use the asset and carries all the risks associated with using that asset. Thus, for example, if a car is purchased on hire purchase, the hirer would be responsible for all the repairs and costs associated with the use of that car in the same way as if they had bought the car directly. At the end of the period of the hire-purchase agreement the ownership of the asset is transferred to the hirer. A normal hire-purchase agreement consists of a deposit and a set number of payments over a number of years.

This type of finance can only be used when a specific asset is purchased, i.e. the finance is for a specified asset purchase and therefore the amount borrowed is limited by the price of the asset. Hire-purchase finance therefore cannot be directly used for financing working capital requirements. The hire-purchase company actually pays the supplier of the asset directly and legally the asset belongs to the hire-purchase company. If repayments are not made in accordance with the hire-purchase agreement, the hire-purchase company has the right to repossess its property. The money borrowed is repaid by monthly instalments which include both a repayment of the capital borrowed and a charge for interest. The rate of interest charged will be dependent on the market rate of interest, but is likely to be higher than the interest on a bank loan.

Hire purchase is available to all businesses and individuals, subject, of course, to the hire-purchase company being satisfied with the credit-worthiness of the person or business.

KEY CONCEPT 9.6

Hire purchase

Hire purchase is for a fixed period. Costs are in the form of interest charges. Ownership of the asset remains with the provider of the finance until all instalments are paid.

Leasing

A lease is an agreement between the person who owns the asset, known as the lessor, and the person who uses the asset, known as the lessee. It conveys the right to use that asset for a stated period of time in exchange for payment but does not normally transfer ownership at the end of the lease period. The period can vary from a very short period to 50 or more years. In common with hire purchase, this form of finance is tied to a specific asset. Thus, its use as a source of finance is limited to the purchase of capital items. Leasing companies will often provide leases tailored to the needs of an industry. For example, in the hospitality industry it is possible to obtain lease finance for the internal telephone system or even the complete furnishing of a hotel.

In general, the cost of leasing is similar to that of hire purchase. The major difference between the two sorts of finance is that, in general, leases tend to be for a longer period and are frequently used as a source of finance for specialized assets. In essence there are two distinct types of leases: operating leases and finance leases. An operating lease is the same in reality as renting the equipment and usually applies to items such as photocopiers.

KEY CONCEPT 9.7

Leasing

Leases are for a fixed period. The costs are in the form of interest charges. Security is related to the asset in question.

The underlying economic substance of a finance lease, on the other hand, is equivalent to borrowing money from a finance company and then using that money to buy an asset. These differences are reflected in the definitions given in Key Concept 9.8.

KEY CONCEPT 9.8

Types of lease

An operating lease

A lease for which the underlying substance of the transaction is a rental arrangement.

A finance lease

A lease for which the underlying substance of the transaction is a financing arrangement.

The reason for emphasizing the difference between the two types of lease is that they are accorded different treatments in the accounts. In broad terms this means that in the case of an operating lease the full amount of the payments made is charged as an expense in the income statement in the same way as we dealt with rent in earlier examples. For a finance lease the treatment is the same as we have already illustrated in earlier chapters, where a loan preceded the purchase of one or more assets. In this case the income statement is only charged with the interest, as would be the case with a loan. An example of some of the disclosure in respect of leases is provided in Case Study 9.2.

A number of variants on leases and hire purchase are available. These include contract hire, lease purchase and sale and lease back. The details of these are beyond the scope of this introduction.

However, it is worth noting that because of the many different types of lease, the accounting treatment of leased assets depends on the type of lease and there is an International Standard on this subject.

CASE STUDY 9.2

BP plc

BP Annual Report and Accounts 2008
Accounting policies

Leases Finance leases, which transfer to the group substantially all the risks and benefits incidental to ownership of the leased item, are capitalized at the commencement of the lease term at the fair value of the leased property or, if lower, at the present value of the minimum lease payments. Finance charges are allocated to each period so as to achieve a constant rate of interest on the remaining balance of the liability and are charged directly against income.

Capitalized leased assets are depreciated over the shorter of the estimated useful life of the asset or the lease term.

Operating lease payments are recognized as an expense in the income statement on a straight-line basis over the lease term.

Commentary

The extracts from the notes to the accounts and the accounting policies statement of BP plc illustrate the disclosure in respect of finance leases. You will see that the accounting policy covers operating leases where the rentals are charged against the profit of the year in which they are incurred. More detail of the actual treatment of the leases, their amount and the charges to the income statement can be found in the notes to the accounts – the relevant extracts of which are reproduced below.

Notes on financial statements

35 Finance debt

$million

	2008			2007		
	Within 1 year	After 1 year	Total	Within 1 year	After 1 year	Total
Borrowings	15 647	16 937	32 584	15 149	15 004	30 153
Net obligations under finance leases	93	527	620	245	647	892
	15 740	17 464	33 204	15 394	15 651	31 045

(Continued)

16. Operating leases

The table below shows the expense for the year in respect of operating leases. Where an operating lease is entered into solely by the group as the operator of a jointly controlled asset, the total cost is included in this analysis, irrespective of any amounts that have been or will be reimbursed by joint venture partners. Where BP is not the operator of a jointly controlled asset, and has not co-signed the lease, operating lease costs and future minimum lease payments are excluded from the information given below. However, where BP has co-signed the lease, BP's share of the lease costs and future minimum lease payments are included.

	$million		
	2008	**2007**	**2006**
Minimum lease payments	**4 870**	4 152	3 647
Contingent rentals	**134**	105	13
Sub-lease rentals	**−201**	−191	−131
	4 803	4 066	3 529

The future minimum lease payments at 31 December, before deducting related rental income from operating sub-leases of $557 million (2007 $618 million), are shown in the table below. This does not include future contingent rentals. Where the lease rentals are dependent on a variable factor, the future minimum lease payments are based on the factor as at inception of the lease.

	$million	
Future minimum lease payments	**2008**	**2007**
Payable within		
1 year	**4 135**	3 780
2 to 5 years	**9 140**	7 660
Thereafter	**5 520**	5 498
	18 795	16 938

Of which, future minimum operating lease commitments relating to drilling rigs are $7730 million (2007 $5688 million).

LONG-TERM FINANCE

The number of alternative sources of long-term finance available is, to some extent, dependent on the type of organization involved. We shall start our discussion with debt finance, such as long-term loans, which are more generally available, and then move on to discuss equity finance. The latter discussion will be subdivided in terms of organization types, i.e. sole proprietorships, partnerships and limited companies, as these affect the type of equity finance available. In respect of limited companies, we shall limit our discussion to private limited companies.

Debt finance

This is the term given to any source of long-term finance that is not equity finance. Often, debt finance is seen exclusively as long-term interest-bearing finance. This is, in fact, a misconception, as all the finance we have discussed so far has been debt finance. We shall look at two broad categories of long-term debt finance, i.e. long-term loans, which are available to all organizations, and debentures and loan stock, which tend to be used by incorporated businesses.

Long-term loans

As we have said, loans can be used for short-term, medium-term or long-term finance. Interest rates are likely to be different for different loan periods as these will need to be adjusted to take into account the higher risk associated with lending money for a longer period. Long-term loans are often for a specific purpose, e.g. the purchase of property, and the period is affected by the life of the asset, the repayments required and the willingness of the lender to lend money. For many small businesses these loans often take the form of a commercial mortgage on property.

Apart from loans related to property, the period of these loans is less in the UK than in Germany and Japan, where longer loan periods are more common. This may reflect reluctance on the part of UK banks and other financial institutions to lend money for long periods. Interestingly, although economic theory would suggest that if there is unsatisfied demand in the market this would be the trigger for new entrants to the market, this has not happened. This is due, in part, to the relatively high costs and low returns in entering this market, although the internet may reduce these costs. The other factor influencing the number of new entrants is the tendency of UK businesses to 'bank' with one organization, i.e. take loans from the bank that holds the business current account. Whether this is a deliberate free choice or a reaction to the banks themselves preferring this type of relationship is not known and is probably in reality a combination of both of those influences. The result is that despite the fact there are many non-UK-based banks operating in the UK there are still limitations on the availability of long-term loans, especially for the purchase of assets other than property. As is the case with all the other types of finance we have discussed, the availability of this source of finance is also heavily dependent on the lender's assessment of the creditworthiness of the prospective borrower.

In the case of large companies, international groups and in particular multinationals, there is also the opportunity to raise funds from the European market and other markets around the world, as is evident from Case Study 9.3. For smaller and medium-sized companies, research by Berry *et al.* (2003) shows that access to the European banks is still very limited.

Debentures and loan stock

These terms refer to particular types of long-term loans to limited companies. They basically mean the same thing and are essentially long-term loan finance. The main difference between these and long-term loans is that interest tends to be at a fixed rate and repayment tends to be at a fixed point in time, rather than over the period of the loan as would be the case for a commercial mortgage or other long-term loan. Debentures and loan stock are issued by the company raising the finance and can usually be traded on what are known as secondary markets. The price at which they can be sold and bought on the secondary market will not be the same as the price at which they were issued. This variation is related to changes in interest rates over time. In virtually all debenture deeds there is a right to repayment or appointment of a receiver if interest is not paid when due. The cost of this type of finance is similar to that for long-term loans and is affected by the market rate of interest, the security available and the risk involved. For this reason, they are more commonly seen in the accounts of larger companies.

Leases and leasehold

As we said in our discussion of leasing as a medium-term source of finance the period of the lease can be extensive and in the case of commercial and residential property the lease can be very long. Indeed the norm for residential leaseholds on flats is 99 years. In the case of flats held on 99-year leases this is generally called a 'leasehold' and this refers to the form of ownership not to the way in which it is financed. So a 'leasehold' is an alternative form of ownership to a 'freehold' and relates to property. However, in the case of commercial property you may simply take out a long lease which would generally be shorter than on residential property and in many of these cases the lease is a form of finance.

CASE STUDY 9.3

BP plc

Extract from the notes to the accounts of BP plc 2008
Finance Debt – extract from note 35

Fair value The estimated fair value of finance debt is shown in the table below together with the carrying amount as reflected in the **statement of financial position**.

Long-term borrowings in the table below include the portion of debt that matures in the year from 31 December 2008, whereas in the **statement of financial position** the amount would be reported within current liabilities.

The carrying amount of the group's short-term borrowings, comprising mainly commercial paper, bank loans, overdrafts and US Industrial Revenue/Municipal Bonds, approximates their fair value. The fair value of the group's long-term borrowings and finance lease obligations is estimated using quoted prices or, where these are not available, discounted cash flow analyses based on the group's current incremental borrowing rates for similar types and maturities of borrowing.

	$ million			
	2008		2007	
	Fair value	Carrying amount	Fair value	Carrying amount
Short-term borrowings	9 913	9 913	11 212	11 212
Long-term borrowings	23 239	22 671	19 094	18 941
Net obligations under finance leases	638	620	908	892
Total finance debt	33 790	33 204	31 214	31 045

Commentary

As you can see from the extract above BP plc classifies it debt by short and long term borrowings and then finance leases which we have already looked at in Case Study 9.2. If you compared the

(Continued)

amount of detail given in respect of maturity with that in the 2003 accounts in the extract below you will see that despite an increase in the number of International Accounting Standards over the intervening years the amount of disclosure in respect of the dates of maturity of debt has diminished.

Extract from the notes to the accounts of BP plc 2003

27 Finance Debt

Analysis of borrowing by year of repayment	2003 Bank loans	2003 Other loans	2003 Total	2002 Bank loans	2002 Other loans	2002 Total
Due after 10 years	–	721	721	–	1 417	1 417
Due within 10 years	–	17	17	1	371	372
9 years	–	337	337	43	310	353
8 years	–	29	291	–	15	15
7 years	–	–	–	–	1 699	1 699
6 years	7	1 700	1 707	–	516	516
5 years	7	938	945	–	1 603	1 603
4 years	8	1 291	1 299	161	344	505
3 years	193	2 593	2 786	19	2 671	1 690
2 years	38	2 636	2 674	120	710	830
	253	10 524	10 777	344	9 656	10 000
1 year	205	9 161	9 366	476	9 526	10 002
	458	19 685	20 143	820	19 182	20 002

KEY CONCEPT 9.9

Debt finance – long term

Long-term debt finance is generally for a fixed period and interest rates can be higher than for short or medium-term finance.

Equity finance

The other major source of long-term finance is equity finance, and here we need to look at organizational types, as this can have a major effect on both the type and the amount of equity finance available.

Sole proprietorships or owner-managed businesses

In the case of a sole proprietorship, as we have seen, the only sources of equity finance are those supplied by the owner and the retained earnings. In many small businesses, the amount of funds that the owner has available to put into the business is often limited. This means that the only source of equity finance is retained earnings. In a fast-growing business it is unlikely that there will be sufficient retained earnings to finance expansion. As such, sole proprietorships, in common with many small businesses, become very reliant on debt finance and, as we shall see, this exposes them to more risk as a downturn in the market, or an increase in interest rates, could have a dramatic impact on their ability to service the debt. Unlike debt finance, equity finance has no limitations in terms of the use to which it is put.

Partnerships

Partnerships, as the name implies, are organizations that are owned, and often managed, by a number of individuals. They are most common among professionals, thus we see doctors, dentists, lawyers, architects and, of course, accountants working in partnerships. In essence, the sources of equity finance for partnerships are the same as for sole proprietorships, i.e. money contributed by the owners and retained earnings. There are, of course, more people involved, so more equity can be raised through contributions by the owners. Partnerships are governed by the legislation contained in the 1890 Partnership Act, the Limited Liability Partnership Act 2000 and the Limited Liability Partnership Regulations 2001, and by case law. In general, the main difference between partnerships and sole proprietorships is that, whereas the sole proprietor is the only person responsible for the debts, in a partnership, except limited liability partnerships, the partners are jointly and severally liable. This means that if a partner cannot pay their share of the debts, the other partners must pay. In the case of limited liability partnerships, which are corporate bodies similar to companies, the partner is only liable for the amount that he or she has agreed to contribute as capital. Although this relatively new form of partnership may encourage more people to take on partnerships and thereby raise the potential pool from which a partnership can raise finance, they are closer to sole proprietorships and other partnerships than to limited companies.

Limited companies

Limited companies have the advantage, from an investor's point of view, that the liability of the owners is limited to the amount they have invested in the company. As with partnerships and sole proprietorships, the major source of equity comes from the owners. However, in the case of limited companies this is through the issue of ordinary shares.

Ordinary shares

In the case of companies, the equity is divided into ordinary shares, which represent contributed capital, and reserves, which represent profits made by the company. Each share normally has a nominal or par value, e.g. 10p or £1. This value has little significance in terms of the price at which the shares are bought and sold on the stock market. It is, however, the figure at which the shares are shown in the accounts. In the case of an existing company any new shares issued after the company has been trading are likely to be issued at a price in excess of the nominal value. The difference between the nominal value and the price at which the share is issued is put to a special account known as the share premium account. This will be separately identified, as Case Study 9.4 illustrates.

As with any other form of organization, the other main source of equity capital is retained earnings. Unlike a sole proprietorship or partnership, a company distributes its profits by way of dividends. The directors decide on the amount of dividend to be paid and the timing of the dividends, and, until a dividend is declared by the directors, the shareholders have no *prima facie* right to a dividend. Dividends can be paid during the year or at the end of the year. If they are paid during the year they are referred to as interim dividends and the dividend at the end of the year is referred to as the final dividend. Dividends are treated differently from drawings, which, as we have seen, are normally deducted from the owner's equity. These differences will be looked at in more detail in Chapter 11. A company has the advantage over a sole proprietorship or a partnership in that it can issue shares to whomever it wishes in whatever proportions it wishes. The owners of the shares, the shareholders, do not have to take part in the management of the company, and in most large companies most shareholders play virtually no part in the management of the company. They merely invest their money and take the risk that they will get better returns, in the form of their share of the profits, than they would by investing in fixed-interest investments. Ultimately, all the profits belong to the shareholders, so if they do not get their share of the profits in the form of dividends, i.e. the profits are retained in the company, their share of the profits and the future earnings is reflected in the price at which they could sell their shares.

CASE STUDY 9.4

Rolls Royce plc

Commentary

The extract from the balance sheet of Rolls Royce plc shows the capital and reserves broken down between the called-up share capital, the share premium account and the other reserves. The user is also referred to a note to the accounts where more details in respect of these subdivisions are given.

Extract from the Group balance sheet of Rolls Royce plc at 31 December 2008

Equity

Capital and reserves	Note	2008	2007
Called-up share capital	18	326	326
Share premiumaccount	19	631	631
Hedging reserves	19	−22	77
Translation reserve	19	660	59
Retained earnings	19	760	2 081
Equity attributable to equity holders of the parent Minority interests		2 355	3 174
Minority interests	19	9	12
Total equity		2 364	3 186

ACTIVITY 9.4

Looking at the information contained in Case Study 9.4 what would you expect to see in the income statement for the year ended 31 December 2008?

Given that the retained earnings had reduced from £2081 million to £760 million you would expect to find a thumping great loss, and you would not be disappointed. The detail of the income statement shows that it made a profit of £862 million before financing charges and tax but after financing and tax it made a loss of £1342 million.

Preference shares

Apart from ordinary shares, a company can also issue preference shares. Unlike ordinary shares, a preference share normally has a fixed dividend and, even if more profits are made, the preference dividend remains the same. In addition, they normally carry a right to preference in the order of payment in the event of the company going into liquidation. They are therefore less risky than ordinary shares and appeal to a different sort of investor. Whether these shares should be classified as equity or debt would depend on the particular type of preference shares in question and the rights attaching to them. Preference shares may be redeemable or non-redeemable. They may carry a right to dividends on a cumulative basis, i.e. if the directors do not pay any dividends in a year the preference shareholders will have a right to be paid that year's dividend and any others that have not been paid before the ordinary shareholders can be paid any dividend. Some preference shares are participating preference shares, whereby they get a share of profits if the profit is over a certain figure.

KEY CONCEPT 9.10

Equity finance

This is long-term permanent finance and comes from two main sources, contributed capital and retained earnings.

OTHER SOURCES OF FINANCE

In addition to the sources of finance mentioned above, depending on their size and other factors, businesses can access money from venture capitalists, business angels and the government. We provide short descriptions of these below.

Venture capital

Larger businesses wishing to get an injection of equity funds can do so by issuing new shares which are sold via the stock exchange. For large small and medium size companies this source is not available. However, there are a number of venture capitalists who will provide long-term finance in the form of shares or of loan finance to these companies. They deal with companies for which the risk is too high for traditional loan financiers, e.g. the banks, and they expect to earn higher returns on their investment. They will provide finance for start-ups, although this is rare, for growth and for management buy-outs or buy-ins, which tend to happen when large businesses wish to sell of parts of their business or family businesses wish to sell out because of problems with succession within the family. They will purchase shares from existing shareholders who may want to realize their investment and they will provide rescue funds to help turn a business around. 3i Group plc is perhaps the best known of these venture capital companies but there are many more, some of which are more specialized than others and concentrate their efforts and expertise in particular sectors.

Business angels

These are often very wealthy individuals who have been successful in business and who are willing to invest in growing other businesses. They not only provide additional finance for smaller firms in which they invest but also provide a wealth of expertise and contacts which can mean the difference between success and failure. The general awareness of business angels has been more apparent in recent years through popular TV shows such as *Dragons' Den*, which provides useful insights into the ways in which these potential investors go about the process of deciding whether or not to invest. Although it used to be difficult for small business owners to find these 'angels' the internet has changed all that – a quick search on the UK alone provided over two million hits – the problem now is finding the right one.

Government assistance

At any point in time there is a plethora of government schemes around to help businesses grow. These range from direct grants, normally although not exclusively, through development agencies and through loan guarantee schemes, grants, tax incentives or rates holidays. All of these can be useful to smaller businesses wishing to grow but lacking the necessary finance to do so on their own. Once again the internet provides a massive amount of information on what is available, to who and where it is available.

FINANCING STRUCTURES AND FINANCIAL RISK

The mix of debt finance and equity finance is known as gearing, and it affects the financial risk of an enterprise. Basically, the more reliant a business is on debt finance, i.e. the more highly geared, the greater is the risk. The risk we are referring to here is that if interest rates go up or the profit margin comes down, the enterprise would not be able to pay the interest or repayments due on its debt finance. There are, of course, advantages in addition to disadvantages in being highly geared, as Example 9.1 illustrates.

EXAMPLE 9.1

Chansit has equity capital consisting of 20 000 ordinary shares of £1 each. It has retained earnings of £10 000 and has £40 000 in loans on which interest at 3% above bank base rate, which currently stands at 5%, is due.

Solidco has equity capital consisting of 40 000 ordinary shares of £1 each. It has retained earnings of £10 000 and has £20 000 in loans on which interest at 3% above bank base rate, i.e. 8%, is due.

Situation 1
Both companies make sales of £100 000 and their net profit before interest is 6% on sales.

The income statements for the two companies would be as shown below.

Income statements (£)

	Chansit	Solidco
Sales	100 000	100 000
Costs	94 000	94 000
Net profit	6 000	6 000
Interest	3 200	1 600
Available for equity shares	2 800	4 400
Earnings per share	0.14	0.11

(Continued)

The earnings per share is arrived at by dividing the profit by the number of shares in issue. Thus, for Chansit the profit of £2800 is divided by 20 000 shares to arrive at the profit per share of 14p. In the case of Solidco, it is £4400 divided by 40 000 shares, i.e. 11p per share. The ordinary shareholders of Chansit are getting a better return than the shareholders of Solidco: 14p per share compared with 11p per share in Solidco. This is despite the fact that both companies have the same sales, costs and net profit. The differences arise as a result of the financing structure, its effect on the interest charges and the remaining profit after interest. In this scenario, Chansit is better off because it has used the money it has borrowed to increase its operating capability and, hence, its profits. This seems sensible but as we will illustrate the apparent advantage can easily be eroded or even removed by a change in costs or interest rates.

Situation 2 – Increased costs

In this situation, instead of making a net profit before interest of 6% of sales, the companies find that they can only make 4%.

In this case, the income statements of the two companies would be as follows.

Income statements (£)

	Chansit	Solidco
Sales	100 000	100 000
Costs	96 000	96 000
Net profit	4 000	4 000
Interest	3 200	1 600
Available for equity shares	800	2 400
Earnings per share	0.04	0.06

In this case, the profit margin of both businesses has fallen by the same amount. As a result, the earnings available for the equity shares have dropped in both cases. However, the effect on the earnings per share is more dramatic in the case of Chansit than it is in the case of Solidco owing once again to the effects of the financing structure. Thus, although in Situation 1 it looked as if Chansit had the better financing structure, we find from a shareholder's point of view that it is more vulnerable to a reduction in the profit margin than Solidco and in this situation Solidco is providing a better return, in the form of earnings per share, to its shareholders.

Situation 3 – Increased interest rates

In this situation, the facts are the same as in Situation 2, i.e. the net profit before interest is 4% on the sales. However, in addition, the bank base rate moves to 7% and therefore the interest on the loans moves up to 10%.

In this case, the income statements of the two companies would be as follows.

Income statements (£)

	Chansit	Solidco
Sales	100 000	100 000
Costs	96 000	96 000
Net profit	4 000	4 000
Interest	4 000	2 000
Available for equity shares	0	2 000
Earnings per share	0.00	0.05

(Continued)

Once again both businesses are affected by the change in circumstances. However, the effect of the rise in interest rates is greater, in terms of the return to the shareholders in Chansit, where the profits are completely used up to pay the interest, than it is in Solidco.

These examples illustrate the effects of high gearing, which are to increase the returns to shareholders but at the same time make them more vulnerable to decreases in the profit margin. In addition, their returns are also affected more by increases in interest rates than those of a low-geared company.

On the other hand, a fall in interest rates is more beneficial to the shareholders of a highly geared company. Hence, there is a trade-off between risk and return.

It is worth mentioning that the lower the share of the business that is financed by equity, the more difficult it is to raise debt finance. Banks in the UK like to see a ratio of one to one, i.e. they will lend money, all other things being equal, so that the debt finance is equal to the equity share. There is often a clause to that effect included in the loan agreement. If the clause limits the amount of borrowing to the equity total, then decisions on how much profit to retain, whether to revalue land and buildings, etc., can have a dramatic effect on a company's ability to raise finance.

SUMMARY

In this chapter, we have considered the main types of short-term, medium-term and long-term finance that are available to all organizations. We have also looked at equity finance in the form of contributed capital and retained earnings. The effects of different organizational forms on the sources of equity finance have been discussed and the effects of the mix of debt to equity finance on the returns to equity shareholders have been discussed and illustrated. It is important to remember that one vital point raised in this chapter was that the type of finance used should relate to the purpose for which that finance will be used.

REFERENCES

Berry, A., Grant, P. and Jarvis, R. (2003) *Can European Banks Plug the Finance Gap for UK SMEs?* ACCA Research Report No. 81, London: Association of Chartered Certified Accountants.

Prest, M. (2007) 'Northern Rock lessons: How did a few dodgy loans in the US housing market lead to a mini-crisis in Britain's banking system?' *Prospect Magazine,* 27th October, Issue 139.

FURTHER READING

Berry, A. (2006) Banks SMES and accountants: an international study of SME's banking relationships. ACCA Research Report No. 95, Association of Chartered Certified Accountants, London.

IASB. (1998) *IAS 17, Leases*: readers should note that this is currently subject to a major discussion on how to improve the reporting of lease-related transactions.

REVIEW QUESTIONS

(✓ indicates answers are available in Appendix A)

1 Why is it important to match the type of finance with the purpose of raising that finance?

✓ **2** What are the forms of short-term finance discussed in the chapter?

3 What are the main differences between equity finance and debt finance?

4 What are the differences between drawings and dividends?

5 What does the term 'highly geared' refer to?

6 What are the advantages and disadvantages of being highly geared?

✓ **7** Which types of short-term finance require a business to provide some form of security?

✓ **8** What form of security is required for each of the forms of short-term finance discussed in the chapter?

PROBLEMS FOR DISCUSSION AND ANALYSIS

(✓ indicates answers are available in Appendix A)

✓ **1** A friend has been to see the bank manager about borrowing some money to finance the acquisition of a new van and a new machine. The bank manager has said that, in view of the current financial structure of the company, the bank would not be prepared to provide funds unsecured. The latest statement of financial position of the company is given below.

Statement of financial position

	Notes	£
Current assets		
Cash		1 500
Inventory		3 600
		5 100
Non current assets		
Vehicles	1	24 000
Equipment	1	45 000
		69 000
Total assets		74 100
Current liabilities		
Bank overdraft		12 900
Trade and other payables		7 500
Taxation		10 800
		31 200
Non current liabilities		
Loan		25 000
		25 000
Total liabilities		56 200
Equity		
Ordinary shares		15 000
Retained profits		2 900
Total equity		17 900
Total equity and liabilities		74 100

Notes:

1   Non-current assets

	Cost £	Depreciation £	£
Vehicles	36 000	12 000	24 000
Equipment	60 000	15 000	45 000
	96 000	27 000	69 000

(a) Advise your friend what alternative sources of finance are available and which would be appropriate for the purpose of buying a van and a new machine.

(b) Explain why, in your opinion, the bank manager was not prepared to lend unsecured.

2   Ben was planning to open a fish and chip shop. He has produced the following projections for the first year, based on his experience of the area and some careful research.

	£
Sales	36 000
Cost of ten-year lease	30 000
Refurbishment	3 000
Equipment	20 000
Inventory of fish etc.	1 000
Rent	2 000
Electricity	900
Wages	8 000
Personal drawings	5 000

Ben estimates that the costs of fish etc., which are required to make the sales target of £36 000 will be £12 000. He says that the equipment will last for five years and has no residual value. He has savings of £40 000 but is reluctant to invest the whole of that. To help buy the lease he has been offered a loan of £20 000 at an interest rate of 10% per annum for the first year, with no repayments required during that year. After the first year the rate will be 4% above base rate. Base rate currently stands at 12%. Alternatively, he can borrow money using a bank overdraft at a rate of 17% per annum.

(a) Calculate what Ben's profit would be if he put in all his own money and borrowed anything else he needs. Hint: the receipts and payments have to be looked at in terms of their regularity and their timing.

(b) Calculate what Ben's profit would be in the first year, assuming he takes the loan.

(c) Calculate what Ben's profit would be in the second year, assuming he does not take the loan and sales and costs are the same as the first year.

(d) Calculate what Ben's profit would be in the second year, assuming he takes the loan.

(e) Ben has asked you to advise him on the choice between the two alternatives. How would you advise him, and what reasons would you give?

CHAPTER 10 CASH FLOW STATEMENTS

LEARNING OUTCOMES

By the end of this chapter you will be able to:

- Understand why cash flow information is important to users of accounts.

- Identify the different types of cash flows and the importance of separating the differing cash flows.

- Explain the importance of operating cash flows and their potential impact on the survival of a business.

- Be able to construct cash flow statements using both the direct and indirect method.

- More fully appreciate the differences between accrual based accounting and cash based accounting.

In this chapter, we explore the importance of cash flows to an organization and show how cash flow statements can be used as an additional mechanism to judge the financial health of an organization.

Throughout the preceding chapters, we have gradually introduced the cash flow statement. In this chapter, we shall consider these cash flow statements in more detail in terms of the information they provide, their format and their uses. At present, cash flow statements are one of three financial statements, the others being the statement of financial position or balance sheet and the income statement. They differ from the other statements insofar as the statement of financial position and income statement are firmly based on a system known as accrual accounting; the cash flow statement is based on actual cash flows. This often causes confusion as the information content is very different and needs to be reconciled in order to see how the three statements fit together to provide a fuller picture of the results of the activities of an enterprise. We shall start with a discussion of the need for cash flow information and then move on to look at the contents and formats of the cash flow statement. Finally, we shall demonstrate how such statements are constructed and how the information is interpreted.

THE NEED FOR CASH FLOW INFORMATION

In Chapter 1, we identified the users of accounts based on the discussion provided in *The Corporate Report* (Accounting Standards Steering Committee, 1975) and since repeated in a wide range of accounting standards including the latest International Financial Reporting Standard for Small and Medium Entities (IFRS-SME; 2009). Apart from identifying the potential users of accounting information, that report also identified the type of information they would need. Amongst other types of information, it clearly identified the need for information on the liquidity of the enterprise. This need was also identified later that year in the report of the Committee on Inflation Accounting, commonly referred to as the Sandilands' report. One of the main users of this statement was expected to be bankers and, as we noted earlier, research (Berry and Robertson, 2006) found that bankers now rated this statement more highly than the statement of financial position or income statement. This was not always the case (Berry *et al.*, 1987; Egginton, 1975) and the reasons for that can be found in the changes in format which have made the statement more useful. The growing importance of the cash flow statement is evidenced by the inclusion of cash flows as one of the main objectives of financial reporting in paragraph 7 of IFRS-SME (2009).

The changes in format and content referred to earlier relate to the users' needs. At its most basic the information contained in the cash flow statement is about where money comes from and how it is used. To be useful, such information needs to differentiate between regular cash flows which are likely to be repeated, e.g. those arising in a retail business from buying and selling goods, paying wages, etc., and other 'one off' cash flows, e.g. new capital being introduced to the business or new fixed assets being purchased or sold. By separating out these two categories of cash flows, the user should be better equipped to arrive at a reasoned judgement about what may happen in the future.

So we now know what type of cash flow information should be provided, but the question that arises is: why, at a general level, is cash flow information important? In answering this it is important to appreciate that in order for a business to be successful it needs two things. The first is that it is profitable and the second is that it is able to pay its debts as they fall due. The income statement helps the user to arrive at a judgement in relation to the profitability of a business and the cash flow statement provides information on the cash inflows and outflows and in so doing provides a part of the answer to the question of whether the debts can be paid when due. Such information can be very revealing. The classic example of why this information is important comes from the start of the 1990s when a company called Polly Peck, which was one of the star performers of the time, went into receivership. In this case despite making a trading profit of £139 million Polly Peck had a net cash outflow from operations of

£129 million and so could not pay its debts! In other words, although it was making a profit it was paying out more than it was getting in. This example underlines the fact that in order to survive, a company needs to be both profitable and solvent. In the case of Polly Peck, the company was profitable but was not solvent, even in the short term.

TYPES OF CASH FLOWS

In earlier chapters when introducing the cash flow statement we identified that there were different types of cash flows. Typical cash inflows would be monies generated from trading, commonly referred to as cash flows from operations, monies from new share issues or other forms of long-term finance and any monies received from the sale of fixed assets. Typical outflows would be monies used to buy new fixed assets, to pay tax and dividends and to repay debenture holders or other providers of long-term capital. As we shall see, the cash flow statement separates these cash flows into various categories. The format we shall follow is that recommended in IFRS-SME (2009), we shall use the example of a cash flow statement shown as Example 10.1 as the vehicle for explaining what a cash flow statement contains. We shall then look at an example of how such a statement is constructed.

EXAMPLE 10.1

Sample cash flow statement

	Notes	This year £000	Last year £000
Net cash from operating activities	x	−700	200
Investing activities			
Payments to acquire fixed assets		−900	−200
Payments to acquire investments			−100
Receipts from disposal of fixed assets		50	
Net cash used in investing activity		−850	−300
Financing activities			
Repayment of loan		−150	
Receipts from issue of ordinary share capital		300	
Net cash used in financing activities		150	0
Decrease in cash in period		−1 400	−100
Cash and cash equivalents at beginning of year		1 350	1 450
Cash and cash equivalents at end of year		−50	1 350

Example 10.1 shows that the cash flow statement provides the details of the change in cash in the year the last figure, £1.4 million outflow this year and £100 000 outflow last year, and reconciles that with the figure for cash and cash equivalents from the statements of financial position. It also divides the cash flows into the business and out of the business under a number of separate headings. These headings or subdivisions are intended to provide information about the source and nature of the cash flow. For example, net cash from

(Continued)

operating activities tells us that the cash comes from the normal continuing operations of the business and these operations and their related cash flows are likely to continue each year. The cash flows under 'Investing activities' and 'Financing activities', on the other hand, are different as they are not likely to recur each year.

ACTIVITY 10.1

Thinking of your own life can you separate the different types of cash flow affecting you?

In answering this you might have thought of the costs of buying food or running a car, petrol, oil, insurance, etc. as regular recurring cash flows and the cost of buying the car as a one-off or non-recurring cash outflow.

Before we move on to looking at the subheadings and what they mean in more detail, we first need to remind ourselves of the definitions of cash flows.

KEY CONCEPT 10.1

Cash flows

Cash inflows are defined as increases in cash. Cash outflows are decreases in cash. Net cash flow consists of the net effect of cash inflows and cash outflows.

Net cash from operating activities

The first subheading in the cash flow statement is net cash from operating activities. If we had kept our business as the simple cash-based model we used up until Chapter 6 (before we introduced year-end inventory, receivables, payables, non-current assets, etc.), the cash flow from operating activities would have been the same as profit. However, as we pointed out from Chapter 6 onwards, this may reflect how the cash has been spent but not the economic activity. This, if you remember, is because some of the spending relates to future years and some to past years. This presents us with a problem because what we have done in effect from Chapter 6 onwards is to adjust the cash figure to arrive at a figure for profit based on the principles of accrual accounting. Therefore, as we illustrated at the end of the Chapter 6 and in the subsequent chapters, if we start with the profit figure, what we have to do is to reverse all those adjustments in order to arrive at the cash flow from operations.

It is very important to your understanding of the cash flow statement and its interrelationship with the income statement and statement of financial position that you understand this process and the reasons for it. We will shortly look at a more comprehensive example which brings together the ideas and explanations you have been introduced to so far. Before that, however, we will remind ourselves in relation to cash from operating activities of the issues we have already looked at. It is worth reminding ourselves of what all the headings mean. Once again we can look at the definitions in IFRS-SME (2009).

The first of these, shown as Key Concept 10.2, defines operating activities. In general, this is fairly straightforward as it relates to the principal activities of the entity and broadly that equates to the entries that we see going through the revenue and expenses account and appearing on the income statement to arrive at the net profit or loss. It would therefore include, in the case of a company, items related trading and to interest and tax.

KEY CONCEPT 10.2

Operating activities

Operating activities are the principal **revenue**-producing activities of the entity. Therefore, cash flows from operating activities generally result from the transactions and other events and conditions that enter into the determination of **profit or loss** (IFRS–SME, 2009, Para 7.4).

In previous chapters, we have seen that in order to reconcile the net profit with the cash from operating activities we had to make adjustments relating to goods purchased during the year but not sold, i.e. increases in inventory and for goods sold during the year that had been bought in previous years leading to decreases in inventory. The treatments of these alternatives, i.e. an increase or decrease in inventory, are summed up in Key Concept 10.3. It is important to note that in this and subsequent explanations we start from the basis of the profit and work to the cash from operations.

KEY CONCEPT 10.3

Increases and decreases in inventory

An increase in the level of inventory must be subtracted from the profit to arrive at the net cash from operations.

A decrease in the level of inventory must be added back to the profit to arrive at the net cash from operations.

ACTIVITY 10.2

Can you explain why an increase in the level inventory should be subtracted from profit to arrive at the cash flow from operations? You might find the equation used to arrive at gross cost of sales and gross profit a useful aid to your thinking so these are reproduced here.

$$\text{Opening inventory} + \text{purchases} - \text{closing inventory} = \text{cost of sales}$$

$$\text{Sales} - \text{cost of sales} = \text{gross profit}$$

An increase in the level of inventory means that we have not sold all of the goods we purchased in the year, which, assuming we had bought them for cash would mean that the cost of sales is lower than the goods we paid for. The lower cost of sales figure in turn increases the profit as that is arrived at after deducting the cost of sales from the sales figure.

Before moving on it is worth just reinforcing the way in which a change in the inventory level causes the cash flow from operations and profit to differ. This is illustrated in Example 10.2.

EXAMPLE 10.2

Assume that a cash-based business Alpha has sales of £100. It has the same £20 opening inventory and £20 closing inventory and made purchases of £60 during the year. So looking at the calculation of cost of sales we see that these are £60 and the profit is £40. It has cash inflow of £100 and an outflow of £60 so a net cash flow from operations of £40.

Opening inventory £20 + purchases £60 – closing inventory £20 = cost of sales £60

Sales £100 – cost of sales £60 = gross profit £40

Cash inflows £100 – cash outflows £60 = cash flow from operations £40

Now assume business Beta has exactly the same opening inventory, sales and purchases as Alpha but that it has £30 in its closing inventory. Beta would have a cost of sales of £50 and a profit of £50 but its cash flow from operations would be exactly the same as Alpha, i.e. £40. So in order to reconcile these two measures we need to reduce the profit by the increase in inventory.

Opening inventory £20 + purchases £60 – closing inventory £30 = cost of sales £50

Sales £100 – cost of sales £60 = gross profit £40

Cash inflows £100 – cash outflows £60 = cash flow from operations £40

Gross profit £50 less increase in inventory £10 = Cash flow from operations £40

We also found in Chapter 7 that the presence of receivables and prepayments in addition to payables and accruals led to differences between the cash flows and the figures included in the income statement. We showed that in some cases the cash flow from sales included money from sales made in the previous year and did not include some cash for the sales in the current year because the money was still owed to the business at the end of the year. In this case our general rule is as set out in Key Concept 10.4.

KEY CONCEPT 10.4

Increases and decreases in receivables and prepayments

An increase in the level of receivables and prepayments must be subtracted from the profit to arrive at the net cash from operations.

A decrease in the level of receivables and prepayments must be added back to the profit to arrive at the net cash from operations.

(Continued)

ACTIVITY 10.3

Assuming business C and business D had the same sales £200 and cost of sales £100 but business C had the same figure £40 for accounts receivable at the start and the end of the year whereas business D was owed £40 at the start of the year but only £30 at the end of the year. What is the effect on the profit and cash flow from operations?

If you had thought about this example you would have realized that as both had the same sales and cost of sales they must both have had the same profit £100 (£200 – £100). The cash flows, however, are different. Business C has cash flows of £200 – £100 = £100, the same as the gross profit. Business D on the other hand has cash flows of £210 (£40 that it was owed at the start of the year plus £170 out of the £200 in sales during the year, as it was still owed £30 at the end of the year). So in this case we would have to add the decrease in accounts receivable to the gross profit to arrive at the cash flow from operations.

So, we have looked at what happens when there is a disparity between cash flows and revenue and expenses which results in a change in the current assets. Also, we have derived a general rule that an increase in current assets should be subtracted from profit and a decrease should be added to profit to find the cash from operations. Let us now look at changes in current liabilities. The general rule here is set out in Key Concept 10.5.

KEY CONCEPT 10.5

Increases and decreases in payables and accruals

An increase in the level of payables and accruals must be added back to the profit to arrive at the net cash from operations.

A decrease in the level of payables and accruals must be subtracted from the profit to arrive at the net cash from operations.

You will see that the rule for increases and decreases in current liabilities is in fact the obverse of that for current assets.

ACTIVITY 10.4

If we now look at businesses E and F which have the same sales £300, cost of sales £200, based on no increase in inventory and purchases of £200, and profit £100. In the case of E the accounts payable remain the same and in the case of E the accounts payable at £30 are £20 more at the end of the year than at the start. What would be the effect on the profit and the cash flow from operations?

In the case of both business E and business F the cash inflow from sales is the same as the figure in the income statement. However, in the case of F the cash outflow in respect of payments to suppliers is different as it has actually paid out the amount it owed at the start of the year £10 plus £170 out of the £200 of goods it purchased during the year, so its cash outflows were £180. So, to reconcile profit with cash flows we would need to reduce the profit £100 by the increase in the amounts owed £20 to get to the cash flow from operations.

(Continued)

In Chapter 8, we dealt with two types of difference between the figures used in the income statement to arrive at profit and their treatment in the cash flow statement. We said that depreciation has no effect on the cash column and as such we had to add back depreciation to the profit to arrive at the cash from operating activity. This is very straightforward. The rule we identified in that chapter in relation to depreciation is reiterated in Key Concept 10.6.

KEY CONCEPT 10.6

Depreciation

The charge for depreciation for the year must be added to the profit to arrive at the net cash from operations.

ACTIVITY 10.5

Business G and business H both have the same profit figure of £300 but business H has charged £40 of depreciation and business G has no depreciation charged in arriving at its profit figure. Assuming all other things are equal how would the cash flow from operations differ? It may be helpful to think about the impact of recoding depreciation in the worksheet.

When you thought about the effect of recording depreciation on the cash/bank column in the worksheet you would have realized that it is not recorded there but it is recorded in the revenue and expenses column. It has to be added back to the profit or loss in order to arrive at the cash flow from operations.

KEY CONCEPT 10.7

Profits and losses on sales of fixed assets

A profit on the sale of fixed assets should be subtracted from the profit to arrive at the net cash from operations.

A loss on the sale of fixed assets should be added to the profit to arrive at the net cash from operations.

You will recall from Chapter 8 that because the depreciation charge is essentially based on estimates – we have to estimate the useful life of the asset and what it might be worth at the end of its useful life – the chances are that if an asset is sold before the end of its useful life a paper profit or loss will arise. This paper profit or loss reflects the difference between what we see the asset for and the estimated carrying amount in the books of account. The paper profit or loss will be charged to the income statement even though it has no effect on the cash received and could be seen as really a correction of the errors in the estimates.

If having read the chapter so far and done the activities you are still not clear about the rules summarized in the Key Concepts to date, it is worth revisiting the appropriate chapters before moving on.

Investing activities

To a large extent, items under this heading are much simpler to deal with as they generally affect the statement of financial position and cash flow in the same way. The heading relates to investment in non-current assets and sales of that category of assets. The only real complication is the one we looked at in Chapter 8, where we illustrated the effect of a sale of a non-current asset on the income statement, statement of financial position and cash flow statement. In that case we dealt with the effect on the income statement, i.e. the paper profit or loss, as part of the reconciliation of the profit with the cash from operating activities and we showed the proceeds of sale as a separate cash inflow. In a published cash flow statement, all payments and receipts in respect of the acquisition and disposal of non-current assets are dealt with under this heading.

FINANCING ACTIVITIES

This heading relates to moneys raised by issuing shares, debentures, loans, etc., and moneys used to redeem shares or debentures or pay back long-term debt. In other words, anything relating to the long-term financing of the business comes under this heading.

Before moving on to work through a full example of how these statements are constructed, it is worth reflecting on what the sample cash flow statement used in Example 10.1 tells us about the business in question. The first item to note is that, like Polly Peck, the business has a negative cash flow from operations. The cash flow statement, under the heading of investing activities, also highlights the fact that the business is investing in fixed assets, and by looking at the information contained elsewhere in the accounts you could arrive at a judgement about whether this is additional capacity or replacement of existing capacity. It is also worth noting that under the heading 'Financing activity' it is raising new long-term capital, which may indicate future expansion. Finally, the fact that there is a decrease in cash needs further investigation. Let us now turn to another example to consolidate what we have discussed and see how the various parts of the statement come together.

EXAMPLE 10.3

We will use the information in this example to produce a cash flow statement from two different starting points. The first of these is to start from the worksheet and produce the cash flow statement directly from the worksheet. This is referred to as the direct method and requires that cash flows are put together in to the major classes of gross cash receipts and payments. The second method is the known as the indirect method and starts with the profit figure and utilises both the statement of financial position and income statement to

(Continued)

produce the cash flow statement. Of course, if we get it right, whichever method is used the resultant answer will be the same. The reason for showing both approaches is that the direct method enables you to see how the information is derived from prime sources (the worksheet representing the firm's accounting records). The indirect method on the other hand helps you to understand the interrelationship between the statement of financial position, the income statement and the cash flow statement.

On 1 April 2010 the statement of financial position of Trypit Ltd, which sold computer components, was as shown below.

Trypit Ltd Statement of financial position at 31 March 2010

Current assets		
Amounts receivable		18 000
Inventory		16 000
		34 000
Non current assets		
Fixed assets – cost	10 000	
– depreciation	2 000	
		8 000
Total assets		42 000
Current liabilities		
Bank overdraft		6 000
Trade payables		14 000
Tax payable		3 000
Dividends payable		5 000
Total liabilities		28 000
Equity		14 000
Retained earnings		0
Total equity		14 000
Total equity and liabilities		42 000

You will note that the statement of financial position in this case is that of a company and includes dividends payable, which are payments due to the owners of the shares in the company, and tax payable which the company has to pay as it is recognized as a separate legal entity.

The transactions for the next twelve months are summarized below.

Paid the year's rent of £6 000 in cash.

Cash sales were £33 000 and credit sales were £30 000.

Cash amounting to £26 000 was received from customers.

They purchased £48 000 of goods on credit and paid their suppliers £34 000.

On 1 October they took out a long-term loan of £3 000 at 10%. Interest was to be paid half-yearly.

Paid wages of £7 000 to an assistant.

Paid the tax due from 2009 of £3 000.

Paid the dividends from 2009 of £5 000.

On the last day of the year they bought and paid for some new plant costing £5 000

(Continued)

At the end of March 2011, the goods included in inventory had a cost price of £18 000.

They depreciate the fittings over five years using the straight-line method.

Their accountant calculated that they would owe corporation tax of £1000 for the year which had not been paid at the year end.

Stage 1

The first stage is to record the transactions on a worksheet. This would appear as shown below.

ACTIVITY 10.6

If you wish to take this opportunity to get more practice in using a worksheet a blank template of the worksheet of Trypit is provided at the end of this chapter before the review questions.

Had you completed the blank worksheet it should look like the one in next page. If not, compare the two and find out what you did wrong and why.

Stage 2

Using the information contained in the worksheet, see next page, we first need to calculate the net cash flow from operating activities. We shall do this using the information contained in the revenue and expenses column and the cash column. We start by identifying those items in the revenue and expenses column that are associated with the calculation of the operating profit, the cash coming into the business (the cash inflows) and cash being paid out of the business (cash outflows).

In terms of the cash inflows, we can see from the cash column that the money received in respect of sales amounted to £59 000, i.e. cash sales of £33 000 plus £26 000 received from the customers in respect of credit sales. In terms of the cash outflows relating to operations, we find that £34 000 was paid to suppliers in respect of inventory purchased during the year. In addition, Trypit paid £6000 for rent and £7000 for wages. The only other figure that affects both cash and the revenue and expenses account is the interest paid. We shall return to the interest paid later.

Going back to the other figures in the revenue and expenses column, you will see that they do not affect the bank column and there is therefore no cash inflow or outflow. From this we can calculate our 'Net cash inflow from operating activities' as follows.

	£	£
Cash from cash and credit sales		59 000
Less:		
Cash paid for purchases	34 000	
Rent	6 000	
Wages	7 000	47 000
Net cash inflow from operating activities		12 000

(Continued)

Worksheet of Trypit for

Description	Bank	Plant	Inventory	Amounts receivable	Equity
		Assets			**=**
Balances	−6 000	10 000	16 000	18 000	14 000
Rent	−6 000				
Sales	33 000				
Sales – credit				30 000	
Debtors	26 000			−26 000	
Stock			48 000		
Creditors	−34 000				
Loan	3 000				
Interest paid	−150				
Wages	−7 000				
Tax paid	−3 000				
Dividend paid	−5 000				
Plant bought	−5 000	5 000			
Balances	−4 150	15 000	64 000	22 000	14 000
Cost of sales			−46 000		
Depreciation					
Balances	−4 150	15 000	18 000	22 000	14 000
Taxation					
Balances	−4 150	15 000	18 000	22 000	14 000

We now need to look for the other cash flows. These are easily identified on the worksheet by looking at the bank column. There is a cash inflow of £3000 when the loan was raised. There is a cash outflow of £150 for the interest on the loan, another cash outflow in respect the tax liability from the previous year of £3000 and a cash outflow of £5000 in respect of the previous year's dividends.

In terms of the International Standard for cash flow statements (IAS 7) the interest and tax are both now treated as relating to operating cash flows and the Standard gives a choice on how to deal with dividends. In the opinion of the authors, it is logical to treat tax and interest in the same way as expenses and this will be the method adopted throughout the examples. There is an argument that dividends should be treated differently because they only exist when the directors declare them whereas interest and tax have to be paid irrespective of actions by the directors. However, there is a counterargument that dividends and interest are both a cost associated with the company using someone else's money to finance its operations. We will simply treat interest, tax and dividends in the same way as part of operating activity. Thus, we can extend our previous calculation as shown below.

(Continued)

ended 31 March 2011

Revenue & expenses	Loans	Trade payables	Tax	Dividend payable	Total depreciation
0		14 000	3 000	5 000	2 000
−6 000					
33 000					
30 000					
		48 000			
		−34 000			
	3 000				
−150					
−7 000					
			−3 000		
				−5 000	
49 850	3 000	28 000	0	0	2 000
−46 000					
−2 000					2 000
1 850	3 000	28 000	0	0	4 000
−1 000			1 000		
850	3 000	28 000	1 000	0	4 000

(Header spanning: *Equity + Liabilities* spans Loans, Trade payables, Tax, Dividend payable)

		£	£
Cash from sales			59 000
Less:			
Cash paid for purchases		34 000	
Rent		6 000	
Wages		7 000	
Interest		150	
Tax paid		3 000	
Dividends paid		5 000	55 150
Net cash inflow from operating activities			3 850

There was also another payment of £5000 for the new plant which we shall show as relating to investing activities and a receipt of £3000 from a loan which is a financing activity. No other amounts affect the cash column, so we can now produce a cash flow statement by classifying the cash flows under appropriate headings. The final statement would be as follows.

(Continued)

Cash flow statement of Trypit Ltd

	£	£
Cash from sales		59 000
Less:		
Cash paid for purchases	34 000	
Rent	6 000	
Wages	7 000	
Interest	150	
Tax paid	3 000	
Dividends paid	5 000	55 150
Net cash inflow from operating activity		3 850
Investing activities		
Acquisition of plant		−5 000
Net cash outflow from investing activity		−5 000
Financing activities		
Long term loan		3 000
Net cash inflow from financing activities		3 000
Net cash flow for the year		1 850
Cash balances at start of year		−6 000
Net cash flow for the year		1 850
Cash balances at end of year		−4 150

The cash flow statement shows the cash flow from operations of £3850 which we calculated above. It then shows the acquisition of plant under investing activities and the receipt of the loan under the heading of financing activities which results in a net increase in cash of £1850. This is the difference between the over-draft shown at the top of the worksheet in the bank/cash colum £6000 and the the £4150 at the bottom of the worksheet.

PRODUCING A CASH FLOW STATEMENT FROM THE INCOME STATEMENT AND STATEMENT OF FINANCIAL POSITION

At the start of Example 10.3, we said that there were two ways of arriving at a cash flow statement. The easiest way is working from a worksheet or the prime records, which is what we have done. The alternative is to work from the information in the final accounts, the indirect method. This method, although applying the same principles, does not rely on having access to the bank and cash accounts, instead it starts from the information in the income statement and statement of financial position and uses some different techniques to arrive at the cash flow statement. In some ways this saves a lot of time summarizing what has happened with the cash flow but it does require a lot more thought. We shall now look at this technique in respect of Trypit Ltd. For this purpose we need to produce the final accounts of Trypit Ltd, as shown below.

Income statement of Trypit Ltd at the year ended 31 March 2011

	Notes	£
Sales		63 000
Cost of sales		46 000
Gross profit		17 000
Net operating expenses	1	15 000
Profit on ordinary activities		2 000
Interest		150
Profit on ordinary activities before taxation		1 850
Taxation		1 000
Profit on ordinary activities after taxation		850
Dividends		3 000
Net loss for the year		−2 150

Trypit Ltd statement of financial position at 31 March 2011

	Notes	2011	2010
Current assets			
Receivables		22 000	18 000
Inventory		18 000	16 000
		40 000	34 000
Non current assets			
Plant at cost	2	15 000	11 000
Plant – depreciation		4 000	3 000
		11 000	8 000
Total assets		51 000	42 000
Current liabilities			
Bank overdraft		4 150	6 000
Creditors		28 000	14 000
Taxation		1 000	3 000
Dividends		0	5 000
		33 150	28 000
Non current liabilities			
Loan		3 000	
		3 000	0
Total liabilities		36 150	28 000
Share capital		14 000	14 000
Retained profits		850	0
Total equity		14 850	14 000
Total equity and liabilities		51 000	42 000

Notes to the accounts
Depreciation of £2 000 is included in operating expenses.
During the year Trypit purchased additional plant for £5 000.

The first figure we need to identify is the cash flow from operations. This we can do by extracting the figures from the income statement and statement of financial position. From the income statement we need the net profit and all those items not involving cash flows, in this case depreciation. These non-cash flow items need to be added back to the profit to get to a figure representing the cash flows. We then need to identify any amounts included in the figures used in arriving at the profit for which a cash flow has not yet taken place. These are sales on credit where the cash has not yet been received, i.e. the increase in receivables and increases in inventory. Similarly, we need to identify any purchases for which no payment has been made – the increase in payables. This can be done from the statement of financial position. A useful technique is to add an extra column to the statements of financial position to show these changes, as shown below.

Balance sheet of Trypit Ltd as at 31 March 2011

	Notes		2011	2010	Changes
Current assets					
Inventory			18 000	16 000	2 000
Receivables			22 000	18 000	4 000
			40 000	34 000	6 000
Non current assets					
Plant – cost	2	15 000			
– depreciation		4 000	11 000	8 000	
			11 000	8 000	3 000
Total assets			51 000	42 000	9 000
Current liabilities					
Bank overdraft			4 150	6 000	–1 850
Payables			28 000	14 000	14 000
Taxation			1 000	3 000	–2 000
Dividends			0	5 000	–5 000
			33 150	28 000	5 150
Non-current liabilities					
Loan			3 000	0	3 000
			3 000	0	3 000
Total liabilities			36 150	28 000	8 150
Equity					
Share capital			14 000	14 000	0
Retained profits			850	0	850
Total equity			14 850	14 000	850
Total equity and liabilities			51 000	42 000	9 000

From the income statement, we know the net profit is £850 and we know from the note that the depreciation charged is £2000. From the changes column in the statement of financial position we can identify that there has been an increase in inventory of £2000 and an increase in trade receivables of £4000. We then find we have an increase in plant of £3000, which from the notes, which are at the bottom of the balance sheet on page 237, we can see is made up of a purchase of £5000 and depreciation of £2000. Looking at the current liabilities, we find an decrease in the bank overdraft of £1850, which is the figure we are trying to reconcile to, an increase in trade payables of £14 000 and decreases of £2000 in tax and £5000 in dividends payable respectively (a net increase of £7000). We can therefore calculate the cash flow from operating activities, as shown.

	£	£
Profit for the year		850
Add:		
Depreciation	2 000	
Increase in payables, tax and dividends payable	7 000	9 000
Less:		
Increase in inventory	−2 000	
Increase in receivables	−4 000	−6 000
Net cash inflow from operating activity		3 850

If we now look at the remainder of the statement of financial position changes column, this will provide us with the basis to complete the rest of the statement. We have identified from the changes column and the notes that there has been an investment of £5000 in plant. Turning to the remaining liabilities, the only item is the £3000 from the loan which we shall bring into the cash flow statement under the heading 'Financing activities'. At this stage our cash flow statement balances and reconciles. However, let us just finish the check of the statement of financial position. In the case of share capital there has been no change, and the movement in respect of profits has already been dealt with in arriving at our cash flow from operations. We are now able to draw up the cash flow statement, which would, of course, be the same as the one already completed as shown below.

Cash flow statement of Trypit Ltd

	£	£
Profit for the year		850
Add:		
Depreciation	2 000	
Increase in payables, tax and dividends payable	7 000	9 000
Less:		
Increase in inventory	−2 000	
Increase in receivables	−4 000	−6 000
Net cash inflow from operating activity		3 850
Investing activities		
Acquisition of plant		−5 000
Net cash outflow from investing activity		−5 000
Financing activities		
Long term loan		3 000
Net cash inflow from financing activities		3 000
Net cash flow for the year		1 850
Cash balances at start of year		−6 000
Net cash flow for the year		1 850
Cash balances at end of year		−4 150

Before leaving the discussion of Trypit Ltd, it is worth returning to the cash flow statement and commenting on what information it gives us.

ACTIVITY 10.7

What additional information can you find in the cash flow statement that was not so obvious from the income statement and statement of financial position?

You should have identified additional information about the cash flow from operations and what Trypit did in terms of investing in the future and how it financed that investment.

We can see that although the business has made a small profit for the year, it has a much larger positive net cash flow during the year. Looking at the reconciliation note we can see that a major reason for this is the increase in current liabilities. This, combined with the raising of the loan, means that Trypit is increasing its financial risk. This may or may not be acceptable, we would have to look at the norms for the industry and other factors in order to make an informed decision on risk.

SUMMARY

In this chapter, we have consolidated our understanding of the cash flow statement and looked at two of the ways in which it can be produced. More importantly, we have tried to give an indication of what information can be obtained from such a statement and why that information is important. Perhaps the major message that the reader should take from this chapter is that a business cannot survive merely by being profitable. It also needs to stay solvent, and this aspect of the business has to be properly managed. We shall be discussing how cash flows can be managed later in this book.

Before leaving cash flow statements, it is worth looking at an example from a set of published accounts, one of which is shown below as Case Study 10.1.

CASE STUDY 10.1

Thorntons plc

Group cash flow statement for the 52 weeks ended 27 June 2009

Commentary

This example came from a set of accounts prepared under the UK Accounting Standard regime and would differ from one prepared under the International Standards, which is the format we have used in the text. The major differences relate to the cash inflow from operating activities, which under the International Standard format would be after taking account of interest income and charges, taxation, dividends, etc., which are shown here in the main body of the statement. The other part of the statement is the reconciliation of the cash inflow from operating with the figures from the income statement and this is shown below. Again, this will differ under the International Standard format as it will start with the net profit retained rather than the profit before interest and tax or as in this case the operating profit.

Reconciliation of operating profit to net cash flow from operating activities

Annual Report and Accounts 2009		Thorntons plc	
	Note	Group 52 weeks ended 27 June 2009 £'000	Group 52 weeks ended 28 June 2008 £'000
Cash flows from operating activities	26a	**17 138**	11 481
Cash flows from investing activities			
Proceeds from sale of property, plant and equipment		**51**	262
Purchase of investments			
Purchase of property, plant and equipment		**−7 112**	−5 680

(Continued)

Net cash used in investing activities		**−7 061**	−5 418
Cash flows from financing activities			
Net proceeds from issue of ordinary shares		**2**	223
Interest paid		**−1 469**	−1 831
Interest received		**27**	37
Capital element of finance lease rental payments		**−3 297**	−3 712
Borrowings (repaid)/advanced		**−1 800**	2 000
Dividends paid	10	**−4 040**	−4 550
Net cash used in financing activities		**−10 577**	−7 833
Net decrease in cash and cash equivalents and bank overdrafts		**−500**	−1 770
Cash and cash equivalents at beginning of period	26b	**1 088**	2 858
Cash and cash equivalents at end of period		**588**	1 088

26 Cash flow from operating activities

a) Cash generated from operations

	Group 2009	Group 2008
	£'000	£'000
Continuing operations		
Operating profit	**9 739**	10 326
Adjustments for:		
Depreciation and amortization	**11 572**	11 246
Amortization of Government grants received	**−21**	−21
Profit on disposal of property, plant and equipment	**−16**	−143
Share-based payment charge	**520**	447
Operating cash flow before working capital movements	**21 794**	21 855
Changes in working capital		
Increase in inventories	**−1 063**	−6 105
Decrease/(increase) in trade and other receivables	**1 072**	−2 520
Increase in payables	**430**	2 309
Increase/decrease in provisions	**198**	49
Decrease in post-employment benefit obligations	**−3 281**	−1 600
Cash generated from operations before taxation	**19 150**	13 988
Corporate taxation	**−2 012**	−2 507
Cash flows from operating activities	**17 138**	11 481

Commentary

Note the proceeds of the sale of non-current assets are shown in the main part of the statement and the profit or loss on those sales is shown in the reconciliation statement. The reconciliation statement also shows the movements on inventories, payables and receivables as we have discussed in the relevant chapters.

ACTIVITY 10.6 FROM EARLIER - BLANK WORKSHEET

Worksheet of Trypit for the year ended 31 March 2011

| Description | Assets | | | | = | Equity + Liabilities | | | | | | |
	Bank	Plant	Inventory	Amounts receivable		Equity	Revenue & expenses	Loans	Trade payables	Tax	Dividend payable	Total depreciation
Balances	−6 000	10 000	16 000	18 000		14 000	0		14 000	3 000	5 000	2 000
Rent												
Sales												
Sales – credit												
Debtors												
Stock												
Creditors												
Loan												
Interest paid												
Wages												
Tax paid												
Dividend paid												
Plant bought												
Balances												
Cost of sales												
Depreciation												
Balances												
Taxation												
Balances												

REFERENCES

Accounting Standards Steering Committee (1975) *The Corporate Report*, London: ASC.

Inflation Accounting Steering Committee (1975) *Inflation Accounting*, Cmnd 6225, London: HMSO.

IASB. (1992) *IAS 7, Cash Flow Statements*. London: IASB.

IASB. (2009) *International financial reporting standard for small and medium sized entities*. London: IASB.

Berry, A., Citron, D. and Jarvis, R. (1987) *The Information Needs of Bankers Dealing with Large and Small Companies*, Certified Accountants Research Report 7, London: Certified Accountants Publications.

Berry, A. and Robertson, J. (2006) 'Overseas bankers in the UK and their use of information for making lending decisions: Changes from 1985'. *British Accounting Review*, 38(1):175–91.

Egginton, D. (1975) 'The changes that Britain's bankers would like to see', *Accountants Magazine*, 27 July:14–15.

REVIEW QUESTIONS

(✓ indicates answers are available in Appendix A)

✓ **1** What is the main aim of a cash flow statement?

✓ **2** What are the claimed advantages of the cash flow statement?

3 How does 'net cash flow from operating activities' differ from operating profit?

4 How does an increase in the depreciation charge affect the operating profit and the 'cash flow from operating activities'?

5 What effect does an increase in inventory have on the difference between the net profit and the cash from operating activities?

PROBLEMS FOR DISCUSSION AND ANALYSIS

(✓ indicates answers are available in Appendix A)

✓ **1** Discuss the impact of each of the items below on the statement of financial position, income statement and cash flow statement, giving reasons for your answer where appropriate.

(a) During the year the company sold a fixed asset with a carrying amount of £5000 for £3000.
(b) The company also revalued its land from its original cost of £130 000 to £200 000.
(c) The building which had cost £90 000 and on which depreciation of £30 000 had been provided was revalued to £100 000.
(d) The company had also made an issue of 100 000 8% £1 shares at a price of £1.20 per share.
(e) The company had paid back a long-term loan to the bank of £80 000.

2 Information on the transactions of Newspurt Ltd in its first year of trading is given below.

May 2010
Issued 50 000 £1 ordinary shares for £50 000.
Purchased a machine for £30 000 and paid immediately.
Bought a delivery van for £10 000 and paid immediately.
Paid tax and insurance on the van of £400.
Paid a quarter's rent in advance of £2000.
Purchased raw materials costing £10 000 on one month's credit.

June 2010 – April 2011
Made sales of £90 000, all on credit.
Purchased raw materials costing £40 000, all on credit.
Paid four quarters' rent in advance, amounting to £8000 in total.
Paid trade payables of £38 000.
Received £70 000 of accounts receivable from customers.
Paid wages of £25 000.
Paid four quarters' rent in advance, amounting to £8000 in total. Paid trade payables of £38 000. Received £70 000 of accounts receivable from customers. Paid wages of £25 000.

Required

(a) Produce a worksheet for Newspurt Ltd.
(b) Produce a cash flow statement for Newspurt Ltd.
(c) Identify any additional information about Newspurt Ltd that the user can get from the cash flow statement that would not have been apparent in the income statement and statement of financial position.

3 The transactions set out below relate to the second year of trading of Manigod Ltd. Its statement of financial position at the start of the year is also given below.

Statement of financial positon of Manigod Ltd at the end of Year one

	£	£	£
Current assets			
Bank			9 100
Receivables and prepaids			22 000
Inventory			3 000
			34 100
Non current assets	*Cost*	*Depreciation*	
Fixtures	40 000	10 000	30 000
Car	10 000	2 000	8 000
	50 000	12 000	38 000
Total assets			72 100
Current liabilities			
Payables			12 000
Total liabilities			12 000
Share capital			50 000
Retained profit			10 100
Total equity			60 100
Total equity and liabilities			72 100

Transactions for year 2

Bought another car for £5000.
Paid general insurance of £1200 of which £1000 relates to the year and £200 is a prepayment
Paid rent £8000.
Received from customers £67 000.
Bought new inventory for £43 000 on credit terms.
Paid £38 000 to suppliers.
Paid wages of £28 000.
Made sales of £99 000 all on credit.
Issued additional shares of £10 000.
Paid other expenses of £2000.
Paid car tax and insurance of £500 for the year.
The policy is to depreciate fixtures and cars at 20% each year straight line.

Required

(a) Prepare a worksheet and statement of financial position for Manigod Ltd up to the end of year 2.
(b) Produce a cash flow statement for Manigod Ltd for year 2.
(c) Comment on Manigod Ltd's cash flow and profitability.

4 The information below relates to Springtime Ltd.

Statement of financial position of Springtime Ltd as at 30 April 2010

	Notes	2010	2009
Current assets			
Cash		5	61
Receivables		1 259	1 004
Inventory	4	1 763	1 194
		3 027	2 259
Non-current assets		£	£
Land & buildings	3	260	260
Fixtures	3	285	320
Motor vehicles	3	221	162
		766	742
Total assets		3 793	3 001
Current liabilities			
Bank overdraft		559	288
Payables		1 370	1 147
Taxation	2	332	332
		2 261	1 767
Non current liabilities			
Loans	5	200	130
Total net assets		200	130
Total liabilities		2 461	1 897
Share capital	6	545	483
Retained profit	6	787	621
Total equity		1 332	1 104
Total equity and liabilities		3 793	3 001

Income statement of Springtime Ltd for the year ended 30 April 2010

	Notes	2010 £	2009 £
Sales		4 814	5 614
Cost of sales	1	4 298	5 039
Operating profit		516	575
Interest charges		156	53
Profit before tax		360	522
Taxation	2	194	292
Retained profit		166	230

Extracts from the notes to the accounts

1   Included in the cost of sales are the following charges:

	£
Depreciation	156
Auditors' remuneration	55
Directors' remuneration	240
Hire of plant	30
Profit on sale of fittings	20

2   Fixed assets:

	Land	Buildings	Fittings	Motor vehicles
Balance at 1 May 2009	120	140	600	440
Additions			100	140
	120	140	700	580
Disposals			90	
Balance at 30 April 2010	120	140	610	580
Depreciation				
Balance at 1 May 2009			280	278
Charge for year			75	81
			355	359
Disposals			30	
Balance at 30 April 2010			325	359
Net book value 2010	120	140	285	221
Net book value 2009	120	140	320	162

5   A long-term loan amounting to £70 was repaid during the year. This was replaced with a new loan of £140 repayable in ten years.

6   Share capital and reserves:

	Share capital	Retained profit
Balance at 1 May 2009	483	621
Share issue	62	
Movements in year		166
Balance at 30 April 2010	545	787

Required

(a) Produce a cash flow statement and notes for Springtime Ltd.

(b) Briefly describe what additional information is disclosed by the cash flow statement and how it would affect your view of the performance of Springtime Ltd in the year in question.

CHAPTER 11
FINAL ACCOUNTS AND COMPANY ACCOUNTS

LEARNING OUTCOMES

By the end of this chapter you will:

- Have been exposed to the system of double entry that is used as an alternative to the worksheet approach.

- Have developed an understanding of the different types of business entity and their advantages and disadvantages.

- Understand the impact of different types of entity on the accounting and financial reporting processes.

- Be familiar with the reporting requirements for small and medium sized companies as laid down by the international accounting standards board.

Having established a base of knowledge about a simple form of organization, this chapter looks at the most common organizational forms, sole proprietorships and companies, and the impacts of each of these on the financial accounts produced. In addition, it examines some of the underlying advantages and disadvantages of different organizational structures and also provides a bridge to other methods of illustrating double-entry systems.

The first section of this chapter has been included to assist readers who wish to continue with their studies using other textbooks. So, for those whose exposure to accounting is not likely to be taken further, this section can be scan-read. More advanced accounting textbooks are likely to use a more traditional approach for explaining accounting and the mechanics of accounting. It will also be helpful to readers who have had some exposure to that traditional approach as an aid to understanding how the exposition in this book and that in other texts relate to one another. In the next part of the chapter we shall move on to look at the trial balance and the final adjustments required before final accounts are extracted from the worksheet. In the remainder of the chapter we consider alternative formats of final accounts and how these relate to different forms of organization. This will involve some consideration of the advantages and disadvantages of the different organizational forms available. It will also require an examination of the ways in which the presentation of accounting information may differ. Before these new areas are discussed, however, we shall examine the traditional approach to accounting found in other textbooks and compare it with the worksheet approach.

THE TRADITIONAL APPROACH

In this approach, instead of using columns to portray the individual accounts in an organization's accounting system, these accounts are represented by T accounts. In many basic book-keeping courses these T accounts form a major part of the course and students are required to spend a lot of time practising entries to these accounts. Often this is done on the basis of rote learning. It is further complicated by the terminology used: 'debits' and 'credits'.

For people studying accounting for the first time, the worksheet approach has been shown to be superior. Moreover, it is more in line with the increasing use of electronic spreadsheets. However, experience has shown that those who have already had some exposure to accounting often experience initial problems in converting from one representation of an accounting system to another. In this chapter, we are going to work through a simple example to illustrate that the difference between the two methods is superficial and does not in any way change the principles involved.

KEY CONCEPT 11.1

The use of T accounts and the worksheet are simply alternative ways of representing the process of double-entry book-keeping. The fundamental principles of accounting and the underlying accounting equation are not in any way altered by the way in which double entry is illustrated.

EXAMPLE 11.1

Brian started a business and during the first year the following transactions took place.

1 Opened a business bank account and paid in £10 000 of his own money.

2 Bought a van for £5000 and paid for it in cash.

3 Bought goods for £35 000 on credit and had paid £33 000 at the end of the year.

4 Sold goods for £45 000 all for cash.

5 Had goods in inventory at the end of the year which cost £4000.

6 Paid expenses on the van of £1000.

7 Paid rent on his premises of £1500.

Let us first see what the worksheet would look like for Brian's business and we shall then see how the same transactions would be represented under the traditional method.

Brian's worksheet version 1

	Assets			=	Equity + Liabilities		
	Cash	**Van**	**Inventory**		**Equity**	**Revenue & expenses**	**Trade payables**
Item 1	10 000				10 000		
Item 2	−5 000	5 000					
Item 3			35 000				35 000
	−33 000						−33 000
Item 4	45 000					45 000	
Item 5			−31 000			−31 000	
Item 6	−1 000					−1 000	
Item 7	−1 500					−1 500	
Balance	14 500	5 000	4 000		10 000	11 500	2 000

You should make sure that you understand the entries on the worksheet before moving on. If you do have problems, refer back to the appropriate chapters. Now we record the same transactions using the traditional approach of T accounts. Note that we have put the asset accounts on the left hand side of the page and the equity and liabilities on the right and separated these by a solid line.

	Assets			**=**		**Equity + liabilities**		

Cash — **Owner's equity**

Item 1	10 000	Item 2	5 000				Item 1	10 000
Item 4	45 000	Item 3	33 000					
		Item 6	1 000		Bal c/d	10 000		
		Item 7	1 500			10 000		10 000
		Bal c/d	14 500				Bal b/d	10 000
	55 000		55 000					
Bal b/d	14 500							

(Continued)

Assets				=	Equity + liabilities			
Van					**Revenue & expenses**			
Item 2	5 000				Item 5	31 000	Item 4	45 000
					Item 6	1 000		
		Bal c/d	5 000		Item 7	1 500		
	5 000		5 000		Bal c/d	11 500		
Bal b/d	5 000					45 000		45 000
							Bal b/d	11 500
							Bal b/d	45 000
Inventory					**Amounts payable**			
Item 3	35 000	Item 5	31 000		Item 3	33 000	Item 3	35 000
		Bal c/d	4 000		Bal c/d	2 000		
	35 000		35 000			35 000		35 000
Bal b/d	4 000						Bal b/d	2 000

Note: c/d, carried down; b/d, brought down.

A careful examination of the two systems will show that they have recorded the same transactions. All that has changed is the way in which the recording has been represented. This will be made clearer if we explain some of the items and the ways in which they have been treated.

For example, with the worksheet approach, to deal with item 1, where Brian puts some money into the business, we opened up a column entitled Cash and one entitled Equity on the other side of the worksheet. We then entered the amount involved, £10 000, in each of these columns. By contrast, under the traditional approach we opened two T accounts: one of these was for cash and the other for equity. We then entered the amount involved, £10 000, in these two accounts. All that is happening is that in contrast with the worksheet which uses columns to represent accounts the alternative T accounts system uses T accounts to represent those same accounts. You need to remember that this does not change the substance of what we are doing, i.e. recording economic transactions, all that has changed is the way in which that process is represented.

Using T accounts, it is perhaps less clear which side of the account the entry should go in. In the case of assets the entry is put on the *debit* side, i.e. the *left-hand* side, and in the case of equity liabilities it is put on the *credit* side, i.e. the *right-hand* side. This can, of course, be related to the accounting equation shown above the T accounts, where asset balances in the worksheet are on the left-hand side of the equals sign and equity and liabilities are on the right-hand side of the equals sign.

KEY CONCEPT 11.2

Debits and credits

Under the traditional approach assets are shown as debit balances and liabilities are shown as credit balances.

We now consider the way in which item 2, the purchase of the fixed asset, is dealt with. We find that using the worksheet approach a new column is opened for the asset on the left-hand side of the equation and the

(Continued)

cash column, also on the left-hand side, is reduced by the amount paid for the new asset, i.e. £5000. The traditional approach also starts in the same way by opening a new account for the new asset, and puts the cost of £5000 on the left-hand side because it is an asset. So far, the methods are essentially similar. The other half of the transaction is perhaps slightly more difficult to follow as we have to reduce the cash balance. This is done by putting the £5000 on the right-hand side of the cash account. This is called crediting an account – in this case we are crediting a cash account.

ACTIVITY 11.1

Look at item 3 and see if you can follow the entries in the worksheet and compare them to those in the T account system.

You should have identified that with item 3 the worksheet shows the goods bought as inventory and the amount owing in the payables column. It then shows the cash/bank column reduced by the amount paid and the payables reduced by that amount.

By contrast the T account method shows the inventory increase on the left-hand side of that account and the increase in payables on the right-hand side of the payables account. It then shows the reduction in the bank and cash by putting the amount on the right-hand side of that account and the reduction in the amounts payable by putting the amount on the left-hand side of that account.

Even at this stage it is perhaps becoming obvious that, although both approaches are based around the accounting equation, the worksheet approach is easier to follow as it relies less on jargon and rote learning than the more traditional approach. Another advantage of the worksheet approach is that we know at the end of the exercise that we have balanced our accounts and if they do not balance the error can be found by working back through the worksheet as described in Chapter 5. In the case of the more traditional approach, we are as yet unsure that our accounts balance and so we would now extract what is commonly known as a trial balance. If having extracted this trial balance we found that it did not balance we would have to check through most if not all of the entries in our accounts to find the error. Hopefully that will not be the case with the trial balance for Brian's business, which would be as follows.

Trial balance of Brian's business

	Debit	Credit
Cash	14 500	
Equity		10 000
Trade payables		2 000
Van	5 000	
Inventory	4 000	
Revenue and expenses		11 500
	23 500	23 500

We can now see that the accounts do balance. You may have noticed that the columns are headed *Debit* and *Credit* and that all the accounts from the left-hand side of the accounting equation, or the left-hand side of our worksheet, the asset accounts, are in the debit column and all the accounts from the right-hand side of the accounting equation and the worksheet, those which relate to what the business owes, are in the credit column. In this case we have not made an error in our double entry as the trial balance balances and so we can move to the next stage. This is where final adjustments are made for accruals, depreciation, etc. These adjustments are often referred to in the accounting literature as end of period or end of year adjustments.

END OF PERIOD ADJUSTMENTS

As we have said, end of period adjustments refer to adjustments such as those required to provide for depreciation, bad debts, accruals and prepayments, etc. These have all been covered in Chapters 6–8 and you should be familiar with the way in which they are dealt with via the worksheet. For the purposes of comparison we shall initially show how they are dealt with through the worksheet, the approach you are familiar with, and we will then look at how they are dealt with through the traditional approach.

EXAMPLE 11.1 (Continued)

At the end of the year Brian decides that the van will have no scrap value and should be depreciated £1000 a year for five years, and he also tells you that the rent is payable quarterly in advance so that only £1200 of the £1500 paid relates to this year.

Entering these adjustments on the worksheet would result in the worksheet shown below. You will notice that we have had to open two new accounts or columns to deal with the changes and then arrive at a new balance.

Brian's worksheet version 2

	Assets				=	Equity + Liabilities			
	Cash	Van	Inventory	Prepaids		Equity	Revenue & expenses	Trade payables	Depre-ciation
Item 1	10 000					10 000			
Item 2	−5 000	5 000							
Item 3			35 000					35 000	
	−33 000							−33 000	
Item 4	45 000						45 000		
Item 5			−31 000				−31 000		
Item 6	−1 000						−1 000		
Item 7	−1 500						−1 500		
Balance	14 500	5 000	4 000			10 000	11 500	2 000	
Adjustment 1							−1 000		1 000
Adjustment 2				300			300		
Balance	14 500	5 000	4 000	300		10 000	10 800	2 000	1 000

In the traditional approach we would also have to create the new accounts as illustrated below and then extract another trial balance. We have bolded and italicized the new entries which are in the two new accounts, depreciation and prepaid, with corresponding entries in the revenue and expenses account, which are also italicized. A comparison of the two methods at this point shows that they are doing the same thing albeit that they are representing it using a different mechanism.

	Assets				=		Equity + liabilities		
		Cash						Inventory	
Item 1	10 000	Item 2		5 000		Item 3	35 000	Item 5	31 000
Item 4	45 000	Item 3		33 000					
		Item 6		1 000					
		Item 7		1 500					
		Bal c/d		14 500				Bal c/d	4 000
	55 000			55 000			35 000		35 000
Bal b/d	14 500					Bal b/d	4 000		

Assets			=	Equity + liabilities		
Van				**Owner's equity**		
Item 2	5 000				Item 1	10 000
		Bal c/d	5 000	Bal c/d	10 000	
	5 000		5 000		10 000	10 000
Bal b/d	5 000				Bal b/d	10 000

Amounts payable				**Revenue & expenses**		
Item 3	33 000	Item 3	35 000	Item 5	31 000	Item 4	45 000
				Item 6	1 000	*Adjustment 2*	*300*
				Item 7	1 500		
Bal c/d	2 000			*Adjustment 1*	*1 000*		
	35 000		35 000	Bal c/d	10 800		
		Bal b/d	2 000		45 300		45 300
						Bal b/d	10 800

Depreciation				**Prepaid**		
		Adjustment 1	*1 000*	*Adjustment 2*	*300*		
Bal c/d	1 000					Bal c/d	300
	1 000		1 000		300		300
		Bal b/d	1 000	Bal b/d	300		

However, there is a short cut which is often shown in textbooks and this involves making adjustments on what is effectively a type of worksheet. The difference between that worksheet and the one we use is that the rows become columns and vice versa. This worksheet is shown below and, as you can see, it merely extends our earlier trial balance to a new trial balance. This type of worksheet is often referred to as the extended trial balance.

The main difference between the two approaches in this respect is that when using the worksheet approach the final adjustments are automatically part of the double-entry system. Under the traditional approach they can be and often are outside the double-entry system. This can, of course, lead to errors and omissions which may be more difficult to trace. Let us look at the extended trial balance of Brian's business.

Extended trial balance of Brian's business

			Adjustments		Final	
	Debit	Credit	Debit	Credit	Debit	Credit
Cash	14 500				14 500	
Equity		10 000				10 000
Trade payables		2 000				2 000
Van	5 000				5 000	
Inventory	4 000				4 000	
Revenue and expenses		11 500	1 000	300		10 800
Depreciation				1 000		1 000
Prepaid			300		300	
	23 500	23 500	1 300	1 300	23 800	23 800

DISCUSSION

We have seen that the differences between the two approaches are not differences of principle. Rather, they are alternative ways of depicting the same entries in the books of account of a firm. In the authors' opinion, the advantages of the worksheet-based approach outweigh the advantages of the alternative approach and make it easier for those coming to the subject for the first time to assimilate the main principles involved in a double-entry book-keeping system. We shall now consider the way in which final accounts are produced and the rules and regulations governing their format.

ACTIVITY 11.2

Have a go at the example below, using the worksheet, T accounts and the extended trial balance method, and comparing your answer with the one we have provided at the end of the chapter after the questions and problems for discussion and analysis.

Sharon opened a business and during the first year had the following transactions:

1   Opened a business bank account and paid in £12 000 of her own money.

2   Bought fixtures and fittings for £8000 and paid for it in cash.

3   Bought goods for £22 000 on credit and had paid £18 000 at the end of the year.

4   Sold goods for £38 000 all for cash.

5   Had goods in inventory at the end of the year which cost £3000.

6   Paid general expenses of £2000.

7   Paid rent on his premises of £900.
    On investigation you find that the fixtures and fittings are likely to last four years and will have no residual value. You also find that the rent paid only covers three quarters of the year.

FINAL ACCOUNTS

Before we look at the regulations and the effects of different organizational forms, we should remind ourselves of the way in which the final accounts, i.e. the statement of financial position, income statement and cash flow statement, are derived from the worksheet. This may be more readily understood if we consider the example of Brian's business. We shall extract the final accounts from the worksheet above.

Income statement for Brian's business for the year ending xx.xx.xx.

	£	£
Sales		45 000
Cost of goods sold		31 000
Gross profit		14 000
Rent	1 200	
Van expenses	1 000	
Van depreciation	1 000	3 200
Net profit		10 800

You will notice that the formal income statement merely summarizes what is contained in the revenue and expenses column of the worksheet. You may also have noticed that it is called the income statement for the period ended on a certain date. This emphasizes that the income statement is a period statement; we can contrast it with the heading of the statement of financial position below. This, as you can see, is at a particular point in time – a snapshot at a point in time.

Statement of financial position of Brian's business as at xx.xx.xx

	£
Current assets	
Cash	14 500
Prepaids	300
Inventory	4 000
	18 800
Non current assets	
Van at cost	5 000
Depreciation	1 000
	4 000
Total assets	22 800
Current liabilities	
Trade payables	2 000
	2 000
Equity	
Owner's equity	10 000
Retained earnings	10 800
Total equity	20 800
Total equity and liabilities	22 800

Cash flow statement for Brian's business for the year ended xx.xx.xx

	£
Cash from operating	9 500
Investing activities	
Purchase of van	5 000
Cash outflow from investing activity	5 000
Financing activities	0
	0
Net cash inflow	4 500

Reconciliation of net profit and cash from operating activities

	£	£
Net profit		10 800
Add:		
Depreciation		1 000
Increase in trade payables		2 000
		13 800
Less:		
Increase in inventory	4 000	
Increase in prepayments	300	4 300
		9 500

You will have noticed that the statement of financial position merely takes the final line of the work-sheet and classifies it under appropriate headings to enable the reader to interpret the information more readily. We shall be dealing with the subject of interpretation in more detail in Chapter 12. Prior to that, however, we need to consider the effect of different forms of organizational structure on the presentation of final accounts.

FORMS OF ORGANIZATION

As we said in Chapter 1, there are many forms of organization possible, from a sole proprietorship, through partnerships, limited liability partnerships, companies and groups of companies to multinational conglomerates. In addition, there are other less common forms such as banks, insurance companies, cooperatives, friendly societies and provident societies. Each of these organizational forms requires slightly different accounts. This may be because the needs of the users are slightly different or because of other factors such as the requirements of legislation or other regulations, e.g. those imposed by the Stock Exchange or other regulatory bodies. Rather than attempting to deal with all the different forms of organizations, we shall concentrate our discussion on the simpler forms of organization: the sole proprietorship and the limited company. The other common form of organization which we find, especially in the professions, i.e. accountants, lawyers, architects, etc., is partnerships. These can be of two types, i.e. an ordinary partnership and a limited liability partnership, which broadly has the same reporting requirements as companies in that it has to conform to the same standards of accounting, file annual accounts, have the accounts audited if it has turnover in excess of £6.5 million etc. However, all partnerships, whether limited or unlimited, have specialized accounting problems as all the partners' inputs and entitlements have to be accounted for. For those who wish to explore these issues in more depth we have included a discussion and worked examples illustrating the problems and solutions in Appendix B.

We shall commence our discussion at the smallest and most common form of business organization: the sole proprietorship.

The sole proprietorship

This is a one-owner business and is very simple to set up. All that is really required is a business bank account. Because it is so simple and because it has little recognition in law, there are no formal guidelines for the format of the accounts.

However, the fact that the business and the owner are not seen as separate legal entities could be a problem if the business gets into difficulties, as the owner is liable for all the debts of the business and may have to sell personal possessions such as the family home to meet them. In addition, as we discussed in Chapter 9, this form of organization relies heavily on the owner for finance and this can lead to problems if and when the business expands as owners tend to have fairly limited funds at their disposal.

Limited companies

Unlike the partnership and the sole proprietorship, a limited company is recognized as a separate legal entity quite distinct from its owners. The debts incurred in the normal course of business are those of the company. In the case of a default in payment, it is the company which has to be sued rather than the owner. The fact that the owners may also be the managers and the only employees has no relevance as in the eyes of the law all these roles are different.

Broadly, companies are set up in a particular form to meet the requirements of the business concerned. For certain non-commercial organizations requiring the legal status of a company, it is normal for the company to be set up as a company limited by guarantee. This is an unusual form of incorporation. The members promise to contribute a guaranteed amount should the company go under, the amount of such a guarantee normally being limited to £1 per member.

For commercial organizations, the more common form of company is one in which shares are issued to the owners. In this case, their liability is limited to the nominal value of the shares. The owners are referred to as shareholders or members. These companies can be either private companies or public companies, and in the latter category they can be listed or unlisted. 'Listed' is a term referring to the fact that the company's shares are traded on a recognized Stock Exchange. We need not dwell on the detailed differences between the various types of company as this is outside the scope of this book. However, we can broadly say that private companies are generally easier to form but their shares cannot be freely traded on a Stock Exchange, whereas public companies (plcs) have shares which are freely transferable. They must also have a share capital in excess of £50 000. Public companies are subject to more restrictions and regulation than private companies and may be subject to other forms of regulation: they must comply with accounting standards and in some cases Stock Exchange requirements. The latter do not apply to private companies.

We shall limit our discussion to private companies and discuss the advantages of this type of organization over those already dealt with. The main advantage has already been mentioned: the limitation on the liability of the owners of the business in the event that the business goes bankrupt. Other advantages come from the ability to arrange distribution of profits and indeed of control of the company by means of the share ownership of the various parties concerned. Although the default position is that ordinary shares generally have votes, it is possible to issue non-voting ordinary shares and as such it is possible to arrange the voting rights, and therefore control, of the company as the founders wish.

There are disadvantages to the limited company as an organizational form, however. This is because they are subject to regulatory legislation. The extent of the legislation, however, varies with the size of the business. Smaller businesses, although required to submit accounts to Companies House, may not need to have them audited and they may be allowed to submit abridged accounts. Similarly, there is now a special international accounting standard for smaller companies. For slightly larger companies the accounts they produce have to be full accounts that comply with the general International Accounting Standards, or their UK equivalent. These accounts have to be audited and a copy of the audited accounts has to be lodged with Companies House. The form of these accounts is subject to the requirements of the Companies Acts in the UK and the equivalent regulatory requirement elsewhere. Now that we have an International Financial Reporting Standard for Small and Medium Sized Entities (IASB 2009) we can use that as the basis for our discussion of what we might expect to see in a set of accounts of a company. The Standard requires that a complete set of financial statements should include the following items.

(a) a statement of financial position as at the reporting date.
(b) either:
  (i) a single statement of comprehensive income for the reporting period displaying all items of income and expense recognized during the period including those items recognized in determining profit or loss (which is a subtotal in the statement of comprehensive income) and items of other comprehensive income, or
  (ii) a separate income statement and a separate statement of comprehensive income. If an entity chooses to present both an income statement and a statement of comprehensive income, the statement of comprehensive income begins with profit or loss and then displays the items of other comprehensive income.
(c) a statement of changes in equity for the reporting period.
(d) a statement of cash flows for the reporting period.
(e) notes, comprising a summary of significant accounting policies and other explanatory information.

We are already familiar with item (a), which we have referred to as the statement of financial position. Similarly the cash flow statement (d) and notes to the accounts (e) are both items we are familiar with.

In addition to these general requirements, there are detailed requirements covering the format and content of the actual accounts and an overarching requirement that they should comply with generally accepted accounting practice, hence the inclusion of the cash flow statement.

Clearly, to go through these requirements in great detail is outside the scope of an introductory text. Instead, we have included below a set of accounts for a private company. The following text highlights areas of difference between the accounts of the limited company and those of the other forms of organization considered. We consider first the balance sheet or statement of financial position.

Statement of financial position of Broll Ltd as at xx. xx. xxxx

	Notes	This year £	Last year £
Current assets			
Cash at bank and in hand		3 500	2 000
Amounts receivable		10 000	4 000
Inventory	1	10 000	7 000
		23 500	13 000
Non current assets			
Tangible assets	2	25 000	20 000
Intangible assets	3	50 000	56 000
		75 000	76 000
Total assets		98 500	89 000
Current liabilities			
Trade payables		4 000	3 000
Taxation	4	2 600	1 400
Dividends	5	1 600	1 100
		8 200	5 500
Non-current liabilities			
Loans	6	15 000	9 000
		15 000	9 000
Total liabilities		23 200	14 500
Equity	7	70 000	70 000
Share capital	8	5 300	4 500
Retained profits		75 300	74 500
Total equity and liabilities		98 500	89 000

The first difference is in the title of the statement: the fact that Broll is a limited company must be stated. In addition, the statement contains comparative figures for the previous year, as well as references to a number of notes. These notes normally contain greater detail than can be shown on the face of the accounts and as such are an integral part of the analysis of the accounts of a company. This will be discussed in more detail in Chapter 12. As you can see, the top half of the statement of financial position is very similar to those we have encountered before, apart from the inclusion of dividends and taxation and the fact that a lot of the detail is left to the notes to the accounts. For example, note 3 would contain details of fixed assets bought and sold during the year and also the depreciation to date and that charged during the year.

The lower half of the statement of financial position is somewhat different as the owners' equity is referred to as share capital and this may consist of different types of share capital. Each type may carry different voting rights etc. This would only be apparent if we looked at the detail contained in the notes. Similarly, there may be a number of different types of reserves such as 'revaluation reserves' – a reserve for revalued assets such as land and buildings. However, in this case the only reserve is the retained profits, which is similar to the account for that purpose in the case of a sole proprietorship. The note to the accounts referred to usually doubles up as the statement of changes in equity required by the standard. In the case of Broll Ltd it would be as follows.

Statement of changes in equity

	Share capital	Retained profits
At start of the year	70 000	4 500
Profit for the year attributable to shareholders		3 400
Dividends		−2 600
At end of year	70 000	5 300

This is a fairly straightforward statement for Broll Ltd but for plcs it can be more complex as Case Study 11.1 illustrates. If the changes are only to the retained profits then this statement can be dispensed with and combined with the income statement (IFRS-SME, 2009, Para 3.18) and this is what we will use in this chapter.

CASE STUDY 11.1

Extract from Annual Report of Thorntons Plc 2009

25 Statement of changes in shareholders' equity continued

Company	Note	Share capital £000	Share premium £000	Retained earnings £000	Total £000
At 30 June 2007	6	68 111	13 551	12 161	32 523
Total recognized income and expense				4 437	4 437
New share capital issued	23	24	199		223
Share-based payment charge				447	447
Effect of tax on share option movement	7			−510	−510
Movement in investment in own shares				18	18
Dividends	10			−4 550	−4 550

(Continued)

Company	Note	Share capital £000	Share premium £000	Retained earnings £000	Total £000
At 28 June 2008		6 835	13 750	12 003	32 588
Total recognized income and expense				3 205	3 205
New share capital issued			2		2
Share-based payment charge				520	520
Effect of tax on share option movement				−171	−171
Dividends				−4 040	−4 040
At 27 June 2009		6 835	13 752	11 517	32 104

Commentary

In the case of Thorntons we find that there are lots of different types of movements. In other cases you may find lots of different classes of shares and lots of different types of reserves.

ACTIVITY 11.3

Why not take a look on the internet at the annual reports of a few major plcs and get a feel of the types of reserves that are there?

You will probably have found that all companies have retained earnings, a lot have a revaluation reserve which arises from revaluations of the assets. You may have found all sorts of other specific reserves, some of which are required by law. This is the case for the capital redemption reserve, which companies need to set up when they buy back their own shares.

Let us now move on to look at the statement of comprehensive income. The first thing we need to do is to define the term comprehensive income as this is new.

KEY CONCEPT 11.3

Comprehensive income

The International Standard makes a distinction between what is essentially revenue and expenses relating to trading which result in a profit or loss and other gains or losses that arise in the normal course of business, examples are gains or losses on sale of fixed assets, foreign currency gains or losses, etc. The combination of these two types of gains or losses, essentially trading and other, create what the standard refers to as comprehensive income.

Having defined comprehensive income let us now look at what a statement of comprehensive income might look like.

Comprehensive income statement of Broll Ltd for the year to xx. xx.xxxx

	Notes	£	This year £	Last year £
Turnover	9		60 000	45 000
Cost of sales			40 000	30 000
Gross profit			20 000	15 000
Other income	10		7 000	7 000
Distribution costs			−8 000	−6 000
Administrative expenses			−11 500	−11 600
Finance costs	11		−1 500	−900
Profit on ordinary activities before tax			6 000	3 500
Tax	12		−2 600	−1 400
Profit on ordinary activities after tax			3 400	2 100
Retained profit at start of year			4 500	3 500
Dividends – interim	13	−1 000		
– final	13	−1 600	−2 600	−1 100
Retained profit at the end of the year			5 300	4 500

We can see that down to gross profit the format is familiar. We then see the other income, i.e. the non trading income, being brought in and separately disclosed. Then the expenses are taken off and there is an option to cluster these under the headings of administrative and distribution costs. The assumption here is that all costs that relate to the manufacture of goods would be included in cost of sales as we saw when discussing inventory, work in progress and finished goods. This grouping of expenses means that a lot of the detail is lost. Although you will find some breakdown of the figure in the note to the accounts, the extent of this detail is likely to be limited to that required to be disclosed under the regulatory framework. It is quite likely that there may also be a heading for other expenses and if there is borrowing, as is the case with Broll Ltd, there will be a separate heading for finance costs.

However, it is from the point at which the net profit is shown that the real differences arise. The most striking of these is that taxation is included in the income statement. This is because the company is recognized as a separate entity for legal and tax purposes and its profits are liable to corporation tax. In contrast, the sole proprietorship and the partnership are not separate legal or taxable entities, and the profit is only taxable as the income of the owners rather than in its own right. Moving on, we find once the profit for the year is arrived at we add the retained profits at the start of the year and then deduct the dividends, which are distributions of profits to the owners, which provides the figure for retained profits at the end of the year. This latter part of the income statement can be seen as a replacement for a statement of changes in equity if the only changes arise from profits made and distributed in the form of dividends. The dividends themselves are in fact a form of distribution to the owners (the shareholders) and are 'pro rata' to the number of shares held. There may be an interim and final dividend in one year but not in the other. This is not unusual: the declaration of any dividend depends upon the needs of the business and the availability of both profits and liquid funds to pay them. An interim dividend is in fact essentially a payment made part way through the year and is also dependent on both profitability and the availability of liquid funds. The final line of the income statement is the sum transferred to reserves: this is the residual balance being transferred to the reserves, and is a profit in this case.

ACTIVITY 11.4

Why do you think it is important to separate out other income from gross profit?

You may have thought about the fact that other income could include 'one-off' sources of gains, e.g. from the sale of fixed assets, and as such it is helpful for readers of the income statement to be aware that this will not be repeated next year whereas the trading income should be.

The next statement to look at is the cash flow statement. Once again you will be familiar with the basic layout and contents.

Cash flow statement of Broll Ltd for the year ended xx.xx.xxxx

Cash flows from operating activity	This year	Last year
Profit for the year	3 400	2 100
Adjustments for non cash income and expenses		
Non cash finance costs	1 500	900
Non cash taxation expenses	1 200	1 600
Depreciation	10 000	8 000
Amortisation	6 000	6 000
Cash flow included in investing activity		
Gain on sale of equipment	−17 000	−7 000
Changes in operating assets and liabilities		
Increase(−)/decrease in receivables	−6 000	2 000
Increase in inventories	−3 000	−1 000
Increase in payables	1 000	400
Net cash from operating activities	7 100	13 000
Cash flow from investing activity		
Proceeds from sale of equipment	14 000	18 000
Purchase of new equipment/patents	−22 000	−21 000
Net cash used in investing activity	−8 000	−3 000
Cash flows from financing activity		
Payment of interest	−1 500	−600
Increase in borrowings	6 000	−7 000
Payment of dividends	−2 100	−1 400
Net cash used in financing activities	2 400	−9 000
Net increase in cash and cash equivalents	1 500	
Cash and cash equivalents at start of year	2 000	3 000
Cash and cash equivalents at end of year	3 500	2 000

As you can see the profit is adjusted by changes in working capital, depreciation and amortization, all of which you are familiar with. The main difference in calculating the cash flow from operations in the case of a company is the inclusion in this section of items relating to interest and to dividends. These you will note are included later in the cash flow statement under the heading of cash flows relating to financing.

ACTIVITY 11.5

Have a look at the cash flow statement and identify those items for which the treatment in terms of cash flows and accrual accounting differ.

You will probably have identified, depreciation, sale of equipment, working capital items, all of which you are familiar with. You may also have identified interest and tax where the charge for the year is added back and then shown elsewhere in the statement. In reality, in this case, because all the interest was paid in the year the treatment is the same it is just classified as a different type of cash flow, i.e. one that relates to the method of financing the firm's activity not the actual activity itself.

ACTIVITY 11.6

Think about why the two figures relating to taxation included in the cash flow statement differ.

The answer here is that as the taxation for the year cannot be determined until the profit has been calculated it will not be paid until the following year. The payments in respect of tax during the year are likely to relate to last year.

The final difference between the final accounts of companies and other entities relates to the requirement to provide information about the accounting policies adopted, e.g. what method is used for arriving at the figure for inventory, first in first out or weighted average cost, and other notes to the accounts. The latter will contain a lot of the detail behind the summary figures included in the financial statements.

Many examples of published accounts are available and Case Study 11.2 provides an illustration of some typical accounting policies and notes to the accounts from a typical published annual report.

CASE STUDY 11.2

Next plc Annual Report 2009

Extracts from the accounting policies
Intangible assets
Intangible assets acquired separately from a business are carried initially at cost. An intangible asset acquired as part of a business combination is recognized outside goodwill if the asset is separable or arises from contractual or other legal rights and its fair value can be measured reliably. Following initial recognition, intangible assets are carried at cost less accumulated amortisation and impairment

(Continued)

losses. Intangible assets with a finite life have no residual value and are amortized on a straight line basis over their expected useful lives as follows:

Brand names and trademarks ten years

Customer relationships four years.

The carrying value of intangible assets is reviewed for impairment whenever events or changes in circumstances indicate the carrying value may not be recoverable.

Property, plant & equipment

Property, plant and equipment are stated at cost less accumulated depreciation and reviewed annually for impairment.

Depreciation is provided to write down the cost of property, plant and equipment to their estimated residual values, based on current prices at the statement of financial position date, over their remaining useful lives by equal annual instalments.

The useful lives generally applicable are summarized as follows:

Freehold and long leasehold buildings 50 years

Plant and fittings:

Plant, machinery and building works 10–25 years

Fixtures and fittings 6–15 years

Vehicles, IT and other assets 2–6 years

Leasehold improvements the period of the lease, or useful life if shorter.

Trade and other receivables

Trade receivables are stated at original invoice amount plus any accrued service charge (in the case of Directory customer receivables).

Where there is objective evidence that there is an impairment loss, the amount of the loss is measured as the difference between the carrying amount and the present value of the estimated future cash flows discounted at the original effective interest rate. The carrying amount of the receivable is reduced through use of an allowance account. Amounts charged to the allowance account are written off when there is no expectation of further recovery.

Commentary

In reality all companies will have a range of accounting policies that need to be disclosed and broadly the number of accounting policies disclosed will vary with the complexity of the business concerned. Note in the accounting policies relating to trade and other receivables Next clearly identifies that it has a policy for dealing with bad debts and those that are expected not to be recovered.

Extract from notes to the accounts of Next Plc

18. Bank loans and overdrafts

	2009 £m	2008 £m
Bank overdrafts and overnight borrowings	46.3	37.7
Unsecured bank loans	75.0	205.0
	121.3	242.7

(Continued)

Bank overdrafts are repayable on demand and bear interest at a margin over bank base rates. Overnight borrowings and unsecured bank loans fall due within one year of the balance sheet date and bear interest at a margin above LIBOR. The unsecured bank loans included £75.0m (2008: £205.0m) drawn by the Company under a medium term bank revolving credit facility committed until November 2010 (2008: September 2009), see Note 30.

19. Trade and other payables

	2009 £m	2008 £m
Trade payables	204.8	175.0
Obligations under finance leases	0.4	0.4
Other taxation and social security	43.6	56.8
Share based payment liability	2.1	–
Other creditors and accruals	234.2	234.4
	485.1	466.6

Trade payables are not interest-bearing and are generally settled on 30-day terms. Other creditors and accruals are not interest bearing

Commentary

As you can see the notes provide much of the detailed information behind the headline figure included in the financial statements. Once again there is a clear relationship between the complexity of the business and the number and extent of the notes and explanations required to provide users of accounts with the information they need to understand the performance of the business and compare it to alternative investments.

SUMMARY

In this chapter, we have introduced you to the idea that different organizational forms require accounts in different forms and to the reasons for them. This is as it should be. The most appropriate form of organization should be governed by sound business considerations rather than by accounting requirements or burdens imposed by legislation.

REVIEW QUESTIONS

(✓ indicates answers are available in Appendix A)

✓ **1** Explain in your own words the meaning of the terms trial balance and extended trial balance.

2 Explain the meaning of the term final adjustments.

3 Explain the difference between a sole proprietorship and a partnership.

4 Why is it advantageous to set a business up as a limited company?

5 What are the differences between a sole proprietorship and a limited liability company?

6 Describe how the choice of organizational form determines the format of the final accounts.

PROBLEMS FOR DISCUSSION AND ANALYSIS

1 Charlie is a wholesaler supplying over 250 retailers in the local region. He employs one driver and a warehouse-man, and does the remainder of the work associated with running the business himself. He has a basic knowledge of book-keeping and keeps the basic records himself right up to trial balance stage, but relies on professional help to get the final accounts drawn up. At the end of the year the following balances appeared in his accounting records.

	£
Warehouseman's wages	18 060
Driver's wages	20 040
Shelving and warehouse equipment	22 000
Depreciation to date	13 200
Van	18 000
Depreciation to date	4 500
Office equipment	8 000
Depreciation to date	6 000
Inventory at the start of the year	62 200
Trade payables	51 400
Electricity	4 800
Business and water rates	7 600
Warehouse rental	42 000
Telephone	3 200
Trade receivables	54 190
Owner's equity at start of year	60 000
Retained earnings at start of year	6 000
Insurances	3 600
Delivery costs	11 400
Administration costs	6 700
Purchases	365 850
Sales	540 000
Cash at bank	3 460
Drawings	30 000

In conversation with Charlie you find the following information.

(a) No depreciation has been charged for this year. The warehouse equipment is being written off over ten years, the office equipment over eight years and the van over four years. In all cases the assumption is that there is no residual value and the straight-line method of depreciation is appropriate.

(b) The electricity bill for the final quarter has not been included so the charge in the accounts represents only three quarters.

(c) £800 of the insurance charges is a prepayment relating to next year.

(d) Included in the trade receivables is an amount of £9600 owed by a shop that has gone bankrupt since the end of the year.

(e) He had £59 700 worth of goods in inventory at the end of the year.

Using either an extended trial balance or worksheet approach, draw up statement of financial position and income statement for Charlie's warehouse.

2 Topper and Co. is an independent high street retailer of gentlemen's clothing specializing in the top end of the city gent's market. It also has a larger mail order business; hence the large amount of trade receivables. At the end of its accounting year the owner has brought you the following information extracted from the books of account.

	£
Shop assistants' wages	36 120
Manager's salary	40 080
Shop fittings	44 000
Depreciation to date	26 400
Car	36 000
Depreciation to date	9 000
Inventory at the start of the year	124 400
Trade payables	22 800
Electricity	9 600
Business and water rates	15 200
Showroom rental	84 000
Telephone	6 400
Trade receivables	28 380
Owner's equity at start of year	120 000
Retained earnings at start of year	12 000
Insurances	7 200
Delivery costs	22 800
Administration costs	13 400
Purchases	731 700
Sales	1 080 000
Cash at bank	10 920
Drawings	60 000

You are also able to obtain the following information.

(a) The electricity bill for the final quarter has not been included so the charge in the accounts represents only three quarters.

(b) £200 of the insurance charges is a prepayment relating to next year.

(c) Included in the trade receivables is an amount of £2400 owed by a customer who has been declared bankrupt.

(d) No depreciation has been charged for this year. The showroom fittings are being written off over ten years and the cars over four years. Topper and Co. uses the straight-line method of depreciation.

(e) Topper and Co. had £99 700 worth of goods in inventory at the end of the year.

Using either an extended trial balance or worksheet approach, draw up statement of financial position and income statement for Topper and Co.

ANSWER TO ACTIVITY 11.2

Sharon's worksheet

| | Assets | | | = | Equity + Liabilities | | | | |
	Cash	Fixtures & Fittings	Inventory		Equity	Revenue & expenses	Trade payables	Accruals	Depreciation
Item 1	12 000				12 000				
Item 2	−8 000	8 000							
Item 3			22 000				22 000		
	−18 000						−18 000		
Item 4	38 000					38 000			
Item 5			−19 000			−19 000			
Item 6	−2 000					−2 000			
Item 7	−900					−900			
Balance	21 100	8 000	3 000		12 000	16 100	4 000		
Depreciation						−2 000			2 000
Accrual						−300		300	
Balance	21 100	8 000	3 000		12 000	13 800	4 000	300	2 000

The same set of transactions depicted through the medium of T accounts would be as follows.

Assets   =   **Equity + liabilities**

Cash

Item 1	12 000	Item 2	8 000
Item 4	38 000	Item 3	18 000
		Item 6	2 000
		Item 7	900
		Bal c/d	21 100
	50 000		50 000
Bal b/d	21 100		

Fixtures and fittings

Item 2	8 000		
		Bal c/d	8 000
	8 000		8 000
Bal b/d	8 000		

Inventory

Item 3	22 000	Item 5	19 000
		Bal c/d	3 000
	22 000		22 000
Bal b/d	3 000		

Owner's equity

		Item 1	12 000
Bal c/d	12 000		
	12 000		12 000
		Bal b/d	12 000

Revenue & expenses

Item 5	19 000	Item 4	38 000
Item 6	2 000		
Item 7	900		
Depreciation	*2 000*		
Accrual	*300*		
Bal c/d	13 800		
	38 000		38 000
		Bal b/d	13 800

Accrual

		Rent	*300*
Bal c/d	300		
	300		300
		Bal b/d	300

Amounts payable

Item 3	18 000	Item 3	22 000
Bal c/d	4 000		
	22 000		22 000
		Bal b/d	4 000

Assets		=	Equity + liabilities	
			Depreciation	
			Charge	*2 000*
	Bal c/d	2 000		
		2 000		2 000
			Bal b/d	2 000

Extended trial balance of Sharon's business

	Debit	Credit	Adjustments Debit	Adjustments Credit	Final Debit	Final Credit
Cash	21 100				21 100	
Equity		12 000				12 000
Trade payables		4 000				4 000
Fixtures and Fittiings	8 000				8 000	
Inventory	3 000				3 000	
Revenue and expenses		16 100	2 000			
			300			13 800
Depreciation				2 000		2 000
Accrual				300		300
	32 100	32 100	2 300	2 300	32 100	32 100

Extended trial balance of Sharon's business

	Debit	Credit	Adjustments Debit	Adjustments Credit	Final Debit	Final Credit
Cash	21 100				21 100	
Equity		12 000				12 000
Trade payables		4 000				4 000
Fixtures and Fittiings	8 000				8 000	
Inventory	3 000				3 000	
Revenue and expenses		16 100	2 000			
			300			13 800
Depreciation				2 000		2 000
Accrual				300		300
	32 100	32 100	2 300	2 300	32 100	32 100

Once again the adjustments at the year end are shown in *italics* and affect the revenue and expenses account, the depreciation account and the accrual account. The extended trial balance shows the adjustments of £2000 for depreciation and £300 for the accrual in respect of the last quarter's rent.

CHAPTER 12
FINANCIAL STATEMENT
ANALYSIS

LEARNING OUTCOMES

By the end of this chapter you will:

- Have revisited the users of accounting information discussed in Chapter 1 and identified their common needs.

- Understood that financial information is only one of a number of sources of information that should be used in analysis.

- Have learned the techniques of eyeballing, trend analysis, common size statement analysis and ratio analysis.

- Understood the limitations of analysis and the limitations inherent in the financial information available for analysis.

The concepts, uses and limitations of financial analysis are explored in this chapter, in which we return to the different users and their needs to provide a framework in which an informed analysis can take place. Some of the basic techniques of analysis are explained and explored through the use of a single case study. Finally, the chapter looks at the limitations of financial analysis, including the impacts of price changes and different accounting choices.

In the previous chapters, we have considered the way in which accounting information is produced and what the components of financial statements mean. In this chapter, we shall concentrate on how we can analyze the information in financial statements to come to judgements about the performance of the business entity. This chapter will offer some guidelines on approaches to performance analysis and introduce some techniques of analysis. We shall start by revisiting the user groups which we introduced in Chapter 1 and looking at their information requirements.

USER NEEDS

Investor group

The investor group was discussed previously as a homogeneous group with similar needs, but there are, in fact, different types of investor. For sole traders and partnerships the investor is the owner or partner. The equivalent of this type of investor in a company is the ordinary shareholder. These investors will be referred to from now on as equity investors. We need to establish what this group has in common, and what distinguishes the equity investor in a large company from the equivalent in a sole proprietorship. In general, equity investors take on all the risks associated with ownership and are entitled to any rewards after other prior claims have been met. For a sole trader the equity investor, i.e. the owner, is also likely to be heavily involved in the management and day-to-day running of the business. Where there is this direct involvement his or her needs are the same as for managers (discussed below). In the case of larger organizations, such as large private companies and all public companies, there is likely to be a separation of ownership and management. For large businesses the final accounts meet the information needs of the shareholders, who are in the main properly characterized by the term 'absentee owners'. In general, the smaller the organization and the greater the direct involvement of the owners in the day-to-day running of the business, the more detail will be required. However, the information required to meet the needs of equity investors is broadly the same irrespective of the type of ownership involved. We therefore suggest that the basic needs of this group of users can be met with information about

- profitability, especially future profitability;
- management efficiency (for example, are assets being utilized efficiently?);
- return on their investment
  - within the firm
  - compared with alternatives;
- risk being taken
  - financial risk
  - business risk;
- returns to owners
  - dividends
  - drawings etc.

Preference shareholders

For investments in companies it is also possible to purchase a share known as a preference share. These shares are generally seen as less risky than ordinary shares and therefore do not normally earn as great a reward. Although it is difficult to generalize on the differences between these shares and ordinary shares (this varies from share to share), normally preference shareholders will be entitled to a fixed rate of dividend and to repayment before ordinary shareholders in the event of the business being 'wound up'. Because of the nature of the shares, these users are likely to be interested in

- profitability, mainly future profitability;
- the net realizable value of the assets;
- the extent by which their dividends are covered by profit.

If we compare the needs of these two groups of investors, we can see that this group is more likely to be interested in the extent to which income is safe, rather than in the growth of the business. This is because in most cases it is only ordinary shareholders who will benefit from such growth. The preference shareholders' return is normally in the form of a dividend at a fixed rate irrespective of the profits made.

In many ways, this type of investment is similar to long-term loans (we shall deal with these in more detail later). The similarity is at a fairly superficial level in that the return is at a fixed rate. There are important differences beyond this superficial similarity, however. In the case of a loan the interest has to be paid whether or not profits are made, whereas preference dividends, like dividends on ordinary shares, are not due to be paid until they are declared by the directors of the company. This is one of the reasons why the interest on loans is treated as an expense in arriving at the profit before taxation, whereas the preference dividend is shown as an appropriation of profit after tax. The differences in the way in which they are dealt with in the accounts also reflect the different treatments in tax legislation. The interest on the loan is allowed for tax purposes. It is an expense in arriving at the taxable profit. Another reason for the difference in treatment is that loans are repayable at some specified point in time whereas, unless specifically stated (as in the case of redeemable preference shares, preference shares are permanent capital). In this way they are more similar to ordinary shares: the capital is only repaid if the business ceases to exist. We can now move on to look at other providers of capital who are also users of accounting information.

Lenders

Lenders, as we saw in Chapter 9, can be conveniently subdivided into three subgroups: short-term creditors, medium-term lenders and long-term lenders.

Short-term creditors are normally trade creditors, i.e. those who supply the business with goods on credit. Their areas of interest would be

- liquidity/solvency, short term;
- net realizable value of the assets;
- profitability and future growth;
- risk (financial and business).

Medium-term lenders may well be bankers and other financial institutions. Their areas of interest would be

- profitability (future profits provide cash for repayment of loans);
- security and the nature of the security;
- financial stability.

Long-term lenders will have the same needs as medium-term lenders, except if they are 'secured' lenders. A secured lender is someone who has a legal charge on the assets of the business and can claim those assets if the business does not repay or service the lending in accordance with the lending agreement. In the case of secured lenders their areas of interest are likely to be

- risk, especially financial risk;
- security – net realizable value of specific assets;
- interest cover – how well their interest is covered by the profits being made.

As can be seen, these different types of lender have broadly the same needs for information. It is the emphasis that changes depending on whether one is looking from a short- or a long-term perspective.

Employees

Employees are interested in judging job security and in assessing their wages, especially their relative fairness. Their areas of interest are likely to be

- profitability – average profits per employee for the purposes of productivity bargaining;
- liquidity – future trends in profits.

There has been considerable debate over the extent to which these needs are met by conventional accounts and whether an alternative statement such as a statement of value added would meet these needs better.

Auditors

Auditors are not normally seen as a user of accounting information. However, in order to carry out an audit efficiently, an analysis of accounts is frequently carried out. As auditors have to express an opinion on whether the company is a going concern they are interested in all aspects of the business. For the purposes of planning and carrying out their audit, the auditors are likely to be interested in

- trends in sales, profit, costs, etc.;
- variations from norms;
- accounting policies.

Management

It is very difficult to describe the needs of managers as they will vary greatly from situation to situation. They will be interested in all the information above, however, as they are likely to be judged on their performance by outside investors or lenders. In addition, they will require detailed information on the performance of the business as a whole and on the parts of the business to enable them to manage the business on a day-to-day basis. This information could include such items as profitability by major product, costs per product and changes in sales or component mix.

The list of users dealt with above is not intended to be comprehensive. We have tried to give the reader a flavour of the differing needs of the various groups discussed and to indicate that some of these will not be provided by the annual accounts. At this stage we need to establish what, if any, needs are common and what other factors need to be considered.

Some common needs which can be readily identified are profitability, liquidity and risk. The problem is how these are measured and how to judge good or bad performance. Before going on to discuss these issues in detail, let us first examine the common needs in more detail and look at the context in which the financial analysis is to be carried out.

Common needs

TABLE 12.1 Common needs

User group	Future profitability	Profitability	Efficiency	Return on investment	Business risk	Financial risk	Riskness of return to investor	Value of assets	Comparability	Liquidity
Owners	×	×	×	×	×	×	×	×	×	
Preference shareholders	×	×			×	×	×			
Lenders	×	×	×		×	×	×	×	×	×
Employees	×	×	×							×
Government		×								
Auditors	×	×	×			×		×	×	×

As is clear from Table 12.1 the most obvious need that virtually all these groups have in common is the need for information about the profitability of the business. This can be divided into two components, one relating to current or past profitability and the other to future profitability. Information relating to the current or past profitability is available from the financial statements but information about future profitability is a matter of judgement. Users have to arrive at their own judgement on this and although information in the annual report may help it is only one part of the picture. Another factor that is common to a number of groups is the requirement for information about financial risk and about 'liquidity' or 'solvency', as it is often called. Other themes that emerge concern the return on the investment in the business. This has associated measures such as the riskiness of the return (dividend cover or interest cover). There are also a number of needs that are more specific to particular user groups. A good example of these is the security measures used by lenders which we have summarized under value of the assets. In reality in small businesses this need for security is more likely to be met from outside the business through personal guarantees from owners and directors or even charges on other property owned by the owner rather than belonging to the business. This may include a charge on the owners' family homes although banks have been more reluctant to use this in recent years as they wish to avoid the unfavourable publicity associated with taking over the family home as well as closing the business if things go badly wrong. We shall examine how the common needs can be analyzed in some detail after we have established the context in which the analysis should take place.

CONTEXT FOR FINANCIAL STATEMENT ANALYSIS

Before doing any analysis it is important to remember that it must be seen in a wider context than merely a mechanical exercise using various techniques. Some of the factors that are directly relevant to any analysis of business performance are as follows.

KEY CONCEPT 12.1

Financial analysis

Good financial analysis requires that the person for whom the analysis is being done is clearly identified together with the purpose of the analysis. It is unlikely to be useful if it does not take into account as many relevant factors as possible.

The size of the business

The fact that a business is the size of IBM makes it less vulnerable to the decisions of others outside the organization. For example, a banker might lend money to a small business at a rate of 10% or more above base rate, whereas for IBM or BP the rate would be much lower. Similarly, the banker is likely to ask for security from the small business whereas with IBM the name itself is enough security.

The riskiness of the business

Apart from size, the nature of the business needs to be taken into account: a gold prospecting business will have a different level of risk and return than a bank although following the recent world banking crisis the latter are no longer considered to be the ultimate safe investment. Other factors which affect the risk, known as business risk, are reliance on a small number of products, the degree of technological innovation and, of course, vulnerability to competition. A good example of an industry with high business risk is that of dot.com companies, where there have been spectacular successes but also spectacular failures.

The economic, social and political environment

Examples of the way in which the economic, social and political environment affects industry can be found in virtually any daily paper. For example, if the pound goes down relative to the euro, this will affect imports and exports and some firms will gain or suffer accordingly. Changes in interest rates often have sharp effects on firms that are financed by a large amount of borrowing (loans or overdrafts). The effects of the social environment tend to be more subtle. A study of recent history shows that although profit is still accepted as the prime motivation for business there is increasing concern with environmental and social effects evidenced by the increase in environmental reporting; carbon accounting is the latest example of this phenomena. Similarly we have seen in recent years a vast increase in the level of corporate social reporting and reporting relating to governance, directors pay and remuneration and bonuses. These social changes frequently coincide with political changes, although the environmental issue is a good example of a social effect which is likely to transcend political changes.

The industry trends, effects of changes in technology

In order to make any judgements about performance and more especially about the future, it is vital to understand the way in which the industry is going. For example, in the late 1970s and early 1980s most of the major British toy manufacturers went bankrupt. This was in part due to changes in the nature of the industry and the product. The industry was being affected by cheap imports, the impact of large buyers, and the high rates of inflation and interest. The product required in the market place was also changing towards electronic toys rather than the traditional die-cast model cars such as Dinky toys. Interestingly, many of the products of companies that went bust are still being manufactured today albeit at a much smaller scale and more clearly aimed at a niche market. So, for those who like sticking pieces of plastic together with glue a bit of searching of specialist outlets will find brand new Airfix model plane kits still being made and sold. A more up-to-date example of the effect of changes in technology can be found in the forms of mobile technology and how these have changed from CD players to MP3 and MP4 players and the increasing sophistication of mobile phones which have made the internet accessible to all who can afford to pay.

EFFECT OF PRICE CHANGES

We have just mentioned high rates of inflation. The effect of price changes may be more specific. For example, even with the slowing down in recent years, the price of property has been rising faster than the general change in prices over decades. There have been a number of proposals for taking account of price changes in corporate reports, none of which has gained general acceptance although there is an increasing emphasis on fair value accounting of late. The fact that the perfect solution has not been found does not mean that the problem can be ignored as even low rates of inflation of 5% or less can mean that what appears to be a gentle growth of sales is in fact a decline. It should be pointed out that, although we normally think of price changes in terms of price rises, there are many examples where the effects of new technology, competition and economies of scale have led to reductions in price. The most obvious examples are in the electronics industries and the computer industry. For example, simply look at how the prices of mobile phones, MP3 and MP4 players and digital cameras have come down in recent years as technological advances make them cheaper to produce and at the same time drive prices of less sophisticated models downwards.

PROJECTIONS AND PREDICTIONS OF THE FUTURE

While we can all take a guess at the future, clearly there is a case for taking into account the opinion of those more closely involved with the business and those who have expertise in the industry and in analyzing likely economic trends. Financial analysis must, after all, relate not only to what has happened but also to what is going to happen. So we need to understand the economy or economies in which the business is operating and this may be many different economies as businesses become more global in their operations. Thus the level of sophistication required to make sound investment decisions is ever increasing. On the bright side, however, information is becoming increasingly accessible.

Having looked at some of the factors which need to be taken into account, it should be clear that, although a set of accounts may contain some of the information, a lot of other information will have to be obtained from other sources. These other sources of information can be conveniently subdivided into sources external to the business and those internal to the business. Some examples of these other sources are discussed below.

Sources external to the business

- *Government statistics* These include the *Monthly Digest of Statistics* (www.statistics.gov.uk) Department for Business Innovation and Skills (www.bis.gov.uk, statistics and The Office of Public Sector Information (www.opsi.gov.uk) publications.

- *Trade journals* These may be specific to the trade or more general professional or business journals such as *Management Today* or *Marketing Week*.

- *Financial press* A lot of information can be gleaned from the financial pages of quality newspapers, from the *Financial Times* and from specialist publications such as the *Investors' Chronicle*.

- *Databases* There are now a number of on-line databases, such as Datastream, Reuters and Bloomberg which can be accessed for information. These contain information about other companies, industry statistics and economic indicators.

- *Specialist agencies* These may provide an industry-wide analysis, general financial reports, credit-scoring services and many other services.

- *The internet* A simple search on the internet using any of the available search engines will provide thousands of hits on virtually any business you care to imagine.

So the difficulty is no longer accessing data. The issue we face now is how we know which data are reliable and provide good information content and what are less reliable or even of dubious authenticity. Remember that it is still the case that many 'open source' data allow open authorship with no checks and balances on what is posted. A good example is Wikipedia, which advertises itself as the encyclopedia anyone can edit! Virtually all these sources are probably available on the internet. Some may provide free access to information while others such as specialist agencies, financial advisers and credit rating agencies may provide a 'taster' and then charge for more detailed reports. In addition the first three of the sources in the list above are likely to be fairly readily accessible in good libraries. The others are more specialized and access may be more limited and much more expensive.

Sources internal to the business

The annual report and accounts

The information contained in the annual report and accounts will vary from company to company, with very small companies and most limited liability partnerships only including the minimum information that they are required to in order to meet their legal obligations and the requirements of the regulatory bodies. Quoted companies, on the other hand, tend to use the annual report as an important part of the public relations and communication process with their shareholders and prospective shareholders. In many cases their reports consist of well over a hundred pages of glossy full-colour information on a wide range of aspects of the business concerned. The BP annual report for 2008 from which we have used extracts in this book consisted of 211 pages of which over half were devoted to the financial statements and financial information. We have seen as we looked at case studies to illustrate various points that the breadth of information is considerable. Of course, not all companies will devote the same amount of space to environmental issues, for example, so in the discussion below we shall deal with those contents that you will find in virtually all annual reports of quoted companies. Before doing that, however, it is worth just glancing at Case Study 12.1, which gives an idea of the contents of a fairly typical annual report for a company listed on the Stock Exchange. For smaller companies it is likely that the reports will be much briefer as much of the disclosure is related to Stock Exchange requirements or is voluntary.

Over recent years in the UK, the contents of the annual report for listed companies have increased with the addition of more and more statements and explanations. We shall divide these contents into two main categories, namely those that are subject to audit and those that are not subject to audit.

Audited contents of annual reports

The audited components can be divided into two components: the main statements of account and the explanatory notes relating to them, and then the supplementary statements. We shall look briefly at these, starting with the main statements with which you are now familiar, namely the income statement, cash flow statement and statement of financial position, or balance sheet as it is called in the case study below.

CASE STUDY 12.1

BP plc

Commentary

The contents of the annual report and accounts of BP plc are provided below to give those unfamiliar with such reports a feel for what they might include. As can be seen the report is very comprehensive and long, 211 pages. It contains a mix of statutory reporting requirements such as the directors' report, financial statements and auditor's report, reports to meet the Stock Exchange listing requirements, e.g. chairman's statement and remuneration report, and 'voluntary' reports such as those relating to safety, employees, etc.

BP Annual Report and Accounts 2008
What's inside?

(Continued)

Additional information for shareholders

Main statements and explanatory material

The income statement This is the statement that summarizes the revenue and expenses for the period. It is probably still the most important statement for users although, as we mentioned earlier, the cash flow statement is gaining in importance with bankers. As with all statements, the information is related to the past and its usefulness is limited by that. Similarly, the fact that the information tends to be summarized information may mean that the performance of the weaker parts of a business is not necessarily readily apparent as it can be offset by the performance of the stronger parts.

The cash flow statement The cash flow statement also relates to the period and provides information about the origin of the cash coming into the business and how that cash was spent. It broadly distinguishes between the cash flows arising out of the normal operations of the business and other cash flows. The latter group is then further subdivided into those relating to investment in the business and those concerned with financing the business. Finally, the statement reconciles these with the movements in the cash balances between the opening and closing statements of financial position.

The statement of financial position or balance sheet This will give information about the position at a point in time. The information is therefore really only valid at that point in time and given that the median time for publication by large companies is over three months after the reporting date and for small companies it is thought to be at least ten months, the information may have very little bearing on the current position. This question of how timely the information is has a major bearing on what can be achieved from an analysis of the accounting information contained in the published accounts.

Notes to the accounts Because by their very nature the main financial statements are summaries of a vast number of often complex transactions, the analyst needs further explanation of the contents of the summarized statements and this can be found in the notes to the accounts. Without the information in the notes the level of analysis possible is likely to be very superficial, especially in complex business organizations. However, users often find that the level of detail contained and the complexity and technical language used are not helpful to their understanding of the treatment of various items in the accounts.

The accounting policies statement As we have seen, there are a number of different ways of dealing with such items as inventory. Is FIFO or weighted average cost being used? For depreciation, is reducing balance or straight line being used? What is the policy regarding bad debts or impairment of the values of assets? Many other items are subject to similar preconditions, so it is vital to understand the basis which has been adopted. This should be stated in the statement of accounting policies. Unfortunately, all too often, these statements are of such generality that they are fairly meaningless. It is not uncommon to find a statement on depreciation which says that 'depreciation is charged on the straight-line method over the useful life of the assets'. The problem with such a statement is that different assets have different lives and different residual values. In fact, it is likely that different businesses will come to different estimates of both of these for the same asset. This leads to problems of comparability between different companies as the basis adopted will affect the profits, asset values, etc. Within the same business the problems are to some extent alleviated by the requirement to follow the basic accounting concept of consistency. This perhaps is one of the reasons why research with users and in particular with bankers finds that the cash flow statement, which is not subject to lots of choices of alternative treatments, is now being given more weight.

KEY CONCEPT 12.2

Consistency

This important concept says that:

An accounting policy once adopted should not be changed from year to year. This is applied fairly rigorously to most limited companies as their financial reports are covered by legislation and are subject to an audit report. For many small companies, limited liability partnerships and unincorporated businesses such as sole proprietorships and other partnerships it is likely to be less rigorously applied.

Subsidiary statements

Statement of comprehensive income This was previously known by various names. In the case of Unilever plc, as you will see in Case Study 12.2, it is called the consolidated statement of recognized income and expense. These statements bring in the total gains not just those arising from trading. The other gains may come from the sale of parts of the business or of the non-current assets or from revaluations of non-current assets to reflect the fair value at the reporting date.

CASE STUDY 12.2

Consolidated statement of recognized income and expense: Unilever plc 2008

Consolidated statement of recognised income and expense for the year ended 31 December

	€ million 2008	€ million 2007	€ million 2006
Fair value gains/(losses) net of tax:			
On cash flow hedges	**(118)**	84	6
On available-for-sale financial assets	**(46)**	2	15
Actuarial gains/(losses) on pension schemes net of tax	**(2 293)**	542	853
Currency retranslation gains/(losses) net of tax(a)	**(1 688)**	(413)	(335)
Net income/(expense) recognized directly in equity	**(4 145)**	**215**	**539**
Net profit	**5 285**	4 136	5 015
Total recognized income and expense 21	**1 140**	4 351	5 554
Attributable to:			
Minority interests	**205**	237	242
Shareholders' equity	**935**	4 114	5 312

(a) Includes fair value gains/(losses) on net investment hedges of €(560) million (2007: €(692) million; 2006: €(779) million).

(Continued)

Commentary

The extract from the annual report of Unilever plc shows the total gains from on-trading activities such as currency gains and losses etc. These are added to the bet profit to arrive at the total gains and losses for the period of report. You will see that among the other gains are losses in the year on hedges on financial assets and a big loss on the actuarial value of the pension fund.

Reconciliation of movements in shareholders' funds This statement shows the major changes in the owners' equity, i.e. the shareholders' funds. It includes any profits or losses made, dividends, new shares issued or shares bought back by the company. An example which includes most of the items mentioned above can be found in Case Study 12.3.

CASE STUDY 12.3

Movements in shareholders' funds: Rolls Royce plc Annual Report 2008

Commentary

As can be seen in the extract from the 2008 annual report of Rolls Royce plc, there is a reconciliation of the movements in shareholders' funds over the year. This combines information from the income statement with information relating to the redemption and issue of new shares.

Rolls Royce plc

Reconciliation of movements in shareholders' funds

For the year ended December 31, 2008

	2008 £m	2007 £m
At January	1 612	1 184
Total recognized gains for the year	(1 240)	514
Transfer from transition hedging reserve	(78)	(149)
Share-based payment adjustments	5	16
Related tax movements	22	47
At December 31	331	1 612

Supplementary information

Chairman's statement or Chief Executive's Review In the case of public companies, this statement is included with the annual accounts. It is a personal overview of the company's financial performance, strategy and future prospects. The information contained should not be taken at face value as it is likely to reflect one point of view which itself may be biased. The statement often highlights only the positive side. As a senior lending banker commented, 'It is as important to ascertain what is left out as it is to ascertain what has been included'.

Review of operations This provides an overview of the business. It would normally contain a review of business environment, the various components of the business and how they are performing, usually against key performance indicators (KPIs). These reviews often include a breakdown of the business either by type of business or by geographical area.

Directors' report This is a statutory requirement for all companies and the Companies Act defines the information which must be disclosed. The statutes, however, lay down a minimum and more and more we find that in the case of public companies this is not the only information given. You will find information on how the business has performed over the period, the business review, information in respect of corporate governance, social responsibility and environmental matters may also be included. For private companies on the other hand the information given is normally the minimum required.

Auditors' report With the exception of smaller companies and smaller limited liability partnerships, up to £5.6 million turnover and a statement of financial position total of £2.8 million or less, every company and limited liability partnership is subject to an annual audit of its accounts. Included in the accounts is a report from the auditors stating whether, in their opinion, the accounts show a 'true and fair' view. As far as financial analysis is concerned, this report is best treated as an exception report: unless it is qualified in some way no account needs to be taken of it. It is worth mentioning that for most bankers it does add credibility to the figures. It does not, however, mean that the accounts are correct in all their details: often the report contains a number of disclaimers in respect of certain figures.

Statement of corporate governance In the last two decades there has been an increasing emphasis on corporate governance and the Stock Exchange now requires that all listed companies include this statement in their annual report. The contents are set out by the Stock Exchange and include risk management, treasury management, internal control, going concern and auditors, in addition to commentary around the directors' remuneration levels and changes.

In addition to the items mentioned above, you will also frequently find other items such as the highlights of the year. These are normally presented separately at the start of the annual report, a five-year historical summary, analysis of share-holdings showing who the major shareholders are, statements of principal subsidiaries, etc.

THE COMMON NEEDS EXPLAINED

We have identified common needs such as profitability, liquidity, financial risk, etc., but before we can carry out any analysis we need to know what is meant by these terms. We shall therefore discuss what each term means and identify what we are trying to highlight with our analysis. For this purpose we shall use the example of Broll Ltd. You are already familiar with this example which we introduced in Chapter 11. It is reproduced below.

EXAMPLE 12.1

Comprehensive income statement of Broll Ltd for the year to xx. xx.xxxx

	Notes	£	This year £	Last year £
Turn over	9		60 000	45 000
Cost of sale			40 000	30 000
Gross profit			20 000	15 000
Other income	10		7 000	7 000
Disturbution costs			−8 000	−6 000
Adminstrative expenses			−11 500	−11 600
Finance costs	11		−1 500	−900
Profit on ordinary activities before tax			6 000	3 500
Tax	12		−2 600	−1 400
Profit on ordinary activities after tax			3 400	2 100
Retained profit at start of year			1 000	0
Dividends -interim	13	−1 000		
-final	13	−1 600	−2 600	−1 100
Retained profit at end of year			1 800	1 000

Profitability

Looking at the first of our needs relating to profitability, it is intuitively obvious that the starting point for this information should be the income statement. Before looking at the information contained in the income statement, we need to establish what information is needed.

We need some sort of relative comparison:

● Is the business more profitable than it was last year?

● Is it more profitable than a similar business, or even a dissimilar business?

Each of these questions requires us to measure the profit relative to something else. The last question cannot be answered by simply looking at one set of accounts. We need to compare a number of different businesses and to do this we have to make sure that the accounts are comparable. Are they depreciating the assets over the same time period? Remember that the shorter the time period the greater the charge, and therefore the smaller the final profit figure. It is for these comparisons that the accounting policies statement is required. Let us look at comparisons over time within our own business. If we look at of the income statement of Broll Ltd we find that the business made more profits this year, when it earned £6000 profit before taxation, than last year, when the figure was only £3500. The question that now arises is whether it is more profitable because it is selling more, i.e. £60 000 this year compared with £45 000 last year, or whether it is more efficient, or whether it is a combination of the two.

We can go some way to answering this by simply working out what the increase in sales was and what the increase in profit was. In this case the sales increased by 33%, i.e.

(Continued)

$$\pounds 60\,000 - \pounds 45\,000 = \frac{\pounds 15\,000}{\pounds 45\,000} \times 100 = 33\%$$

The profit, however, increased by over 70%, i.e.

$$\pounds 6\,000 - \pounds 3\,500 = \frac{\pounds 2\,500}{\pounds 3\,500} \times 100 = 71\%$$

Thus, we have discovered that not only is Broll Ltd making more profit by selling more but it is also making a greater profit on each sale. However, we do not know whether this seemingly favourable change is because this year was a good year or last year was a bad year or whether we have had to invest a lot of money in order to increase the profitability. The former question can only really be answered satisfactorily by comparisons over a longer period of time than two years and by comparing Broll Ltd with a similar business in the same industry. The second question can perhaps be answered in the case of a small company by looking at what return the profit represents relative to the amount invested. This then begs the question of what the amount invested is. Often in the case of small businesses the major investment made by the owner is the time spent in the business. In the case of a public company, on the other hand, there is normally very little relationship between the amount shown in the accounts under share capital and reserves and the amount you would have to invest to buy the company through the purchase of shares on the Stock Exchange.

Although not ignoring the above problems, for the present we can look at the statements of financial position as a rough guide in the absence of anything better. We can see that in this case the equity investment in the form of capital and reserves has hardly changed, £74 500 last year and £75 300 this year. Therefore, we can be reasonably certain that there is a real increase in efficiency from last year.

Statement of financial position of Broll Ltd as at xx. xx. xxxx

	Notes	This year £	Last year £
Current assets			
Cash at bank and in hand		3 500	2 000
Amounts receivable		10 000	4 000
Inventory	1	10 000	7 000
		23 500	13 000
Non current assets			
Tangible assets	2	25 000	20 000
Intangible assets	3	50 000	56 000
		75 000	76 000
Total assets		98 500	89 000
Current liabilities			
Trade payables		4 000	3 000
Taxation	4	2 600	1 400
Dividends	5	1 600	1 100
		8 200	5 500
Non-current liabilities			
Loans	6	15 000	9 000
		15 000	9 000

(Continued)

	Notes	This year £	Last year £
Total liabilities		23 200	14 500
Equity	7	70 000	70 000
Share capital	8	5 300	4 500
Retained profits		75 300	74 500
Total equity and liabilities		98 500	89 000

Before leaving the question of profitability, we need to discuss the future profitability of the business, as this was identified as a common need for many users. The fact that a company has been profitable is comforting but if you want to make a decision about whether to buy into a business or sell up you need information about the future, not the past. This information is not contained in the income statement, although it could be argued that information on the past is the best guide to the future. In practical terms, the only way you can form an opinion about the future is by using a combination of information including past profits, knowledge of the industry, predictions about the economy and many other factors.

Profitability summary

- Profitability requires comparisons:
  - over time
  - with other businesses.
- Profitability relates to:
  - the past for evaluation
  - the future for prediction.

Liquidity and financial risk

We shall deal with these two together as they are both related to the financing of the business. The area of financial risk or solvency is of vital importance as there are many cases where a business has gone bankrupt because of cash flow problems even though it was profitable. There are also cases where two companies in the same line of business produce dramatically different results purely because of the way they are financed. For example, if you make a return of 15% on every pound invested and can borrow money at 10%, it is worth borrowing money because the excess return goes to the owners. However, there is some risk involved in such a course of action as you will lose if the interest rate rises to, say, 17% and you are still only making 15%. A way of measuring the financial risk is to look at the statement of financial position and identify the amount of debt finance, i.e. loans, debentures, bank overdrafts and other borrowing, and to compare this with the amount of equity finance, i.e. owners' capital plus reserves.

In the UK, in general, debt finance does not normally exceed the equity finance, although the extent to which this generalization holds true is to some extent dependent on the size of the business. This is largely as a result of the banks' policies of lending on a pound-for-pound basis, i.e. for each pound of your money that you put in the business the bank will lend a pound. Although this is not a hard and fast rule, it is effectively used as the benchmark by bank managers in the clearing banks in the UK. It is interesting that different countries seem to adopt different benchmarks. For example, banks in Germany and Japan tend to lend well above the one-for-one norm.

In the case of Broll Ltd, there is some long-term borrowing and this has increased from £9000 to £15 000. This may not be a good thing as in the case of Broll Ltd the company is only making £6000 on the capital invested of over £75 000. This is less than the 10% being paid on the loan – we can find this rate by looking at the amount of the loan in the statement of financial position £15 000 and comparing it to the finance cost in the income statement, £1500. If a company is reliant on borrowing as a source of finance it must ensure that it is earning a greater return than it is costing to borrow that money. Looking now at liquidity: what is generally understood by this is; can you meet your commitments as they fall due? In general, the major area for concern is the short term, which is often taken to be a year. This is convenient as it fits in with the definition used for current assets and current liabilities, and so we have a suitable measure simply by looking at the statement of financial position. For example, Broll Ltd has current assets of £23 500 and current liabilities of only £8200. This means that it should get enough money in during the next year to pay what it is currently due to pay out in that year.

One of the problems that arise with this apparently simple measure is that current can mean due tomorrow or in twelve months or even more. In the case of some current assets, for example inventory, it first has to be sold and then the money has to be collected. Another problem is the question of what the correct liquidity level for the business is, for example, if there is a lot of cash in the bank that is hardly an efficient use of resources. In the case of Broll Ltd the amount of £3500 in the bank may be far in excess of its true needs. There is also the question of whether £10 000 tied up in trade receivables is excessive on sales of £60 000, it is in excess of 16% of sales and if we compare this with last year where the comparative figures were £4000 and £45 000, less than 9% we can see that there may be an issue that needs further exploration.

ACTIVITY 12.1

Can you think of reasons why the percentage of sales that have not been paid for should have gone up?

You may have thought that this is because of a big sale near the year end, a deliberate policy to extend credit in order to increase the total sales, both of which may be positive, or it could be that the company is less efficient at collecting money or customers are less able to pay, both of which would be bad signs for Broll Ltd.

Other problems with interpreting the information may arise if we try to compare different businesses. For example, an aircraft manufacturer will have different needs from a food wholesaler. Even within the same industrial sector, the needs will differ. For example, a whisky distiller will have different needs from a brewery, as the former has a product that has to be matured over years whereas the latter has a product that is produced in a few months and has a fairly limited shelf life.

Financial risk summary

- Financial risk involves long-term and short-term solvency.
- Requirements and norms differ widely from industry to industry.

The importance of considering the type of industry is aptly illustrated by the statements of financial position contained in Case Study 12.4.

CASE STUDY 12.4

Financial statements – comparisons over time: Next plc (2009) and BP plc (2008)

Consolidated balance sheet of Next plc
As at 24 January

	Notes	2009 £m	2008 £m
ASSETS and LIABILITIES			
Non-current assets			
Property, plant & equipment	9	612.8	610.6
Intangible assets	10	55.4	36.2
Interests in associates	12	3.5	2.9
Other investments	13	1.0	1.0
Other financial assets	16	14.1	0.5
		686.8	651.2
Current assets			
Inventories	14	318.7	319.1
Trade and other receivables	15	639.6	591.5
Other financial assets	16	84.4	12.6
Cash and short term deposits	17	47.856	56.0
		1 090.5	979.2
Total assets		1 777.0	1 630.4
Current Liabilities			
Bank overdrafts	18	(46.3)	(37.7)
Unsecured bank loans	18	(75.0)	(205.0)
Trade and other payables	19	(485.1)	(466.6)
Other financial liabilities	20	(15.8)	(55.0)
Current tax liabilities		(85.9)	(92.4)
		(708.1)	(856.7)
Non-current liabilities			
Corporate bonds	21	(567.8)	(539.7)
Net retirement benefit obligation	23	(69.1)	(45.8)
Provisions	24	(13.1)	(9.4)
Deferred tax liabilities	6	(34.2)	(22.6)
Other financial liabilities	20	(2.4)	(12.3)
Other liabilities	25	(226.0)	(223.0)
		(912.6)	(852.8)
Total liabilities		(1 620.7)	(1 709.5)
Net assets/liabilities		156.6	(79.1)
EQUITY			
Share capital	26	19.7	20.1
Share premium account	27	0.7	0.7
Capital redemption reserve	27	10.2	9.8
ESOT reserve	27	(48.7)	(54.8)

(Continued)

	Notes	2009 £m	2008 £m
Fair value reserve	27	69.6	11.3
Foreign currency translation reserve	27	9.7	2.6
Other reserves	27	(1 443.8)	(1 443.8)
Retained earnings	27	1 539.30	1 374.90
Shareholders equity		156.7	(79.2)
Minority request	27	(0.1)	0.1
Total equity		156.6	(79.1)

Approved by the Board on 26 March 2009
S A Wolfson Director
D W Keens Director

Consolidated financial statements of the BP group
At 31 December

	Note	$ million 2008	2007
Non-current assets			
Property, plant and equipment	23	103 200	97 989
Goodwill	24	9 878	11 006
Intangible assets	25	10 260	6 652
Investments in jointly controlled entities	26	23 826	18 113
Investments in associates	27	4 000	4 579
Other investments	29	855	1 830
Fixed assets		152 019	140 169
Loans		995	999
Other receivables	31	710	968
Derivative financial instruments	34	5 054	9 741
Prepayments		1 338	1 083
Defined benefit pension plan surpluses	38	1 738	8 914
		161 854	155 874
Current assets			
Loans		168	165
Inventories	30	16 821	26 554
Trade and other receivables	31	29 261	38 020
Derivative financial instruments	34	8 510	6 321
Prepayments		3 050	3 589
Current tax receivable		377	705
Cash and cash equivalents	32	8 197	3 562
		66 384	78 916
Assets classified as held for sale	4	—	1 286
		66 384	80 202
Total assets		228 238	236 076
Current liabilities			
Trade and other payables	33	33 644	43 152
Derivative financial instruments	34	8 977	6 405

(Continued)

	Note	$ million 2008	2007
Accruals		6 743	**6 640**
Finance debt	35	15 740	**15 394**
Current tax payable		3 144	**3 282**
Provisions	37	1 545	**2 195**
		69 793	**77 068**
Liabilities directly associated with the assets classified as held for sale	4	—	**163**
		69 793	**77 231**
Non-current liabilities			
Other payables	33	3 080	**1 251**
Derivative financial instruments	34	6 271	**5 002**
Accruals		784	**959**
Finance debt	35	17 464	**15 651**
Deferred tax liabilities	20	16 198	**19 215**
Provisions	37	12 108	**12 900**
Defined benefit pension plan and other post-retirement benefit plan deficits	38	10 431	**9 215**
		66 336	**64 193**
Total liabilities		136 129	**141 424**
Net assets		92 109	**94 652**
Equity			
- Share capital	39	5 176	**5 237**
- Reserves		86 127	**88 453**
BP shareholders equity	40	97 303	**93 890**
Minority interest	40	806	**962**
Total equity	40	92 109	**94 652**

P D Sutherland Chairman Dr A B Hayward Group Chief Executive

Commentary

In this example you will note that both of the balance sheets shown are titled Consolidated Balance Sheet. This signified that it is the balance sheet (statement of financial position) of a group of companies rather than a single company. A group exists where a number of companies are owned by another company, referred to as the parent company or holding company. Most of the companies quoted on the Stock Exchange are in fact groups of companies taking advantage of the protection offered by setting up individual companies with limited liability, so that if one part has a problem it does not automatically bankrupt the rest of the operation.

If you were to contrast the balance sheets of BP with those of Next plc you would see that there are structural differences. For example, BP is involved in a lot of joint ventures; it has a higher proportion of its total assets in the form of non-current assets whereas Next Plc has mainly current assets. These differences arise because of the nature of the industries in which these two very different companies operate.

ACTIVITY 12.2

Look at the balance sheets of BP plc and Next plc and identify their relative reliance on borrowing. What conclusions might you draw about the financial risk inherent in these two companies?

You probably noticed that Next Plc is heavily reliant on borrowing with £1620.7m of total liabilities as compared to £156.6m of equity. It is therefore more risky in purely financial terms than BP plc. The reason for the low equity in Next plc is because of the negative figure for 'other reserves' and if you went to note 27 you would find that this all relates to a capital reconstruction dating from 2002.

Once again, the general conclusion to be drawn is that on its own the analysis of the financial statements is only a small part of the story and that analysis needs to be put into a wider context of knowledge of the industry and the environment. It is also clear from the statements of financial position or balance sheets that without the notes to the accounts you will only have a superficial view of the business. The maxim that a little knowledge is a dangerous thing applies equally to business analysis as it does elsewhere. With that firmly in mind, we can now move on to look at some of the techniques that can be used to analyze the financial information.

TECHNIQUES OF ANALYSIS

Many techniques are used in financial analysis, from simple techniques such as studying the financial statements (in a manner similar to the exercise we have just done) and forming a rough opinion of what is happening to sophisticated statistical techniques. It should be pointed out that this rough analysis based on 'eyeballing' the accounts is vital as it forms the base on which the more sophisticated techniques can be built. If, for example, we fail to notice that a business has made a loss for the past few years the application of the most sophisticated techniques will not help as we have failed to grasp an essential point.

We shall limit ourselves to an examination of some simple techniques and the more commonly used ratio analysis. The choice of technique is once again a function of what you are trying to do and the purpose of your analysis. For example, managers and auditors may be interested in establishing any variations from past norms and explaining these and, where necessary, taking appropriate action. However, for a shareholder in a large company such an analysis, even if it were possible, would be inappropriate as no action could be taken and the level of detail is too specific.

Comparison of financial statements over time

With limited data a simple comparison of the rate and direction of change over time can be very useful. This can be done both in terms of absolute amount and in percentage terms. Both are normally required in order to reach any meaningful conclusions. For example, a 50% change on £50 000 is more significant than a 50% change on £1000. However, if you only have £1000 to start with a change of £500 may well be significant. Hence, it is not only the absolute figure but also the amount relative to other figures that is important.

The period chosen is also worth considering. Too short a time period will not be very meaningful. This was the case with Broll Ltd where we could only say that the profit had increased but had no idea about whether that was part of a trend or whether it was because last year was a particularly bad year. Similarly, one has to be careful not to take too long a period as the nature of the business or the environment may have altered drastically. Finally, it must be borne in mind that there may be other changes which have affected the figures; for example, the business may have decided to depreciate its vehicles over three years instead of four. Having taken account of these warnings, let us now look at how we could do the comparisons.

TREND ANALYSIS

Trend analysis is normally used for time periods in excess of two to three years in order to make the results easier to understand and interpret. It involves choosing a base year and then plotting the trend in sales or profits or whatever from there on.

KEY CONCEPT 12.3

Trend analysis

In trend analysis the choice of an appropriate base year is vital. If the base year chosen is not typical the resultant analysis will at best be extremely difficult and at worst actually misleading.

EXAMPLE 12.2

ABC Ltd

ABC Ltd income statement summary

	2010 £000	2011 £000	2012 £000	2013 £000	2014 £000
Sales	12 371	13 209	16 843	14 441	13 226
Cost of sales	9 605	9 981	12 807	9 858	10 812
Gross profit	2 766	3 228	4 036	4 583	2 414
Operating expenses	1 689	1 783	2 274	2 311	2 116
Net profit before interest	1 077	1 445	1 762	2 272	298
Interest	215	252	460	768	676
Net profit after interest	862	1 193	1 302	1 504	−378
Taxation	464	529	875	579	98
Net profit after tax	398	664	427	925	−476
Dividends Retained profits	164	185	336	337	112
	234	479	91	588	−588

If we take the cost of sales figures it is clear from a casual examination that it rises in 2011 to a peak in 2012, after which it falls in 2013. If we plotted that on a graph it would look like Figure 12.1.

(Continued)

FIGURE 12.1   ABC Ltd cost of sales

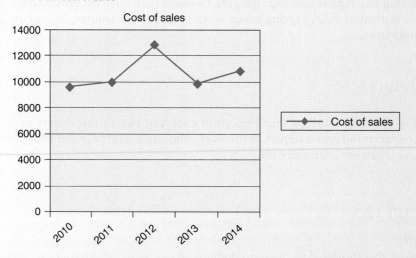

As you can see, the information contained is fairly limited; it merely reflects what we have already found. To make any sensible comment we need to see how these costs are behaving in relation to something else. This could be in relation to another item in the income statement such as sales or in relation to the costs in a comparable company. To do the latter comparison, however, we first have to find some common means of expression as the companies being compared are unlikely to be exactly the same size. One way of doing this is to use index numbers to express the figures we are looking at and the way in which they change from year to year.

Index number trends

As with other forms of trend analysis, this technique is normally used for periods in excess of two to three years. It is intended to make the results easier to understand and interpret. It does this by choosing a base year, setting that base year to 100 and expressing all other years in terms of that base year.

If, for example, we used 2010 as the base year and set that at 100, we would be able to calculate the sales trend as follows:

$$\frac{2011}{2010} \times 100 = \frac{13\,209}{12\,371} \times 100 = 107$$

For 2012 the calculation would be:

$$\frac{2012}{2010} \times 100 = \frac{16\,843}{12\,371} \times 100 = 136$$

Using the same formula we can find the index for each of the other years and we can then look at the trend. In this case the figures are as follows:

2010	2011	2012	2013	2014
100	107	136	117	107

(Continued)

We could do the same for the cost of sales and the profit figures and then these could be analyzed. In the case of sales we can see that the sales peaked in 2012 and then declined to the same level as in 2011. This can be seen more easily in Figure 12.2, which shows the sales and the cost of sales.

FIGURE 12.2   ABC Ltd sales and cost of sales

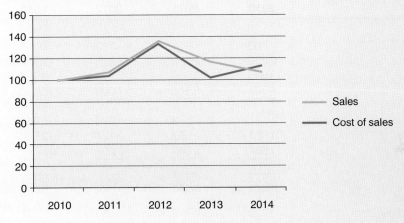

Figure 12.2 is therefore much more informative as it relates sales to cost of sales; in addition, the use of index numbers allows us to compare this company with another irrespective of size. The graph in this case shows that both sales and cost of sales peak in 2012. After that, however, we see that although sales fall in both 2013 and 2014 the cost of sales rises again in 2014. The fact that we have used indexes means that we can compare these two trends even though the figures underlying them are different.

Percentage changes

Another technique often used in trend analysis is to identify the percentage change from year to year and then examine the trends in this. For example, if we look at the sales we find that the change from 2010 to 2011 was 7%, whereas that from 2011 to 2012 was 27%. These figures are calculated using the following formula:

$$\frac{\text{this years's sales}}{\text{last year's sales}} \times 100 = \frac{13\,209}{12\,371} \times 100 = 107 \text{ or } 7\% \text{ up}$$

Once again it should be pointed out that these trends are of most use if they are compared with other trends, either in the business itself or in the industry. You should also bear in mind that these percentage increases are often illusory as they merely reflect the increase that would be expected as a result of the rate of inflation in the particular period and the particular country concerned.

COMMON SIZE STATEMENTS

A technique which can be used to turn the large numbers we often encounter in accounts into more digestible information is 'common size' statements. This technique, as the name implies, deals with the problem of comparisons of differently sized companies. It involves expressing the items in the statement of financial position, for example, as percentages of the total assets. Once again this is best illustrated by looking at ABC Ltd whose statements of financial position are reproduced below. We can derive

EXAMPLE 12.2 ABC Ltd (Continued)

ABC Ltd summary statements of financial position

	2010	2011	2012	2013	2014
Current assets					
Bank and cash	400	464	183	15	41
Receivables	2 259	2 389	3 012	2 776	2 508
Inventory	3 645	3 952	3 903	3 289	3 255
	6 304	6 805	7 098	6 080	5 804
Non current assets					
Intangible assets			470	451	460
Tangible assets	1 964	2 063	2 127	2 596	2 553
	1 964	2 063	2 597	3 047	3 013
Total assets	8 268	8 868	9 695	9 127	8 817
Current liabilities					
Bank loans and overdraft	0	3	86	427	663
Payables	3 701	3 706	4 842	3 311	4 277
Taxation	110	415	186	44	48
Dividends	121	137	224	225	1
	3 932	4 261	5 338	4 007	4 989
Non current liabilities					
Loans	1 219	991	620	796	92
	1 219	991	620	796	92
Total liabilities	5 151	5 252	5 958	4 803	5 081
Ordinary share capital	1 447	1 459	1 471	1 476	1 476
Share premium account	137	145	163	157	157
Retained profits	1 533	2 012	2 103	2 691	2 103
	3 117	3 616	3 737	4 324	3 736
Total equity and liabilites	8 268	8 868	9 695	9 127	8 817

The problem when looking at standard statements of financial position is that the figures often disguise what is really happening. If, however, we convert the statements to some common measure the underlying trends become clearer. We could take, for example, the share capital for 2010 and express it as a percentage of the total figure for equity and liabilities or assets. We find that it is 18% in that year compared with 16% in 2011. To calculate this we simply divided the share capital figure by the total for equity and liabilities and then multiplied the result by 100. Thus for 2012 we would have:

$$\frac{\text{Share capital}}{\text{Total capital}} \times 100 = \frac{1\,471}{9\,695} \times 100 = 15.2\%$$

Following this procedure for all items in the statements of financial position produces common size statements as follows. Note that there will be rounding errors in the figures.

(Continued)

ABC Ltd summary statements of financial position

	2010	2011	2012	2013	2014
Current assets					
Bank and cash	5	5	2	0	0
Receivables	27	27	31	30	28
Inventory	44	45	40	36	37
	76	77	73	67	66
Non current assets					
Intangible assets	0	0	5	5	5
Tangible assets	24	23	22	28	29
	24	23	27	33	34
Total assets	100	100	100	100	100
Current habilities					
Bank loans and overdraft	0	0	1	5	8
Payables	45	42	50	36	49
Taxation	1	5	2	0	1
Dividends	1	2	2	2	0
	48	48	55	44	57
Non current liabilities					
Loans	15	11	6	9	1
	15	11	6	9	1
Total liabilities	62	59	61	53	58
Ordinary share capital	18	16	15	16	17
Share premium account	2	2	2	2	2
Retained profits	19	23	22	29	24
	38	41	39	47	42
Total equity and liabilities	100	100	100	100	100

One of the things that we can see from an analysis of these statements is that the current assets have shown a decline over the period from 76% of the total in 2010 to only 66% in 2014. We can see that the company has paid off its long term loans and is using short term finance in the form of a bank overdraft and higher levels of payables to replace that finance. We can also see that 2013 was not a typical year, e.g. the receivables and payables levels were out of line with other years. It should be noted that with this technique the choice of the base year is just as important as it was with trend analysis.

The technique of common size statements can be applied just as easily to the income statement. In the case of the income statement it is normal to express all items as a percentage of sales as illustrated below.

ABC Ltd common size income statement summary

	2010 £000	2011 £000	2012 £000	2013 £000	2014 £000
Sales	100	100	100	100	100
Cost of sales	78	76	76	68	82
Gross profit	22	24	24	32	18
Operating expenses	14	13	14	16	16

(Continued)

	2010 £000	2011 £000	2012 £000	2013 £000	2014 £000
Net profit before interest	9	11	10	16	2
Interest	2	2	3	5	5
Net profit after interest	7	9	8	10	−3
Taxation	4	4	5	4	1
Net profit after tax	3	5	3	6	−4
Dividends	1	1	2	2	1
Retained profits	2	4	1	4	4

Apart from the obvious rounding errors which occur when working in whole numbers, the statement above is fairly self-explanatory. An item that is worth highlighting is that the cost of sales and operating expenses in 2014 have squeezed the operating profit down to only 2% return on sales in a year when the interest charges are seen to be 5% of sales. This illustrates the risk of high gearing, in the case of ABC equity is around 40% of the total finance used by the business and the increase in cost of sales which we identified and illustrated in Figure 12.2 led to the gross profit margin being squeezed and a position where the net profit of £298 000 was not enough to cover the interest charge of £676 000 resulting in a loss for that year.

ACTIVITY 12.3

If you have forgotten the way in which gearing affects the relative return to the shareholders go back and work through Example 9.1 Chansit on pages 217–219

Common size statements and the other techniques that we have examined so far have largely ignored the relationship between the components of the financial statements of a business. The effect of this is that we have not been able to extract everything we could from the information available. Other techniques of analysis are available which look at the relationship between items in the statement of financial position and items in the cash flow and income statement. The most common of these techniques is known as ratio analysis and is explored more fully below.

certain information and questions from just looking at the various statements of financial position, but it is not easy to identify exactly what is happening. Where did the intangible assets come from, and what are they? These questions can often be answered, in part at least, by using the detailed information contained in the notes to the accounts.

RATIO ANALYSIS

Although ratio analysis is seen in virtually every accounting textbook, most students, although having little difficulty in calculating ratios, find extreme difficulty in understanding what they mean once they have been calculated. Because of this we shall not deal extensively with all the possible ratios that can be calculated but instead we shall look at the more commonly used ratios and try to concentrate on the relationships that we are trying to express through the ratios we calculate. This approach will increase your understanding of the reasons for calculating these ratios and will therefore enable you to interpret the results from a sound basis of understanding. We shall look at what we are trying to measure and then the ratios that can be used to measure that particular aspect of an enterprise's operations. Before doing that, we need to understand exactly what a ratio is. This is defined in Key Concept 12.4.

KEY CONCEPT 12.4

Ratio

A ratio R is quantity A divided by quantity B:

$$R = \frac{A}{B}$$

In essence a ratio is merely a shorthand notation for the relationship between two or more things. It is the relationship that it is expressing that must be understood. Without that understanding, the ratio, no matter how precisely calculated or sophisticated, is meaningless.

Apart from understanding the relationship underpinning the ratio, we also need to examine ratios in a wider context. For example, if we want to work out how many police we need to police a football match, we could work on the basis of one policeman to a number of spectators. If we found that we needed 200 police for a crowd of 40 000 spectators the ratio would be one to 200 or 1:200.

Obviously this ratio is meaningless on its own as it does not tell us whether we are using the right number of police. To decide this we would need to establish whether there were still problems of violence, whether they were associated with the home team or certain visiting teams or, if there was no record of violence, whether we could achieve the same result with fewer police. The former problem would require additional information whereas the latter could perhaps be judged, in part at least, by looking at what other football clubs do and what ratio of police to spectators they use. This simple example serves to illustrate the fact that the ratio on its own cannot tell us very much. It needs to be looked at in the context of other information and experience.

On the other hand, ratios do allow us to deal with changes over time in absolute amount and to compare different sized businesses.

Classification of ratios

As we have already said, the important point to bear in mind is what the ratio is attempting to illustrate. For example, if we go back to our policing example we could calculate the ratio of police to catering staff – it would, of course, be very difficult to get any meaning from such a ratio. Broadly, ratios can be classified into groups dealing with aspects of performance such as profitability, efficiency, financial risk and returns to investors.

Profitability ratios

In our discussion of the needs of users we identified that one of their major concerns was with profitability and future profitability. This is because the shareholders or owners can only get a return on their investment if the business is making a profit. Hence, they need to find out not only whether the business is making a profit, which they can find by looking at the income statement, but also whether it is more or less profitable than it was and more or less profitable than other alternative investments. A look at the income statement can tell us if it has made more profit in absolute terms but it does not tell whether it is making the same percentage profit on sales; to find that out, we need to do some calculations. The most common ratios that give information on profitability are the gross profit and net profit margin. These compare the profit made with the sales figures. They are defined below together with the calculations of these ratios in relation to ABC for 2013:

$$\text{gross profit margin} = \frac{\text{gross profit}}{\text{sales}} \times 100 \qquad \frac{4\,583}{14\,441} \times 100 = 32\%$$

$$\text{net profit margin} = \frac{\text{net profit}}{\text{sales}} \times 100 \qquad \frac{925}{14\,441} \times 100 = 6\%$$

If you look back at ABC, you will see that in the case of the gross profit margin this is straight forward, whereas in the case of the net profit we could have looked at the net profit before interest or before tax or after tax; we chose the latter as this is more likely to allow cross company comparisons. These ratios, if compared year on year, tell us whether the margins are changing or not and if they are changing we might want to investigate further to see if they are improving relative to what we are using to generate those profits. This can be done by combining information from the statement of financial position in terms of the assets (capital employed) we use to generate profits with information from the income statement, i.e. the profits made. There are many alternative ways of looking at this and to some extent the choice of ratio may relate to the perspective being taken. For example, the management may be concerned with the total return irrespective of how the assets were financed; the shareholders may be concerned with the return to them or perhaps in a comparison of the two. One important thing to remember when using ratios which combine figures from a flow statement, i.e. the income statement or cash flow statement, with those from a static statement, i.e. the statement of financial position, is that it is better to use the average of the opening and closing statement of financial position figures as that takes account of the changes in the 'stock of wealth' being used to generate those profits or cash flows.

ACTIVITY 12.4

Calculate the gross profit and net profit margin for 2014 and think about what a comparison with the 2013 ratios tell you.

You will have found that in each case the ratio shows a drop in the profit margin. If you go back to the common size income statement you will see that this is apparently due to an increase in the cost of sales but could it be something else?

KEY CONCEPT 12.5

Ratios which combine figures from statements which measure flows of profits or cash over a period should use the average of the relevant figures from the statement of financial position to make the ratio more meaningful.

The most common ratio used for measuring the profitability relative to the capital employed to generate those profits is the return on capital employed. This is defined below and calculated for ABC for 2013:

$$\text{return on capital employed} = \frac{\text{profit before tax and interest}}{\text{average shareholder's funds} + \text{loans}} \times 100$$

$$= \frac{2\,272}{4\,739} \times 100 = 48\%$$

Although this gives a picture of how the business as a whole is doing from the point of view of the shareholders, they may be more interested in how they are doing so they may want to see the return that is available for them. In this case they may look at the return on equity, which is defined as follows and calculated for ABC for 2013:

$$\text{return on equity} = \frac{\text{profit after tax and interest}}{\text{average shareholder's funds}} \times 100$$

$$\frac{925}{4\,031} \times 100 = 23\%$$

If you compare the components of the two ratios you will find that in the former case the net profit before interest and tax is used and compared to the average total finance employed, whereas in the latter the net profit after tax and interest is used and compared with the average shareholders' funds. These differences simply reflect the fact that in the latter case the amount available to shareholders is after all other claims on the profits have been met. The reason for using the profit before interest and tax in the return on capital employed is that you can then compare different companies with different financing structures and different taxes due.

You should also note that on their own they tell us very little. We need to compare what is happening from year to year or from business to business to extract any meaning from the ratios. We shall look at some comparisons over time when we look at the efficiency ratios below.

ACTIVITY 12.5

Calculate the return on equity for 2014.

You will have noticed that the return on equity is now negative as the firm made a substantial loss in 2014. You might therefore conclude that where there is a loss calculating ratios like return on equity and return on capital employed is meaningless – in fact there was a return on capital employed albeit minimal so in this case that might have been worth calculating but generally where there is a loss these ratios are meaningless.

Efficiency ratios

These ratios are in some ways similar to return on capital employed insofar as they are trying to measure how the business assets are used to create profits. If, for example, we looked at our use of our own car then we could measure the number of miles we did in a year. Clearly, the more we use the car the more miles we will do and arguably the more miles we do the more efficient is our utilization of the car. In the case of businesses we can look at the efficiency with which they use their assets by comparing the average assets from the statements of financial position with the appropriate figures from the income statement. The more common of these efficiency ratios are discussed below and illustrated with figures taken from ABC's 2013 accounts.

Inventory turnover: This measures the number of times the inventory is turned over each year. You will remember from the chapter on inventory that we discussed the costs of holding inventory which included warehousing costs and the costs of financing the level of inventory in addition to the cost of the inventory itself. Therefore, the faster you turn the inventory over the less money you have tied up in this at any point in time and the cheaper your inventory holding costs are. The ratio can be expressed either in the number of times the inventory is turned over each year or the number of days that inventory is held. The ratios for each are given and it is once again important to note that we are using average figures from the two statements of financial position at the start and end of the year and comparing these with the cost of sales as, like the cost of inventory in the statements of financial position, that figure excludes any profit element whereas the sales figure includes profit. The reason for using average figures is that it makes some allowance for changes in prices during the year in addition to changes in volume of activity. Clearly, if we sell more we would expect the inventory held to go up in absolute amount but we would not necessarily expect them to have to hold more days' inventory.

$$\text{inventory turnover} - \text{times} = \frac{\text{cost of sales}}{\text{average inventory}} \quad \frac{9\,858}{3\,596} = 2.7 \text{ times}$$

$$\text{inventory turnover} - \text{days} = \frac{\text{average inventory}}{\text{cost of sales}} \times 365$$
$$\frac{3\,596}{9\,858} \times 365 = 133 \text{ days}$$

ACTIVITY 12.6

Calculate the inventory turnover in days for 2014.
  Your answer should be the same as that given below.

If we calculated the days' inventory held for other years we would find the following results:

$$2011: \frac{(3\,645 + 3\,952)/2}{9\,981} \times 365 = 139 \text{ days}$$

$$2012: \frac{(3\,952 + 3\,903)/2}{12\,807} \times 365 = 111 \text{ days}$$

$$2013: \frac{(3\,903 + 3\,289)/2}{9\,858} \times 365 = 133 \text{ days}$$

$$2014: \frac{(3\,928 + 3\,255)/2}{10\,812} \times 365 = 110 \text{ days}$$

This tells us that there is no clear pattern to the level of inventory being held. On the face of it, this ratio also tells us that the business was doing better in 2014 than in 2013, but beware of false conclusions because if you return to look at the income statements and common size statements for those years you will see that in 2014 the cost of sales has risen and the gross profit has fallen. In fact, after taking off the interest and tax charges, ABC was making a loss in 2014 – hardly an improvement on 2013 when it was making a profit!

Receivables and payables turnover: These ratios provide us with a measure of how quickly we are collecting money from our customers and how quickly we are paying our suppliers. They are calculated below measured in days rather than times a year and you will notice that in the case of receivables we use the sales, i.e. including the profit element, whereas in the case of payables we use the cost of sales, thus comparing like with like.

$$\text{receivables turnover} - \text{days} = \frac{\text{average receivables}}{\text{sales}} \times 365$$

$$\frac{2\,894}{14\,441} \times 365 = 73 \text{ days}$$

$$\text{payables turnover} - \text{days} = \frac{\text{average payables}}{\text{cost of sales}} \times 365$$

$$\frac{4\,077}{9\,858} \times 365 = 151 \text{ days}$$

ACTIVITY 12.7

Calculate the receivables and payables turnover in days for 2014.
Your answers should be the same as those given below.

If we looked at the trends in the ratios for payables, receivables and inventory turnover for the four years we would find the following pattern:

Year	Payables turnover (days)	Receivables turnover (days)	Inventory turnover (days)
2011	135	63	139
2012	121	57	111
2013	151	73	133
2014	256	73	110

This provides us with some interesting information as it shows that ABC is taking longer to collect the money due to us from customers. More importantly the time ABC is taking to pay its suppliers has increased dramatically in 2014. This may indicate that we have cash flow or liquidity problems, so we can now turn to look at some ratios that deal with liquidity under the more general heading of financial risk.

ACTIVITY 12.8

What connections have been made in the commentary on the efficiency ratios?
Inventory turnover was connected to changes in gross profit and cost of sales. The changes in payables and receivables turnover have been connected to liquidity and financial risk.

Financial risk ratios

In Chapter 9, we introduced the idea of gearing and financial risk. In a nutshell, what we were saying was that if you could borrow money at a rate of interest that was less than the percentage profit the firm was making this would be advantageous for the equity investors. However, we identified that there was a risk in doing this as it could have a negative effect if the interest rate rose or the profit dropped. We also noted in Chapter 9 that if interest was not paid on long-term loans and debentures the lenders had the right to petition the court to appoint a receiver who could wind the firm up. We will discuss some ratios which measure financial risk and liquidity. We will now look first at long-term risk.

The most common measure of long-term financial risk is the ratio of long-term debt to long-term capital. This can be expressed in terms of debt either as a percentage of total long-term finance or in relation to equity. For ABC these ratios for 2013 are

$$\text{gearing ratio:} \quad \frac{\text{long-term debt}}{\text{long-term debt + equity}} \qquad \frac{796}{5\,120} = 16\%$$

$$\text{debt equity ratio: long-term debt:equity} \qquad 796 : 4\,324 = 18\%$$

These show that long-term debt is less than 20% of equity. These ratios, although being useful, may only show part of the picture as they only relate to long-term borrowing. Hence, it is always advisable to look at the ratio of total debt to total long-term finance. For ABC in 2013 this is

$$\text{full gearing ratio:} \quad \frac{\text{total debt}}{\text{total debt + equity}} \qquad \frac{4\,803}{9\,127} = 53\%$$

This ratio gives us a clue that although ABC is not heavily reliant on long-term debt it is reliant on short-term debt.

ACTIVITY 12.9

Calculate the debt equity ratio and the full gearing ratio for 2010 and think about what it tells you about ABC.

You will have found that the debt equity ratio for 2014 is 2.4% but the full gearing ratio is now nearly 58% which again suggests that there is heavier reliance on short term debt.

The reliance on short-term debt we can see from the statement of financial position is mainly trade payables and relying on this as a source of finance may not be a problem if it is covered by receivables. This of course assumes similar collection and payment periods. We therefore need to look at ratios which tell us something about the short-term liquidity of the firm. The most common of these are the current ratio and the acid test or quick ratio. These are defined below and are calculated for ABC for 2013:

$$\text{Current ratio:} \quad \frac{\text{current assets}}{\text{current liabilities}} \qquad \frac{6\,080}{4\,007} = 1.5 : 1$$

$$\text{Acid test or quick ratio:} \quad \frac{\text{current assets} - \text{inventory}}{\text{current liabilities}} \qquad \frac{2\,791}{4\,007} = 0.7 : 1$$

The ratios tell us that we can cover our current liabilities from our current assets if we include stock but if we exclude stock the acid test ratio tells us we only have 67p coming in to cover each £1 we are due to pay out. To decide whether this is normal or not we need to know what the industry norm is, e.g. supermarkets will tend to be cash rich as they tend to sell for cash, whereas a furniture retailer may have large receivables as they often have deals offering people credit. The other information we need is the trend in the firm concerned. If we calculated these ratios for all years we would find the following.

ACTIVITY 12.10

Calculate the current ratio and acid test for 2014 and compare your answer with that given in the table below.

Year	Current ratio	Acid test
2010	1.6:1	0.7:1
2011	1.6:1	0.7:1
2012	1.3:1	0.6:1
2013	1.5:1	0.7:1
2014	1.2:1	0.5:1

Looking at the trends here we can see that they mirror the trends in our turnover ratios and suggest that by 2014 ABC is encountering problems with liquidity. One difficulty with these ratios based on the statement of financial position ratios is that as they relate to one point in time they are potentially open to manipulation. However, if we combine this with what we know from our efficiency ratios, which are based on the flows over time, we can see that not only does ABC not have enough to cover its payables but it is taking longer and longer to pay them. A further ratio based on flows over time which could be calculated is the cash flow from operations to the current liabilities. In the case of ABC we have not produced a cash flow statement for each year but for 2014 the cash flow statement is as shown below.

ABC cash flow statement for 2014	
Net loss	−588
Add: Depreciation	43
Increase in payables	966
Decrease in tax and dividends	−220
Decrease in inventory	34
Decrease in receivables	268
Net cash from operating activity	503
Investing Activities	
Payments to acquire fixed assets	−9
Net cash used in investing activity	−9

Financing activity

Repayment of loan	−704
Net cash used in financing activity	−704
Decrease in cash in period	−210
Cash and cash equivalents at beginning of year	−412
Cash and cash equivalents at end of year	−622

The cash flow from operations for 2014 was £503 000 so the ratio is

$$\text{cash flow ratio:}\quad \frac{\text{average current liabilities}}{\text{cash flow from operations}}\qquad \frac{4\,498}{503}\times 365 = 3\,264 \text{ days}$$

This confirms that ABC has liquidity problems as it tells us that if it continues to operate as it did in 2014 it would take 3264 days or nearly nine years to pay its current liabilities, i.e. those due to be paid within a year!

Returns to investors

The major ratios that are useful to the investor relate either the earnings per share to the share price, the price earnings ratio, or the dividend per share to the share price, the dividend yield. These ratios rely on knowing the share price and except for quoted companies this will not be readily available. We will therefore look at alternative ratios that we can derive from a set of accounts. These are earnings per share, which we encountered in Chapter 9, and dividend cover, which tells us how many times the dividend is covered by profits available to pay the dividend, i.e. profits after tax. For lenders, interest cover is a similar ratio that provides a measure of how 'at risk' their interest payments are. These ratios are defined below and are calculated for ABC for 2013:

$$\text{earnings per share:}\quad \frac{\text{profit after interest and tax}}{\text{number of ordinary shares in issue}}\qquad \frac{925}{1\,476} = 63\text{p}$$

$$\text{dividend cover:}\quad \frac{\text{profit after interest and tax}}{\text{ordinary dividends}}\qquad \frac{925}{337} = 2.7 \text{ times}$$

$$\text{interest cover:}\quad \frac{\text{profit before interest and tax}}{\text{interest}}\qquad \frac{2\,272}{768} = 3.0 \text{ times}$$

Once again these ratios on their own are fairly meaningless and we would need to compare them over time or against other businesses to make any sense of them. The following table provides details over time.

Year	Earnings per share (p)	Dividend cover (times)	Interest cover (times)
2010	28	2.4	5
2011	46	3.6	5.7
2012	29	1.3	3.8
2013	63	2.7	3
2014	−32	−4.2	0.44

We can see that 2013 is not a typical year and also that in 2014 things look very difficult as ABC is not even earning enough profit to cover its interest charges. We can also see that the trend in interest cover has been getting worse from 2011 onwards, which indicates there is increased financial risk in the business.

Before moving on let us summarize what we have learned about ABC. The first thing we found was that in 2014 it was making a thumping loss. Using the information from the common size statements and the ratios we found that there was a problem with profitability. For 2014 the gross profit and net profit margin had declined to 18% and 2% respectively and the interest was greater than the net profit. In Activity 12.4 we asked whether this decrease which seemed to be related to the cost of sales could be attributed to anything else. The answer is, 'yes, it could be a reduction in sales price caused by competition which could indicate long-term problems'. So we have a loss-making business perhaps operating in a difficult or declining market which is heavily reliant on short-term borrowing to finance its operations. It has dramatically increased the time taken to pay its suppliers, its acid test ratio is getting worse and based on the cash flow from operations it would take over nine years to pay of its current liabilities. Would you invest in ABC?

SUMMARY OF MAJOR ISSUES

There is no point in using sophisticated techniques for analysis without an understanding of the following:

- The wider context: The economic social and political pressures, the type of industry and where the industry as a whole is going.

- The organization: What type of organization we are dealing with. Is it a charity? Is it big or small? How are these factors affecting the information that is being presented and the way in which that information is presented, and how should they affect our analysis?

- Who the analysis is for: As we have seen, different users have different needs in terms of analysis and, even when their needs appear to overlap, the emphasis is frequently different from group to group.

- How good the base data are: In this case we are dealing with analysis based on historic cost accounts, which assume that prices do not change, when in practice this is not the case. Even if we overcome that problem, there is the question of how up to date or out of date the information is. There are also issues of comparability because different accounting policies are adopted and because the size of the organization affects norms.

Finally, we need to be clear what the point of the analysis is. Are we providing the base for a decision about the future actions of a user of accounting information and, if so, what alternatives in terms of decisions is that user facing? Having identified in our case that ABC seems to have some problems, we now need to identify what, if any, action can be taken to solve some of those problems. In general, the role of the outside user is probably limited to that of problem identification as in most cases there is little that the outside user can do in terms of problem solving. This is a task that should be carried out by the management of the company.

In order for management to be able to carry out this task, as we have already suggested, they will need more detailed information and often they will also require different forms of information. For example, the fact that the costs are rising does not help as they need to know which costs are actually rising. They also need to know whether the problem is due to the fact that at a lower level of sales they are losing the economies of scale. Then they need to know the level of sales and costs they would expect in 2015 and thereafter so that they can take appropriate actions to improve the performance of their business. In the next chapters we shall consider these additional needs of managers and how they are met through the analysis of past information, whether it is in the form we have already seen or in a different form. We shall also consider what other information is needed for planning, decision making and control, where this is obtained, and how it is used.

Before moving on to that discussion; here are some of the key features and limitations of financial statement analysis.

Key features

- Financial analysis has to be looked at in the wider context of the industry, the environment, etc.
- Financial analysis has to be targeted to meet the needs of the user of the analysis.
- Financial analysis is only as good as the base information that is being analyzed.
- Financial analysis involves both inter-temporal and inter-firm comparisons, and this imposes limitations.

These key features point to some limitations that have to be borne in mind when discussing financial analysis. These can be usefully summarized under three headings as follows.

Key limitations

Information problems

- The base information is often out of date, i.e. timeliness of information leads to problems of interpretation.
- Historic cost information may not be the most appropriate information for the decision for which the analysis is being undertaken.
- Information in published accounts is generally summarized information and detailed information may be needed.
- Analysis of accounting information only identifies symptoms, not causes, and therefore is of limited use.

Comparison problems – inter-temporal

- Effects of price changes make comparisons difficult unless adjustments are made.
- Changes in technology affect the price of assets, the likely return and the future markets.
- A changing environment affects the results and this is reflected in the accounting information.
- Potential effects of changes in accounting policies on the reported results.
- Problems associated with establishing a normal base year to compare other years with.

Comparison problems – inter-firm

- Selection of industry norms and the usefulness of norms based on averages.
- Different firms have different financial and business risk profiles, and this affects the analysis.
- Different firms use different accounting policies.
- Impacts of the size of the business and its comparators on risk, structure and return.
- Different environments affect results, e.g. different countries, home based versus multinational firms.

Hence, there are a number of issues that you need to bear in mind when carrying out your analysis and interpreting and reporting the results. They should not, however, be used as a reason not to attempt the analysis.

FURTHER READING

Pendlebury, M., Fanning D., and Groves, R. (2003) *Company Accounts Analysis, Interpretation and Understanding*, London: Cengage.

REVIEW QUESTIONS

(✓ indicates answers are available in Appendix A)

✓ **1** Identify the main user groups and their common needs in terms of financial analysis.

2 How do the needs of long-term lenders differ from those of equity investors?

✓ **3** What factors do we need to take into account in order to put our analysis in context?

4 What sources of information outside the business are available to you and how would you use this information in your analysis?

5 What information would you derive from reading the Chairman's statement?

6 What other parts of the annual report would you use in your analysis?

✓ **7** What is the difference between financial risk and business risk?

8 How would you measure financial risk in the short and long term?

9 What are the limitations to analysis which are inherent in the accounting data?

10 What is a ratio and what should you bear in mind when interpreting ratios?

PROBLEMS FOR DISCUSSION AND ANALYSIS

(✓ **indicates answers are available in Appendix A**)

✓ **1** Metaltin

The information below relates to Metaltin Ltd

Income statement of Metaltin Ltd for the year ended 30 April 2010

	Notes	2010	2009
Sales		4 814	5 614
Cost of sales	1	4 299	5 039
Operating profit		515	575
Interest charges		156	53
Profit before tax		359	522
Taxation	2	193	292
Retained profit		166	230

Statement of financial position of Metaltin Ltd as at 30 April 2010

	Notes	2010	2009
Current assets			
Cash		5	61
Receivables		1 259	1 004
Inventory	3	1 763	1 194
		3 027	2 259
Non-current assets			
Motor vehicles	4	221	162
Fittings	4	285	320
Land and buildings	4	360	227
		866	709
Total assets		3 893	2 968
Current liabilities			
Bank overdraft		676	255
Trade payables		1 370	1 147
Taxation	2	215	332
		2 261	1 734
Non current liabilities			
Loans	5	200	130
		200	130
Total liabilities		2 461	1 864
Share capital	6	545	483
Retained profit	6	787	621
Revaluation reserve	6	100	0
Total equity		1 432	1 104
Total equity and liabilities		3 893	2 968

Cash flow statement of Metaltin Ltd for the year ended 30 April 2010

Net profit	166
Add: Depreciation	123
Increase in payables	106
	395
Less: Profit on sale of fixed assets	20
Increase in inventory	569
Increase in receivables	255
Net cash from operating activity	−449
Investing Activities	
Payments to acquire fixed assets	−240
Payments to acquire investments	0
Receipts from disposal of fixed assets	80
Net cash used in investing activity	−160

Financing activity

Issue of loan	140
Repayment of loan	−70
Receipts from issue of ordinary share capital	62
Net cash used in financing activity	132
Decrease in cash in period	−477
Cash and cash equivalents at beginning of year	−194
Cash and cash equivalents at end of year	−671

Extracts from the notes to the accounts:

1 Included in the cost of sales are the following charges:

	£
Depreciation	123
Auditors' remuneration	55
Directors' remuneration	240
Hire of plant	30
Profit on sale of fittings	20

2 Fixed assets

	Land	Buildings	Fittings	Motor vehicles
Balance at 1 May 2009	120	140	600	440
Additions			100	140
Revaluations	60	40		
	180	180	700	580
Disposals			90	
Balance at 30 April 2010	180	180	610	580
Depreciation				
Balance at 1 May 2009		33	280	278
Charge for year		−33	75	81
Disposals		0	355	359
Balance at 30 April 2010			30	
		0	325	359
Carrying amount 30 April 2010	180	180	285	221
Carrying amount 30 April 2009	120	107	320	162

3 A long-term loan amounting to £70 was repaid during the year. This was replaced with a new loan of £140 repayable in ten years.

4 Share capital and reserves.

	Share capital	Retained profit	Other reserves
Balance at 1 May 2009	483	621	
Share issue	62		
Movements in year Balance at		166	100
30 April 2010	545	787	100

(a) Produce a common size statement of financial position and income statement for Metaltin Ltd and comment on each of these statements.

(b) Calculate the percentage changes in the statement of financial position and the income statement from 2009 to 2010 and comment on what this analysis reveals.

(c) Using all the information and techniques available to you, comment on the performance of Metaltin Ltd as reflected in the accounts and the cash flow statement.

2 Thones

The financial statements of Thones are given below.

Statement of financial position of Thones at the end of year two

	Note	Year 2 £	Year 1
Current assets			
Bank		3 400	9 100
Receivables and prepaids		54 200	22 000
Inventory		4 000	3 000
		61 600	34 100
Non current assets			
Car	1	10 000	8 000
Fixtures	1	20 000	30 000
		30 000	38 000
Total Assets		91 600	72 100
Current liabilities			
Payables		17 000	12 000
		17 000	12 000
Total liabilities		17 000	12 000
Share capital		60 000	50 000
Retained profit		14 600	10 100
Total equity		74 600	60 100
Total equity and liabilities		91 600	72 100

Income statement of Thones for year 2

Sales		99 000
Cost of sales		42 000
Gross profit		57 000
Expenses		
Insurance	1 000	
Rent	8 000	
Wages	28 000	
Other expenses	2 000	
Car tax etc.	500	
Depreciation: fixtures	10 000	
Depreciation: car Net profit	3 000	52 500
		4 500

Cash flow statement of Thones for year 2

Net profit	4 500
Add:	
Depreciation - fixtures and cars	13 000
Increase in payables	5 000
	22 500
Less:	
Increase in inventory	1 000
Increase in receivables and prepaids	32 200
Cash flow from operations	−10 700
Investing activity	
Purchase of fixed assets	−5 000
Net cash used in investing activity	−5 000
Financing activity	
Proceeds of issue of shares	10 000
Net cash inflow from financing activity	10 000
Net cash inflow	−5 700
Cash at start of year	9 100
Cash at end of year	3 400

Notes

1 Non-current assets

	Car	Fixtures	Total
At start of year	10 000	40 000	50 000
Purchases during year	5 000		5 000
At end of year	15 000	40 000	55 000
Depreciation at start of year	2 000	10 000	12 000
Charge for year	3 000	10 000	13 000
	5 000	20 000	25 000
Carrying amount at end of year 2	10 000	20 000	30 000
Carrying amount at end of year 1	8 000	30 000	38 000

Required

(a) based on the financial statements of Thones, identify which ratios would be useful to calculate and which would not.

(b) calculate the ratios identified in (a) above.

(c) comment on what your analysis tells you about the performance of Thones.

3 Keaton Ltd

Keaton Ltd summarized statements of financial position

	2006 £000s	2007 £000s	2008 £000s	2009 £000s	2010 £000s
Current assets					
Bank and cash	4 698	6 801	7 839	3 273	9 747
Receivables	17 589	24 693	60 270	48 987	66 768
Inventory	20 031	23 034	53 091	74 823	99 606
	42 318	54 528	121 200	127 083	176 121
Non current assets					
Intangible assets	5 247	5 220	7 305	9 969	10 674
Tangible assets	20 175	23 130	43 920	43 740	69 255
	25 422	28 350	51 225	53 709	79 929
Total assets	67 740	82 878	172 425	180 792	256 050
Current liabilities					
Bank loans and overdraft	10 581	4 026	18 180	29 316	37 638
Trade payables	16 197	24 588	55 659	41 130	72 831
Taxation	459	768	4 302	2 712	3 444
Dividends	801	1 812	3 339	3 738	3 672
	28 038	31 194	81 480	76 896	117 585
Non current liabilities					
Loans	14 793	15 477	35 241	35 430	67 844
	14 793	15 477	35 241	35 430	67 844
Total liabilities	42 831	46 671	116 721	112 326	185 429
Ordinary share capital	2 229	2 829	3 396	6 792	7 077
Share premium account	2 931	7 530	14 598	11 247	12 387
Retained profits	19 749	25 848	30 975	43 692	41 734
Revaluation reserve			6 735	6 735	9 423
Total equity	24 909	36 207	55 704	68 466	70 621
Total equity and liabilities	67 740	82 878	172 425	180 792	256 050

Summarized income statements of Keaton

	2006 £000	2007 £000	2008 £000	2009 £000	2010 £000
Sales	93 930	116 232	259 470	278 340	372 753
Cost of sales	65 751	82 525	197 197	208 755	294 475
Gross profit	28 179	33 707	62 273	69 585	78 278
Operating expenses	17 022	21 398	36 830	35 130	59 881
Net profit before interest and tax	11 157	12 309	25 443	34 455	18 397
Interest	2 727	2 652	7 707	10 167	14 082
Net profit after interest and tax	8 430	9 657	17 736	24 288	4 315
Taxation	2 517	1 746	9 270	7 833	2 601
Net profit after tax	5 913	7 911	8 466	16 455	1 714
Dividends Retained profits	801	1 812	3 339	3 738	3 672
	5 112	6 099	5 127	12 717	−1 958

Notes:

1 During 2010 some of the freehold properties were revalued.

2 Loans amounting to £22 million were repaid during 2010.

3 No fixed assets were disposed of during the year.

(a) From a review of the information, identify the areas which you would concentrate on in your analysis of the position of Keaton Ltd.

(b) Complete the common size income statement for the five years and analyze these statements with particular reference to the profitability of Keaton.

Common size income statements of Keaton

	2006 %	2007 %	2008 %	2009 %	2010 %
Sales	100	100	100	100	100
Cost of sales	70	71	76		
Gross profit	30	29	24		
Operating expenses	18	18	14		
Net profit before interest and tax	12	11	10		
Interest	3	2	3		
Net profit after interest and tax	9	8	7		
Taxation	3	2	4		
Net profit after tax	6	7	3		
Dividends Retained profits	1	2	1		
	5	5	2		

(c) Calculate the trends in the sales and cost of sales, and comment on the information disclosed by your analysis.

(d) Using whatever form of analysis you consider appropriate, comment on the financial risk profile of Keaton Ltd for the five years under review.

(e) Based on your analysis write a brief report for the bank advising them on whether to continue to provide finance for Keaton Ltd.

(f) Apart from the information arising from your analysis what other information would you advise the bank to consider when making their decision?

(g) Discuss how your analysis would have been altered if you were carrying out the analysis on behalf of a prospective shareholder.

PART II
MANAGEMENT
ACCOUNTING

CHAPTER 13
INTERNAL USERS AND INTERNAL INFORMATION

LEARNING OUTCOMES

By the end of this chapter you will:

- Have understood some of the needs of management and how accounting information can be used to satisfy some of those needs.

- Have a greater appreciation of the roles of managers as planners and decision makers, as controllers of the activities and the need for them to have and develop tools that will allow them to carry out those roles more efficiently.

- Have a clearer understanding that although financial accounting and management accounting are often viewed as being completely separate they in fact frequently draw upon the same source information and use the same techniques to enable the end user to make more informed decisions.

- Have thought about and understood the impacts of the type of business, its size and complexity on the management accounting systems that are needed.

Having been concerned in previous chapters with external reporting and the needs of external users, we now return to internal users and their needs. Their needs are discussed under the headings of decision making, planning and control. The impacts of organizational size and structure on these needs are then examined to provide a context for the remainder of the book.

At the start of this book and again in Chapter 12, we discussed external users of information, their information needs and introduced some techniques through which they could analyze the accounting information available. As we pointed out in Chapter 12 the accounting information was only one source of information that these external users could access and use to arrive at their decisions. The accounting information they were using was derived from the financial reports via the annual accounts of the enterprise being analyzed. As we saw in Chapter 5 and onwards the underlying information for these financial reports comes from the organizations' accounting system. We illustrated the accounting system using fairly simple examples and building levels of complexity as we proceeded through the chapters until finally we had built up the information to produce a set of final accounts. In reality the accounting system of an organization may be fairly simple or extremely sophisticated depending on the size and complexity of the business. If the business is large or complex then the information needed to control and manage it on a day-to-day basis will need to be up to date and complete and as such it will rely on a sophisticated accounting system. The management, especially of bigger enterprises, is unlikely to be carried out by the owners. Instead they will appoint people to manage the business for them. This might be done through a board of directors in the case of a company with reporting being very formally undertaken through the medium of the annual report and the annual general meeting to which all the shareholders are invited. In any case in all organizations there will be a group of people directly involved in the management of the activities and it is the needs of this group of users and how they might be met that we will be examining in the remainder of this book. In Chapter 1 we identified that management, as users of financial information, would need more detailed information than that normally contained in the financial accounts but also more up-to-date information, and indeed some different types of information.

ACTIVITY 13.1

Can you think why the management of a retail business with two retail outlets would need more detailed and up-to-date information and what they would need it for?

You will remember that in Chapter 12 we said that the annual accounts took anything up to ten months to be produced and audited so they are not helpful for decisions. In the case of the retail business with two outlets you may have come up with lots of ideas of what management would need to know. Some examples you might have thought of were what inventory was held in each branch, what was selling and what wasn't, what the cash flows were and whether the managers were controlling costs and using the resources of the business effectively. They would want information that would help them make planning decisions about the future, how much to order, whether they were making enough profit to expand, whether each branch was equally profitable and if not why not.

As you might imagine some of the information you identified in Activity 13.1 would also potentially be useful to other users that are external to the enterprise. It may, in fact, be very useful to them if they had it, but on the other hand it could be that there is too much information for their needs. After all, as an investor you only want to decide between investing in BP, Total or Shell and you are not necessarily interested in how many petrol stations they have and whether some are more profitable than others. In addition many of the external users we discussed in Chapter 12 do not have the power to demand access, as for example in the case of the larger public companies such as Rolls Royce plc and indeed there are strict rules about when information is made public to avoid some investors or potential investors profiting at the expense of others because they had access to privileged information that was not publicly available. At the other end of the spectrum the enterprises are too small and their internal accounting system too unsophisticated to produce any information other than that which underpins the annual accounts, as would be the case with, for example, your local fish and chip shop.

We shall now examine the needs of management in terms of the information they may require in order to make decisions between alternative opportunities, to plan the enterprise activities and to ensure that the plans are carried out. It is this information which is primarily prepared for internal users that may be available to external users if they have sufficient power to demand and obtain access.

MANAGEMENT'S INFORMATION NEEDS

Management need to be able to ascertain the impact of their past decisions, make decisions about future actions, evaluate alternative ways of deploying the resources of the enterprise, make decisions about future investments and evaluate outcomes. If we look at what we have covered so far and its adequacy for management purposes we will see that it is lacking in many ways. Looking back to Chapter 4 we identified that the contents of an income statement related to sales revenue and to costs. If you think about sales to start off with you will realize that the sales figure in reality is an amalgamation of lots of individual sales. Each of these sale lines may have different costs associated with them and as such the gross profit percentage made on, for example, greengrocery may be vastly different from that on tinned produce or frozen meals and in order to maximize profit it may be that a different sales mix should be strived for. Similarly, if we consider the costs or expenses in the income statement, we recognize that some relate to a period of time, e.g. rent, and some to activity, e.g. delivery costs, some will be more or less fixed no matter what the level of activity and others will vary either directly with activity or at a certain level. You can only make so many deliveries with one van; at some point you will need another van or another driver, so there is a point at which costs will step up.

ACTIVITY 13.2

Thinking about your time at university where you are involved in attending lectures, seminars, tutorials and other activities what different costs can you identify that the university might incur in delivering a business course and how might these differ from those associated with a course in computer science?

You might have identified some examples of costs that are incurred despite the level of activities, e.g. there would need to be a building, lecture theatres, library, staff offices, etc. There would be other costs such as those associated with delivering lectures and tutorials that will vary with the number of students, as would the paper for handouts. If we took the computer science course would they need more computers, or perhaps more sophisticated computers and computer software and if they did need more computers would they need more computer technicians to keep them going?

At this point we have identified that management is likely to need different information than external users. They will need more up-to-date information, that is often more detailed, and they will need this more frequently than external users as they have to manage the day-to-day running of the business and adjust the activities to ensure that they deliver the service that their customers want and potentially to maximize profit.

Returning to the annual accounts, clearly in a situation where management has already decided on the course of action to follow then they would be interested in the outcomes of those past decisions and they could obtain certain information from the annual accounts in respect of the outcomes. The information is unlikely to be sufficient even for this purpose because the annual accounts often only contain summarized and simplified information: it tells management what the outcome is, i.e. where they have got to, but it tells them little about the journey to get there, i.e. what has worked and what has not. This is almost certainly true in anything other than the smallest of enterprises. This summarized information may alert management to the fact that profit is lower than anticipated, but it is unlikely to be sufficiently detailed to identify the cause of this variation. This means that for management purposes there is almost invariably a need for more detailed information about the results of their past decisions and actions than that which is contained in the annual accounts.

In addition as the name implies, annual accounts are only drawn up once a year, and this is another reason why they are unlikely to be sufficient to meet the needs of managers, who need more regular and up-to-date information. The fact that annual accounts are only produced at the year end means that even if they are able to establish why the results have varied from those anticipated it may well be too late to take appropriate action. The fact that the time span between the year end and the actual production of the annual accounts varies from about three to four months for quoted companies to periods in excess of ten months for smaller enterprises does not help. What managers need is more frequent and more timely information.

KEY CONCEPT 13.1

Management information needs

More detailed information.
Up-to-date information.
Frequent information.
Decision-relevant information.

The reason why management is likely to require information more frequently is so that they can monitor the results of their actions and decisions, and fine tune the business as and when required. This is not to imply that none of the needs of managers are met by the financial information system on which the annual accounts are based. If you think back over what we have covered in the chapters to date you will start to see the connections and also recognize that if management is to use the information to make decisions, control the business and plan for the future there will be a need for more information that is up to date and is available on a regular basis. We started that journey with working out that the income statement could provide management with the information about what has happened over a period, what has been sold, what costs incurred and what, if any, profit had been made. However, the question that arises is whether that result is what was expected and we found in Chapter 12 that external users compare the results with what has happened in the past and what others in a similar industry and having a similar size are doing. For management this information is also useful as after all they will be judged by the owners on how they are doing compared to others.

However, managers have one big advantage over external users: they know what they planned to do. Therefore, they can look at their plans and their achievements and see if they have achieved what they intended. If not, they can then carry out some analysis to find out why they have not achieved their goals. This process can be undertaken at the end of the period but is more likely to be done via a management control system throughout the period with milestones being identified, targets set and variations from target, known in accounting jargon as variances, being identified and action taken to correct either the original assumptions or the way in which the business is actually operating. Chapter 14 deals with this process of planning, control, identification of variances and its **implications** for action in some detail.

ACTIVITY 13.3

Think of what information from the income statement of a mature business you might use to formulate plans for next year and what other information you might want to take into account when formulating your plans.

You might have thought that you could use the sales and cost of sales as a measure of 'normal activity' to form the base for your plans and then thought about what might happen if you could expand or if the market was declining. You might then have looked at the expenses in detail and considered which would change with the level of activity and which ones would stay fairly stable. In doing this you would need to be aware of what was happening in the economy, was the economy buoyant, were people spending money, what was happening to wages, etc.

You will have realized, having thought about Activity 13.3, that the information in the income statement has provided you with a starting point to come to some broad forecasts of what might happen. From there you might have added external information and analyzed the internal information in more detail. You would have thought about the way in which the costs relate to the levels of activity and realized that some vary directly with activity, e.g. the inventory sold must relate directly to the sales unless there is waste or pilferage. Others, like the rent of a retailer, will not vary with activity but instead will relate to time, i.e. the longer the period the more rent will be due. This leads you to the idea that although the income statement contains lots of costs or expenses, these are not all the same. Some are more variable and some are more fixed.

Thinking back to Chapter 6, where we dealt with inventory, you might realize that in general in that chapter and throughout the book to date we have dealt with single product businesses. Whilst this has been useful as a simplifying assumption it is unlikely to be the case in reality. Businesses will have multiple products probably with different costs attached and with some shared costs. In Chapter 6 we introduced the idea of marginal costs and absorption costing and saw that absorption costing allocated some indirect costs to the product in the form of foreman's wages etc. As you will appreciate, if you have multiple products, while you may be able to work out the direct labour costs associated with a product the 'overheads' included in an absorption costing system become more and more an estimate. If you are using absorption costing as the basis for your decisions this could have dire consequences if your estimates are wrong. On the other hand, if you only deal with the direct costs how do you ensure that you have enough activity and profit to cover your overheads? This whole area will be covered in more detail in Chapter 15 where we will be discussing the relationships between the costs, the level of activity and profits and starting to think about the costs of a unit of inventory in a very different way. We will explore this further in Chapters 16, 17 and 18.

ACTIVITY 13.4

If you consider a restaurant, a bar and a car manufacturer to what extent do you think it would be appropriate to look at an absorption costing system like that introduced in Chapter 6 and what, if any, other measures or systems might you think might be more appropriate?

You may have realized that in the case of a car manufacturer there are lots of components that can be directly connected to the car being made whereas in the case of a bar it is much more difficult to connect the bar staff with the cost of the drinks sold as they may be collecting glasses, washing up, etc. Similarly in a restaurant some of what is sold has identifiable ingredients, e.g. a glass or bottle of wine served with the meal, while the meal itself not only has identifiable ingredients but also takes time to prepare and serve. So it should be clear that a one size fits all approach to costing is not optimal. We may want to look at what drives the costs and what impact additional activity has on the costs as alternative ways of thinking about the business and build systems that assist management in the decisions relating to the particular size and nature of the business.

Moving on from inventory we then looked in Chapter 7 at amounts receivable and payable and the idea of trade credit given and received. We showed in that chapter that the levels of credit given could lead to serious differences, positive or negative, between the profit for the period and the cash flows for that same period. In Chapter 12 we introduced the idea of looking at efficiency ratios such as the number of days credit taken and given, how long it took to turn over the inventory, etc. From an external user's point of view we showed that these ratios could be used to look at trends over time and evaluate how efficient management had been in managing the business. We pointed out throughout the first section of the book that businesses, especially new small businesses, can often be profitable but get into trouble because they cannot or do not manage their cash flows and in particular their short-term cash flows. In Chapter 19 we will be looking at how management can use budgets as early warning systems that things are not working as they should be. These budgets can take the form of cash budgets, or budgets for jobs, areas of activity, etc. depending on the sort of business, the way in which it is organized and the needs of management. In Chapter 21 we will be returning to and extending the analytical tools we introduced in Chapter 12 and discussing how these can be utilized for more efficient management of working capital. By using these tools, management can identify and chase late payers and take corrective action when things are going wrong, rather than waiting until the end of the year when the financial accounts are drawn up or the bank calls in their overdraft by which time the damage has been done and it is a lot more difficult to put right.

ACTIVITY 13.5

If a business has an inventory turnover of 45 days and sells all its goods on credit which it takes 50 days to collect how long would it take to turn one unit of inventory into cash?

The answer is 95 days so you would have to be able to find the finance for that unit of inventory you sold for over three months. This could be done in part by the business taking advantage of credit terms it is offered. This will be explained in more detail in Chapter 21.

Returning to the first part of this book, we found that in Chapters 8 and 9 we were discussing long-term, 'non-current', assets and the ways in which these could be financed such as by the injection of equity, by medium to longer term loans or even by simply not buying them and instead leasing them. In effect we were looking at how we financed the investment in long-term assets. Athough we intimated that there were choices in the ways of financing an asset we did not explore this in any detail. In Chapter 20 we will be revisiting the whole idea of investing in long-term income generation and discussing techniques for deciding between alternative opportunities and ways of financing those opportunities. In reality the financial accounting system contains a lot of the information management requires, for example, it records who owes them money and how long they have owed it. So, in some cases the techniques you will be introduced to draw directly on financial accounting information and in some cases they draw on the base information, e.g. the underlying costs included in the inventory valuation, and use that information in a different way.

ACTIVITY 13.6

Think back to the methods of depreciation and their impact on profit and on cash flows and consider what impact that might have on differing investment appraisal methods.

You will probably have thought that different methods of depreciation will affect the profit more than the cash flow as they are added back to the profit to arrive at the cash flow. Therefore it may be that eliminating these estimates for depreciation and the impact of the differing methods provides the basis for a more sensible method for evaluating different alternative investment opportunities.

We could use other examples of information contained within the accounting system that, if presented and used in different ways from that required to draw up annual accounts, would meet management needs better. The decision about whether to make more of one product or another could be informed by the costs and relative profitability of the products in question, by the ability to make more of one product or the other, by the market or by a combination of all of these factors. So management may be turning to their marketing and sales departments to get ideas on what could be sold, to their production departments to see what could be produced and to their purchasing and even personnel departments to see if there are any problems in getting a steady supply of the materials and labour necessary to produce the different products.

Having said that management needs other information, it is important to understand that the base information used to produce the annual accounts could also be used as the source for many different reports that are provided to meet the specific needs of management. It should be borne in mind that, as with the other users referred to in Chapter 12, for management purposes financial information is only one of a number of types of information needed in order to make decisions about the future direction and actions of the business. It is not our intention to deal with these other types of information as they are outside the scope of this text, but they could include marketing information and employment legislation. We shall continue our discussion of management's information needs within the relatively narrow confines of financial information.

The discussion to date has suggested that management needs more frequent and more detailed information, and that information may be required in a different format than that contained in the annual accounts. We suggested that this information was used to monitor progress and take appropriate actions to fine tune the business, i.e. planning, control and decision making. Implicit in this process of monitoring is that the results are judged against some expectations. These expectations may be rough plans carried in the head of the owner of a small business or detailed plans and budgets in the case of a larger enterprise or the previous years' results contained in the annual accounts. We have identified that management needs information for planning the next year's activities, for controlling those activities and for making longer term investment decisions. In the remaining chapters of the book, we will be looking at how we plan, how we set objectives, issues about goal congruence, and techniques for controlling and reporting on activities so management can carry out their duties.

It is worth remembering that most if not all of this information may also be useful to users other than managers. However, some of the information is commercially sensitive and achievement of the goal of an enterprise may be dependent on its plans being kept secret from its competitors. Thus, not all external users will be able to demand access to the information and the question of whether they have access will depend not only on who they are but also upon their importance to the enterprise. We shall now consider why these external users may need some of the additional information that is available to management, what those needs may be, and the factors, such as relative power, competition and confidentiality, which determine their access or lack of access to internal information.

EXTERNAL USERS' INFORMATION NEEDS

One external user group who can demand access to internal accounting information is the taxation authorities. The nature of the information they require will vary but will normally be either more detailed breakdowns of particular expense headings or details of the timing of purchases and sale of fixed assets. The reason for this is that the taxation system is based upon a different set of rules for arriving at the taxable profit from those used to arrive at the accounting profit. The taxation authorities, which include, in the UK, both the Inland Revenue and Customs and Excise, who deal with value-added tax (VAT), have a statutory right of access to information.

Another external user which often is in a sufficiently powerful position to demand and obtain further information is the enterprise's bankers. The information they demand will, of course, depend on the circumstances. For example, if the enterprise is doing well the information demanded will be different from what would be required if the enterprise had problems. We shall discuss at a general level some of the additional information they may require and why this is required before going on to examine what determines whether or not this information is available to these external users.

In general, the information demanded by an enterprise's bankers (in addition to information on the movements on the bank accounts which the bank already has) can be divided into two categories: that required for routine monitoring and that enabling judgements to be made about the future needs of the enterprise. The former category would include regular management accounts such as monthly income statements, an analysis of debts in terms of how old they are (this is known as an 'aged debt analysis') and other up-to-date information such as the amount owed by the enterprise, i.e. the monthly trade payables balance. All this information is required to monitor the health of their customer's business on a more regular basis than would be possible if they had to rely on the information provided by annual accounts, which, as we have already said, are likely to be a few months out of date when they are produced.

Bankers also require other information to make judgements about the future needs and prospects of the enterprise in order to ascertain whether to lend money, when it is likely to be repaid and the risk involved. The information on future prospects is normally required in the form of projected cash flow statements and income statements, but would also include information about other loans that the enterprise may have and their due dates for repayment. The financial information is, of course, only part of the information that the banker may require; this could also include future orders, plans, analysis of competitors, etc.

As we have already indicated, there are circumstances where, like other external users such as shareholders and competitors, the banker cannot get access to this additional information. We shall examine those circumstances in our discussion of the impact of organizational size and structure on the information produced for management purposes, which is, of course, one factor that determines what these external users have access to.

IMPACTS OF ORGANIZATIONAL SIZE

We have discussed the needs of management in terms of information to make decisions about the future, to plan future actions and to control the business on a day-to-day basis. It should be clear that the more complex and sophisticated the business is, the more likely it is that it will require additional information. For example, the local garage owner may be able to carry in his head all the information needed to enable the business to be run effectively on a day-to-day basis. This is because the business is sufficiently small and the proprietor, who in this situation is, of course, also the manager, is directly involved in the running of the business and is on the spot to take whatever action is necessary.

On the other hand, in a large and complex business there is a need for a more formalized system for a number of reasons. First, the amount of information required in, for example, a multi-product firm is such that it is unlikely that the management would be able to carry, in their heads, all the detail necessary to run the business effectively. (A fuller discussion of the problems faced by multi-product firms and the techniques available to solve those particular problems is contained in Chapter 18, where we look at the effects of resource constraints and at 'make or buy' decisions.) Second, with larger businesses it is probably the case that the larger the business the more the senior managers will be removed from the day-to-day operations. This will not only change their information needs to requiring information of a more strategic type, but will also impose a requirement for additional information to control the activities and actions of those below them.

Hence, the size of the organization will influence the information needs of its managers and the way in which these needs are met, i.e. the need for more formal systems as the size of the business increases. We have also suggested that the nature of the business has an effect on the information needs – thus a multi-product business will require more sophisticated information systems than a single-product business. Consider, for example, the different information required to run a restaurant where the only product is food, compared with that required to run a hotel. In the latter case, not only do you need information about the food operation, but also information is required on bed occupancy rates, the bar profit, etc.

However, in discussing the information needs of managers, it has to be borne in mind that information is not cost free. In general, the more sophisticated the information system the more it costs to set up and run. Hence, the need for better and more up-to-date information always has to be balanced against the costs and benefits of obtaining that information. However, as we point out in Chapter 14, although there is considerable literature on cost–benefit analysis, the practical implementation of such an approach is fraught with difficulties. We should also remember that more up-to-date information is not in itself better *per se* as it also needs to be relevant to the use to which it is to be put. A fuller discussion of what constitutes relevant information in relation to costs and benefits, and how these relate to short-term decisions, is contained in Chapter 17. This issue of obtaining relevant information at a reasonable cost is part of the explanation of why in the case of many small businesses there is little in the way of formal management information. In many of these cases the information if it exists at all is held in the owner–manager's head in a form that is not readily accessible to others. In these situations, bankers are often able to exercise considerable influence as a major provider of finance; however, in the end, no matter how much pressure is exerted they cannot access information that does not exist. They therefore have to rely on the annual accounts and such other information as is available.

We have shown that the information available is influenced not only by the needs of managers but also by the size and complexity of the organization's products. We have also suggested that the nature of the product or products can influence the information systems. There are, of course, many other factors which will have an influence on what is required and what is produced. Consider, for example, the differing needs of high-technology industries and the impacts of flexible manufacturing systems and of management techniques such as just-in-time. These, like the particular industry, will lead to specific needs. A full discussion of these is outside the scope of this book, although in subsequent chapters we have tried to look at different industries in both the manufacturing and service sectors. Rather than pursuing the effects of differing industries further, we shall now consider a more general influence upon the information needs of managers, i.e. the structure of the organization.

IMPACTS OF ORGANIZATIONAL STRUCTURE

It is clear from looking at a few well known examples that different organizations have different structures and this means that their information needs may also differ. If we consider retailing, it is obvious that a business such as Marks & Spencer that operates both within the UK and abroad is going to need information relating to an overseas branch that may be different from that for a London branch, if for no other reason than the effect of different currencies. Thus, in general, an organization that has a multinational operation will have different information requirements than one whose operations are solely in the domestic market.

Similarly, many department stores such as Debenhams are organized round departments as profit centres and the departments' profits are identified separately. This implies that both the cost records and the takings from sales have to be identified and recorded by department. It may well be the case in such organizations that management is rewarded on the basis of schemes such as profit sharing, or by comparing profits achieved against predetermined targets. In such circumstances the information system would have to be designed to meet the structural requirements of the organization. These and similar matters are touched on in the discussion of department and divisional accounting in Chapter 17, and the impact and uses of budgets in Chapter 19.

We could, of course, find many more examples of different organizational structures apart from those referred to above as the organizational structure will depend on and to some extent be determined by the product, the market in which a business operates and the competitive environment, in addition to more mundane factors such as geography and location of its component parts or outlets. To do so would be extremely time consuming and outside the requirements of this text, but in general terms the more decentralized an organization is the more complex the information system will be.

SUMMARY

In this chapter, we have looked at the information needs of internal users. We have shown that the broad term management covers a wide range of people in the organization who may each have differing information needs. These will vary from the detailed information needs of the manager of a department within a store to the more strategic needs of the general manager of the whole department store. This analysis can of course be applied to other organizations where there are multiple layers of management ranging from those involved in the day-to-day running up to the board of directors. We have also indicated that the size and complexity of the organization and its structure will affect the information requirements of those within the organization and the relative availability of this information to those external users who may have the power to access such information. However, the common thread that runs throughout is that management needs detailed up-to date information for the purposes of planning, decision making and control of organizations. It is to a more detailed examination of these areas that we turn in the following chapters.

REVIEW QUESTIONS

(✓ indicates answers are available in Appendix A)

✓ **1** What are the main reasons why management would require additional information to the annual accounts?

2 One of the major improvements that bankers wish to see in respect of financial information is an improvement in the timeliness of information. Explain what this means and why it is important to bankers. How might this differ from managers?

3 What is likely to be the major impact of organizational size on the information needs of managers?

4 What useful management information is available from the accounting system from which the annual accounts are produced?

5 What additional information would bankers wish to have and what purpose would they use this for?

PROBLEMS FOR DISCUSSION AND ANALYSIS

(✓ indicates answers are available in Appendix A)

1 Would the way in which managers use the information you have identified in your answer to question 5 above differ from the way it is used by bankers and, if so, how would it differ?

✓ **2** In each of the situations outlined below identify what you believe your information needs would be.

Situation 1
You are the manager of a local branch of a national retail organization. All buying is done centrally and prices are fixed. You are in charge of the day-to-day management and hiring and firing of staff. Your annual remuneration is fixed.

Situation 2
The situation is the same as above except that in addition to your annual salary you receive a bonus of £1 for each £100 profit made above that expected.

Situation 3
As in situation 2 above except that you are able to decide on the selling price yourself.

Situation 4
You have been so successful as a branch manager that the company has promoted you to the position of regional manager in charge of 20 shops all of whose managers work under the conditions outlined in situation 3 above.

3 You work for an organization primarily involved in health care which runs a number of nursing homes for the elderly and has a head office staff consisting of yourself and two owner directors. Each of the nursing homes has a matron in charge who looks after the day-to-day running of the nursing home, but the advertising of the service etc., is carried out by one of the directors whilst the other director looks after the billing of the patients and collection of monies due. The overall profitability of your organization has fallen drastically in the last year and you have been asked to investigate the situation.

Identify what information you would need and what level of detail would be required in order for you to start your investigation.

CHAPTER 14
PLANNING AND CONTROL

LEARNING OUTCOMES

By the end of the chapter you will be able to:

- Understand the need for organizations to plan and control their businesses.

- Recognize that there are four stages in the planning and control process.

- Recognize the critical importance of setting objectives.

- Understand the importance to consider the cost and benefits of generating accounting information.

- Appreciate the importance of the impact of the size of the organization and the environment in the planning and control process.

This chapter examines the planning and control process, which is divided into four stages: the setting of objectives; making strategic decisions; making operating decisions; and monitoring and corrective action. Those factors that will affect the design and application of the planning and control process are also considered.

To be able to make decisions wisely, individuals and organizations need to have some vision about the future. A decision made without any thought to the future may well result in undesirable consequences; this is particularly so in the business context. For example, one of the main reasons identified for the failure of small businesses is the lack of planning of cash requirements. These businesses often fail despite the fact that they trade profitably. Apart from the need to make plans, there is also a need to monitor actual performance to ensure that the plans are being attained. This monitoring activity is an essential part of the control exercised by organizations to help secure their survival and efficiency.

In this chapter, we examine the planning and control process using a framework which not only explains the process itself but also provides an essential foundation for the analysis of discussions in subsequent chapters.

It is important to recognize that the planning and control process cannot be examined in isolation. There are a number of factors that will influence its design and application. In this chapter, we also discuss some of the more significant factors, such as technology, that may influence the design of accounting information systems in the context of the planning and control process, and it is appropriate here to consider some of the main limitations inherent in the application of the process.

THE PLANNING AND CONTROL PROCESS

KEY CONCEPT 14.1

Planning and control

Planning involves the determination of objectives and expressing how they are to be attained. The control process is the means of ensuring that the plans will be achieved.

A number of stages have been identified in the planning and control process:

Stage 1   Setting of objectives.

Stage 2   Making strategic decisions.

Stage 3   Making operating decisions.

Stage 4   Monitoring and possible corrective action.

We will begin by considering the four stages in the planning and control process before turning to the technical aspects of this process and factors that may influence the design of the accounting system within the process.

Objectives

From both a practical and a theoretical perspective, the determination and setting of objectives are probably the most complex stage of the planning and control process in a business organization.

However, in the absence of any explicit objectives there is no basis for management to evaluate whether the business is succeeding, or any criterion for choosing between alternative business opportunities.

Organizations themselves do not have objectives *per se*; the objectives of the organization will reflect those of the people involved with that organization. These individuals will each have their personal goals and it is likely that some may conflict with other participants. A sales manager's objective may be the maximization of sales, in volume terms, without any strong consideration to profitability. This may conflict with the objectives of the financial management of the firm whose primary concern could be to maximize profits through the introduction of higher prices with lower volumes of sales. This conflict in objectives is more commonly referred to as a lack of goals congruence.

The problem of goal congruence is more acute in large business organizations because of the number of participants and their varying vested interests. In the case of a large company, it is likely that employees would find an increase in remuneration desirable and possibly one of their personal goals. However, this may conflict with the interest of shareholders if it reduces the amount available to them for payment of dividends.

KEY CONCEPT 14.2

Goal congruence

Goal congruence is the alignment of organizational goals with the personal and group goals of the individuals within an organization.

From a wider social perspective, there is a growing awareness of the need to recognize the interests of parties external to the organization itself when it sets its objectives. In particular, customers, government and the local community will all have an interest in the survival and the activities of the organization. For example, in recent years there has been growing public concern about environmental issues. Through public pressure, a number of firms have had to change policies regarding their production activities. A good illustration of this is the change in policy of petrol companies to produce unleaded petrol.

If a business organization's objectives are to be effective there must be congruence of goals. Horngren *et al.* (1999) suggest that 'Goal congruence exists when individuals and groups work towards the organization goals that top management desires – that is, managers working in their own best interest take actions that further the overall goals of top management'. When an organization sets its objectives, the interests of all the participants will need to be recognized and common goals identified.

A number of academics maintain that it is not important to consider the goals of each individual, since their major interests will tend to converge to form group objectives. For example, it is likely that more pay will be a common goal for all employees. However, for an organization, there still remains the problem of identifying and setting objectives that satisfy all interested groups.

Lowe and Chua (1983) suggest that by looking at the common ground shared by the participants it is possible to establish organizational goals. They start by designating the possibilities open to organizations as 'activity spaces', which are defined by the interests of the varying groups involved with the organization. For example, the activity space for shareholders of a company might be to reduce labour costs, whereas that of employees (and possibly of governments) would be to maintain jobs and wage levels. Figure 14.1 shows the activity space for each interested group.

Where the boundaries of the activity space for each group overlap in Figure 14.1 there are regions where the acceptable activity is common to more than one group. The area where the activity spaces for all groups overlap is described as the 'feasible region'. Lowe and Chua argue that it is the task of management of an organization to confine its activities within this 'feasible region'.

FIGURE 14.1

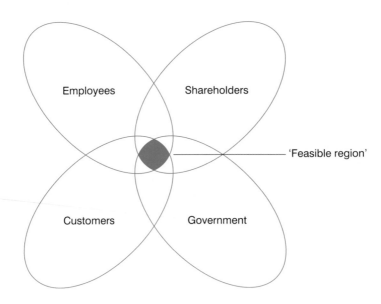

The most obvious activity in the 'feasible region' for a business organization in a capitalist economy is the making of profit. Where markets are, by and large, unregulated and competitive, profit making it an essential element in ensuring a firm's survival. Profits are by nature quantifiable and targets can readily be set in terms of formulating objectives. The quantifiable nature of profits also means that they are measurable. This attribute is very attractive to managers as deviations from the set objectives during an accounting period can easily be identified. This feature is particularly important in the control process, which will be discussed later in the chapter. It is common, in practice, to find the profit objective stated, more precisely, in terms of maximization of profits.

Qualitative objectives, in contrast with those of a quantitative nature, suffer from the problems associated with measurement. For example, the quality of a product (in meeting its purpose and customer requirements) is far more difficult to define in measurable terms, and difficulties also arise when comparing the objective set with actual performance in the control process. Although product or service quality is often cited as a prime objective of a business, in reality it is often disregarded or assessed inappropriately through movements in sales revenue.

Because of the difficulty often faced in setting unquantifiable goals, such as a quality definition or social responsibilities, most firms tend to compromise on the easier option of profit setting as the major (or sole) criterion for expressing their objectives. Although this gives a simple version of the firm's objectives, it has the disadvantage of conferring a blinkered view of the interactions which take place with various other interests. This can effectively undermine the firm's performance and even, paradoxically, threaten the profit which the company has put in esteem.

These problems with regard to unquantifiable goals are particularly pertinent to non-profit-making organizations, e.g. local authorities and charities. Frequently the objective for such organizations will be expressed in terms of the amount of the service rendered and the quality of that service. These objectives are inherently difficult or impossible to express in quantitative terms. However, a considerable amount of research has been carried out over recent years in an attempt to overcome these problems associated with non-profit organizations. A detailed discussion of the potential ways in which qualitative objectives can be effectively employed in such organizations is outside the scope of this introductory text.

KEY CONCEPT 14.3

Strategic decisions

Strategic decisions are those that determine the long-term policies of the firm and that are necessary if the firm is to meet its objectives.

Making strategic decisions

Strategic decisions in a business organization will invariably relate to policy changes in respect of the products or services that are currently being offered and the markets where they are sold.

The nature of the environment in which businesses operate is uncertain and outside the control of management. Some typical examples of the uncertain variables that can confront an organization are changes in taste, high inflation, recession and competitiveness. If organizations remain static and do not consider alternative policies in such an environment, it is likely that their objectives will not be met, which could threaten their survival in the long term. Often, strategic decisions have been made to maintain long-term profitability by diversifying, which has also made businesses less dependent on their traditional markets. For example, Ladbrokes, who primarily concentrated in the betting shop market, have invested in hotels and the leisure industry.

Drury (2000) suggests that to make effective strategic decisions management should be proactive in 'identifying potential opportunities and threats in its current environment and take specific steps immediately so that the organization will not be taken by surprise by any developments which may occur in the future'. He argues that firms should be constantly searching for alternative courses and developing

- new products for sale in existing and new markets;
- new markets for existing products.

ACTIVITY 14.1

Although there is a recognition that an organization's objectives will inevitably reflect a number of stakeholders' objectives it is common to find maximization of profits being the driving force in business decision making. Describe a situation where a business might make a decision that will not maximize profits.

A common example in retailing comes to mind – the pricing of a product as a loss leader. This encourages customers into the shop to purchase a number of products that have significant profit margins as well as the product that is a loss leader.

KEY CONCEPT 14.4

Operating decisions

Operating decisions are decisions that focus on the efficient use of the resources available to the firm in the short term.

It is also maintained that because of the importance of strategic decisions they will tend to be taken at the higher levels of management of organizations. These decisions are of a long-term nature, and this is one of the features that differentiates them from operating decisions.

Making operating decisions

The majority of operating decisions in an organization will be concerned with pricing and output, e.g. price setting and the determination of the level of service to be offered.

To be effective, the decisions must be made with deference to the objectives and strategic policies of the organization. However, as these decisions are taken in the current economic environment, often there will be constraints on the levels of sales and production. These constraints may prevent an organization, in the short term, from meeting its objectives. For example, an organization may be confronted with shortages of skilled labour which will effectively constrain output levels in the short term. If the maximization of profits is an objective of the organization in this situation, the constraint will also effectively result in limiting the extent to which the objective can be met in the short term. In the long term usually these constraints can be relieved. In the case of shortages in labour skills, training can be given. In circumstances where resource constraints exist, although the long-term objectives cannot be satisfied, it is still important to allocate scarce resources efficiently. Management accounting techniques have been developed to allocate scarce resources efficiently in these circumstances and they will be considered in detail in a later chapter.

The long-term plans of an organization, as previously mentioned, will be formulated through the making of strategic decisions with reference to the overall objectives of the organization. In cases where, in the short term, the targets embodied within the long-term plans cannot be met, there may be a need to amend or revise these plans in the light of the current economic situation. The process of re-examining long-term plans, in such circumstances, is an important feature of managing organizations effectively in a dynamic economic environment.

Operating decisions will be translated into a short-term plan which is referred to as a budget. Budgets are simply plans of action expressed in money terms. The process of aggregating operating decisions into a plan compels management to look ahead and coordinate their activities. Without forward plans that coordinate activities, the business may drift along meeting undesirable situations, such as not having enough suitable staff to provide a service that should have been anticipated and avoided. The budget also acts as a basis for judging performance, through comparison between actual and budgeted figures. This comparison can help to highlight strengths and weaknesses within the organization. It is important that budgets should be communicated to personnel in an organization so that they are aware of the planned (budgeted) targets. This will enable them to act in accordance with the plan.

The degree of sophistication and detail given to these budgets will depend inevitably on the size of the organization and the needs of internal users within the organization. Often the budgets will cover a period of one year and be broken down into monthly intervals. Primarily the reason for periodic monthly budgets is for control reasons, to allow a comparison of budget and actual activity at regular intervals so that timely monitoring of the plan is facilitated.

The process of preparing budgets and the types of budgets that are commonly employed will be examined in detail in Chapter 19.

Monitoring and corrective action

Essentially, monitoring and corrective action are the major parts of the control activities of any organization. The first element in this stage is the monitoring of actual performance against budget. Inevitably, from this comparison, differences (commonly referred to as 'variances') will be identified – it is unlikely that the actual performance will be exactly the same as the budget. The reason for this is that the operating decisions embodied in the budget will normally be determined well in advance of actual performance, and the process of forecasting cost and revenues in a dynamic economic environment is surrounded by uncertainty.

KEY CONCEPT 14.5

Monitoring and corrective action

Monitoring is the process of comparing actual performance with a predetermined target (plan). It provides the basis from which corrective action can be planned and taken.

To monitor performance effectively, personnel in an organization who incur expenditure and generate revenues will be identified and made responsible for these costs and revenues. The underlying approach adopted here is known as 'responsibility accounting'. The approach recognizes various decision centres throughout an organization, and traces cost and revenues to individual managers who are primarily responsible for making decisions and controlling the cost and revenues of the centre. The manager's knowledge of the centre places him or her in a relatively advantageous position, within an organization, to ensure that budget targets are achieved. These responsibility centres will normally take the form of departments or divisions within an organization.

In effective responsibility accounting systems, managers will, to some extent, also participate in the preparation of their own budgets. There is evidence from research suggesting that in certain circumstances participation by responsible managers in the setting of budgets enhances the probability that an effective planning and control system is employed within an organization.

There is a need for a reporting system, in an organization, to communicate relevant information to support a system of responsibility accounting effectively. The reports should show the actual performance, the budget and the deviations (variances) from budget. The model in which budgeted and actual costs and revenues are collected and then reported, e.g. by product, labour or material input costs in a manufacturing organization, will be determined by management. The major factors influencing management in deciding on the extent and sophistication of the reporting system will be the costs of installing such a system compared with the benefits generated from the system. A more detailed discussion of the cost and benefits of information systems will be covered later.

When variances have been identified, it is necessary to determine the reason for them in order that corrective action may be taken. If deviations from budget, assuming the budget reflects realistic targets, are not corrected it could be harmful to the organization in the long run. For example, material usage in a production process may exceed the budget in a particular control period, which could result in losses and consequently threaten the profitability of the organization if action is not taken.

Whilst the methods for identification of variances and their causes are outside the scope of this text, it is appropriate that you have some insight into the general nature of the causes of variances.

Traditionally, texts have tended to concentrate on variances that have been caused through operating problems, e.g. the prices of raw materials are greater than anticipated in the budget, perhaps because of inefficient buying practices by buyers. A number of academics, in particular Demski (1982) and Bromwich (1980), have argued that there could be other causes of variance that have tended to be overlooked in the control process. Basically they identify three causes of variances:

1   Operating variances are related to human or mechanical factors that result in the budget targets not being achieved.

2   Random variances are caused by divergences between actual and planned costs that arise at random, i.e. they occur by chance and there is no means of controlling these variances. For example, in some chemical processing the output can vary per unit of input because such variations are inherent in the process; in particular, evaporation often occurs in these types of process, and this is difficult to measure.

3   Planning variances will occur if plans are not realistic at the time of actual performance, even if operations have been efficiently carried out. Put simply, the plans may be out of date. For example, during the planning stage material costs may have been set with due care, but because of rapid inflation these planned costs are out of date in the control period and therefore do not represent realistic budget targets to compare actual and planned activities.

You should now read Case Study 14.1 on variances.

CASE STUDY 14.1

Mark plc variances

Mark plc employs a budgeting system to control costs. The original budget for 2008 included material A, which was estimated to cost £5 per kilogram. It was anticipated that 1 000 kg would be used during the year. Therefore, the budget in total cost terms was £5 000. During the year, however, although 1 000 kg was used, the cost was £6 000.

Traditionally, the analysis of the variance between actual and budget would be presented as follows:

	Actual £	Budget £	Variance £
Material A 1 000 kg	6 000	5 000	(1 000)

The parentheses around the variance of £1 000 indicate that it is 'unfavourable', i.e. actual costs exceed budget (plan).

This analysis, however, does not give any indication as to the cause of the variance. For example, it could be because of inefficient buying practices by the purchaser of the materials or because prices have increased through inflation during the year. The former cause implies that the variance is due to operating problems and actions may be taken in the future to ensure that more efficient buying practices are used. In contrast, if the variance is caused through inflation since the price was set in the

(Continued)

original budget, it implies that the variance is because the plan is out of date. In this case it is unlikely that the firm can take any action to prevent such variances occurring again.

Let us now assume that the firm has information at the end of the year 2008 indicating that a realistic planned price taking account of inflation during the year would be £5.50 per kilogram. The variances could then be analyzed as follows:

	Actual £	Budget £	Variance £
Variance caused through inefficient operations	6 000	5 500	(500)

	Original budget £	Updated budget £	Variance £
Variance caused by the plan being out of date	5 000	5 500	(500)

In this analysis, the causes of the variance are clearly identified, i.e. £500 relates to operating problems and £500 is because the original budget was out of date. The information presented in this way is more informative and useful for management purposes.

Although the analysis of operating, random and planning variances is on the whole theoretically sound, there are a number of practical problems, which may explain its limited use in practice. For example, in Case Study 14.1 the up-to-date budget of £5 500 was established at the end of the year. In other words, this budget was established in hindsight after the purchase of the material. To establish a realistic budget reflecting the recent past operating conditions these budgets, by their nature, must be determined after the event. Although such budgets are useful for variance analysis purposes, they do not give any targets for management to work to during the actual production period. This is a major deficiency in the use of these types of budgets. There are a number of other major criticisms, the most critical commentator being Lloyd Amey (1973).

In the context of this book, as has already been mentioned, it is not necessary for us to delve too deeply into the details of the causes of variances or to examine the criticisms in detail. It is important, however, to recognize, from the work of Demski and Bromwich in this area, the limitations of traditional variance analysis, which can restrict the effectiveness of the planning and control process in its practical application.

Another effective limitation to this stage of the process is the cost of investigating the cause of variances. The activity of investigation can be costly. It may be considered not worth the time and money to carry out such an investigation for the benefits derived.

THE CONTROL SYSTEM

The accountant's control system, the monitoring and corrective action stage of the process, is often compared with those of an engineer, using the analogy of a central heating system. Figure 14.2 is a relatively simplistic diagram of a central heating system. In this system, the desired temperature is set and the comparator compares this with the actual room temperature. If there is any deviation from the set temperature, action is automatically taken by the system to fuel the boiler to enable it to compensate for any temperature variance. This system thus involves the process of monitoring actual output against a desired output, and when a variance is identified corrective action will automatically be taken.

FIGURE 14.2

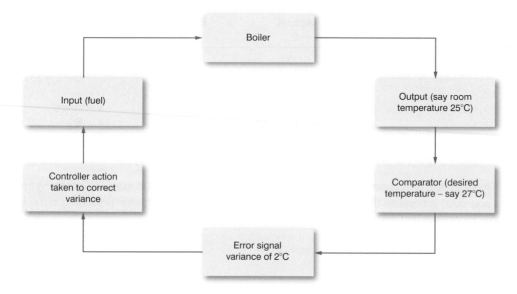

Earlier, when we were examining the planning and control process, very similar stages were identified and described. However, there are a number of interesting differences between the two systems, some of which will give us greater insight into the limitations of the planning and control process.

An important difference is that the central heating model is a physical system where there are automatic responses to outputs. That is, corrective action is taken to obtain the desired temperature automatically, and without any reference to operatives. In contrast, the control model, within the planning and control process, is normally dependent upon humans. In this system, the response to deviations from the budget is not taken automatically. Time lags will be experienced in all accounting reporting systems and people will have to be motivated to respond to variances and take corrective action if it is perceived to be necessary.

The extent of these time lags in reporting will depend on the sophistication of the accounting information system. In the case of some large companies, the monitoring of performance will be on a weekly basis and, with computerization helping to speed up the reporting process, the capability of taking corrective action is relatively quick. However, in the majority of organizations, control reports will normally be generated on a monthly basis. The main restriction to implementing more timely systems will be the installation and running cost, which once again relates to the cost and benefits of information systems, i.e. an information system should only be installed if the benefits generated from the system exceed the cost of installing the system. The variances that are reported in an accounting information system can, of course, only be used to guide future operations. An organization cannot remedy past mistakes.

It is now well recognized that the effectiveness of accounting information systems is very much dependent upon the attitudes of individuals associated with the organization. Although a considerable amount of attention is now correctly given to the influence of individuals on accounting information systems, there is still considerable scope for further research as well as the appreciation in practice that human behaviour can distort the effectiveness of accounting systems.

In the context of the control systems, the process of setting targets will be influenced and affected by the behaviour of individuals. For example, a sales manager may respond negatively if he is set a target that, in his opinion, he is unable to achieve. Another example is the required action to correct further undesirable variances: this action will very much depend on the reaction and motivation of the responsible manager and his subordinates. If a manager perceives that targets are unrealistic, it is unlikely that he or she will be motivated to take corrective action to ensure that they are met in the future. The accountant's control system is therefore limited in its application by the motivation of individuals in setting budgets and taking action on variances that have been identified.

THE COST AND BENEFITS OF ACCOUNTING INFORMATION SYSTEMS

An accounting information system is a commodity in much the same way as household goods such as detergents, soap and food. That is, there is a cost, often considerable, in installing and running the system. The benefits from employing the system should exceed the cost or otherwise it would be questionable whether the system should be installed.

The optimal system for any organization will be the system that generates the greatest amount of benefits net of costs. Horngren *et al.* (1999) contrast this approach with choosing a system because it is more accurate or a truer approximation of economic reality. The cost–benefit approach does not use accuracy as a criterion but focuses on the net benefits derived from alternative systems, giving preference to the system that generates the greater net benefits.

The practical implementation of the cost–benefit approach, however, is rather complex. Although it may be feasible to determine the cost of alternative systems, the benefits, e.g. the quality of information, are invariably difficult to measure as they tend to be qualitative. Although this is a problem, the cost–benefit approach is relevant in the choice of systems and is particularly relevant to the systems within the planning and control process described earlier.

ORGANIZATIONAL AND ENVIRONMENTAL CONTEXT

A number of writers and researchers argue that the installation of effective planning and control processes in businesses requires consideration of individual and organization factors. Earlier we briefly examined individual behavioural considerations with reference to the setting of budgets and the motivation required to take corrective action to maintain control of costs and revenues within the organization. Now we briefly consider other organizational and environmental issues.

Businesses are affected by and dependent on their environment. Emmanuel *et al.* (1990) stress that a firm's 'ultimate survival is determined by the degree to which it adapts and accommodates itself to environmental contingencies (uncertain events)'. Therefore, the design of planning control systems must be carefully tailored to match their environment and the organizational context in which the system will be employed. This approach is not new in practice; it has been implicitly recognized by accountants for a number of years.

Traditionally, writers of texts have suggested that there is one best way in which a particular task can be carried out regardless of the environment in which the organization operates, e.g. the nature of the market and the production process. Accounting information systems as illustrated in texts have invariably adopted this approach, and have not differentiated the various needs of accounting for different organizations. This approach very much follows the classical management and scientific management theories propounded by, for example, Taylor (1947). The contingency theory of organizations, in contrast, accepts that different types of organization will require differing types of accounting information to enable them to function effectively.

Emmanuel *et al.* identify three major classes of contingent factors:

1   technology, e.g. the nature of the production process – labour-intensive vis-à-vis machine-intensive operations;

2   environmental, e.g. the degree of competition and the degree of predictability;

3   structural, e.g. the size and type of the organization.

These contingent factors will affect the accounting information systems and, in particular, the effectiveness of the planning and control process. For example, in the context of planning, businesses that are in a relatively risky market will tend to invest more in planning in an attempt to predict outcomes and analyze alternative opportunities to lessen their risk. The design of planning and control systems should take account of these wider issues if a firm is to survive and cope in its environment.

USERS OF PLANNING INFORMATION AND THE IMPACT OF ORGANIZATIONAL SIZE

Very little reference has been made to small businesses vis-à-vis large businesses, so far, in the context of installing and employing planning and control systems. Clearly, there are constraints for small businesses in their use and choice of such systems. One of the major constraints relating to the cost and benefits of installing these systems was described earlier. Nevertheless, there is increasing evidence to suggest that there is a greater chance of survival if small firms do use budgets to plan their future and employ control mechanisms to ensure that these plans are met. The reason often cited for the high failure rate in the UK of this size of firm is the lack of planning and control of cash resources. Therefore, some of what has been said so far regarding the need for planning and control it would appear is relevant to this size of enterprise.

SUMMARY

For organizations to operate efficiently in a dynamic and uncertain environment, there is a need for them to plan and control their businesses. Four important stages of the planning and control process were identified and examined in this chapter.

The setting of objectives is clearly critical to the process. The other stages in the process are very dependent on clear objectives being set and communicated to personnel within an organization.

In the uncertain environment that confronts business organizations, it is important that they constantly make and review strategic decisions to maintain their position in the market place and to exploit the opportunities for growth. In the short term, organizations must manage their resources efficiently in their day-to-day operating decisions which are embodied within short-term plans known as budgets. If an organization is to ensure that it is meeting its objectives in the long and short term, it is necessary to monitor results and take corrective action when relevant. This was examined in the last stage of the process.

A number of problems were also identified relating to these four stages in the planning and control process. Potentially these problems can limit the effectiveness of the process. However, there is growing evidence that the more successful organizations invest heavily in planning and control information systems.

REFERENCES

Amey, L. (1973) 'Hindsight vs expectations in performance measurement', in L. Amey (ed.) *Readings in Management Decisions*, London: Longman.

Bromwich, M. (1980) 'Standard costing for planning and control', in J. Arnold, B. Carsberg and R. Scapens (eds.) *Topics in Management Accounting*, London: Philip Allan.

Demski, J.S. (1982) 'Analyzing the effectiveness of traditional standard cost variance model', in A. Rappaport (ed.) *Information for Decision-Making*, 3rd edn, Upper Saddle River: Prentice Hall.

Drury, J.C. (2000) *Management and Cost Accounting,* 5th edn, London: International Thomson Business Press.

Emmanuel, C.R., Otley, D.T. and Merchant, K. (1990) *Accounting for Management Control*, London: International Thomson Business Press.

Horngren, C., Bhimani, A., Foster, G. and Datar, S. (1999) *Management and Cost Accounting*, Upper Saddle River: Prentice Hall.

Lowe, E.A. and Chua, W.F. (1983) 'Organizational effectiveness and management control', in E.A. Lowe and J.L.F. Machlin (eds.), *New Perspectives in Management Control*, London: Macmillan.

Taylor, F.W. (1947) *Scientific Management,* New York: Harper and Row.

FURTHER READING

For those who wish to examine the importance of strategy in practice and its relationship with planning and control an excellent journal to read is *Strategic Change* published by Wiley.

REVIEW QUESTIONS

(✓ indicates answers are available in Appendix A)

✓ **1** There are a number of stages in the planning and control process. Identify these and give a brief description of each stage.

2 In recent years external users of accounting information have required from firms their internal management accounting information. Explain why such information is useful to these users.

3 Define responsibility accounting with reference to the planning and control process.

PROBLEMS FOR DISCUSSION AND ANALYSIS

(✓ indicates answers are available in Appendix A)

✓ **1** Discuss the main differences between the control models of accountants and engineers. Detail any limitations to the planning and control process that can be identified through this comparison.

2 Give illustrations of how the behaviour of individuals can affect the planning and control process.

3 For plans to be effective, management should consider the wider environmental factors that relate to the firm. Discuss.

4 Describe why it is important to set objectives in the firm and comment on the problems of setting objectives.

CHAPTER 15
COST BEHAVIOUR AND COST–VOLUME–PROFIT ANALYSIS

LEARNING OUTCOMES

By the end of this chapter you will be able to:

- Understand the nature of fixed and variable costs.

- Appreciate the way in which costs behave over activity levels.

- Explain how past costs are measured to predict future costs.

- Use cost–volume–profit (CVP) analysis in decision making.

- Appreciate the limitation and assumptions underpinning the determination of future costs and revenues.

To be able to predict future costs for planning and decision making, it is necessary to understand how costs behave in relation to activity levels. The chapter begins by examining the nature of cost behaviour, classifying costs into fixed and variable. This classification is then employed within the context of cost–volume–profit analysis.

For managers to be able to choose between alternative business opportunities, they need information regarding future costs and revenues, and the way in which these may vary at different levels of activity. In order to use this information effectively, in the business environment, they also need to understand how costs are determined and the way in which costs and revenues behave.

In this chapter, we begin by examining cost behaviour and the ways in which costs are predicted, and then we consider the application of this information to decision making using the technique of cost–volume–profit (CVP) analysis. This technique examines the interrelationships between cost, volume and profits at differing activity levels to aid managers in their decision making. We also critically appraise the traditional methods and models that are used and the underlying assumptions.

COST BEHAVIOUR

To understand how costs behave, it is first necessary to understand the nature of costs. Some costs are essentially fixed in nature, e.g. the standing charge for the domestic telephone service. Others vary with usage or activity, e.g. the cost of each telephone call made. These costs are known as variable costs. Unfortunately, not all costs fall neatly within these categories and therefore it may be necessary to make some simplifying assumptions about how costs behave for the purpose of decision making.

Before examining fixed and variable costs and how they behave it is worthwhile to start with the examination of cost functions.

KEY CONCEPT 15.1

Variable costs

Variable costs are the same per unit of activity and therefore total variable costs will increase and decrease in direct proportion to the increase and decrease in the activity level. The activity level may be measured in terms of either production/service output or sales output. The choice will depend on what is being measured.

KEY CONCEPT 15.2

Fixed costs

A cost is fixed if it does not change in response to changes in the level of activity.

ACTIVITY 15.1

Think of a plumber who works for himself from a rented lock-up garage and travels to jobs in a van he purchased. Detail examples of fixed and variable costs that the business will incur.

The following are likely variable and fixed cost that would be related to such a business:

Variable:

- the labour cost
- materials/components
- fuel for a van.

Fixed:

- rent for the garage
- insurance for the van and garage
- depreciation on the van
- electricity for the garage.

Linear cost functions

A basic notion of science is the idea that one thing will depend on another according to some mathematical relation. It is likely that in your study of economics you have come across the application of this concept. For example, when considering the relationship between the total spending (c) of a nation on all consumption goods in one year and the total income (y) of all persons in the nation in one year economists use the expression:

$$c = f(y)$$

This expression states that consumption is a function of the level of income. That is, the level of consumption in one year will be dependent upon the level of income.

Similarly, this basic notion is also applied in accounting in order to understand the functional relationships between cost and activity levels.

There are two important variables involved in the construction of cost functions. (We shall use the example of the cost of travelling to illustrate the nature of these variables and their interrelationship.)

- The dependent variable y is the cost to be predicted – the total cost for an activity, e.g. the cost of petrol for a journey.

- The independent variable x is the level of activity, e.g. the number of miles to be travelled on the journey.

The dependent variable is expressed as a function of the independent variable:

$$y = f(x)$$

FIGURE 15.1 The total cost of petrol for a journey is a function of (or dependent on) the number of miles travelled

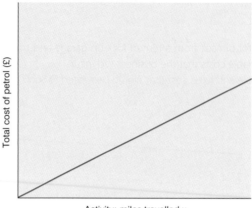

Activity: miles travelled *x*

In our example, similar to the functional relationship of consumption and income described above, this relationship can be expressed as shown in Figure 15.1.

In this relationship, we have assumed that there is only one independent variable, i.e. the number of miles travelled. However, in this example, and in general, there is more than one independent variable. In the case of the cost of petrol for a journey the consumption of petrol and therefore cost will also be dependent upon, for example, the speed at which the vehicle travels.

In the relationship between the dependent and independent variables illustrated in Figure 15.1, the vertical axis is the dependent variable, measuring total cost of petrol, and the horizontal axis is the independent variable, measuring the activity, i.e. the miles travelled. The cost for the number of miles travelled can be plotted on the graph to produce a cost function. The function may be linear or non-linear. Traditionally, accountants assume cost functions to be linear, which is not necessarily a realistic assumption as often costs behave in a non-linear fashion.

KEY CONCEPT 15.3

Linear cost functions

Mathematically we can express the linear cost function as follows:

$$Y = a + bx$$

where Y is the total cost to be predicted, a is a constant, i.e. the element of cost that remains unchanged whatever the activity level (in accounting terminology this is known as the 'fixed cost', e.g. the road tax payable on a car), b is the cost that will be the same for each unit of activity, and therefore as the activity varies so will the cost (this cost is known as the variable cost, e.g. the cost of petrol), and x, as before, is the level of activity, measured in units of output.

Figure 15.2 illustrates a linear cost function of a telephone bill. Point a represents the fixed costs, which remain the same for any level of activity – in our example the standing charge. The line bx

FIGURE 15.2

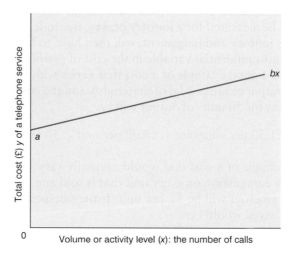

illustrates the variable cost b (the cost per call), rising in proportion to increases in activity x (the number of calls made).

We can determine the total cost of the use of the telephone using the above expression if we know the cost of the standing charge, the cost per call and the number of calls to be made:

$$\text{standing charge } a = £14$$
$$\text{cost per call } b = 4\text{p}(£0.04)$$

The number x of calls to be made is 1500. Hence, if Y is the total cost of the bill,

$$Y = £14 + £0.04 \times 1\,500 = £74$$

If the number of calls increases to 1800, the total cost of the bill will be:

$$Y = £14 + £0.0 \times 41\,800 = £86$$

To help you to understand this expression and its usefulness you should examine a recent telephone bill for your household and calculate the total cost of the bill if the number of calls made increased by say 50%. This exercise may also result in your spending less time on the telephone!

The choice of the independent variable

Often, as previously mentioned, there will be more than one independent variable that will affect the total cost of an activity. The speed at which the vehicle travels, in addition to the miles travelled, was cited as a variable that can affect the amount of petrol consumed and thus the total cost of petrol for a journey. However, invariably it is too complex to take account of all independent variables that affect total costs. Because of this, the independent variable that is chosen, when there is more than one, should be the most influential variable in relation to the movement of cost. In the case of the cost of petrol for a journey, it is likely, in general, that the most influential variable will be the miles travelled rather than, for example, speed.

In some cases the selection of the most influential variable will be obvious. However, in other cases it may not be so obvious. In such cases past costs should be examined at different activity levels to establish which of the independent variables are most influential. In the example of the cost of a journey, the consumption of petrol could be measured for a journey of, say, five miles at differing speeds. A decision, based on the evidence of this journey and judgement, will then have to be made as to whether the miles travelled or the speed is the most influential variable in the cost of petrol for the journey.

The cost of raw material is a good example of a cost that varies with the level of production output. For example, if one unit of output requires 2 kg of material A and the cost per kilogram of the material is £1.50, then the material cost for 50 units of output will be:

$$2 \text{ kg} \times £1.50 \text{ per kilogram} = £3.00 \text{ per unit} \times 50 \text{ units} = £150$$

Sales commission is an example of a cost that would normally vary with sales output. For example, if a salesperson receives 10% commission on every unit that is sold and the selling price per unit is £20, the commission that will be received will be £2 per unit. If the salesperson sold 3000 units during the year the total commission received would be:

$$2 \times 3\,000 \text{ units} = £6\,000$$

Labour paid on a hourly basis is conventionally classified as a cost that varies with production output. In reality, however, this category of labour will invariably be paid a fixed wage which bears no direct relationship to output levels. There may be some incentive bonus included in the pay structure that will be linked with output, but primarily the main proportion of the remuneration will be fixed for a fixed working week. Nevertheless, for decision-making purposes it is assumed that this category of labour is variable because, physically (ignoring the basis of remuneration), production levels will normally be a function of the labour input.

Figure 15.3 illustrates the movement of variable costs over activity levels. In this illustration you will see that at the intercept, in which the cost function meets the vertical axis, costs and activity are zero. This is because variable costs relate directly to activity levels; hence, if activity is zero the variable costs will be zero and as activity increases the variable cost function (i.e. the total variable cost) will increase. This can be compared with Figure 15.2, where the fixed costs were also included in the illustration.

FIGURE 15.3

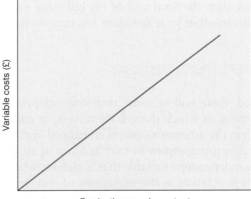

Production or sales output

FIGURE 15.4

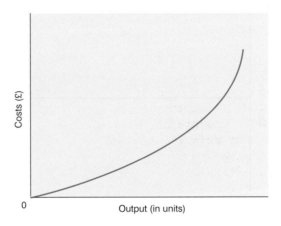

In reality, it is unlikely that costs that are traditionally classified as variable will behave strictly in a linear fashion. The variable cost function therefore tends to be curvilinear. The following examples illustrate some of the reasons why variable costs are not strictly linear.

- In the case of raw materials purchased at certain stages of activity, manufacturers are likely to benefit from bulk discounts.

- Prices of resources tend to increase as a scarcity arises due to demand.

- Diminishing returns: for example, attempts to sell more units may well entail transporting the extra units over longer distances to reach more distant markets and therefore distribution costs may increase at a faster rate than activity. Assuming that selling prices are constant, these greater distribution costs will result in diminishing profit margins.

Figure 15.4 shows a variable cost function with diminishing returns.

Fixed costs

Examples of costs that will normally be classified as fixed are rent, rates, salaries of administrators and the standing charge for a telephone service referred to earlier. Fixed costs of this type will normally also be classified as overhead costs, which are described in Chapter 16. Figure 15.5 illustrates the traditional graphical representation of the way in which fixed costs behave over activity levels.

However, the concept that fixed costs are constant over all levels of activity is not realistic. In reality, a fixed cost will only be fixed over a limited range of output. For example, in the case of a telephone, the standing charge is fixed if only the basic service is used; if voicemail is required the standing charge increases. Similarly, a factory has a limited capacity; if production were to exceed that capacity, another factory would be required and therefore the costs would increase. Hence, these types of cost tend to behave in a stepped fashion. Figure 15.6 illustrates a stepped cost function in the case of renting a factory. The rent is £2000 for one factory which has a capacity in output terms of 1000 units. Another factory will be required for output levels exceeding 1000 units, and the total rent will increase to £4000 (assuming that the rental and the capacity are the same). This cost will remain at £4000 up to 2000 units, when another factory will be required and costs will increase in the same fashion, and so on.

FIGURE 15.5

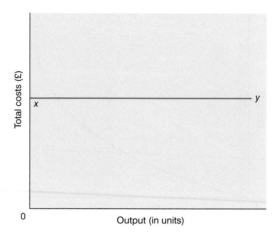

FIGURE 15.6

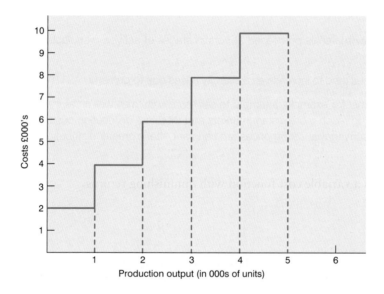

ACTIVITY 15.2

In the case of the plumbing business in Activity 15.1, detail typical cost which is not strictly fixed nor variable.

The following cost may come to mind: The cost of a mobile phone where the rental charge is fixed but the call charge is likely to variable or stepped.

The relevant range of activity

In predicting future cost behaviour, assuming that the intention is to operate in the relevant range of activity, we can be reasonably confident about the pattern of cost behaviour. This confidence is important to managers as the information regarding the way in which costs behave will be the basis for future decision making. If the costs do not behave as predicted, this could lead to decisions being taken that may jeopardize the organization's future.

KEY CONCEPT 15.4

The relevant range of activity

The relevant range of activity relates to the levels of activity that the firm has experienced in past periods. It is assumed that in this range the relationship between the independent and dependent variables will be similar to that previously experienced.

Outside the relevant range we cannot be confident that the relationship between the variables will hold. Figure 15.7 shows a cost function in the relevant range of activity and other cost functions outside this range, which are not of a similar pattern. Therefore, if an organization is intending to operate at an activity level not experienced before, it must be extremely cautious in the prediction of future costs, relying more on forecasting methods than on predicting costs on the basis of past behaviour. The examination of forecasting methods is outside the scope of this text; you can find references to the methods in most advanced management accounting texts.

Conventionally, for convenience, graphical representations of the relations between cost and volumes do show cost functions that are the same for all levels of activity, i.e. the same pattern of costs is shown inside and outside the relevant range of activity. This is the case in all the graphical representations showing cost functions illustrated before Figure 15.7 in this chapter.

FIGURE 15.7

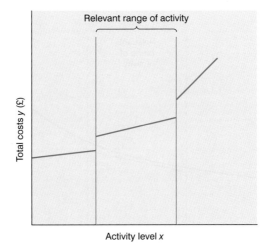

Cost behaviour assumptions and limitations

As we have already mentioned, accountants conventionally employ cost functions that are linear for use in making operating decisions. This practice is based on a number of assumptions and we have discussed most of them. For clarity, however, they are summarized below.

- all costs can be divided into either fixed or variable costs;

- fixed costs remain constant over different activity levels;

- variable costs vary with activity but are constant per unit of output;

- efficiency and productivity remain constant over all activity levels;

- cost behaviour can be explained sufficiently by one independent variable.

From our earlier analysis, it will be recognized that these assumptions are rather simplistic and tend to be approximations of reality. Therefore, the question arises: are the cost functions used by accountants justified? The answer to this question is often difficult to establish with much confidence. Primarily this is a cost–benefit question (this approach was generally considered in Chapter 14): are the net benefits greater when accountants' linear cost functions are used compared with the more sophisticated cost functions such as curvilinear functions? The non-linear functions will invariably be more costly to establish because of their sophistication. Although the cost and benefits of an information system, as previously mentioned, are difficult to establish, it is theoretically a sound concept, and therefore should be borne in mind when deciding in practice what models to employ. It is also the case that the relatively recent developments in information technology have tended to reduce the cost of developing and using these more sophisticated models.

Arnold and Turley (1996) argue that the use of a linear cost function 'is not unreasonable as statistical studies have presented evidence which suggests that within specified output limits [the relevant range of activity], organizations do have cost functions which are approximately linear'. Figure 15.8 shows how a curvilinear cost function approximates to a linear function within the relevant range of activity.

FIGURE 15.8

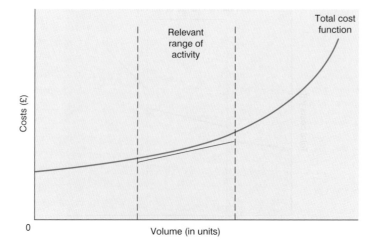

ACTIVITY 15.3

Which of the following costs are fixed, variable, or a mixture of both:

1 Depreciation on a car

2 Power to operate a drill

3 Advertising

4 Sales commissions

5 Fuel used for a lorry

Answers:

1 Fixed

2 Variable

3 Variable

4 Variable

5 Variable

KEY CONCEPT 15.5

Cost estimation

Cost estimation relates to methods that are used to measure past (historical) costs at varying activity levels. These costs will then be employed as the basis to predict future costs that will be used in decision making.

Cost estimation

There are many methods of cost estimation. Detailed knowledge of each of these methods is not necessary at this stage of your studies. However, it is important that you appreciate the basic principles and limitations of cost estimation. For a detailed examination of the methods see Horngren *et al.* (2005).

The methods of cost estimation that can be used range from those that are simple to others that are mathematically complex. The essential factor is to choose the estimation technique that generates the greatest benefits net of the costs of deriving the information. This to a great extent will depend on the size of the organization. The smaller the organization, the less likely it is that a sophisticated method will be employed, as the costs will be relatively high compared with the benefits that will be generated from the use of such a method.

Cost estimates will be based on historical cost accounting data, i.e. on the costs of past production, service and sales activity. One of the simplest methods is the account classification method, which involves simply observing how costs behave in a previous period from past accounting data and classifying these costs as fixed or variable. The method relies on much subjective judgement and, hence, is limited in its ability to predict the future behaviour of costs accurately.

A more sophisticated method of cost estimation is regression analysis. The linear regression model involves making a number of observations from past cost behaviour and statistically analyzing the data to produce a line of best fit. Figure 15.9 shows graphically a number of points that have been determined from past cost behaviour at varying levels of activity, and a line of best fit is established using the mathematical technique of regression analysis. A clear pattern of behaviour, i.e. where the points are closely clustered together over the ranges of activity, indicates a high correlation between cost and output (activity), whilst a widely dispersed arrangement of points indicates a low correlation. For further explanation see a text on quantitative methods, such as *Quantitative Methods for Business Decisions* by Curwin and Slater (2008). In the example illustrated in Figure 15.9, there is a fairly clear pattern of behaviour, and thus we can conclude that there is a relatively high correlation between cost and output.

FIGURE 15.9

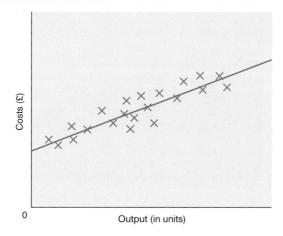

There are more sophisticated statistical techniques using regression analysis for estimating costs. These include multiple regression, which takes account of more than one independent variable, and curvilinear regression.

The use of past data to determine future costs and the way in which they behave does have its problems. The following briefly summarizes some of these.

- Relevant range of activity: As previously mentioned, little confidence can be placed in cost estimates beyond the range of activity from which the data have been derived. It is therefore dangerous to extrapolate cost trends well beyond the levels of output previously experienced.

- The number of observations: It is important in statistical analysis to derive many observations of output and cost levels in order to be able to make accurate predictions about future behaviour. The greater the number of observations, the higher is the accuracy of the estimate and therefore the better the prediction.

- Changes in prices: Past costs may not reflect current price levels and they will bias the estimates downwards. There is therefore a need to adjust these prices to current levels.

- Changes in technology: Only observations made under current production procedures should be included in the analysis. Costs of work practices using, for example, machinery that is no longer used is irrelevant to future decisions.

- Incorporating past inefficiencies: If operations were performed in an inefficient manner in the past and cost estimates are derived from this past period, they will incorporate inefficiencies.

With the development of more sophisticated techniques, there is increasing use of industrial engineering methods in measuring future costs. Using time and motion studies, input and output analysis, and production control productivity surveys it is possible to specify relatively accurately the relationship between labour time, machine time, materials and physical output. These techniques look to the future physical levels of resources and then convert them into money values instead of using past data as the basis of estimating future costs.

COST–VOLUME–PROFIT ANALYSIS

Organizations are constantly faced with decisions relating to the products and services they sell such as the following:

- Should we change the selling price, and if so what would be the effect on profit?

- How many units must be sold to break even?

- How many units must be sold to make a specified target profit?

- Should more money be spent on advertising?

> **KEY CONCEPT 15.6**
>
> **Cost–volume–profit (CVP) analysis**
> CVP analysis is a tool used by organizations to help them make decisions by examining the inter-relationships between cost, volume and profits.

The cost data used in CVP analysis will be derived from the prediction of future costs discussed earlier in this chapter.

Sales revenue

It is normally assumed in CVP analysis that sales revenue, like costs, behaves in a linear fashion over varying output levels. That is, the sales price per unit sold will be the same for all levels of output. Figure 15.10 illustrates a sales revenue function; the vertical axis represents the total sales revenue and the horizontal axis is the sales output levels. It can be seen that the sales revenue function increases in direct proportion to sales output. This is because the selling price is the same for every unit sold.

The assumption that the selling price will remain constant for all levels of sales is rather unrealistic. For example, often you will find quantity discounts being offered with consumable foods at supermarkets, e.g. if you buy one tablet of soap the price is 30p, whereas if you buy two tablets the price is 50p (i.e. 25p each). This limitation to the application of CVP analysis will be considered in more detail later.

CVP analysis: the equation

CVP analysis is based on the following relationship that can be expressed as an equation:

$$\text{profit} = \text{sales} - (\text{fixed cost} + \text{variable cost})$$

FIGURE 15.10

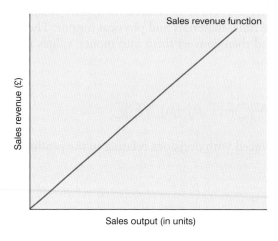

or:

$$P = Sx - (FC + VCx)$$

This expression can be rearranged as follows:

$$Sx = VCx + FC + P$$

where S is the selling price per unit, x is the number of units to be sold, VC is the variable cost per unit, FC is the fixed cost and P is the expected profit. The nature of this equation is very similar to the cost functions considered earlier. You will notice that only one independent variable is being accounted for: the activity, measured in units. Also, the fixed and variable costs are expressed in a similar way and when added together are equal to total cost. The only additional variables are sales price, which was discussed above, and profit, profit being the difference between sales revenue and total costs.

To illustrate the application of CVP analysis in decision making we consider the example of Boycott Industries.

EXAMPLE 15.1

Boycott Industries

Boycott Industries produce only one product. The following revenues and costs have been estimated for the forthcoming month:

Selling price	£70 per unit
Variable costs	£40 per unit
Fixed cost	£ 2 400

(Continued)

The management of the firm wish to know the following:

1. How many units need to be sold to break even (i.e. to make neither a profit nor a loss)?
2. How many units must be sold to make a profit of £600?
3. Would it be a worthwhile policy to introduce advertising at a cost of £1200 and to increase sales output from 300 to 350 units?
4. Should the selling price be to make a profit of £4320 on sales of 120 units?

Solution

1. The number of units to break even is obtained from the equation:

$$Sx = VCx + FC + P$$

To break even $Sx = VCx + FC$; we drop P (profit) from the original equation because at the breakeven point profits will be zero. Using the data given we have the following equation:

$$70x = 40x + 2\,400$$

Therefore, $x = 80$ units.

Proof

	£	£
Sales (£70 × 80 units) *Less costs:*		5 600
Variable cost (£40 × 80 units)	3 200	
Fixed costs	2 400	5 600
Profit		0

2. For the number of units that have to be sold to make a profit of £600,

$$Sx = VCx + FC + P$$

Using the data given we have the following equation:

$$70x = 40x + 2\,400 + 600$$

Therefore, $x = 100$ units.

3. Advertising costs £1200; sales output increases from 300 to 350 units. Rearranging the equation in 1 above:

$$P = Sx - (VCx + FC)$$

The profit for 300 units is therefore:

$$\text{Profit} = 70 \times 300 - [40(300 + 2\,400)]$$
$$= £6\,600$$

(Continued)

Advertising costs will increase fixed costs by £1200 and the profit for 350 units will be:

$$Profit = 70 \times 350 - [40(350) + 3\,600]$$

Therefore, the profit is £6900. Presumably the firm will go ahead and advertise the product as it generates greater profits.

4. For the selling price to make a profit of £4 320 on sales of 120 units, we again use:

$$Sx = VCx + FC + P$$
$$S(120) = 40(120) + 2\,400 + 4\,320$$

Therefore, $S = £96$.

The breakeven chart

A useful method of illustrating the relationship between cost, volume and profits is through the medium of what is commonly referred to as a breakeven chart.

The relationship between these variables is plotted on a graph. The cost functions and the sales revenue function, which in previous illustrations have been shown separately, are now included together in the breakeven chart.

Figure 15.11 shows the breakeven chart for Boycott Industries, using the data given earlier. You will notice that in the construction of this particular chart the variable costs are plotted above the fixed costs, resulting in a total cost function that rises from the intercept at £2400 and increases at the rate of £40 per unit. There is another way of constructing the total cost function in breakeven charts which will be illustrated later. The main advantage of the chart to management is that from the chart the breakeven

FIGURE 15.11

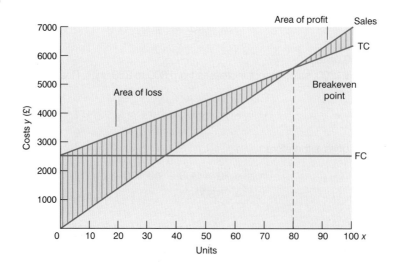

point and the areas of loss and profit can clearly and quickly be identified. This enables management to establish the effect of varying output levels that they may wish to consider. For example, the profit at an output level of 90 units can easily be read from the chart without the need to solve an equation.

The contribution margin method

The contribution margin is equal to the sales price per unit less the variable cost per unit. It is also common to find the contribution margin described as the contribution per unit. Using the data from Boycott Industries the contribution margin is as follows.

	£
Sales price per unit	70
Less: Variable cost per unit	40
Contribution margin	30

Figure 15.12 is another version of the breakeven chart, once again using the data relating to Boycott Industries.

The total cost function is constructed by first plotting the variable costs and then the fixed costs. By constructing the total cost function in this way we can identify the contribution margin, i.e. the difference between the sales and variable cost functions, as shown on the chart.

The interesting point to notice is that each unit sold will make a contribution of £30. The contribution initially reduces the loss incurred by fixed costs by £30 per unit. When fixed costs have been covered by the contribution generated by sales at the output level of 80 units (i.e. at the breakeven point) every unit sold thereafter contributes £30 to profits. For example, at the origin (i.e. no sales) a loss is made of £2400, which is the sum of the fixed costs. When one unit is sold it contributes £30, thereby reducing the loss to £2370 (2400 – 30). As sales output increases, the loss will be reduced by £30 per unit to the breakeven point where the fixed costs are now totally covered. After the breakeven point, each unit sold increases profit by £30 per unit; therefore, if 81 units are sold a profit of £30 would be made.

FIGURE 15.12

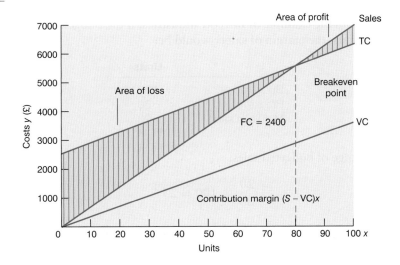

The contribution margin is an important concept and is used widely in accounting to aid managers in making decisions. We shall be examining the concept in more detail in Chapters 17 and 18.

Using the contribution margin approach, we can answer the problems posed earlier, e.g. the break-even point for Boycott Industries:

$$Sx = VCx + FC + P$$

Rearranging this expression in terms of the contribution margin, where $Sx - VCx$ = contribution margin C, we have $Cx - FC + P$, and for the breakeven point $Cx = FC$ and it follows that $x = FC/C$. Using the data from Boycott Industries, $x = 2400/30 = 80$ units.

ACTIVITY 15.4

If the selling price is £10, the variable costs are £6, the fixed cost are £400 and the desired profit is £1200 what is the number of units necessary to break-even?

$$Sx = VCx + FC + P$$
$$Sx - VCx = FC + P$$
$$£10x - £6x = £400 + £1\,200$$
$$£4x = £1\,600$$

Therefore x, the number of units to breakeven is 400.

Margin of safety

The margin of safety is the amount by which actual output, normally measured in terms of sales, may fall short of the budget without incurring a loss. It may be expressed as a percentage of budgeted sales. It is, therefore, a crude method of measuring risk that the business might make a loss if it fails to achieve budget. Using the data from the example of Boycott Industries, if the budgeted sales were 100 units and the breakeven point 80 units, the margin of safety would be:

	Units
Budgeted sales	100
Breakeven point	80
Margin of safety	20

Expressed as a percentage of budgeted sales:

$$\frac{20}{80} \times 100 = 25\%$$

A further illustration is provided in Case Study 15.1, Amex Sounds Ltd.

CASE STUDY 15.1

Amex Sounds Ltd

Amex Sounds Ltd is a company which specializes in the sale of domestic electronic sound equipment. The company purchases goods from manufacturers and sells them to the retail trade. A high proportion of the goods they sell are manufactured abroad and imported. Since starting up five years ago they have been very successful, in terms of sales and profit growth. The managing director has recently been offered an exclusive contract to sell a CD player that is manufactured in South Korea. Although it has been sold successfully in the USA it has yet to be sold in the European market.

   The company is currently assessing whether or not to enter into the contract. The following gives information relating to the estimated costs and revenues of the contract.

- A market survey has been completed with the help of a marketing consultant. At a price of £40 per CD player the estimated sales in the first year would be 9 500 units. This is considered to be the most realistic price and volume level in the forthcoming year taking account of competition.

- The price paid for each CD player will be £19.50. This includes the cost of packaging and shipment. The contract specifies that this price will be fixed for one year from the contract date.

- Variable costs, other than the cost of the recorder, are estimated to be £3.00 per CD player sold.

- The company is currently trading from a rented warehouse in Islington. However, there is very little space for further expansion. After due consideration of location and costs, it is decided that if the contract is accepted a warehouse in Peterborough will be rented and used exclusively for the sale of these CD players. Peterborough has been chosen primarily because of the relatively lower cost of renting premises and the better employment situation. The rent of this warehouse will be £46 000 per year and it is estimated that salaries will be £65 000 per year.

- Other fixed costs are anticipated to be £15 000.

The following summarizes the costs that will be incurred in selling the CD players.

	Costs per unit £
Variable costs	
Purchase price of a CD player	19.50
Other variable costs	3.00
	22.50
Fixed costs (per year)	
Rent of warehouse	46 000
Salaries	65 000
Other fixed costs	15 000
	126 000

(Continued)

In the decision whether or not to accept this contract, CVP analysis will be a useful aid. We shall therefore begin by determining the profit at the estimated output level of 9500 and the breakeven point employing the equation method and the notation used earlier:

$$Sx = VCx + FC + P$$

We can rearrange the equation in terms of profits and contribution per unit where $S - VC$ is the contribution per unit:

$$P = x(S - VC)FC$$
$$P = 9\,500(40 - 22.50) - 126\,000 = £40\,250$$

The contribution per unit is therefore £17.50 (40 – 22.50).

To determine the breakeven point in terms of units sold, we rearrange the equation using the contribution per unit approach.

The breakeven point is given by: contribution $(x) = FC$:

$$17.50x = 126\,000$$

Therefore, the breakeven point is 7200 units.

The difference between the breakeven point and the estimated sales in terms of units is 9500 – 7200 = 2300 units; this would give the company a margin of safety in percentage terms of (2300/9500 × 100) or 24% approximately.

Clearly, the information derived from our analysis will be useful in the assessment of this contract. In particular, the determination of the breakeven point gives the management of the company a basis to evaluate an element of the risk associated with the contract. Knowledge that there is a margin of safety of 2300 units will be useful in this assessment.

We now extend our analysis to consider an advertising scenario. It will be assumed that costs and revenues above remain constant with the exception of any effect on costs and revenues associated with advertising.

The company consults an advertising firm regarding the sales of the CD player. Two separate strategies are proposed:

- expenditure on advertising of £16 000 will increase the sales volume in the year to 10 300 units, or

- expenditure of £30 000 will increase the sales volume in the year to 11 500 units.

These two strategies will be considered separately and compared with the original analysis above taking into account the profit and breakeven levels.

Advertising costs £16 000, sales volume 10 300 units

The advertising costs would be classified as fixed costs; therefore, fixed costs will now be £126 000 + £16 000 = £142 000. Using the equation method we can determine the profit:

$$P = x(S - VC)FC$$
$$P = 10\,300 \times 17.50 - 142\,000$$

Therefore, the profit is £38 250. The breakeven point is given by contribution $(x) = FC$:

$$17.50x = 142\,000$$

Therefore, the breakeven point is 8 114 units (to the nearest whole number).

This proposal, we can safely say, will not be attractive to the company as profits are £40 250 – £38 250 = £2000 lower than the original proposal and the risk is greater as the breakeven point will be higher by 8114 – 7200 = 914 units.

Advertising costs £30 000, sales volume 11 500 units

Fixed costs will now increase to £126 000 + £30 000 = 156 000.

$$P = x(S - VC)FC$$
$$P = 11\,500 \times 17.50 - 156\,000$$

Therefore, profit will be £45 250. The breakeven point is given by contribution $(x) = FC$:

$$17.50x = £156\,000$$

Therefore, the breakeven point is 8 914 units (to the nearest whole number).

In this case, the decision whether to use advertising is somewhat more complex. First, the profit will increase by (£45 250 – £40 250) = £5000, which presumably will be attractive to the company. However, the risk measured in terms in breakeven analysis is greater as the breakeven point has risen from 7200 to 8914 units.

The analysis of these advertising strategies, in terms of profit and breakeven points, is clearly useful in determining whether the company should use advertising. However, it is important to appreciate that this information will only be a part of the total information necessary to evaluate proposals. For example, it will also be necessary to consider the effect on cash flows. It is likely that the company will require additional investment to support an advertising campaign and this should be taken into account.

CVP analysis: linear function – the assumptions and limitations

The cost–volume–profit model that has been examined and illustrated in this chapter has been assumed to be linear. The assumptions and limitations of a linear cost function were described earlier in the section relating to cost behaviour, and these are relevant to the CVP model.

The sales function, as was previously discussed, is also assumed to be linear and therefore it is assumed that the sales price will remain constant over all levels of activity. Empirical evidence suggests that this is unlikely for the majority of goods and services. A more realistic sales function would be represented by a curvilinear pattern. However, although the assumption of a linear function seems to be too simplistic, there is evidence that within the relevant range of activity the sales function, like cost, does approximate to a linear pattern.

The choice of employing a linear or a non-linear function to represent sales in the analysis will once again depend on the costs and benefits of the information.

In the examples of the application of CVP analysis we have assumed a one-product firm (Boycott Industries). In reality, the majority of firms produce more than one type of product. This assumption has been made because there are particular problems associated with the application of CVP analysis in multi-product firms.

There may be interdependences between the production and demand of two or more of the firm's products. For example, the demand for one product, e.g. the sales of butter, may be affected by the demand for another product, e.g. margarine. In these cases, it will be necessary to examine the CVP relationships together. This will not cause a problem if the sales mix (the proportion of sales volumes of the interdependent products) and the profit margins are the same. If the mix changes the overall volume targets may be achieved but the effects on profits will depend on whether the product with the higher or lower margin predominates in the mix.

Fixed costs represent another problem in the application of CVP analysis in multi-product firms. If the fixed cost can be identified with particular products there is no cause for concern. However, if fixed costs are of a general nature, e.g. head office expenses, these costs will have to be apportioned and/or allocated on some fairly arbitrary basis. This could be misleading and lead to inaccurate decisions.

If one or more of the resources available to a firm is scarce, there will be a constraint on the potential total sales output. The problem is how the resources should be allocated among the products. This will depend on how effectively each product uses the resource. We shall be examining this problem in more detail in Chapter 18.

SUMMARY

In this chapter, we examined the nature of fixed and variable costs, and the way in which these costs behave over activity levels. We explained the way in which these costs are measured for use in predicting future costs. In practice, important decisions will be made by organizations based on the understanding of cost behaviour and the ability to predict future costs accurately. However, it was stressed that often rather simplistic assumptions were made in deriving this information. Although the adoption of these assumptions limits the accuracy of the information, invariably we can derive reasonable approximations of the real world by using methods that may not be considered wholly realistic. CVP analysis was examined. This is an extremely useful technique in the decision-making process of organizations, although it is also limited by the rather simplistic assumptions underlying the determination of future costs and revenues over varying activity levels.

REFERENCES

Arnold, J. and Turley, S. (1996) *Accounting for Management Decisions*, 3rd edn, Upper Saddle River: Prentice Hall.
Curwin, J. and Slater, R. (2008) *Quantitative Methods for Business Decisions*, 6th edn, Andover: Cengage Learning.
Horngren, C., Bhimani, A., Datar, S. & Foster, G. (2005) *Management and cost accounting.* 3rd ed. Upper Saddle River: Prentice Hall.

FURTHER READING

For a more detailed analysis of methods of cost estimation reference can be made to Drury, C. *Management Accounting for Business,* 4th edn. Cengage Learning.

REVIEW QUESTIONS

(✓ indicates answers are available in Appendix A)

1 It is often assumed that there is only one independent variable in cost behaviour. Explain the nature of independent variables and why this assumption is made.

✓ **2** Explain what is meant by the relevant range of activity and its significance in CVP analysis.

3 Variable and fixed costs are traditionally assumed to be linear. Explain why this assumption is unrealistic.

4 What are the problems associated with CVP analysis in a multi-product firm?

PROBLEMS FOR DISCUSSION AND ANALYSIS

(✓ indicates answers are available in Appendix A)

1 In the table below, fill in the blank spaces:

Sales £	Variable Costs £	Fixed costs £	Total costs £	Profit £	Contribution £
1 000	700		1 000		
1 500		300		500	
	500		800	1 200	
2 000		300		200	

✓ **2** Clean-it plc makes washing machines and with its existing plant capacity the maximum production possible is 1 000 units per year.

Fixed costs are estimated at £18 000 per annum and the selling price of each machine is £120. Sales for the next year are expected to drop to 800 units.

The cost of each washing machine is calculated as follows:
Direct material cost £20
Direct labour cost 5 hours at £8 per hour

(a) Calculate (i) the breakeven point, (ii) the maximum profit and (iii) the profit at an estimated sales level of 800 units.

(b) alter by the following proportions:
Direct materials increase by 20%
Fixed costs come down by £6000
Direct labour costs increase by £2 per hour.
What will be (i) the new breakeven point and (ii) the new profit at the estimated sales level of 800 units?

3 Cords plc manufactures a style of corduroy trousers that it sold last year at £18 a pair. The cost specifications for these trousers were as follows:

Variable costs per pair of trousers	£
Materials	6.50
Labour	3.50
Fixed overheads per month	26 400

Cords plc made a profit of £11 040 each month.

(a) How many pairs of trousers did Cords plc sell each month?

(b) Cords plc is now planning next year's operations. The sales director is proposing to boost sales by reducing the selling price to £17 and spending an additional £3000 per month on advertising. She estimates that these actions will enable the company to sell 5 800 pairs of trousers each month. Evaluate the sales director's proposals taking into account their expected impact on profits and on the breakeven point. State any assumptions you need to make.

(c) If the managing director of Cords plc were to require that next year's profit show a 15% increase over last year's performance, how many pairs of trousers would have to be sold each month, (i) assuming that the sales director's policies were adopted and (ii) assuming that they were not.

4 The following is a summary of the profit and loss account for the latest financial year of Arnold Ltd:

	£000	£000
Sales revenue	(25 000 units at £20)	500
Cost of goods sold		
Direct material	£105	
Direct labour	£185	
	£290	
Fixed overheads Profit	£200	490
		10

The Chief Executive of Arnold Ltd is unhappy with the above results and is considering alternative policies.

(a) Calculate the current breakeven point in units

(b) Calculate the following that would be required under (i) and (ii) to:

- maintain the current profit level, and
- increase profit to £50 000.
    (i) Sales units required if price was decreased by 10%.
    (ii) The amount of additional advertising expenditure to increase sales to 27 500 units at a sales price of £20.

CHAPTER 16
ACCOUNTING FOR OVERHEADS AND PRODUCT COSTS

LEARNING OUTCOMES

By the end of this chapter you will be able to:

- Distinguish between traditional full costing, activity based costing and marginal costing and the way in which overheads are accounted for in product costing.

- Understand the importance of sharing overheads to product cost on an equitable basis using activity based costing and absorption costing.

- Recognize the impact on profits in using absorption costing, activity based costing and marginal costing.

This chapter focuses on how overhead costs are dealt with in determining the cost of products. Three costing methods are examined: absorption costing; activity based costing; and marginal costing.

The income statement summarizes all the costs and revenues of an organization over a defined period of time. Although this information is extremely useful in determining the overall profitability of the organization, there is also a need to determine the costs and the profitability of individual products.

We shall examine a number of the reasons why management requires product costing information.

- **To control costs**: Product costs will be compared with planned costs. If the actual costs deviate from the plan, management may need to take corrective action so that predetermined management targets are met in the future.

- **To aid planning**: Product costs are a useful base for estimating future product costs in the planning process. But when using past costs for this purpose, management must be careful to take account of any potential changes in the level of costs in the future, due to inflation.

- **For valuing inventories**: Product costs need to be determined so that the value of products that are complete (finished goods) and products that are partially complete (work in progress) can be established at the end of each accounting period for inclusion in the balance sheet and the income statement.

- **To aid the setting of selling prices**: The cost of products may influence the setting of prices. From a marketing viewpoint it can be argued that the price will be determined through market forces, i.e. from consideration of what the market can bear. However, in a number of situations, particularly where there is little or no competition, prices will often be set with reference to the cost.

- **To ascertain the relative profitability of products**: In times of scarce resources when a firm is constrained as to its level of output, it is likely that management will favour selling only its most profitable products. In these circumstances, knowledge of product costs is essential.

When firms only manufacture one product the process of product costing is relatively straightforward. This is because all the costs of the business are directly attributable to the single product that is produced by the firm. The complexity of product costing occurs when an organization produces more than one product. In these types of organizations, known as multi-product firms, management is confronted with two main problems. First, it is necessary to set up a system to account for those costs that can be directly attributed to individual products. These costs are known as direct costs. For example, the amounts of raw materials used to produce individual products can normally be identified and a system is required to account for this direct cost. The second problem, which is more complicated, is to account for costs that are not directly attributed to any one product. There are two terms in accounting terminology that are used to describe these types of costs – indirect or overhead costs. An example of an indirect cost is the cost of renting a factory in a multi-product firm where it is impossible to attribute the cost to individual products directly.

KEY CONCEPT 16.1

Direct and indirect costs

A direct cost is one that is traceable, and thus attributable, to a product. Indirect costs (also known as overhead costs) are those that cannot be easily and conveniently identified with a particular product.

In this chapter, we consider the main approaches used in the determination of product costs in multi-product firms; namely marginal costing and full costing. Under the marginal costing approach it is only direct costs that are included in the cost of the product. Costs that are not directly identifiable with products (indirect costs) are excluded from the cost of individual products. In contrast, the full costing approach includes not only direct costs but also indirect costs. It is argued, by those who favour the full costing approach, that to facilitate the fair and equitable computation of product costs, overheads must be included.

Before examining these approaches, it should be stressed that the need to identify the costs and revenues is not restricted to manufactured products but extends to services provided and to organizations that are purely service oriented. An insurance broker, for instance, should identify costs of selling different types of policy, for example car insurance and life assurance, to determine the profitability of the varying policies that are sold. This information may influence what policies are sold and the mix of policies. For the purposes of our analysis, we shall tend to focus on manufacturing organizations.

Under the full costing approach we will consider two methods of apportioning overheads – absorption costing and activity-based costing. Activity-based costing is commonly referred to as ABC.

We begin our analysis by examining the principles of full costing before separately considering absorption costing and activity-based costing.

FULL COSTING

Definitions of full costing

In a manufacturing organization, the costs incurred in producing and selling a product consist of production costs and other business expenses such as administration, selling and distribution expenses. The costs to be included in the full costing approach may include all these costs or just some, e.g. the production costs. The definition of full costing adopted will depend on the purpose for which the full costing of products is being used and the preferences of management. For management purposes, accounting information, as has already been emphasized, is not regulated by any external forces, such as the law or accounting standards set by the professional accountancy bodies. Management may adopt definitions and use accounting data at their discretion to meet their organization's requirements.

For the purposes of our analysis, we shall adopt the definition of full costing that only includes production costs. This is the definition of full costing that is conventionally used for the purpose of valuing finished goods and work in progress, which was discussed in Chapter 6. In the context of inventory valuations, it is argued that it is only appropriate to include those costs that are incurred prior to sale of the inventory. Normally, these costs will consist of only those related to production.

Figure 16.1 shows the flow of costs associated with the manufacturing organization when the full costing approach is adopted, where 'full cost' represents only those costs associated with production, whether they are direct or indirect costs. Here materials and labour are classified as both direct and indirect costs. For example, in the case of manufacturing labour the arrows are directed to both work in progress (i.e. directly into the production process, thereby indicating that they are a direct cost) and indirect production costs (i.e. indicating they can be indirect cost). The classification of these costs into direct and indirect, not surprisingly, will depend on whether the cost can be identified directly with products or not.

KEY CONCEPT 16.2

Full costing

The full cost of a product consists of the direct and indirect costs of production.

On some occasions, it may be more convenient to classify a cost as indirect although it would be possible to identify the cost directly with a product. Consider, for example, the labour costs of a supervisor who is responsible for a group of employees working on a number of different products. An elaborate system would have to be set up to record the time supervising each employee and then to relate this time (and thus costs) to particular products. In this case it may be considered more cost effective and convenient simply to classify supervision costs as indirect.

An example of indirect material cost is the cost of machine lubricant. Indirect costs, other than materials and labour, can typically be in the form of costs related to heating, lighting, training and the depreciation of machinery and premises (if owned). All indirect production costs will be included in product costs, so that at any point in time the value of work in progress and finished goods will consist of materials, labour and indirect costs. The cost of goods sold will be matched with the revenue from the sales of these goods in the income statement. When full costing is applied, as in our definition, the cost of goods sold will consist of both direct and indirect production costs, as indicated in Figure 16.1.

Product and period costs

Before examining the methods of full costing that are used, it is appropriate to consider another classification of costs, namely period costs. Any costs not categorized as product costs will normally be classified as period costs.

Product costs, as we have already mentioned, will only be recognized in the income statement when the product is sold. Prior to the sale, the cost of products will be shown as an asset (either as work in progress or finished goods) in the balance sheet, thereby indicating that these items have some future benefit to the business. The principle adopted here is the accruals concept. Period costs, in contrast, are seen as costs that relate to the current period in question. They are therefore viewed as costs that cannot justifiably be carried forward to future periods because they do not represent future benefits or because the future benefits are so uncertain as to defy measurement. Hence, period costs will be recognized in income statement in the accounting period when they are incurred. The distinction between product

FIGURE 16.1

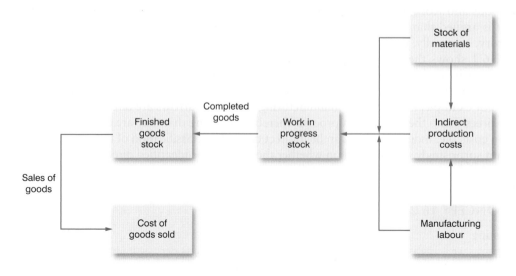

ACTIVITY 16.1

Messina Company is a manufacturing firm that produces three products. The following are the major source of costs of producing these products:

- components
- electricity
- depreciation
- production labour costs
- insurance.

Classify these costs into direct and indirect costs.
The costs would normally be classified as:

- components – direct
- electricity – indirect
- depreciation – indirect
- production labour costs – direct
- insurance – indirect.

and period costs is important in the valuation of inventory and the determination of income. We shall be examining the effect of this categorization of costs in further detail later in this chapter when we analyse the differences between marginal costing and full costing.

ACTIVITY 16.2

If Messina Company was a single product company how would the costs in Activity 16.1 be classified?
All the costs would be classified as direct.

ABSORPTION COSTING

We have already mentioned that a system has to be devised to trace direct costs to individual products. This process is relatively straightforward because direct costs can be identified precisely with a particular product. For example, when materials are obtained from inventory, the cost of these materials will be recorded against product and accounted for as a cost to the product. The complexity arises when we are to share out indirect costs to products. The objective is to share out costs equitably. The method adopted should therefore take into account the amount of indirect services used to support the manufacture of products. Traditionally, the method used to share out overhead costs to products and services was absorption costing.

FIGURE 16.2

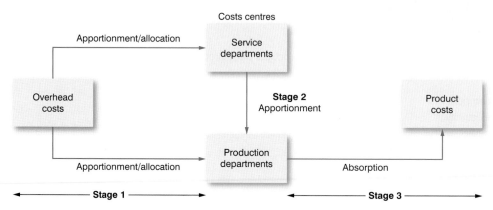

Production overhead costs will be incurred by cost centres that support the production activity. The cost centres can be divided into two categories – production and service cost centres. Production cost centres are departments where the manufacturing activity physically takes place, e.g. an assembly department. Service cost centres are primarily engaged in servicing the production function, but are not directly involved in the production activity. A 'goods in' department, whose function it is to ensure that goods and materials received from suppliers are of the standard and quantity ordered, is a typical example of a service cost centre in a manufacturing organization. The overhead costs of both the production and service cost centres must be absorbed into the product to establish the full cost of products.

At this stage it is appropriate to summarize the stages in the absorption of overheads. Figure 16.2 shows the three stages in this process.

The following is a further explanation of the stages.

Stage 1

The first stage in the absorption of overhead costs is to identify and collect overhead costs associated with both the production and service cost centres. Some of these costs can be relatively easily 'allocated' to particular cost centres. The word allocated, in the context of product costing, means that the cost can be directly traced to a cost centre. For example, in a drawing office, classified as a service cost centre because it provides a service to a number of production cost centres, the salaries of draughtsmen can be identified with the centre by recording the salary payment from the payroll against the cost centre. In contrast, the cost of heating and lighting consumed by the drawing office may not be so easy to establish. The cost of heating and lighting may, for example, be billed for the whole building, in which the drawing office is only one of many occupant cost centres. In such cases, because the cost is difficult, if not impossible, to identify accurately with any one cost centre a method of 'apportioning' these costs on a fair and equitable basis must be adopted. The term apportioning describes the sharing out of overhead costs that cannot be directly traced to a cost centre. A reasonable method of apportioning heat and lighting costs that relates to the benefits (i.e. heating and lighting) enjoyed by the drawing office may be on the basis of the area that the office occupies. For example, if the total cost of heating and lighting is £15 000 and the area used by the drawing office is, say, 6000 out of a total area of the building of, say, 30 000 square metres, the cost apportioned to the drawing office would be:

$$£15\,000 \times 6\,000/30\,000 = £3\,000$$

Stage 2

When all the overhead costs, allocated and apportioned, have been established for each service cost centre, it is then necessary to charge these costs to the production cost centres. Once again some method of apportionment will have to be used. The reason for this is that the service cost centres will normally be servicing more than one production cost centre and the costs of the service are unlikely to be easily identified with any one production cost centre. Using the example of the drawing office again, it is likely that the service supplied by this office will spread over a number of production cost centres and it may well be impractical to identify the accurate cost of this service with production departments. In these circumstances, a method of apportionment has to be adopted that fairly and equitably charges the service cost to the production cost centres.

Prior to moving to stage 3 of the process of absorbing overhead costs into products it is appropriate, at this point of our analysis, to consider an example that illustrates the allocation and apportionment of costs to production cost centres.

EXAMPLE 16.1

The allocation and apportionment of overhead costs to production cost centres

In this example, costs for various overhead 'items' are first identified and shown under 'Total amount'. The costs are then allocated or apportioned to production and service cost centres. In the case of indirect labour and materials the costs are allocated to these cost centres as they can be directly identified to the centres. With reference to the following table 'Allocation and apportionment of costs', of the total amount of indirect materials consumed (£20 000), £8000 has been directly identified with production cost centre A. In contrast, the costs related to power, rent and rates and insurance cannot be directly identified with the cost centres. Therefore, these costs will be apportioned to the centres using some equitable basis reflecting the benefits the centres have enjoyed. In the case of the cost of power, for example, the number of machine hours consumed by the cost centres is considered an equitable basis for apportionment. If you refer to the information relating to the use of machine hours in the example you will notice that machinery was only used in the two production cost centres. Of the total of 110 000 machine hours, 50 000 were consumed by production cost centre A and 60 000 hours by cost centre B. The cost of power for each of these production cost centres is then calculated with reference to the consumption by the two departments; the following shows the calculation:

Production cost centre		£
A	50 000 hours/110 000 hours × £22 000	= 10 000
B	60 000 hours/110 000 hours × £22 000	= 12 000
Total cost of power		22 000

Therefore, the apportioned charge to production cost centre A is £10 000 and to B is £12 000.

Similar calculations using different assumptions are made to establish the apportioned charge to the cost centres for rent and rates and insurance.

(Continued)

Allocation and apportionment of costs

Item	Basis	Total amount £000	Production cost centres		Service cost centres	
			A £000	B £000	X £000	Y £000
Indirect materials	Allocated	20	8	4	5	3
Indirect labour	Allocated	30	14	6	4	6
Power	Machine hours	22	10	12	–	–
Rent and rates	Area	10	2	5	2	1
Insurance	Book value	8	3	2	3	–
Total overheads		90	37	29	14	10
Service X to Prod	No. of employees		5	9	(14)	–
Service Y to Prod	DL hours		8	2	–	(10)
Total overheads		90	50	40	–	–
Units produced			10 000	10 000		

Data used for apportioning overheads

Item			Quantity			
Machine hours (h)	110 000	50 000	60 000	–	–	
Area (sq ft)	30 000	6 000	15 000	6 000	3 000	
Book value fixed assets (£)	96 000	36 000	24 000	36 000	–	
No. of employees	7 000	2 500	4 500			
Direct labour hours (h)	20 000	16 000	4 000	–	–	

The costs relate to one year.

After allocating and apportioning the overheads to the production and service cost centres, the next stage is to apportion the service centre costs to the production cost centres. The basis of apportionment chosen, in the case of the costs of service cost centre X, is the number of employees in each production cost centre. The number of direct labour (DL) hours worked by employees in the production cost centres is the basis of apportionment used for service centre Y. As previously mentioned, the basis of apportionment should reflect the benefits enjoyed by the consuming production cost centres. For example, it may be that service cost centre X is the works canteen. If so, the number of employees in each production cost centre may be a reasonable basis for calculating the amount of use made of this facility by each of the two production cost centres. The calculation of the apportioned charge to the production cost centres is very similar to the calculation described above for apportioning power costs. Hence, in the case of service cost centre X the calculation will be as follows:

Production cost centre		£
A	2 500/7 000 × £14 000	5 000
B	4 500/7 000 × £14 000	9 000
Total cost of service cost centre X		14 000

It can be seen that the whole of the costs of service centre X are now apportioned to the two production cost centres. Similar calculations will be made to apportion the cost of service cost centre Y to the two production cost centres. Finally, the overhead costs are aggregated for each of the two production cost centres as can be seen in the final line in the example.

Stage 3

As has been mentioned previously, the production cost centres are where the manufacturing activity actually takes place. Units of products will physically pass through these cost centres in the course of the manufacturing cycle. As the products pass through the centre a proportion of the overhead cost is charged to the product (or absorbed into the product). The objective here, once again, is to charge out overheads to units of production on some equitable basis. Normally an absorption rate is used for this purpose. The absorption rate is determined by the following formula:

$$\frac{\text{total overheads of a production cost centre}}{\text{level of activity}}$$

We have already discussed how the numerator in this formula is determined in stage 2 above. The denominator, the level of activity, will be chosen with reference to the types of products passing through the production cost centres and the main activities of these centres. If, for example, the particular products passing through the centre are homogeneous, i.e. similar in construction, the appropriate activity to be chosen is likely to be the number of units worked on in the production centre. In these circumstances, the activity, units of production, should represent an equitable basis for absorbing the overheads as the benefits enjoyed by each unit from the expenditure of overheads should be equal or very similar. For example, if it was estimated that 10 000 units were to be worked on in the year by production cost centre A, in Example 16.1 above, and assuming that the products were homogeneous, the absorption rate would be £50 000/10 000 units = £5 per unit. This rate would then be applied to each unit of production worked on in the cost centre and would represent a reasonable share of the overhead cost appropriate to each product.

In contrast, if the products are not homogeneous it is then necessary to choose an activity measure that corresponds more closely with the overhead expenditure of each production cost centre. If, for example, overhead expenditure of a production cost centre is mainly incurred in supporting the direct labour function, the measure chosen should be based on this activity. In these circumstances, the number of direct labour hours would probably be a suitable measure.

In practice, the most common activity measures used to absorb overheads into product costs are chosen from the following list:

- direct labour hours;
- direct labour cost;
- machine hours;
- cost of materials;
- units produced.

The following shows the calculation of the absorption rate with reference to the data given in Example 16.1 for production cost centre A assuming that machine hours is the appropriate activity measure:

$$\frac{\text{total overheads of cost centre A}}{\text{level of activity}} = \frac{\text{£50 000}}{\text{50 000 machine hours}}$$

Therefore, the absorption rate is £1 per machine hour. This rate will be applied to units of product passing through cost centre A. For example, if one of the products passing through cost centre A uses up 40 machine hours in the manufacturing process, the charge to the product will be:

$$40 \text{ hours} \times \text{£1 per machine hour} = \text{£40}$$

Predetermined overhead absorption rates

In practice, overhead absorption rates are normally determined once a year in advance of the actual cost being incurred. Hence, the two elements of the above formula will be estimates; that is, the total overheads of each production cost centre and the level of activity chosen will be based on estimates rather than actual costs.

There are a number of reasons why estimates are used rather than actual costs. Two of the main reasons are as follows. First, some overhead costs are only known some months after they have been incurred. For example, electricity costs are normally billed to consumers every quarter in retrospect. Therefore, an organization would have to wait three months before it could determine this overhead cost, and only then could it charge the cost to products that may have already been manufactured and sold. Clearly, such a delay in determining costs would have a detrimental affect on the timeliness of management information. Second, a number of overhead costs are seasonal, for example, heating costs. Seasonal variations can distort the costing of products. For example, if a product is manufactured in the summer, the cost of heating absorbed into the product cost is likely to be zero. In contrast, if the product is manufactured in the winter the cost would include a charge for heating. Hence, the cost of a product could then depend on when it was produced. It can be argued that such circumstances would distort the costing of products and would also require a firm to set up complex costing systems to reflect these seasonal variations.

The use of estimates in determining the overhead absorption rate does create problems. The actual overheads incurred in a period may not be equal to the overheads that have been absorbed into product costs because the absorption rate is based on estimates. Therefore, the amount of overheads absorbed over a period will only be the same as the cost actually incurred if the actual overhead cost of the production cost centre is equal to the estimates cost (the numerator in the formula) and the actual level of activity is equal to the estimated activity level (the denominator in the formula). Normally, any difference between the total overheads absorbed and the actual overheads incurred during a period will be directly charged to the income statement for that period. These differences in costs will not be allocated or apportioned to products, but will be classified as a period cost. The reason for this is that it is generally seen as impractical and too costly to identify these differences with individual products, but large differences may need to be investigated.

Example 16.2 illustrates the process of absorbing overheads into units of production where the actual overhead cost is different from the original estimates on which the absorption rate was based.

EXAMPLE 16.2

The following are estimates relating to the manufacture of a number of similar products for the forthcoming year 2008:

Estimated units to be produced during the year 100 000

Estimated overhead cost during the year £150 000

Therefore, the overhead absorption rate will be

$$\frac{£1\,50\,000}{100\,000\ \text{units}} = £1.50\ \text{per unit}$$

(Continued)

The actual number of units produced in 2008 was 110 000; hence, the charge to products passing through the cost centre will be 110 000 units × £1.50 (the absorption rate) = £165 000.

However, the overheads actually incurred during 2008 were £176 000. Hence, the difference between actual overhead costs and what was absorbed during the year is £176 000 − £165 000 = £11 000. This £11 000 will be charged to the income statement as an 'under-recovery of overhead' during the year, and therefore will be classified as a period cost because it is not identified with any of the units of production produced during the year.

In this example, the cost and the activity level were underestimated during the year. Differences between estimates and actual costs and activity levels will often occur, in practice, because it is very difficult to estimate precisely what the actual costs and activity levels will be in advance of the event.

Case Study 16.1 illustrates a number of the procedures and principles regarding the absorption of overheads that have been discussed above.

CASE STUDY 16.1

PHJ Machines Ltd

PHJ Machines Ltd has organized its production cost centres by the types of machines that it uses to manufacture its products. There are four production cost centres which are known by the machine type – machine type 1, 2, 3 and 4. The company desires to establish an overhead absorption rate for each of these cost centres based on a machine hour rate. The company also wishes to determine the cost per unit of one of its products XDC.

The management of the company have made the following estimates for the forthcoming year 2010.

	£	£
Indirect materials		
Machine type 1	300	
Machine type 2	600	
Machine type 3	700	
Machine type 4	400	2 000
Maintenance costs		
Machine type 1	700	
Machine type 2	800	
Machine type 3	1 200	
Machine type 4	900	3 600
Other overhead expenses		
Power		1 400
Rent and rates		3 200
Heat and lighting		800
Insurance of buildings		800

(Continued)

	£	£
Insurance of machinery		1 000
Depreciation of machinery		10 000
Supervision		4 800
Total overheads		27 600

Other relevant information (based on estimates)

Machine type	Effective horse power	Area occupied (square metres)	Book value of machinery £	Working hours
1	10	400	5 000	2 000
2	15	300	7 500	1 000
3	45	800	22 500	3 000
4	30	500	15 000	2 000
	100	2 000	50 000	8 000

To determine the machine hour rate, we must first allocate costs that can be directly identified with the four cost centres, i.e. the indirect materials and the maintenance costs. We then need to apportion those overheads that cannot be directly identified with a cost centre, i.e. those described in our example as 'other overhead expenses'. This has to be carried out by sharing out these overheads to the cost centres based on some equitable method that reflects the use made of these resources. The following sets out the apportioning of costs to the four cost centres. The basis of apportionment is indicated in parentheses against the cost item.

	Type of machines			
	1 £	2 £	3 £	4 £
Costs allocated				
Indirect materials	300	600	700	400
Maintenance costs	700	800	1 200	900
Costs apportioned				
Power (effective horse power)	140	210	630	420
Rent and rates (area)	640	480	1 280	800
Light and heating (area)	160	120	320	200
Insurance – building (area)	160	120	320	200
Insurance – machines (book value of machine)	100	150	450	300
Depreciation of machines (book value of machine)	1 000	1 500	4 500	3 000
Supervision (working hours)	1 200	600	1 800	1 200
Total overheads	4 400	4 580	11 200	7 420

(Continued)

The calculation of the apportioned costs to the cost centres in this example is similar to that shown in Example 16.1. To illustrate this computation further, the calculation of the apportioned costs of rent and rates to cost centres is shown below.

Cost centre machine type		£
1	400 m²/2 000 m² × £3 200 =	640
2	400 m²/2 000 m² × £3 200 =	480
3	800 m²/2 000 m² × £3 200 =	1 280
4	500 m²/2 000 m² × £3 200 =	800
Total cost of rent and rates apportioned		3 200

The basis of apportionment for each type of overhead cost, we can assume, has been chosen because it represents a reasonable method for sharing out the cost and reflects the benefits enjoyed by the cost centre from the resource. For example, the supervision cost has been apportioned on the basis of working hours and it is likely that this basis would reasonably reflect the benefits enjoyed from this resource by each cost centre.

Now that the total overheads have been collected for each of the four cost centres we can divide these costs by the estimated working hours of each machine to obtain the absorption rate.

Machine type		Machine hour rate
1	£4 400/2 000 h =	2.20
2	£4 580/1 000 h =	4.58
3	£11 200/3 000 h =	3.73
4	£7 420/2 000 h =	3.71
		(to the nearest penny)

An alternative system that could be adopted by the company would be to absorb the total overhead cost by the total estimated machine hours. In this case, it would not be necessary to allocate and apportion costs over individual cost centres because the same rate would be applied to all cost centres. The overhead absorption rate would therefore be:

$$\text{total costs/total working hours} = £27\,600/8\,000\text{ h}$$
$$= £3.45\text{ per machine hour}$$

This rate would then be charged to all items of production passing through all cost centres. Although this method is appealing, in that far less time is spent in calculating the overhead absorption rate, it does not take account of the resources consumed by the individual cost centres in the production process. It is therefore likely that such a system would excessively distort the costing of individual products.

Turning now to the product costs of XDC, the following information is also given: 2000 units were produced in the year. The direct costs incurred were:

	£
Direct material	870
Direct labour	940

(Continued)

The machine hours actually worked in the year producing 2 000 units of XDC were as follows:

	Hours
Machine type 1	400
Machine type 2	400
Machine type 4	200

To determine the cost per unit, we first need to determine the total cost associated with the manufacture of the product. The direct costs are given above. The overhead costs to be absorbed into the product will be based on the overhead absorption rate, the machine hour rate and the actual hours worked in these cost centres on the product. The total cost of product XDC is as follows:

		£
Direct material		870
Direct labour		940
Machine type 1	400 h × £2.20	880
Machine type 2	400 h × £4.58	1 832
Machine type 3	200 h × £3.71	742
Total cost		5 264

It is now necessary to divide the total cost by the number of units produced to determine the cost per unit:

£5264/2000 units = £2.63 per unit (to the nearest penny)

ACTIVITY-BASED COSTING (ABC)

In the use of absorption costing, as shown in Case Study 16.1, an overhead absorption rate is determined. This rate is calculated by dividing the overhead cost of a production department by a selected volume of activity. In the case of Case Study 16.1 the activity chosen was machine hours.

The absorption costing approach was developed at a time when overhead costs were only a small fraction of total costs; direct labour and direct material costs accounted for the largest proportion of the costs. Accuracy in apportioning overhead costs, because they were not so significant, was therefore not too critical in, for example, pricing decisions and inventory valuation. The situation today is very different where overhead costs tend to be more important, particularly with the advent of advanced manufacturing technology. Often in these modern manufacturing environments direct labour accounts for less than 5% of product costs. Similarly, often direct material costs are not as important as they were in traditional manufacturing environments. In today's business environment it therefore appears difficult to justify the use of direct labour or as a basis for allocating and apportioning overheads. The relative significance of overhead costs means that it is important to more accurately allocate these costs to products.

In addressing this problem, Cooper and Kaplan (1987), by obtaining a greater understanding of cost behaviour, developed an alternative approach for tracing costs from costs centres to products – activity-based costing (ABC).

KEY CONCEPT 16.3

Activity-based costing

Activity-based costing recognizes the complexity of business activities, the nature of the overheads and what drives or causes them.

Absorption costing, as illustrated earlier in this chapter, allocated to products the costs of resources that are used in proportion to the number of units produced of a particular product. Such resources include labour, materials and machine-related costs such as power and lubricants. Many resources, however, are used in non-volume-related support activities, such as setting up, production scheduling, quality control and inspection. These support activities assist in the efficient manufacture of a wide range of products and are not, in general, affected by changes in production volume. They tend to vary in the long term according to the range and complexity of the products manufactured rather than the volume of output.

The wider the range and the more complex the products, the more support services will be required. Kaplan and Cooper illustrate this relationship with an example of two identical plants. One plant produces 1 000 000 units of product A. The second plant produces 100 000 units of product A and 900 000 similar units of 199 similar products. The first plant has a simple manufacturing environment and requires limited manufacturing support facilities. Set-ups, expediting inventory movements and schedule activities are minimal. The other plant has much more complex production activities. The 200 products must be scheduled through a production plan, and this requires frequent set-ups, inventory movements, purchase activities and inspections. To handle this complexity, the support departments must be larger and more sophisticated, which results in higher costs. An absorption costing system assumes that all products consume all resources in proportion to their production volumes and tend to allocate too greater a proportion of overheads to high-volume products (which cause relatively little diversity and, hence, use fewer support services) and too small a proportion of overheads to low-volume products (which cause greater diversity and therefore use more support services).

The main ideas that underpin activity based costing are:

- Activities cause costs – activities include ordering, materials handling, machining, assembly, production scheduling and despatching.

- Producing products creates demand for activities.

- Costs are assigned to a product on the basis of the products consumption of the activities.

Steps in calculating product costs:

Step 1: Identify major activities, e.g. machining, production runs and orders.

Step 2: Collect the overhead costs in a cost pool for each major activity.

Step 3: Determine the cost drivers for each activity:
  machining – cost per machine hour;
  production runs – cost per set-up;
  number of orders – cost per order.

Step 4: Trace the cost of the activities to the product, using the cost drivers as a measure of demand.

  For example: the cost for the ordering activity totalled £100 000 and there were 10 000 orders (the cost driver). Each product would therefore be charged with £10 (£100 000/10 000 orders) for each order it required.

The following example illustrates the way in which ABC is used, and contrasts this method of full costing with absorption costing.

EXAMPLE 16.3

Johnkap Ltd manufactures two products, X and Y. The manufacturing processes for producing the two products are very similar. The following details the production data for these two products for 2011:

	X	Y
Units produced	5 000	7 000
Direct labour hours per unit	1	2
Number of set-ups	10	40
Number of orders	15	60
Machine hours	3	1

Overhead costs:	£
Cost of setting up	20 000
Cost of handling orders	45 000
Costs relating to machine activity	2 20 000
Total overhead costs	2 85 000

The company wishes to determine the cost per unit in respect of overhead costs using:

(a) absorption costing: absorbing costs on the basis of direct labour hours and machine hours; and
(b) ABC using suitable cost drivers to trace overheads to cost.

(a) Absorption costing:

Direct labour hour basis	Total direct labour hours
Product:	
X (5 000 units × 1 h)	5 000
Y (7 000 units × 2 h)	14 000
Total	19 000
Total overhead costs	£2 85 000

Therefore, the overhead absorption rate is

$$\frac{£2\,85\,000}{19\,000\,hours} = £15\,per\,direct\,labour\,hour$$

The overhead absorbed into each unit of:

$$X \quad 1\,h \times £15 = £15\,per\,unit$$
$$Y \quad 2\,h \times £15 = £30\,per\,unit$$

(Continued)

Machine hour basis	Total machine hours
Product:	
X (5 000 units × 3 h)	15 000
Y (7 000 units × 1 h)	7 000
Total	22 000
Total overhead costs	£2 85 000

Therefore, the overhead absorption rate is

$$\frac{£285\,000}{22\,000\text{ hours}} = £12.95 \text{ per machine hour}$$

The overhead absorbed into each unit is as follows:

$$\text{X}\quad 3\text{ h} \times £12.95 = £38.85$$
$$\text{Y}\quad 1\text{ h} \times £12.95 = £12.95$$

(b) Activity-based costing:

The appropriate cost drivers in this example are those which relate to the way in which overhead costs were incurred. Overhead costs are those relating to machine activity, production run set-ups and the number of orders handled.

The overhead costs will be absorbed into products based on the following cost drivers:

Machining costs £2 20 000/22 000 h = £10 per machine hour
Set-up-driven costs £20 000/50 setups = £400 per set-up
Order-driven costs £45 000/75 orders = £600 per order

Products costs:

X		£
Machine costs (15 000 h × £10)	=	150 000
Set-up costs (10 × £400)	=	4 000
Order costs (15 × £600)	=	9 000
Total	=	163 000
Unit cost £163 000/5 000 × £32.60		

Y		£
Machine costs (7 000 h × £10)	=	70 000
Setup costs (40 × £400)	=	16 000
Order costs (60 × £600)	=	36 000
Total	=	122 000
Unit cost £122 000/7 000 = £17.43		

Commentary

(i) Direct labour hour basis: None or very little of the overhead costs appears to be incurred in support of the direct labour activity. That is, overhead costs are not driven by the direct labour activity. Using direct

(Continued)

labour hours as the basis for apportioning overhead costs in these circumstances could distort the costs apportioned to individual products. From the example, it can be seen that product Y, relatively under the direct labour hour basis, absorbs an unrealistic amount of overhead costs. This is simply because more direct labour hours are worked on Y as compared with X.

(ii) Machine hour basis: Although this basis for absorbing overheads clearly takes account of the main cost driver – machine-related costs – it does ignore other cost drivers associated with overhead costs, namely handling and set-up costs.

(iii) Activity-based costing: A more realistic basis for absorbing costs because it takes account of all the significant cost drivers.

The major criticisms of ABC are:

● The resources required to introduce the system.

● The assumption is that it is activities that cause cost. It could be argued, however, that decisions cause cost or that the passage of time causes cost.

● It is easier to measure quantifiable drivers of cost because they are easily identifiable compared with qualitative drivers of cost. For example, the number of purchase orders may be identified as a cost driver and the more crucial negotiating ability of different purchasing personnel may be ignored.

ACTIVITY 16.3

The Wren Company uses predetermined department overhead rate on a labour cost basis for its Department A and a Machine Hour basis for Department B. An extract of the budget for these two department shows:

	Department A	Department B
Direct labour costs	£320 000	£ 70 000
Factory overheads	£280 000	£300 000
Direct labour hours	26 000	60 000
Machine hours	2 000	40 000

What predetermined overhead rates should be used in Departments A and B?
The following rates should have been calculated:
Department A £280 000/£320 000 = 0.875 times or 87.5% (for every £1 of labout cost).
Department B £300 000/6 000 hours = £5.00 per hour

DIFFERENT TYPES OF PRODUCTION PROCESSES

In the examination of full costing above, we have discussed the general principles of costing systems that take into account direct and indirect costs. In practice, there are a number of different types of costing systems that are contingent on the type of technology used in the production process and the type of product being produced. Traditionally, the systems are classified into two categories: job costing and process costing.

At this stage of your studies, it is not necessary to examine these two systems in detail. However, it is appropriate to give you some insight into the systems. Job costing systems will be used when the costs of each unit of production, or a batch of units, can be identified at any time in the manufacturing cycle. The examples we have looked at earlier closely mirror the job costing system. In contrast, in a system of process costing, individual products cannot be identified until the manufacturing process is complete. A number of similar products will be manufactured at the same time within the process. Costs are accumulated on a process or departmental basis and are then divided by the number of units produced to obtain an average unit cost. In such cases product costs will represent the average unit costs of production.

MARGINAL COSTING

In this chapter, so far no specific reference has been made to fixed and variable costs. Variable costs, as previously defined, vary proportionally with production. The term marginal cost refers to the change in total costs resulting from the production of one more (or less) unit of production. Invariably the marginal cost will be synonymous with the variable cost of a product and in the context of product costing we shall assume that these two terms have the same meaning.

The classification of costs that we have tended to concentrate on in this chapter is direct and indirect costs. We have defined a direct cost as one that is traceable, and thus attributable, to a given cost objective, in our case a product. In the context of a multi-product firm the only direct costs that can be identified with a product will be those costs that change when production increases or decreases, i.e. marginal costs. Indirect costs will therefore normally only consist of fixed costs, i.e. costs that do not change as production increases or decreases.

KEY CONCEPT 16.4

Marginal costing

Only direct production costs are included as product costs in marginal costing.

Earlier, when we defined product costs, in the case of full costing we said that both direct and indirect costs of production should be included in the cost. It follows that product costs, in this case, will include both fixed and variable costs of production in absorption costing. The process of absorbing overheads, and in particular the apportionment of costs, although based on clearly identified criteria, is relatively arbitrary. Often a number of bases for apportioning overhead costs are available, each having the quality that they are equitable. However, the use of these different bases will invariably result in differing amounts of costs being apportioned to products. In Case Study 16.1, heating and lighting costs were apportioned on the basis of area occupied. It could have been argued that working hours would have been just as equitable as a base for apportioning these costs. The result, in terms of the amount of costs that are apportioned to the four cost centres, however, would be very different. The cost of a product will therefore often depend on the choice of the basis used to apportion costs. Similarly, activity-based costing, although described as a more realistic method for absorbing overheads, relies on a certain amount of judgement and can also be relatively arbitrary in the way in which costs are apportioned.

It is not difficult to appreciate the argument that the use of the full costing method can distort costing and the value placed upon products. Those who support this argument advocate that the only costs that should be classified as product costs are those that are direct, which we are assuming in this analysis are only marginal costs. All other production costs, i.e. fixed overheads, are classified as period costs.

In the following chapters relating to decision making, it will be argued that fixed costs should normally be ignored in the decision-making process, i.e. they are irrelevant to the decision. This is another argument in support of marginal costing vis-à-vis full costing.

Although the argument for marginal costing of products is attractive and convenient, it implies that fixed costs are not incurred in the production process. This is clearly not true. Expenditure on fixed costs is just as essential in the manufacture of products as marginal costs. In recent years, the case for inclusion of fixed costs in product costs has gained further momentum as the proportion of fixed costs incurred in the manufacture of products has grown as a result of automation. The majority of the costs associated with automation, such as the cost of machinery, are of course fixed costs. Another argument in support of full costing is that if fixed costs are ignored the cost of products will be seen to be undervalued. For example, if the costs of a unit of production consist of £2 of marginal costs and £10 of fixed costs, the value given to this product for inventory valuation purposes under the marginal costing regime will be just £2. The cost of resources employed in the production of this unit, and hence its true value, is clearly more than £2! It is therefore not surprising that in practice firms tend to favour full costing for inventory valuation purposes.

The arguments for and against these methods of costing all have their virtues and it is not easy to resolve which method is preferable. To some extent, the method preferred is dependent on its application. For example, in the case of future decision making the arguments in favour of marginal costing as the preferred method are well documented, as we shall see in Chapters 17 and 18. However, the preference is not so clear when other applications are considered. We can therefore only conclude that the preferred method will depend on individual subjective judgements regarding the strengths and weaknesses of the two methods.

Perhaps the most controversial debate regarding the use of full and marginal costing relates to inventory valuation and its effect on income measurement. It is therefore appropriate to examine these two methods of product costing in more detail. In this analysis, absorption costing will be compared with marginal costing.

INCOME MEASUREMENT AND INVENTORY VALUATIONS

In Case Study 16.2, for clarity, we consider a firm that produces only one product. In such a situation, all the costs would by definition be identifiable with the one product and therefore would be classified as direct costs whether or not they are fixed or variable. However, in practice, the distinction between these two classifications will still be valid in this situation. The reason for this, as was previously mentioned in the discussion on overhead absorption rates, is that many of the indirect costs will only be known some months after they have been incurred. For management purposes it is often preferable to absorb these costs using estimates rather than wait until the actual cost can be determined. In Case Studies 16.2 and 16.3 we treat fixed factory overheads in a similar way to their treatment in a multi-product firm.

We will now consider Case Study 16.3, where there is a movement in inventories over the two-year period. Here the units produced are greater (2009) or less (2010) than those sold.

From the case studies we can summarize the differences between the methods as follows:

- When sales equal production (i.e. when there is no movement in inventory), marginal and absorption costing will yield the same profit. The amount of fixed costs charged to the income statement will be the same.

- When production exceeds sales (i.e. when inventories are increasing), absorption costing will show a higher profit than does marginal costing. Under absorption costing a portion of the fixed production costs is charged to inventories and thereby deferred to future periods.

- When sales exceed production, absorption costing shows a lower profit than does marginal costing. This is because the fixed costs included in the inventories are charged to the later period in which the inventories are sold.

In the long run, the profit figures disclosed by the two methods must even out because sales cannot continuously exceed production, nor can production continuously exceed sales.

The differences in profits derived from the application of the two methods can be reconciled by the following arithmetic expression:

$$\text{fixed overhead absorption rate} \times \text{the movement in inventories}$$
$$\text{during a period} = \text{difference in profits}$$

CASE STUDY 16.2

The Foot Lighting Company

The Foot Lighting Company Ltd manufactures and sells one design of desk lamp. The following are the costs of production for 2008:

Marginal costs (direct cost) £3.00 per unit

Fixed factory overhead absorption rate £2.00 per unit.

The fixed factory overhead rate is based on estimates of overhead costs of £40 000 and an activity level of 20 000 units. Actual fixed overheads incurred in 2008 were £40 000. The sales price is £8.00 per unit.

Sales and production data for 2008 in units are as follows.

	Units
Opening inventory of finished goods	1 000
Production	20 000
Sales	20 000
Closing inventory of finished goods	1 000

During 2008, selling expenses were £1600 and administration expenses not associated with production were £1000.

We shall begin by producing an income statement for 2008 using the absorption costing approach and assume that any over- or under-absorption of overheads is charged or credited to the income statement as a period cost.

Income statement for 2008 (using absorption costing)

	£	£
Sales (£8 × 20 000)		160 000
Less cost of goods sold		
Opening inventory of finished goods (£5 × 1 000)	5 000	
Plus production (£5 × 20 000)	100 000	
Cost of goods available for sale	105 000	
Less closing inventory of finished goods (£5 × 1 000)	5 000	100 000
Gross profit		60 000

(Continued)

	£	£
Period costs:		
Administration	1 000	
Selling	1 600	
Over- or under-absorption of overheads	–	2 600
Net profit		57 400

Commentary

The production and the opening and closing inventory of finished goods in this statement, using the absorption costing approach, are costed at the full cost of the product, i.e. the direct costs of £3 and the overheads absorbed at £2 per unit. You will also note that there are no movements in the opening and closing inventories during the year. This is because the units produced are equal to those sold.

The period costs are represented by selling and administration expenses; hence, they are not included in the product cost.

There is no over- or under-absorption of overheads. This is because the total overheads absorbed [£2 per unit multiplied by the number of units produced (20 000), i.e. £40 000] are the same as the actual overheads incurred during the year.

Income statement for 2008 (using marginal costing)

	£	£
Sales		160 000
Less cost of goods sold		
Opening inventory of finished goods (1 000 × £3)	3 000	
Production (20 000 × £3)	60 000	
Cost of goods available for sale	63 000	
Less closing inventory of goods sold (1 000 × £3)	3 000	60 000
Contribution		100 000
Less period costs		
Fixed factory overheads	40 000	
Administration	1 000	
Selling	1 600	42 600
Net profit		57 400

That is, the net profit is the same in both cases.

From the above statement, it can be seen that the main differences between absorption and marginal costing are as follows:

- The product costs: the production costs and the values of opening and closing inventories of finished goods consist only of the direct costs of £3 per unit.

- Fixed factory overheads are classified as period costs under the marginal costing approach and are not included as product costs.

- The summation of sales revenue less cost of goods sold represents the contribution; contribution was earlier defined as sales less marginal costs (see Chapter 15).

- Both methods of costing in this case study produce the same profit figure.

(Continued)

CASE STUDY 16.3

The Foot Lighting Company

We shall assume that the costs and sales price are the same as in Case Study 16.2 for the following years 2009 and 2010.

The sales and production data, in terms of units, for 2009 and 2010 are as follows:

	2009 Units	2010 Units
Opening inventory of finished goods	1 000	6 000
Production	22 000	16 000
Sales	17 000	21 000
Closing inventory of finished goods	6 000	1 000

We shall also assume that the overhead absorption rate, actual overheads incurred, administration and selling expenses are the same as in Case Study 16.2.

We begin our analysis by considering the absorption costing method.

Income statement (using absorption costing)

2009	£	£
Sales (17 000 × £8)		136 000
Less cost of goods sold		
Opening inventory of finished goods (1 000 × £5)	5 000	
Production (22 000 × £5)	110 000	
Cost of goods available for sale	115 000	
Less closing inventory of finished goods (6 000 × £5)	30 000	85 000
Gross profit		51 000
Less period costs		
Over-absorption of overheads (see note below)	(4 000)	
Administration costs	1 000	
Selling costs	1 600	(1 400)
Net profit		52 400

Over-absorption of overheads

	£
Overheads absorbed during the year 22 000 units × £2 =	44 000
Actual overheads incurred during the year	40 000
Over-absorption of overheads	4 000

(Continued)

The £4000 represents the amount that we have overcharged to products during the period. That is, we have charged £44 000 through applying the absorption rate, which is based on an estimate, whilst the actual overhead costs were £40 000. The difference will therefore be credited to the income statement.

2010	£	£
Sales (21 000 × £8)		168 000
Less cost of goods sold		
Opening inventory of finished goods (6 000 × £5)	30 000	
Production (16 000 × £5)	80 000	
Cost of goods available for sale	110 000	
Less closing inventory of finished goods (1 000 × £5)	5 000	105 000
Gross profit		63 000
Less period costs		
Under-absorption of overheads (see note below)	8 000	
Administration	1 000	
Selling	1 600	10 600
Net profit		52 400

Under-absorption of overheads	£
Overheads absorbed during the year 16 000 × £2	32 000
Actual overheads incurred during the year	40 000
Under-absorption of overheads	8 000

In this case we have absorbed less than we estimated by £8000 and this amount will therefore be charged to the income statement as a period cost.

Income statement (using marginal costing)

2009	£	£
Sales		136 000
Less cost of goods sold		
Opening inventory of finished goods (1 000 × £3)	3 000	
Production (22 000 × £3)	66 000	
Cost of goods available for sale	69 000	
Less closing inventory of finished goods (6 000 × £3)	18 000	51 000
Contribution		85 000
Less product costs		
Fixed factory overheads	40 000	
Administration	1 000	
Selling	1 600	42 600
Net profit		42 400

(Continued)

2010	£	£
Sales		168 000
Less cost of goods sold		
Opening inventory of finished goods (6 000 × £3)	18 000	
Production (16 000 × £3)	48 000	
Cost of goods available for sale	66 000	
Less closing inventory of finished goods (1 000 × £3)	3 000	63 000
Contribution		104 000
Less period costs		
Fixed factory overheads	40 000	
Administration costs	1 000	
Selling	1 600	42 600
Net profit		61 400

The following summarizes the differences between the net profits of the methods used above.

	2009 £	2010 £
Marginal costing	42 400	61 400
Absorption costing	52 400	52 400
Net profit difference	(10 000)	9 000

The difference in net profit over these two years is a direct result of the methods used. In the case of absorption costing fixed costs are classified as product costs and are therefore included in the valuation of inventories. When there is an increase in inventories during a period (i.e. in year 2009) the fixed costs associated with these inventories will be included in the inventory value rather than being included (recognized) as a cost in the 'cost of goods sold' computation. In contrast, when there has been a decrease in inventory during a period (i.e. in year 2010), which means a proportion of the goods sold (5000 units in our example) has been obtained from the opening inventories rather than production, the fixed costs related to these inventories are released as expenses and matched against sales. In the case of the marginal costing approach, all fixed costs during a period, because they are classified as period costs, will be charged in the income statement in the period in which they are incurred.

Movement in finished inventories	2009 Units	2010 Units
Opening	1 000	6 000
Closing	6 000	1 000
Difference	5 000	(5 000)

The following summarizes the movement in inventories over the two-year period.

(Continued)

In 2009 there has been an increase in inventories of 5000 units. Under the absorption costing approach, the fixed cost element of these inventories (5000 units × £2 absorption rate = £10 000) will not be included as a cost in the period. However, in the case of a marginal costing approach these fixed costs (£10 000) will be charged, as a period cost, to the income statement in 2009, i.e. when they were incurred. The net profit in the case of absorption costing is £10 000 more than the profit under the marginal costing approach.

The reverse situation arises in 2010. In this year the fixed costs associated with the decrease in inventories, under absorption costing, are released as costs and matched against the sales during the period. Thus, 5000 units × £2 absorption rate = £10 000 is now recognized as a cost in the cost of goods sold. These fixed costs are excluded in the case of marginal costing because they were not incurred during the year as they relate to the previous year. Therefore, the net profit calculated under absorption costing will be £9000 less than the profit under the marginal costing method.

SUMMARY

The determination of product costs for management information purposes is clearly critical in the planning, control and decision-making process of organizations. However, the values given to products depend very much on the form of costing method adopted. Three methods have been examined in this chapter – traditional full costing, activity-based costing and marginal costing. The main difference between the methods is the way in which production overheads are accounted for.

Under the full costing and activity-based costing methods, production overheads are included as a product cost. In multi-product firms overheads will always be difficult if not impossible to trace directly to products. There is therefore a need to adopt some system that equitably shares out the overheads to products. In this chapter, we examined both absorption costing and activity-based costing as a means of sharing out overhead costs to products. It is important to recognize the advantages and the problems associated with the adoption of these methods.

The marginal costing method, in contrast, treats overheads as a period cost, and it follows that the only expenses that are included in product costs are direct costs. Although this method overcomes the problems associated with absorbing overheads, it does ignore a significant element of the production cost in the valuation of cost of sales and inventories.

An example of the application of marginal and absorption costing was illustrated at the end of the chapter, applying both of these costing methods to inventory valuations. The example showed the differences in values and net profit obtained when these two methods were applied. It is important that you understand the reasons for these differences and appreciate the arguments for and against the application of the methods to product costing.

REFERENCES

Cooper, R. and Kaplan, R.S. (1987) 'How cost accounting systematically distorts product costs', in W.J. Bruns and R.S. Kaplan (eds.) *Accounts and Management: Field Study Perspectives,* Harvard: Harvard Business School.

Drury, C. and Tayles, M. (1994) Product costing in UK Manufacturing organizations, *The European Accounting Review* 3(3):443–70.

FURTHER READING

A further detailed explanation on product costing, and particularly activity-based costing can be found in the following issues of *Management Accounting:*

Drury, C. (1989) Activity-based costing, September.

Gering, M. (1999) Activity-based costing: focusing on what counts, February.

Gering, M. (1999) Activity-based costing and performance improvement, March.

Gering, M. (1999) Activity-based costing and the customer, April.

Gering, M. (1999) Activity-based costing: lessons learned implementing ABC, May.

REVIEW QUESTIONS

(✓ indicates answers are available in Appendix A)

1 Explain why it is important to determine the cost of products.

2 Define direct and indirect costs.

✓ 3 Give examples of expenditure that would be classified, in a manufacturing organization, as direct costs and indirect costs.

4 What are period costs?

5 Explain why it is necessary to use estimates in determining an absorption rate.

6 Discuss the advantages and disadvantages of applying marginal costing for product costing.

7 Explain the weaknesses of absorption costing when applying the direct labour methods of absorption in an advanced manufacturing technology environment, and suggest how activity-based costing can overcome some of those weaknesses.

PROBLEMS FOR DISCUSSION AND ANALYSIS

(✓ indicates answers are available in Appendix A)

✓ 1 Barclay plc uses a predetermined overhead rate in applying overheads to product costs on a direct labour cost basis for cost centre X and on a machine hour basis for cost centre Y. The following details the estimated forecasts for 2008:

	X	Y
Direct labour costs	£100 000	£ 35 000
Production overheads	£140 000	£150 000
Direct labour hours	16 000	5 000
Machine hours	1 000	20 000

(a) Calculate the predetermined overhead rate for cost centres X and Y.

(b) BNH is one of the products manufactured by Barclay. The manufacturing process involves the two cost centres X and Y. The following data relate to the resources that were used in the manufacture of the product during 2008:

	X	Y
Direct materials	£20 000	£40 000
Direct labour	£32 000	£21 000
Direct labour hours	4 000	3 000
Machine hours	1 000	13 000

Determine the total production cost for product BNH using full costing.

(c) Assuming that product BNH consists of 20 000 units, what is the unit cost of BNH?

(d) At the end of the year 2008 it was found that actual production overhead costs amounted to £160 000 in cost centre X and £138 000 in cost centre Y. The total direct labour cost in cost centre X was £144 200 and the machine hours used were 18 000 in cost centre Y during the year. Calculate the over- or under-absorbed overhead for each cost centre.

2 Drawrod plc has three manufacturing cost centres: Punching, Stamping and Assembly. In addition, the company has two service cost centres: Maintenance and Inspection.

The following details the estimated production overhead expenses for the year to 31 December 2009:

	£	£
Indirect materials		
Punching	12 000	
Stamping	14 000	
Assembly	10 000	
Maintenance	8 000	
Inspection	4 000	48 000
Indirect labour		
Punching	24 000	
Stamping	30 000	
Assembly	14 000	
Maintenance	36 000	
Inspection	10 000	114 000
Other overhead expenses		
Power	56 000	
Rent and rates	128 000	
Heat and light	32 000	
Insurance of buildings	32 000	
Insurance of machines	40 000	
Depreciation of machines	40 000	328 000
Total		490 000

The following are additional estimates relating to manufacturing for the year ended 31 December 2009:

	Punching	Stamping	Assembly	Maintenance	Inspection	Total
Area occupied (sq. metres)	18 000	12 000	24 000	3 000	3 000	60 000
Working hours	52 500	45 000	30 000	15 000	7 500	150 000
Book value of machines	2 00 000	1 40 000	60 000	–	–	400 000
Machine hours	51 200	64 000	44 800	–	–	160 000
No. of employees	180	150	240	30	60	660

The costs of the service cost centre are to be apportioned as follows:

	Maintenance (%)	Inspection (%)
Punching	40	20
Stamping	30	30
Assembly	30	50
	100	100

The company's bases for the absorption of overheads are as follows.

Punching	Machine hours
Stamping	Machine hours
Assembly	Working hours

(a) Calculate the absorption rates for the Punching, Stamping and Assembly cost centres (calculations to the nearest penny).

(b) Specify and explain the factors to be considered in determining whether to use a single factory-wide overhead absorption rate for all factory overheads or a separate rate for each manufacturing cost centre, with reference to the system applied to Drawrod plc.

3 The management of Absent Ltd has been studying the first three years' results of this newly formed company and are a little concerned with the figures produced. They tend to think of profits as being directly related to the volume of sales and find it confusing that for one year the reported sales are higher than those of the previous year but the reported net profit is lower.

The following figures are applicable to the years under consideration:

	2008	2009	2010
Actual sales (units)	36 000	50 000	60 000
Actual production (units)	58 000	35 000	53 000

In each of the years the estimated production volume was 45 000 units and the estimated fixed overheads were £67 500.

The selling price was £4 per unit and variable costs were £1.50 per unit for all three years.

Actual costs equalled estimated costs in all years. Selling and administrative expenses for each year were £10 000. The company had no opening inventory. The management accountant was having considerable difficulties explaining to management that fluctuations in profits resulted from differences between volume of sales and the volume of production within an accounting period, together with the system of product valuation used.

(a) Prepare income statements for Absent Ltd using marginal costing and absorption costing for each of the three years to aid the management accountant's explanation.

(b) Reconcile the net profit reported under the costing methods.

(c) Which costing method would you recommend for management decision-making purposes and why?

4 Saltwhistle plc is a manufacturing company which deals in specialist pottery products. These products vary in degree of fragility. The company makes three products – fruit bowls, table lamps and china teacups. These items are stored, after completion, then packed and distributed.

Budgeted information has been gathered for the month of June 2011 as follows:

	Fruit bowl	Table lamp	China cups
Production and sales units	6 000	9 000	6 000
Raw material usage (kg)	1.5	2.5	0.6
Raw material cost (3 per kg)	12	15	25
Direct labour (hours)	2	4	1
Direct labour (cost)	4	6	5
Number of production runs	60	135	105

Overhead costs:

- Indirect labour: the basic rate of pay is £4 per hour. Overtime is paid at time and a half, on incremental hours, when total hours in a month exceed 40 000. During June 2011, 50 000 hours are expected to be worked.

- Packaging materials: £126 000. These packaging materials are used to protect the pottery in transit. The amount used for each fruit bowl, table lamp and china cup is in the ratio 2:3:4, respectively. The ratio is linked to the relative fragility of the goods being distributed.

- Set-up costs: £120 000

- Establishment costs: £320 000

- Administration costs: £150 000

The management of Saltwhistle at present use a plant-wide overhead recovery rate, based on direct hours. However, as they price their goods on a cost plus basis, they have decided to investigate an activity-based costing approach to overhead allocation.

Additional information for the period has been estimated as follows:

(i) Indirect labour, establishment and administration costs have been identified as being attributable to each of three work areas, as follows:

	Quality control (%)	Storage (%)	Packing (%)
	Cost allocation proportions		
Indirect labour – basic	10	15	75
Indirect labour – overtime	50	10	40
Establishment	10	80	10
Administration	60	10	30

(ii) The fragility of the three products affects the time needed for quality control and packing. The storage required is related to the different size of the units. The relevant requirements per unit have been estimated as follows:

	Fruit bowl	Table lamp	China cup
Quality control (minutes)	4	7	14
Storage (square metres)	0.2	0.7	0.1
Packing (minutes)	3	6	10

Required

(a) Calculate the budgeted cost per unit for a fruit bowl, a table lamp and a china cup, under the following circumstances:

   (i) where only the basic forecast budget information is used;
   (ii) where the additional information enables an activity-based costing approach to be applied.

(b) Explain, making reference to the figures calculated in (a), how activity-based costing and the use of cost drivers may help to improve cost data in Saltwhistle plc.

5 Victoria Jonson is the marketing director of a AS Ltd, a manufacturing company that produces two products, cogs and wats. At a recent management meeting Victoria observed from the management accounts that both products have a very healthy profit margins. The company currently uses absorption costing techniques charging overheads to products at £2 per direct labour pound.

Suzy Arthurs, the new management accountant, argues that there are problems using absorption costing to charge out overheads between cogs and wats because the system unfairly allocates overheads to these products and distorts the profit margins. In particular, she argued:

● The overhead costs for machining had nothing to do with the direct labour hours. These costs were more likely to vary with the number of machine hours.

● The indirect labour included allowances for benefits, break periods and costs related to supervision and engineering staff. This overhead was indirect to the products but was related to the direct labour costs.

● The set-up overhead was generated by changing jobs at particular periods in the production process and should be related to the set-up hours rather than the direct labour hours.

● The assembly overheads are related to costs incurred in the assembly of parts. The more parts needed to be assembled, the higher is the overhead cost. Therefore, the correct cost driver should be the number of parts.

● The inspection overhead cost arose from checking the finished goods. The higher the number of finished units, the higher is the inspection cost. The appropriate cost driver should be the number of hours spent on the inspection.

The following relevant data have been made available:
Details of product costs and units sold:

		Cost per unit (£)		
Product	Units sold	Direct material	Direct labour	Selling price per unit
Cogs	4 000	20	8	70
Wats	40 000	10	5	40

Overhead activities and cost drivers:

Overhead activities	Cost drivers
Machining	Machine hours
Indirect labour	Direct labour cost
Machine set-up time	Set-up hours
Assembly	Number of parts
Inspection	Inspection hours

Estimated overhead costs and activities:

Nature of activity	Overhead cost (£)	Total activity (cost drivers)	Cogs	Wats
Machining	160 000	10 000	1 500	8 500
Indirect labour	81 200	232 000	32 000	200 000
Machine set-up time	68 000	2 500	1 000	1 500
Assembly	88 550	402 500	192 500	210 000
Inspection	66 250	4 000	1 600	2 400
Total	464 000			

Required

(a) Calculate the profit margin in terms of unit and total costs for both cogs and wats using absorption costing.

(b) Calculate the profit margin as in (a) above but using activity-based costing (ABC).

(c) Comment on the profitability of the two products from the above analysis.

CHAPTER 17
ACCOUNTING FOR DECISION MAKING: WHEN THERE ARE NO RESOURCE CONSTRAINTS

LEARNING OUTCOMES

By the end of the chapter you will be able to:

- Understand how businesses make decisions when there are no constraints of physical resources.

- Appreciate that traditional costing methods are not appropriate when making future decisions as their application will not maximize future cash flows.

- Explain the meaning and the elements of relevant costs and why they should be employed in future decision making.

- Recognize the limitation to quantitative information that is used in these decisions and appreciate the importance of qualitative elements in making such decisions.

In terms of decision making, the relevant costs and benefits which relate to the decision are future costs and benefits. These future costs can be categorized into incremental costs and benefits, opportunity costs, avoidable costs and replacement costs. In this chapter, we consider these categories of costs in relation to business problems where there are no resource constraints.

For planning, management will need to make decisions about future business opportunities to ensure that the organization's objectives are met. A large proportion of these decisions will relate to the short term and will be expressed in financial terms in the organization's budget (see Chapter 19). Management will also be required to make decisions of a more immediate nature which relate to opportunities that were not anticipated at the planning stage. To ignore profitable opportunities because they have not been specifically included in the budget would clearly be irresponsible in a dynamic business environment. These decisions can be categorized as follows:

- Decisions where there are no resource constraints: In these circumstances organizations will be free to make decisions, knowing that the decision will not affect other opportunities, e.g. the decision to introduce a new product, where the decision will not affect, in any way, the demand and production levels of other products. These decisions can also be simply described as 'accept or reject' decisions.

- Decisions where there are resource constraints: This situation occurs when an organization experiences a shortage of physical resources, e.g. a shortage of a particular material. In such cases, an organization will be unable to accept all potential desirable opportunities. To decide which of these opportunities to choose it will be necessary to implement a priority (ranking) system.

- Mutually exclusive decisions: These are decisions where the acceptance of one opportunity will mean that the others will be rejected, e.g. in choosing a particular design for building a bridge; the acceptance of one design results in the others being rejected. Mutually exclusive decisions can include situations both with and without resource constraints.

In this chapter, we shall be examining the methods used by accountants to provide information for management to make efficient short-term decisions and the application of these methods to different types of decision when there are no resource constraints. Decisions where an organization is subject to resource constraints and the make or buy type of decision will be considered in the next chapter.

The reference to the short term will be interpreted to mean decisions that will affect the firm within a period of a year. This is the convention. It will be assumed that the values of cash inflows and outflows throughout the year will be of an equivalent value. This tends to be a little naïve in that clearly all individuals and firms will prefer to receive, for example, cash today rather than in 11 months' time. For clarity, however, it is convenient in our analysis to make this assumption, as complexities arise when we begin to take account of the time value of money in the decision-making process which is considered later on in Chapter 20.

ACTIVITY 17.1

What is the effect of a short resource constraint?

The answer is: you cannot do what you want to because of a shortage of a resource that in the short term cannot be relieved. This may, for example, mean that because of shortages of skilled labour a firm may be restricted in the amount it can produce over a definitive time period.

RELEVANT COSTS AND BENEFITS

Decision making

Decisions relate to the future, and the function of decision making is to select courses of action for the future that satisfy the objectives of the firm. There is no opportunity to alter the past, although past experience may help us in future decisions. For example, the observation of past cost behaviour may help to determine future levels of cost.

Relevant costs and benefits can therefore be defined as those costs and benefits that will result from making a specific decision. A more precise definition will be established after we have examined the underlying principles of relevant costs and benefits, and considered some examples of the application of these principles.

The relevant costs for decision making are different from those used in accruals accounting. This is not surprising as the principles of traditional costing (e.g. overhead absorption methods) evolved from the need to report historical events, rather than to determine future costs and benefits. A number of methods adopted by accountants to account for decisions about the future are derived from economic theory and therefore may be familiar to you.

We now consider the principles underlying relevant costs for decision making and the application of these principles to specific types of decisions. The differences between the application of relevant costs and traditional costing will also be discussed in this analysis.

Future and past (sunk) costs

Costs of a historical nature, which are normally referred to as sunk costs, are incurred as a result of a past decision and are therefore irrelevant to future decisions and should be ignored.

KEY CONCEPT 17.1

Sunk costs

Sunk costs or past costs can easily be identified in that they will have been paid for or they are owed under legally binding contracts. The firm is committed to paying for them in the future.

CASE STUDY 17.1

Wellings plc

A firm has an obsolete machine that was purchased and paid for two years ago. The net book value of the machine, as shown in the accounts of the firm, prior to its becoming obsolete is £72 000. The alternatives now available to the firm are

- to make a number of alterations to the machine at an estimated cost of £20 000 and then to sell it for £40 000, or

- to sell it for scrap, the estimated selling price being £15 000.

(Continued)

The net book value of £72 000 represents the original cost of purchasing the machine less the accumulated depreciation (charge for depreciation over the two year period). The original cost is the result of a past decision. It was incurred two years ago and therefore it is a sunk cost. It is irrelevant to the future decision whether they alter the machine and sell it, or sell it for scrap. The depreciation is also based on the original cost of the machine and is thus irrelevant to this future decision. The only relevant costs and benefits in this example are those related to the future; we can analyze these as follows.

	Alter £	Scrap £
Future benefits	40 000	15 000
Future costs	20 000	–
Future income	20 000	15 000

From the analysis of relevant costs and benefits, it can be seen that the firm will be £5000 better off altering the machine and selling it rather than selling it for scrap.

Differential (incremental) costs

Another important principle in the determination of relevant costs and benefits is that only differential (incremental) costs and benefits are relevant to future decisions. The application of the principles underlying differential costing will be illustrated by considering in Case Study 17.2 the opportunity offered to a firm, which has spare capacity, to accept a special order. Through a comparison of the costs and benefits associated with the opportunities available to the firm, we are able to identify differential costs and benefits. It is these costs and benefits that are relevant to decisions between competing opportunities.

KEY CONCEPT 17.2

Differential costs

Differential (incremental) costs are the differences in costs and benefits between alternative opportunities available to the organization. It follows that when a number of opportunities are being considered, costs and benefits that are common to these alternative opportunities will be irrelevant to the decision.

Avoidable and unavoidable costs

An alternative way of determining whether a cost is relevant or irrelevant in decisions (such as the special order for the dressing gowns illustrated in Case Study 17.2), instead of using the differential analysis, is by asking the question: will a cost be avoided if the company did not proceed with the special order? If the answer is positive the cost is relevant and should be included. For example, consider this question with regard to the cost of plant hire for the special order above: will the cost of plant hire be avoided if the company does not proceed with the order? The answer is yes, i.e. the cost is relevant to the decision as it will only be incurred if the order is accepted. Alternatively, a cost is described as unavoidable if the cost will be incurred whether or not the decision is to accept or reject, i.e. the cost is irrelevant to the decision.

CASE STUDY 17.2

Haslemere plc

Haslemere plc manufactures dressing gowns. The current capacity is 120 000 gowns per year. However, it is predicted that in the forthcoming year sales will only be 90 000 gowns. A mail order firm offers to buy 20 000 gowns at £7.50 each. The acceptance of this special order will not affect regular sales and will take a year to complete. The managing director is reluctant to accept the order because £7.50 is below the factory unit cost of £8 per gown.

The following gives the predicted total income and the predicted income per unit, in a traditional costing format, if the order were not to be accepted.

	£	Total £	£	Per unit £
Sales: 90 000 gowns at £10 each		900 000		10.00
Less factory expenses				
Variable	540 000		6.00	
Supervision	90 000		1.00	
Other fixed costs	90 000	720 000	1.00	8.00
Gross profit		180 000		2.00
Selling expenses				
Variable	22 500		0.25	
Fixed	112 500	135 000	1.25	1.50
Profit		45 000		0.50

The management accountant with the production and sales manager is requested to review the costs of taking on the special order. These are their conclusions:

1 The variable costs of production relate to labour and materials and these will be incurred at the same rates as for the production of their normal production units.

2 There will be a need for additional supervision. However, it is anticipated that four of the current supervisors can cover this requirement if each of them works overtime of five hours per week. Supervisors are paid £10 per hour and overtime is paid at a premium of £2 per hour. There are 48 working weeks to the year. Therefore the additional costs will be

$$5\,h \times £12\,per\,hour \times 48\,weeks \times 4\,supervisors = £11\,520$$

3 Other fixed costs relate to costs such as factory rent and the depreciation of plant. It is anticipated that these will remain the same if the order is accepted.

(Continued)

4 There will be a need to hire an additional machine costing £10 000 if the contract is accepted.

5 The variable sales costs relate to salespersons' commission, and this cost will not be incurred on the special order.

6 The fixed sales expenses relate to the administering of sales. These costs will remain the same except that it is anticipated that a part-time clerk will be required to help with the additional workload if the special order is accepted. The salary will be £6000 per year.

Using the differential costing approach, we can compare the total income for the year for Haslemere plc if the order is accepted or rejected.

	Accept £	Reject £	Differential cost and revenue £
Sales	1 050 000	900 000	150 000
Factory expenses			
Variable costs	660 000	540 000	120 000
Supervision	101 520	90 000	11 520
Other fixed costs	90 000	90 000	–
Hire of plant	10 000	–	10 000
	861 520	720 000	141 520
Sales expenses			
Variable costs	22 500	22 500	–
Fixed costs	118 500	112 500	6 000
Total costs	1 002 520	855 000	147 520
Profit	47 480	45 000	2 480

From the differential analysis, it can be seen that Haslemere plc will be £2480 better off if the special order is accepted. Also, it can be observed that a number of the costs are irrelevant in the decision analysis. That is, they are the same whether or not the order is accepted; for example, 'other fixed costs' are £90 000 for both the accept and the reject decisions. Therefore, the analysis of data could have been simplified by only considering the differential costs and revenues related to the special order. If the differential analysis of costs and revenues results in a profit, from a purely quantitative perspective, the order should be accepted.

KEY CONCEPT 17.3

Opportunity cost

The opportunity cost of a resource is normally defined as the maximum benefit which could be obtained from that resource if it were used for some alternative purposes. If a firm uses a resource for alternative A rather than B, it is the potential benefits that are forgone by not using the resource for alternative B that constitute the opportunity cost. Therefore, the potential forgone benefits, the opportunity cost, are a relevant cost in the decision to accept an alternative.

Opportunity cost

The economists' concept of opportunity cost has been adopted by accountants for decision-making purposes. This concept relates to the cost of using resources for alternative opportunities.

The following is an example of the concept of opportunity costs: Basil Sums, a qualified accountant, is a sole practitioner. He works 40 hours per week and charges clients £20 per hour. Basil is already overworked and will not work any extra hours each week. A circus offers Basil £1000 per week to become a lion tamer. In the decision to become a lion tamer Basil must consider the benefits he would forgo from his accounting practice, i.e. £20 × 40 hours = £800 per week; this is the opportunity cost of Basil's becoming a lion tamer. Assuming that Basil is only concerned with financial rewards, he will accept the offer as he will be £1000 – £800 = £200 per week better off.

ACTIVITY 17.2

A firm of solicitors rents an office to carry out its work. Is there an opportunity costs in using the office?

A possible answer is: The revenue of renting the office to another firm is an opportunity cost of using the office. It is what is foregone by employing the resource.

Replacement costs

In cases where a resource was originally purchased for some purpose other than an opportunity currently under consideration, the relevant cost of using that resource is its replacement cost. This cost has come about as a direct result of the decision to use the resource for a purpose not originally intended and the need to replace the resource. The following example will help you to understand the application of this principle.

Hicks Bats Ltd has been approached by a customer who would like a special job done. The job would require the use of 500 kg of material A. Material A is used by Hicks Bats for a variety of purposes. Currently, the company holds 1000 kg in inventory which was purchased one month ago for £6 per kilogram. Since then, the price per kilogram has increased to £8. If 500 kg were used on this special job it would need to be replaced to meet the production demand from other jobs.

The relevant cost of using material A on this special job is the replacement cost 500 kg × £8 = £4000. This is because the material will need to be replaced and as a result of its use the replacement will cost £4000. The cost of £4000 will have arisen as a direct result of accepting the special order and therefore is relevant to the decision. It should be noted that the original cost of £6 per kilogram is irrelevant to the decision as it relates to a past decision and has already been incurred (i.e. a sunk cost).

Case Study 17.3 illustrates the application of the principles of relevant costs described above compared with traditional costing methods.

CASE STUDY 17.3

Hutton plc

Hutton plc is considering whether to accept the offer of a contract to undertake some reconstruction work at a price of £73 000. The work would begin almost immediately and will take about a year to complete. The company's accountant has submitted the following statement.

	£	£
Contract price		73 000
Less costs		
Cost of work already incurred in drawing up detailed costings		4 700
Materials		
A	7 000	
B	8 000	15 000
Labour		
Direct	21 000	
Indirect	12 000	33 000
Machinery		
Depreciation on machines owned	4 000	
Hire of special equipment	5 000	9 000
General overheads		10 500
Total cost		72 200
Expected profit		800

The management of the company is rather apprehensive as to whether it is advisable to incur the inevitable risks involved for such a small profit margin. On making further enquiries the following information becomes available:

1 Material A was bought two years ago for £7000. It would cost £8000 at today's prices. If not used on this contract, it could be sold for £6500. There is no alternative use for this material.

2 Material B was ordered for another job but will be used on this job if the contract is accepted. The replacement for the other job will cost £9000.

3 The trade union has negotiated a minimum wage agreement, as a result of which direct wages of £21 000 will be incurred whether the contract is undertaken or not. If not employed on this contract, it is thought that these employees could be used to do much needed maintenance work, which would otherwise be done by an outside contractor at an estimated cost of £18 500.

4 The indirect labour is the wage of a foreman who will have to be taken on to supervise the contract. A suitable person is ready to take up the appointment at once.

5 The machine which is already owned is six years old. £4000 is the final instalment of depreciation required to write off the balance on the asset account. There is no alternative use for the machine and its scrap value is negligible because of the high cost of dismantling and removal.

6 The general overhead absorption rate is 50% of direct labour. Overheads are expected to rise by £4000 if the contract is accepted.

(Continued)

With reference to the above information and the principles of relevant costs discussed earlier, we can now consider the individual items of costs that should be accounted for in the decision whether to accept or reject the contract.

1 Material A: The £7000 originally paid for the material is a sunk cost and is therefore irrelevant. We are told that the current replacement cost is £8000. However, the company can only obtain £6500 if it was sold, i.e. the net realizable value. This is the benefit the company forgoes (the opportunity cost) by using the material on this contract. Hence, £6500 is the relevant cost.

2 Material B: The fact that this material has already been ordered means that the company is legally committed to pay the supplier of the material. Hence, this cost of £8000 can also be considered as a sunk cost and is irrelevant to the decision. The only alternative is to use the material on the other job. If so the company would have to purchase some more material at a cost of £9000. This is the opportunity cost of using the material on this contract.

3 Direct labour: These employees will be paid whether the contract is accepted or not; therefore, this cost is unavoidable and irrelevant. However, if they were not employed on this contract the company would save £18 500 in fees to the outside contractor for maintenance. The £18 500 is therefore a relevant cost as this is the opportunity cost of using them on the contract.

4 Indirect labour: The cost of £12 000 for employing the foreman is an incremental cost, i.e. it will only be incurred if the contract is accepted, and therefore is relevant to the contract.

5 Depreciation on the machine owned: The cost of depreciation relates to a past cost (i.e. sunk cost) and is thus irrelevant to the decision. A relevant benefit would be the machine's scrap value. However, as this is negligible it is ignored.

6 The hire of special equipment: The cost of £5000 will only be incurred if the contract is accepted and therefore the cost is an incremental cost and is relevant to the decision.

7 General overhead: The only cost that is relevant is the increase in cost of £4000 if the contract is accepted. That is, this cost is incremental and is thus relevant to the decision. All the other costs related to general overheads are unavoidable and therefore irrelevant.

8 Cost of work already incurred in drawing up costings (£4700, detailed at the beginning of the schedule): This cost is irrelevant to the contract as it is a sunk cost and therefore should be excluded.

We are now in a position to draw up an amended statement of costs for the contract.

Relevant costs and benefits

	£	£
Contract price		73 000
Less costs		
Materials:		
A	6 500	
B	9 000	15 500
Labour		
Direct	18 500	
Indirect	12 000	30 500
Hire of special equipment		5 000

(Continued)

	£	£
Overheads		4 000
Total costs		55 000
Expected profits		18 000

In this particular case study, it is apparent that by considering only costs that are relevant the contract is more attractive to the company. In the original schedule of costs and revenues, which were based on traditional costing methods, the expected profit was only £800 compared with £18 000. It should be stressed that the higher profits yielded from the analysis of relevant costs and benefits compared with the traditional analysis will not always be the rule. The result depends on the particular circumstances of the firm making the decisions.

The principles underlying the relevance of costs and benefits to decisions, described and illustrated in Case Study 17.3, tend to focus on costs rather than revenues. However, the same principles apply to revenues. That is, only those revenues that will be generated as a result of the decision should be brought into the decision model and are therefore relevant to that decision. Relevant benefits by their very nature relate to the future. All benefits that have been received or are due to be received from a prior commitment are irrelevant to future decisions.

The meaning of relevance

Earlier in this chapter, relevant costs and benefits were defined, in general terms, as those costs and benefits that will result from a specific decision. We are now in the position to derive a more precise definition.

There are also costs and revenues that are incurred or generated by an organization that will not be relevant to a decision, i.e. will not be affected by a decision. It is important to be able to identify these costs and benefits so that we can eliminate them from our analysis.

KEY CONCEPT 17.4

Relevant costs and benefits

Relevant costs and benefits are those that relate to the future and are additional costs and revenues that will be incurred or result from a decision.

Costs that are relevant to a decision may also be:

- the cost of replacing a resource that was originally purchased for some other purpose;
- the opportunity cost of using a resource that could be used for some alternative purpose.

FIXED AND VARIABLES COSTS, AND THE CONTRIBUTION APPROACH TO DECISION MAKING

The concept of contribution was introduced in Chapter 15. The contribution is the difference between the sales revenue and the variable costs. We reintroduce the concept here in the context of relevant costs and decision making.

It is normally assumed that costs will behave in a linear fashion. That is, fixed costs are constant over all volumes and variable costs will vary in direct proportion to volume. Therefore, in a number of situations in decision making, fixed costs will be irrelevant to decisions as they will remain the same whether or not the decision is accepted or rejected, i.e. they are unavoidable. Hence, when there are no scarce resources in the making of a decision and the sales revenue exceeds the relevant variable costs, an accept decision will be made. This decision rule is applicable to a number of types of decisions.

A word of caution: there will be some situations when costs will not necessarily behave in a linear fashion, and so variations in unit variable costs or in fixed cost levels might occur. For example, the cost of new machinery specifically purchased for a future contract would be classified as a fixed cost, but it is relevant to the contract as it is avoidable. When fixed costs are directly attributable to opportunities they will be relevant to the accept/reject decision. However, unless you are given a clear indication to the contrary, you should always assume that costs do behave in a linear fashion. It should be noted that this assumption was also adopted in Chapter 15.

The contribution approach can be applied to a number of types of decisions that management must take in the course of running a business. The following examples illustrate the concept.

ACTIVITY 17.3

A research student in a business school has proposed carrying out a research project on the budgeting process of small firms. A professional accounting body is very keen to sponsor this research. However, they have stipulated that they are only willing to fund the student's expenses and travel costs in carrying out the research. These, they argue, are the only costs that directly relate to the research. The head of the business school, however, insists there should be included in this research fee a 25% mark up on top of this cost to cover the school's overheads. What are the issues to be considered in making the decision to proceed or not with the research proposal applying economic decision rules?

The following issues are relevant:

- Only the costs directly related to the research are incremental costs and therefore relevant.
- The 25% fee is likely to be based on costs that are unavoidable and further likely to be fixed costs and therefore irrelevant to the decision.

THE RANGE OF PRODUCTS TO BE MANUFACTURED AND SOLD

The management of an organization will be confronted with a number of opportunities each year and will have to decide which opportunities should be embodied within their plans. In Case Study 17.4, the products are independent of each other. We can derive a simple rule from this study: if a product makes a positive contribution it is worth considering for acceptance within the firm's production programme. The fixed costs have been apportioned to products. This is the convention under absorption costing which was described in Chapter 16. It is where overheads are absorbed into products using predetermined rates based on budgeted figures for overhead costs and activity levels. Normally these overhead costs will be unavoidable and thus not relevant, as in the example above. Overhead costs will only be relevant if they are incremental in nature.

CASE STUDY 17.4

Nelson's Oil and Fat Products plc

A firm has the opportunity to manufacture and sell three products, A, B and C, in the forthcoming year. The following is a draft summary of the profit or loss on the products.

	Total £	A £	B £	C £
Sales revenues	200 000	30 000	20 000	150 000
Variable costs	136 000	21 400	13 200	101 400
Fixed costs	44 000	3 400	7 400	33 200
Total costs	180 000	24 800	20 600	134 600
Profit (loss)	20 000	5 200	(600)	15 400

The fixed costs of £44 000 represent overhead costs which have been apportioned to the products and will remain the same whether or not all or some of the products are sold during the year.

Because of the loss shown by product B, the management propose to eliminate that product from its range.

The firm would be making a profit of £20 000 if all three products are manufactured and sold. However, if only A and B were sold, as the management suggest, the profit would be reduced.

	Total £	A £	C £
Sales	180 000	30 000	150 000
Variable costs	122 800	21 400	101 400
Contribution	57 200	8 600	48 600
Fixed costs	44 000		
Profit	13 200		

This reduction in profit is because product B makes a contribution of £6800 (£20 000 – 13 200) and the fixed costs remain the same at £44 000 whether or not A, B or C are manufactured and sold.

CLOSING AN UNPROFITABLE DEPARTMENT/DIVISION

In a dynamic business environment, organizations will inevitably need, at times, to appraise the economic viability of their departments and divisions. Although the decision whether or not to close or keep open a department/division is a very different decision from those involved in the determination of the range of products to be manufactured and sold (described above), the same underlying principles of relevance are adopted.

Invariably, in practice, there are a number of costs that are allocated to departments which are outside their control and relate to overheads that are incurred by the firm as a whole. A typical example is head office expenses, which relate to the administrative costs of running the business. These types of cost are irrelevant as they are unavoidable.

The rule to be applied in such decisions is that if a department makes a positive contribution, i.e. revenue exceeds variable costs, the department should remain open and vice versa. However, when there are fixed costs that are directly attributable to a department, and therefore are avoidable, the rule can be amended and expressed as follows: if the revenue generated by a department exceeds the costs directly attributable to that department, it should remain open and vice versa. An example of such a decision is given in Case Study 17.5.

CASE STUDY 17.5

Recaldin Engineering plc

The following are the costs and revenues of three departments, X, Y and Z, summarized in a traditional costing format.

	X £000	Y £000	Z £000	Total £000
Revenue	80	40	60	180
Department costs	24	15	46	85
Apportioned costs	20	10	20	50
Total costs	44	25	66	135
Profit/(loss)	36	15	(6)	45

The apportioned costs of £50 000 in total are unavoidable and relate to head office overhead costs.

From the way in which the data are presented, it could be argued that department Z should be closed down as it makes a loss of £6000. Currently, the total profit of the three departments is £45 000. However, if department Z were closed the profit would be reduced.

	Total £000	X £000	Y £000
Revenue	120	80	40
Department costs	39	24	15
Departmental profit	81	56	25
Apportioned costs	50		
Profit	31		

Unfortunately, in practice a number of organizations still persist in ignoring the principles of relevant costs and benefits in making future decisions. This can only distort decision making and result in organizations taking wrong courses of action.

SUMMARY

In this chapter, we have considered decisions that organizations are required to make regarding future opportunities where there are no constraints in respect of physical resources. In the context of all the types of decisions considered, it is clear that the application of traditional costing methods will not result in organizations satisfying the assumed objective of maximizing future cash flows. It was illustrated that the maximization of cash flows will only be satisfied when the principles of relevant costs are applied to such decisions. The costs and benefits that are relevant were described and are summarized below:

- future costs and benefits;
- differential and incremental costs and benefits;
- avoidable costs;
- replacement costs;
- opportunity costs.

The main limitation to the analysis is that only quantitative information has been considered. In practice many of these decisions will be made on the basis of qualitative criteria. This will be discussed at the end of Chapter 18 after examining the methods used to make decisions where there are scarce resources.

REVIEW QUESTIONS

(✓ indicates answers are available in Appendix A)

1 Discuss the reasons why accrual accounting methods are not appropriate to future decision making.

✓ 2 In the context of decision making explain the meaning of:

- sunk costs;
- differential costs;
- avoidable and unavoidable costs;
- opportunity costs.

3 Depreciation is an important concept in the determination of profit. Discuss why it is classified as an irrelevant cost in decision making.

4 In the majority of cases fixed costs will be irrelevant in decision making, but on some occasions they may be relevant. Describe the circumstances when fixed costs are relevant to future decisions.

PROBLEMS FOR DISCUSSION AND ANALYSIS

(✓ indicates answers are available in Appendix A)

✓ **1** Calculators plc manufacture and sell pocket calculators. The sales price of these calculators is £22. The company's current output is 40 000 units per month, which represents 90% of the company's productive capacity. Noxid, a chain store customer which specializes in selling consumable electronic goods, offers to buy 2000 calculators as a special order at £16 each. These calculators would be sold under the name of Noxid.

The total costs per month are £800 000, of which £192 000 are fixed costs.

(a) Advise Calculators plc whether they should accept the special order.

(b) Would your advice change if Noxid wanted 5000 calculators?

2 Spinks Ltd produce three products, A, B and C. The following is an estimate of costs and revenues for the forthcoming year:

	A £	B £	C £
Sales	32 000	50 000	45 000
Total cost	36 000	38 000	34 000
Net profit (loss)	(4 000)	12 000	11 000

The total cost of each product comprises one-third fixed costs and two-thirds variable costs. Fixed costs will be constant whatever the volume of sales.

The managing director argues that as product A makes a loss the production of this product should be discontinued.

Comment on the managing director's argument.

3 Eatitnatural Ltd is a company which specializes in the manufacture and sale of health foods. The company has just completed market research on a new type of organic toothpaste called Abrasive. The budget estimate derived from the market research for one year's production and sales, which was presented to the board by the marketing manager, is as follows:

	£	£
Cost of production (100 000 kg)		
Labour		
Direct wages	50 000	
Supervisory	30 000	80 000
Raw materials		
Ingredients X	17 000	
Ingredients Y	7 000	
Ingredients P	9 000	
Ingredients Z	1 000	34 000
Other variable costs		10 000
Fixed overheads (60% of direct labour)		30 000
Research and development		20 000
Total costs		174 000
Sales (100 000 kg at £1.60 per kg)		160 000
Loss		(14 000)

The board of directors are very disappointed with this budget in view of the research and development costs already incurred of £20 000 and the need to make use of the spare capacity in the factory. Fred Sharpe, the managing director, suggests bringing in a consultant to examine the costs of the new product.

The following additional information is available.

(i)   60% of the direct labour requirement would be transferred from another department within the company. The monthly contribution of this department (£5000), subject to introduction of a special machine into the department at a hire cost of £4000 per year, would fall by only 20% of its current level as a result of the reduction in the labour force. The remainder of the direct labour requirement would have to be recruited. It is anticipated that their wages will be the same as those transferred from the other department. In addition, it is estimated that the cost of recruitment, e.g. advertising, will cost £3000.

(ii) Two supervisors would be required at a cost of £15 000 per year each. One would be recruited; the other, Reg Raven, would remain at work instead of retiring. The company will pay him a pension of £5000 per year on his retirement.

(iii) Inventories of ingredient X are currently available for a whole year's production of Abrasive, and are valued at their original cost. The price of this ingredient is subject to dramatic price variations, and the current market price is double the original cost. It could be resold at the market price less 10% selling expenses or retained for use later in another new product to be manufactured by the company, by which time it is expected that the market price will have fallen by about 25%.

(iv) Ingredient Y's price has been very stable and is used for other products currently manufactured and sold by the company. There are no stocks available for the production of Abrasive.

(v)   Ingredient P is another commodity with a fairly static price. Half of the annual requirement is in inventory and the other half will have to be purchased during the year at an estimated cost of £4500. The materials in inventory could be resold for £4000 less 10% selling expenses, or could be used to produce another product after some further processing. This processing, which would take 2000 hours in the mixing department where labour is paid £12 per hour, would save the company additional purchasing costs of £5000. The mixing department has sufficient idle capacity to do this amount of work only.

(vi) Ingredient Z was bought well in advance and is held in inventory. It has no alternative use. Fred Sharpe is beginning to regret the decision to buy this ingredient in advance as it will deteriorate in store and may become dangerous before the end of the budget period. It cannot be sold and will cost the company £500 to dispose of it if it is not used to produce Abrasive.

(vii) The other variable costs can all be avoided if the contract is not accepted.

(viii) Fixed overheads of the company are expected to increase by £2000 per year as a result of manufacturing and selling Abrasive.

As the consultant employed by the company, you are requested to re-examine this statement, taking account of the additional information, and to recommend any necessary action. Clearly state any assumptions that you make.

4 Eno Man Ltd is currently tendering for a contract to supply Wilson Components 10 000 units of a new product Innova.

To complete the production, Eno Man Ltd would use its present surplus capacity. The company accountant has produced the following statement as a basis for establishing the tender price for the 10 000 units of Innova.

Costs	£000	£000
Material X – note (i)		50
Labour		
Production – note (ii)	74	
Supervisors – note (iii)	56	124
Variable overhead – note (iv)		12
Fixed overhead – note (v)		37
Total cost		223
Normal mark-up (10%)		22.3
Tender price		245.3

Notes:

(i) The company have enough material X in stock to produce all the requirement for the order. The material was bought two years ago at a cost of £55 000. £5000 worth of this stock has been subsequently damaged. The remaining stock cannot be sold or used for any other product.

(ii) Additional labour would need to be recruited for production purposes at a cost of £54 000. Another worker whose annual salary is £20 000 per annum would be transferred from the existing labour force. This would not affect normal production.

(iii) The additional supervisors would be required if the product were to be manufactured. One would have to be recruited from outside the company on a one-year contract, at a salary of £25 000 and a recruitment cost of £6000. The other supervisor, whose present salary is also £25 000, would be transferred from existing production personnel. As a result, the existing workshop would incur £4000 in supervision overtime. If the new product were not to be manufactured, the supervisor would remain with the company.

(iv) 80% of variable overheads totalling £6000 varies in proportion to output. The rest represents the straight-line depreciation of the machines to produce the new product. If the contract is not accepted the machines will be sold for £5000. If the machines are used to manufacture Innova then the scrap value at the end of the year will be zero.

(v) The fixed overhead charge out is based on 50% of the production labour costs. The rate covers costs such as rates, estimating and administration. Administration costs are expected to rise by £5000 if the order is accepted.

Required

Comment on the accountant's statement, making revisions which you think are appropriate and your reason for making them. State clearly any assumptions you make.

CHAPTER 18 ACCOUNTING FOR DECISION MAKING: RESOURCE CONSTRAINTS AND DECISIONS WHICH ARE MUTUALLY EXCLUSIVE

LEARNING OUTCOMES

By the end of this chapter you will be able to:

- Explain the meaning of opportunity cost and apply the concept in decision making.

- Distinguish between external and internal opportunity costs.

- Understand how to determine an optimal production plan when resources are scarce.

- Understand how to carry out a make or buy decision.

This chapter examines decision making within a business environment when resource constraints exist. Qualitative factors, that can play a significant part in decision making, are considered.

In Chapter 17, we examined the principles of relevant costs and the application of these principles in making accounting decisions. These decisions related to situations where there were no resource constraints and their acceptance or rejection did not affect the demand or production levels of any other products. In practice, however, a decision taken by an organization will often necessitate giving up other opportunities, either because of the lack of resources or because the decision is mutually exclusive (i.e. where the acceptance of one opportunity will mean that others will be rejected). In this chapter, we shall be examining decisions where there are resource constraints and the make or buy decision. The make or buy decision is probably the most common type of mutually exclusive decision that confronts organizations.

In the case of decisions where there are resource constraints, we shall be restricting our analysis to the problem when there is only one scarce resource. Decision making when there are two or more scarce resources is outside the scope of this introductory text. However, the same principles apply to this type of decision in the determination of an optimal solution. The main difference is that when there are two or more scarce resources, more complex mathematical skills are required in the computation of the solution.

In Chapter 17, in our analysis of short-term decisions, we assumed that only quantitative factors (e.g. cost and revenues) are relevant in the decision-making process. Initially, in the consideration of decision making in this chapter we shall continue with this assumption. Often in reality, however, qualitative factors will also be influential in the decision-making process. It is appropriate, therefore, to conclude our examination of short-term decision making by considering the nature of qualitative factors and some examples that will often be influential in the decision-making process in practice.

DECISION MAKING WITH CONSTRAINTS

For the situation where there are no constraints and fixed costs are unavoidable (i.e. irrelevant), as described in Chapter 17, we derived a decision rule:

All opportunities should be accepted if they make a positive contribution to fixed costs and profits.

KEY CONCEPT 18.1

Decision making with constraints objective

When there are resource constraints, the objective that should be applied is to establish the optimum output within the constraints to maximize contribution and therefore profits.

If the availability of one or more resources is restricted, however, an organization will be unable to accept every opportunity that yields a positive contribution. It is therefore necessary to derive a decision-making rule that takes account of these resource constraints to enable organizations to maximize profits.

Before considering this process to determine the optimum output, it is appropriate to examine the nature of constraints that an organization may be subjected to in the context of its operations.

Traditionally, in accounting texts, the constraints that are usually considered relate to shortages of manufacturing resources, such as particular types of materials, labour skills and the size of manufacturing plant. However, organizations in the service sector could similarly be restricted in their earning capacity as a result of such constraints. For example, it could be the case that an accounting practice is restricted as to the number of clients it can accept for audit work because of the shortage of qualified accounting staff available to the practice. The principles to be applied, when there are constraints, will be same for both manufacturing and service sectors.

The constraints described relate to the short term and can invariably be eliminated in the long term. For example, a firm has the opportunity to manufacture and sell two products, X and Y, both of which yield a positive contribution per unit. However, owing to a shortage of skilled machine operators, the firm cannot satisfy the demand for these products. Clearly, this constraint is only a short-term phenomenon as the firm could train machine operators now to ensure that there will not be a shortage in the long term. However, in the short term this will be an effective constraint on production and ultimately income.

THE CONTRIBUTION APPROACH WITH ONE SCARCE RESOURCE

In determining the optimum output, as detailed in Key Concept 18.2, it should be noted that the analysis only takes account of quantitative factors. However, it is often the case that qualitative factors will also be influential in the decision process. For example, unprofitable products may be included in the range offered to customers to maintain customer loyalty to all products sold by the firm. This should always be borne in mind when making such decisions.

Example 18.1 illustrates the stages of the process described above.

KEY CONCEPT 18.2

The optimum output with one constraint

To determine the optimum output with one constraint, we must first determine the contribution of all opportunities and eliminate those that yield a negative contribution. Second, we must establish the contribution per unit of the constraint for all those opportunities that yield a positive contribution. For example, say product A yields a positive contribution of £16 per unit and takes four labour hours to produce; assuming that labour is the only effective production constraint, then the contribution per labour hour in producing product A is £16/4 hours = £4 per labour hour. This provides the crucial information about the efficiency of the use of the constrained resource in terms of contribution and thus profitability. The next stage is to rank these opportunities, preferring those that yield the highest contribution per constraint. If, for example, product B generates a positive contribution per labour hour of £3, product A will be ranked higher, in the absence of other factors, as it yields a contribution of £1 more per labour hour. The optimum plan can then be derived within the total resources available. In the example above this will be total labour hours available to the firm in a defined period.

EXAMPLE 18.1

The directors of Fame plc are in the process of drawing up the production plan for the forthcoming year. There are five products that are under consideration: A, B, C, D and E. The following statement of the contribution per unit of these opportunities has been prepared by the company's accountant.

(Continued)

	A £	B £	C £	D £	E £
Selling price	10	24	48	13	22
Variable costs					
Materials	7	3	2	3	2
Labour	4	7	10	2	5
Total variable costs	11	10	12	5	7
Contribution per unit	(1)	14	36	8	15
Estimated demand in units	800	700	800	600	400
Labour hours per unit	4	7	10	2	5

All labour is paid at the rate of £1 per hour. The total of fixed costs for the year is estimated to be £14 990 and will not vary with the range of products actually produced and sold.

The labour position has become very difficult and it is anticipated that only 7000 hours will be available next year.

We begin our analysis to determine the optimum production plan, within the labour constraint confronted by Fame plc, by accepting all opportunities that yield a positive contribution and rejected those that yield a negative contribution. All the opportunities with the exception of product A yield a positive contribution. Product A, which has a negative contribution, will therefore, at this stage, be eliminated from the company's possible future range of products.

Before we continue, it is wise to check whether the labour constraint of 7000 hours is an effective constraint on the company's activities. We can do this by calculating the total labour hours required to meet the demand of the four products identified that yield positive contributions. We will begin with product B and follow alphabetical order:

Product	Demand in units	Per unit	Labour hours total	Cumulative
B	700	7	4 900	4 900
C	800	10	8 000	12 900

It can be seen from the cumulative labour hours column that if we satisfied the demand of only products B and C the company would exceed the labour hours it has available (i.e. 7000 hours). Hence, we can conclude that labour hours are an effective constraint on the company's level of production and that the company will be unable to accept all the opportunities available to it.

We can now calculate, for the four remaining opportunities, the contribution per labour hour by dividing the labour hours per unit into the contribution per unit and ranking the opportunities in order of the highest contribution per labour hour:

	B	C	D	E
Contribution per labour hour	£14/7 h = £2	£36/10 h = £3.60	£8/2 h = £4	£15/5 h = £3
Ranking	4	2	1	3

From the table above, it is apparent that product D is ranked first as it yields the highest contribution per labour hour (£4), followed by product C with a contribution of £3.60 per labour hour and then products E and

(Continued)

B. This priority ranking can now be applied to determine the products that will be included in the optimum plan and to establish the total contribution that is generated from this plan:

		Labour hours		Contribution (£)	
Product	Demand units	Per unit	Total	Per unit	Total
(1) D	600	2	1 200	8	4 800
(2) C	580	10	5 800	36	20 880
			7 000		25 680

It can be seen that the company is able to satisfy the total demand for product D, which was ranked first, within the labour constraint, leaving 7000 – 1200 = 5800 hours available for the production of other products. Product C is the next product preferred within the ranking order and the total demand for C is estimated to be 800 units. However, to satisfy the demand for C will use up 800 units × 10 hours per unit = 8000 hours and we only have 5800 hours available. Therefore, the company will be restricted to producing 5800 hours/10 hours = 580 units of product C because of the shortage of labour. Products B and E are excluded from the plan as there are no more labour hours available.

This is the optimal plan because it takes account of two important variables, contribution and the scarce resource – labour hours. If the production plan had been based on a priority ranking scheme that only took account of the contribution, ignoring the constraint, the ranking order in terms of the highest contribution per unit would be as follows.

Ranking	Product
1	C
2	E
3	B
4	D

The total contribution that would be yielded from this ranking order would have been as follows:

		Labour hours		Contribution (£)	
Product	Demand units	Per unit	Total	Per unit	Total
C	700	10	7 000	36	25 200

It can be seen that only product C, which was ranked first using the ranking order based on the highest contribution per unit, will be produced and sold by the company. This is because the maximum demand for product C is 800 units and because of the restriction on labour hours available only 700 units can be produced (i.e. 10 hours × 700 units = 7000 hours). The important point to recognize, however, is that the contribution of £25 200 generated from this ranking order is less than the contribution (£25 680) from using the order of ranking based on contribution per labour hour described earlier. The comparison of profitability using these two approaches clearly shows that if an organization is to maximize its profits and when there are resource constraints, these constraints must be included within the decision process.

ACTIVITY 18.1

In Activity 15.1 and 15.2 we considered the costs structure of a plumber. What do you think is likely to be the main resource constraint of this plumber and assuming that this constraint is the only one what should be the decision rule be for accepting of jobs?

The hours the plumber is willing to work is likely to be the main resource constraint to the business. Therefore the decision rule for accepting jobs should be based on the contribution per labour hour. That is, accepting the jobs within the constraint that generates the highest contribution per labour hour.

THE CONTRIBUTION PER UNIT OF SCARCE RESOURCE AND THE INTERNAL OPPORTUNITY COST

The use of the contribution per unit of scarce resource in establishing an organization's optimum production plan leads us to some interesting insights into the measurement of the opportunity cost of scarce resources. In Chapter 17, we defined the opportunity cost of a resource as 'the maximum benefit which could be obtained from that resource if it was used for some alternative purpose'. Invariably, the opportunity cost of a resource that is scarce will be greater than its purchase price. This is because there will be competing opportunities for the resource within the organization. A number of examples were shown in the last chapter where the relevant cost of using a resource (the opportunity cost) exceeded the purchase price of the resource.

The concept of opportunity cost can also be applied in the selection of products to be included in an organization's optimum production plan. We shall continue with the example of Fame plc to illustrate the application and to help us to understand further the concept of opportunity costs in this type of decision.

In the case of Fame plc labour hours were scarce, and there were competing alternative opportunities for this resource within the company. In particular, there were only enough labour hours to satisfy the demand for product D and partially to satisfy the demand for C, producing 580 units out of a total demand of 800. The contribution per labour hour of product C was £3.60 and only opportunities that yield a higher contribution per labour hour would therefore be preferred. In the case of products B and E, the contribution per labour hour was less; hence, C was preferred.

Indeed, if any new opportunities became available to Fame plc they would only be included in the optimum production plan if they generated a contribution per labour hour greater than £3.60.

Product C can therefore be described as the marginal product within the production plan and the contribution per labour hour of £3.60 as the marginal return on one hour of labour. That is, if Fame plc had one more labour hour available the return on this hour would be £3.60, or conversely, if one hour fewer was available the company would lose £3.60, in terms of contribution. In terms of the production of product C, an extra labour hour will produce one-tenth of one C, as it takes ten hours to produce one unit. Therefore, we assume here that product C is divisible, i.e. that we can make and sell one-tenth of a unit more or less of C. The following shows the increase in contribution from one more hour used in producing one-tenth of C:

	£
Selling price (£48/10)	4.80
Less costs	
Materials (£2/10)	0.20
Labour (£10/10)	1.00
Total variable costs	1.20
Increase in contribution	3.60

This computation would be the same if one less hour were to be available, but would result in a loss in contribution of £3.60.

At this stage, it is appropriate to summarize the three main points that have been derived from our analysis so far and to examine their implications.

1   If one more labour hour becomes available it will contribute £3.60 per hour. In the case of Fame plc, the contribution of £3.60 per hour will be generated from an additional 2200 hours, if these hours were available. These 2200 hours represent the number of hours that would be used in making another 220 units (220 × ten hours per unit) of product C, the unsatisfied demand of C (total demand 800 units minus 580 units that are planned to be produced within the original labour constraint). If more than 2200 hours became available, assuming there were no new opportunities, labour would then be used to produce product E, which would generate £3 per hour. The number of units of E produced would clearly depend upon how many hours became available; 2000 hours would be required to satisfy the total demand for E. If any more hours were available, these would be employed on the least preferred product B.

   This information at the planning stage can be extremely useful to managers in considering scenarios. For example, management may be unsure as to the exact number of hours it may have available, and could ask the question: if 300 additional labour hours became available, in the coming year, what would be the increased contribution? This can be quickly calculated when the contribution per labour hour is known, by simply multiplying the contribution per labour hour by the number of hours; in this example £3.60 × 300 hours = £1080.

2   If one less hour is available, Fame plc would lose £3.60 per hour in contribution.

   The loss in contribution of £3.60 per hour would continue for every hour lost up to 5800 hours; 5800 hours (580 hours × ten hours per unit) are the total hours required to satisfy the original constrained demand of 580 units of product C. This information, similarly, could be useful to management at the planning stage in considering scenarios. For example, what would be the loss in contribution if 600 labour hours were lost due to machine breakdowns during the year? Knowing the loss in contribution for every labour hour lost, the calculation is simple and quick, i.e. 600 hours × £3.60 = £2160.

3   If future opportunities became available they would have to contribute at least £3.60 per labour hour before they would be considered for inclusion in the future production plan.

   It would not be necessary, in such cases, to recalculate the contribution from each product and then to rank each product etc., in coming to this conclusion. All that is necessary is to calculate the contribution per labour hour for any additional opportunities that become available. These should then be compared with the contribution per labour hour generated from the current opportunities included in the optimum plan. If these new opportunities yield a higher contribution per labour hour they will displace those currently in the plan. Once again this information will be extremely useful to management.

From the point of view of planning the future profitability of an organization, we can therefore conclude that the knowledge of contribution from the use of con strained resources is extremely useful to management in making decisions.

The contribution per labour hour is also known as the internal opportunity cost of labour. The term internal opportunity cost is more appropriate when it is used in examining the efficient use of resources within an organization. In the example of Fame plc, labour was paid £1 per hour, but there is the additional cost of labour (i.e. the internal opportunity cost of £3.60 per hour) that relates to its use within the organization because there are competing opportunities for the use of the scarce resource. The cost of labour per hour is therefore represented by two elements of costs:

1   the cash cost of employing the labour, which can be described as the 'external opportunity cost';

2   the internal opportunity cost, which reflects the cost of using the resource within the organization itself due to competing opportunities.

These costs can be summarized in a table as follows:

	£
Cash cost of employing labour (the external opportunity cost)	1.00
Internal opportunity cost for the use of labour in the organization	3.60
Total cost of labour	4.60

The determination of the internal opportunity cost is extremely useful as it indicates how much Fame plc would be willing to pay to obtain one more labour hour.

For example, to release more labour hours to produce additional units of product C, the company may decide to offer overtime to their employees at a premium, but are unsure what premium to offer. The total opportunity cost of £4.60 per hour is the maximum the company should be willing to pay for an additional labour hour. The payment of a higher rate will result in a loss. On the basis of this information the company may decide to offer its employees £3 per hour (i.e. a premium of £2 per hour) for any overtime worked, which is £1.60 less than the maximum they can afford to pay. The contribution generated from one labour hour to produce one-tenth of product C will then be as follows:

	£	£
Selling price (one-tenth of £48)		4.80
Less costs		
Materials (£2/10)		0.20
Labour		
External opportunity cost	1.00	
Premium for overtime	2.00	3.00
Total costs		3.20
Contribution		1.60

If the company anticipated that their employees would be willing to work 350 hours of overtime during the period the additional total contribution will be £1.60 × 350 hours = £560.

In this analysis we have used the example of a labour constraint. However, the principles applied in this example are relevant to any situation where a resource is scarce: we must determine the opportunities that use these resources most efficiently.

KEY CONCEPT 18.3

Make or buy decisions

A make or buy decision involves the problem of an organization choosing between making a product or carrying out a service using its own resources, and paying another external organization to make or carry out a service for them.

MAKE OR BUY DECISIONS

An example of a make or buy decision is the decision as to whether an organization should design and develop their own new computer system or whether an external software house should be hired to do the work.

The 'make' option should give the management of the organization more direct control over the work. However, an external contractor will often have specialist skills and expertise for doing the work. As with the majority of decisions considered in this chapter, make or buy decisions should not be made on the basis of cost alone. Factors other than the costs and benefits of a decision, which are normally referred to as 'qualitative factors', will be considered in more depth at the end of this chapter.

We begin our analysis by first examining whether to make or buy when an organization has spare capacity. We shall then consider the situation when capacity is restricted because of shortages of resources.

Where there is spare capacity

We assume an organization is not working at full capacity and therefore has enough resources available to make a product or component, if it so wishes, without affecting the production of other products.

Example 18.2 illustrates the principles that should be applied to make and buy decisions.

EXAMPLE 18.2

Hughes plc is a company that is confronted with the problem of whether to make or buy three components, A, B and C. The respective costs are as follows:

	A (£)	B (£)	C (£)
Production units	*1 000*	*2 000*	*4 000*
Variable costs per unit			
Materials	4	5	2
Labour	10	12	5
Total variable cost	14	17	7

The fixed costs per annum that are directly attributable (avoidable costs) to the manufacture of the components and are apportioned (unavoidable costs) to components are as follows:

Avoidable costs	£
A	1 000
B	5 000
C	13 000
Apportioned fixed costs	30 000
	49 000

A subcontractor has offered to supply units of A, B and C for £12, £21 and £10, respectively.

The relevant costs to be taken into account in this decision are the differential costs associated with making or buying. In this example the differential costs are the differences in unit variable costs and the directly attributable fixed costs. The following is a summary of the relevant costs.

(Continued)

	A £	B £	C £
Variable cost per unit, making	14	17	7
Cost per unit, buying	12	21	10
Additional cost per unit of buying	(2)	4	3
Production units per annum	1 000	2 000	4 000

	£	£	£
Additional total variable cost of buying	(2 000)	8 000	12 000
Fixed costs saved by buying	1 000	5 000	13 000
Additional total cost of buying	(3 000)	3 000	(1 000)

The organization would therefore save £3000 per annum by subcontracting component A (this is because the variable cost per unit to make the component is greater than the purchase price) and £1000 per annum by subcontracting component C (this is due to the saving of £13 000 of fixed costs directly attributable to making the component). In the case of component B, the organization will be £3000 better off making the component.

It should also be noted that the apportioned fixed costs are irrelevant because they are unavoidable to this decision.

In such decisions there will normally be another consideration that is relevant. If components A and C are to be purchased from a subcontractor it is likely that the organization will have spare capacity. It is also likely that this spare capacity has some value to the organization; for example, it may decide to let the space to an outside party which would generate additional income. This additional income should then be included as a relevant cost of making the components as the revenue will be forgone if the component is made. It is an opportunity cost.

As mentioned previously, in these types of decisions there will inevitably be other qualitative factors that should be taken into account. In this example, the organization may be apprehensive about the quality of the work of the subcontractor. This factor may lead the organization to favour making components A and C, although in cost terms this policy would be unprofitable.

Where there is no spare capacity

A firm may be confronted with the decision whether to make or buy a component when it is currently working at full capacity. To make the component, it will be necessary for the firm to stop or restrict its current production output. In such cases the cost of making must include not only the costs directly attributed to making but also the loss in contribution of the production that has been displaced by the decision to make. The loss in contribution is the internal opportunity cost, which was discussed earlier.

Example 18.3 illustrates the application of the concept of the internal opportunity cost in the make or buy decision when capacity is restricted.

EXAMPLE 18.3

Lee plc is in the process of deciding whether to make or buy a component that is to be embodied in one of the products it manufactures and sells. Labour is in short supply and the factory is currently working at full capacity. The following are the estimated costs per unit to make the component:

(Continued)

	£
Direct labour (5 hours at £4 per hour)	20
Direct material	15
Fixed overheads	5
Total cost per unit	40

The fixed overhead costs are apportioned to the product and will be unavoidable whether or not the component is made. Hence, the cost is irrelevant to the decision whether to make or buy. All the other costs are directly attributable to the cost of producing the component and are therefore relevant. The relevant cost associated with making the component is therefore £35.

The alternative is to buy in the component from another firm. The cost of buying the component is £38 per unit.

If labour was not in short supply, the firm should make the component rather than buying it because the relevant costs of making (£35) are less than the purchase price of buying (£38).

However, in view of the shortage of labour, we must consider the contribution forgone by the decision to make. To do so we must account for the contribution generated from the current production activity that is to be restricted in opting to make the component. The following data relate to the revenue and cost per unit associated with a product that is to be displaced by producing (making) the component:

	£	£
Selling price		26
Less costs		
Direct labour (3 hours at £4 per hour)	12	
Direct material	8	20
Contribution per unit		6

The contribution per hour of labour generated from this product is £2 (i.e. contribution £6 divided by 3 hours of labour time). This is the internal opportunity cost of using the labour on the manufacture of this product. If labour is to be efficiently diverted to making the component instead of this product it must therefore yield a contribution of at least £2 per hour. We can also conclude that the effective cost of labour employed on making the component consists of two elements: the cash paid to employees for their labour of £4 per hour (i.e. the external opportunity cost) plus the internal opportunity cost of £2 per hour. These two elements of cost should therefore be included in the calculation to decide whether to make or buy the component. The following summarizes all the relevant costs in making the components:

	£	£
Direct labour		
Cash paid to employees (the external opportunity cost) £4 × 5 hours	20	
Internal opportunity cost £2 × 5 hours	10	30
Direct materials		15
Total relevant costs		45

The inclusion of the internal opportunity cost as a relevant cost to the decision to make has resulted in a cost for making the component of £45. This exceeds the buying price of £38; hence, purely on financial grounds the decision should be to buy rather than make.

The principle that the internal opportunity cost should be included in the relevant costs of a make or buy decision applies to all situations where there is no spare capacity because resources are scarce.

QUALITATIVE FACTORS

In our analysis of decision making in this and the last chapter, all the decisions made were based only on financial criteria. Often, however, qualitative factors will be of great influence in such decisions. Indeed, on some occasions an opportunity would be rejected on purely quantitative (financial) criteria but for other reasons, primarily of a qualitative nature, the opportunity is accepted.

Qualitative factors are factors which cannot be quantified in terms of costs and income. They may stem from either non-financial objectives or factors which could be quantified in money terms but have not been because there is insufficient information to make a reliable estimate.

The nature of these qualitative factors will vary with the circumstances under consideration. The following are some examples of qualitative factors that may influence decisions.

Customers

The inclusion or exclusion of a product from the range offered or the quality of the product and after-sales service will invariably affect demand for the product and customer loyalty. For example, the exclusion of one product from a range because it is uneconomic to produce and sell could affect the demand for other products. Products manufactured by firms are often interdependent and this interdependence can be calculated before a decision is made.

Employees

Decisions involving the closure of part of a firm or relocation or changes in work procedures will require acceptance by the employees. If the changes are mishandled, bad labour relations could lead to inefficiencies and losses.

Competitors

In a competitive market, decisions by one firm to enhance their competitive advantage may result in retaliation by competitors. For example, the decision to reduce selling prices in order to raise demand will not be successful if all competitors take similar action.

A firm may decide to produce an unprofitable product or to offer a service at a loss because otherwise it would be leaving the market for competitors to enjoy. The firm considers that continued service to customers will eventually affect the demand for its other products.

Legal constraints

An opportunity may occasionally be rejected because of doubts about pending legislation. The decision to open a hotel, for example, may be influenced by pending legislation on safety requirements that would result in additional costs which are too complex to estimate.

Suppliers

A firm may rely heavily on a good relationship with a particular supplier for the prompt delivery of supplies. Some decisions may affect that supplier and the relationship must be considered in any decision.

ACTIVITY 18.2

In Example 18.3, Lee plc was making a decision on whether to make or buy in a component. What other factors other than cost and price should the company take into account in making the decision?

The following are some of the factors that are likely to influence the company in making the decision:

- The quality of the bought in component.
- The possibility of losing the skills and know how of making the component.
- The good relationship with the company's suppliers could be affected by the decrease in purchases of parts and materials due to the production in-house of the component.
- The possibility that the supplier of the component cannot deliver on time and meet orders.

SUMMARY

In this chapter, we have developed a number of the concepts introduced in Chapter 17. In particular, the concept of opportunity cost was examined and the two elements of cost – the external and internal opportunity costs – were identified.

The concept of opportunity cost was shown to be a very powerful tool in determining the optimal production plan when an organization is experiencing a shortage of resources. In particular, it ensures that scarce resources are used efficiently.

Lastly, in this chapter we examined the nature of the qualitative factors that may influence decisions. A number of examples were given which illustrate their importance in the decision-making process.

FURTHER READING

An excellent analysis of decision making when there is more than one constraint can be found in Chapters 10 and 11 of *Accounting for Management Decisions* by J. Arnold and S. Turley (Prentice Hall International, 3rd edn, 1996).

REVIEW QUESTIONS

(✓ indicates answers are available in Appendix A)

✓ 1 Many organizations, at particular times, will be subject to shortages of resources. These shortages will effectively restrict their ability to meet the demand for their products or services. Describe four examples of these types of constraints, two from a manufacturing firm and two from a service firm.

2 Explain why a shortage of resources in an organization is a short-term phenomenon.

3 Discuss the importance and usefulness of the concept of internal opportunity cost in the making of decisions.

4 The opportunity cost of a resource, in some circumstances, may be higher than the resource's purchase price. Explain why this may be the case.

5 Qualitative factors are often influential in the decision-making process. Describe the nature of qualitative factors and give three examples that may influence a decision to make a component rather than buying it from another firm.

PROBLEMS FOR DISCUSSION AND ANALYSIS

(✓ indicates answers are available in Appendix A)

✓ **1** Coyle plc at present manufactures all the components that go to make up its finished products. A salesman from a components supplier has just offered to provide the firm's requirements for two components, the BC100 at £7.75 each and the BC200 at £2.00 each. If the firm buys in components the capacity utilized for these components at present would be unused. The firm currently manufactures 50 000 units of each component and the current costs of production are as follows:

	BC100 £	BC200 £
Materials	2.50	1.00
Labour	3.00	1.25
Fixed overheads	3.50	1.75
Total cost per unit	9.00	4.00

(a) On a quantitative basis, should the firm continue to manufacture BC100 and BC200 or should it buy in both or either of the components?

(b) Discuss the qualitative factors which are likely to have an influence on this decision.

✓ **2** Pigeon Proprietary Ltd proposes a production plan for 2008, aiming to maximize profits. The following details are available:

Product	A £	B £	C £	D £	E £	F £
Selling price	20	28	8	36	16	40
Costs Direct labour	4	4	1.2	2.4	2.8	1.6
Direct materials	4	6	2.4	8.8	3.6	3.2
Fixed overheads	4	6	2.4	8.8	3.6	3.2
Total cost	12	16	6.0	20.0	10.0	8.0
Profit	8	12	2.0	16.0	6.0	32.0
Labour hours per unit	6.4	7	4	9	5	12
Machine hours per unit	3	2	1	3	1	8
Maximum demand	2 500	1 200	700	1 100	900	2 900

Fixed overhead, which is estimated to cost £10 000 irrespective of what is produced and sold, is applied at 100% of direct labour cost.

A maximum of 64 000 direct labour hours is expected to be available.

(a) Calculate the optimal profit-maximizing production plan and explain the reasons for your choice.

(b) Explain the following hypothetical internal opportunity costs:

- direct labour hours £2.40;
- machine hours £1.70.

3 You have recently been appointed as a consultant to the Murphy Manufacturing Company. The management of the company had prepared a report showing certain data concerning the two products, Mox and Tox. The following information has been extracted from this report.

	Mox £	Tox £
Selling price	3.0	1.5
Costs		
Direct materials	0.8	0.5
Direct labour	1.0	0.2
Fixed overheads	1.4	0.5
Total cost	3.2	1.2
Profit/(loss)	(0.2)	0.3
Monthly sales in units	1 000	2 000

In view of the poor results shown by Mox, the following changes have been proposed by the management:

(i) Abandon the production of Mox and buy in 1000 per month for £2800. The quality is identical and selling price will remain unchanged.

(ii) Use the spare capacity to make Tox. It is estimated that 1000 units could be sold at £1 each. Material costs are £0.40 per unit and labour costs £0.20.

All overheads are fixed and are not expected to change from the present cost of £2000 per month. No stocks are held.

(a) Comment on the suitability of the management's statement for assessing product profitability and indicate any ways in which you think it could be improved.

(b) Prepare a monthly profit and loss statement for the present and proposed new programmes. Do the proposed changes appear to be profitable? Explain the reasons for any misunderstandings which may have arisen as a result of the management's proposal.

4 Burco Ltd produces and sells two products, X and Y. During the last year 700 labour hours were worked and the operating results were as follows.

	X 1 000	Y 1 000	Total 2 000
Units sold	**£**	**£**	**£**
Sales	1 000	2 000	3 000
Variable costs			
Labour	200	500	700
Materials	550	900	1 450
Total variable costs	750	1 400	2 150
Contribution	250	600	850
Fixed costs			600
Net income			250

All variable costs are a linear function of output. The material used for X is completely different from that used for Y but both may be produced with the same labour force.

Five units of X can be made in one labour hour, whereas only two units of Y can be made in one labour hour. Labour hours are expected to be limited to 800 next year.

The following information about the market for X and Y for next year is available:

	X	Y
Maximum quantity that may be sold next year (units)	1 100	1 200
Minimum quantity that must be sold next year to retain market (units)	600	800

(a) Assuming plant capacity is fully used, what is the optimum mix of X and Y?

(b) Assuming that the price of material for Y decreases by 20%, what is the optimal mix of X and Y? Do not assume any change in the price of X or Y.

(c) Assuming that the cost of labour increases by 20%, prices can only be put up by 10% without affecting sales limits and the number of labour hours available is reduced to 600, what is the optimal mix of X and Y?

(d) What is the net income in each case for scenario (a), (b) and (c) above?

(e) Discuss the limitations of your analysis.

CHAPTER 19
BUDGETS

LEARNING OUTCOMES

By the end of this chapter you will be able to:

- Understand the main purposes of budgets.

- Explain the relationship between the various conventional budgets.

- Construct budgets for various planning objectives.

- Understand the role of flexible budgets in the planning and control process.

- Appreciate that budgets can create conflicts between personnel in the business.

The main focus of this chapter is on short-term planning. Budgets are the medium by which these short plans are operationalized within a business environment. The budget process is examined with associated contingent factors such as the level and type of technology. Finally, the chapter considers the concept of flexed budgets which are a important element of the control process.

In Chapter 14, Planning and control, four stages of the planning and control process were identified. The third stage, which was described as 'Making operating decisions', focused on the use of resources and the individual decisions necessary to use these resources consistently within the overall objectives of an organization. In this stage it was also stated that the decisions would be translated into a short-term plan, normally referred to as a 'budget'. Budgets were defined as 'plans of action expressed in monetary terms'. In this chapter, we shall be examining the purpose of budgets, the budgeting process with the context of preparing budgets. Budgets are also the starting place in the control process as explained in Chapter 14. This chapter also examines the flexing of budgets so that they can be effectively used in the control process.

It should be stressed that different types of organization will require different types of budgets to enable them to function effectively. The budget must match the organization's particular situation. In Chapter 14, we mentioned the application of contingency theory to all accounting information systems. The major contingency factors identified were technology, the environment and the structure of the organization. Similarly, these factors will affect the type of budget to be employed in an organization. To illustrate this point, we can briefly compare the information content and design of a retail organization's budget with that of a manufacturing organization. In a retail organization, the budget will deal mainly with the level of consumer sales and the purchases of goods necessary to satisfy these sales. In contrast, the budget of a manufacturing organization will tend to focus on the sales of products that will be manufactured and the production activity necessary to meet these sales. However, there will be some similarities between the two types of budget and a common basis for preparing the budget of different types of organization. We shall concentrate, in this chapter, on large manufacturing organizations, which traditionally have relatively sophisticated budgets.

THE PURPOSE OF BUDGETS

Below are listed a number of the traditional purposes of budgets. Although we said earlier that budgets, and thus the purpose of budgets, will depend on the type of organization, those given below are appropriate to most organizations.

To compel planning

The introduction of budgets within an organization forces management to look ahead and set short-term targets. By looking to the future, management are then in a good position to anticipate potential problems. For example, the identification of shortages of cash at particular times in the budget period will give management the opportunity to ensure that provisions are made to supplement this shortage, e.g. to negotiate an overdraft facility with their bank.

Coordination of the different functions within an organization

The preparation of budgets will tend to increase the coordination between different departments and units within an organization as it is essential that the individual plans of managers are integrated. The managers are therefore forced to consider the relationships between various departments. For example, it is important that a purchasing department is aware of the material requirements for manufacture so that buying and inventory levels are maintained to service the needs of the manufacturing activity during the budget period.

Communication

A budget will often be a useful means by which top management can formally communicate their objectives and strategies for the forthcoming budget period. This function will be reinforced, normally periodically, through a control mechanism, which will be referred to later, that reviews actual performance against the budget during the budget period.

To provide a basis for responsibility accounting

Individual managers are identified with their budget centres and are made responsible for achieving the stated budget targets. These targets may be in terms of expenditure, income and output that are considered to be within the manager's control. Responsibility accounting was previously outlined in Chapter 14. Within the context of budgets responsibility accounting represents an important feature of the delegation of responsibility within an organization.

To provide a basis for a control mechanism

The budget may be used as a basis for comparing actual performance with a plan and identifying any deviation from that plan. The identification of these deviations gives management the opportunity to take corrective action so that such deviations do not persist in the future. When budgets are used in the context of a control mechanism the term 'budgetary control' is normally used.

Authorization of expenditure

The budget may act as a formal authorization of future expenditure from top management to those individuals who are responsible for the expenditure. The fact that an item of expenditure, for example, is contained in the budget that has been approved by the top management of the organization implies that the item has been approved and no further approval will normally be required.

A means to motivate employees to improve performance

The budget may be used as a target to motivate employees to reach certain levels of attainment. For example, in a previous budget period a salesperson may achieve sales of products to the value of £30 000; management may in the next period set a target of, say, £40 000 believing, rightly or wrongly, that this new target will motivate the salesperson to reach higher levels of attainment than in the previous period.

It is also the case that budgets may mean different things to different people within an organization. For example, whilst a budget may be introduced by management in an organization with the aim of monitoring production costs, production managers may perceive the main purpose of the budget as a device to monitor their performance. Budgets can therefore lead to much misunderstanding, frustration and friction within an organization.

ACTIVITY 19.1

Think about and describe something you wish to purchase that incurs a significant cost of money. You decide to take a loan out for a period of time to pay for this purchase. How would you determine and plan to pay back the loan each year?

An example, could be considering taking out a loan from a bank for £12 000 to buy a car to be paid back over three years. I think I can afford to pay back about £3500, the capital sum plus interest, in each of the three years. To ensure this is the case I need to make a plan – a budget – over the forthcoming year of all significant expenditure and income:

- My rent on the flat I live in
- Insurances for the car and other possessions
- Food
- Gas and electricity
- Membership to health club
- My annual subscription to Southend United F.C.
- Travelling to away football matches
- Salary from employment.

After taking account of the above expenses and perhaps leaving a small margin for amounts I have not planned for, I am in a good position to know if I can afford to pay the yearly payment of loan.

KEY CONCEPT 19.1

The budget process

The term 'the budget process' refers to the sequence of operations necessary to produce a budget for a particular organization. The sequence of operations will depend upon the type of organization and its perceived requirements for planning and control.

THE BUDGET PROCESS

The following analysis focuses on the main features of the budget process.

The products that will be manufactured and sold, in a budget period, will be determined via the operating decisions, as previously described in Chapters 17 and 18. These decisions are initially made in isolation from a number of functions within an organization that are there to support the manufacture and sales of the products that have been chosen in the decision-making process. In the context of a manufacturing organization these supportive functions will normally relate to purchasing, production, marketing, administration and finance. Each of these functions will also require investment in resources, such as personnel necessary to perform the support function. It is at the beginning of the budget process that consideration is given to the operating decisions collectively and their interrelationships with these functions. At this stage, the resource implications of the decisions are analyzed to determine the extent to which they will draw upon the functions that were described above. From this analysis, guidelines will be formulated for the preparation of the budgets. The guidelines represent a framework for the preparers of budgets, identifying the overall levels of activity and the organization's policies on performance criteria, e.g. productivity. The personnel involved at this stage will be the top management of the organization. These managers will include those who have overall responsibility for the sales and production activities and those who are responsible for ensuring that the activities are coordinated, e.g. an accountant who has responsibility for the coordination of the accounting information input, often referred to as the budget accountant. Thus, the vitally important management task of coordination of the various interrelated aspects of decision making begins in the budgeting process.

In a manufacturing organization, for example, the main task of coordination will inevitably be concerned with the overall policy on the level of sales and production activities. The coordination of these activities will involve ensuring that the level of production output is sufficient to meet the sales demand for products and any inventory of finished goods that is also required by management. For example, if the sales demand for a product is 150 units and the desired closing finished goods inventory level is 30 units, assuming there are no opening inventories of finished goods available, 180 units will have to be manufactured to meet the sales and inventory requirements in the budget period. The functions such as marketing and finance necessary to support these levels of output will also be considered at this stage, and so will the formulation of management policies on the levels of performance for the budget period.

When top management have determined the output levels and associated policies, they must then be communicated to the preparers of the budgets. As mentioned, previously the preparers will be given guidelines and it will be the responsibility of these preparers to formulate the budgets within these guidelines. Budgets will be prepared for individual responsibility centres which have been defined by the organization's hierarchy. These centres will be managed by personnel who are responsible for particular functions within the organization, e.g. generating sales, producing products, and those supporting the sales and production functions.

There is some debate on the extent to which managers who are responsible for spending and income-generating departments should be involved in the preparation of their own budgets. It is normally the case, however, that managers of these responsibility centres will have some influence over the content of the budget. The extent of influence will vary from organization to organization and will depend on the management style of the organization. For example, the top management of some organizations may adopt a regime of imposing rules on subordinates without any discussion with them. The problem is that if managers are solely responsible for the preparation of the budget it is likely that the budget will reflect a bias in favour of the manager which may not be in the best interests of the organization as a whole. For example, it is likely that a manager who is responsible for the sales of a particular product range will set a budget that can easily be attained. The attainment of such targets will invariably be looked upon favourably by the manager's superiors. It is likely, however, that a manager of a responsibility centre will have a greater degree of knowledge and understanding of the operation of his own centre than any other personnel within the organization, and this knowledge is important in the formulation of budgets. Hence, there, is a strong case for at least some involvement by the manager of a responsibility centre in the preparation of the centre's budget.

Typically, in the budgeting process of an organization, individual budgets for each responsibility centre will be the subject of negotiations before approval and adoption by the organization. The parties in this negotiation stage will normally include the manager of the responsibility centre, the preparer of the budget (if not the manager) and the manager's superior. The accountant who is responsible for budgets within the organization will normally act as an intermediary in this negotiation process. Often in large organizations the negotiation process will be in a number of stages as the budget moves up the management hierarchy for approval. Figure 19.1 illustrates a typical hierarchy for the production management of an organization and the stages of negotiation of the production budget for three products that collectively represent a range of products.

FIGURE 19.1

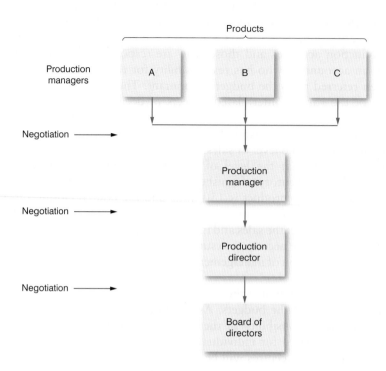

In the figure, the production budgets in terms of costs and output levels would be determined for products A, B and C. It has been assumed here that a product manager is responsible for the production of each of the products. As mentioned above, it is likely that the product manager will prepare his or her own budget or at least be influential in its content. When the budgets have been prepared, the first stage in negotiation will take place between the individual product managers and the production manager who has overall responsibility for the production of this range of products. After the individual budgets have been agreed, the combined budgets for the range are then negotiated with the production director, who has responsibility for all production of the organization. The last stage of negotiation of the production budget will be at Board level where eventually the budget will be approved.

At each stage of the negotiation process, as described, bargains are struck between the managers responsible for the budget and their immediate superiors. The negotiations between managers in the hierarchy of an organization in effect therefore represent a bargaining process where the individual goals of managers are formulated for a forthcoming budget period.

At Board level, the final fine tuning of the respective budget will take place. This process involves ensuring that all the budgets are consistent with each other, e.g. that the required material inventory levels are sufficient to meet the production requirement throughout the year. When all the individual budgets have been finalized and approved at this level they are summarized into what is commonly referred to as a master budget. The master budget will normally take the form of a budgeted balance sheet and income statement for the budget period. The information within the master budget is in effect a summary of all the individual budgets referred to earlier. Hence, the master budget represents the overall plan for an organization. It is useful as it clearly sets out the targets for the organization in an easily understandable form and can be compared with the actual balance sheet and income statement.

After the final approval at Board level, the budgets will be passed down the organization to the respective responsibility managers. It will be these managers who will be delegated to carry out the plans contained within each individual budget.

Plans in the form of budgets are extremely useful to an organization. A number of the purposes identified earlier for budgets highlight their usefulness. For example, they compel organizations to look ahead and thereby anticipate any particular problems that may arise in the future. The nature of budgeting that has been described so far tends to be rather static, in the sense that the planning process is based upon certain assumptions and events that will occur in the forthcoming budget period. However, the business environment in reality tends to be dynamic, and events may therefore not turn out as anticipated in the budget. It may well be that deviations from the budget are harmful to the organization; for example, the cost of producing a product may be greater than that anticipated in the budget and losses may be made. It is therefore important that these actual events in a budget period are monitored against the budget so that action may be taken to alleviate any undesirable situations.

Deviations from the budget in a period, however, may be due to events within the control or outside the control of the organization. For events that are within its control, the organization can take action, if they are undesirable, to ensure that such deviations will not occur in the future. In contrast, events outside the control of the organization, such as a downturn in the economy, may mean that it will be necessary for the organization to reconsider its plans. Typically, this will often result in organizations 'trimming' their operations to lower levels of activity or diversifying into other markets. The point here is that undesirable situations may be averted if an efficient system of control is imposed, and if the actual and budgeted performances are compared sufficiently frequently.

THE BUDGET TIME PERIOD

At this point of our analysis, it is appropriate to consider the budget period. The budget period normally employed by organizations is one year. The reason for a period of a year appears to relate to the periodic reporting requirements for published accounts regulated by the law. Public companies, for example, are required by law, with few exceptions, to publish accounts annually. It should also be recognized that there is normally a link between the information content of budgets and the annual accounts. For example, an organization's budget will normally include the planned total sales for the period whilst the annual accounts will show the actual sales achieved in the same period. Mainly for control purposes, the budget for the year will be broken down into quarterly, monthly and weekly periods. The extent to which the budget is broken down to these shorter periods will depend on the needs of the particular organization and the state of the economy. For example, if an organization operates in a very competitive market it is likely that management will desire to monitor performance on a fairly regular basis to ensure that the organization is maintaining its competitive position, as reflected in actual revenues, costs and output.

ACTIVITY 19.2

In Activity 19.1 You created a budget of your annual expenditure to ensure that you could afford to make yearly payment to pay back a loan to buy a car. To ensure you keep within your budget how will you breakdown your budget over the year so you can check your actual expenditure with your budget and explain the rationale for doing so?

For example, you may decide to break down your budget on a quarterly basis and compare it with actual expenditure because your bills for your rent on the flat, insurance, gas and electricity are paid quarterly and these are the main regular periodic outflows of expenditure.

KEY CONCEPT 19.2

Master budget

The master budget will normally consist of the budgeted income statement and balance sheet, representing a summary of the individual functional budgets of the organization as a whole.

PREPARATION OF BUDGETS

The master budget

The master budget is extremely useful to management as it clearly sets out the objectives and the targets for the forthcoming budget period, and is in a form that is easy to comprehend. It also provides a basis for coordinating individual functional budgets. The importance of coordination was emphasized earlier in this chapter. In a medium to large manufacturing organization these functional budgets will normally consist of sales, production, administration, distribution and cash budgets.

For small organizations, frequently the income statement, balance sheet and cash budget will be sufficient for the organization's management requirements. The information contained in these three budgeted statements can provide management with a reasonable base to analyze the forthcoming period. In particular, a number of ratios and indicators can be derived such as those relating to profitability, liquidity and financing. The use of these ratios and indicators was discussed in Chapter 12.

We shall begin, for clarity, by considering the preparation of an income statement, balance sheet and cash budget for a small firm just starting up (Example 19.1).

EXAMPLE 19.1

Sivraj Ltd was formed on 1 July 2008 with a share capital of £40 000. £24 000 of this capital was immediately invested into fixed assets, leaving £16 000 cash.

The fixed assets, it is estimated, have a ten-year life, and will have no value at the end of ten years. The company have decided to depreciate these assets using the straight-line method of depreciation. Therefore the depreciation charge per year will be £24 000/10 years = £2400, or expressed in monthly terms £2400/12 months = £200.

Prior to starting, business plans have been formulated for the first six months of the first year of operations. These plans are set out below.

Sales for the six months are estimated to be £600 000. However, the company operates in a seasonal market and will also be allowing some of its customers to take credit. The company anticipates the following receipts of cash over the six-month period from sales:

	Sales receipts £
July	40 000
August	50 000
September	50 000
October	70 000

(Continued)

Sales receipts
£

November	120 000
December	170 000
	500 000

From this breakdown of the anticipated cash received over the six-month period, it is apparent that at the end of the period there will be money owing from customers (i.e. receivables) of £600 000 – £500 000 = £100 000.

The materials required to meet the demand for sales are estimated to be £240 000. To enable the company to maintain an inventory (to ensure against any shortages), £260 000 worth of materials will be purchased in the period. However, because of the production cycle and the credit that the company will be obtaining from its suppliers the pattern and amount paid to suppliers will be as follows:

Payment to suppliers for materials
£

July	60 000
August	60 000
September	20 000
October	20 000
November	20 000
December	20 000
	200 000

At the end of the six-month period, the company have purchased materials costing £260 000 but have only paid £200 000 for them; thus, the company will owe (i.e. have payables of) £60 000 at the end of December 2008.

The estimated labour cost that will be incurred over the six months will be £180 000. In addition, the firm anticipates that overheads (excluding depreciation) of £138 000 will also be incurred over this period. Overheads and wages will be paid evenly over the six-month period.

We shall also assume that any cash deficits are financed by a bank overdraft.

To ensure that sufficient cash resources are available, the company wishes to calculate a cash budget (forecast) on a monthly basis in addition to a budgeted profit and loss account for the period and a balance sheet at the end of the period.

We shall begin by constructing the three budgeted statements from the information given. This will be followed by a commentary concerning the usefulness of these statements to management. The cash budget will be considered first (Table 19.1).

It can be seen from the cash budget for Sivraj Ltd that the inflows and outflows of cash are recorded in the budget statement when the cash is actually received or paid. There are a few main points to remember when constructing a cash budget:

- The dates of receipt and payment of cash, not the date of sale or purchase, are relevant; thus, allowance must be made for any credit period given or received. For example, in the case of Sivraj Ltd the relevant sales are when the cash is actually received and not when the sales are earned in the period.

- Provisions should be excluded as they do not affect cash flows; for example, depreciation on fixed assets is excluded as the cash flow associated with fixed assets occurs when the asset is paid for. Thus, the relevant cash outflow is £24 000, which was paid out for the fixed asset when it was purchased. The depreciation charge is irrelevant and should be ignored.

(Continued)

- Any inflows of capital and outflows such as drawings, payment of tax and dividends must also be included. In the example of Sivraj Ltd the only relevant item of this nature is the capital which was injected into the business on start-up.

- The format of the cash budget is very similar to the worksheets which were introduced in an earlier chapter. In the case of cash budgets the horizontal headings should relate to the discrete time period chosen for the budget. Thus, in this example, the requirement is monthly for six months to the end of December 2008. The company could have chosen weeks, however; in such a case there would be a column for each week of the six-month period. The time dimension will depend on the requirements of the managers of the organization.

TABLE 19.1   Cash budget for six months for Sivraj Ltd

	July £	August £	September £	October £	November £	December £
Cash inflows						
Share capital	40 000					
Sales receipts	40 000	50 000	50 000	70 000	120 000	170 000
Total cash inflows	80 000	50 000	50 000	70 000	120 000	170 000
Cash outflows						
Materials	60 000	60 000	20 000	20 000	20 000	20 000
Wages	30 000	30 000	30 000	30 000	30 000	30 000
Overheads	23 000	23 000	23 000	23 000	23 000	23 000
Fixed assets	24 000					
Total cash outflows	137 000	113 000	73 000	73 000	73 000	73 000
Net cash flow	(57 000)	(63 000)	(23 000)	(3 000)	47 000	97 000
Balance brought forward	–	(57 000)	(120 000)	(143 000)	(146 000)	(99 000)
Balance carried forward	(57 000)	(120 000)	(143 000)	(146 000)	(99 000)	(2 000)

The income statement, for convenience, has been constructed in a summary form rather than through the use of a worksheet (Table 19.2). Unlike the cash budget, the income statement is constructed by applying the concept of accruals accounting (i.e. matching revenues with costs associated with the revenues) rather than cash flow accounting. Thus, in our example, the material cost is the cost of materials included in the sales rather than the cash paid for the materials. The depreciation charge for the six months is calculated by taking the monthly charge of £200 and multiplying by six.

The balance sheet, similarly to the income statement, has been constructed without the use of a worksheet (Table 19.3). The following is a brief explanation of how the value of some of the assets and liabilities has been derived.

The inventory figure represents the difference between materials purchased (£260 000) and those materials consumed in the sales over the six-month period (£240 000). Receivables of £100 000 is the difference between the sales in the period and the cash received. The sum of £60 000 for payables is the difference between the materials purchased (£260 000) and the cash paid at the end of the six months (£200 000). The bank overdraft is derived from the cash budget and is the balance at the end of December 2008.

(Continued)

TABLE 19.2 Profit and loss account for the six months ending 31 December 2008

	£	£
Sales		600 000
Cost of sales		
Materials	240 000	
Wages	180 000	420 000
Gross profit		180 000
Less		
Depreciation	1 200	
Overheads	138 000	139 200
Net profit		40 800

TABLE 19.3 Balance sheet as at 31 December 2008

	£	£	£
Fixed assets			
Cost			24 000
Less depreciation			1 200
			22 800
Current assets			
Inventory		20 000	
Debtors		100 000	
		120 000	
Less current Liabilities			
Creditors	60 000		
Bank overdraft	2 000	62 000	58 000
			80 800
Share capital			40 000
Profit and loss a/c			40 800
			80 800

The use of worksheets, as described in earlier chapters, in the construction of the income statement and the balance sheet illustrates the interrelationships between these statements. Although worksheets were not used in this example, the interrelationships between these statements should still be apparent.

From a brief glance at these three budgeted statements for Sivraj Ltd, their usefulness should be apparent to you for planning. For example, it is predicted that although the company anticipates making a profit of £40 800 for the six months, which appears reasonably healthy, there will be large deficits of cash during this period. The problem for Sivraj Ltd is the pattern of cash payments and receipts. High material costs are incurred in the first two months in addition to the payment for the fixed assets. In contrast, sales, the major source of cash, are higher in the later part of the period. Identifying this situation prior to trading is extremely

(Continued)

useful as it may be possible to take action to reduce these cash deficits whilst trying to obtain some additional funding. For example, it may be possible to get receipts from sales in earlier, either by restricting the credit given to customers or by encouraging customers to pay more quickly by offering a discount for prompt payment. This would result in cash being received earlier and would thereby reduce the cash deficit each month.

By identifying cash shortages at this stage, Sivraj Ltd will also be in a better position to finance any deficits. For example, the bank would look more favourably on an application for an overdraft after having some insight into the future profitability of the company. This situation can be contrasted with the negative attitude of the bank when an application for funding is made after a firm has gone into debt without any prior communication with the bank. Another possible alternative action to relieve this potentially undesirable situation could be to raise additional share capital to fund the cash deficits of the business.

In the analysis of the budgets of Sivraj Ltd, our main concern has, not surprisingly, been focused on the cash deficits. It could have been the case that Sivraj Ltd had budgeted cash surpluses rather than deficits during the budget period. In these circumstances, the identification of these surpluses would also be useful to the business. By identifying surpluses at this early stage the firm would be in a better position to plan the investment of such funds, e.g. in short-term deposits, to obtain the maximum amount of interest.

As previously mentioned, a number of other characteristics of the business can be analyzed through the use of ratio analysis. However, in general the major benefit to budgets of this nature to an organization such as Sivraj Ltd is that events can be anticipated and action taken for the best interests of the organization.

External funding organizations will always require budgeted information from firms, similar to that produced in the case of Sivraj Ltd, before any agreement to lend money. This is particularly the case when small businesses, such as Sivraj Ltd, apply for funding from banks.

The sales and production budgets

The sales and production budgets will normally be prepared for manufacturing organizations and will reflect the respective targets for these functions in the forthcoming budget period. As mentioned previously, the summation of these budgets will be embodied within the overall income statement and balance sheet. Also, as these functions will involve cash payments and receipts they will also be the source for the overall cash budget.

In Example 19.2, we shall concentrate on the sales and production budgets and subsequently determine a budgeted income statement. We shall also emphasize the importance of coordinating these different functions within an organization, in particular the production output level necessary to support the sales volume and desired inventory levels.

EXAMPLE 19.2

Nadia plc has gathered the following data about future sales and production requirements for the year 2008.

	Estimated sales:			
Product	Units	Price	Opening inventory 1 January 2008 Units	Desired closing inventory 31 December 2008 Units
A	20 000	£55	8 000	10 000
B	50 000	£50	15 000	14 000
C	30 000	£65	6 000	6 000

(Continued)

Materials used in manufacture:

		Amount used per unit of production		
Inventory no.	Unit	A	B	C
54	Component	3	–	5
32	Metres	2	1	3
44	Kilograms	–	2	–

Estimated purchase price of materials:

Inventory no.	
54	£3 per component
32	£2 per metre
44	£4 per kilogram

Inventory levels of materials:

Inventory no.	Opening inventory 1 January 2008	Closing inventory 31 December 2008
54	21 000 components	25 000 components
32	17 000 m	23 000 m
44	10 000 kg	8 000 kg

Labour requirement:

Product	Hours per unit	Rate per hour
A	4	£7
B	5	£5
C	5	£6

Production overheads are estimated at £500 000 per year. For internal management purposes, Nadia plc adopts a marginal costing system, and therefore treats these overheads as a period charge (see Chapter 14).

In this example, we presume that the sales demand, in terms of volume, is the constraining factor. Hence, the production volume will be dependent upon the sales demand.

The management of Nadia plc require the following budgetary information for the forthcoming budget period:

- sales budget in money terms;

- production budget in units;

- materials purchased budget in units;

- materials purchased budget in money terms;

- materials cost per unit manufactured and sold;

(Continued)

- the total labour hours worked during the period and the cost, plus the cost of labour per unit manufactured and sold;
- the unit contribution of each product;
- the profit or loss for the budget period;
- the value of closing finished inventory at the end of the budget period.

Sales budget in money terms

We have been given the price per unit and the volume of units that it is estimated will be sold. To calculate the total sales revenue generated from these sales we simply need to multiply these two variables:

Product	Units × price (£)	Sales revenue (£000)
A	20 000 × 55	1 100
B	50 000 × 50	2 500
C	30 000 × 65	1 950
Total		5 550

Production budget in units

The production level during the budget period not only must satisfy the sales demand but also must ensure that the inventory levels are sufficient for the period. In the case of Nadia plc the opening and closing inventory levels have been estimated, and we have been given the sales demand; from this information, and with the help of a simple equation, we shall be able to determine the production level to satisfy this demand.

The equation we shall use, sometimes referred to as the inventory formula, is as follows (measured in units):

$$\text{production} + \text{opening inventory} = \text{sales} + \text{closing inventory}$$

This equation states that the units produced during the budget period plus what is in inventory at the beginning of this period are equal to the units to be sold plus the units required as inventory at the end of the period.

For our purposes, as there is only one unknown quantity (production), we need to rearrange this formula:

$$\text{sales} + \text{closing inventory} - \text{opening inventory} = \text{production}$$

Applying this equation to the figures for Nadia plc, measured in units, we obtain the following:

Product	Sales	+	Closing inventory	−	Opening inventory	=	Production
A	20 000	+	10 000	−	8 000	=	22 000
B	50 000	+	14 000	−	15 000	=	49 000
C	30 000	+	6 000	−	6 000	=	30 000

(Continued)

Materials purchased budget measured in units

Three types of materials described by inventory numbers (inventory number 54, 32 and 44) are used in the production of A, B and C. Before determining how many units of these item will need to be purchased in the period, we must first calculate the number of units of inventory necessary to satisfy production requirements:

Product	Units	Inventory no. 54	Inventory no. 3	Inventory no. 44
A	22 000	(×3) 66 000	–	(×5) 110 000
B	49 000	(×2) 98 000	(×1) 49 000	(3) 147 000
C	30 000	–	(×2) 60 000	–
Total		164 000	109 000	257 000

The figures in parentheses represent the number of units of material required for each product. For example, in the case of product A, three units of inventory no. 54 are required to make one unit of A.

The purchase of materials required for the forthcoming budget period can now be calculated using a similar equation to that used in determining the production level:

$$\text{purchases} + \text{opening inventories} = \text{production} + \text{closing inventories}$$

Purchases, etc., in the equation will be measured in terms of material units, e.g. components in the case of inventory no. 54.

The equation states that the materials required for production during the period and closing inventory at the end of the period will be met from the purchase of materials and the inventory that is available at the beginning of the period.

From the information that is given in this example, we are told the opening and closing inventory requirements and we have calculated above the materials required for production. Therefore, three of the four variables in the equation are known to us, and by rearranging the equation we shall be able to calculate the purchases figure:

$$\text{production} + \text{closing inventory} - \text{opening inventory} = \text{purchases}$$

Applying this equation to the information that has been given for the three inventory numbers, we obtain the following:

Inventory no.	Production	+	Closing inventory	–	Opening inventory	=	Purchases
54	164 000	+	25 000	–	21 000	=	168 000
32	109 000	+	23 000	–	17 000	=	115 000
44	257 000	+	10 000	–	8 000	=	259 000

It should be remembered that the above purchases figures represent the units for the respective materials; thus, for example, in the case of inventory no. 54, the purchases requirement will be 168 000 components.

Materials purchased budget in money terms

The calculation of purchases, measured in money terms, is relatively straightforward. We simply multiply the purchases in terms of units by the cost per unit which was given at the beginning of the example:

(Continued)

Inventory no.	Purchases (units)		Cost per unit £	Total cost £
54	168 000	×	3	504 000
32	115 000	×	2	230 000
44	259 000	×	4	1 036 000
				1 770 000

Materials cost per unit manufactured and sold

This information may be required by management in the determination of the profitability of each of the products sold and for inventory valuation purposes. All the relevant information regarding this calculation has been given and it just remains for us to perform the calculation; for each unit of product we need to multiply the cost per unit of material by the amount of the material required to manufacture each product:

		Products		
Inventory no.	Cost per unit of inventory (£)	A £	B £	C £
54	3	(×3) 9	–	(×5) 15
32	2	(×2) 4	(×1) 2	(×3) 6
44	4	–	(×2) 8	–
Material cost per unit sold		13	10	21

The figures in parentheses represent the number of units of material required for each product.

The total labour hours worked during the period and the cost, plus the cost of labour per unit manufactured and sold

We begin by computing the labour cost per unit of goods manufactured and sold. This information will provide management with data that is useful to assess profitability and for inventory valuation purposes. The arithmetic for the calculation is relatively simple to obtain the total labour cost per unit we need to multiply the hours per unit by the rate per hour:

Product	Hours per unit £	Rate per hour cost per unit	Total labour £
A	4	7	28
B	5	5	25
C	5	6	30

For calculation of the total labour hours, the production units must be multiplied by the hours per unit. If we then multiply the total labour by the rate per unit we can determine the total cost. It is important to appreciate why production units are used in these calculations rather than sales units. The reason is that the objective here is to determine how many hours were actually worked and the cost of those hours during the year. If sales units were used we would be establishing the total hours that have been consumed in producing the sales. If there are changes between the opening and closing levels of finished inventories the units produced will not equal the sales units sold. This was the case for both products A and B, as can be seen when we determined the production levels for these two products earlier. In contrast, for product C the finished inventory level remained unchanged and thus the production units and the sales units were the same, i.e. 30 000 units.

(Continued)

Product	Production units	Hours per unit	Total hours	Rate per hour £	Total cost £
A	22 000	4	88 000	7	616 000
B	49 000	5	245 000	5	1 225 000
C	30 000	5	150 000	6	900 000
			483 000		2 741 000

The unit contribution of each product

We have used the concept of contribution in earlier chapters relating, for example, to cost behaviour and cost volume profit analysis. To remind you, the contribution per unit is equal to the sales price per unit less variable costs per unit. The only variable costs we have in this example are materials and labour. These variable costs, you will remember, have been determined earlier. Thus, the contribution per unit for these three products will be as follows:

		A £		B £		C £
Sales price		55				65
Less variable costs						
Material	13		10		21	
Labour	28	41	25	35	30	51
Contribution per unit		14		15		14

The profit or loss for the budget period

We shall begin by determining the total contribution for the three products and then deduct the overhead cost, which is the convention under the marginal costing regime.

Product	Contribution per unit £	No. of units sold	£
A	14	20 000	280 000
B	15	50 000	750 000
C	14	30 000	420 000
Total contribution			1 450 000
Less overheads			500 000
Profit			950 000

The value of closing finished inventory at the end of the budget period

Under the marginal costing regime finished inventory will be valued at marginal cost (variable cost). From the information already obtained we know the variable costs of each product and we therefore need to multiply this cost by the number of units of finished inventory which was given at the beginning of this example:

Product	Finished inventory in units	Marginal cost £	Value of finished inventory £
A	10 000	41	410 000
B	14 000	35	490 000
C	6 000	51	306 000
Total value of finished inventory			1 206 000

(Continued)

The budgets prepared above will act as a source of information in the construction of the income statement, balance sheet and cash budget.

The budgets constructed in this example will always be broken down further to responsible departments, thus enabling the management of these departments to identify clearly the plans purely associated with their departments.

It should also be stressed that the budgets prepared for Nadia plc will not necessarily be common to all manufacturing organizations. The form and design of the budgetary system will depend upon the particular organization's management requirements. However, the example does illustrate the main principles in the preparation of budgets for manufacturing organizations.

In the example of Nadia plc, overheads were given as one figure, i.e. £500 000 per year. Normally, as previously mentioned in the section on the budgeting process, organizations will also prepare detailed budgets for overhead expenditure. These will represent the planned costs associated with expenses budgets associated with supporting the manufacturing function, such as machine maintenance, administration and sales. It should also be mentioned that as new technology and automation are being introduced into the manufacturing environment, overhead costs are tending to grow as a proportion of the total cost of an organization's operations. Hence, organizations should be placing more emphasis on planning and control of these types of costs. However, many of the systems that are in use have not been efficiently designed to cope with this phenomenon. There is considerable debate, at present, as to the methods of costing and budgeting that should be introduced to monitor overhead costs.

ACTIVITY 19.3

An income statement is more important than a cash budget. List three major advantages of a cash budget and comment on this statement.

The following are three main advantages of a cash budget:

- It helps to ensure the organization overall is solvent and can therefore pay its bills over the year.
- It identifies surplus so that this may be deposited in an interest bearing account.
- It helps in making trade credit decision; for example, whether to extend credit to customers.

Both budgets – the income statement and the cash budget are of equal importance. They are used to help plan and control different aspects of the business. For example, the budget income statement acts as a performance target for an organization whilst the focus of a cash budget is on liquidity.

FLEXIBLE BUDGETS

The budgets we have been considering up to now in this chapter are fixed budgets. That is, they are prepared on the basis of an estimated activity level. This activity level may be in terms of the estimated volume of sales or estimated volumes of production or any other activity relevant to the operations of the organization. A fixed budget is a fundamental part of the planning process. However, in terms of monitoring performance the actual activities levels are likely to differ from the fixed budget levels. In terms of identification of variances caused through the actual performance differing from the budget, fixed budgets are not helpful but they are an important starting place in the control process.

To address the this problem of fixed budgets in terms of using them as a part of the control monitoring process, the budget can be 'flexed' to the actual output level whether it is higher or lower than the fixed budget. Only the variable costs and sales will be affected and by definition the fixed costs will not be subject to the flexing process because they do not vary with output. The concept of flexible budgeting is illustrated in Example 19.3.

EXAMPLE 19.3

Priddy Ltd. is a manufacturing company and employs a fixed budget for monitoring of the company's performance. The following is a performance report is in respect of the production department for May:

	Budget	Actual	Variance
Production (units)	20 000	18 000	2 000
	£	£	£
Direct labour (£1/ per unit)	20 000	19 500	500 (FAV)
Direct materials (4p per unit)	800	1 000	200 (ADV)
Variable overheads (20p per unit)	4 000	3 600	400 (FAV)
Fixed overheads	18 000	17 500	500 (FAV)
Total costs	42 800	41 600	1 200 (FAV)

(FAV) = favourable variance
(ADV) = adverse variance,

The above report suggests that the production department has been efficient with an overall £1200 favourable variance. Only the material cost has an adverse variance and is above the budget. But clearly the report is misleading! What the above analysis shows is that the budget based on a higher output level has estimated higher costs than that of the actual lower output. This is of course not surprising and is misleading for comparative purposes. If any of the production costs are variable it must be expected that producing less than budget is likely to cost less in terms of labour, materials and variable overheads consumed. It could well be the case, however, that the price of these elements of production could have exceeded budget but this would not be apparent from this performance report.

A flexible budget will provide us with a more informative analysis. A flexed budget is created on the basis of the fixed budget costs per unit but based on the actual output of 18 000 production units. The following shows the amend performance report using a flexed budget:

	Original fixed budget	Flexed budget	Actual	Variance
Production (units)	20 000	18 000	18 000	2 000
	£	£	£	£
Direct labour (£1/unit)	20 000	18 000	19 500	1 500 (ADV)
Direct material (4p/unit)	800	720	1 000	280 (ADV)
Variable overheads (20p/unit)	4 000	3 600	3 600	–
Fixed overheads	18 000	18 000	17 500	500 (FAV)
Total costs	42 800	40 320	41 600	1 280 (ADV)

(Continued)

In constructing the flexed budget the variable costs per unit are now multiplied by the flexed output, that is, the actual output. In the case of direct labour, for example, the cost of £1 per unit is multiplied by the output of 18 000 units, the flexed budgeted estimated total cost being £18 000 which is then compared with the actual cost total cost of labour being £19 500, giving an adverse variance of £1500. If this is compared with the favourable variance of £500 from the difference between the fixed budget and actual costs it is then amply apparent that this is misleading. It follows that for both the other variable costs of direct materials and variable overheads the same misleading outcomes can be noted when comparing the two performance reports. Therefore the use of flexible budgets makes the control process much more realistic and useful.

The analysis of the variances should not stop at just the comparison between the flexed and actual costs. Traditionally, variances are further broken down in terms of efficiency, how well the resources have been used, and by cost, the cost paid for the resource. Both adverse and favourable variances should be investigated as the result could lead to future decisions that will benefit the organization. Further details of this analysis are beyond the scope of this book but references to other specialist management accounting texts (e.g. Drury, 2009) to 'Standard Costing' or simply 'Variance Analysis' deal with the subject in detail.

It should also be noted that these traditional analyses of variances have their limitations. This was discussed in Chapter 14, an introductory chapter on planning and control.

ACTIVITY 19.4

Think about planning for the cost of petrol you will consume travelling in your car next year. What are the two main elements of cost in determining a budgeted cost of travelling for the year at the beginning of the planning period?

At the end of the year the total cost is unlikely to match your original fixed budget. Why not?

How would you identify through analysis the reasons for this cost variance from the original budget?

Some suggested answers:

- Two elements of cost are the miles travelled and the cost of petrol.
- It is likely that the miles originally budgeted differ from the actual miles travelled. The cost of petrol is also likely to have differed during the year.
- Variance analysis – flex budgeted miles to actual miles and multiple by cost of petrol per mile originally budgeted. This will result in a flexed budget. If the flexed budget was to be compared with the actual cost the difference would be how much more or less you paid for petrol for the year.

SUMMARY

We began this chapter by considering the main purposes of budgets. They were described under the following headings:

- to compel planning;

- coordination of different functions;

- communication;

- to provide a basis for responsibility accounting;

- to provide a basis for a control mechanism;

- authorization of expenditure;

- a means to motivate employees to improve performance.

From this list, it is apparent that budgets are introduced and used for a variety of reasons. Although it may appear initially that the introduction of budgets can only be to the advantage of the organization, they can create conflicts within the organization. For example, management may have introduced budgets for a positive reason, to motivate employees, but employees may see the budget in a negative light which has a demotivating effect. However, it will always be necessary to monitor performance.

A sequence of operations is needed to implement a planning system such as budgets effectively. This sequence of operations is known as the budget process. It is important to understand this process as it links the reasons for the implementation of the budget and the preparation of budgets. It was also stressed that the budget process and form of budgets would be dependent upon a number of contingent factors such as the type of technology employed by the organization.

Two examples of preparing budgets were examined, both of which illustrated how the process of preparing budgets effectively coordinated the plans of separate functions of the organization, e.g. the sales budget and its relationship with the production and inventory budgets. A number of principles, such as those underlying cash budgets, were stressed in the preparation of different budgets. It is important that you should understand these principles in order to be able to prepare budgets.

Finally, flexible budgets were introduced that link the planning stage in the budgeting process with the control function within the organization.

REFERENCES

Drury, C. (2009) *Management Accounting for Business*, 4th edn. Andover: Cengage Learning.

FURTHER READING

Organizational issues, in respect of budgeting, are well represented by *Accounting for Management Control*, Chapters 6 and 7, by C. Emmanuel, D. Otley and K. Merchant, 2nd edn (International Thomson Business Press, 1990).

REVIEW QUESTIONS

(✓ indicates answers are available in Appendix A)

1 What is a budget?

✓ **2** What are the main reasons for an organization to introduce budgets?

3 Explain why budgets may mean different things to different people within an organization, giving reasons.

4 Describe the main differences in the budgeting process for a small retail firm and a large manufacturing firm.

5 Discuss the interrelationships between the sales budget and the production budget in a manufacturing organization.

6 Explain, giving examples, the main advantages of identifying cash surpluses and deficits in a cash budget.

7 What determines the budget time period?

8 What is a master budget? Describe its role in relation to other budgets.

PROBLEMS FOR DISCUSSION AND ANALYSIS

(✓ indicates answers are available in Appendix A)

1 With reference to the example of Sivraj Ltd, prepare a income statement and balance sheet from the data using worksheets.

✓ **2** CJH Ltd is preparing its annual budget. The following data are available:

Product	Estimated sales (units)	Opening inventory (units)	Closing inventory (units)
X	18	8	10
Y	50	15	15
Z	30	6	6

Material	Cost per unit £	Units of material used per unit of product			Opening inventory (units)	Closing inventory (units)
		X	Y	Z		
A	3	3	–	5	21	25
B	2	2	1	3	17	23
C	4	–	2	1	10	15

(a) Prepare the production budget in units.
(b) Give the total budgeted cost of materials used in the production of X, Y and Z.
(c) Give the total cost of materials A, B and C purchased.

3 Faraday Ltd is a wholesaler. The management has been extremely worried about the firm's cash position over the last few years. In January 2008 they seek your advice and ask you to prepare a cash budget for the forthcoming months of April, May and June 2008. In addition, they have asked you to write a report on the cash position over this period, and in particular on ways in which you think it could be improved.

The following data are made available to you regarding the firm's operations:

(i) Estimated sales for the six months to June 2008:

Month	Credit sales £	Cash sales £
January	122 000	12 900
February	137 000	14 500
March	142 000	17 700
April	148 000	20 100
May	134 000	15 000
June	126 000	12 600

Cash is received immediately on cash sales. The firm allows customers one month's credit on sales other than for cash.

(ii) Purchase of goods for resale are made on credit. The firm receives two months' credit on these purchases. The purchases for the six months to June 2008 are as follows:

Month	£
January	62 000
February	58 000
March	71 000
April	80 000
May	54 000
June	48 000

(iii) An inventory check at the end of the last year has revealed £45 000 of inventory, valued at cost, is considered obsolete. The firm is currently negotiating the sale of this inventory for £9500 and anticipates payment in May 2008.

(iv) Faraday's manufacturing overheads are estimated to be £12 000 per month. This includes a charge for depreciation of £2000 per month. The company takes one month to pay these expenses.

(v) Selling and distribution expenses are estimated to be £50 400 per year and are incurred evenly over the year. One month's credit is taken.

(vi) The firm is currently negotiating an advertising programme with an agency. The cost will be £6300 in May and £7700 in June. Payment will be made in cash.

(vii) In June the firm anticipates paying £3880 tax to the Inland Revenue.

(viii) The firm has agreed to purchase new stock-handling equipment. The cost of £105 200 is payable in two equal instalments in April and May 2008.

(ix) The firm expects in June to be able to take advantage of adjacent property (cost of £150 000) to expand their operation.

(x) It is estimated that the cash balance at 1 April will be £16 000.

4 Borough Equipment plc produces two products, Main and Pain, for sale to electrical wholesalers. The following information relates to the six months ending 31 December 2010:

Product	Budgeted sales units	Price per unit (£)	Budgeted inventories 1 July 2010 (units)	Budgeted inventories 31 December 2010 (units)
Main	16 200	14.35	5 100	8 100
Pain	11 800	12.20	2 600	6 600

Components bought in and used in manufacture:

	Amount used per unit of product	
Component	Main	Pain
X	5	3
Y	2	4

Component	Price £	Expected inventories 1 July 2010	Expected inventories 31 December 2010
X	0.68	38 000	46 000
Y	0.24	13 500	19 500

Labour:

Product	Hours per unit	Rate per hour (£)
Main	2	4.50
Pain	1	4.00

Overheads for the six months are anticipated to be £25 000. The company adopts a marginal costing system and treats overheads as a period cost.

Prepare the following:

(a) sales budget;
(b) production budget;
(c) purchases budget in terms of components;
(d) purchases budget in pounds;
(e) the total labour hours and cost for the period;
(f) the contribution per unit;
(g) the profit or loss for the period.

Comment on the usefulness of these budgets for planning, decision making and control.

5 Warpaint plc is a wholesale company specializing in the purchase and sale of different brands of paint. The company's year ends on 31 March. You have been requested in early February 2011 to assist in the preparation of the cash budget for the period 1 April 2011 to 31 March 2012. The following information is available regarding the company's operations during this period:

(i) It is anticipated that the cash balance at the 31 March 2011 will be £25 000.

(ii) The sales management of the company forecast that the volume and pattern of sales in the year ended 31 March 2011 will be the same next year. They do, however, intend to increase the selling price of all products by 10% of the current sales price.

The following details the actual and estimated sales for the year ended 31 March 2011:

Month	£000
April 2010	90
May 2010	100
June 2010	150
July 2010	130
August 2010	120
September 2010	100
October 2010	80
November 2010	140

Month	£000
December 2010	120
January 2011	100
February 2011	150
March 2011	200

Sales collections are normally made as follows:

During the month of the sale	60%
In the first subsequent month	30%
In the second subsequent month	10%

(iii) Creditors it is estimated will represent 50% of the sales value each month but will not be paid by the company until the following month.

(iv) Overheads which have been running at £40 000 per month during the year 2010/11 are paid in the month they are incurred. It is anticipated that in the year 2004/05 this monthly expenditure will increase by 10% with the exception of depreciation. £10 000 of these overhead expenses represent depreciation on fixtures and fittings, etc.

(v) A £40 000 payment in respect of corporation tax is due in April 2012.

(vi) The marketing department intends to start up an advertising campaign from April 2011 for two months. This will require cash payments of £5000 in May and £8000 in June.

(vii) The salary bill each week is approximately £4000 per week and paid on Friday at the end of the week. This was the level in 2003/4, and it is anticipated that a 10% increase will be negotiated in July 2011.

Required

Prepare a cash budget for the first three months of the year beginning 1 April 2012. Assume there are four weeks to each month.

CHAPTER 20
INVESTMENT
DECISIONS

LEARNING OUTCOMES

By the end of this chapter you will be able to:

- Understand and distinguish between four methods of investment appraisal – accounting rate of return, payback, net present value and internal rate of return.

- Understand the process of discounting.

- Use these methods in making long-term decisions.

- Explain the importance of time value for money.

- Calculate perpetuities.

This chapter examines the four main methods of investment appraisal within a business decision-making environment: net present value; the internal rate of return; the accounting rate of return; and payback methods.

In this chapter we shall be examining how managers of businesses make long-term investment decisions vis-à-vis short-term decisions. The main difference between long and short-term decisions is that the benefits in the case of long-term decisions will accrue over a longer period, usually well over one year, and often much longer. This difference in time dimension has important implications in terms of the value of money. The value of money over time will be an important feature in the evaluation of the differing methods of investment appraisal available to managers, and will be considered later.

By their nature, long-term decisions tend to be strategic. This means that resources are committed for a long period of time and these decisions determine the long-term policies of the firm that are necessary to meet its objectives.

The methods of investment appraisal we will be considering are designed primarily to satisfy one objective, that is, to maximize profits of the firm. The maximizing of profits can also be translated into maximizing the value of shareholders' wealth. The shareholders are the owners of the firm, to whom the management of the firm are accountable. The link between the investment decision and the finance necessary to fund the investment is that the return from an investment must adequately satisfy those providing the finance. Therefore, the criteria that are to be applied in terms of accepting or rejecting individual investment opportunities will reflect the demands of those who finance the firm.

Risk will play an important part in determining the return demanded by those funding the business. The higher the risk, the greater is the return that those funding the business will demand. Differing investment opportunities have different risk profiles. The main factors that affect risk are the structure of the market and industry, changes in technology and tastes and exposure to macroeconomic variables.

It should be recognized, however, that there are other criteria than maximizing profits that a firm may adopt in determining whether to invest. It may be that a firm's objective at a particular point in time is, for example, to maximize market share, which may be in conflict with the maximization of profits. It is likely that in such cases, the methods of investment appraisal that we will be considering would then be inappropriate.

In this chapter, we will be examining and evaluating the following methods of investment appraisal:

- the accounting rate of return (ARR) method;

- the payback method;

- discounted cash flow (DCF) methods, namely:
    - the net present value (NPV) method; and
    - the internal rate of return (IRR) method.

ACCOUNTING RATE OF RETURN (ARR)

A long-term investment project may be assessed by calculating its estimated accounting rate of return (ARR) and comparing it with a predetermined target ARR, the target being set by management and presumably reflecting their objectives in terms of a satisfactory return. The ARR is sometimes also referred to as return on investment (ROI). In principle, these two measures are the same. There is a difference, however, between ARR and return on capital employed (ROCE). ROCE is used normally to describe the return on investment of a reporting entity as a whole, for example, a company, rather than of one individual project, as in the case of ARR.

Unfortunately, and confusingly, there are several different definitions of ARR. One of the most popular is:

$$ARR = \frac{\text{estimated average profit}}{\text{estimated average investment}} \times 100\%$$

The other definitions include:

$$ARR = \frac{\text{estimated total profit}}{\text{estimated initial investment}} \times 100\%$$

and:

$$ARR = \frac{\text{estimated average profit}}{\text{estimated average investment}} \times 100\%$$

There are various arguments in favour of each of the above definitions. The most important point is, however, that the method adopted should be used consistently, thereby ensuring that like is compared to like.

The profit figure in this measure is the accounting profit based on accruals accounting principles and is normally taken after depreciation but before taxation. Taxation is ignored as the variation in taxes over time, which may be outside the control of the firm, can distort the measure from one period to another. This would be problematic for the appraisal of investment projects, as there would not be a consistent basis upon which to compare investments.

The use of the ARR method of appraisal involves estimating the ARR on the proposed project and comparing it with a target ARR. If the estimated rate of the proposed project exceeds the target rate, the project should be undertaken. Conversely, if the estimated return is less than the target, the proposed project should be rejected.

ACTIVITY 20.1

In making long-term capital decisions what decision criteria should companies employ and why?

The decision criterion that should be adopted is to maximize shareholders' wealth, assuming this is the company's objective.

KEY CONCEPT 20.1

Accounting rate of return (ARR) decision rule

Compare the estimated ARR of a proposed project with the target ARR. If the estimate exceeds the target, accept the project; if it is lower, reject the project.

CASE STUDY 20.1

Hilditch Environmental Consultants Ltd

Hilditch Environmental Consultants Ltd are currently appraising an investment opportunity. The company uses the accounting rate of return for such purposes. The target ARR for the company is 20%. The following details relate to the proposed investment:

Investment: cost of the asset £80 000

Estimated life: four years

Estimated profit before depreciation:

	£
Year 1	20 000
Year 2	25 000
Year 3	35 000
Year 4	25 000

If the asset were to be depreciated on a straight-line basis and the asset has a nil residual value, the annual depreciation charge will be £80 000/4 years = £20 000 per year. The annual profits after depreciation, and the mid-year net book value of the asset for each year, would be as shown in Table 20.1.

TABLE 20.1

Year	Profit after depreciation	Mid-year net book value	ARR in the year
1	0	70 000	0
2	5 000	50 000	10
3	15 000	30 000	50
4	5 000	10 000	50

The mid-year net book value in Table 20.1 is the value at the mid-point between the beginning of each year and the end of the year; for example, the value of the asset at the beginning of year 1 was £80 000 and at the end £60 000 (after deduction of depreciation of £20 000); the mid-year net book value therefore being £70 000.

From Table 20.1, it can be seen that the ARR, from a yearly perspective, is low in the early years of the project. This is partly because of low profits in year 1, but in the main it is due to the net book value of the asset being much higher in the early years. The relatively higher net book value of assets in early years is a characteristic of the straight-line depreciation method which we discussed in Chapter 8.

The project does not achieve the target ARR of 20% in its first two years, but exceeds it in years 3 and 4. This begs the question of whether the project should be accepted.

(Continued)

When the ARR from a project varies from year to year, it makes sense to take an overall view, which was implied earlier, when definitions of the method were being discussed. Using the most common definition cited earlier, that is:

$$\text{ARR} = \frac{\text{estimated average profit}}{\text{estimated average investment}} \times 100\%$$

where:

$$\text{estimated average profit} = \frac{\text{total profit}}{\text{number of years}} = \frac{£25\,000}{4} = £6250$$

Estimated average investment over the four-year period = £(80 000 + 0)/2 = £40 000 (the average investment being the average value of the asset at the beginning of its life, £80 000, and at the end of its life, in this case £0). Therefore,

$$\text{ARR} = £6250/40\,000 \times 100 = 15.63\%$$

As the estimated ARR is less than the target rate of 20%, the project should be rejected.

Although ARR adopts accounting measures which can be manipulated more easily than, say, simple inflows and outflows of cash, the measure is consistent with the way in which organizations report in their annual accounts. That is, both ARR and financial accounting information reported in the annual accounts are based on accruals accounting. Therefore, if the ARR of a project is estimated, some reasonable assessment may be made as to the effect of a proposed project on future reported profits.

The main criticism of the ARR is that it does not take account of the timing of profits generated from the investment. The model therefore assumes that the profits earned in the first year, for example, are equivalent in terms of value to profits earned in later years. That is, ignoring inflation, £1 today is assumed to be the same as £1 in ten years' time. Intuition will lead us quickly to the conclusion that this is not so! This assumption therefore ignores the concept of the time value of money. The theme of time value of money will be considered in more detail later in this chapter when considering the methods based on discounted cash flow.

THE PAYBACK METHOD

KEY CONCEPT 20.2

Definition of payback
Payback is normally defined as the period, usually expressed in years, which it takes the cash inflows from an investment project to equal the cash outflows.

It should be noted that in this definition of payback, the term 'cash flow' is used rather than accounting profit. Therefore, this method is not based on accruals accounting concepts and, hence, does not, for example, take account of depreciation.

Example 20.1 illustrates the use of the payback method where there are two mutually exclusive investment opportunities available to a firm, that is, where only one opportunity can be accepted.

EXAMPLE 20.1

Project	A £	B £
Cost of investment	50 000	50 000
Cash inflows		
Year 1	10 000	40 000
Year 2	15 000	30 000
Year 3	20 000	10 000
Year 4	25 000	5 000
Year 5	60 000	5 000

Following the definition of payback in Key Concept 20.2, Project A will pay back the investment after the third year. By the end of year 3, it has paid back £45 000 (£10 000 + £15 000 + £20 000) and the other £5000 will be paid back during year 4. When the actual payback occurs during a year, it is the convention to express this point in time as a fraction of a year, or in months. For example, in the case of Project A in the fourth year £25 000 is received, but only £5000 is necessary to add to previous year's cash inflows to pay back the original investment; this £5000 can then be expressed as a fraction of the total for that year £5000/£25 000, i.e. one-fifth of the year, or in months £5000/£25 000 × 12 months = 2.4 months.

In contrast, Project B pays back the investment in one year and four months. This project therefore would normally be preferred under the payback criteria.

It should be noted that in calculating the fraction of the year or the month in which payback takes place, as in the example above, it has been assumed that the cash flows are received evenly throughout the year. Owing to the inevitable uncertainty involved in long-term investment appraisal, this is a reasonable assumption. It would normally be very difficult and problematic to estimate precisely the spread of cash flows within years.

When examining two mutually exclusive projects, as in the case of Projects A and B above, the usual decision is to accept the one with the shortest payback, assuming the payback period satisfies some preconceived target. However, when only one investment opportunity is being examined, the payback of that opportunity will be compared with a target payback. This concept of a target payback could be employed in the case of Projects A and B above, assuming that these two projects were not mutually exclusive, that is we could, if we so wished, accept both investment opportunities. For example, if our payback target was four years, Project B would be accepted because it pays back after one year and four months. Project A would also be accepted, because its payback of three years and 2.4 months is less than the target.

Much of the perceived risk associated with investment projects is related to uncertainty due to the time span in which benefits in terms of cash flows are received. The longer the time period for receipt of cash, the greater the risk. Therefore, by differentiating projects in terms of the period to pay back the investment, the payback method measures this type of risk. Thus, in terms of Example 20.1, Project B could be seen as less risky than Project A, because the payback period is shorter.

The method is relatively simple to understand and to calculate. Not surprisingly, the method is often used as a first screening method in the appraisal of investment opportunities, before any other of the more sophisticated methods are employed. Hence, in this context the first question to ask in assessing an investment proposal is: 'How long will it take to pay back its cost?' The organization may, for example, have a policy that only projects that pay back within four years will be appraised using other more rigorous methods of appraisal.

There are two important criticisms of the payback method. The first is clearly fundamental and relates to the fact that cash flows after the payback period are ignored. Hence, it could be the case that whilst a project produces a large net cash flow (i.e. where cash inflows significantly exceed outflows), they are generated in the later part of the project and may be ignored as this is after the payback period. For example, in the case of Projects A and B in Example 20.1, Project B was preferred because of its shorter payback period, but overall Project A generates more cash inflows, totalling £130 000 compared with only £90 000 in the case of Project B. However, Project A's cash inflows were mainly earned in the later years. The second criticism of the payback method relates to the method not taking account of the time value of money, similarly to the ARR. This criticism is not entirely valid as the method can be adapted to take account of the timing of cash inflows, which will be considered later.

DISCOUNTED CASH FLOW (DCF)

To recap, the ARR method of investment appraisal ignores the timing of cash flows and the opportunity cost of capital. Payback considers the time it takes to recover the original investment cost, but ignores total cash flows over a project's life.

Discounted cash flow (DCF) is an investment appraisal technique which takes into account both the time value of money and also total cash flows over a project's life. It is therefore often argued with much credence that DCF is a superior method to both ARR and payback as a method of investment appraisal.

From the term 'discounted cash flow', two important characteristics can be identified about the method:

1   The timing of cash flows is taken into account by a process of discounting. The effect of discounting is to give a bigger value per £1 for cash flows that occur in earlier years. For example, £1 earned after one year will be worth more than £1 earned after two years, which in turn will be worth more than £1 earned after ten years. The process of discounting involves selecting a discount rate that reflects an individual's or an organization's time value of money.

2   Cash flows are accounted for in the appraisal, rather than cost and revenues as used in the accruals accounting convention. The reason for this is that in accounting for cash flows, receipts and payments are recognized when they occur. This is not the case for the majority of costs and revenues when employing accruals accounting. For example, the cost of an investment will be accrued over the life of the investment employing a system of depreciation. In contrast, the whole of the cost of the investment when accounting for cash flows would be recognized when the payment is made. This was illustrated in Chapter 10, Cash flow statements. In taking account of the time value of money, it is important that the cost and benefits of an investment are recognized when they are actually paid and received, rather than when they are recognized as a debt or liability or are accrued, as in the case of capital investment expenditure, over the life of the asset.

The process of discounting

Discounting is compounding in reverse. The following example explains the relationship between discounting and compounding.

EXAMPLE 20.2

Suppose that a company invests £10 000 to earn a return of 10% (compound interest). The value of the investment with the interest will accumulate as follows:

$$
\begin{array}{ll}
\text{After one year } £10\,000 \times (1.10) & = £11\,000 \\
\text{After two years } £10\,000 \times (1.10)^2 & = £12\,100 \\
\text{After three years } £10\,000 \times (1.10)^3 & = £13\,310
\end{array}
$$

and so on. This is compounding. The formula for the future value of an investment including accumulated interest earned after n time periods is:

$$FV = PV(1 + r)^n$$

where:

FV   is the future value of the investment with interest.

PV   is the initial or present value of the investment.

r is the compound rate of return (reflecting the time value of money) per time period.

n is the number of time periods; normally measured in years.

Discounting converts future values to present values and is the reverse of compounding. For example, if a company expects to earn a (compound) rate of return of 10% on its investments, how much would it need to invest now (the present value of the future sum) to have an investment of:

£11 000 after one year? or

£12 100 after two years? or

£13 310 after three years?

The answer is £10 000 in each case, and we calculate it by discounting, as follows:

$$\text{After one year, } £11\,000 \times \frac{1}{1.10} = £10\,000$$

$$\text{After two years, } £12\,100 \times \frac{1}{(1.10)^2} = £10\,000$$

$$\text{After three years, } £13\,310 \times \frac{1}{(1.10)^3} = £10\,000$$

The discounting formula to calculate the present value of a future sum of money at the end of n time periods is 1:

$$PV = FV \frac{1}{(1 + r)^n}$$

KEY CONCEPT 20.3

The definition of present value

Present value can be defined as the cash equivalent now of a sum of money receivable or payable at the stated future date, discounted at a specified rate of return.

Discounting can be applied both to money receivable and also to money payable at a future date. Hence, by discounting all payments and receipts from a capital investment to a present value, they can be compared on a common basis at a value which takes account of when the various cash flows will take place. Example 20.3 illustrates the use of the discounted cash flow method in investment appraisal.

EXAMPLE 20.3

Harvey Ltd is investigating an investment opportunity which will generate £40 000 after two years and another £30 000 after three years. Its target rate of return is 12%. The present value of these cash inflows is

Year	Cash flow	Discount factor 12%	Present value £
2	40 000	$\dfrac{1}{(1.12)^2}$	31 880
3	30 000	$\dfrac{1}{(1.12)^3}$	21 360
Total PV			53 240

The present value of the total future inflows of cash, discounted at 12%, is £53 240. This means that if Harvey Ltd can invest now to earn a return of 12% on its investments, it would have to invest £53 240 now to earn £40 000 in two years' time plus £30 000 in three years' time.

In the application of DCF to investment decisions, only future cash flows are relevant. Therefore, the principles detailed in Chapters 17 and 18 relating to decision making are also applicable to long-term investment decisions. Thus, for example, past costs are not relevant because they are sunk, whilst opportunity costs are relevant.

In relation to the payback method of investment appraisal, as examined earlier, the yearly cash flows can be discounted. Therefore, by discounting the cash flows the payback method would then take account of the time value of money. When discounting is applied to the payback method, the term 'discounted payback' is commonly used.

We will now consider the two main methods of using DCF to appraise investment opportunities, namely the net present value (NPV) method and the internal rate of return (IRR) method.

The net present value method

Net present value (NPV) is the value obtained by discounting all cash outflows and inflows of an investment opportunity by a chosen rate of return. It was said earlier that the rate of return was directly associated with an individual's or, in the context of business, a firm's time value of money which will reflect a shareholder's opportunity cost. The opportunity cost in this context is the rate of return shareholders and other providers of capital forgo by investing in the firm. This opportunity cost is commonly referred to as the 'cost of capital'.

The present value of cash inflows minus the present value of the cash outflows is the NPV. Therefore, if the NPV

- is positive, it means that the cash inflows from the investment will yield a return in excess of the cost of capital, and therefore the investment project should be undertaken; in this situation, it can be seen that the business can pay its providers of capital the necessary returns and still have cash to employ in the business;

- is negative, it means that the cash inflows from the investment will yield a return less than that required to satisfy the providers of capital, and therefore the opportunity should be rejected;

- is exactly zero, it means that the investment has generated exactly the required returns to satisfy the providers of capital, without any surplus to employ in the business.

The discount factor that was calculated using the formula $1/(1\ r)^n$ can be more conveniently determined by simply using discount tables. The discount tables for the present value of £1, for differing values of r and n, are given in Appendix C.

Example 20.4 illustrates the use of the NPV method using present value tables.

EXAMPLE 20.4

Benaud Ltd is considering a capital investment, where the estimated cash flows are

Year	Cash flow £
0 (i.e. now)	(100 000)
1	60 000
2	80 000
3	40 000
4	30 000

The company's cost of capital is 15%. What is the NPV of the proposed project, and should it be undertaken?

Solution

Year	Cash flow £	Discount factor at 15%	Present value £
0	(100 000)	1.000	(100 000)
1	60 000	0.870	52 200
2	80 000	0.756	60 480
3	40 000	0.658	26 320
4	30 000	0.572	17 160
NPV			56 160

(*Continued*)

The present value of cash inflows exceeds the present value of cash outflows by £56 160, which means that the project produces a DCF yield in excess of 15%. The project should therefore be undertaken.

In using DCF methods for investment appraisal, there are some important conventions to note regarding the timing of cash flows:

1 A cash flow at the beginning of an investment project, described in the example above as 'now', is assumed to occur in year 0. The present value of £1 now, in year 0 is:

$$\frac{1}{(1+r)^n} = \frac{1}{(1+r)^0} = £1$$

regardless of the value of r. Therefore, as in the example above, the discount factor to use for cash flows arising in year 0 is 1.0.

2 A cash inflow or outflow that occurs during the course of a year rather than at the year end is assumed to happen at the end of the year. For example, £2000 received half-way through the year is assumed to be received at the end of that year. This convention is adopted because of the complexity of discounting sums throughout time periods. Given the uncertainty relating to the future, it is considered that whilst the calculation does not result in an absolutely precise present value, it is a reasonable approximation of reality.

Annuities

Where there are constant cash flows arising at annual intervals for a number of years (known as annuities), time can be saved by using annuity tables, which are given in Appendix C. Example 20.5 illustrates the use of annuity tables and some of the other aspects that are pertinent to decision making using DCF techniques.

EXAMPLE 20.5

Marsh plc is a manufacturing company whose management are currently appraising the production and sale of a new product. This would involve the purchase of a new machine costing £240 000 in addition to using an old machine purchased for £80 000 five years ago, which currently has a net book value of £60 000.

Annual sales of the product would be 5000 units at a selling price of £32 per unit. Unit costs would be

	£
Direct labour (two hours at £4 per hour)	8
Direct materials	7
Fixed costs including depreciation	9
	24

The project would have a five-year life, after which the new machine would have a residual value of £10 000. The fixed overhead absorption rate is estimated to be £4.50 per direct labour hour, but actual expenditure would not alter should the company decide not to produce this new product.

(Continued)

Working capital requirements would be £10 000 at the beginning of the first year, rising to £15 000 in the second year and remaining at this level until the end of the project, when it would be recovered.

The company's cost of capital is 20%. Ignore taxation. Should the company accept this opportunity?

Solution

The NPV is calculated as follows:

Year	Equipment £	Working capital £	Contribution £	Net cash flow £	Discount rate	Present value £
0	(240 000)	(10 000)		(250 000)	1.000	(250 000)
1		(5 000)		(5 000)	0.833	(4 165)
1–5			85 000	85 000	2.991	254 235
5	10 000	15 000		25 000	0.402	10 050
NPV						10 120

Notes and commentary

1 The NPV is positive and therefore should be accepted.

2 Purchase of the new machine in year 0 for £240 000 is an incremental cost which is therefore a relevant cost.

3 The cost of using the old machine is nil – the original cost and the current net book value are irrelevant costs as they are sunk and there appears to be no opportunity cost associated with using this machine.

4 The investment of working capital is a relevant cost because the company will forgo the possibility of being able to invest this money elsewhere for the life of the project. The amount invested as working capital is £10 000 at the beginning of the project, rising to £15 000 at the beginning of year 2. That is £5000 additional investment at the beginning of year 2, which for discounting purposes we can assume arises at the end of year 1. The full £15 000 is recoverable at the end of the project's life.

5 The contribution from the new product is 5000 units × £17(£32 − 15) £85 000 per year. The fixed costs, because they are unavoidable and will not change whether the project is accepted or rejected, are irrelevant. This cash inflow will not change over the five-year period and therefore we can use the annuity tables in determining the present value of these cash flows.

6 The annuity discount factor can be obtained from the table – the present value of an annuity; where n is five years and r is 20%, the factor is 2.991. This discount factor is simply the sum of the individual factors for each of the five years where r is 20% from the present value tables. By multiplying the annual contribution of £85 000 per annum, we obtain the present value of this annuity.

Perpetuities

A perpetuity is an annuity which is expected to last indefinitely – for example, undated government stocks where a fixed rate of interest is received annually but where the capital is unlikely to be repaid. Often perpetuities are used to approximate perceived long time spans, for example for calculating the present value of anticipated returns on an investment that will be held for the foreseeable future. Another example is the revenue generated from the toll on the Dartford tunnel and bridge, which will continue for the foreseeable future.

The present value of any perpetuity is given by the annual receipt or payment, divided by the relevant discount rate. For example, the *PV* of £1 per annum in perpetuity at a discount rate of 10% would be £1/0.10 = £10. Similarly, the present value of £1 per annum in perpetuity at a discount rate of:

$$15\% \text{ would be } \frac{£1}{0.15} = £6.67$$

$$20\% \text{ would be } \frac{£1}{0.20} = £5$$

To apply the present value of £1 per annum in perpetuity to an investment evaluation, we simply multiply the total cash outflow or inflow by the sum of present value of £1 per annum in perpetuity. Therefore, if it is anticipated that the revenue from the tolls at the Dartford tunnel and bridge are to generate inflows of cash of say £10 million pounds per annum for the foreseeable future at a discount rate of 15%, the present value of these streams of cash flows would be:

$$\frac{£1}{0.15} \times £10 \text{ million} = £66.7 \text{ million.}$$

ACTIVITY 20.2

Using the annuity tables in Appendix C and assuming a cost of capital of 10% what is the NPV of an annuity of £2000 for a period of five years but the first payment is received at the end of year 2?

£2000 × 3.7908 (annuity factor for five years) = £7581.60 less £1818 (.909 [annuity factor for year 1] × £2000) = £5763.60.

Internal rate of return (IRR) method

The internal rate of return (IRR) is the second investment appraisal method based on discounted cash flow techniques. Although a number of the principles applicable to IRR are similar to the NPV method, there is a notable difference in the final outcome and the decision criteria. In the application of the IRR method, it is necessary to calculate the exact DCF rate of return which an investment opportunity is expected to achieve, that is the rate of return at which the NPV is equal to 0, and compare this with a target rate, which should be the project's cost of capital. If the expected rate of return exceeds the target rate of return, the project should be undertaken. Conversely, if the expected rate of return is less than the target the opportunity should be rejected.

Without a computer or a programmed calculator, the calculation of the internal rate of return is made by a trial and error technique called interpolation. The first step is to calculate two present values, both as close as possible to zero. The closer to zero, the more accurate will be the end result. Ideally, in applying these two rates the result should be one NPV being positive and the other negative. It is then necessary to use interpolation to establish the rate where NPV is 0. Example 20.6 illustrates the process.

EXAMPLE 20.6

A company is investigating an opportunity to buy a machine for £80 000 now which, it is anticipated, will save £20 000 per annum for five years. It is also anticipated that the machine will have a resale value of £10 000.

We begin by selecting a trial rate, say 9% (note that in this calculation we can use both the PV tables and the annuity tables):

Year	Cash flow £	PV factor at 9%	Present value £
0	(80 000)	1.0	(80 000)
1–5	20 000	3.890	77 800
5	10 000	0.650	6 500
NPV			4 300

£4300 is fairly close to 0, considering the amounts we are computing. We can therefore use 9% as one of the two rates necessary for the calculation of the IRR.

In addition, the NPV is positive, which means that the real rate of return, where NPV is 0, is higher than 9%. We could now try, say, 12%:

Year	Cash flow £	PV factor at 12%	Present value £
0	(80 000)	1.0	(80 000)
1–5	20 000	3.605	72 100
5	10 000	0.567	5 670
NPV			2 230

This NPV is also fairly close to zero but is negative. The real rate of return is therefore greater than 9% (NPV +4300) but less than 12% (NPV = – 2230).

The interpolation method assumes that the NPV rises in a linear fashion between the two NPVs. The formula to apply is:

$$\text{Rate of return} = A + \left[\frac{P}{P+N} \times (B - A) \right]$$

Where:

  A is the (lower) rate of return with a positive NPV.
  B is the (higher) rate of return with a negative NPV.
  P is the amount of the positive NPV.
  N is the amount of the negative NPV.

Now, applying this formula to the data calculated for the project we can calculate the IRR:

$$\text{IRR} = 9\% + \left[\frac{4300}{4300 + 2230} \times (12 - 9) \right]\% = 10.975\%$$

If the cost of capital is, say, 10% we would accept the project because its IRR is greater; if, on the other hand, the cost of capital is 15%, we would not accept this project.

The concept of accounting for the time value of money through using the cost of capital as a discount rate is appealing from a number of perspectives. There are, however, problems in determining the correct discount rate. The cost of capital for an individual project should take account of the risk associated with the project. It is often difficult to measure precisely the risk for individual projects. A detailed discussion of the ways in which the cost of capital can be determined and in particular their problems can be found in a number of financial management texts, including Lumby and Jones (2000).

Case Study 20.2 examines an investment opportunity and employs all four investment appraisal methods in determining an outcome.

It was stated earlier that the accounting rate of return (ARR) and the payback methods of investment appraisal each suffer from serious disadvantages. One ignores the timing of cash flows while the other does not take account of all the relevant cash flows, that is, after the payback period. The DCF methods which we have examined both take account of the timing of cash flows and all the relevant cash flows.

By discounting relevant cash flows by the cost of capital and only accepting opportunities that exceed this return, both DCF methods ensure that shareholders' wealth is maximized. Research suggests that of these two DCF methods of investment appraisal, in practice IRR is favoured. The main explanation given for this preference is that managers appear to prefer to talk in relative percentage terms, rather than absolute sums of money, as in the outcome for NPV decisions. However, although in the majority of situations both the NPV and IRR methods of appraisal will give the same decision, there are occasions, namely when considering mutually exclusive projects, where the two methods are incompatible. In these circumstances the NPV should be used. A full discussion of why the NPV method is preferred can be found in Lumby and Jones (2000).

It can be argued, however, that all the methods have certain attributes, although the DCF methods are arguably the most rigorous from a theoretical perspective.

In many situations, long-term opportunities will be either accepted or rejected, based purely on financial criteria, through the employment of one or more of the methods that we have examined in this chapter. However, it will also be the case that qualitative factors, that is factors which cannot be explicitly quantified in money terms, will be influential and sometimes overriding in a situation. Examples of qualitative factors are given in Chapter 18. Although this chapter has focused on short-term decision making, the nature of the qualitative factors is likely to be similar.

ACTIVITY 20.3

The following are the cash flows in pounds sterling from two opportunities which are mutually exclusive, that is, you can invest in one of the opportunities. It is anticipated that both of these investment opportunities will generate income over a 5-year period. The required investment is £10 000 for each:

Opportunities	Alpha	Gamma
Year 1	3 000	4 000
Year 2	3 000	4 000
Year 3	3 000	2 000
Year 4	8 000	2 000
Year 5	8 000	2 000

Using the payback decision rule of accepting the investment opportunity that pays back the quickest, which opportunity would you accept adopting this decision rule?

Now determine which opportunity you would prefer using the NPV rule based on a 10% discount rate? Using the information you have from these two calculation state which is preferred and why.

Using the payback decision rule Gamma would be preferred because it pays back at the end of the third year. Now using the NPV method at 10% discount rate Alpha will be preferred as it has the highest NPV.

Alpha should be chosen because it satisfies the organization's assumed objective of maximizing shareholders' wealth. The payback method does not take account of payback of cash flows after the payback period has been met

CASE STUDY 20.2

Holefoods Ltd

Holefoods Ltd, an expanding catering firm, are considering tendering for a local authority contract to supply school meals. If they decide to tender and are successful, this will be their first contract in the public sector. The contract is for a period of five years.

The company has spent £2500 on a feasibility study related to this contract. From this study, they have obtained the following estimates of costs, revenues and volumes.

1   The initial cost of the investment for the necessary cooking equipment will be £30 000. This sum will be payable at the beginning of the contract.

2   Selling price of meals: £1.00 per meal for the first three years, then £1.20 for years four and five.

3   Cost of meals: £0.60 per meal for the first three years, then £0.70 for years four and five.

4   Rent of premises is estimated to be £2000 per year.

5   Forecast of the number of meals to be sold:

Year	No. of meals
1	30 000
2	32 000
3	32 000
4	33 000
5	33 000

6   Transport costs: £2000 per year.

7   The company uses straight-line depreciation and intends to charge £1500.

8   The company's cost of capital is 14%.

9   The company expects a payback within four years and its target accounting rate of return is 25%.

Calculate: the NPV, IRR, payback period (undiscounted and discounted) and the ARR.

(Continued)

Solution
NPV

The £2500 spent on the feasibility study is considered to be irrelevant to the decision.

	Year					
	0	**1**	**2**	**3**	**4**	**5**
	£	**£**	**£**	**£**	**£**	**£**
Cost of equipment	(30 000)					
Sales		30 000	32 000	32 000	39 600	39 600
Cost of meals		(18 000)	(19 200)	(19 200)	(23 100)	(23 100)
Transport costs		(2 000)	(2 000)	(2 000)	(2 000)	(2 000)
Rent		(2 000)	(2 000)	(2 000)	(2 000)	(2 000)
Cash flow	(30 000)	8 000	8 800	8 800	12 500	12 500
Cost of capital 14%	1.00	0.877	0.769	0.675	0.592	0.519
Net cash flow	(30 000)	7 016	6 767	5 940	7 400	6 487
Total NPV = + 3 610						

Therefore under the NPV decision rule, accept the proposed project.

IRR

At 14% the NPV was positive £4389; therefore, the IRR, where the NPV is 0, must be greater than 14%; so let us try 20% (note that we only need to discount the cash flows):

	Year					
	0	**1**	**2**	**3**	**4**	**5**
Cash flow	(30 000)	8 000	8 800	8 800	12 500	12 500
Cost of capital 20%	1.00	0.833	0.694	0.578	0.482	0.402
Net cash flow	(30 000)	6 644	6 107	5 086	6 025	5 025
Total NPV = + 1 113						

Using interpolation

$$\text{IRR} = 14\% + \left[\frac{£3610}{£3610 + 1113} \times (20\% - 14\%) \right] = 18.59\%$$

The IRR of the project exceeds the cost of capital, therefore the project will be accepted.

Payback
Undiscounted:

Year	Cash flows £	Cumulative cash flow £
0	(30 000)	(30 000)
1	8 000	(22 000)
2	8 800	(13 200)
3	8 800	(4 400)
4	12 500	8 100

(Continued)

Therefore, the project pays back in the third year; more precisely, £4440/£12 500 × 12 months = 3 years 4.2 months (assuming the cash flows arise evenly throughout the year). As this period is less than four years, the target payback period, we would accept the project.

Discounted: using the discounted cash flow figures in the NPV calculation above based on a 14% cost of capital, the payback profile is as follows:

Year	Cash flows £	Cumulative cash flow £
0	(30 000)	(30 000)
1	7 016	(22 984)
2	6 767	(16 217)
3	5 940	(10 277)
4	7 400	(2 877)
5	6 487	3 610

Therefore, the project pays back in the fifth year; more precisely, £3610/£6487 × 12 months = 4 years and 6.7 months.

ARR

Depreciation based on straight-line depreciation convention: £30 000/five years = £6000 per annum; £6000 needs to be deducted from the undiscounted cash flows per annum, £30 000 (£6000 × five years) over the total life of the project. The sum of the undiscounted cash inflows from the project is £50 600 less £30 000 = £20 600, and the average annual return = £20 600/5 years £4120.

The average investment is £15 000 [(£30 000 + 0)/2], hence

$$ARR = \frac{£4\,120}{£15\,000} \times 100 = 27.5\%$$

The ARR of 27.5% is greater than the target of 25%, therefore the project is acceptable under this criterion.

SUMMARY

In this chapter, we have examined the four main financial methods of investment appraisal: accounting rate of return, payback, net present value and the internal rate of return. For each of the methods we looked at the use of the methods within a business decision-making environment. The attributes of all the methods were considered. It was argued that all the methods have some use within the decision-making process; this explains why a number of companies employ all four methods.

The concept of the time value of money was discussed and the processing of discounting was examined within the context of long-term decision making. Although discounted cash flow methods are relatively more theoretically rigorous, there are problems in determining the cost of capital, the discount rate.

REFERENCE

Lumby, S. and Jones, C. (2000) *Corporate Finance Theory and Practice,* 6th edn, London: Thomson Learning.

FURTHER READING

An interesting analysis of the use of investment appraisal methods in the UK is Arnold, G.C. and Hatzopoulos, P.D. (2000) in the *Journal of Business Finance and Accounting*, 27(5) and (6) pp. 603–26.

REVIEW QUESTIONS

(✓ indicates answers are available in Appendix A)

✓ **1** Explain the main differences between DCF methods of investment appraisal and ARR.

2 Discuss the main attributes of the ARR and payback methods.

3 What is the meant by discounting cash flow? Why is it necessary to discount cash flows?

4 In the employment of DCF investment appraisal methods, explain why cash flows are used rather than accounting profits.

5 What is the effect on the value of the firm and shareholders' wealth if an investment opportunity with an NPV of £5000 is accepted?

PROBLEMS FOR DISCUSSION AND ANALYSIS

(✓ indicates answers are available in Appendix A)

✓ **1** (a) Find the net present value of the following cash flows using a 10% cost of capital:

	Cash flows (£)		
Year	Project A	Project B	Project C
0	(1 500)	(500)	
1	1 300	200	
2	650	200	
3	900	200	
4	2 700	200	
5		200	200
6		200	200
7			200

(b) Find the NPV of £3000 received at the end of each year forever. The first payment is due at the end of the first year and the appropriate discount rate is 10%.

2 The management of Boon and Border plc are in the process of examining the company's investment opportunities. There are six opportunities; the following details provide the relevant information regarding these opportunities.

Project A would cost £29 000 now, and would generate the following cash flows:

Year	£
1	8 000
2	12 000
3	10 000
4	6 000

The equipment included in the cost of the investment could be resold for £5000 at the start of year 5.

Project B would involve a current outlay of £44 000 on capital equipment and £20 000 on working capital. The profits from the project would be as follows:

Year	Sales £	Variable costs £	Contribution £	Fixed cost £	Profit £
1	75 000	50 000	25 000	10 000	15 000
2	90 000	60 000	30 000	10 000	20 000
3	42 000	28 000	14 000	8 000	6 000

Fixed costs include an annual charge of £4000 for depreciation; all the other fixed costs are avoidable. At the end of year 3 the working capital investment would be recovered and the equipment would be sold for £5000.

Project C would involve a current outlay of £50 000 on equipment and £15 000 on working capital. The investment in working capital would be increased to £21 000 at the end of the first year. Annual cash profits would be £18 000 per annum for five years, at the end of which the investment in working capital would be recovered.

Project D would involve an outlay of £20 000 now and a further outlay of £20 000 after one year. Cash profits thereafter would be as follows:

Year	£
2	15 000
3	12 000
4–8	8 000 p.a.

Project E is a long-term project involving an immediate outlay of £32 000 and annual cash profits of £4500 p.a. in perpetuity.

Project F is another long-term project, involving an immediate outlay of £20 000 and annual cash profits as follows:

Years	£
1–5	5 000
6–10	4 000
11 in perpetuity	3 000

The company discounts all projects of ten years' duration or less at a cost of capital of 12%, and all longer projects at a cost of 15%.

Required

(a) Calculate the NPV of each project, and determine which should be undertaken by the company.
(b) Calculate the IRR of projects A, C and E.
(c) Calculate the discounted and non-discounted payback periods of project A.
(d) Calculate the accounting rate of return.

3 The Waugh Electronics Company Ltd is thinking of buying, at a cost of £22 000, some new quality control equipment that is expected to save £5000 in cash operating costs. Its estimated useful life is ten years, and it will have a zero disposal value.

Calculate:

(a) Internal rate of return.

(b) Net present value if the cost of capital is 16%.

(c) Payback period.

(d) Accounting rate of return based on initial investment and on average investment.

4 Dr Oliver has £1000 which he will decide to invest if he can be reasonably confident that his investment will earn at least 10% p.a. He is considering three projects, each of which would cost £1000 to begin:

(a) Project A would earn £1090 at the end of the first year.

(b) Project B would earn £1250 at the end of the second year.

(c) Project C would earn £700 at the end of the first year, and another £700 at the end of the second year.

Advise Dr Oliver.

CHAPTER 21
MANAGEMENT OF
WORKING CAPITAL

LEARNING OUTCOMES

By the end of this chapter you will be able to:

- Understand the importance of managing working capital and optimizing the individual levels of current assets and trade payables.

- Explain the working capital cycle.

- Appreciate the importance of case management.

- Calculate inventory optimizing models.

- Manage trade payables and credit.

Management of working capital is critical to the survival and development of all business entities. In this chapter, we will consider why it is so important and examine the main elements of working capital.

All organizations that produce and sell goods and services will need to invest in current assets. Current assets represent assets held in the short term to ensure that day-to-day operations can effectively be carried out. Although, the investment in various types of current assets will depend on the particular demands of the business and the goods and services sold, typically the investments will include receivables, inventory and the maintenance of a cash balance.

The main source of finance for current assets will normally be from short-term credit sources. Short-term credit sources were discussed in Chapter 9 and will normally include trade credit and bank overdrafts. They are conventionally described as accounts payable or creditors.

Working capital is the difference between the monetary value of current assets and current liabilities. If the difference is positive, that is when current assets exceed current liabilities, working capital is said to be 'positive'. For example, if total current assets add up to £3000 and current liabilities total £1200, the difference £1800 is 'positive' working capital and thus will be additionally financed from sources other than by short-term credit. Where current liabilities exceed current assets, this is known as 'negative' working capital. This means that short-term sources of finance are also financing non-current assets which may be seen as imprudent.

KEY CONCEPT 21.1

Definition of working capital

Working capital is the difference between current assets and current liabilities, measured in monetary terms.

As we have pointed out in previous chapters, the nature of the business is likely to be very influential on the type and extent of the assets and the working capital employed in a business. For example, a manufacturing firm is likely to have high levels of raw materials, work in progress (WIP) and finished goods; it will sell goods on credit while receiving credit from suppliers of the raw materials. In the case of a retail business the working capital requirements are likely to be very different. For example, retailers will only have one category of inventory, goods for resale, and are unlikely to give their customers credit, but you can always ask! What this tells us is that the resources employed in the management of working capital should reflect the needs of the business.

A business's liquidity is closely linked with working capital. Liquidity refers to the ability of the business to meet debts when they fall due, which is clearly critical if it is to survive. In Chapter 12, Financial statement analysis, liquidity was examined primarily from an external user perspective. Here we will consider liquidity from a slightly different perspective, that of management.

The various types of working capital tend to be related and have implications for other aspects of the business. The decision, for example, to increase the period of credit given to customers is likely to increase the level of receivables and increase the volume of sales. The level of inventory is also likely to rise to support these extra sales. These increases will inevitably have an effect on the financing of the firm, in particular its liquidity.

We begin the chapter by examining why the management of working capital is important. This is followed by looking more closely at the working capital cycle. Each element of the cycle is examined to assess the opportunity to minimize the investment while maintaining a sufficient level of investment to carry out day-to-day operations. Finally, the main types of working capital are examined separately in a business context supported by mini case studies. In this chapter, we will be drawing upon a number of concepts and techniques that have already been studied in earlier chapters in the book. When this is the case, references will be made to the relevant chapter.

THE IMPORTANCE OF MANAGEMENT OF WORKING CAPITAL

The need to manage current assets

For most businesses, the investment in current assets is significant and essential to carry out day-to-day operations. Current assets will normally be financed by a mixture of those who supply short-term funding, for example trade payables and banks, and the business itself. It is the portion of current assets that is financed by the businesses that is categorized as working capital. Working capital is therefore a part of the business's capital which is represented by investments by the owners, who in the case of a company would be shareholders. The owners of a business will expect a return, but, unlike other assets, current assets in the main do not generate monetary returns and as such tight management of working capital is vital if the business is to maximize returns. It is also important for businesses to manage their short-term sources of funds as the suppliers may wish to restrict the credit given. In the case of banks, they may restrict or increase the charge for the facility. Another important reason why current assets need to be managed is to ensure that they are sufficient to support the day-to-day operations of the business. For example, too tight a control of inventory could lead to shortages of items and a loss of customer goodwill.

It is to the firm's advantage to keep this investment in working capital to a minimum but at the same time invest sufficiently in current assets to be able to carry out day-to-day trading activities efficiently. This balance between the cost and the level of working capital must be carefully managed. As we have said, if, for example, inventory is kept at too low a level this may result in running out of goods, which may lead to the business losing custom. On the other hand, investing too much in inventory will increase the direct costs of the business in addition to incurring opportunity costs.

The cost of investing in working capital

We now examine in more detail the concept of the cost of investing in working capital. The cost of investing in working capital, as mentioned above, is the direct costs plus the opportunity cost (the concept of opportunity cost is generally defined in Key Concept 17.3). The direct cost is the cost of the capital invested in working capital, e.g. the interest on the additional debt finance needed to sustain a higher level of working capital. In the context of working capital, the opportunity cost is represented by the returns forgone by investing in current assets rather than in some alternative investment opportunity. For example, the opportunity cost of investing in inventory is the returns received for investing the money elsewhere. There may, of course, be a number of opportunities. When this is the case the opportunity cost is the alternative that renders the greatest return.

KEY CONCEPT 21.2

Opportunity cost of working capital

The returns forgone by investing in working capital rather than some alternative investment opportunity.

Financing working capital and the type of business

The way in which businesses finance themselves and particularly their working capital needs are important. There are alternative sources of finance available but there is a need to take account of their cost and maturity. Sources of finance were examined in Chapter 9 and you may wish to revisit that chapter to refresh your knowledge of the various types of finances available.

Businesses face particular working capital funding problems when they are subject to seasonal trading variations. In such circumstances, it is likely that the size of the investment in current assets will reflect this seasonality and the funding will also have to mirror these trading variations. Businesses, therefore, need to plan and determine their working capital needs. These plans will normally and wisely be translated into the businesses budget. The cash budget as discussed in Chapter 19 plays a significant part in the management of working capital.

Liquidity

In terms of liquidity, the management of working capital is critical. Businesses must ensure they have enough liquid resources to meet any demands upon them. For example, if a business starts to expand quickly and has to invest heavily in current assets to support this expansion, they may find themselves overstretching their cash resources. This is often referred to as overtrading and can lead to the businesses going into liquidation.

KEY CONCEPT 21.3

Overtrading

Overtrading describes the situation where a business has expanded its turnover to a level not supported by its investment in working capital.

In cases where there is negative working capital, that is when the short-term payables are financing current assets and a proportion of fixed assets, it may be the case that the firm is unable to obtain liquid funds quickly to pay off payables, thus creating a liquidity crisis. This is not to say that when a business has negative working capital that it will result in insolvency or financial distress. The financial report for 2003 for Sainsbury plc, the supermarket chain, for example, shows a negative working capital of £621 million. Sainsbury has the benefit of a high level of trade credit but a very low level of receivables. They also have very large cash resources in hand and at the bank, both of which are common to this type of business. It is clear that although Sainsbury plc has a large negative working capital, it is unlikely that the company will experience any serious short-term liquidity problems as it is normal practice for retail organizations to have a negative working capital balance.

External users

It is important that management are aware that external parties to the business will also be monitoring the company's management of working capital and in particular their liquidity. Management therefore not only have to make decisions regarding working capital which they perceive are important for effective operating of the business itself, but must also take account of external parties' perceptions of the businesses management of working capital. For example, when banks make lending decisions, they will normally closely examine an applicant's management of working capital. This is likely to give the bank some indication of how well the applicant's business is managed and provide information for the bank's decision whether to lend or not. For quoted companies, analysts are also likely to examine working capital management of firms. Poor working capital management may lead analysts to 'mark down' the share price.

THE WORKING CAPITAL CYCLE

The working capital cycle – sometimes referred to as the 'cash cycle' or the 'operating cycle' – is utilized to determine the time from any investment outlay or investment in current assets to the inflow of cash derived from the investment. The measure is usually in terms of days, that is the number of days it takes to transform current assets into cash, less the number of day's credit allowed by suppliers of goods and services. Differing industrial sectors will tend to have different cycles measured in days. In some circumstances the cycle can be negative. This is likely to be the case with supermarkets such as Sainsbury plc, cited earlier, which have a negative cycle because they tend to sell for cash and therefore have very low receivables but will have taken advantage of the large amounts of trade credit available to them. This, of course, means that suppliers, in this case, are financing the whole of the current assets in addition to a proportion of longer term assets.

Figure 21.1 illustrates the flows of cash within the cycle.

KEY CONCEPT 21.4

The working capital cycle

The working capital cycle is the period of time from the investment into current assets to the inflow of cash derived from the investment.

FIGURE 21.1

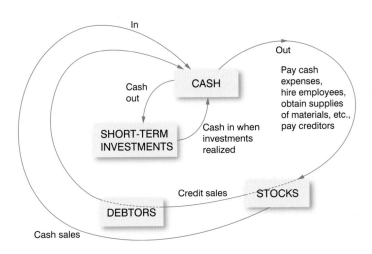

Figure 21.1 shows that payments relating to operating expenses and other costs are continually made and this subsequently results in the inflow of cash through sales. The diagram also shows cash inflows and outflows in respect of short-term investments. Businesses often use facilities at their banks and other institutions to invest surplus cash in the short term. There are some liabilities that are paid periodically throughout the year, say on a quarterly basis or even once a year, as in the case of business taxes. In these circumstances cash reserves should ideally be built up during the year to meet these debts and these should be placed in short-term interest paying bank accounts. There are, of course, other types of payments which are not explicitly referred to in the diagram, such as the purchase of fixed and other non-current assets. These payments must also be carefully managed.

We will use an example to illustrate and explain the analysis needed to determine the length of the working capital cycle.

EXAMPLE 21.1

Bugg Ltd is a medium-sized manufacturing company. The owner, who also manages the business, has recently read in the financial pages of a business magazine that management should regularly monitor the business's working capital cycle; that is, the time lag between paying for raw materials and recovering from your customers the value of the sales.

The following information is relevant for determining the working capital cycle for Bugg Ltd. All customers are given credit.

	2008 £
Inventory:	
Raw materials	20 000
Work-in-progress	14 000
Finished goods	16 000
Purchases on credit	96 000
Cost of goods sold	140 000
Sales on credit	160 000
Receivables	32 000
Payables	16 000

The working capital cycle in days is calculated based upon turnover ratios, some of which you will remember from Chapter 12. These are as follows:

	No. of days
Raw materials turnover	
$= \dfrac{\text{raw materials}}{\text{purchase on credit}} \times 365 = \dfrac{20\,000}{96\,000} \times 365$	76
Less: credit from suppliers (payables turnover)	
$= \dfrac{\text{payables}}{\text{purchase on credit}} \times 365 = \dfrac{16\,000}{96\,000} \times 365$	$\dfrac{61}{15}$

(Continued)

	No. of days
Production period (WIP turnover)	
$= \dfrac{\text{work in progress}}{\text{cost of goods sold}} \times 365 = \dfrac{14\,000}{1\,40\,000} \times 365$	37
Finished goods inventory (finished goods turnover)	
$= \dfrac{\text{finished goods}}{\text{cost of goods sold}} \times 365 = \dfrac{16\,000}{1\,40\,000} \times 365$	42
Credit taken by customers (receivables turnover)	
$= \dfrac{\text{accounts receivable}}{\text{sales}} \times 365 = \dfrac{32\,000}{1\,60\,000} \times 365$	$\dfrac{73}{167}$

(i) 365 days represent the number of days in the year.

(ii) Entries under No. of days have been rounded to whole numbers.

Therefore, the working capital cycle for Bugg Ltd is 167 days, which can be described as the approximate time span from the purchase of supplies of materials to the receipt of cash from customers.

The individual calculations can be interpreted as follows:

1 Inventory of raw materials – 76 days: the number of days inventory of supplies held by the company.

2 Credit from suppliers – 61 days: the number of days it takes, on average, for the firm to pay suppliers. Normally, this period will reflect the contract conditions between the supplier and their customer. The number of day's credit is conventionally deducted from the number of day's inventory in hand because it is the suppliers who, through the provision of trade credit, are partially financing the investment in inventory.

3 Production period – 37 days: this relates to work in progress and represents the average time it takes to produce goods.

4 Finished goods inventory – 42 days: this inventory is ready for sale and represents a buffer to meet customers demand for goods.

5 Receivables – 73 days: this represents the average length of the credit taken by customers. It may well be that the contractual credit given is less than 73 days, this would mean customers are abusing the contract conditions. The subject of late payment will be considered later in the chapter.

It can be seen from the example that in general the longer the cycle, the greater is the investment in working capital and vice versa. There is, as mentioned previously, a balance to be achieved between having too much invested in working capital, the opportunity cost, and having too little which could, for example, result in losing customers. Because there may be insufficient goods available for sale, management has to think through alternative ways to manage the working capital cycle and the impacts of their actions. For example, they could reduce the time given to customers to pay their debts and this will clearly reduce the length of the cycle and thereby free cash resources for alternative profitable employment. However, the potential cost of reducing the credit period is that customers will go elsewhere and find suppliers who will offer relatively more attractive credit terms.

Some other possible ways of decreasing the working capital cycle are as follows:

● Reduce the inventory of raw materials and finished goods. However, management will have to be cautious in pursuing such policies as they may result in stock-out costs. For example, not having sufficient finished goods to meet customers demands which could result in customers taking their trade elsewhere. Similarly, there are stock-out costs for raw material inventory as this can have a detrimental effect on the business by stopping production of goods because of the lack of materials and having to wait for deliveries while still incurring other costs, e.g. wages, overheads.

● Delay payments to suppliers. This will increase the credit taken in number of days which will ultimately reduce the operating cycle. This, however, can be a dangerous strategy as it could lead to a loss of goodwill from suppliers, for example the supplier refusing to trade with the business or trading on the basis of cash or strict credit terms.

It should be apparent from these examples that there is a critical balance between the costs and benefits in deciding upon the level of individual current assets and liabilities. A number of models have been developed that give companies a reasonable indication of the optimum levels of working capital, some of which will be examined in more detail in this chapter.

The use of the working capital cycle measure is a useful tool for management in the overall control and management of working capital. In particular, comparisons may be made historically, e.g. by comparing the current year with previous years, and by comparing the firm's cycle with industry averages.

TRADE CREDIT

The nature of trade credit

Trade credit is one of the most important sources of short-term finance for most businesses and is characterized by one business entity extending credit to another on the purchase of goods or services. The advantage in employing trade payables for short-term finance is that it is free, that is there are no explicit costs. This is not the case with any other sources of finance, for example bank loans.

Although there are no direct costs associated with employing trade payables as a source of funding, the level must be carefully managed. The balance between short-term payables and liquid assets or nearliquid assets such as short-term investments is critical to any business. Liquidity problems for a business could result in not having enough cash to pay suppliers when the debt falls due. In these circumstances, a supplier's initial response is likely to be a refusal to supply the business with any future credit purchases. Ultimately, non-payment could result in suppliers applying for a court order to wind up the business. The management must therefore carefully monitor and manage the level of their payables.

Another reason why trade payables should be managed carefully is that in November 1998, the UK government introduced legislation to give businesses a statutory right to claim interest from other businesses for late payment of commercial debt. Further details of this legislation can be found at www.payontime.co.uk.

Interested parties from outside the business will often be concerned about the balance of trade payables and liquid resources, and use this information for judging the status of the business from their perspectives. For example, a bank, in making lending decisions, is likely to examine closely a business's ability to remain trading for the foreseeable future and to examine the client's capability to repay the loan and interest. The demands from suppliers in the form of trade payables could well be critical to the firm's ability to meet such repayments.

Measuring the level of trade credit

An important measure used in determining the level of trade payables at any point in time is the payables turnover ratio, which was calculated earlier in the working capital cycle computations. The ratio computes the time taken by the business to pay suppliers (measured in days).

KEY CONCEPT 21.5

Payables turnover ratio.

$$\frac{\text{trade payables}}{\text{credit purchase}} \times 365 \text{ days}$$

Ideally, the denominator in this ratio should only include costs relating to purchases of goods and services on credit as indicated by the term 'credit purchases'. For internal purposes, information relating to goods and services purchased on credit is likely to be available and accessible. For external parties, in examining the business from an outsider's perspective, this will not always be the case. In such cases, surrogate information may be used, for example, the cost of goods/services sold shown in the annual financial report. The cost of goods/services sold may not exclusively relate to supplies/services purchased on credit. Other costs may be included such as wages and salaries, which are not related to trade purchases on credit. In the case of most UK companies, the 'Notes to the accounts' will invariably give a breakdown of the cost of goods/services sold. From these notes, a reasonable estimate can be made of what goods are purchased on credit and those costs, such as salaries, that do not involve credit. In these circumstances judgement must be employed in deciding how appropriate it is to use the ratio.

In terms of management's control and monitoring of liquidity the payables turnover ratio can be usefully employed with other ratios such as the quick ratio and the current ratio. It is important, however, to recognize that the information derived from these ratios should be used historically and comparatively in terms of industry averages. From this analysis trends may be established which will help management make informed decisions.

Another useful tool for managing trade payables is a schedule of aged debts. This schedule lists payables outstanding based on the age of the debt. From this management can see the amounts they owe to individual suppliers and the period for which these debts have been owed. Most accounting software packages automatically produce such schedules.

Cash discounts

A number of suppliers of goods and services who offer credit terms often also offer discounts for earlier payment than that stipulated in the contract. These circumstances create a choice for businesses. Do they take the whole credit period to pay the debt or do they pay earlier and receive a discount? The offer may be put in the following terms: 30 days' credit on receipt of services rendered; a cash discount of 1% of the invoice price if the debt is paid within ten days. The benefit of accepting the cash discount must be balanced by the cost of not having the credit available from the supplier over the normal credit period. If the cash discount is not taken there is a benefit foregone which is an opportunity cost.

EXAMPLE 21.2

The following details relate to a debt of £1000 incurred by Coyle plc. The terms of trade are 2% cash discount if the invoice is paid within ten days, the normal terms of payment being within 30 days. Assume that the company currently has a bank overdraft on which interest is payable at 14% per annum. Should Coyle plc accept or reject the offer of a cash discount?

(Continued)

Cost if the cash discount is accepted:

$$£980(£1000 - 2\%)$$

Therefore, this option would save £20.

Cost if cash discount is rejected:
The payment of £1000 will be made to the supplier on the thirtieth day. However, the company would have a period of 20 days extra (30 – 10 days) to employ the money; in this case the overdraft we can assume will be reduced by this amount for 20 days. This would save the company:

$$£980\,20 \times 365 \times 14\% = £7.51$$

Therefore, by rejecting the discount the net affect of paying the supplier £1000 in 30 days and employing this money to reduce the overdraft, saving £7.51, will be £1000 – £7.51 = £992.49.
The company should, on the basis of this information, accept the cash discount because there are greater savings (£20 – £7.51 = £12.49).

TRADE RECEIVABLES

Giving credit to customers is an important way of securing sales. Some industries have norms in terms of the days of credit given; for example, it could be that 45 days is the norm in terms of credit given across a specific industry sector. If a business entity in this sector were not to offer credit it is likely to reduce their chances of selling any goods or services because by not offering credit the price of the goods or services are effectively higher than the competitors are charging. However, it should be remembered that many types of industry sectors do not traditionally allow trade credit. For example, retail shops normally trade based on cash or debit and credit cards. This is demonstrated in Sainsbury plc's annual financial report for the year ended 29 March 2003, where in the balance sheet their debtors (trade receivables) balance is £297 000 and their cash and bank balance is just over £3 m. The efficient management of receivables is concerned with the problem of achieving an optimum level of investment into this current asset.

The optimum level of receivables

In deciding a policy for determining the optimum level of receivables the following should be taken into account:

- The trade-off between:
  - extending credit in order to increase the volume of sales and profits and
  - the opportunity cost and administrative costs of carrying increased receivables, as well as the potential increase in bad debts.
- The level of risk a business is prepared to extend to individual customers wishing to purchase goods/services on credit. This risk can be identified through an analysis of individual customers.
- The investment in debt collection management.

Debt collection policies

The overall debt collection policy of a firm should be set where the margin between the benefits from the profits generated from the sales of goods and services and the administrative and other costs incurred in debt collection is at its greatest.

It is common to find that extra spending on debt collection management will reduce bad debts and reduce the average collection period. This in turn will reduce the cost of the investment in receivables (that is, the opportunity cost of this investment). However, beyond a certain level of expenditure on debt collection management the saving from a reduced level of bad debts and the reduction in the average collection period will not be sufficient to justify the extra administrative costs.

Credit control – individual accounts

An important aspect of the management of trade receivables is the initial investigation of potential credit customers and the continuing control of outstanding accounts. The main points to consider in these two processes are as follows:

- References from, for example, banks regarding a potential customer's financial standing.

- Checking a customer's credit rating with agencies such as Dun and Bradstreet.

- Initially adopting a conservative credit policy. This may include the amount of credit allowed in money terms and the period allowed for payment. If the customer consistently pays on time and generally behaves reasonably, the firm may then decide to increase the level of credit.

- The annual accounts of customers, if available, may be a useful source of information to assess customers' creditworthiness.

- Aged receivables (aged debtors) lists should be produced periodically, detailing outstanding debt by customers, and the time these debts have been outstanding. This list should be monitored regularly and action if necessary taken in respect of breaches of the credit allowed to individual customers.

- Press comments should be checked, in particular information relating to the creditworthiness of current and potential future customers.

- Debt judgements given by the County Court against businesses or individuals is available on a Register of County Court Judgements which is maintained for six years. This register is available for the public to inspect for a small fee and it may be appropriate to check if a potential new customer has had any judgements against them prior to deciding whether or not to give credit.

ACTIVITY 21.1

In a recession name and describe three working capital issues that management need to monitor closely.
  The following are three issues:

- Cash levels: this may be addressed by a detailed cash budget that needs to reviewed constantly to ensure liquidity and a rigorous monitoring system.
- Late payment.
- Stock levels: to ensure stock levels reflect the lower level demand that is normally experienced in a recession.

Total credit given

An important decision that management of businesses must make is the level of total credit to be maintained and whether this level should be extended. In determining whether it is profitable to extend credit, the following should be taken into consideration:

- the extra sales that a more generous credit policy would stimulate;

- the profitability of extra sales;

- the extra length of the average debt collection period;

- the required rate of return (opportunity cost) on the investment in additional receivables;

- the increase in bad debts that would normally result from an increase in volume of sales which would follow the introduction of a more generous credit policy;

- additional administration costs in managing additional credit sales.

The average debt collection period can be measured by the receivables turnover ratio.

KEY CONCEPT 21.6

Receivables turnover ratio.

$$\frac{\text{trade receivables}}{\text{credit sales}} \times 365 \text{ days}$$

Example 21.3 examines a decision to extend credit.

EXAMPLE 21.3

The Ovraj Company

The Ovraj Company is a manufacturing company. The company is considering whether to adopt a more liberal credit policy as a means of increasing sales above the present monthly level of £40 000. The current average collection period is one month with no bad debts. If the credit period is lengthened, however, it is anticipated that sales will increase and some bad debts will be incurred. The following details two options:

Increase in credit period	Increase in sales above £40 000 per month	% bad debts
½ month	£2 000	1
1 month	£3 200	2

(Continued)

The price of the only product manufactured is only £1 per unit with a variable cost of £0.60, which is anticipated to remain constant as production increases. Fixed costs are estimated to be £96 000 per annum.

It is anticipated that it will not be necessary to increase inventory even if the volume of sales increase. All investment in receivables will be financed from retained earnings; taxes can be ignored. Total investment in the company's net assets, excluding receivables, is fixed at £1 400 000.

The following analysis shows the credit policy that will maximize reported profits:

	Current policy (1 month)	Increase in credit period by ½ month (to 1½ months)	Increase in credit period by 1 month (to 2 months)
Sales per month	40 000	42 000	43 200
Sales per annum	480 000	504 000	518 400
Variable costs	288 000	302 400	311 040
Contribution	192 000	201 600	207 360
Bad debts	–	5 040	10 368
Net contribution	192 000	196 560	196 992
Fixed costs	96 000	96 000	96 000
Profit	96 000	100 560	100 992

Notes:

1 Sales p.a. = sales per month × 12

2 Variable costs per annum = sales p.a. × £0.60.

3 Bad debts = sales × % bad debts; representing what is foregone by Ovraj if receivables become bad.

The above analysis shows that the most profitable option in terms of reported profits is to increase the credit period by one month to two months – a profit of £100 992. This solution, however, ignores the additional investment required in receivables to support this increase in sales, which represents the opportunity cost of increasing sales.

The following analysis examines the above results taking into account this opportunity cost for each of the options assuming that the company has a expected return on investment of 20% per annum. The criteria will then be to select the option that has the highest profit after charging the opportunity cost of this increase in receivables.

	Current policy (1 month)	Increase in credit period by ½ month (to 1½ months)	Increase in credit period by 1 month (to 2 months)
Receivables	40 000	63 000	86 200
Reported profits (as above)	96 000	100 560	100 992
Opportunity cost (20% × receivables)	8 000	12 600	17 280
Net profit	88 000	87 960	83 712

Notes:

1 Receivables = sales per month × the number of months credit, e.g. two months' credit £43 200 two months £86 400.

If the opportunity cost of the investment in receivables is taken into account the preferred option would remain at one month.

INVENTORY

The word 'inventory' is the term which is used in the USA and included in international accounting standards. In the UK 'stock' is the term that has traditionally been used and will continue to be used for some time. Both of these terms mean the same.

Categories of inventory

The industrial sector that a business operates in will be very influential in determining the importance of inventory in monetary terms and operational terms. For example, in manufacturing industries inventory is important from both perspectives, that is it will normally represent a large proportion of the current assets and in operation terms it is critical that it is efficiently managed. Normally, in manufacturing businesses there will be three categories of inventory – raw materials, work in progress (WIP) and finished goods. The cost element of each of these categories will differ. The value of raw material will normally contain the cost of raw material and any cost bringing the raw material to its destination, whereas WIP will consist of raw materials and other direct costs that have been incurred at that stage of production and will also include a proportion of overhead costs. Finished goods, on the other hand, will include all the costs of production plus other administrative costs of bringing these goods to the present state.

A retail business, in contrast, is likely to have one category of inventory – that for resale. Service industries will vary in what is included in their inventory; for example, a firm of accountants is likely to have work in progress at any point in time which will similarly be the case with other professional services such as solicitors. The value of the inventory in these latter cases is likely to be very significant in proportion to the overall value of these businesses and therefore will need to be well managed.

Terms and definitions

There are a number of key terms and definitions used in the management of inventory. The following are the main terms and definitions:

- Stock-outs: these arise when there is a requirement for an item of inventory, but none is available at that particular time, i.e. the business is temporarily out of inventory or stock.

- Lead time: the time which elapses between the placing of an order for inventory and delivery.

- Buffer stock or inventory: this is the level of inventory held in case of unexpectedly high demand and/or the inventory required to meet demand during the lead time.

- The order quantity: the number of units of an item in one order.

- The reorder quantity: the balance of units remaining in inventory at which will be triggered an order for additional inventory.

The reasons for businesses holding inventory

The principal reasons why a business may hold inventory are as follows:

- Inventory acts as a buffer when there is an unusual high demand.

- Holding inventory enables businesses to take advantage of quantity discounts by buying in bulk.

- Any delay in production caused by a lack of materials or parts is kept to a minimum.

- To ensure the business is not forced to purchase inventory at a higher price than may otherwise have been necessary simply because it needs to replenish inventory quickly.

- The loss of customer goodwill from not being able to meet demand.

- To take advantage of seasonal and other price fluctuations.

Inventory costs

We have already reflected on the benefits of inventory in terms of the reasons why businesses hold inventory. As was the case with trade receivables and trade payables, there are also costs of holding inventory. Inventory costs are conventionally categorized into four groups:

The costs of the inventory itself

- raw materials;

- direct labour;

- associated indirect costs (e.g. supervisor's wages).

Holding costs

- the capital tied up in inventory (the opportunity cost);

- warehousing and handling costs;

- deterioration costs;

- obsolescence;

- insurance;

- pilferage.

Ordering costs

- costs of raising orders;

- delivery costs.

Stock-out costs

- loss of sales;

- loss of customers' goodwill;

- cost of lost production;

- extra cost of having to replenish inventory quickly, possibly at higher prices.

Although the references to inventory costs above tend to focus on manufacturing industries, similar costs are incurred by other types of business such as retail shops, especially loss of goodwill and customers, which in 2004 led to changes in the top management at Sainsbury plc.

Inventory control

The management of inventory in a business is important, particularly where the investment is large in proportion to the total assets of the business. Therefore, efficient systems and procedures are critical and these need to be reinforced with periodic inventory checks.

Control of inventory levels is often achieved by collecting, for each inventory item, details of the amounts used in an average period (average), an exceptionally busy period (maximum) and exceptionally slack period (minimum). The supplier's delivery period or lead time would be analyzed in a similar way, identifying the average, maximum and minimum delivery times. Having this information at hand it is possible to calculate a level of inventory (a reorder level) that will trigger a fresh purchase. If stock-outs are to be avoided, a very conservative level may be set as follows:

$$\text{reorder level} = \text{maximum delivery period} \times \text{maximum usage}$$

It will also be necessary to determine a reorder quantity, that is the quantity of inventory for a particular inventory item which should be ordered when inventories have fallen to the reorder level. There are relatively sophisticated inventory management models, in particular the economic order quantity (EOQ) model, which can determine the optimum reorder quantity taking account of the holding and ordering costs. This model will be examined later after considering a less sophisticated model. For small values, less sophisticated models are more appropriate as they focus on choosing a level of inventory which will minimize the administrative inconvenience of frequent reordering without leading to excessive high levels of inventory being held.

EXAMPLE 21.4

Reorder level and reorder quantity

Miles plc uses circuit boards for the manufacture of its washing machines. These boards are one of hundreds of low-value inventory items that are stored. Usage of the boards is expected to be at a rate of about 30 000 per year. Management estimates that the maximum weekly usage is about 750 and minimum weekly usage about 400. Experience has shown that suppliers deliver on average three weeks after an order is placed, but it can be as much as four weeks or as little as two weeks.

Suggest a reorder quantity for the circuit boards.

The following analysis details a reorder level and quantity:

Average weekly usage of boards 30 000 p.a./50 weeks = 600 per week (assuming a 50 working week year).

The average usage between the time an order is placed and the time the goods are received is 600 boards × 3 weeks = 1800 boards.

However, the maximum usage during the supplier's lead time is 750 boards × 4 weeks = 3000 boards.

A cautious management may decide to keep 3000 boards in inventory at any point. It follows that the company should reorder no later than when the inventory level reaches 3000 in order to avoid a stock-out and the associated costs of such an event.

The above analysis ignores a number of important factors, particularly the holding costs and inventory order costs.

Economic order quantity

The economic order quantity (EOQ), which is also referred to as economic batch quantity (EBQ), is the order quantity for an item of inventory which minimizes costs.

There are a number of assumptions underpinning the basic EOQ model:

- Demand for the inventory item is certain, constant and continuous over time.

- The supply lead time is constant and certain, or else there is instantaneous resupply.

- No stock-outs are permitted.

- All prices are constant and certain, and there are no bulk purchases discounts.

- The cost of holding inventory is proportional to the quantity of inventory held.

Notation

D = the usage in units; C the cost of placing an order;

H = holding costs;

Q = the reorder quantity.

The assumptions set out above lead to a regular pattern of usage as shown below where an average inventory $Q/2$ can be determined and the inventory is replenished just at the point when existing inventory run out to point Q, which will be at the maximum inventory level (Figure 21.2).

As H is the holding cost per unit of inventory, the cost of holding the average inventory for one time period is:

$$\frac{Q}{2} \times H$$

The number of orders for inventory made in a time period depends upon the annual usage D. The number of orders made in a time period will equal:

$$\frac{D}{Q}$$

If the cost of making one order is C, then the total ordering costs for the time period will equal:

$$\frac{C \times D}{Q}$$

Therefore, the total cost per time period T, equals:

$$\frac{Q}{2} \times C + \frac{C \times D}{Q}$$

FIGURE 21.2

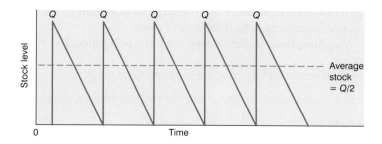

The objective is to minimize T.

As there are no stock-out costs, no buffer inventory and no bulk purchase discounts, these are the only costs which vary with size of the order.

The formula

The formula for economic order quantity (EOQ), i.e. Q, can be derived from the above total cost per time T using calculus. For your studies here, you should simply accept the following formula as the basis for determining EOQ:

$$Q = \sqrt{\frac{2CD}{H}}$$

EXAMPLE 21.5

The demand for a commodity is 40 000 units per year, used at a constant rate throughout the year. It costs £20 to place an order and 40p to hold a unit for a year. The following details the computation to determine the order size at the minimum costs, the number of orders placed each year and the length of the inventory cycle:

$$Q = \sqrt{\frac{20 \times 20 \times 40\,000}{0.4}}$$

$= 2\,000$ units (the economic order quantity that minimizes costs)

Hence, the orders per year that should be made:

$$= \frac{40\,000}{2\,000} = 20 \text{ orders per year}$$

and it follows that the stock cycle is:

$$\frac{52 \text{ weeks}}{20 \text{ orders}} = 2.6 \text{ weeks}$$

The variability of costs with the order size can be represented by the graph shown in Figure 21.3.

(Continued)

FIGURE 21.3

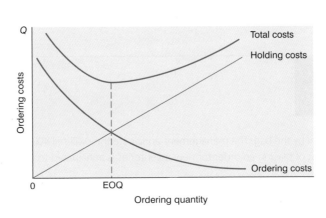

At the EOQ order size, ordering costs per period will equal inventory holding costs:

$$\frac{Q}{2} \times H = \frac{C \times D}{Q}$$

In the example above where the EOQ was 2000 units; costs were as follows:

	£
Annual ordering costs £20 × 20	400
Annual inventory holding costs 2 000 × £0.40	400
Total annual costs of inventory	800

It must be remembered that the relevant costs to use in these computations are the additional costs that would be incurred if one more unit of inventory were to be held for one additional time period. For ordering costs these should equal be equal to the extra costs that would be incurred if one more order was placed.

Just in time (JIT)

In response to challenges that the manufacturing industry has experienced over the last 30 years a number a innovative production systems have been introduced many of which focus on inventory. These include just in time (JIT), total quality control (TQC) and materials requirement planning (MRP) systems. However, perhaps the most popular has been JIT, which originated in the Toyota Motor Corporation. We will therefore spend a little time examining this technique.

The Chartered Institute of Management Accountants (CIMA) Official Terminology defines JIT as 'a technique for the organization of work flows, to allow rapid, high-quality, flexible production whilst minimizing manufacturing waste and inventory levels'.

The aim is to have zero inventories. Not surprisingly, therefore, much of the emphasis is given to the relationship with the suppliers. Classically in JIT systems there tends to be relatively fewer suppliers; this reduces costs. The supplier is regarded as an extension of the manufacturing process. Therefore, sharing information with suppliers regarding future purchasing requirements is the key to JIT, as ideally supplies are delivered only when production requires them.

JIT embraces more than just inventory issues. It is a management philosophy running throughout a business. Much of the emphasis in the design of JIT systems is on quality and flexibility which, it is argued, make this approach so popular in manufacturing industry.

ACTIVITY 21.2

Saltwhistle plc sells charcoal by the bag. The management anticipate they will sell 4000 bags next year and the price per bag will be £8. The cost of placing an order for new inventories is anticipated to be £150. Calculate the EOQ for bags of charcoal.

$$\text{EOQ} = \text{square root of } 2 \times 2\,000 \times 150/8 = 274 \text{ (to the nearest bag)}$$

CASH MANAGEMENT

The emphasis that a business entity places on cash is dependent on a number of factors. The main factors are the industrial sector and size of the business. In terms of sectors clear differences in emphasis on the management of cash and the systems employed are easily recognized between retail businesses, which do not offer credit, and say typical manufacturing industries where credit is normally given to customers. Inherent in some sectors is seasonality of the business. This often results in the inflows of cash not coinciding with the way in which expenditure is spread over the year. Therefore, at varying points of the year there will be large cash surpluses and at other times large cash deficits in these businesses.

Research strongly indicates that cash management is more critical in small than in large businesses. The evidence suggests that small businesses have generally a higher level of business and financial risk compared with their larger counterparts. This makes them more vulnerable to insolvency, particularly in times of economic recessions.

The reasons for holding cash

John Maynard Keynes, the economist, in his most famous publication, the *General Theory of Employment, Interest and Money*, published in 1936, identified three main reasons for businesses to hold cash. These are still relevant in today's business context:

- **The transaction motive** – to be able to meet payments when they fall due. It should be remembered that often the inflows and outflows of cash in business operations tend not to synchronize, which means that cash has to be carefully managed.

- **The precautionary motive** – cash should be kept by a business in order to meet any unexpected outgoings. The nature of business lends itself to uncertainties which may mean that expenditure cannot always be anticipated. The larger the near-liquid assets which can be quickly transformed into cash, the less the amount of cash that needs to be held.

- **The speculative motive** – cash should be kept to take advantage of any unexpected beneficial opportunity.

The cost of holding cash

The benefits of holding cash have been identified above. Inevitably, however, there is a cost to holding cash – the opportunity cost. This is the profit foregone by not employing the cash elsewhere, for example the return from investing the money in short-term investments or in less liquid assets, such as new equipment.

The management of the business therefore has to balance the benefits of holding cash against the costs. Put another way, management has to balance the advantages of liquidity against the profitability of employing the cash in some investment opportunity.

Cash and cash equivalents

In general, the term 'cash' in this text is used in the context of receipts and payments for goods and services, and includes cash equivalents such as payments and receipts from credit cards and cheques. However, there is normally an additional opportunity cost when using cash equivalents. This cost relates to the time it takes administratively to recognize the payment or receipt. For example, for cheques paid or drawn outside the City of London area, a minimum of three working days is needed for clearance. The firm receiving the cheque has first to deposit it at its own bank. This bank will then present the cheque to the bank named on the cheque (i.e. the drawing bank). Only when the drawing bank transfers the funds to the bank at which the cheque was deposited does the firm which receives the cheque technically benefit from the receipt of funds. This delay in recognizing cheques into an account creates an opportunity cost, as the cash could alternatively be employed elsewhere during this delay. The following simple example illustrates the calculation of the opportunity cost in such circumstances.

EXAMPLE 21.6

Suppose a customer pays £10 000 by cheque and the cheque takes five days to clear. If bank interest payable on a bank deposit account is 10% p.a., the opportunity cost of accepting a cheque rather than cash is

$$£10\,000 \times \frac{5 \text{ days}}{365 \text{ days}} \times 10\% = £13.70$$

It is assumed there are 365 days in the year.

The opportunity cost of accepting a cheque for £10 000, in this example, rather than cash is £13.70, assuming that the next best alternative is to deposit the £10 000 in a bank deposit account. There are also other direct costs that may be charged at varying rates for banking cheques and credit card transactions.

There are inevitably benefits in accepting or paying with cheques and other forms of 'cash equivalents' as compared with cash. Probably the most important is security. Security, in terms of cash management, is an important issue and should therefore be an important consideration in deciding on the means of payment that is acceptable.

The frequency of banking cash – the decision

A problem for a number of businesses, particularly retail businesses, is the decision about how frequently they should bank their cash receipts. Example 21.7 illustrates the problem and provides a method for identifying a solution.

EXAMPLE 21.7

Chris Raven owns a chain of greengrocery shops in the Surrey area which are open during the day, Monday to Saturday, 52 weeks per year.

Takings are currently banked once per week on Friday mornings. As Chris's business has expanded he has been incurring what he considers to be high bank overdraft charges at a rate of 11%. He has been advised by a consultant that if he is to reduce this charge he should bank his receipts daily, except on Saturdays. Friday's and Saturday's takings could be banked on the following Monday. He has forecast that the total turnover will amount to £1.95 million next year. It is estimated that the bank will charge £12 for each banking receipt.

To evaluate this option with current banking arrangements we need to examine the costs and benefits of both situations and then choose the minimum cost option. We will examine the problem in six discrete stages.

1 The calculation of the overdraft rate per day if the annual rate of charges is 11%:

$$\frac{11 \text{ days}}{365} \times 100 = 0.03\% \text{ per day}$$

2 Daily takings (assuming takings are evenly distributed over the working week), if annual takings are £1 950 000, amount to:

$$\frac{£1\,950\,000}{312 \text{ days}} = £6250 \text{ per day}$$

(NB. The number of working days in the year 52 weeks 6 days 312 days)

3 The cost of holding the daily takings, £6250, for one day instead of banking it would be:

$$£6\,250 \times 0.03\% = £1.875 \text{ per day}$$

4 The number of days' delay incurred by only banking one day per week, i.e. Friday, is:

Takings on	Days on which receipts could be banked	Number of days' delay incurred by Friday banking
Monday	Tuesday	3
Tuesday	Wednesday	2
Wednesday	Thursday	1
Thursday	Friday	0
Friday	Monday	4
Saturday	Monday	4
Total days		14

(Continued)

(It is assumed that the takings on each day could be banked at the start of the next day, with the exception of Friday's and Saturday's takings, which as mentioned previously will be banked on Monday morning.)

In one week, the total number of days' delay incurred by only banking on a Friday is therefore 14. At a cost of £1.875 per day, the weekly cost of Friday banking is £26.25 (£1.875 × 14 days), and it follows that the annual cost of banking only on a Friday £1365 (£26.25 × 52 weeks). Therefore, in terms of bank overdraft charges, Chris could save £1365 per year, assuming that the overdraft rate remains at 11% and turnover remains constant.

5 The total incremental cost of banking on a daily basis:

$$£12 \text{ per visit} \times \text{additional visits}$$

Additional number of visits per week = 5 – 1 visit previously = 4
Therefore annually the additional visits are 208 (4 × 52).

$$£12 \times 208 \text{ visits} = £2496$$

6 The costs and benefits of banking daily:

	£
Benefits – less bank charges	1 365
Costs – incremental cost of visits	2 496
Loss	(1 131)

Therefore, of the options available, it is less costly to bank once a week rather than daily.

The example has been used to illustrate the type of decisions related to the management of cash, and some of the costs and benefits that should be accounted for in such circumstances. However, in practice, all possible options should be identified and examined, for example the effect on costs if the firm were to bank twice a week, in addition to other potential additional costs such as additional insurance costs for holding varying amounts of cash.

In these types of decisions, it is often the case that some costs and benefits are difficult to identify and measure. In the above example, it is likely that the incremental costs of visiting the bank would be difficult to measure. The process of banking includes the employee's time in going and returning from the bank and also the time taken to prepare the documentation, that is counting the various denominations of currency and filling in banking forms and the firm's own records. It is likely that much of this process cannot be precisely measured. In practice, a pragmatic approach will invariably be taken, such as only including costs that are judged to be significant, and estimating the costs based on judgement and experience.

Cash budget and cash levels

A major question to be resolved by those businesses which permanently or for long periods of time hold a cash balance is: how much cash should be held purely in liquid form and how much should be invested in short-term securities? If a business has too little cash, as previously explained, it may experience liquidity difficulties. On the other hand, if a business holds too much cash it is missing opportunities to earn profits. The management challenge is to balance these factors.

An associated decision to be taken when investing in securities is: what should the balance be between securities with different maturity dates? Remember that normally, the longer is the time to maturity, the greater are the returns.

In some industries, as we have said, the majority of businesses will have substantial cash balances permanently or for relatively long periods of time. Examples are retail shops such as Tesco, Sainsbury and Marks and Spencer. Referring back to the Sainsbury 2003 Annual Financial Report shows that 'cash at bank and in hand' represented just over 15% of the total assets of the company. It is therefore important for this type of businesses to spend time trying to get their cash balances at the right levels to maximize profits while at the same time being sufficiently liquid. Many of these large businesses employ corporate treasurers whose specific skills include managing cash.

The key to getting the right balance between profitability and liquidity is planning. Planning and cash budgets were discussed in Chapter 19. Through the cash budget, businesses can identify surplus funds, the size of the funds, and when and how long they will be available. From this information informed decisions can be made whether to invest these balances in short-term securities and, if so, for how long.

One ratio that has been discussed before which is useful in assisting management in this decision relating to cash balances is the ratio of cash balances to the level of current assets:

$$\text{proportion of cash held} = \frac{\text{cash balances}}{\text{current assets}}$$

This ratio gives a rough guide to the level of cash balances that a firm should hold. The use of the ratio requires judgement on the part of management in deciding what a desirable proportion of cash held to current assets is. This judgement will be influenced by past experiences as well as looking to the future cash commitments indicated in the cash budget. The ratio may be used historically, that is in comparison with past ratios and in comparison with industry averages.

ACTIVITY 21.3

Describe what is likely to happen to the level of cash if a company experience movements in terms of an increase and a decrease in the following working capital items:

- Inventories
- Trade receivables
- Trade credit.

Inventories:
    Increase: cash level will decrease
    Decrease: cash level will increase

Trade receivables
    Increase: Cash levels go down
    Decrease: Cash levels go up

Trade credit
    Increase: Cash levels go up
    Decrease: Cash levels go down.

SUMMARY

In this chapter, we have considered the need for working capital and the methods for optimizing the individual levels of current assets and trade payables.

The needs of individual businesses, in terms of the need to manage working capital, will be dependent, to a great extent, on which industrial sector they operate in. For example, a high street retailer or supermarket is likely to have very little, if any, trade receivables, but a relatively level high of inventory, which is likely to be mainly financed from trade payables. A very different picture emerges in manufacturing businesses. The level of trade receivables and inventory in manufacturing industries are likely to be significant and the business will not be as liquid as many other industrial sectors. The resources employed into managing particular categories of working capital will reflect these needs.

FURTHER READING

Arnold, G. (2008) *Corporate Financial Management*, FT Prentice Hall, 4th Edition.

REVIEW QUESTIONS

(✓ indicates answers are available in Appendix A)

1 What are the main costs and benefits associated with holding inventory?
2 What does the working capital cycle measure?
3 List the reasons why it is important to manage the level of working capital?
✓ 4 What are the motives for holding cash?
5 What are the variables that should be considered when deciding upon the frequency of banking cash?
6 What are the hidden costs of late payment?
7 What are the main considerations in deciding whether to extend the credit period given to customers?
8 What is the economic order quantity?

PROBLEMS FOR DISCUSSION AND ANALYSIS

(✓ indicates answers are available in Appendix A)

1 AJB Restaurants is a small chain of slow food restaurants operating on the south coast. It is estimated that their sales receipts for the next year will be £14 million. These receipts will be spread evenly over the following 50 working week year. The restaurant is open only five days per week: Tuesday, Wednesday, Thursday, Friday and

Saturday. The pattern of receipts within each week is that the daily rate of receipts on Friday and Saturday is twice that experienced on Tuesday, Wednesday and Thursday.

Receipts for the whole week are normally banked on Saturdays of each week but this practice is being reconsidered. It is suggested that banking should be carried out either daily or twice weekly, on Wednesday and Saturday. The incremental cost to AJB Restaurants of each banking is £50. AJB Restaurants always operates on a bank overdraft and the current overdraft rate for the company is 14%. This interest charge is applied on a simple daily basis.

Required

Advise AJB Restaurants on the best policy amongst the three alternatives for banking receipts. Indicate the annual amount by which AJB Restaurants will be worse off if it pursues the worst, rather than the best, of the three policies for banking receipts.

✓ **2** LWJ plc requires advice on its debt collection policy. The current policy and two alternative options are detailed below:

	Current policy	Option 1	Option 2
Cost of debt collection p.a. (£)	240 000	300 000	400 000
Bad debts (% of sales)	3	2	1
Average collection period (months)	2	1.5	1

Current sales are £4.8 million per year, and the company requires 15% return on its investments. Should the company discard the current policy in favour of Option 1 or 2?

3 A study of receivables of MEJ plc has shown that it is possible to classify all receivables into certain categorizes with the following characteristics:

	Average collection period (days)	Bad debts (%)
A	15	0.5
B	20	2.5
C	30	5.0
D	40	9.5

The average profit schedule for the company's range of products is as follows:

	£	£
Selling price		2.50
Less:		
Materials	1.00	
Wages	0.95	
Variable overheads	0.30	
Fixed overheads	0.05	2.30
Profit		0.20

The company has the opportunity of extending its sales by £1 000 000 split between categories C and D in the proportions 40:60. The company maintains an overdraft with the bank. The current rate of interest on the overdraft account is 11%.

Discuss the factors to be considered in the formulation of policy for credit control management and use the above data in your discussion.

4 Compute the economic order quantity for an inventory item with the following relevant data:

- annual demand 20 000 units;

- ordering costs £16;

- inventory holding costs £0.10 per unit.

5 Nelson plc is a restaurant supplier that sells a number of products to various restaurants in the local area. One of their products is a special meat cutter with a disposable blade.

　The blades are sold in packages of 12 blades for £20 per pack. The demand for the replacement blades is at a constant rate of 2000 packages per month. The packages cost Nelson's £10 each from the manufacturer and require a three-day lead time from the date of the order. The holding cost is 10% per annum of the cost of the blades excluding packaging. The order cost is £1.20 per order.

(i) Calculate:

(a) the economic order quantity;
(b) the number of orders needed per year;
(c) the total cost of buying and holding blades for the year.

(ii) Assuming there is no reserve (e.g. safety inventory) and that the present inventory level is 200 packages, discuss when the next order should be placed.

(iii) Discuss the problems that most firms would have in attempting to apply the EOQ formula to their inventory problems.

APPENDIX A: ANSWERS

CHAPTER 1

Review questions

1 (a) To help them control the level of their expenditure, to assist in planning future levels of expenditure, to help them raise additional finance (for example, mortgages, hire purchase, etc.), and to help them decide the best way to spend their money.

   (b) To control the activities of the organization, to plan future activities, to assist in raising finance and to report upon the activities and performance of the enterprise to interested parties.

2 In general for external users the answer to this is the annual report or accounts. Where specific reports such as the statement of financial position or income statement are mentioned in the body of the text these are shown below.

Management – various reports including specialist reports

Owners – annual report Lenders – cash flow statement, income statement, statement of financial position

Suppliers – annual report, statement of financial position

Customers – income statement, statement of financial position

Employees – profitability, therefore income statement

Government – income statement

The general public – profitability, therefore income statement, also environmental and other information therefore specialist reports plus the narrative part of the annual report.

4 ● That the information is only a part of that necessary to make 'effective decisions'.

   ● That accountancy is as yet an inexact science and depends on a number of judgements, estimates, etc.

   ● That the end result of the accounting process can only be as good as the inputs and in times of rising prices some of these inputs are of dubious value.

   ● That accounting systems can be counter-productive, for example the maximization of a division's profit may not always ensure the maximization of enterprise profit.

Problems for discussion and analysis

1 (a) Examples are: selling price, costs of manufacture, set-up costs, marketing costs, etc.

   (b) Examples are: size of market, competitors, technical specifications, etc.

CHAPTER 2

Review questions

1 Your answer should encapsulate the idea of the static nature of a stock measure, and the way in which that differs from the dynamic nature of measures covering periods of time.

2 The alternatives and the drawbacks identified were: original cost: identification of original cost as cost to whom

   ● historic cost: reductions in value, increases in prices

   ● replacement cost: specialist items, changes in technology leading to non-replacement

   ● economic value: problems of forecasting the future, the choice of appropriate discount rates

   ● net realizable value: do we want to sell, is it a forced sale or at open market value?

Problems for discussion and analysis

1   The way in which this question is designed is to allow students to think through the alternatives and for the tutor to tease out some of the underlying assumptions and test the students' understanding. It also serves to reinforce the idea that if accounting is to reflect economic reality it is unlikely to be able to do so using only one cost/value measure.

(a)   Freehold shop – This could be economic value or historic cost. Students' attention should be drawn to the problems inherent in calculating the economic value of a business that has not started and to the problems with historic cost in changing economic conditions. This may lead to the conclusion that net realizable value based on open market value may be more appropriate.

(b)   Hanging display rail for clothes – This is likely to have limited, if any, usefulness to the new business and therefore it is likely to be sold, thus under these assumptions net realizable value is likely to be most appropriate.

(c)   A two-year-old car which is essential for the business – The fact that it is essential for the business would seem to rule out net realizable value whilst the fact that it is two years old would suggest that original cost is inappropriate. This leaves as possible choices economic value, which may be difficult to ascertain, replacement cost of a similar vehicle, written-down cost, and historic cost. In the case of the latter it is important that students are made aware of which historic cost is appropriate; i.e. cost to the restaurant business and not cost to the clothes shop.

(d)   New restaurant tables and chairs – In this case replacement cost is likely to equal historic cost so either of these would be acceptable, as would economic value. In the case of net realizable value the tutor can use this as an opportunity to explain that there are costs associated with sale which will mean that this value is lower than the price paid for the tables and chairs. This is of course exacerbated by the fact that they are now second hand.

(e)   Cash till – Like the car and the freehold property this can be used in the new business, so net realizable value is unlikely to be appropriate. The example is chosen because, unlike the freehold and the car, the market for used cash tills is not so visible and as such establishing replacement cost of a used till may not be so easy. This example can also be used to illustrate the problems associated with establishing historic cost and written-down cost; what is the economic life of a till?

(f)   Quantity of fashion garments that were not sold in the closing-down sale – At first sight the basis that looks obvious is the net realizable value. However, students' attention should be drawn to the fact that these were not sold in the closing-down sale, so open market value may not be appropriate even if it could be established.

CHAPTER 3

Review questions

1   ● Future benefits
   ● Accruing to the entity
   ● Resources controlled by the entity
   ● Resulting from past events

2   ● The asset must be capable of measurement
   ● The measurement can and will be done in monetary terms.

Problems for discussion and analysis

1 (a)

Statement of financial position of the business

	£
Current assets	
Cash	500
Inventory	6 500
	7 000
Non-current assets – Tangible	
Delivery van	3 200
Office furniture	2 300
Fixtures and fittings	7 600
Fixed assets – Freehold land and buildings	34 000
	47 100
Total assets	54 100
Current liabilities	
Bank overdraft	20 700
	20 700
Non-current liabilities	
Mortgage	29 000
	29 000
Total liabilities	49 700
Owners equity	4 400
Total equity	4 400
Total equity and liabilities	54 100

(b) You will have noticed that the current liabilities exceed the current assets. This means that the business may not be able to pay what it owes from what it has in short term assets. This increases the riskiness of the business. You may also have noticed that there is no plant and machinery but it does have a building and has cash in tills so this is likely to be a retailer rather than a manufacturing business. It is quite feasible when looking at the statement of financial position to come to some general conclusions about the nature of the business – how it is financing its activities and therefore how much risk there is. As you will see in later chapters a business that relies heavily on borrowing is more prone to major impacts if the interest rates change.

CHAPTER 4

Review questions

1 The important point to make is that revenue relates to inflows from normal activities. You should think about why money received from for example the sale of the firm's premises should not be included as revenue in the same way as sales that arise as a result of trading.

2 ● When the earnings process is substantially complete *and*
   ● When payment is reasonably certain.

7 An asset gives a future benefit, whereas with an expense the benefit is used up.

Problems for discussion and analysis

1 (a) In most cases the service, i.e. the provision of the room for the night is provided in advance of payment. The payment is generally immediate in the case of casual bookings but may be some time later in the case of account customers, tour operators, etc. A possible model could be:

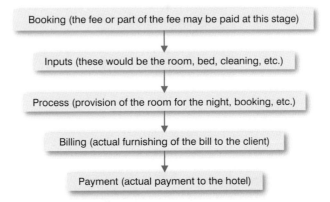

In most situations the point of recognition would be at the point of billing. The point at which payment is made may be at any time from booking on. It is worth spending a few moments thinking about whether you should recognize income at an earlier point if, for example, the payment accompanies the booking. What would be the hotel's position if the customer subsequently cancels the booking and asks for a refund?

   (b) In this case the money is paid in advance of receiving the service and indeed the service that will be used is not known as some or all of the available services could be used. In reality, unless overnight stops were involved or the entrance fee covered more than one visit, the problem of when to recognize revenue is largely academic as it would be recognized at the end of each day. The model is likely to be:

   (c) Here the situation is clearer and in fact the process is more akin to the manufacturing model in the chapter. The point of recognition would be after provision of the service, in this case meals, as long as there was reasonable certainty regarding payment. In most cases the short time span between completion of service and payment would mean that these points were effectively one and the same.

   (d) In this case the money is likely to come in two phases, an initial deposit and then the balance. In virtually all cases this would occur prior to the client going on the tour. However, it could be argued that the agent has provided the service as soon as the tour is booked and as such revenue in the form of the travel agents' fee could be recognized at an earlier point. The process is likely to be:

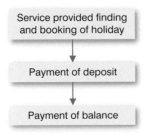

(e)   Here the customers are likely to have paid in advance of the service being provided. The question that has to be discussed is when the earnings process is substantially complete. A possible model is:

CHAPTER 5

Review questions

2   (a)   Increase the bank column and increase the owner's equity column.

(b)   Reduce the bank column by £100 and open up a new asset column for the new asset, a desk, and put £100 in that column.

(c)   Here we have to assume that the goods have been paid for. In this case we decrease cash by £200 and open a new asset column for the goods bought and put £200 in there.

(d)   If we assume the rent is paid in arrears then the entries would be to reduce cash and charge an expense of £300.

(e)   No entry is required as the earnings process is not substantially complete.

(f)   Reduce bank column and charge as an expense in the revenue and expense column.

(g)   Increase the bank column by £350 and increase the revenue and expense column by £350 for sales as in this case the earnings process is complete and receipt of money is certain.

Answer to Activity 5.6

Bill's worksheet for month 1

| Description | Assets | | = | Equity + Liabilities | |
	Bank/cash	Goods		Equity	Revenue & expenses
Opening balance	3 000			3 000	
Goods bought	−2 000	2 000			
Van hire	−300				−300
Rent	−100				−100
Sales	6 500				6 500
Balances	**7 100**	**2 000**		**3 000**	**6 100**
Cost of goods sold		−2 000			−2 000
Final balance	**7 100**	**0**		**3 000**	**4 100**

Answer to Example 5.2

Worksheet for Jill's business

	Assets				=	Equity + Liabilities		
	Cash	**Cars**	**Rent**	**Furniture**		**Equity**	**Loans**	**Revenue & expenses**
Day 1	5 000					5 000		
Day 2	6 000						6 000	
Day 3	−300		300					
Day 4	−9 900	9 900						
Day 5	−220			220				
Day 6	−30							−30
Day 8	−120							−120
Day 9	3 800							3 800
Day 9*		−3 000						−3 000
Day 10	3 900							3 900
Day 10*		−3 100						−3 100
Day 11	−4 000	4 000						
Day 12	−10							−10
Day 15	−60							−60
Day 17	−75							−75
Day 18	−300		300					
Day 20	4 300							4 300
Day 20*		−3 800						−3 800
Day 22	5 200							5 200
Day 22*		−4 000						−4 000
Day 23	−4 300	4 300						
Day 24	−40							−40
Day 25	−75							−75
Day 26	−500						−500	
Day 29	−500							−500
Day 30	4 700							4 700
Day 30*		−4 300						−4 300
Day 31	−40							−40
Balance	**12 430**	**0**	**600**	**220**		**5 000**	**5 500**	**2 750**
Day 31**			−600					−600
Balance	**12 430**	**0**	**0**	**220**		**5 000**	**5 500**	**2 150**

*You will notice that every time we sold a car we immediately transferred the cost of that car from our 'Cars' column to 'Revenue and expenses' as an expense. This transfer was carried out because, having sold the car, we no longer expected a future benefit and therefore we no longer had an asset. An alternative treatment would be to do this exercise at the end of the month.

**When we complete our worksheet, it is important to review our assets and ask ourselves the question, is there a future benefit and if so are these still assets? If, as in this case, the answer is no, then we need to transfer their cost to revenue and expenses of the period.

Transaction summary

We have set out below the transactions that took place together with the treatment of those transactions on the worksheet and, where appropriate, explanations of that treatment and acceptable alternatives. If there are any items that you still do not understand you should try to examine them in terms of the basic definitions referred to in Chapters 3 and 4.

Day 1   Opened a business bank account and paid in £5000 of her own money.
         Here we have created a business asset in the form of cash and have also opened an account to show the owner's stake in the business under the heading of owner's equity.

Day 2   Paid into the bank £6000 that she had borrowed from her parents for use by the business.
         Once again the business has acquired an asset as it will get a future benefit from the cash. It has also acquired an obligation to pay some body some money and as such has a liability for the amount borrowed.

Day 3   Found a suitable showroom and paid a fortnight's rent of £300.
         We have already discussed this transaction in the main body of the chapter. Our treatment has been to reduce our asset cash in the bank and to record an asset of the prepaid rent from which we will derive a *future benefit*.

Day 4   Went to the car auction and bought the following cars for cash:

         Ford for £3000
         Toyota for £3100
         Mazda for £3800

         Clearly, by paying out £9900 we have reduced our cash at the bank and so that is one side of the entry. The other side is to record the cars as an asset as we shall get a future benefit from these.

Day 5   Bought some office furniture for £220.
         This is exactly the same as the previous transaction. We have merely exchanged one asset, cash, for another, furniture which will provide the business with a *future benefit* from its use.

Day 6   Employed a teenager who was on the dole to clean cars for her at the rate of £10 per car and paid out £30.
         In this case one side of the transaction is clear in as much as the cash has clearly been reduced by £30. The question that then arises is whether there is an asset or an expense. We have shown the cost of the car cleaning as an expense because we are uncertain that any *future benefit* will arise from this particular expenditure. The fact that a car is cleaned does not add any intrinsic value and in fact it is probably necessary to clean all the cars in the showroom regularly because customers expect to buy clean cars.

Day 8   Placed adverts for all three cars in the local paper. The cost of advertising was £20 per day for each car. She decided that all three should be advertised for two days, and so the total cost was £120.
         You should refer back to the text for a detailed discussion of the reasons for our treatment of this item. What we have done is to apply the *prudence principle*, treated the item as an expense and charged the item to the revenue and expenses account at the same time as we reduced our cash by £120.

Day 9   Sold the Ford for £3800 cash.
         Clearly, we have another £3800 in our bank and so we increase our cash column. We also have a sale which accords with our definition of revenue and so we bring that revenue into the revenue and expenses column.

Day 9*   Cost of sales
         Here we have reduced our assets by the cost of the car we sold and charged that cost, i.e. the cost of the *expired benefit* to the revenue and expenses column.

Day 10   Sold the Toyota for £3900 cash.
         See the explanations for day 9 above. If you have got these wrong, make sure you understand why, and then correct your worksheet for all similar items before reading on.

Day 11   Returned to the car auction and bought a Renault for £4000.
         This is in essence the same as the transaction on day 4. If you have made an error, you should reread that explanation and check that your treatment of the transaction on day 23 is correct before moving on.

Day 12   Employed her teenage friend to clean the Renault for £10.
         This is in essence the same as the transaction on day 6. If you have made an error, you should reread that explanation and check that your treatment of the transaction on day 24 is correct before moving on.

Day 15   Readvertised the Mazda for three days at £20 per day, total cost £60.
         See the explanation for day 8.

Day 17   Advertised the Renault using a special block advert which cost £75 in total.
          See the explanation for day 8.

Day 18   Paid rent of showroom for the next fortnight amounting to £300.
          This is in essence the same situation as day 3. The entry should therefore be the same. At this stage you could also reduce the rent column by the rent for the first two weeks and charge this to the revenue and expenses column as the benefit has now expired. We have not done this because we wished to illustrate the importance of the final review before a statement of financial position and income statement are finally drawn up.

Day 19   Was offered £4300 for the Mazda.
          There is no need to record this as the transaction is not substantially complete at this stage and so we would not recognize revenue. If you have shown a sale at this stage reread the definition of revenue given in Chapter 4.

Day 20   Accepted the offer for the Mazda and was paid £4300.
          Now we have a sale and revenue can be recognized as in day 9 above.

Day 22   Sold the Renault for £5200.
          Once again we have a sale and revenue can be recognized.

Day 23   Went to the car auction and bought a Fiat for £4300.
          See day 4 for explanation of the treatment.

Day 24   Had the Fiat professionally valeted at a cost of £40.
          This is the same as the cleaning. The fact that it was done professionally does not alter the argument set out in respect of day 6 above.

Day 25   Advertised the Fiat using the special block advert at a cost of £75.
          This should be treated in the same way as previous adverts for the same reasons.

Day 26   Decided that as things were going so well she would repay her parents £500.
          This is a different transaction from any of the ones we have dealt with so far. Those dealt with expenditure of cash for either a past or a future benefit. In this case we have reduced our cash in order to pay back an amount that the business owes, i.e. we have used some cash to reduce our liability. Hence, we reduce the amount shown as owing in the loan column by the £500 and we reduce the amount of cash we have by £500.

Day 27   Took the Fiat on a test drive with a customer and seized the engine.
          Although an economic event has happened, we cannot account for it as at this stage the effect of that event cannot be adequately expressed in monetary terms.

Day 29   Had Fiat repaired at a cost of £500.
          We are now in a position to account for the event as we know the effect in monetary terms. However, we are left with the question of whether the expenditure is going to provide a future benefit or whether it is an expense. We need to ask ourselves whether the expenditure added to the asset. If it has then there is no problem in recognizing the transaction as one which creates an asset. If, however, the expenditure merely restores the asset to the state that it was in previously, then it is doubtful that it relates to an asset and applying the prudence principle we would be safer to charge it to the revenue and expenses account as an expense, which is what we have done. In essence this is a shorthand way of recording two events. The first is that the engine blew up, so reducing the future benefit we could expect from the asset. If we knew the extent of this reduction we could have charged that as a past benefit. If we had done that then the repairs could legitimately be viewed as enhancing the future benefit to be obtained in respect of the reduced asset. This whole process is in fact cut short because we do not know what the loss in value of future benefits was; we are therefore in effect using the cost of repairs as a surrogate for that loss in value.

Day 30   Sold the Fiat for £4700. See previous transactions of this type on days 9, 10, etc.

Day 31   Paid electricity bill of £40 for the month.
          Here we have a reduction of the cash in respect of the use of electricity over the past month. The benefit has clearly expired and we therefore have an expense.

CHAPTER 6

Review questions

1 Raw materials, work in progress, finished goods.

3 As the cost of the goods sold, especially with a small business, is often calculated by taking the opening inventory plus purchases less closing inventory, the effect would be to reduce the cost of sales figure and thereby increase profit.

5 If the net realizable value is less than cost then to use cost would overstate the future benefits; on the other hand, if it is higher, to include the higher figure would mean that unrealized profits were being taken which would be contrary to the prudence principle.

9 FIFO, LIFO and average cost. The effects in times of rising prices are tabulated below.

Method	Statement of financial position (balance sheet)	Income statement (profit and loss account)
FIFO	Up-to-date value	Out-of-date values – overstated profit
LIFO	Out-of-date value	Up-to-date values – understated profit
Average	Understated value – mid point	Understated value – mid-point profit

Problems for discussion and analysis

4 (a) FIFO

Model 2

	Purchases		Sales		Inventory	
	Units	Cost	Units	Cost	Units	Cost
Quarter 1	80	£50	80	£ 4 000	0	
Quarter 2	100	£55	100	£ 5 500	0	
Quarter 3	60	£55	40	£ 2 200	20	£1 100
Quarter 4						
Cost of goods sold				£11 700		
Closing inventory						£1 100

Model 3

	Purchases		Sales		Inventory	
	Units	Cost	Units	Cost	Units	Cost
Quarter 1						
Quarter 2						
Quarter 3	80	£60	80	£ 4 800	0	
Quarter 4	160	£65	100	£ 6 500	60	£3 900
Cost of goods sold				£11 300		
Closing inventory						£3 900

(b)   Average cost

Model 2

| | Purchases | | Total | Sales | Inventory | |
	Units	Cost	cost	cost	Units	Cost
Quarter 1	80	£50	£ 4 000			
Quarter 2	100	£55	£ 5 500			
Quarter 3	60	£55	£ 3 300			
Quarter 4						
Average cost	240	£53.33	12 800			
Cost of goods sold (220)				£11 733		
Closing inventory					20	£1 067

Model 3

| | Purchases | | Total | Sales | Inventory | |
	Units	Cost	cost	cost	Units	Cost
Quarter 1						
Quarter 2						
Quarter 3	80	£60	£ 4 800			
Quarter 4	160	£65	£10 400			
Av cost	240	£63.33	£15 200			
Cost of goods sold (180)				£11 400		
Closing inventory					60	£3 800

(c)   Values in statement of financial position

	Cost	Net realizable value	Statement of financial position
FIFO			
Model 2	£1 100	£1 000	£1 000
Model 3	£3 900	£5 400	£3 900
AVCO			
Model 2	£1 067	£1 000	£1 000
Model 3		£5 400	

CHAPTER 7

Review questions

1   A trade payable represents an amount owing by an enterprise to a third party. They arise when goods or services are supplied in advance of payment being made.

2   In the former case an invoice for the goods or services supplied has been received, whereas in the latter no invoice has been received at the time the accounts are drawn up; therefore an estimate of the amount owing for the goods or services provided is made.

3   Because they will change their form in the next year, in the former case to cash and in the latter normally to services.

Problems for discussion and analysis

1 (a) Record in the inventory column and in a trade payables column.

Statement of financial position – increase assets and liabilities.

Income statement – no effect.

Cash flows – no effect until payment is made.

(b) Record an asset and reduce the asset bank.

Statement of financial position – increase one asset and reduce another.

Income statement – no effect.

Cash flows – cash outflow.

(c) Increase the asset bank and reduce the asset trade receivables.

Statement of financial position – increase one asset and reduce another.

Income statement – no effect.

Cash flows – cash inflow.

(d) Reduce a liability, the loan, and reduce the asset bank.

Statement of financial position – reduce an asset and a liability.

Income statement – no effect.

Cash flows – cash outflow.

(e) This is more open to a debate about how to deal with research expenditure. The area of debate is whether or not there is a future benefit and how certain that benefit is. If it is reasonably certain that a future benefit will arise the answers below apply:

● Reduce the asset bank and record an asset.

● Statement of financial position – reduce one asset and increase another.

● Income statement – no effect.

● Cash flows – cash outflow.

If, however, it is *not possible* to say with any certainty there will be a future benefit then the answers below are appropriate:

● Reduce the asset bank and record an expense.

● Statement of financial position – reduce the asset bank.

● Income statement – record an expense.

● Cash flows – cash outflow.

(f) Record an asset trade receivables and record revenue in the Income statement.

Statement of financial position – increase the asset trade receivables.

Income statement – record sale as revenue.

Cash flows – no cash flow until money is received.

(g) Record a reduction in the liability, trade payables, and reduce the asset bank.

Statement of financial position – reduce an asset and a liability.

Income statement – no effect.

Cash flows – cash outflow.

(h) Reduce the asset bank and record an expense in the Income statement account.

Statement of financial position – reduce the asset bank.

Income statement – charge the expense wages.

Cash flows – cash outflow.

(i)   Reduce the asset bank and record an expense in the Income statement account.

Statement of financial position – reduce the asset bank.

Income statement – charge the expense wages.

Cash flows – cash outflow.

(j)   Reduce the asset bank and charge the interest expense to Income statement account.

Statement of financial position – reduce an asset.

Income statement – charge the expense interest.

Cash flows – cash outflow.

(k)   Reduce the asset bank and reduce the liability accruals.

Statement of financial position – decrease an asset and a liability.

Income statement – no effect.

Cash flows – cash outflow.

(l)   Record an asset prepayments and reduce the asset bank.

Statement of financial position – increase one asset and reduce another.

Income statement – no effect.

Cash flows – cash outflow.

(m)   Reduce the asset bank and reduce the owner's equity.

Statement of financial position – reduce an asset and the owner's equity.

Income statement – no effect.

Cash flows – cash outflow.

(n)   Record an asset in the bank and increase the owner's equity.

Statement of financial position – increase an asset and the owner's equity.

Income statement – no effect.

Cash flows – cash inflow.

(o)   Reduce an asset inventory and reduce the owner's equity.

Statement of financial position – reduce an asset and reduce the owner's equity.

Income statement – no effect.

Cash flows – no effect.

(p)   Reduce the asset trade receivables and charge the bad debt as an expense.

Statement of financial position – reduce an asset.

Income statement – charge bad debt as an expense.

Cash flows – no effect.

CHAPTER 8

Review questions

1   Broadly matching revenue with cost incurred in earning that revenue. The chapter also discusses the International accounting standard and the idea of spreading the original cost over the useful life of the asset and depreciation as a measure of the wearing out of an asset.

3   Technological advances, past experience, the factors that cause the asset to wear out.

Note: It is important to realize that at best this is only a best estimate.

5   This describes the figure arrived at after taking the accumulated depreciation away from the historic cost.

Problems for discussion and analysis

1   (a)   The land is normally not depreciated as it is assumed not to wear out. The building should be depreci-ated and a stronger case can be made for the use of the straight-line method than the reducing balance method.

     (b)   In this case it would seem that for the cars they should be depreciated over four years as they are unlikely to do 60 000 miles. The vans, on the other hand, should be traded in after three years purely on the basis of mileage. The question is then; do we use up more future benefit in the earlier years than in later years? It may be the case that an argument can be put up suggesting that the wearing out process is even over the life of the assets and the incidence of repair costs is greater in later years. This argument would indicate that straight line is the more appropriate method of depreciation. However, if we looked at the total costs of using the vehicles one could argue that by using reducing balance the repair costs in later life would be compensated by the additional depreciation in earlier years so achieving a matching of costs and revenues over the asset's life.

     (c)   Depreciate over five years on the basis of prudence. No particular method is clearly more appropriate.

     (d)   The facts suggest that if we apply the same argument as we outlined for vehicles then reducing balance would be the choice.

     (e)   It may be that the appropriate method is usage-related in this case. Apart from that there is no strong reason for one method rather than another although, as the first year has lower production than later years, it would be difficult in terms of wearing out to argue for the reducing balance method.

CHAPTER 9

Review questions

2   Trade credit, factoring and bank overdrafts.

7   Bank overdrafts and factoring.

8   For factoring the security is normally provided by the debts that are factored. In reality factoring companies will only advance money against customers who they believe are good credit risks. Bank overdrafts can be secured on the assets of the business or on those of the owners. In the case of limited companies the security may take the form of directors' guarantees.

Problems for discussion and analysis

1   (a)   In this situation, the type of finance that would be appropriate is medium-term finance. This could be a loan, hire purchase or leasing. As the bank manager has indicated that the bank is not particularly interested in lending the money, it looks as if the alternatives are likely to be leasing or hire purchase. The choice between these would depend upon their availability, the life of the assets, the repayments, and the com-pany's cash flows.

     (b)   The reason the bank manager is not prepared to lend the money unsecured is probably because of the high gearing, the high exposure of the bank currently, and the fact that the business is under-capitalized.

CHAPTER 10

Review questions

1   The main aim is to provide information to users regarding liquidity and the cash received and spent during the period.

2   ● It provides information on the liquidity of the business.

   ● It helps the user to identify where money has come from and how it has been used.

   ● It provides some indication about cash flows which are recurrent and those which are less likely to recur.

Problems for discussion and analysis

1   This question is designed to ensure that you think through the difficult areas before they get into the calculation and production of a cash flow statement.

   (a)   The statement of financial position – the non-current assets are reduced by £5000 and the cash is increased by £3000.

   The income statement – profit is reduced by £2000 loss on the sale of the non-current asset.

   The cash flow statement – the cash flow from investing activities will show a cash inflow of £3000.

   (b)   The statement of financial position – the carrying amount of the land is increased by £70 000 and the same amount is credited to a revaluation reserve.

   The income statement – no effect as the gain is not realized.

   The cash flow statement – no effect as no cash flow has occurred.

   (c)   The statement of financial position – the carrying amount of the building will be increased to £100 000. The revaluation reserve will be credited with £40 000, i.e. £100 000 less the previous carrying amount of £60 000, The income statement – there will be no effect.

   The cash flow statement – there are no cash flows involved in either the revaluation or the depreciation adjustments.

   (d)   The statement of financial position – increase issued share capital by £100 000 and the share premium account by £20 000.

   The income statement – no effect.

   The cash flow statement – cash flows from financing would show an inflow of £120 000, i.e. 100 000 shares at £1.20 each.

   (e)   The statement of financial position – reduce the non-current liabilities by £80 000 and reduce the bank balance by a similar amount.

   The income statement – no effect, as we are merely using an asset to discharge a liability.

   The cash flow statement – the financing section of the cash flow statement would show a cash outflow of £80 000.

CHAPTER 11

Review questions

1   Your answer should show that you understand that the initial trial balance is equivalent to the first balance on the worksheet, and the extended trial balance as the final balance on the worksheet i.e. including the end of year adjustments.

CHAPTER 12

Review questions

1 The groups identified in the chapter are equity investors, i.e. shareholders and their representatives, lenders, employees, auditors and management. The common needs identified are past and future profitability, information relating to financial risk and solvency, return on investment and risk.

3 The purpose of the analysis, size of business, risk of the type of business, economic, social and political environment, industry trends, technological change, price rises and their effects.

7 Financial risk relates to the mix of owners' equity and debt financing, whereas business risk refers to the type of business or trade in which the enterprise is engaged.

Problems for discussion and analysis

1

Common size income statement of Metaltin Ltd 2010

	Notes	2010	2009
Sales		100	100
Cost of sales	1	89	90
Operating profit		11	10
Interest charges		3	1
Profit before tax		7	9
Taxation	2	4	5
Retained profit		3	4

The common size income statements show that most of the relationships remain fairly constant, with the exception of interest charges which have moved from 1% to 3% of the sales.

Common size statements of financial position of Metaltin Ltd as at 30 April 2010

	Notes	2010	2009
Current assets			
Cash		0%	2%
Receivables		32%	34%
Inventory	3	45%	40%
		78%	76%
Non-current assets			
Motor vehicles	4	6%	5%
Fittings	4	7%	11%
Land and buildings	4	9%	8%
		22%	24%
Total assets		100%	100%
Current liabilities			
Bank overdraft		17%	9%
Trade payables		35%	39%
Taxation	2	6%	11%
		58%	58%

	Notes	2010	2009
Non current liabilities			
Loans	5	5%	4%
		5%	4%
Total liabilities		63%	63%
Share capital	6	14%	16%
Retained profit	6	20%	21%
Revaluation reserve	6	3%	0%
Total equity		37%	37%
Total equity and liabilities		100%	100%

Broadly the structure of the business has remained the same in relation to non-current and current assets, although it should be noted that inventory is a higher proportion of the total assets in 2010 than in 2009. On the liabilities side the important items to note are the major increase in the overdraft and, to a lesser extent, the increase in trade payables falling due after one year.

CHAPTER 13

Review questions

1   Annual accounts contain summarized information – more detail may be required. More regular and more up-to-date information is needed to take action. The information in the annual accounts may not be suitable for decisions to be made in respect of planning, control, investment, etc.

Problems for discussion and analysis

2   **Situation 1**

On the face of it you may not need much financial information as you are not judged on profitability, over which you have little control as selling prices and buying prices are fixed. You do have some control over the costs in the form of wage bills so you may require information about that area, and your daily cash takings and some idea of inventory turnover to control for pilferage of goods or cash.

Situation 2
Here you would need the information contained in the projections which provide the profit target, so that you could attempt to improve on the profit either by increasing sales or adjusting the staffing of your outlet to reduce the costs and thereby increase the profit. Other issues such as profit by product and changes in sales mix could also be explored.

Situation 3
Some of the additional information you would need relates to cost by product, potential sales volume by product, price elasticity of demand, competitor prices, etc.

Situation 4
Here the question moves the student into a senior management position which would need information for control purposes, such as profitability by branch, turnover by branch, branch cash flows, etc.

CHAPTER 14

Review questions

1   **Stage 1:** *Setting objectives* – This involves detailing the objectives of the organization in the long and short term. Organizations do not have objectives *per se*; the objectives will reflect the objectives of those people involved in the organization. These objectives can be in quantitative terms, e.g. the growth rate of profits, or in qualitative terms, e.g. statements about public responsibility.

Stage 2: *Making strategic decisions* – Strategic decisions are those which determine the long-term policies of the firm and are necessary if the firm is to meet its objectives, e.g. policy changes relating to the range of products that are sold.

Stage 3: *Making operating decisions* – Operating decisions are those that focus on the efficient use of resources available to the firm in the short term and will be embodied in plans, conventionally referred to as budgets.

Stage 4: *Monitoring and possible corrective action* – Monitoring is the process of comparing actual performance with a predetermined plan. It provides the basis from which corrective action can be planned and taken.

Problems for discussion and analysis

1   The main differences between the models is that the engineer's model is a physical model which generates automatic responses whilst the accountant's model is dependent upon humans for corrective responses. A number of limitations can be identified primarily due to this particular difference in the systems. First, with the accountant's control model there tend to be time lags in the reporting of variances because of the nature of accounting systems; and secondly people, rather than the mechanical system, will have to be motivated to respond to variances, identify the cause of the variance and take corrective action.

CHAPTER 15

Review questions

2   The relevant range of activity refers to the level of activity the firm has experienced in past accounting periods. The significance of this range is that cost behaviour, the relationship between the dependent and independent variables, can be established with a certain amount of accuracy. This is because the firm has experienced cost behaviour in this range before and can observe the relationship between cost and activity levels. This information is useful in predicting future costs for decision-making purposes. Outside this range cost behaviour in the past is not known and is therefore more difficult to predict.

Problems for discussion and analysis

2   (a)   (i)   Breakeven point: using the breakeven equation, where x is the number of units to breakeven:

$$S(x) = VC(x) + FC$$
$$120(x) = 60(x) + 18\,000$$
$$x = 300 \text{ units}$$

(ii) Maximum profit where output is 1000 units: using the above equation where P equals profit:

$$S(x) = VC(x) + FC + P$$
$$120(1000) = 60(1000) + 18\,000 + P$$
$$120\,000 = 60\,000 + 18\,000 + P$$
$$P = £42\,000.$$

(iii) Profit at the sales level of 800 units:

$$120(800) = 60(800) + 18\,000 + P$$
$$96\,000 = 48\,000 + 18\,000 + P$$
$$P = £30\,000.$$

(b) Costs alter by the following proportions:

Direct materials increase by 20%.

Fixed costs come down by £6000.

Direct labour costs increase by £1 per hour.

(i) The new breakeven point: increase in costs:'

Direct materials £20 + 20% of £20 = £24

Direct labour ten hours at £5 per hour = £50

Therefore total variable costs will be £74

Fixed costs 18\,000 – 6000 = £12\,000

$$S(x) = VC(x) + FC$$
$$120(x) = 74(x) + 12\,000$$
$$x = 261 \text{ units (to the nearest whole number).}$$

(ii) The new profit at the estimated sales level of 800 units:

$$120(800) = 74(800) + 12\,000 + P$$
$$96\,000 = 59\,200 + 12\,000 + P$$
$$P = £24\,800.$$

CHAPTER 16

Review questions

3 The following are typically categorized as direct costs in a multi-product firm.

- Direct labour.
- Direct materials.
- Components specifically purchased for the production of products.
- Any other costs that are directly traceable to products and services.

The following are examples of indirect costs in a multi-product firm.

- Supervision.
- Inspection.
- Maintenance.
- Personnel services.

Problems for discussion and analysis

1 (a) Cost centre X based on direct labour cost basis:

£140 000/£100 000 = £1.40 per £ of direct labour cost

Cost centre Y based on machine hour basis:

£150 000/20 000 hours = £7.50 per machine hour.

(b)

	X £	Y £
Direct labour costs	100 000	35 000
Direct material	20 000	40 000
Direct labour	32 000	21 000
Overheads:		
X £1.40 × £32 000	44 800	
Y £7.50 × 13 000 hrs		97 500
	96 800	158 500

Total cost of production:

	£
X	96 800
Y	158 500
	255 300

(c) Total cost of production/number of units

$$\frac{£2\,55\,300}{20\,000} = £12.27 \text{ per unit}$$

(d)

	X £
Actual cost	160 000
Absorbed overheads:	
X £144 200 × £1.40	201 880
Over-absorbed overhead	41 880

	Y £
Actual cost	138 000
Absorbed overheads:	
Y 18 000 hours × £7.50	135 000
Under-absorbed overhead	3 000

	£
X over-absorbed	41 880
Y under-absorbed	(3 000)
Total over-absorbed	38 880

CHAPTER 17

Review questions

2 ● Sunk costs

Sunk costs are costs of a historical nature and therefore are incurred as a result of a past decision. It follows that these costs are irrelevant to future decisions. Sunk costs can be easily identified in that they will have been paid or are subject to legally binding contracts and the firm is committed to paying for these contracts in the future.

● Differential costs

Differential costs, sometimes referred to as incremental costs, are differences in costs and benefits of alternative opportunities available to the organization. If the costs and benefits do not differ for alternative opportunities under consideration these costs and benefits will be irrelevant to decisions. On the other hand, if there are differences between costs and benefits these will be classified as relevant to the decision.

● Avoidable and unavoidable costs

An avoidable cost is a cost that can be avoided if an opportunity is not taken up. These costs are relevant because they are directly attributable to the decision to take up an opportunity. In contrast, an unavoidable cost is one that is going to be incurred whether or not the decision related to a particular opportunity is accepted or rejected. This cost, by its nature, is irrelevant in decision making.

● Opportunity costs

An opportunity cost is defined as the maximum benefit which could be obtained from a resource if it were used for some alternative purpose than the opportunity under consideration. The opportunity cost of resources are therefore relevant costs in decision making.

Problems for discussion and analysis

1 (a) Check on the number of units that can be manufactured at full capacity:

Capacity at 90% = 40 000 units; therefore 100% capacity is equal to 40 000 × 100/90 = 44 444 units (to the nearest round number).

Therefore the company could increase their capacity by another 4444 units if they so wished.

Variable cost per unit :
Total costs − fixed costs = total variable costs
£800 000 − £192 000 = £608 000

Therefore variable cost per unit = £608 000/40 000 units = £15.2 per unit.

Contribution per unit if special order is accepted:

£16 − £15.2 = £0.80 per unit;
Total additional contribution = £0.80×2000 units = £1600

Calculators plc should accept the special order, assuming that fixed costs are irrelevant, because it would increase their total contribution by £1600.

(b) The company, due to its limited capacity, can only make 4444 additional units. Assuming that Noxid will only accept a contract for not less 5000 pocket calculators Calculators plc can:

(i) Sell the 5000 units to Noxid and reduce their other sales of units that sell for £22 by 556 units; this would result in a total contribution as follows.

	Contribution £
Sales to Noxid (5 000 × £0.80)	4 000.00
Other sales (40 000 − 556) 39 444	
units × (£22 − £15.20) £6.8	268 219.20
	272 219.20

or:

(ii) Reject the order from Noxid and sell 40 000 at £22 per unit; the total contribution for this option would be as follows.

$$£6.8 \text{ per unit} \times 40\,000 \text{ units} = £272\,000$$

In purely financial terms option (i) above is preferable to Calculators plc by (£272 219.20 − £272 000) = £219.20.

It should be noted that there is possibly another option; for the company to increase its capacity. However, it is likely that fixed costs would increase, but we have no available information to assess this possible option.

CHAPTER 18

Review questions

1 (a) Manufacturing – Two typical constraints that are often experienced in manufacturing industry are shortages of particular labour skills and space for machinery. The shortage of skilled labour will often occur when there are competitive local labour markets. Available space is often the cause of restricting the number of machines that can be installed in a factory and thereby the production capacity.

(b) Service sector – For professional firms in the service sector a typical resource constraint is the lack of the necessary professionally qualified staff needed to meet client demand. Another example of resource constraints in the service sector is the shortage of storage space required by garages to ensure that cars are available for mechanics to work on as they finish the previous job. This constraint would effectively limit the amount of vehicles that a firm could service.

Problems for discussion and analysis

1 (a) We will assume that fixed costs are unavoidable. The relevant costs of the make-or-buy decision:

	BC100 £	BC200 £
Cost of buying in	7.75	2.00
Relevant costs of making	5.50	2.25
Extra cost of buying in	2.25	
Saving if bought in		0.25
Decisions	**Make**	**Buy-in**

(b) Discuss the qualitative factors which are likely to have an influence on this decision.

Answer guide: The following are a number of qualitative factors which may be influential in the make-or-buy decision:

- The opportunity cost of the use of spare capacity.
- Reliability of supplies.
- Control over quality.

2 (a)

		Product				
	A £	B £	C £	D £	E £	F £
Selling price	20	28	8	36	16	40
Costs						
Direct materials	4	4	1.2	2.4	2.8	1.6
Direct labour	4	6	2.4	8.8	3.6	3.2
Total variable costs	8	10	3.6	11.2	6.4	4.8
Contribution	12	18	4.4	24.8	9.6	35.2
Labour hours per unit	6.4	7	4	9	5	12
Contribution per labour hour £	1.88	2.57	1.1	2.76	1.92	2.93
Ranking	5	3	6	2	4	1

Optional production plan

Product	Quantity units	Labour hours		Contribution £
		Per unit	Total	
F	2 900	12	34 800	102 080
D	1 100	9	9 900	27 280
B	1 200	7	8 400	21 600
E	900	5	4 500	8 640
*A	1 000	6	6 400	12 000
			64 000	171 600
Less: Fixed costs				10 000
Profit				161 600

*The number of units of product A that can be produced will be restricted to 1000 due to the constrained labour hours.

Fixed costs are unavoidable and are therefore irrelevant in the decision.

(b) Direct labour hours (£2.40) can be interpreted in the following ways:

- the contribution a firm would forego by losing one hour of labour
- the contribution gained if the firm could release one more hour
- the maximum the firm would be willing to pay to release one more hour.

Machine hours (£1.70) – The additional contribution if one more machine could be released. Thus it is also the maximum additional cost that the company would be willing to pay to secure one more machine hour. It can also be interpreted as the contribution the company would forego by losing a machine hour.

CHAPTER 19

Review questions

2 (i) Budgets compel management to look ahead and set short-term targets. By looking ahead management are then in a good position to anticipate potential problems.

   (ii) The introduction of budgets encourages greater co-ordination of the functions within the organization. For example, a production budget can only be constructed with knowledge of the forthcoming period's sales and desired inventory levels.

(iii) Budgets may be introduced to force management to communicate their objectives and strategies formally in the forthcoming periods. Communications are also enhanced within the organization when budgets are compared periodically with actual expenditure. Discussions through this control mechanism will invariably occur regarding future actions.

(iv) Budgets provide a basis for identifying those responsible for differing functions within an organization and a basis for measuring their performance.

(v) If an organization wishes to implement control mechanisms the budget is an important part of these mechanisms. Budgets in such cases will act as a benchmark that can be compared with actual performance of managers and operatives.

(vi) Budgets may be introduced as a medium for which expenditure is authorized. If expenditure is contained within a budget it implies that it has been approved by top management and no further approval is required.

(vii) A reason for introducing budgets in an organization may be to motivate employees. In this sense the budget is once again being primarily used as a target to motivate employees to reach certain levels of attainment.

Problems for discussion and analysis

2 (a)

	X	Y	Z
Sales	18	50	30
Less: Opening inventory	8	15	6
	10	35	24
Plus: Closing inventory	10	15	6
	20	50	30

(b)

	Material		
	A	B	C
Products			
X (20 units)	60	40	
Y (50 units)		50	100
Z (30 units)	150	90	30
Units of material	210	180	130
Cost per unit of material	£ 3	£ 2	£ 4
Total cost of materials purchased for production	£630	£360	£520

(c)

	Material		
	A	B	C
Units to be purchased			
Production	210	180	130
Plus: Closing inventory	25	23	15
	235	203	145
Less: Opening inventory	21	17	10
Purchases	214	186	135
Cost per unit of material	£ 3	£ 2	£ 4
Total cost of purchases	£642	£372	£540

CHAPTER 20

Review questions

1   The main differences are that DCF methods take account of the time value of money and account for relevant inflows and outflows of cash associated with an investment decision. In contrast, the ARR method does not take account of the time value of money and therefore presumes that the value of £1 received or paid in sometime in the future has the same value as £1 received or paid now (today). The ARR method also accounts for costs and revenues based on the accruals accounting convention rather on cash flow.

Problems for discussion and analysis

1   (a)   Project A

Using present value tables

Year	Cash flow	Discount factor 10%	Present value £
0	(1 500)	1.0	(1 500)
1	1 300	0.909	1 182
2	650	0.826	537
3	900	0.751	676
4	2 700	0.683	1 844
		NPV	+2 739

Accept project because it has a positive NPV.

Project B

Using annuity tables

Year	Cash flow	Discount factor 10%	Present value £
0	(500)	1.0	(500)
1–6	200 pa	4.355	871
		NPV	+371

Accept project because it has a positive NPV

Project C

Using annuity tables

Year 7 4.868

Less   Year 4 (3.170)

1.698 × £200 = £340 NPV

(b)   A perpetuity

$$\frac{\text{Annuity}}{\text{Cost of capital}} = \text{Present value of the annuity in perpetuity}$$

$$\frac{£3000}{0.10} = £30\ 000$$

CHAPTER 21

Review questions

4   There are three main reasons for holding cash:

- To be able to meet payments when they fall due (transaction motive)
- In order to meet any unexpected outgoing (precautionary motive)
- Take advantage of any unexpected opportunities (speculative motive)

Problems for discussion and analysis

2

	Current policy (£)	Option 1 (£)	Option 2 (£)
Average receivables (see note 1)	800 000	600 000	400 000
Opportunity cost 15% (see note 2)	120 000	90 000	400 000
Bad debts (based on sales value)	144 000	96 000	48 000
Cost of receivables collection	240 000	300 000	400 000
Total cost of payable policies	500 000	486 000	508 000

Note 1: Average receivables = Sales × collection period/12 months, e.g. current policy average receivables £4.8 m × 2/12 = £800 000

Note 2: The opportunity cost calculation is based on the average receivables multiplied by the 15%; e.g. current policy 15% of £800 000 = £120 000.

Option 1 will be preferred as it is the option with the least cost.

Total assets employed and return on assets

	Current policy (1 month)	Increase in payables period by 1/2 month (1.5 months)	Increase in payables period by 2 months (2 months)
	£	£	£
Receivables (note 3)	40 000	63 000	86 400
Other assets	1 400 000	1 400 000	1 400 000
Total Assets	1 440 000	1 463 000	1 486 400
Return on assets (see note 4)	6.67%	6.87%	6.79%

Note 3: Receivables = monthly sales × the number of months that receivables are outstanding; e.g. when receivables are outstanding for two months and sales are £43 200 per month the receivables at any point in time will be £86 400 (2 × £43 200)

Note 4: Return on Assets = Profit divided by Total assets × 100.

On the basis of return on assets the preferred option will be (if only very marginally) an extension of payables by 1/2 a month, i.e. option 1.

APPENDIX B:
PARTNERSHIPS

A partnership exists where two or more people enter into an agreement to run a business together. This can have a number of advantages: the additional person may bring new finance to the business or new skills or contacts, etc. In essence, partnerships are fairly simple organizations and are similar to a sole proprietorship in that there are no rules governing the format of accounts, and so these can be tailored to meet the needs of the users of those accounts. However, as you can imagine, there is more potential for conflict where there is more than one owner, and because of this there is considerable case law on partnerships as an organizational form.

For our purposes, all we need to do is to look at some of the more common issues arising in accounting for partnerships. We shall start, however, by considering the most basic situation where two people enter into an equal partnership, each putting in the same amount to the business and sharing profits equally. For accounting purposes all we need to do is to open a separate owner's equity account for each owner. These are generally referred to as 'partner's capital' accounts. We also need to open another account for each owner, or partner, to record other more short-term transactions. These are commonly referred to as 'partner's current accounts'. They record such things as the partner's entitlement to profit and their drawings. It is important in law that the capital transactions and other transactions are separated as different legal treatments may be applied to each of these amounts if the partnership were to be dissolved or cease to exist. For our purposes, we can work on the basis that the capital account relates only to deposits and withdrawals of capital from the business, and all other items are recorded via the current accounts. Let us use a simple example to illustrate how straightforward partnership accounting should be.

EXAMPLE 1

Jane and John (Part 1)

Jane and John go into business together, sharing profits equally. Jane put in £1000 to the business and John put in £9000. They buy some fixed assets for £6000, some inventories for £2000 and put the rest into a business bank account.

Before going on to the transactions of the period, let us first examine how we would record the information to date on our worksheet.

Worksheet of Jane and John partnership version 1

| | Assets | | | = | Equity + Liabilities | |
	Cash	Fixed assets	Inventory		Jane's equity	John's equity
Item 1	10 000				1000	9 000
Item 2	−6 000	6 000				
Item 3	−2 000		2 000			

As you can see, all that we have had to do is to open a separate account for each partner, which we have called Jane's equity and John's equity. More correctly, these should be referred to as capital rather than equity.

EXAMPLE 10

Jane and John (Part 2)

During the first year they sold goods for cash amounting to £30 000 and bought additional inventory for £13 000; other expenses amounted to £4000 and they had goods in hand at the end of the year amounting to £3000. The fixed assets are to be depreciated over five years, using straight-line depreciation, with no residual value.

Recording the above on the worksheet we find that at the end of the year there is a profit of £12 800 to be divided between the two partners. You will see that on the worksheet reproduced below we have opened partners' current accounts and have put their shares of the profits in their current accounts.

Worksheet of Jane and John partnership version 2

| | Assets | | | = | Equity + Liabilities | | | | |
	Cash	Fixed assets	Inventory		Jane's capital	John's capital	Revenue and expenses	Jane's current account	John's current account
Cash in	10 000				1 000	9 000			
Fixed asset	−6 000	6 000							
Goods	−2 000		2 000						
Sales	30 000						30 000		
Goods	−13 000		13 000						
Expenses	−4 000						−4 000		
Depreciation		−1 200					−1 200		
Cost of sales			−12 000				−12 000		
Balance	15 000	4 800	3 000		1 000	9 000	12 800		
Distribution							−12 800	6 400	6 400
	15 000	4 800	3 000		1 000	9 000	0	6 400	6 400

You should also have noticed that because the profit has been distributed to the partners via their current accounts, the final balance on the revenue and expenses column is nil.

As you can see, the principles involved are very simple. It is really only a question of separating the various transactions. What often makes it more complex is the nature of the partnership agreement itself. For example it may require that interest is paid on the balances on the partners' accounts, or just on the balances on the capital accounts. It might require that certain partners get paid salaries or a bonus, and each of these may happen before or after profits are split. Finally, a partnership agreement may require that profits are split according to some formula other than equal shares. Each of these situations can be easily handled if the partnership agreement is well drafted. All one does is follow the instructions contained in it.

Before we look at an example to illustrate how this is done, let us examine some of the reasons why these requirements are included in partnership agreements.

INTEREST ON CAPITAL

Interest on capital is usually included in a situation where the partners contribute uneven amounts. For instance, in the above example, since Jane has put in £1000 to John's £9000, they may decide to compensate him for the fact that he has more money at risk by giving interest on the capital before dividing the profit. If this was the case and they decided that interest at 10% would be charged, the new worksheet would appear as shown on the next page.

Worksheet of Jane and John partnership after interest at 10%

	Assets			=	Equity + Liabilities				
	Cash	Fixed assets	Inventory		Jane's capital	John's capital	Revenue and expenses	Jane's current account	John's current account
Cash in	10 000				1 000	9 000			
Fixed asset	−6 000	6 000							
Goods	−2 000		2 000						
Sales	30 000						30 000		
Goods	−13 000		13 000						
Expenses	−4 000						−4 000		
Depreciation		−1 200					−1 200		
Cost of sales			−12 000				−12 000		
Balance	15 000	4 800	3 000		1 000	9 000	12 800		
Interest							−1 000	100	900
Distribution							−11 800	5 900	5 900
	15 000	4 800	3 000		1 000	9 000	0	6 000	6 800

You can see by comparing this with the previous worksheet that the only effect is on the amount in each partner's current account (interest and distribution of profits).

PAYMENT OF SALARIES OR BONUS

A payment of salary or bonus is often done to reward particular partners for getting new business or for putting in more work in the business than the other partners. If, for example, Jane worked in the business every day of the week whereas John was rarely involved in the day-to-day running of the business, they may decide that Jane should receive a salary of £5000 before interest was paid and before the profit was divided up. The resultant worksheet would be as shown on the next page. Once again it is important to notice that the amount of the profit has not changed but the partners' shares of the profit have been altered to reflect their various inputs to the business. As before, the final balance on the income statement after the distributions is nil.

Worksheet of Jane and John partnership after interest and salaries

	Assets			=	Equity + Liabilities				
	Cash	Fixed assets	Inventory		Jane's capital	John's capital	Revenue and expenses	Jane's current account	John's current account
Cash in	10 000				1 000	9 000			
Fixed asset	−6 000	6 000							
Goods	−2 000		2 000						
Sales	30 000						30 000		
Goods	−13 000		13 000						
Expenses	−4 000						−4 000		
Depreciation		−1 200					−1 200		
Cost of sales			−12 000				−12 000		
Balance	15 000	4 800	3 000		1 000	9 000	12 800		
Salaries							−5 000	5 000	
Interest							−1 000	100	900
Distribution							−6 800	3 400	3 400
	15 000	4 800	3 000		1 000	9 000	0	8 500	4 300

UNEVEN SHARES OF PROFIT

Because partners bring different skills, expertise and connections to a business venture, it is not uncommon for partners to decide to share profits in some other ratio than equally. If, for example, Jane and John decided that, because John had a number of contracts which were the backbone of the business, he should take 60% of the profit and Jane would have the other 40%, then the worksheet would be as follows:

Jane and John partnership after interest and salaries and profit split 40:60

	Assets			=	Equity + Liabilities				
	Cash	**Fixed assets**	**Inventory**		**Jane's capital**	**John's capital**	**Revenue and expenses**	**Jane's current account**	**John's current account**
Cash in	10 000				1 000	9 000			
Fixed asset	−6 000	6 000							
Goods	−2 000		2 000						
Sales	30 000						30 000		
Goods	−13 000		13 000						
Expenses	−4 000						−4 000		
Depreciation		−1 200					−1 200		
Cost of sales			−12 000				−12 000		
Balance	15 000	4 800	3 000		1 000	9 000	12 800		
Salaries							−5 000	5 000	
Interest							−1 000	100	900
Distribution							−6 800	2 720	4 080
	15 000	4 800	3 000		1 000	9 000	0	7 820	4 980

As before, the only alteration is to the distribution of the profit. The calculation of the profit itself is unaffected; this change in profit sharing arrangements, like the previous ones, only affects the balance on the partners' current accounts. It is worth noting while we are on the subject of current accounts that these accounts are used not only to record distributions of profits etc., at the end of the year but also to record withdrawals from the business. These take place throughout the year.

PARTNERSHIP FINAL ACCOUNTS

Before leaving the subject of accounting for partnerships, we should compare the format of the partnership final accounts with those of a sole proprietorship. The important aspects of partnership accounts which are reflected in the final accounts are: (a) that each partner's equity should be separately identified; and (b) that a split should be made between capital and other amounts due to the partners. The majority of the non-capital transactions will be reflected in the balances on the current accounts, although other kinds do occur, for example a partner may make a loan to the partnership. This would be dealt with separately, in the same way as any other loan, rather than being included in the partner's current account.

Income statement of Jane and John's partnership for the year

	£	£
Sales		30 000
Cost of goods sold		12 000
Gross profit		18 000

(Continued)

	£	£
Expenses	4 000	
Depreciation	1 200	5 200
Net profit		12 800
Distributions		
Salary – Jane		5 000
		7 800
Interest – Jane	100	
– John	900	1 000
		6 800
Profit share – Jane	2 720	
– John	4 080	6 800
		0

If you compare the format of this income statement with the one for Brian's sole proprietorship in the main text, you will see that the only difference is that the partnership income statement has a 'distribution statement' added at the end. Although this is often shown as part of the income statement, there are no hard and fast rules. The way in which the accounts are presented is largely up to the partners involved. The statement of financial position of the partnership would appear as follows:

Statement of financial position of Jane and John's partnership at end of year

	£	£
Current assets		
Inventory		3 000
Cash		15 000
		18 000
Non current assets		
Fixed asset	6 000	
Depreciation	1 200	4 800
Total assets		22 800
Financed by		
Partners capital accounts		
Jane	1 000	
John	9 000	10 000
Partners current accounts		
Jane	7 820	
John	4 980	12 800
		22 800

We can see that the major difference in the statement of financial position from that of a sole proprietor is in the section relating to how the business is financed. The owners' equity is divided between the owners and subdivided according to its permanency. The more permanent investment is in the capital accounts and the less permanent is in partners' current accounts.

SUMMARY

Partnership accounting can appear to be very complex but in reality it is a question of following a logical progression and splitting the profits or losses among the partners in accordance with the partnership agreement. As we have seen, the partnership agreement can be varied to reflect the uneven amount of work, capital and involvement of partners in the running of the business, and the accounting process can also be changed to reflect this.

PROBLEMS FOR DISCUSSION AND ANALYSIS

The information below forms the basis for the questions which follow.

Susan sets up a business on her own as a sole proprietorship and has the following balance sheet at the end of year 1:

Statement of financial position of Susan's business at the end of year 1

Current assets		
Receivables		6 500
Inventory		7 000
		13 500
Non-current assets		
Vehicle at cost	6 000	
Depreciation	1 500	4 500
Equipment at cost	12 000	
Depreciation	2 400	9 600
		14 100
Total assets		27 600
Current liabilities		
Payables		6 000
Bank overdraft		4 500
		10 500
Equity		
Owner's equity		10 000
Profit for year	12 000	
Less: Drawings	4 900	7 100
Total equity		17 100
Total equity and liabilities		27 600

At the end of the first year, Susan realized that, although the business was profitable, she could hardly take out enough money to live on because she was heavily reliant on her bank and creditors already. She also found that a lot of her time which could have been used to produce more goods was being taken up selling goods, collecting debts and generally doing administrative work.

She therefore decided at the start of the second year to take in a partner who would put an additional £5000 into the business and would be able to do some of the selling and other tasks after Susan had trained him. The agreement was a verbal agreement only on the first day of the new year and the two of them agreed to share profits equally.

In the second year the summarized transactions of the business were as follows.

Sales, all on credit, £70 000; monies received from customers, £62 000; purchases £40 000, all on credit; monies paid to suppliers, £38 000; monies introduced by new partner, Bob, £5000; other expenses incurred and paid, £7000; drawings by Susan £7000 and by Bob £5000; goods in inventory at the end of the year, £9000.

1   The current partnership agreement between Susan and Bob has the advantage of being simple. If you were advising Susan, would you suggest any alternatives to the present agreement and, if so, why?

2   What, if any, additional accounts need to be opened in the second year to cope with the fact that the business is now a partnership and for what reason are they needed?

3   Explain how you propose to deal with the following:

- the balance of £7100, i.e. the profit after drawings;
- the drawings from the business by Susan and Bob in year 2;
- the money introduced by Bob in year 2.

4   Produce the final accounts of the partnership for year 2 in a form suitable for a partnership.

5   Discuss what changes would need to be made if Susan and Bob decided to form a company to take over the business to protect both partners' interests as they stand under the current partnership agreement.

APPENDIX C:
PRESENT VALUE AND
ANNUITY TABLES

Present value of £1 at compound interest: $(1 + r)^{-n}$

Period interest rate (r) (%)

(n)	1	2	3	4	5	6	7	8	9	10	11	12	13	14	15
1	0.9901	0.9804	0.9709	0.9615	0.9524	0.9434	0.9346	0.9259	0.9174	0.9091	0.9009	0.8929	0.8850	0.8772	0.8696
2	0.9803	0.9612	0.9426	0.9246	0.9070	0.8900	0.8734	0.8573	0.8417	0.8264	0.8116	0.7972	0.7831	0.7695	0.7561
3	0.9706	0.9423	0.9151	0.8890	0.8638	0.8396	0.8163	0.7938	0.7722	0.7513	0.7312	0.7118	0.6931	0.6750	0.6575
4	0.9610	0.9238	0.8885	0.8548	0.8227	0.7921	0.7629	0.7350	0.7084	0.6830	0.6587	0.6355	0.6133	0.5921	0.5718
5	0.9515	0.9057	0.8626	0.8219	0.7835	0.7473	0.7130	0.6806	0.6499	0.6209	0.5935	0.5674	0.5428	0.5194	0.4972
6	0.9420	0.8880	0.8375	0.7903	0.7462	0.7050	0.6663	0.6302	0.5963	0.5645	0.5346	0.5066	0.4803	0.4556	0.4323
7	0.9327	0.8706	0.8131	0.7599	0.7107	0.6651	0.6227	0.5835	0.5470	0.5132	0.4817	0.4523	0.4251	0.3996	0.3759
8	0.9235	0.8535	0.7894	0.7307	0.6768	0.6274	0.5820	0.5403	0.5019	0.4665	0.4339	0.4039	0.3762	0.3506	0.3269
9	0.9143	0.8368	0.7664	0.7026	0.6446	0.5919	0.5439	0.5002	0.4604	0.4241	0.3909	0.3606	0.3329	0.3075	0.2843
10	0.9053	0.8203	0.7441	0.6756	0.6139	0.5584	0.5083	0.4632	0.4224	0.3855	0.3522	0.3220	0.2946	0.2697	0.2472
11	0.8963	0.8043	0.7224	0.6496	0.5847	0.5268	0.4751	0.4289	0.3875	0.3505	0.3173	0.2875	0.2607	0.2366	0.2149
12	0.8874	0.7885	0.7014	0.6246	0.5568	0.4970	0.4440	0.3971	0.3555	0.3186	0.2858	0.2567	0.2307	0.2076	0.1869
13	0.8787	0.7730	0.6810	0.6006	0.5303	0.4688	0.4150	0.3677	0.3262	0.2897	0.2575	0.2292	0.2042	0.1821	0.1625
14	0.8700	0.7579	0.6611	0.5775	0.5051	0.4423	0.3878	0.3405	0.2992	0.2633	0.2320	0.2046	0.1807	0.1597	0.1413
15	0.8613	0.7430	0.6419	0.5553	0.4810	0.4173	0.3624	0.3152	0.2745	0.2394	0.2090	0.1827	0.1599	0.1401	0.1229
16	0.8528	0.7284	0.6232	0.5339	0.4581	0.3936	0.3387	0.2919	0.2519	0.2176	0.1883	0.1631	0.1415	0.1229	0.1069
17	0.8444	0.7142	0.6050	0.5134	0.4363	0.3714	0.3166	0.2703	0.2311	0.1978	0.1696	0.1456	0.1252	0.1078	0.0929
18	0.8360	0.7002	0.5874	0.4936	0.4155	0.3503	0.2959	0.2502	0.2120	0.1799	0.1528	0.1300	0.1108	0.0946	0.0808
19	0.8277	0.6864	0.5703	0.4746	0.3957	0.3305	0.2765	0.2317	0.1945	0.1635	0.1377	0.1161	0.0981	0.0829	0.0703
20	0.8195	0.6730	0.5537	0.4564	0.3769	0.3118	0.2584	0.2145	0.1784	0.1486	0.1240	0.1037	0.0868	0.0728	0.0611
25	0.7798	0.6095	0.4776	0.3751	0.2953	0.2330	0.1842	0.1460	0.1160	0.0923	0.0736	0.0588	0.0471	0.0378	0.0304
30	0.7419	0.5521	0.4120	0.3083	0.2314	0.1741	0.1314	0.0994	0.0754	0.0573	0.0437	0.0334	0.0256	0.0196	0.0151
35	0.7059	0.5000	0.3554	0.2534	0.1813	0.1301	0.0937	0.0676	0.0490	0.0356	0.0259	0.0189	0.0139	0.0102	0.0075
40	0.6717	0.4529	0.3066	0.2083	0.1420	0.0972	0.0668	0.0460	0.0318	0.0221	0.0154	0.0107	0.0075	0.0053	0.0037
45	0.6391	0.4102	0.2644	0.1712	0.1113	0.0727	0.0476	0.0313	0.0207	0.0137	0.0091	0.0061	0.0053	0.0027	0.0019
50	0.6080	0.3715	0.2281	0.1407	0.0872	0.0543	0.0339	0.0213	0.0134	0.0085	0.0054	0.0035	0.0022	0.0014	0.0009

	16	17	18	19	20	21	22	23	24	25	26	27	28	29	30	
1	0.8621	0.8547	0.8475	0.8403	0.8333	0.8264	0.8197	0.8130	0.8065	0.8000	0.7937	0.7874	0.7812	0.7752	0.7692	1
2	0.7432	0.7305	0.7182	0.7062	0.6944	0.6830	0.6719	0.6610	0.6504	0.6400	0.6299	0.6200	0.6104	0.6009	0.5917	2
3	0.6407	0.6244	0.6086	0.5934	0.5787	0.5645	0.5507	0.5374	0.5245	0.5120	0.4999	0.4882	0.4768	0.4658	0.4552	3
4	0.5523	0.5337	0.5158	0.4987	0.4823	0.4665	0.4514	0.4369	0.4230	0.4096	0.3968	0.3844	0.3725	0.3611	0.3501	4
5	0.4761	0.4561	0.4371	0.4190	0.4019	0.3855	0.3700	0.3552	0.3411	0.3277	0.3149	0.3027	0.2910	0.2799	0.2693	5
6	0.4104	0.3898	0.3704	0.3521	0.3349	0.3186	0.3033	0.2888	0.2751	0.2621	0.2499	0.2383	0.2274	0.2170	0.2072	6
7	0.3538	0.3332	0.3139	0.2959	0.2791	0.2633	0.2486	0.2348	0.2218	0.2097	0.1983	0.1877	0.1776	0.1682	0.1594	7
8	0.3050	0.2848	0.2660	0.2487	0.2326	0.2176	0.2038	0.1909	0.1789	0.1678	0.1574	0.1478	0.1388	0.1304	0.1226	8
9	0.2630	0.2434	0.2255	0.2090	0.1938	0.1799	0.1670	0.1552	0.1443	0.1342	0.1249	0.1164	0.1084	0.1011	0.0943	9
10	0.2267	0.2080	0.1911	0.1756	0.1615	0.1486	0.1369	0.1262	0.1164	0.1074	0.0992	0.0916	0.0847	0.0784	0.0725	10
11	0.1954	0.1778	0.1619	0.1476	0.1346	0.1228	0.1122	0.1026	0.0938	0.0859	0.0787	0.0721	0.0662	0.0607	0.0558	11
12	0.1685	0.1520	0.1372	0.1240	0.1122	0.1015	0.0920	0.0834	0.0757	0.0687	0.0625	0.0568	0.0517	0.0471	0.0429	12
13	0.1452	0.1299	0.1163	0.1042	0.0935	0.0839	0.0754	0.0678	0.0610	0.0550	0.0496	0.0447	0.0404	0.0365	0.0330	13
14	0.1252	0.1110	0.0985	0.0876	0.0779	0.0693	0.0618	0.0551	0.0492	0.0440	0.0393	0.0352	0.0316	0.0283	0.0254	14
15	0.1079	0.0949	0.0835	0.0736	0.0649	0.0573	0.0507	0.0448	0.0397	0.0352	0.0312	0.0277	0.0247	0.0219	0.0195	15
16	0.0930	0.0811	0.0708	0.0618	0.0541	0.0474	0.0415	0.0364	0.0320	0.0281	0.0248	0.0218	0.0193	0.0170	0.0150	16
17	0.0802	0.0693	0.0600	0.0520	0.0451	0.0391	0.0340	0.0296	0.0258	0.0225	0.0197	0.0172	0.0150	0.0132	0.0116	17
18	0.0691	0.0592	0.0508	0.0437	0.0376	0.0323	0.0279	0.0241	0.0208	0.0180	0.0156	0.0135	0.0118	0.0102	0.0089	18
19	0.0596	0.0506	0.0431	0.0367	0.0313	0.0267	0.0229	0.0196	0.0168	0.0144	0.0124	0.0107	0.0092	0.0079	0.0068	19
20	0.0514	0.0433	0.0365	0.0308	0.0261	0.0221	0.0187	0.0159	0.0135	0.0115	0.0098	0.0084	0.0072	0.0061	0.0053	20
25	0.0245	0.0197	0.0160	0.0129	0.0105	0.0085	0.0069	0.0057	0.0046	0.0038	0.0031	0.0025	0.0021	0.0017	0.0014	25
30	0.0116	0.0090	0.0070	0.0054	0.0042	0.0033	0.0026	0.0020	0.0016	0.0012	0.0010	0.0008	0.0006	0.0005	0.0004	30
35	0.0055	0.0041	0.0030	0.0023	0.0017	0.0013	0.0009	0.0007	0.0005	0.0004	0.0003	0.0002	0.0002	0.0001	0.0001	35
40	0.0026	0.0019	0.0013	0.0010	0.0007	0.0005	0.0004	0.0003	0.0002	0.0001	0.0001	0.0001	0.0001	0.0000	0.0000	40
45	0.0013	0.0009	0.0006	0.0004	0.0003	0.0002	0.0001	0.0001	0.0001	0.0000	0.0000	0.0000	0.0000	0.0000	0.0000	45
50	0.0006	0.0004	0.0003	0.0002	0.0001	0.0001	0.0000	0.0000	0.0000	0.0000	0.0000	0.0000	0.0000	0.0000	0.0000	50

Amount of £1 at compound interest: $(1 + r)^n$
Period interest rate (r) (%)

(n)	1	2	3	4	5	6	7	8	9	10	11	12	13	14	15
1	1.0100	1.0200	1.0300	1.0400	1.0500	1.0600	1.0700	1.0800	1.0900	1.1000	1.1100	1.1200	1.1300	1.1400	1.1500
2	1.0201	1.0404	1.0609	1.0816	1.1025	1.1236	1.1449	1.1664	1.1881	1.2100	1.2321	1.2544	1.2769	1.2996	1.3225
3	1.0303	1.0612	1.0927	1.1249	1.1576	1.1910	1.2250	1.2597	1.2950	1.3310	1.3676	1.4049	1.4429	1.4815	1.5209
4	1.0406	1.0824	1.1255	1.1699	1.2155	1.2625	1.3108	1.3605	1.4116	1.4641	1.5181	1.5735	1.6305	1.6890	1.7490
5	1.0510	1.1041	1.1593	1.2167	1.2763	1.3382	1.4026	1.4693	1.5386	1.6105	1.6851	1.7623	1.8424	1.9254	2.0114
6	1.0615	1.1262	1.1941	1.2653	1.3401	1.4185	1.5007	1.5869	1.6771	1.7716	1.8704	1.9738	2.0820	2.1950	2.3131
7	1.0721	1.1487	1.2299	1.3159	1.4071	1.5036	1.6058	1.7138	1.8280	1.9487	2.0762	2.2107	2.3526	2.5023	2.6600
8	1.0829	1.1717	1.2668	1.3686	1.4775	1.5938	1.7182	1.8509	1.9926	2.1436	2.3045	2.4760	2.6584	2.8526	3.0590
9	1.0937	1.1951	1.3048	1.4233	1.5513	1.6895	1.8385	1.9990	2.1719	2.3579	2.5580	2.7731	3.0040	3.2519	3.5179
10	1.1046	1.2190	1.3439	1.4802	1.6289	1.7908	1.9672	2.1589	2.3674	2.5937	2.8394	3.1058	3.3946	3.7072	4.0456
11	1.1157	1.2434	1.3842	1.5395	1.7103	1.8983	2.1049	2.3316	2.5804	2.8531	3.1518	3.4785	3.8359	4.2262	4.6524
12	1.1268	1.2682	1.4258	1.6010	1.7959	2.0122	2.2522	2.5182	2.8127	3.1384	3.4985	3.8906	4.3345	4.8179	5.3503
13	1.1381	1.2936	1.4685	1.6651	1.8856	2.1329	2.4098	2.7196	3.0658	3.4523	3.8833	4.3635	4.8980	5.4924	6.1528
14	1.1495	1.3195	1.5126	1.7317	1.9799	2.2609	2.5785	2.9372	3.3417	3.7975	4.3104	4.8871	5.5348	6.2613	7.0757
15	1.1610	1.3459	1.5580	1.8009	2.0789	2.3966	2.7590	3.1722	3.6425	4.1772	4.7846	5.4736	6.2543	7.1379	8.1371
16	1.1726	1.3728	1.6047	1.8730	2.1829	2.5404	2.9522	3.4259	3.9703	4.5950	5.3109	6.1304	7.0673	8.1372	9.3576
17	1.1843	1.4002	1.6528	1.9479	2.2920	2.6928	3.1588	3.7000	4.3276	5.0545	5.8951	6.8660	7.9861	9.2765	10.7613
18	1.1961	1.4282	1.7024	2.0258	2.4066	2.8543	3.3799	3.9960	4.7171	5.5599	6.5436	7.6900	9.0243	10.5752	12.3755
19	1.2081	1.4568	1.7535	2.1068	2.5270	3.0256	3.6165	4.3157	5.1417	6.1159	7.2633	8.6128	10.1974	12.0557	14.2318
20	1.2202	1.4859	1.8061	2.1911	2.6533	3.2071	3.8697	4.6610	5.6044	6.7275	8.0623	9.6463	11.5231	13.7435	16.3665
25	1.2824	1.6406	2.0938	2.6658	3.3864	4.2919	5.4274	6.8485	8.6231	10.8347	13.5855	17.0001	21.2305	26.4619	32.9190

	16	17	18	19	20	21	22	23	24	25	26	27	28	29	30	
1	1.1600	1.1700	1.1800	1.1900	1.2000	1.2100	1.2200	1.2300	1.2400	1.2500	1.2600	1.2700	1.2800	1.2900	1.3000	1
2	1.3456	1.3689	1.3924	1.4161	1.4400	1.4641	1.4884	1.5129	1.5376	1.5625	1.5876	1.6129	1.6384	1.6641	1.6900	2
3	1.5609	1.6016	1.6430	1.6852	1.7280	1.7716	1.8158	1.8609	1.9066	1.9531	2.0004	2.0484	2.0972	2.1467	2.1970	3
4	1.8106	1.8739	1.9388	2.0053	2.0736	2.1436	2.2153	2.2889	2.3642	2.4414	2.5205	2.6014	2.6844	2.7692	2.8561	4
5	2.1003	2.1924	2.2878	2.3864	2.4883	2.5937	2.7027	2.8153	2.9316	3.0518	3.1758	3.3038	3.4360	3.5723	3.7129	5
6	2.4364	2.5652	2.6996	2.8398	2.9860	3.1384	3.2973	3.4628	3.6352	3.8147	4.0015	4.1959	4.3980	4.6083	4.8268	6
7	2.8262	3.0012	3.1855	3.3793	3.5832	3.7975	4.0227	4.2593	4.5077	4.7684	5.0419	5.3288	5.6295	5.9447	6.2749	7
8	3.2784	3.5115	3.7589	4.0214	4.2998	4.5950	4.9077	5.2389	5.5895	5.9605	6.3528	6.7675	7.2058	7.6686	8.1573	8
9	3.8030	4.1084	4.4355	4.7854	5.1598	5.5599	5.9874	6.4439	6.9310	7.4506	8.0045	8.5946	9.2234	9.8925	10.6045	9
10	4.4114	4.8068	5.2338	5.6947	6.1917	6.7275	7.3046	7.9259	8.5944	9.3132	10.0857	10.9153	11.8059	12.7614	13.7858	10
11	5.1173	5.6240	6.1759	6.7767	7.4301	8.1403	8.9117	9.7489	10.6571	11.6415	12.7080	13.8625	15.1116	16.4622	17.9216	11
12	5.9360	6.5801	7.2876	8.0642	8.9161	9.8497	10.8722	11.9912	13.2148	14.5519	16.0120	17.6053	19.3428	21.2362	23.2981	12
13	6.8858	7.6987	8.5994	9.5964	10.6993	11.9182	13.2641	14.7491	16.3863	18.1899	20.1752	22.3588	24.7588	27.3947	30.2875	13
14	7.9875	9.0075	10.1472	11.4198	12.8392	14.4210	16.1822	18.1414	20.3191	22.7374	25.4207	28.3957	31.6913	35.3391	39.3738	14
15	9.2655	10.5387	11.9737	13.5895	15.4070	17.4494	19.7423	22.3140	25.1956	28.4217	32.0301	36.0625	40.5648	45.5875	51.1859	15
16	10.7480	12.3303	14.1290	16.1715	18.4884	21.1138	24.0856	27.4462	31.2426	35.5271	40.3579	45.7994	51.9230	58.8079	66.5417	16
17	12.4677	14.4265	16.6722	19.2441	22.1861	25.5477	29.3844	33.7588	38.7408	44.4089	50.8510	58.1652	66.4614	75.8621	86.5042	17
18	14.4625	16.8790	19.6733	22.9005	26.6233	30.9127	35.8490	41.5233	48.0386	55.5112	64.0722	73.8698	85.0706	97.8622	112.4554	18
19	16.7765	19.7484	23.2144	27.2516	31.9480	37.4043	43.7358	51.0737	59.5679	69.3889	80.7310	93.8147	108.8904	126.2422	146.1920	19
20	19.4608	23.1056	27.3930	32.4294	38.3376	45.2593	53.3576	62.8206	73.8641	86.7362	101.7211	119.1446	139.3797	162.8524	190.0496	20
25	40.8742	50.6578	62.6686	77.3881	95.3962	117.3909	144.2101	176.8593	216.5420	264.6978	323.0454	393.6344	478.9049	581.7585	705.6410	25

Present value of an annuity of £1: $\{(1 + r)^{-n} r\}$

Period interest rate (r) (%)

(n)	1	2	3	4	5	6	7	8	9	10	11	12	13	14	15
1	0.9901	0.9804	0.9709	0.9615	0.9524	0.9434	0.9346	0.9259	0.9174	0.9091	0.9009	0.8929	0.8850	0.8772	0.8696
2	1.9704	1.9416	1.9135	1.8861	1.8594	1.8334	1.8080	1.7833	1.7591	1.7355	1.7125	1.6901	1.6681	1.6467	1.6257
3	2.9410	2.8839	2.8286	2.7751	2.7232	2.6730	2.6243	2.5771	2.5313	2.4869	2.4437	2.4018	2.3612	2.3216	2.2832
4	3.9020	3.8077	3.7171	3.6299	3.5460	3.4651	3.3872	3.3121	3.2397	3.1699	3.1024	3.0373	2.9745	2.9137	2.8550
5	4.8534	4.7135	4.5797	4.4518	4.3295	4.2124	4.1002	3.9927	3.8897	3.7908	3.6959	3.6048	3.5172	3.4331	3.3522
6	5.7955	5.6014	5.4172	5.2421	5.0757	4.9173	4.7665	4.6229	4.4859	4.3553	4.2305	4.1114	3.9975	3.8887	3.7845
7	6.7282	6.4720	6.2303	6.0021	5.7864	5.5824	5.3893	5.2064	5.0330	4.8684	4.7122	4.5638	4.4226	4.2883	4.1604
8	7.6517	7.3255	7.0197	6.7327	6.4632	6.2098	5.9713	5.7466	5.5348	5.3349	5.1461	4.9676	4.7988	4.6389	4.4873
9	8.5660	8.1622	7.7861	7.4353	7.1078	6.8017	6.5152	6.2469	5.9952	5.7590	5.5370	5.3282	5.1317	4.9464	4.7716
10	9.4713	8.9826	8.5302	8.1109	7.7217	7.3601	7.0236	6.7101	6.4177	6.1446	5.8892	5.6502	5.4262	5.2161	5.0188
11	10.3676	9.7868	9.2526	8.7605	8.3064	7.8869	7.4987	7.1390	6.8052	6.4951	6.2065	5.9377	5.6869	5.4527	5.2337
12	11.2551	10.5753	9.9540	9.3851	8.8633	8.3838	7.9427	7.5361	7.1607	6.8137	6.4924	6.1944	5.9176	5.6603	5.4206
13	12.1337	11.3484	10.6350	9.9856	9.3936	8.8527	8.3577	7.9038	7.4869	7.1034	6.7499	6.4235	6.1218	5.8424	5.5831
14	13.0037	12.1062	11.2961	10.5631	9.8986	9.2950	8.7455	8.2442	7.7862	7.3667	6.9819	6.6282	6.3025	6.0021	5.7245
15	13.8651	12.8493	11.9379	11.1184	10.3797	9.7122	9.1079	8.5595	8.0607	7.6061	7.1909	6.8109	6.4624	6.1422	5.8474
16	14.7179	13.5777	12.5611	11.6523	10.8378	10.1059	9.4466	8.8514	8.3126	7.8237	7.3792	6.9740	6.6039	6.2651	5.9542
17	15.5623	14.2919	13.1661	12.1657	11.2741	10.4773	9.7632	9.1216	8.5436	8.0216	7.5488	7.1196	6.7291	6.3729	6.0472
18	16.3983	14.9920	13.7535	12.6593	11.6896	10.8276	10.0591	9.3719	8.7556	8.2014	7.7016	7.2497	6.8399	6.4674	6.1280
19	17.2260	15.6785	14.3238	13.1339	12.0853	11.1581	10.3356	9.6036	8.9501	8.3649	7.8393	7.3658	6.9380	6.5504	6.1982
20	18.0456	16.3514	14.8775	13.5903	12.4622	11.4699	10.5940	9.8181	9.1285	8.5136	7.9633	7.4694	7.0248	6.6231	6.2593
25	22.0232	19.5235	17.4131	15.6221	14.0939	12.7834	11.6536	10.6748	9.8226	9.0770	8.4217	7.8431	7.3300	6.8729	6.4641
30	25.8077	22.3965	19.6004	17.2920	15.3725	13.7648	12.4090	11.2578	10.2737	9.4269	8.6938	8.0552	7.4957	7.0027	6.5660
35	29.4086	24.9986	21.4872	18.6646	16.3742	14.4982	12.9477	11.6546	10.5668	9.6442	8.8552	8.1755	7.5856	7.0700	6.6166
40	32.8347	27.3555	23.1148	19.7928	17.1591	15.0463	13.3317	11.9246	10.7574	9.7791	8.9511	8.2438	7.6344	7.1050	6.6418
45	36.0945	29.4902	24.5187	20.7200	17.7741	15.4558	13.6055	12.1084	10.8812	9.8628	9.0079	8.2825	7.6609	7.1232	6.6543
50	39.1961	31.4236	25.7298	21.4822	18.2559	15.7619	13.8007	12.2335	10.9617	9.9148	9.0417	8.3045	7.6752	7.1327	6.6605

n	16	17	18	19	20	21	22	23	24	25	26	27	28	29	30
1	0.8621	0.8547	0.8475	0.8403	0.8333	0.8264	0.8197	0.8130	0.8065	0.8000	0.7937	0.7874	0.7812	0.7752	0.7692
2	1.6052	1.5852	1.5656	1.5465	1.5278	1.5095	1.4915	1.4740	1.4568	1.4400	1.4235	1.4074	1.3916	1.3761	1.3609
3	2.2459	2.2096	2.1743	2.1399	2.1065	2.0739	2.0422	2.0114	1.9813	1.9520	1.9234	1.8956	1.8684	1.8420	1.8161
4	2.7982	2.7432	2.6901	2.6386	2.5887	2.5404	2.4936	2.4483	2.4043	2.3616	2.3202	2.2800	2.2410	2.2031	2.1662
5	3.2743	3.1993	3.1272	3.0576	2.9906	2.9260	2.8636	2.8035	2.7454	2.6893	2.6351	2.5827	2.5320	2.4830	2.4356
6	3.6847	3.5892	3.4976	3.4098	3.3255	3.2446	3.1669	3.0923	3.0205	2.9514	2.8850	2.8210	2.7594	2.7000	2.6427
7	4.0386	3.9224	3.8115	3.7057	3.6046	3.5079	3.4155	3.3270	3.2423	3.1611	3.0833	3.0087	2.9370	2.8682	2.8021
8	4.3436	4.2072	4.0776	3.9544	3.8372	3.7256	3.6193	3.5179	3.4212	3.3289	3.2407	3.1564	3.0758	2.9986	2.9247
9	4.6065	4.4506	4.3030	4.1633	4.0310	3.9054	3.7863	3.6731	3.5655	3.4631	3.3657	3.2728	3.1842	3.0997	3.0190
10	4.8332	4.6586	4.4941	4.3389	4.1925	4.0541	3.9232	3.7993	3.6819	3.5705	3.4648	3.3644	3.2689	3.1781	3.0915
11	5.0286	4.8364	4.6560	4.4865	4.3271	4.1769	4.0354	3.9018	3.7757	3.6564	3.5435	3.4365	3.3351	3.2388	3.1473
12	5.1971	4.9884	4.7932	4.6105	4.4392	4.2784	4.1274	3.9852	3.8514	3.7251	3.6059	3.4933	3.3868	3.2859	3.1903
13	5.3423	5.1183	4.9095	4.7147	4.5327	4.3624	4.2028	4.0530	3.9124	3.7801	3.6555	3.5381	3.4272	3.3224	3.2233
14	5.4675	5.2293	5.0081	4.8023	4.6106	4.4317	4.2646	4.1082	3.9616	3.8241	3.6949	3.5733	3.4587	3.3507	3.2487
15	5.5755	5.3242	5.0916	4.8759	4.6755	4.4890	4.3152	4.1530	4.0013	3.8593	3.7261	3.6010	3.4834	3.3726	3.2682
16	5.6685	5.4053	5.1624	4.9377	4.7296	4.5364	4.3567	4.1894	4.0333	3.8874	3.7509	3.6228	3.5026	3.3896	3.2832
17	5.7487	5.4746	5.2223	4.9897	4.7746	4.5755	4.3908	4.2190	4.0591	3.9099	3.7705	3.6400	3.5177	3.4028	3.2948
18	5.8178	5.5339	5.2732	5.0333	4.8122	4.6079	4.4187	4.2431	4.0799	3.9279	3.7861	3.6536	3.5294	3.4130	3.3037
19	5.8775	5.5845	5.3162	5.0700	4.8435	4.6346	4.4415	4.2627	4.0967	3.9424	3.7985	3.6642	3.5386	3.4210	3.3105
20	5.9288	5.6278	5.3527	5.1009	4.8696	4.6567	4.4603	4.2786	4.1103	3.9539	3.8083	3.6726	3.5458	3.4271	3.3158
25	6.0971	5.7662	5.4669	5.1951	4.9476	4.7213	4.5139	4.3232	4.1474	3.9849	3.8342	3.6943	3.5640	3.4423	3.3286
30	6.1772	5.8294	5.5168	5.2347	4.9789	4.7463	4.5338	4.3391	4.1601	3.9950	3.8424	3.7009	3.5693	3.4466	3.3321
35	6.2153	5.8582	5.5386	5.2512	4.9915	4.7559	4.5411	4.3447	4.1644	3.9984	3.8450	3.7028	3.5708	3.4478	3.3330
40	6.2335	5.8713	5.5482	5.2582	4.9966	4.7596	4.5439	4.3467	4.1659	3.9995	3.8458	3.7034	3.5712	3.4481	3.3332
45	6.2421	5.8773	5.5523	5.2611	4.9986	4.7610	4.5449	4.3474	4.1664	3.9998	3.8460	3.7036	3.5714	3.4482	3.3333
50	6.2463	5.8801	5.5541	5.2623	4.9995	4.7616	4.5452	4.3477	4.1666	3.9999	3.8461	3.7037	3.5714	3.4483	3.333

INDEX